macromedia® FLASH® MX 2004

jen dehaan

training from the source

Macromedia Flash MX 2004: Training from the Source

Jen deHaan

  Published by Macromedia Press, in association with Peachpit Press, a division of Pearson Education.

Macromedia Press
1249 Eighth Street
Berkeley, CA 94710
510/524-2178
800/283-9444
510/524-2221 (fax)
Find us on the World Wide Web at:
http://www.peachpit.com
http://www.macromedia.com

To report errors, please send a note to errata@peachpit.com

Printed and bound in the United States of America

ISBN 0-321-21342-4

9 8 7 6 5 4 3 2 1

CREDITS

Macromedia Press Editor: Angela C. Kozlowski

Editor: Robyn G. Thomas

Technical Editor: James Talbot

Production Coordinator: Myrna Vladic

Copy Editor: Nancy Sixsmith

Compositors:
Rick Gordon, Emerald Valley Graphics
Debbie Roberti, Espresso Graphics

Indexer: Joy Dean Lee

Cover Production: George Mattingly, GMD

BIO

Jen deHaan is a Calgary-based Flash "deseloper" (designer/developer) who, in addition to talking about herself in the third person, likes to write books and make things with Macromedia Flash. Jen has been involved in writing for and editing many books, usually on Macromedia products such as Flash, ActionScript, ColdFusion and Dreamweaver. She has also contributed a series of tutorials featured on the Macromedia Developer Center on building an application using Flash.

Jen is the friendly web person championing several sites, including www.flash-mx.com and www.flash2004.com. You can find her personal portfolio and rants at www.ejepo.com or www.deseloper.com, and her forums at www.flashmx2004.com. Jen has dreams of managing a 7-11 to obtain free Slurpees. Surprisingly, she says, few people can spell "deHaan."

ACKNOWLEDGMENTS

It has been a long exhaustive haul, and I'd like to take this opportunity to thank the following people.

A big thank you to the friendly and tireless people at Macromedia Press: Robyn Thomas, Angela Kozlowski, James "Hollywood" Talbot, Nancy Sixsmith, and the layout people for all of their help in making this book. Ben Forta deserves kudos for generously hosting some of the files for this book, and the ingenious Joey Lott for his amazing technical insight. I'd like to acknowledge Carole McClendon at Waterside Productions for her help and assistance. Aral Balkan gets thanks for confirming our suspicions and Robin Debreuil simply for being funny. Thanks to mom and dad for sending provisions and food for those weeks that we did not leave the house. Thanks to the makers of the Family Guy for helping with the stress, and Andrew Welch at Ambrosia for making some fine screen capture software. To the Macromedians Nivesh "component boy" Rajbhandari, Brad Becker, Gary Grossman, Lucian Beebe: thanks for your attention, help, and Flash for that matter. Thanks go to Eric Thompson for getting me up and running again on several occasions (and for your patience with my inquisitive nature and paranoid emails). A round of applause goes to the Flash community for the amazing help and guidance provided, daily, for nothing in return but love. Thanks to the staff at the local Starbucks for making a fine cup of coffee, and to Tim Hortons for selling coffee the other 8 hours a day and helping some haggard and bewildered author at 4am make it through the multi-day shifts.

A special mention goes to Peter for helping every step of the way and going through each and every exercise on every single page more than once with no obligation to do so. Your patience is amazing, but anything wrong with this book is equally your fault.

DEDICATION

This book is dedicated to Nate M. Weiss,
because it was a double-dare.

table of contents

introduction

Macromedia Flash MX 2004 and Macromedia Flash MX Professional 2004 are multimedia applications that allow designers and developers the freedom to create rich and engaging applications, presentations, animations, and Web sites. These applications can be created by integrating images, drawings, audio, video, and text. Flash enables you to create content for a wide variety of platforms and devices. Files that you publish from Flash can be displayed on many different computer operating systems, handheld devices, phones, and even television. Flash can be viewed by almost every online visitor you might have to a Web site because the Flash Player is installed on a majority of computers today. Flash is considered to be a standard for displaying rich content on the Web, and this book shows you many different ways of doing so.

Flash consists of two different editions: Flash MX 2004 and a Pro edition known as Flash MX Professional. The Professional edition includes a number of additional features such as specialized Data Components, a form-based application-authoring environment, specialized video export, and data binding. These extra tools in the Professional environment speed up your workflow and enable you to rapidly develop applications with data connectivity and robust components. Flash MX 2004 contains a wide toolset, enabling you to create similar applications by adding a bit more ActionScript (Flash's scripting language). This book provides a firm foundation in authoring and scripting Flash content, no matter what edition you choose to work with.

PREREQUISITES

Macromedia Flash MX 2004: Training from the Source helps you establish a foundation in either edition of Flash. Most of the book concentrates on the features and workflow of Flash MX 2004. Several Flash MX Professional features are detailed in a few exercises. However, the exercises that use Flash MX Professional features are followed by an equivalent exercise for Flash MX 2004 readers. You can complete the entire application and all its functionality, no matter what version of Flash you are using.

OUTLINE

You will quickly discover that this book details relevant examples that you will find useful for the Web sites you build following the completion of each exercise. You will learn how to create buttons and links, draw and animate in Flash, format text, load data into the application, use ActionScript concepts, and much more. This Macromedia training course steps you through the projects in each lesson, presents the major features and tools in Flash MX 2004, and guides you toward developing the skills you need to create Flash applications and Web sites.

This curriculum should take approximately 22 hours to complete and includes the following lessons:

Lesson 1: Learning the Basics
Lesson 2: Creating Graphics
Lesson 3: Using Text
Lesson 4: Creating and Editing Symbols
Lesson 5: Creating Animation
Lesson 6: Adding Basic Interactivity
Lesson 7: Adding Video and Sound
Lesson 8: Using Screens
Lesson 9: Creating Forms Using Components
Lesson 10: Incorporating Dynamic Data
Lesson 11: ActionScript Basics
Lesson 12: Optimizing Flash Content
Lesson 13: Publishing Flash Documents

THE PROJECT SITE

Macromedia Flash MX 2004: Training from the Source includes a vast number of comprehensive tutorials aimed at showing you how to create a complete application using Flash MX 2004 or Flash MX 2004 Professional. You will create an "online bookstore" application (without a shopping cart) that loads text, images, and a video presentation into the Web site. It also contains a couple of feedback forms that connect to Web Services, some audio, and even a partially animated map providing directions to the fictitious store.

By the end of 13 hands-on lessons, you will complete building an entire Web site using either edition of Flash. You will begin by creating the graphical user interface, which includes imported graphics, drawings you create right in Flash, as well as different kinds of animations. You will edit and then import a video into a Flash document and learn about video compression. Then you will create an interactive presentation using screens (Flash MX Professional) or using ActionScript and the Timeline (Flash MX 2004).

This project includes learning the fundamentals of ActionScript: from the meaning of the scripting terminology to some of the better practices for completing a task and working with code. Even if you are uneasy with writing scripts or any kind of code in general, you will probably find the coding examples that are used both easy and intuitive. Finally, you will optimize your application so it is appropriate for the Web and then publish the files so they can be uploaded and placed online.

STANDARD ELEMENTS IN THE BOOK

Each lesson in this book begins by outlining the major focus of the lesson at hand and introducing new features. Learning objectives and the approximate time needed to complete all the exercises are also listed at the beginning of each lesson. The projects are divided into short exercises that explain the importance of each skill you learn. Every lesson will build on the concepts and techniques used in the previous lessons.

Tips: Alternative ways to perform tasks and suggestions to consider when applying the skills you are learning.

Notes: Additional background information to expand your knowledge, as well as advanced techniques you can explore in order to further develop your skills.

Boldface terms: New vocabulary that is introduced and emphasized in each lesson.

Italicized text: Words that appear in italics are either for emphasis or are text that you must type while working through the steps in the lessons.

Menu commands and keyboard shortcuts: There are often multiple ways to perform the same task in Flash. The different options will be pointed out in each lesson. Menu commands are shown with angle brackets between the menu names and commands: Menu › Command › Subcommand. Keyboard shortcuts are shown with a plus sign between the names of keys to indicate that you should press the keys simultaneously; for example, Shift+Tab means that you should press the Shift and Tab keys at the same time.

Appendixes: This book includes three appendixes. Appendix A,: Installing Extensions, includes information on how to install and use the Macromedia Extension Manager and where to find extensions. Appendix B, Resources, contains links to valuable online resources. And Appendix C, Keyboard Shortcuts, lists shortcuts in Flash MX 2004 and Flash MX Professional.

CD-ROM: The CD-ROM included with the book includes all the media files, starting files, and completed projects for each of the lessons in the book. Any time you want to reference one of the files being built in a lesson to verify that you are correctly executing the steps in the exercises, you will find the files organized on the CD-ROM under the corresponding lesson. For example, the files for Lesson 4 are located on the CD-ROM in the Lesson04 folder.

The directory structure of the lessons you will be working with is as follows:

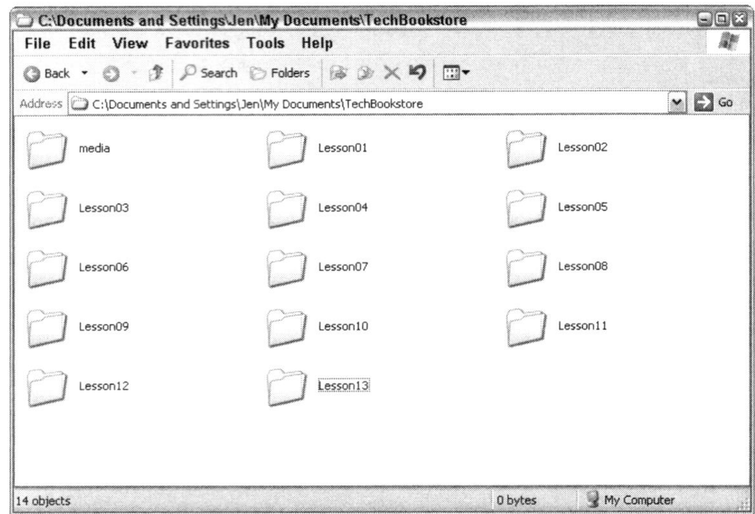

File structure of lesson folders in the project site

For additional practice with the skills you will learn in each lesson, try recreating the starting files that have been provided for you in the lesson files.

MACROMEDIA TRAINING FROM THE SOURCE

The Macromedia Training from the Source and Advanced Training from the Source series are developed in association with Macromedia, and reviewed by the product support teams. Ideal for active learners, the books in the Training from the Source series offer hands-on instruction designed to provide you with a solid grounding in the program's fundamentals. If you learn best by doing, this is the series for you. Each Training from the Source title contains hours of instruction on Macromedia software products. They are designed to teach the techniques that you need to create sophisticated professional-level projects. Each book includes a CD-ROM that contains all the files used in the lessons, completed projects for comparison and more.

MACROMEDIA AUTHORIZED TRAINING AND CERTIFICATION

This book is geared to enable you to study at your own pace with content from the source. Other training options exist through the Macromedia Authorized Training Partner program. Get up to speed in a matter of days with task-oriented courses taught by Macromedia Certified Instructors. Or learn on your own with interactive, online training from Macromedia University. All of these sources of training will prepare you to become a Macromedia Certified Developer.

For more information about authorized training and certification, check out `www.macromedia.com/go/training1`.

WHAT YOU WILL LEARN

You will develop the skills you need to create and maintain your own Web sites as you work through these lessons.

By the end of the course, you will be able to:

- Navigate and use the toolset found in the Flash authoring environment
- Use assets to create an engaging user interface
- Create animation using several different animating techniques
- Import media such as PNG and video files
- Use the built-in component set to create forms to capture data from a visitor
- Use behaviors to instantly add ActionScript to a document
- Use Web Services to collect a visitor's data and send it to a server
- Use screens to rapidly build a presentation
- Understand how ActionScript works with your Flash documents and make components work
- Organize your FLA files so you can optimize and publish your Flash files

MINIMUM SYSTEM REQUIREMENTS

Windows

- 600 MHz Intel Pentium III processor or equivalent
- Windows 98 SE, Windows 2000, or Windows XP
- 128 MB RAM (256 MB recommended)
- 275 MB available disk space

Macintosh

- 500 MHz PowerPC G3 processor
- Mac OS X 10.2.6
- 128 MB RAM (256 MB recommended)
- 215 MB available disk space

* Some features require QuickTime 6.3 or QuickTime Pro 6.3

* Flash MX 2004 and Flash MX Professional 2004 require product activation over the Internet or by phone.

The Studio MX 2004 line of products is extremely exciting, and we're waiting to be amazed by what you will do with it. With a strong foundation in Flash, you can grow and expand your skillset quickly. Flash is really not too difficult to use, no matter what your background might be. With a little bit of initiative and effort, you can fly through the following lessons and be building your own custom applications and sites in no time.

learning the basics

LESSON 1

Macromedia Flash MX 2004 and Macromedia Flash MX Professional 2004 are tools that help you create engaging animations, stream interactive media on the Web such as video, build e-commerce sites, and put together Rich Internet Applications (RIAs) that sometimes include most or all of those elements combined. You can also create CD-ROMs, games, desktop applications, or software for mobile devices. While you follow along and finish the lessons in this book, you will discover that Flash is extremely versatile while being easy and intuitive to use!

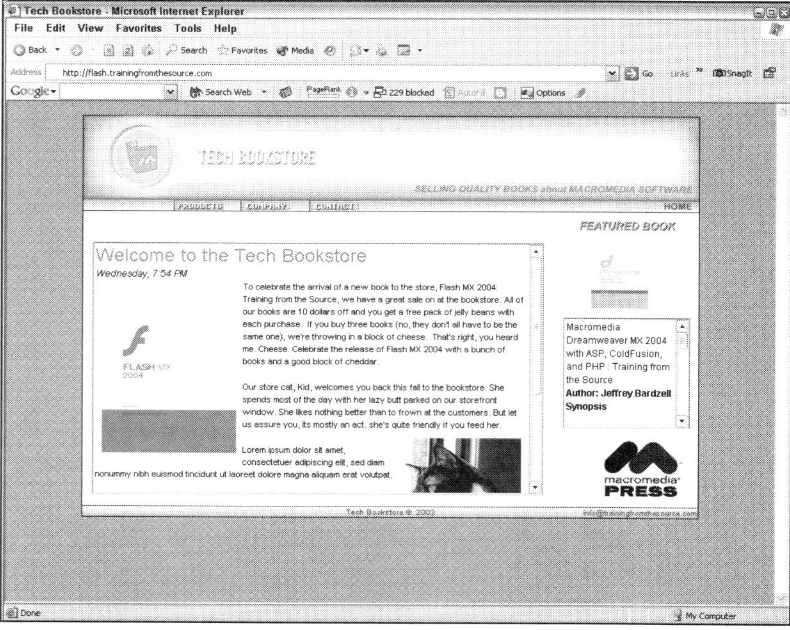

The completed Tech Bookstore Web site.

The first thing to do before you start to work in Flash is to learn how to navigate around the workspace. If you learn how to work using the Flash interface, creating documents is much easier and can be finished quickly. In this lesson, you will learn how to publish your Flash documents and test them in the Flash testing environment or a browser window. You will complete the lesson by exploring the finished version of the project you work on throughout this book.

WHAT YOU WILL LEARN

In this lesson, you will:

- Learn what Flash can do
- Discover the Flash workspace
- Create and save a new Flash document
- Use panels, menus, the Stage, and the Library to navigate in Flash
- Learn how to find help
- Modify your document and customize your preferences and settings
- Test a SWF file
- Take a look at the final project

APPROXIMATE TIME

This lesson takes approximately one hour to complete.

LESSON FILES

Media Files:

None

Starting Files:

None

Completed Project:

Lesson01/bookstore3.fla

INTRODUCING MACROMEDIA FLASH MX 2004

Macromedia Flash MX 2004 is a software application containing tools used to create animations, vector graphics, applications, software, presentations or Web sites. Flash publishes *SWF* files, which are economical on file size and are cross-platform so a majority of people can view them by using the *Flash Player 7*. Flash exports files with the SWF extension that contain the application you built using Flash. It is then played using the Flash Player 7.

NOTE *The Flash Player (in version 7 at the time of writing) is a small piece of software used to play SWF files generated by Flash and is a typical "viewer" application. SWF files are played either in a browser window or a standalone player, and the player ensures the Flash content can be viewed regardless of the platform it is playing on.*

Flash is a well-established application for building multimedia files. You can import many kinds of media into Flash, including text, graphics, video, vector files (including Illustrator and Freehand), PDFs, and audio. You can load Flash SWF files, images, text (including HTML formatted text), and video files into Flash when it is running in a Flash Player. The Flash Player allows you to connect SWF files to a database, XML file, or even a Web Service. You can make your files interactive and dynamic, entertaining and intuitive. The diverse tools in Flash allow you to maximize your creative skills or follow established standards: Flash accommodates and fuses design and development so you can create just about anything.

WHY IS FLASH SO USEFUL?

Flash's SWF files can be viewed by a wide online audience because of the wide distribution of the Flash Player used to view them. The player, which has been installed by millions of people, is also included on most computers out of the box. The small file size of the Flash Player encourages users to download updated versions of the player when they become available. You can also create SWF files that are accessible to visually impaired people using a screen reader with a browser, which expands your audience even further.

You can integrate Flash with other software, such as the Macromedia Studio MX 2004 suite and many third-party applications. Software integration allows you to author Flash documents in a powerful way and incorporate additional elements directly into Flash, such as 3D and complicated vector drawings. Flash is an extensible software application, meaning you will discover many new things to install right into Flash, such as extensions and components. Go to `www.macromedia.com` and this book's Web site at `www.TrainingFromTheSource.com` for the latest information on what Flash extensions are available.

THE POWER AND EASE OF USING FLASH

Flash uses a scripting language called ActionScript, which is a powerful and standards-following language based on ECMAScript and similar to JavaScript and Java. ActionScript is currently in version 2.0, although Flash MX 2004 files can be created using either version of the language. Both versions of ActionScript enable you to create complex and powerful applications. Even though Flash has a scripting language, you don't need a lot (or any) code to build an interactive application. You can essentially drag and drop functionality into your Flash documents using components and behaviors. You will learn how to use both of these features later on in the book.

Flash has many tools in place to help you keep file sizes low and sites running fast, so you do not need to have an extended "loading" phase. You can create shared libraries of assets that you can share across several SWF files. Incorporating large amounts of dynamic data into a SWF is not difficult to do. By dynamically loading content, you allow users to choose what information they want to download instead of the entire application at once.

LOOKING AT THE FLASH WORKSPACE

The Flash workspace, also known as the authoring environment, has a series of *panels* situated around a *Stage*. Flash files are based on *timelines*, which is where all of your assets (such as graphics and text) are organized. A playhead moves along the Timeline when a file plays in the Flash Player. Look at the general Flash layout that follows. You will learn more about how each part of the workspace (or *authoring environment*) functions later in this lesson and the book.

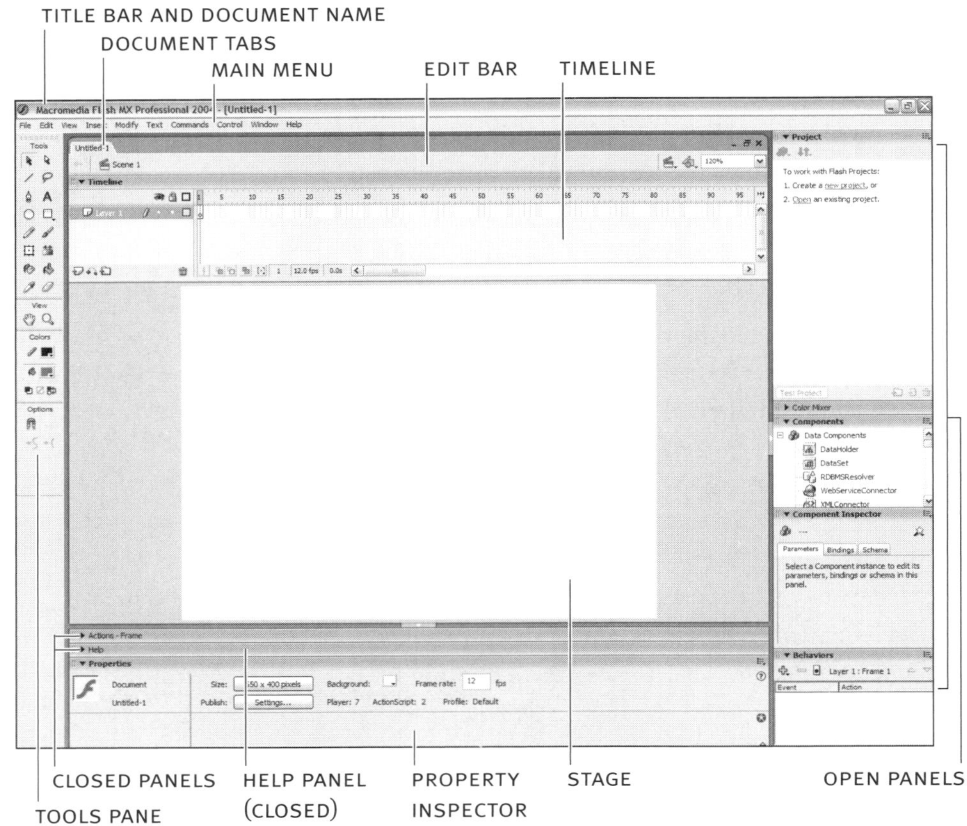
TITLE BAR AND DOCUMENT NAME
DOCUMENT TABS
MAIN MENU
EDIT BAR
TIMELINE
CLOSED PANELS
TOOLS PANE
HELP PANEL (CLOSED)
PROPERTY INSPECTOR
STAGE
OPEN PANELS

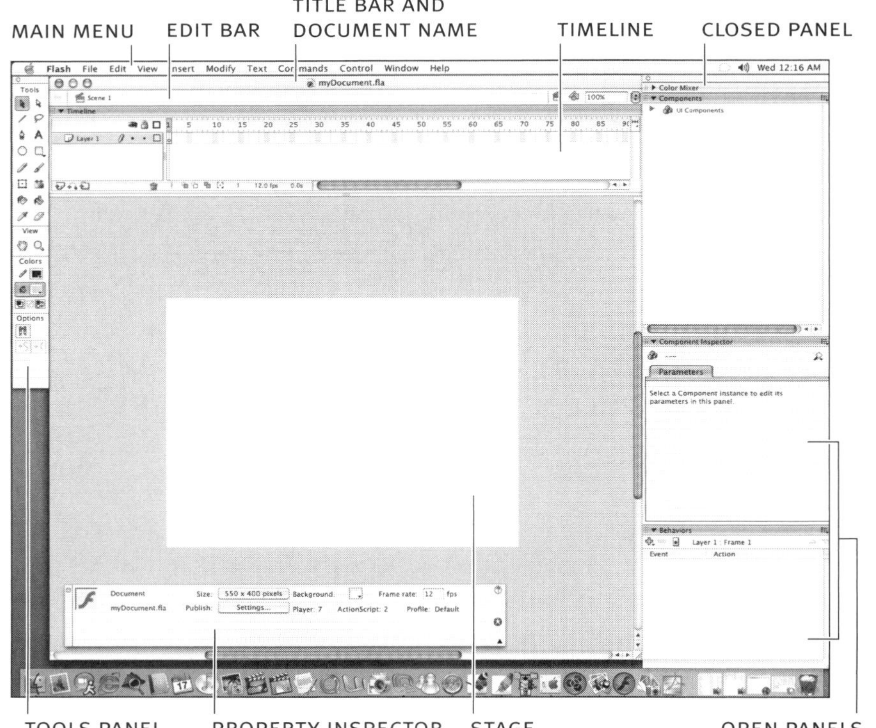
MAIN MENU
EDIT BAR
TITLE BAR AND DOCUMENT NAME
TIMELINE
CLOSED PANEL
TOOLS PANEL
PROPERTY INSPECTOR
STAGE
OPEN PANELS

The authoring environment can be divided into several large sections based on their functionality. Each section also contains many different controls that you will learn about later on in the book.

Menus: Menus in Flash are much like menus in most other software packages you use. Flash menus contain common commands such as Save, Copy, Paste and Help alongside commands specific to the software.

Timeline: SWF files can play on a Timeline, revealing Flash's history as an animation-based program. A Timeline is made of a series of frames in a row. Frames can be empty, can contain content, or can be a keyframe. The Timeline is made of one or more stacked layers containing the elements and code that make up the SWF. Each layer has a row of frames. A playhead is used to navigate the Timeline and choose the current frame you are working on.

Panels: Panels help you put together documents in Flash because they provide control over almost anything you need to create or edit an application. You can open and close panels using the Window menu, so you can have many panels open at once or just a few. The Tools pane contains a great number of tools used to select, create or modify content in the document.

Stage: In the middle of these panels is the *Stage*, which serves as the visible area of your application. The Stage is where you place your media such as graphics, buttons, animations, and interactive form text fields.

Document Tabs and the edit bar: In Windows, every file you have open has a Document Tab associated with it. Document Tabs help you navigate between documents that are open in Flash. The edit bar directly below the Document Tabs helps you navigate through elements of your Flash file. One of the drop-down menus on the edit bar controls the magnification of the Stage, and the other is used to directly choose an element on the Stage to edit.

NOTE *The Document Tabs feature is only available in Windows. On the Mac, the edit bar is located directly below the Timeline by default. To change the location of the Document Tabs to above or below the Timeline, press Shift+Alt and double-click (or Command+Shift and double-click on the Mac).*

NOTE *You cannot see Document Tabs if you are working on a PC and do not have the Stage area maximized. If you don't see Document Tabs after you open a new document, click the Maximize button in the Stage title bar.*

Property inspector: The Property inspector is a context-sensitive panel that displays information about and has editable properties for whatever is currently selected on the Stage. If nothing is selected (or just the Stage is selected), you can change the properties of the Stage and the open document itself. By default, the Property inspector opens below the Stage. If the Property inspector isn't open, open it by choosing Ctrl+F3 (or Command+F3 on the Mac).

CREATING YOUR FIRST FLASH DOCUMENT

There are several different kinds of documents you can build using Flash. You can create media documents, like the SWF files you see with animation and video, which can include many kinds of assets and code. Or, you can create documents that contain only code that helps Flash run.

In this exercise, you will create a new FLA document that eventually serves as the main document for the book's application. This document serves as a *container* for other content that will be loaded into it, such as text, graphics, video, and other SWF files.

NOTE *FLA files are the native file format in Flash, because you can only edit FLA files using Flash. SWF files, the files you export from Flash that we discussed earlier, is an open format so it can be exported by other programs and played in different players.*

This exercise begins with creating a new file in Flash. You will then change the document's properties using the Property inspector and the Document Properties dialog box, and then save the FLA and SWF files to your hard drive.

1) Open Flash either by double-clicking the Flash icon on your desktop, choosing Start > All Programs (Windows XP only) > Macromedia > Macromedia Flash MX 2004 (Windows), or find Flash installed within your `Applications` **folder and double-click the Flash MX 2004 icon (Mac) inside the Macromedia Flash MX 2004 folder.**

NOTE *If you have just installed Flash on your computer and you are opening it for the first time, you need to activate the software. This simple process requires you only to follow the steps and fill in some basic information. For more information on software activation, refer to Macromedia's information at* `www.macromedia.com/software/activation`.

Flash launches with the Start page open by default. The Start page is where you can choose to create a new Flash document or open a new document from a template. After you have created a Flash document, you can open a file you have recently worked on using the Start page.

2) Create a new Flash document by clicking the Flash Document link under the Create New heading.

The Start page has several options to choose from, organized into three lists. All you need to do is click and choose an option, just as you would click a hyperlink on a Web page. Click the *Flash document* link under the *Create New* heading.

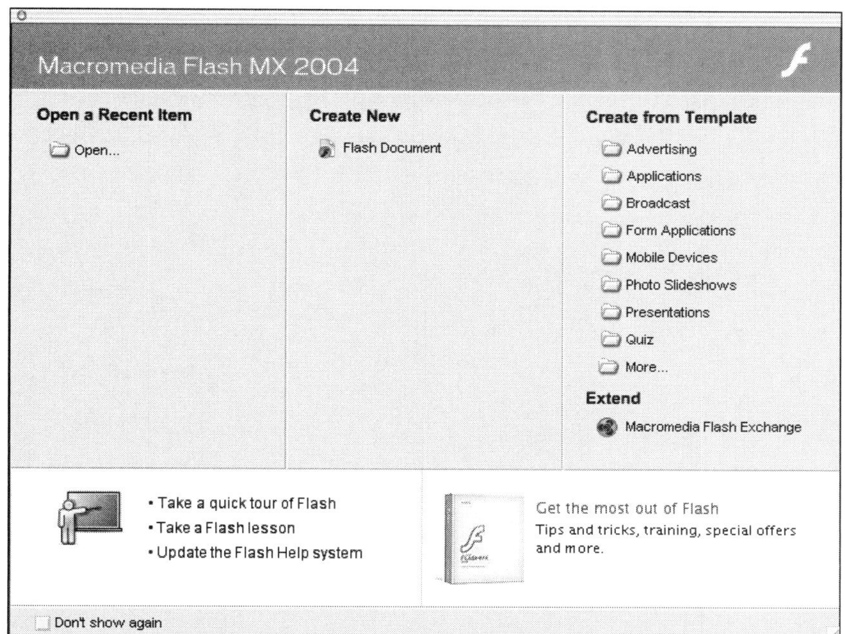

TIP *When you create any new Flash document, the document opens with the default settings. You can change these settings and make them the default so every new document opens with your own custom settings.*

If the Start page is not visible when you open Flash, choose File > New instead. Then click Flash document from the Type list and click OK to create the document. You can use this command whenever you need to create a new document when Flash is already open and running, or you can press Ctrl+Alt+N (or Command+Option+N on the Mac) to directly open a new FLA file.

NOTE *If you are using Flash MX 2004, you can create new FLA files. However, if you're using Flash MX Professional 2004, you have several additional file formats available when choosing File >New, such as new ActionScript file or new Flash Project.*

NOTE *If you don't want to see the Start page again, check the Don't show again check box at the bottom of the dialog box. If you check this option you can also set preferences to launch Flash with a new document, last documents open, or no document at all. Preferences are discussed later in the lesson.*

3) Change the dimensions of the Stage to *780* pixels by *520* pixels in the Document Properties dialog box.

Use the Property inspector to change the dimensions of the Stage. Choose Ctrl+F3 (or Command+F3 on the Mac) to open the Property inspector if it isn't already open. Click the button next to *Size:* in the Property inspector, which opens the Document Properties dialog box.

TIP *If you do not see the Size button, click anywhere on or around the Stage so the Property inspector associates itself with the Stage.*

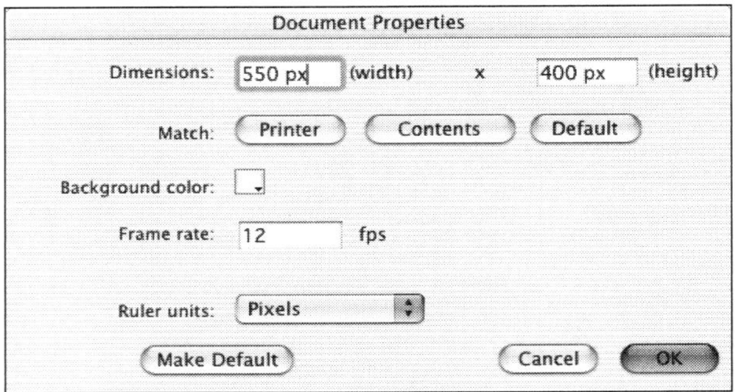

Enter *780 px* into the Width text field, and enter *520 px* into the Height text field. Click OK when you are finished, and the Stage automatically updates in the authoring environment. If you look at the Property inspector again, notice how the dimensions of the Stage are modified. These dimensions are what size the SWF file will be in a browser window.

4) Change the frames per second for the document to *21* FPS in the Property inspector.

Return to the Property inspector again, but this time look at the text field next to Frame rate. Change the default value (12) to *21*. Your SWF file will then play 21 frames every second, and because the SWF plays faster, the animations you make later on will appear to play quite smoothly. (The frame rate is also referred to FPS, which stands for "frames per second.")

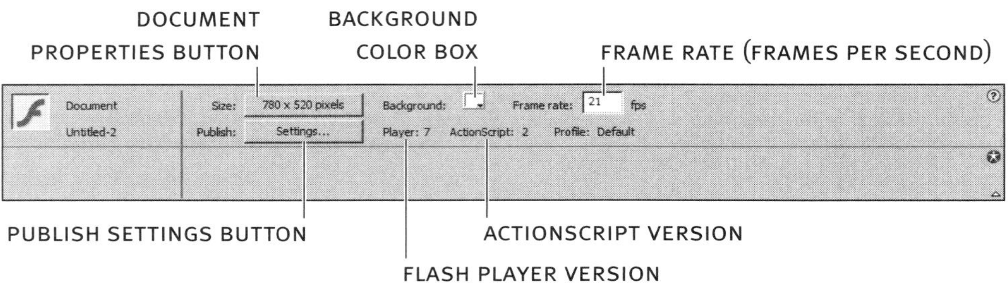

You can choose to change the background color and also view the current Publish settings, such as what Flash player version and ActionScript version the SWF is exporting for. If you need to change these settings, click the Settings button. If you want to change the background color of a SWF, click the Background Color box in the Property inspector; when the palette pops up, choose a color swatch by clicking it.

5) Choose File > Save to save the file as an FLA.

The Save dialog box opens after you choose the Save menu command. You should see Untitled-1.fla in the *File Name* text field (or Save As text field on the Mac).

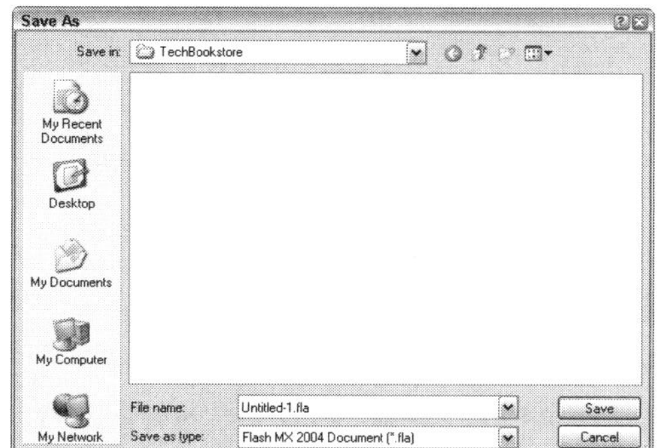

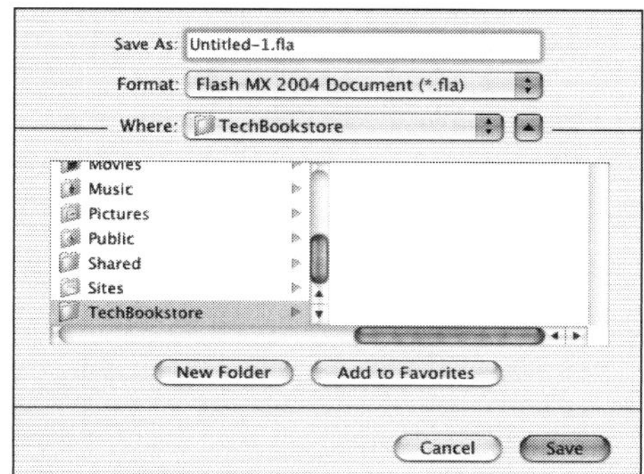

Type *bookstore1.fla* into the File Name text field, and make sure that Save as Type is set to Flash MX 2004 Document (*.fla). Note that you are saving as the Flash MX 2004 FLA file type, which is the default option. The other available option is to save as Flash MX, which enables people using Flash MX (version 6) to open your documents using the older software.

NOTE *If you have Flash MX 2004 elements in your file and try to save as a Flash MX file type, the Flash MX 2004 data will be lost. You see a warning before this happens, and are given the option to cancel the save. Even if you lose some data, you can still open the file you save in Flash MX.*

You can use the browser in the Save dialog box to navigate through your hard drive to find a suitable place to save the files you build while using this book. When you find a place to save your work, create a new folder called *TechBookstore* to save your files in. Click the Save button to save the file. Notice that `bookstore1.fla` is now displayed in the Flash title bar above the workspace.

NOTE *All the files you create for this book should be saved in the* `TechBookstore` *folder.*

6) Choose File > Close to close the document you just saved.

This command closes the open file. If you have not saved the document yet, Flash asks whether or not you want to save the changes you have made.

TIP *If you have not yet saved the changes you made to the document, you see an asterisk next to the file's Document Tab. After you save, the asterisk disappears. This feature is very useful for reminding you to save often!*

WORKING WITH PANELS

In the previous exercise, you learned what panels are and even used the Property inspector (which is a panel) to change the size of the Stage and frame rate of the Flash document. Taking a look at the features and parts of panels found in the authoring environment is important, so you can learn all about what you can create and manipulate in Flash. However, first you need to learn how to open, move, and use a panel. In this exercise, you learn more about how to open, arrange, and use panels in the workspace. In the following lessons, you will use different panels all the time to modify your work.

1) Choose File > Open, and open the `bookstore1.fla` **document from your hard drive.**

When you want to open an FLA file that's already on your hard drive, use the File > Open command to locate and open a file. The Open dialog box opens displays, where in which you can browse through files on your hard drive.

Click the file you want to open, (`bookstore1.fla`), and then click Open. The file opens in Flash.

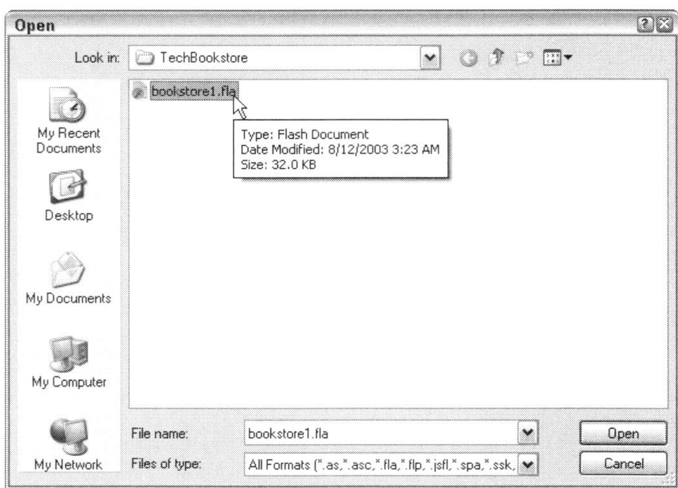

TIP *If you are opening a file in Flash MX 2004 that was previously edited using Flash MX Professional 2004 features, you might see an alert box with the following warning: This file contains Flash MX Professional data. The message also lists what kind of Flash MX Professional data is contained in the file. The document still opens and can be saved in Flash MX, but you will not be able to edit the Flash MX Professional features saved in the file. If you are using Screens, the Flash MX Professional file will not open at all in Flash MX 2004.*

2) Choose File > Save As to save a new version of `bookstore1.fla`**.**

After choosing File > Save As from the main menu, the Save As dialog box opens. Type *`bookstore2.fla`* into the File Name field and click Save when you are finished. Any changes you now make to the open document are saved to the `bookstore2.fla` on your hard drive.

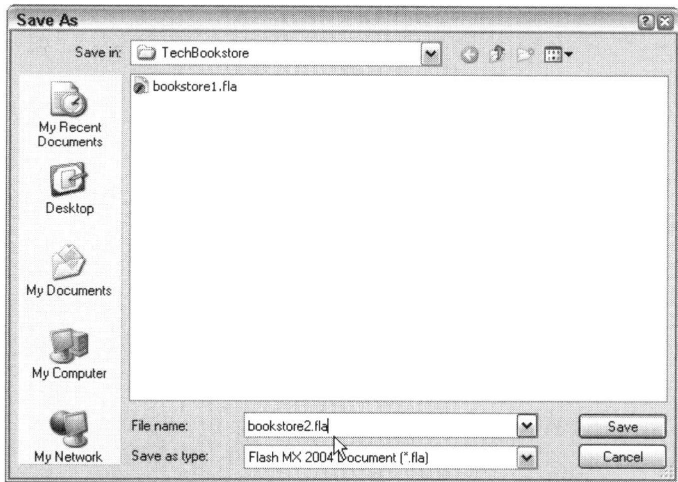

3) Open additional panels to add to the user interface from the Window menu.

Flash opens with a default panel set. The default set does not include many panels, so you will almost certainly want to add more panels to the workspace. You can open panels by selecting panels from the three sub-menus of panels (Design Panels, Developer Panels and Other Panels) under the Window menu.

Choose Window > Design Panels > Color Mixer to open the Color Mixer panel. When the panel opens it's probably not *docked* to the user interface like the other panels in the default panel set (particularly if you are using a Windows system.) Currently, the panel is *floating* because you can move it all around the Flash workspace. Docked panels are snapped to the workspace and can minimize and maximize, but can be undocked from the workspace only by dragging the panel using a specific part of its title bar. If you are on a Macintosh, you only have the option of using floating panels, which can be freely moved around the workspace using the area above its title bar. You can snap panels together into a large floating column in the Mac workspace, discussed following Step 4.

4) Dock the Color Mixer panel to the Flash workspace (Windows only) using the Gripper cursor.

Move your mouse cursor over the upper-left corner of the panel's title bar, and a four-way arrow appears. The four-way arrow cursor is called the *Gripper*.

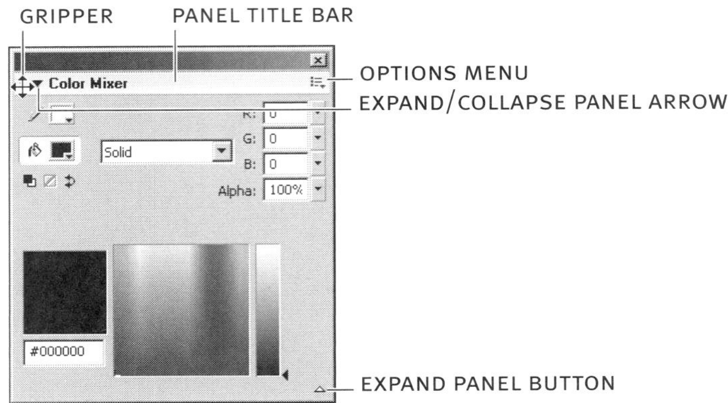

When your mouse is over the Gripper, click and drag the panel to the column of panels to the right of the Stage. When a black outline highlights a part of the workspace, it means that the panel will redock at the current location. Release the mouse button when the area you want the panel to be docked is highlighted. The panel is docked to the workspace in that area.

You can move around any docked panel using the Gripper. If you want to undock a panel, you can drag the panel using the Gripper to anywhere in the workspace and release the mouse button.

NOTE *In the Mac workspace, you can use a cursor similar to the Gripper to grab a floating panel and snap it to a column of panels. The cursor looks like a hand instead of like a four-way arrow. When you drag a panel over a set of panels using this special cursor, a highlight appears where the panel will snap just like in Windows when you dock a panel. Release the mouse button and the floating panel attaches to the column.*

5) Minimize the Color Mixer panel by clicking the panel's name.

When you click the Color Mixer panel name the Color Mixer panel minimizes (or *collapses*). You can also click the arrow next to the name to do the same thing. If you are using Windows, the other panels that are docked resize accordingly. Minimizing panels is useful if you have a lot of panels open in the workspace.

Maximize (or *expand*) the Color Mixer panel by clicking the Color Mixer title a second time.

6) Maximize the Components panel and view the panel's Options menu.

Click the Options menu button on the far-right side of the Components panel's title bar.

NOTE *The Options menu is available only if a panel is maximized.*

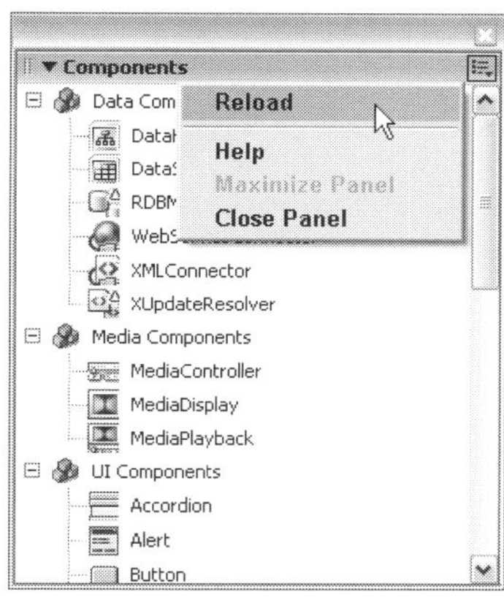

The Components panel should be open as part of the default panel set. If you do not see it open, choose Window > Development panels > Components. The menu contains the option to *Reload* the Components panel. This is useful if you are installing new components into Flash because an updated list of components will appear in the panel after you choose the menu option. Other panels, such as the Library, have many additional and very useful tools in the Options menu, such as creating new symbols, editing properties, and setting linkage. Don't forget to open the Options menu to see what tools are available when you add a new panel to the workspace.

7) Add a Button component to the document from the Components panel and then center the component on the Stage using the Align panel.

Click the Button component in the Components panel, drag it onto the Stage and release the mouse button to add the component to the application.

Open the Align panel by choosing Window > Design Panels > Align. This panel is used to center the component on the Stage. Click the To Stage button, which means you are aligning anything selected on the Stage (such as this component) relative to the dimensions of the Stage itself. If you don't have this button selected, selected items on the Stage are aligned to one another.

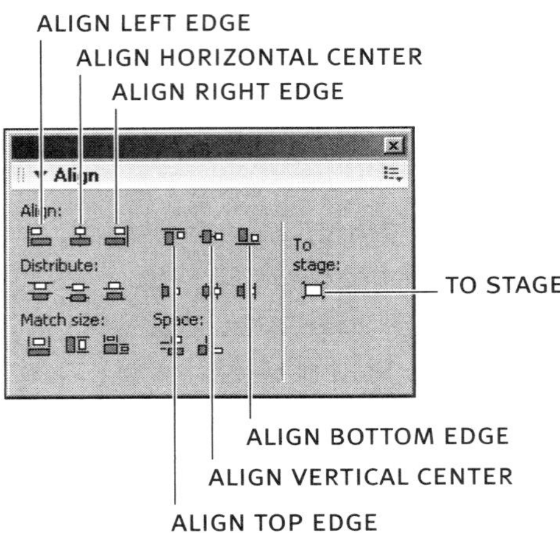

Make sure that the component is selected. If it isn't selected, select the Selection tool and click the component to select it. If it is selected, it has a blue outline around it called a *bounding box*. It also has a crosshair in the upper-left corner.

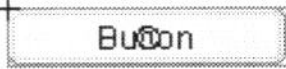

Now click the Align Horizontal Center button and then the Align Vertical Center button in the Align panel. Both of these buttons are under the Align heading in the panel (the top row), and have a small line running through the middle of the object in the icon graphic. These icons are quite helpful for making sure you choose the correct option for aligning the selected object(s) with the Stage. After you click these buttons, the component automatically moves to a new position on the Stage. It should now be centered in the middle of the Stage.

When you finish, dock the Align panel on the right side of the workspace.

8) Open more panels to author with from the Window menu.

You need several additional panels in Flash to build the Web site. Return to the Window menu, and open the following panels:

- Window > Development Panels > Actions
- Window > Development Panels > Web Services (Professional only)
- Window > Other Panels > History
- Window > Library

Repeat the process in Step 4 to dock these panels to the Flash workspace. It does not matter whether or not these panels are left open or closed in the authoring environment for now. You will set a default panel layout in the next step, and you can choose how the panels will be organized in the workspace.

9) Save the panel layout as a new panel set by choosing Window > Save Panel Layout.

The Save Panel Layout dialog box opens. Type *TechBookstore* in the Name field, and click OK. This procedure saves your workspace with all the additional panels you just opened every time you open Flash. If you return to the default layout, you can change to the `TechBookstore` panel set any time by choosing Window > Panel Sets > TechBookstore. You can set up other custom panel sets by using this option. This feature also remembers whether you have panels open or closed, and also saves these settings in your panel layout. If you decide you want panels in a particular panel set open or closed by default (or even want to add or delete certain panels), you can always overwrite the panel set. Simply choose Window > Save Panel Layout and type in the same name for your layout. Flash allows you to overwrite the old set with the new version of it.

USING THE TIMELINE AND FRAMES

All the content you work with in a SWF file is placed and organized somewhere on a Timeline. A *playhead* moves along the Timeline and shows the current frame. You move the playhead around the Timeline in order to edit your Flash document. The Timeline is a succession of *frames* or *keyframes* that exist over time, and they can be empty or filled. A document might span across many frames; however, many designers and developers only use one single frame in the authoring environment. Frames can also be *stacked* on top of one another if you include more than one layer in the FLA. Stacked layers help you separate content or create a layering effect in the document. You learn more about layers in the next exercise.

Keyframes are where changes occur on a Timeline. You might have new content in a keyframe or change a part of an animation. A keyframe can also hold ActionScript. Frames are used between keyframes to fill in parts of an animation or the Timeline. You do not define changes in frames, or else they are turned into keyframes.

Most Flash documents have more than one Timeline. Just as there are many frames, there can be many Timelines in "mini-movies" that you create *within* the Flash document. You will find out more about how there can be more than one Timeline nested within one another in Lesson 4.

In this exercise, you learn how to use the Timeline and select, move, and delete frames. You can continue using `bookstore2.fla` for this exercise.

1) If the Timeline is not open, choose Window > Timeline. The Timeline should have one layer by default, called Layer 1.

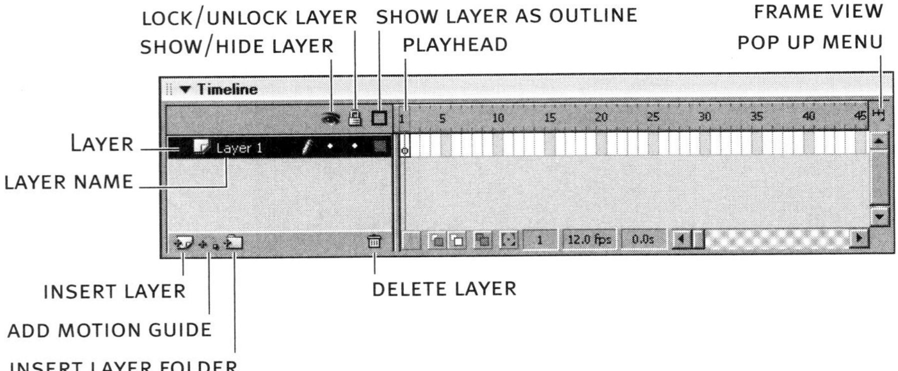

The playhead is located at frame 1. The row numbers running along the top of the Timeline represents the frame numbers along the Timeline. Frames can be referenced by number or by name using *frame labels*. You will add frame labels to a frame in the next task.

2) Lengthen the area to view the layer names by resizing the Timeline.
Drag the bar separating the layer names and frames to resize the area for viewing layer names. When you mouse over the bar, a double-ended arrow cursor appears. When this appears, you can click the bar and drag it to the right to make the layer name area larger, so you can read the entire layer name.

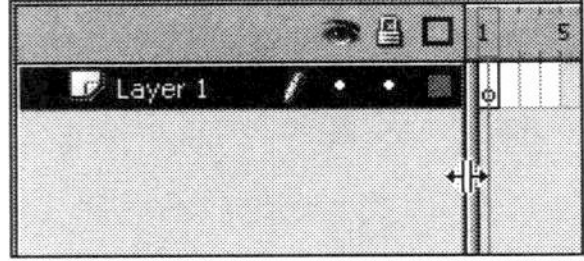

You can also display more layers by dragging the bar separating the Timeline from the application window vertically if the panel is docked. If it isn't, use the lower-right corner of the Timeline to resize the panel.

3) Choose a different frame view from the Timeline's frame view pop-up menu, or leave the default view you have been working with.

You can change the way you view frames in the Timeline. Choose the frame view pop-up menu in the upper-right corner of the Timeline.

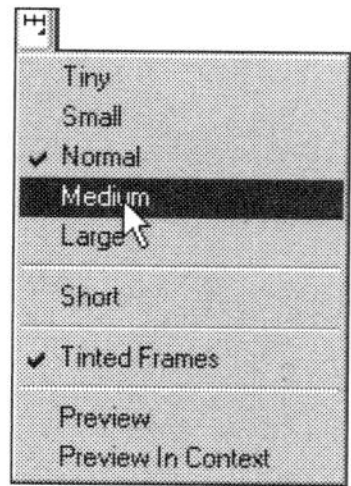

The menu allows you to change the size and appearance of frames in the Timeline. Change the width of frames by selecting Tiny, Small, Normal, Medium, or Large. Frame height is changed by selecting or deselecting the *Short* option. The grey shading you see on some frames can be turned off by selecting or deselecting *Tinted Frames*.

You can even preview content that you have in frames. Preview allows you to view the content of each frame within the Timeline. If you want to display thumbnails of each filled and empty frame, select *Preview in Context*. This feature is useful when you are creating animations because you can view how it progresses over time.

For this project, you will use the default settings of *Normal* sized frames and leave *Tinted Frames* on (selected).

4) Create a new keyframe and a frame on Layer 1 by choosing Insert > Timeline > Keyframe.

A new document has an empty keyframe in frame 1 of `Layer 1`. When you added the component onto the Stage in the previous exercise, the empty keyframe (hollow dot) turned into a keyframe (filled dot).

NOTE *You can add content to the Timeline only if a frame or keyframe is selected. If there are no frames on the layer you have selected, you must first create a keyframe to add content to.*

You can create frames and keyframes using menu commands or keyboard shortcuts. From the menu, you can create a new keyframe by choosing Insert > Timeline > Keyframe or create a frame by choosing Insert > Timeline > Frame. You can also right-click (or control-click on the Mac) on a frame and use the contextual menu to add new frames or keyframes.

NOTE *This book uses the keyboard shortcuts F6 (Keyframe) and F5 (Frame) to insert new frames on the Timeline instead of using the menu. Using shortcuts is a much quicker way of inserting new frames, and it is a good habit to develop.*

Select frame 2 with your mouse and press F6. Another filled keyframe is created, which is exactly the same as the keyframe in frame 1. If you modify this keyframe, perhaps by selecting and then moving the component, the keyframe will differ from frame 1.

Select frame 3 and press F5 to create a new frame. If you change the content in this new frame, the changes will be reflected in frame 2 because content can change only in keyframes.

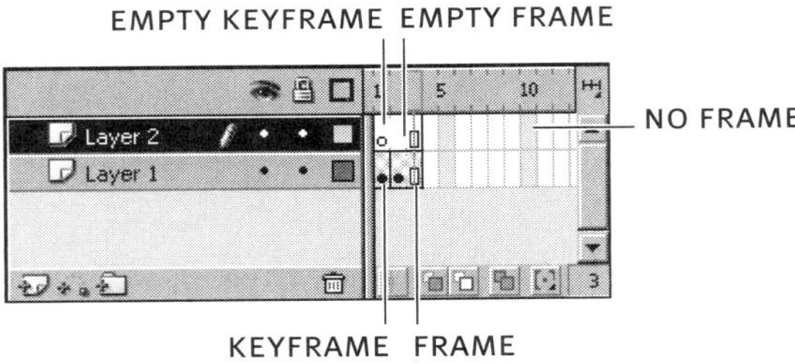

5) Select, move, and delete frames on the Timeline by using your mouse and the Shift key.

You have already selected a frame in Step 4 by clicking on the frame. You can select multiple frames in a row by clicking on the first frame, and then hold the Shift key while clicking on the last frame. If you don't want to select continuous frames, hold the Ctrl or Command keys while clicking individual frames. To select all the frames on the Timeline, right-click (or control-click on the Mac) and choose Select All Frames from the contextual menu.

Select the frame 2 and 3 of Layer 1 and then drag the selection to frames 4 and 5. You are moving these two frames to a new location.

Notice that frame 1 now extends to frame 3. If you want to copy and then move a keyframe instead, simply hold down the Alt or Option keys while dragging the selected keyframe to a new frame.

NOTE *If you select a keyframe on the Timeline, everything on that keyframe is selected on the Stage. If you select an element on the Stage, its associated keyframe is selected on the Timeline.*

6) Delete the Button component and frames by selecting them and pressing the Backspace or Delete keys.

Because you do not need a Button component at this time, delete the component from the Stage. Select the Button component and then press the Backspace or Delete key. You can also delete things from the Stage by right-clicking or control-clicking and choosing Cut from the contextual menu.

The Timeline changes after you delete the component from the Stage. Your keyframe is now an empty keyframe, represented by an empty circle where it used to be filled.

Select all the empty frames on the Timeline except for frame 1. To delete them, right-click (or control-click on the Mac) and choose Remove Frames from the contextual menu.

7) Save the changes you have made to the document by choosing File > Save from the main menu.

UNDERSTANDING LAYERS

Now that you understand Timelines, you should learn more about how to use layers on the Timeline. Layers are in the Timeline and are *stacked* on top of one another. You can create many new layers by using the Insert Layer button in the Timeline. The elements on these layers such as graphics, text and components, appear to be stacked; however, all the unfilled (blank) area is transparent.

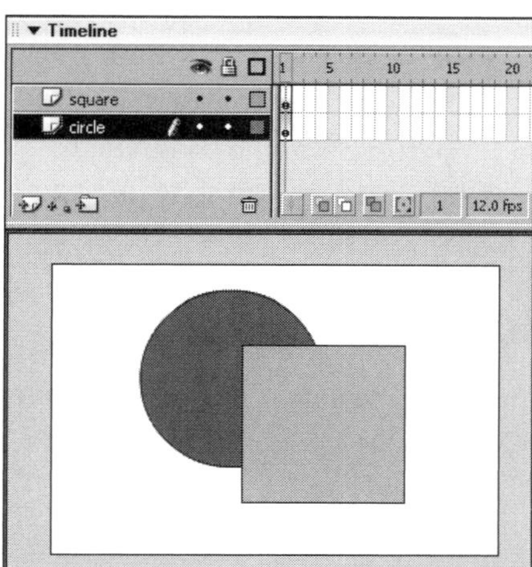

Flash designers and developers tend to organize similar elements onto layers, using them to organize FLA files. It is a great habit to get into! For example, a designer might put all of his or her components on one layer and sound on a different layer. An advantage of using multiple layers is that you can create and modify elements in Flash on one layer, and it doesn't affect content on other layers. Another advantage is that it helps you find elements in your document quickly and easily. You will create many layers throughout the course of this book.

TIP *It is good practice to put all ActionScript in its own layer whenever possible, called actions. Many people who work with Flash make sure that this layer is always on the top of the layer stack, so it is easy to find and does not conflict as much with other parts of the SWF file.*

Layers can be organized into folders. Layer folders are typically used to hold several layers that are related to one another. Folders can be named, and you can open and close the folder to view or hide the layers contained within. There are several kinds of layers that you can use in Flash documents as well. You can have guide layers that include information about the Flash document helping you draw or edit the FLA, or information for other Flash developers to whom you pass the FLA for further editing. Motion guide layers include information for animating particular graphics and creating special effects. The contents of guide layers are not included in the published SWF. You will use motion guide layers in Lesson 5.

In this exercise, you will learn how to add and name new layers and change their properties. You also learn how to organize layers into layer folders. You should still be using `bookstore2.fla` for this exercise.

1) If the Timeline is not already open, choose Window > Timeline from the main menu.

A new document opens with a single layer called Layer 1. You can change the name of the layer by double-clicking it and typing in a new name or right-clicking (control-clicking on the Mac) the layer name and choosing Properties from the contextual menu. The name, type, and height of the layer are among the things Flash allows you to change using this dialog box.

2) Rename `Layer 1` by double-clicking the layer's name and typing in *background*.

After you double click the layer's name (`Layer 1`), the name becomes editable and you can type in a new name for the layer. Press Enter after you finish typing `background` as the new name for `Layer 1`.

TIP *It is always a good idea to give each layer a descriptive name. After your documents get large with many layers, it is easy to forget what items are on that particular layer.*

3) Add a new layer by clicking the Insert Layer button and rename the layer *labels*.

A new layer called `Layer 2` is added after you click the Insert Layer button. Double-click the `Layer 2` name, and then type in *labels*. Press Enter after you finish typing the new layer name.

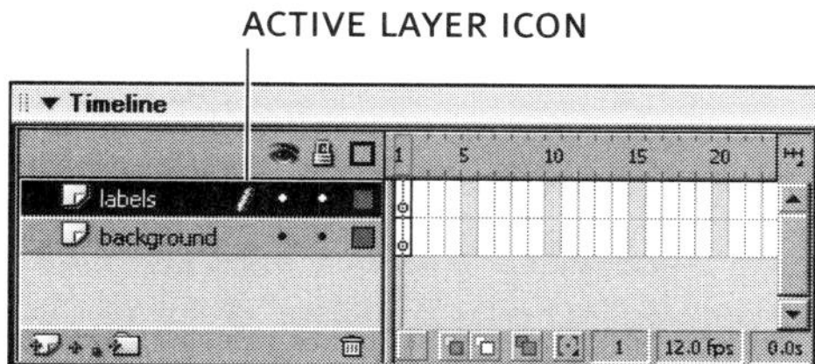

The active layer has a small pencil icon next to its name. Click the `background` layer now. If anything is created or dragged onto the Stage, it is placed on the active layer. Any edits or changes you make to a layer are made to the active layer.

4) Add a frame label to the new `labels` layer by entering a name into the `<Frame Label>` field in the Property inspector.

Frame labels are used to name a particular frame number. They can be referenced using ActionScript, so you do not have to enter a frame number into the code. Frame labels can be moved around the Timeline by clicking and dragging them to a new location.

Click the labels layer to highlight it and make it active. Maximize the Property inspector and make sure that the playhead is at frame 1. In the text field marked `<Frame Label>`, type *home*. Now frame 1 in the labels layer is represented by a small red flag, meaning that the frame is labeled.

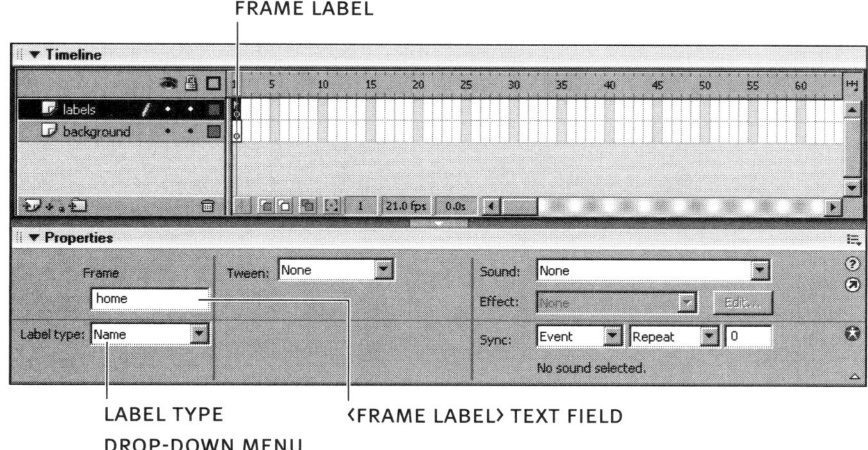

5) Lock the `label` layer by clicking the Lock Layer button.

Click the dot that is under the Lock Layer icon, and a small icon of a lock replaces the dot. Clicking the dot locks the `label` layer so you cannot add anything to the Stage on the layer unless it is unlocked first. Clicking the Lock Layer icon next to a layer name unlocks that layer.

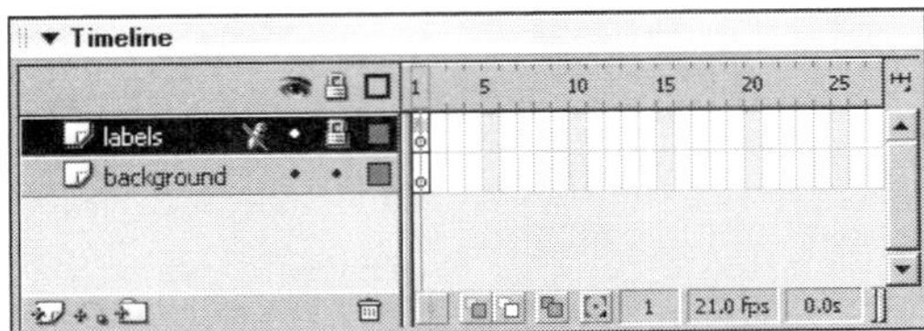

Locking layers is very useful when you want to control your selections and to avoid accidentally placing elements on the Stage in a layer into which you do not want to enter new content. An example of a good layer to lock is one that contains code. Sometimes having elements such as graphics on a layer containing code can cause conflicts. You can avoid placing anything on these layers; yet still add code and labels.

You can also change the *visibility* of a layer by using the small dot under the Show/Hide layer icon that looks like an eye. When you click the Show/Hide layer icon, a red X replaces the dot, and everything on that particular layer is hidden.

6) Create a layer folder by clicking the New Layer Folder button.

Folders help you organize layers into related content. Select the `background` layer and then click the New Layer Folder button. A layer folder, called `Folder 1`, is created above the `background` layer. Double-click the folder name and rename it *graphics*. The folder does not have any contents. Click the `background` layer and, while holding the mouse button, drag it on top of the `graphics` folder. Notice that the `background` layer is now indented underneath the `graphics` folder, which means that the layer is now inside the `graphics` folder.

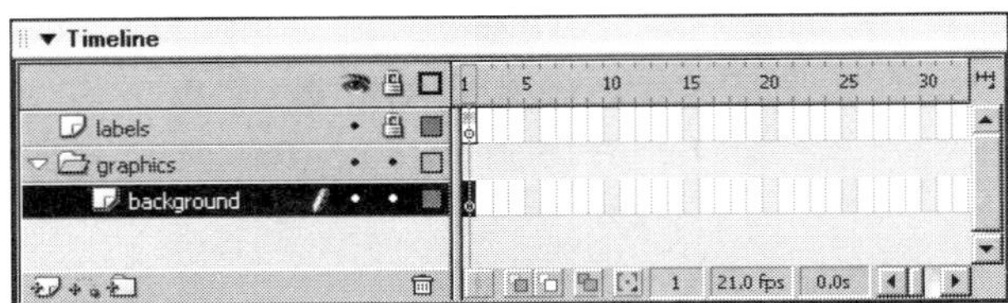

If you click the arrow next to a folder's name, it toggles the folder between open and closed. If a folder is open, the arrow points downwards. Try clicking the arrow to toggle the `graphics` folder between open and closed. After you have finished toggling the folder, leave the folder open (arrow pointing downwards).

7) Create a new layer and then create a shape on the Stage using the Rectangle tool.
Click the `background` layer and then press the Insert Layer button, which creates a new layer directly above the `background` layer. Double-click the layer's name and rename it as *temp*. With the `temp` layer selected, choose the Oval tool in the Tools pane.

Click and drag the cursor diagonally anywhere on the Stage by using this tool. While you are dragging, you can see an outline of what the oval will look like when it is created. When you have a shape that you like, release the tool to create an oval.

8) Create a shape on the `background` layer.
Select the `background` layer and then choose the Rectangle tool from the Tools pane.

Click and drag diagonally across the Stage, just like when you created the oval. Make sure some of the Rectangle overlaps the oval shape you just created. Release the mouse button to form the rectangle. You should see how the oval is layered on top of the rectangle.

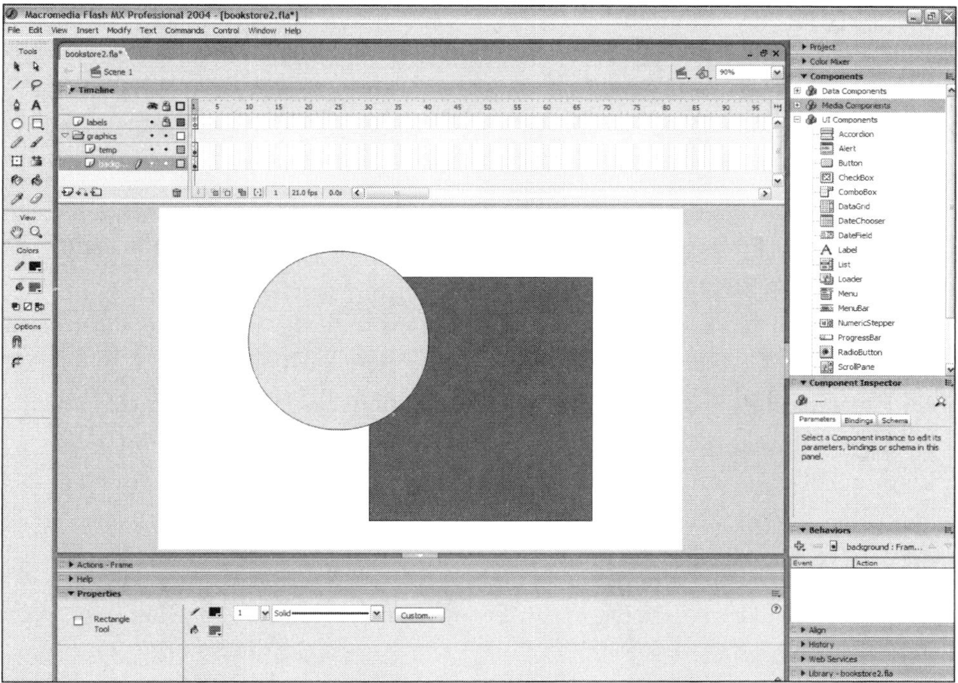

9) Change the order the `background` and `temp` layers are stacked in.

Now, click the `temp` layer on the Timeline and drag it underneath the `background` layer. You see a thick line beneath the `background` layer, which means that the `temp` layer will be moved to that location. Release the mouse button, and the layering of the rectangle and oval is reversed.

This example shows you how layering works in Flash. You won't actually be using these particular graphics in the final document, but hopefully it gives you an idea about how you will layer elements in the following lessons. Select the keyframe in the `background` layer and press the Backspace or Delete key, which deletes everything on that frame.

10) Delete the `temp` layer by clicking the Delete Layer button.

Because you do not need the `temp` layer for the final document, you can delete it from the Timeline. Select the `temp` layer so it is active and then click the Delete Layer button. You can also right-click (control-click on the Mac) the selected layer and choose Delete Layer from the contextual menu.

11) Save your changes by choosing File > Save from the main menu.

SETTING YOUR PREFERENCES

Preferences allow you to control many parts of Flash, from general editing to vector graphics to ActionScript settings. The Preferences dialog box allows you to change settings for the document you are working on or set the changes you make to be the default settings for each file you create in Flash. This exercise shows you what the many preference settings do, so you can choose which ones to change and which ones to leave at the default settings.

1) Choose Edit > Preferences (or Flash > Preferences on the Mac) from the main menu to open the Preferences dialog box.

There are several tabs in this dialog box, allowing you to change many different sections of Flash at once. Each of these tabs covers a different area of Flash. The General tab covers basic settings that are used to control authoring files. The Editing tab contains settings for drawing, vectors, and text. The Clipboard tab is used to control image settings, such as the way gradients are affected and Freehand text. The Warnings tab allows you to choose what warnings appear in Flash. The ActionScript tab lets you make settings for the code editor and class paths.

Click each tab and explore some of the settings that you can change using this dialog box.

2) Change Undo levels value to *150* in the General tab.

The number of Undo levels sets the number of times you can choose to undo your creations, modifications and commands in Flash. You can "undo" by choosing Edit > Undo from the main menu. By entering *150* into the Undo levels text field in the General tab, you allow yourself to "undo" 150 times. The higher the value you have for this field means that more system resources will be used, so do not set the number too high.

3) Change *On Launch* to *Last Documents Open*, or leave it at Start Page and check the other General tab settings.

The General tab also gives you the option of changing how Flash launches. You can either use the Start page (which provides links to choose what files you want to open), or you can set Flash to automatically open the documents that were most recently used in Flash. If you are sharing a computer with other people using Flash, this might not be the best option to choose! If you are sharing a computer or working on other projects, you might want to leave the setting at the Start page, which gives you the most control over what opens.

Make sure that your other settings are the same as seen in the following figure. You should have Shift Select and Show Tooltips options selected, which allows you to hold the Shift key while adding objects to a selection and tooltips will show when you mouse over parts of the workspace. Leave the Highlight color and Font mapping settings at the default settings. Then choose the Show Start Page radio button under On Launch, which means the Start page will appear each time you start up Flash.

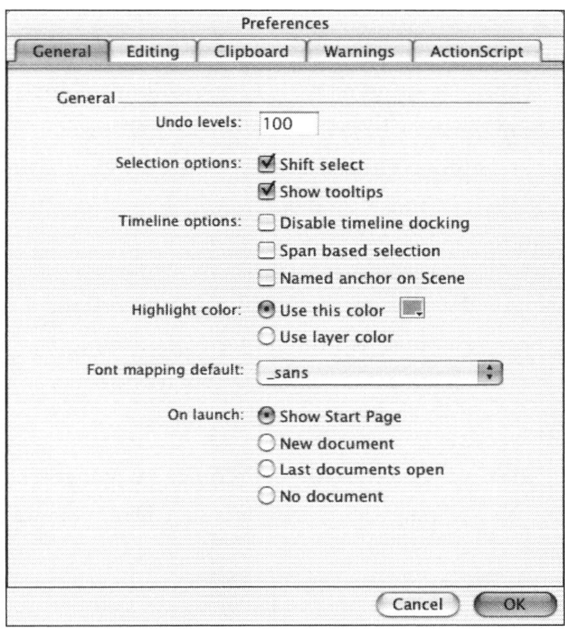

4) In the Editing tab, change the default drawing settings.

Make sure that you have made the following changes to the default drawing settings in the Editing tab. Choose the *Normal* setting for Connect lines, Smooth curves and Click accuracy. Turn Recognize lines and Recognize shapes to the *Off* setting for now (you won't need assistance from Flash in drawing shapes on the Stage.)

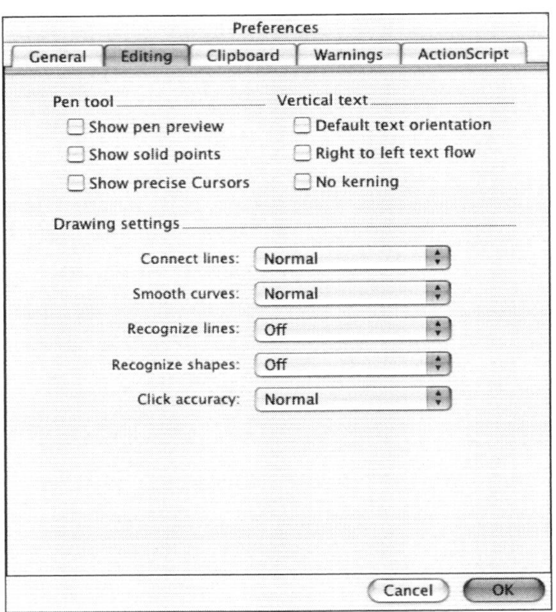

These settings affect how the drawing tools, such as the Pencil tool, make lines. *Connect lines* determines how close two line ends have to be before they snap together to make a single line. *Smooth curves* determines how much smoothing is applied to a line. Smoothing removes the jagged edges that are in most hand-drawn lines. This setting is useful because any lines you might draw by hand are usually improved with a bit of smoothing applied. Besides improving the look of your drawings, it also manages to optimize the application slightly because there are fewer shapes for Flash to render when you put the SWF file online.

If *Recognize lines* is applied, Flash changes a hand-drawn line that is close to straight into a line that is absolutely straight. *Recognize shapes* is similar in that a drawing that is close to a common shape (such as a circle or square) is changed into a perfect rendition. You do not need these options, so they can be turned off for now.

Click accuracy refers to how close the cursor must be to an object for it to be recognized as clicked and selected. Set this option to Normal, which is an accuracy level you are probably used to.

5) Choose Edit > Customize Tools Panel to customize the Tools panel.

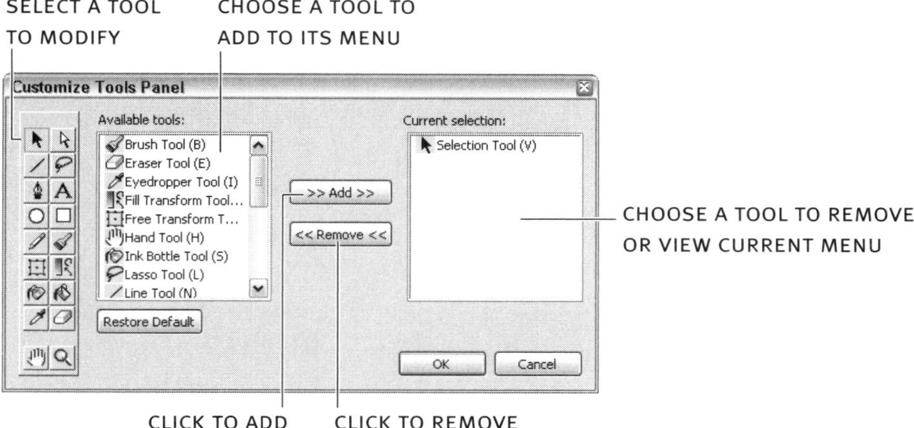

The Customize Tools Panel dialog box is used to rearrange the Tools panel or add extra tools that you might have installed into Flash as part of an extension. To use this dialog box, select a tool on the far left to modify. This tool now shows in the *Selected tool* pane on the far right. If you want to add a tool to a drop-down menu for this button, select a tool from the *Available tools* pane and click the Add button. That tool is now added to the list on the far right.

When you have more than one tool chosen for a button, a small arrow shows up next to the button icon in the Tools panel. Click the button in the Tools panel; a menu drops down from that tool where you can make a selection.

TESTING YOUR FLA

A Flash document cannot be shared online without publishing it into a format that works online. However, before you publish something to upload, you probably want to test it out to see whether all the features in your FLA actually work! Lesson 13 has detailed information on publishing Flash documents and putting them on the Web, but this exercise will walk you through the basics.

1) Choose File > Save As with `bookstore2.fla` **open, and save a new version as** `bookstore3.fla`**.**

Save a new version of `bookstore2.fla`. Make sure you save it in the `TechBookstore` folder on your hard drive.

2) Select the `background` **layer and then drag a Button component from the Components panel to the Stage.**

Drop the Button component anywhere on the Stage on the `background` layer. You simply need something on the Stage so you don't have to test an empty document.

3) Choose Control › Test Movie from the main menu to test the FLA.

The testing environment opens, and your file is displayed as a SWF. When you mouse over the Button component, notice that it glows around the button, which means your document is currently playing in a Flash player.

This is how your SWF file would appear online when it is playing in the Flash player; however, you haven't even left the Flash application.

4) Click the *X* button at the upper-right corner of the Stage (Win) or the upper left of the window (Mac) to close the testing environment.

You can also choose File > Close to close the testing environment. The test movie closes and you are taken back to the authoring environment.

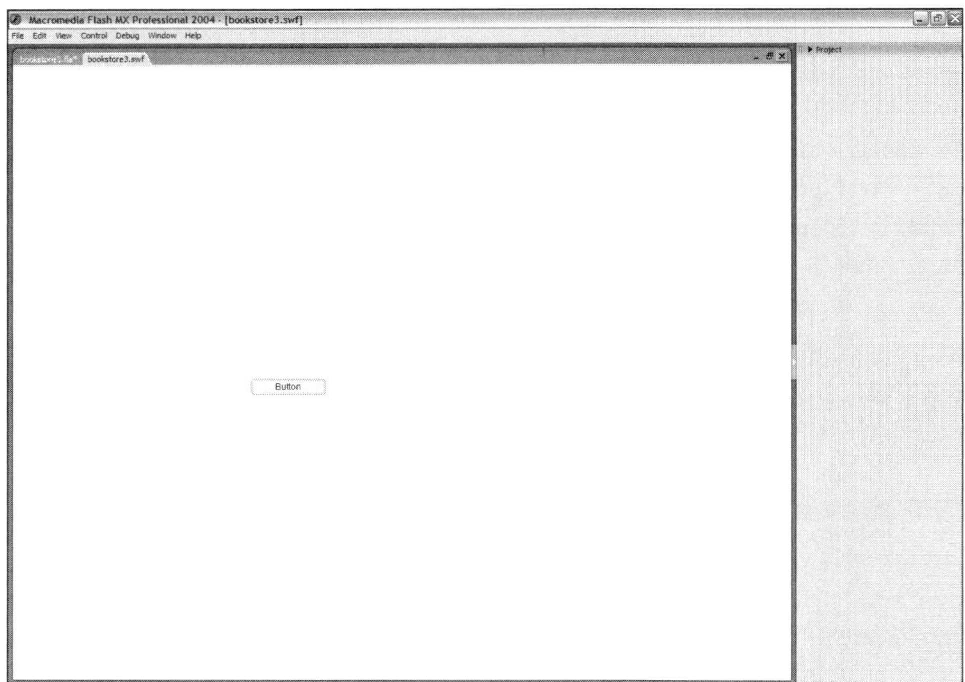

5) Choose File › Publish to publish the FLA file and then find it on your hard drive.

You will briefly see the Publishing dialog box while your document is publishing to the folder where the FLA is saved. When you publish an FLA, a SWF file and HTML file are created by default. This is the file that is played using a browser version of the Flash player when you embed it in an HTML page or the player itself. The SWF file is a compiled version of your FLA that includes all of the graphics and code along the Timeline contained in one small file. You need to at least upload the SWF file for your document for it to be visible online.

Open the `TechBookstore` folder you saved on the hard drive and find `bookstore3.html` and `bookstore3.swf`.

6) Double-click the `bookstore3.html` file and double-click the `bookstore3.swf` file.

The HTML file opens in your default Internet browser, and the SWF file opens in the Flash Player.

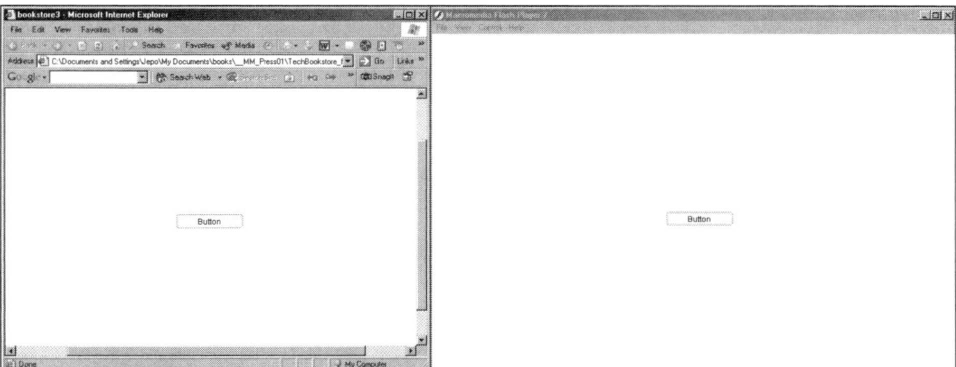

The `bookstore3` SWF file is embedded into the `bookstore3` HTML code using the `<object>` and `<embed>` tags that are created when you publish the FLA. You will learn much more about publishing Flash documents in Lesson 13. Close each of these files and return to Flash.

7) Delete the component from the `background` layer.

Select the Button component on the Stage and press the Backspace or Delete key to remove it from the Stage.

8) Save the changes you made to the file by choosing File > Save.

FINDING HELP

Flash has a very sophisticated Help system. The Help panel has two tabs—the Help tab and the How Do I tab—each containing different kinds of documentation organized into several books. The Help tab includes the *ActionScript Dictionary*, *ActionScript Reference Guide*, *Getting Started with Flash*, *Using Components* and *Using Flash*. The Help documentation might contain some answers you have when you get stuck with a project, or allow you to learn new things in Flash. The *ActionScript Dictionary*, which has documentation on all parts of the ActionScript language, gives you a short description of the way each action works. The *ActionScript Reference Guide* teaches you about ActionScript syntax and coding conventions. *Getting Started with Flash* contains information about using the authoring environment, and *Using Components* and *Using Flash* help you learn how to create Flash documents and also link to parts of the documentation on ActionScript.

TIP *If you are using Flash MX 2004, not all parts of the Help system will apply to you. Both versions of Flash use the same Help documentation. You can tell whether a feature is available only in Flash MX Professional if it says "Flash Professional Only" in the title of the topic.*

The How Do I tab contains three books called *Quick Start*, *Basic Flash* and *Basic ActionScript*. These books contains tutorials that help you learn how to create basic documents using Flash.

1) Choose Help > Help or press F1 to open the Help panel.

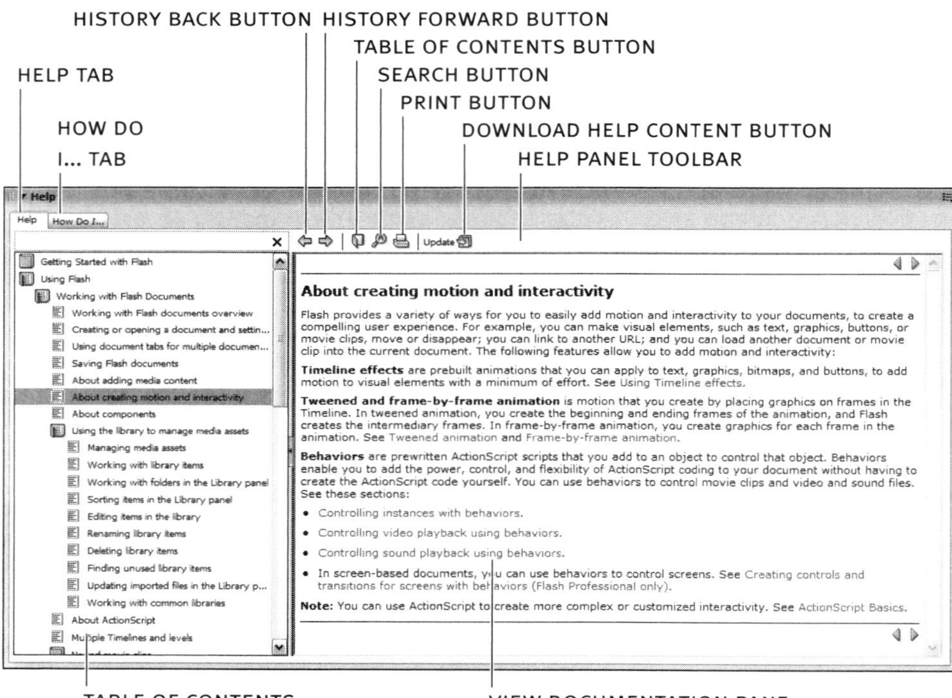

If you do not see the Table of Contents on the left side of the panel, click the Table of Contents button in the Help panel's toolbar. When it opens, you see a series of books containing many topics to choose from. If you click the How Do I tab, you see several different books available for browsing that are different from those in the Help tab.

If you click one of these books in either tab, the Table of Contents expands to include a list of topics in each book. Clicking a topic opens the documentation in the Help panel. Take a second to browse through some of the books in the Help tab.

2) Click the Download Help Content in the Help panel toolbar.

When you click the Download Help Content button (next to the word Update), any new additions to Flash documentation are downloaded from Macromedia's servers and added to the documentation on your computer. You have to make sure that your computer is online before you press the button, so you can connect to Macromedia. If no new content is available, you will see an alert saying that no new help content is available after you click the Update button.

TIP *It is a good idea to get into the practice of seeing whether you can download new help content on a regular basis.*

3) Click the Search button in the Help panel toolbar to open a text field to perform searches in.

A text field used to enter search queries opens above the Table of Contents pane. When you search a topic, only documents from the books in the current selected tab are returned. Meaning that if you search for the word `brush` in the Help tab, it returns documents only from the books listed in the Help tab's Table of Contents.

Type *brush* into the Search field after you select the Help tab, and a series of topics are returned to the Table of Contents. Click The Pen tool in this list, and the content shows up in the pane to the right. Notice that there are two arrow buttons at the bottom of the content area. These buttons enable you to navigate to the previous and next topics in the current book.

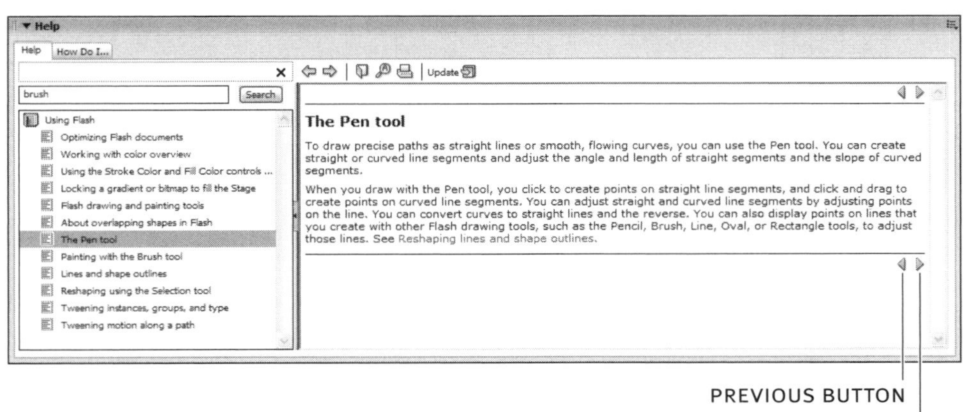

NOTE *If you did not find a search topic, [No Entries were Found] displays in the Table of Contents.*

4) Find some help online.

You don't always have to look within Flash to find help: You can also go online to find your answers. A great place to begin is at `www.macromedia.com`, in which you can find Tech Notes, a Support area, the Development Center with many helpful articles and tutorials, and links to inspirational and helpful Web sites.

Also, use a search engine to enter keywords of the subject you are having trouble with. There are many community Web sites out there that show up with helpful hints and forums, email lists, and people willing to help you solve a Flash problem. Remember to go to this book's Web site at `www.TrainingFromTheSource.com` to find help and resources as well!

EXPLORING THE PROJECT

You will create a fully working Web site by the end of this book. The techniques you learn can be applied to any Web site or project you build in Flash. Many parts of this site can be recycled into your own projects.

You can see the finished Web site online at `http://flash.TrainingFromTheSource.com`.

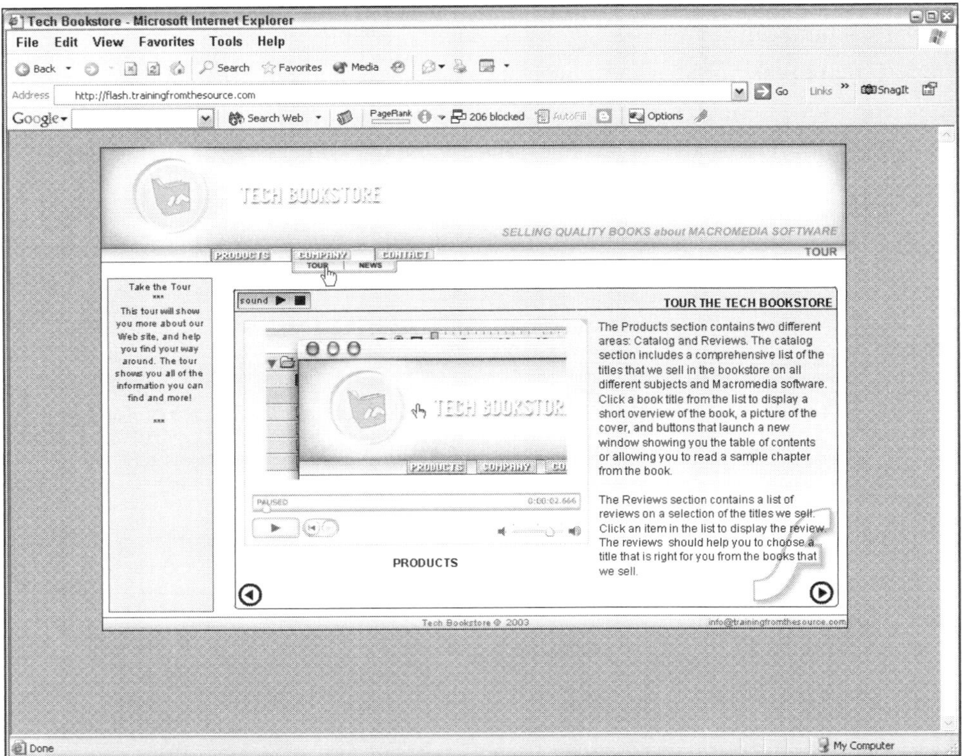

The Web site is a SWF that is embedded in an HTML page. The HTML page has some modification, so it is centered on the page with a custom background pattern. Click the three buttons near the top to explore the various areas in the Web site. The site includes various amounts of dynamic data loaded into many of the different components that ship with Flash MX 2004 and Flash MX Professional 2004. Notice all the graphics, animation, presentation, video, dynamic, and sound elements within this single Web site.

Because these components use some of the features specific to Flash Player 7, anyone viewing the site will need that player version (or greater) to view the Web site. If you don't have Flash Player 7 or greater, go download and install the latest player from: `www.macromedia.com/go/getflashplayer`.

WHAT YOU HAVE LEARNED

In this lesson, you have:

- Discovered the Flash authoring environment (pages 9–11)
- Learned how to create and save a new document (pages 12–16)
- Learned how to modify document settings (pages 12–16)
- Worked with panels (pages 16–21)
- Used and modified frames and layers on the Timeline (pages 21–25)
- Gained an understanding of layers (pages 25–30)
- Set and customized your preferences (pages 30–33)
- Found out how to solve problems using the Help panel (pages 35–38)
- Taken a look at the book's project (pages 38–39)

creating graphics

LESSON 2

To make a document in Flash, you do not need graphics, animation, or even more than one frame! However, SWF files that do not contain graphics or animation can sometimes lack some visual interest. Typically, you have to create or include some kind of visual element to create an appealing SWF file. The drawing tools and the capability to import various kinds of media help you put together presentations that can engage viewers. Flash also provides tools that help you with layout and visual editing. You have a lot of control over what you can create using Flash.

In this lesson, you will learn how to create most of the graphics needed by the main Flash document used for this book's project. The graphics you create and import will be used for the main layout, the logo animation, and the menu system. You will also discover how to manipulate these graphics, and create and use a mask layer. All these skills help form the foundation of Flash as a graphics and animation tool!

The finished background.

WHAT YOU WILL LEARN

In this lesson, you will:

- Navigate the Tools panel
- Use the drawing tools to create graphics
- Use guides and snapping
- Create and use a mask layer
- Use strokes
- Learn about the Library and assets
- Import and optimize bitmaps
- Import vector drawings
- Work with colors and fill
- Create and manipulate graphics

APPROXIMATE TIME

This lesson takes approximately 1 hour and 30 minutes to complete.

LESSON FILES

Media Files:

company_down.png
company_up.png
contact_down.png
contact_up.png
products_down.png
products_up.png
title.png
logo.png
map.FH11

Starting Files:

Lesson02/bookstore4.fla

Completed Project:

Lesson02/bookstore6.fla

USING THE TOOLS PANEL

You already used a few tools from the Tools panel (also known as the toolbar and the toolbox) in Lesson 1. In this lesson, you will learn a lot more about what you can do with the drawing tools. There are four main parts of the Tools panel: Tools, View, Colors, and Options. Hovering the mouse over a button makes a tooltip appear that contains the name of the tool. Simply click one of the buttons to select a tool. A tool button can also have a menu attached to it. If so, there is a small black arrow next to the button's icon. Click and hold the button to open the menu and then select a tool from the menu that appears.

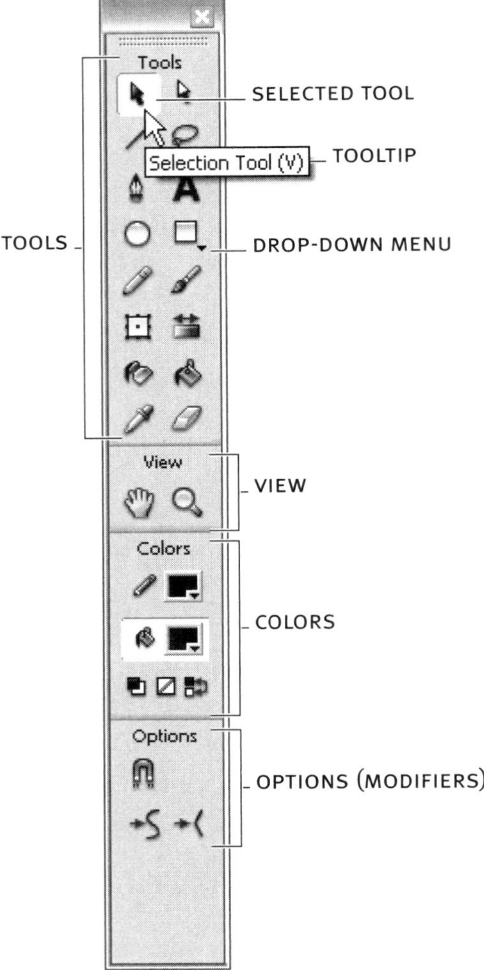

The Tools panel contains tools for selecting, creating and manipulating graphics; and for changing the view of the Stage. Some tools might also have several options available, which appear in the lower section of the Tools panel when the tool is selected (if they are available).

When you have a tool selected, the contents of the Property inspector change to reflect what tool is being used. When the Text tool is selected in the Tools panel, as shown in the earlier graphic, the Property inspector changes to display the text properties you can edit. Most tools work by simply clicking and dragging the tool on the Stage area.

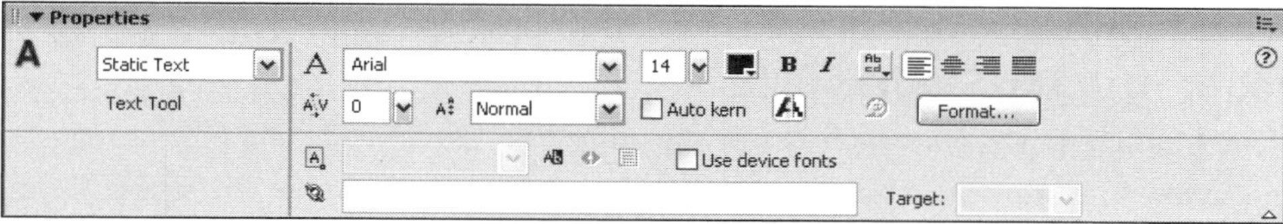

Now let's take a look at the tools in the Flash Tools panel.

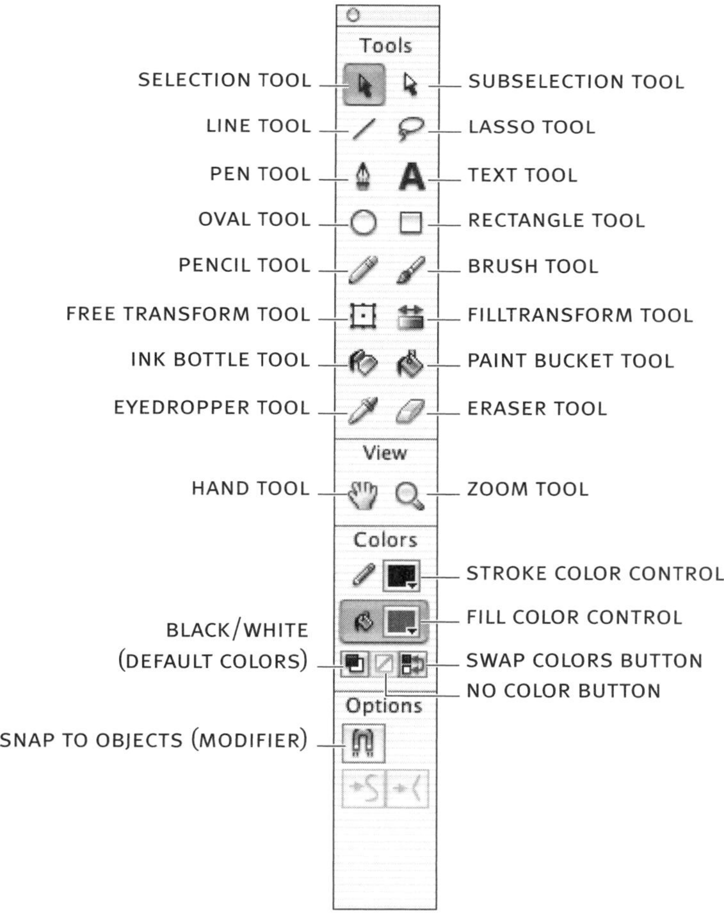

The Selection (arrow), Subselection, and Lasso tools are used to select elements on the Stage. The Line, Pen, Text, Oval, Rectangle, Pencil, and Brush tools are used to create graphics. The Free and Fill Transform tools; Ink Bottle, Paint Bucket, Eyedropper, and Eraser are for modifying graphics. In the View area, the Hand and Zoom tools are used to move the Stage around (Hand) or to magnify or minimize the Stage (Zoom). The Colors area is used to choose stroke or fill colors when you create shapes. Remember that there are additional settings for each tool in the Options area and/or Property inspector.

About Fills and Strokes

Some tools create *strokes*, which can be the outline around a shape or a line you draw on the Stage. A stroke can be of varying thickness defining the edge of a shape. Or, a stroke might be a line on the Stage that doesn't outline a shape. For example, it might be a spiral or a curve drawn *freehand* using a pencil. A stroke can have properties such as color, style (dotted or rippled, for example), or thickness.

Other tools, such as the Oval, Rectangle and Paint Bucket, create shapes that have a *fill* or add a fill to an existing shape. A fill is the area *inside* a closed or open shape. It can be a solid color, gradient or bitmap (image). A fill can be inside a shape that has gaps, as long as those gaps aren't too large. When you create a shape with a fill and a stroke, the two parts are not grouped together, which helps keep the SWF file size a bit lower. You can select both fill and stroke together by double-clicking the fill. You can use the Options area in the Tools panel to make settings about how big the gaps can be. Or, you can set a shape to have no fill at all. The Brush tool creates brushstrokes that are made of fill color.

Sometimes it takes a little time to get used to using fills in your work when working with drawings *on the same layer*. When you create a fill on the Stage, a stroke cutting through it divides the fill you created into two separate regions.

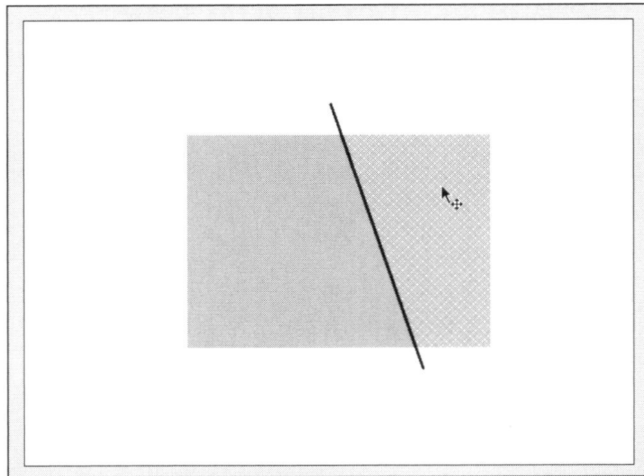

All touching fills or strokes that have exactly the same color will be selected as a single element. And as you saw earlier, if part of that fill or stroke is intersected by a differently colored fill or any color of stroke, the element is broken into regions that are separately selected. If you place one shape on top of another that is a different color, the shape layered underneath is lost. This is seen in the following figure, where a green triangle was placed over a blue circle and then moved.

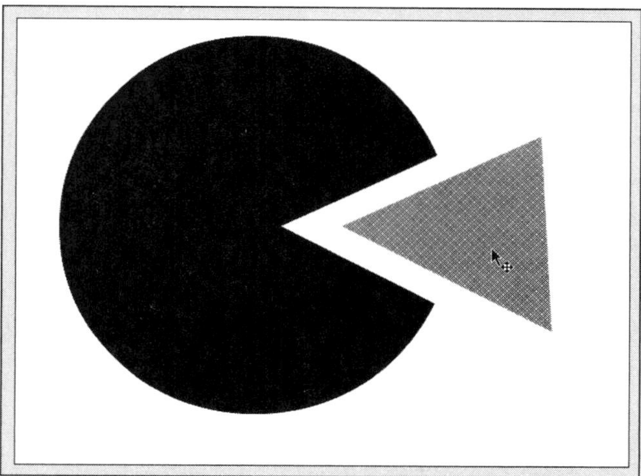

To avoid having a fill break apart when you pass a stroke across it, or join colors that are the same, use layers to break apart your drawings. Layers will keep the different elements separate, so you can move them individually using the Selection tool.

Using Vector and Bitmap Images

The drawings that you create in Flash are made up of *vectors*, which is the native graphics format in Flash. Vector graphics are made up of lines and curves that are defined by mathematical calculations, whereas *bitmap* images (that you might import into Flash) are made up of many pixels on a grid. Because a vector graphic is made up of calculations, it usually means the image is lower in file size.

When vector graphics are resized, the calculations are remade for the new proportions and the vector recreates the drawing on the Stage. This means when vector drawings are scaled, you do not lose image quality like you do when you scale bitmap images. When a bitmap image is resized on the Stage, the pixels are resized, so the image might become distorted and lose quality.

ABOUT COLOR

Color in Flash relies on palettes that contain swatches. There are different kinds of palettes available for you to use, or you can even create and save your own by using the Color Swatches panel. For the Tech Bookstore Web site you're creating, you will choose colors from the default Web-safe palette that contains 216 colors. This palette contains only the colors that can be viewed on most peoples' monitors. It is possible to add custom colors to the palette using the Color Mixer panel. All you need to do is choose a fill or stroke color anywhere in Flash or on the desktop using the Eyedropper tool and then choose Add Swatch from the Options menu. The selected color is added as a swatch to the bottom row of the palette you have open.

You use the swatch colors from palettes to choose colors for filling shapes, drawing, applying to lines, or changing the background color of the Stage. Colors can be defined in several different ways. You can choose or change colors using RGB (*R*ed, *G*reen, *B*lue) or HSB (*H*ue, *S*aturation, *B*rightness) modes. These color modes simply have different ways of representing a color, and you can switch between the modes using the Color Mixer panel's Options menu. RGB mode adds three numerical values to define a color, and HSB mode uses a value for the degree of rotation on the color wheel, and percentages for saturation and brightness to define a color. You can also choose a color using a hexadecimal value, which is a base-16 system that uses a combination of six numbers and letters to define a color. You might be familiar with this color mode if you have written HTML because it is a color mode used on the Web. This lesson and book will provide hexadecimal values for colors, but the same colors can also be found by choosing swatches in the default color palette.

You can choose a fill and stroke color using the *color controls* in the Tools panel. The color controls are the two color swatches you see in the Color section of the Tools panel. When you click a fill or stroke color control, the color pop up window appears and the Eyedropper tool replaces the cursor. You can click the Eyedropper tool on a color in the palette, on the Stage, or on the desktop to select a color to replace the current selected color. The Eyedropper tool in the Tools panel is used the same way. You can use the Eyedropper to help match colors with one another or quickly pick up a color from a layout you designed in Fireworks.

TIP *To access colors using the Eyedropper outside of the Flash authoring environment, click a color control square in the Tools panel, but do not release the mouse button. Move the Eyedropper anywhere on the desktop. When you find the color you want, release the mouse button! The Eyedropper is now loaded with the selected color which can now be used in your document. If you are selecting a fill color, you can only apply that new color to other fills. If you are selecting a stroke color, the selected color can only be applied to other strokes.*

CREATING GRAPHICS WITH DRAWING TOOLS

The first graphics you will create for the Tech Bookstore application use the basic drawing tools to create shapes on the Stage. Basic tools allow you to create nice and simple layouts. Combined with components, you can create attractive presentations simply by using the drawing tools in Flash.

NOTE *If you want to create more complex designs, you should probably consider integrating with Fireworks or FreeHand. These applications offer filters and advanced editing controls to help create effects not possible in Flash. However, many beautiful Web sites have been made using the drawing tools Flash offers!*

You will learn how to use some of the basic drawing tools in Flash and also discover how to choose colors for the shape's stroke and fill. You will also learn how to select these shapes and change the dimensions using the Property inspector.

1) Open `bookstore3.fla`**, created in Lesson 1 and found in the** `Lesson02` **folder, and save it as** `bookstore4.fla` **in the** `TechBookstore` **folder, or open** `bookstore4.fla` **from the** `Lesson02` **folder on the CD-ROM. Open the Publish Settings dialog box, and deselect the HTML check box in the Formats tab.**

You need to save a new version of the file because you will be making some major changes to the bookstore during this lesson. If you decide that it might be easier to revert to the starting file, you can simply close your new file and then reopen and resave `bookstore3.fla`. Open the Publish Settings dialog box by choosing File > Publish Settings. In the Formats tab, deselect the HTML check box so an HTML file is not generated for each bookstore FLA files you create. You will create an HTML document for the final FLA near the end of this book.

2) Set the fill color to #CCCCCC and the outline to #666666 in the Tools panel. Then select the Rectangle tool in the Tools panel, and create a rectangle on the Stage.

Change the fill and stroke settings in the Tools panel. Click the stroke color control in the Tools panel and use the Eyedropper to choose the grey with the hex color of *#666666* from the color pop-up window. You can also enter the number manually into the text field at the top of the color control and press Enter to make the color selection. Repeat this process with the fill color control, but this time set the color to *#CCCCCC*.

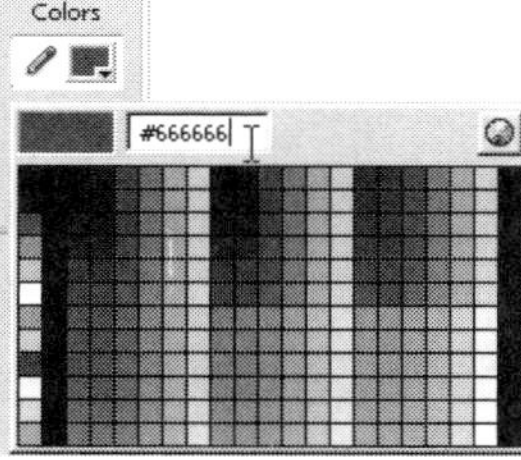

When you finish setting the fill and stroke colors, choose the Rectangle tool from the Tools panel and then click in the Stage. Create a small rectangle on the Stage by clicking and dragging the cursor diagonally across part of the Stage. It doesn't matter yet what the exact measurements are. Select the entire rectangle by double-clicking within the fill area. This action selects both the fill and the stroke at the same time, and a hatched pattern covers the rectangle.

TIP *To select only the fill, single-click within the fill area. To select an entire stroke, you need to double-click on the stroke itself. To select only one segment of the stroke, single-click the segment you want to select.*

3) Change the dimensions of the rectangle to *779* W by *15* H in the Property inspector.

With the rectangle fill and stroke selected, you need to change the dimensions so they are the correct size for the document's layout. Open or maximize the Property inspector and enter new values into the W (width) and H (height) text fields: *779* for width and *15* for height. Press Enter after you have entered each value into the Property inspector.

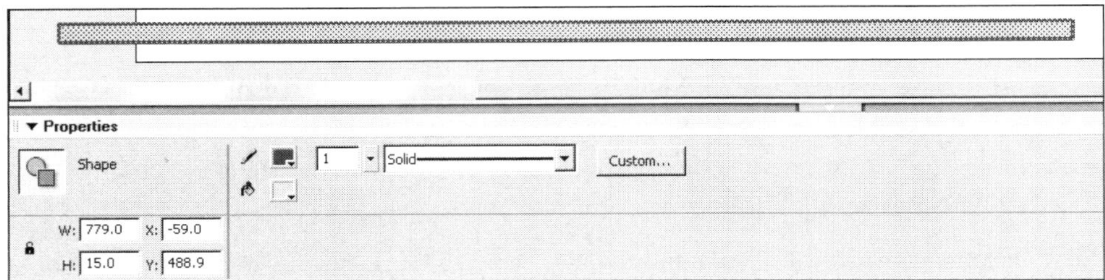

The rectangle updates its dimensions automatically on the Stage. Now that you have created one of the graphical elements for the main layout, you will create a graphic for the logo animation.

4) Create a graphic using the Oval tool that will be used for a glow animation.

The logo animation combines graphics that you create in Flash with a bitmap image file that you will import later in this lesson. The first graphic created in Flash for the logo is an oval that will be used for a glow animation.

Select the Oval tool in the Tools panel and then set your fill color to *#999999* using the fill color control and stroke color to No Color. No Color means that a stroke will not be added to the shape. The No Color button, which looks like a white square with a red line through it and is located right on the Tools panel. You must have the Oval tool selected and the stroke color control selected before you can set the stroke to No Color.

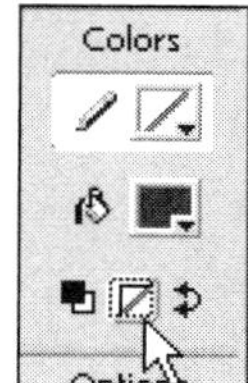

Create a small circle on an empty part of the Stage. To create a circle, hold the Shift key down while clicking and dragging on the Stage. This procedure constrains the shape so the circle has an equal height and width. You will change the grey-colored fill to a more exciting look later in the lesson.

Finally, choose the Selection tool and click the circular shape. Maximize the Property inspector and look at the settings for W and H: They show the current values for the width and height of the selected graphic. Change the W to *130* and the H to *100* to create an oval that fits behind the logo image.

5) Save the Flash document.

Choose File > Save from the main menu to save the changes you've made.

TIP *You can also draw using the Pencil and Brush tools in the Tools panel. It is a lot like drawing with a pencil on paper... except with your mouse. You don't need to do any freehand drawing for this Web site, but you might want to try. Open a new FLA file and explore these two drawing tools. If you have a tablet attached to your computer, Flash has a special feature that allows you to take advantage of pressure sensitivity and tilt of the tablet's pen. When you select the Brush tool, look in the Options area of the Tools panel for the Pressure and Tilt modifiers.*

USING GUIDES, GRIDS, COORDINATES, AND SNAPPING

Flash files have a lot to do with coordinates. Each document has an X and Y coordinate system that can be used to precisely lay out objects on the Stage. You can even use ActionScript to find out or change the X and Y coordinates on the Stage. X refers to the horizontal axis, and Y refers to the vertical axis. If you are in symbol-editing mode, the center of the editing area is at zero when you first open it; numbers then increment from that point. Symbol-editing mode is an area in Flash where you can directly edit symbols, away from the main Stage. You will learn more about symbols and symbol-editing mode in Lesson 4.

Guides, grids, coordinates, and snapping help you place graphics in a correct position on the Stage. These tools are useful because you do not have to try to manually place graphics in a particular spot using only your hand/eye coordination. You can use vertical and horizontal guides to position graphics because they snap in place on the guide. However, the guide lines appear only when you are in the Flash workspace, not when you publish or export the SWF file.

You can change the guide settings by choosing View > Guides > Edit Guides.

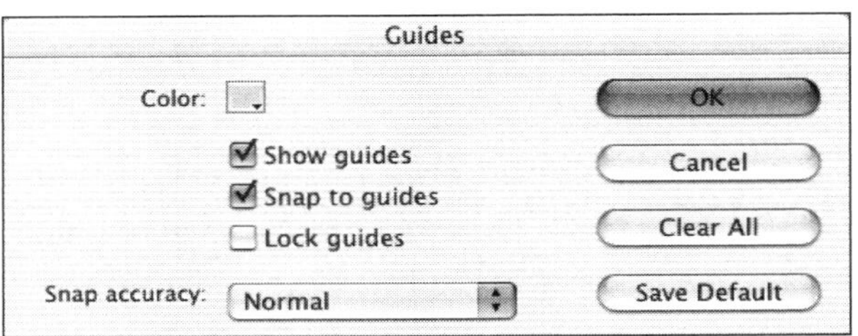

In this dialog box, you can change the color of the guide lines, set whether they are visible, have objects snap to them, and lock the guides so they cannot be accidentally moved. You can also set how close an object has to be to a guide before the object snaps to it. When an object snaps to a guide, it aligns its edge or bounding box to the guide. Snapping and guides help you precisely place objects on the Stage.

NOTE *Make sure that you leave Snap to guides selected.*

A special cursor appears when you mouse over a guide on the Stage, which means you can click and drag the guide to a new location. You have to be careful not to accidentally move a guide when you intend to move a graphic! If you are finished placing guides on the Stage, you might want to lock them by choosing View > Guides > Lock Guides from the main menu.

CREATING A NEW GRAPHIC

In this exercise, you will create the background for the drop-down menus on the Web site by creating a *graphic symbol.* A graphic symbol is a static image that can be reused many times in an FLA file. There are three menus in the Web site, and each one shares the same background graphic. By creating a symbol, you can reuse the graphic in each of the menus. You will learn a lot more about when and how to use symbols in your documents in Lesson 4.

You need to use the Rectangle tool again, but this time you have to set the Corner Radius to make rounded corners. You will learn how to use fill colors, tools, rulers and guides in this exercise.

TIP *By creating a graphic symbol, you can also create more than one layer to achieve graphic effects in a better way than using layers on the main Timeline and Stage. As you learned in Lesson 1, layers are created in a Timeline, and you can stack graphics on top of one another. The Web site's menu uses this process to create a particular look. You will learn a lot more about symbols in Lesson 4.*

1) Open `bookstore4.fla` **in Flash, and save a new version of the document as** `bookstore5.fla`**. Make sure that you have Snap to Objects selected.**

You want to save a new version of this project because you will be making some major changes to the document. Choose File > Save As from the main menu and then enter *bookstore5.fla*. Click the Selection tool and then select Snap to Objects at the bottom of the Tools panel. This enables snapping.

2) Create a new graphic symbol by choosing Insert > New Symbol and then create three new layers by clicking the Insert New Layer button.

For now, you will use a graphic symbol so you can use more than one layer to create the menu background and reuse it several times later on. Choose Insert > New Symbol to open the New Symbol dialog box and then click the Graphic radio button.

Enter *menubg_gr* into the Name text field. When you finish, click OK. At this point, the workspace enters the graphic symbol-editing mode. Don't worry too much about this editing mode at this point because you will learn all the details about symbols in Lesson 4.

When you open the new symbol, there should be one layer on the symbol's Timeline called `Layer 1`. Insert three more layers by clicking the Insert Layer button three times. You should now have four layers total. Double-click `Layer 1` and rename the layer *outer*. Repeat this process to rename `Layer 2` to *middle*, `Layer 3` to *inner* and `Layer 4` to *gradient*. When you finish, the layers should appear similar to the following graphic.

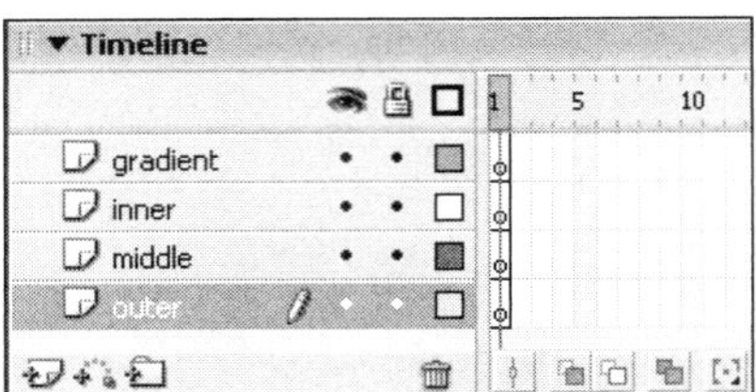

3) Zoom to 800% using the drop-down menu in the edit bar, and set up the outer guides for the menu.

You need to set up a series of guides for the menu background, which will have several colors for an outline, to create a border effect. You will use a series of rounded rectangles layered on top of one another with differing colors to create the effect and use guides to help you layer the rectangles in the symbol.

Turn on rulers by choosing View > Rulers. Rulers automatically appear above and to the left of the editing area. You need to use the rulers to place the guides here, and you can add guides only while the rulers are visible. Zoom in to 800% so it is easier to place the guides. Choose 800% from the drop-down menu in the edit bar, which is directly above the Timeline.

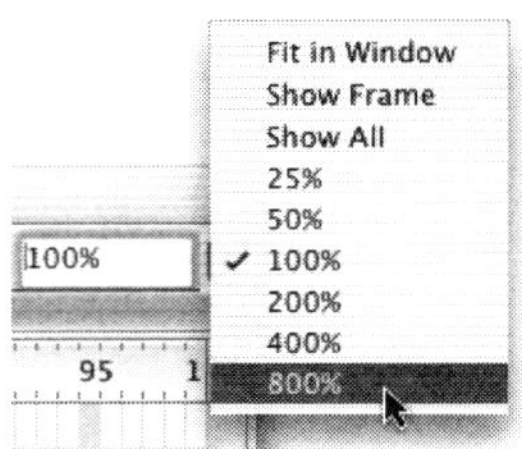

The menu is 110 pixels wide and 15 pixels tall. Click the vertical ruler to the left of the editing area, drag your mouse to 0 on the horizontal ruler, and release the mouse button. A green guide line should appear in the editing area. You can move a guide after you have released the mouse button by clicking it and dragging the line again. A special cursor icon appears when you do this.

Repeat this process, but this time set a guide at 110 pixels on the horizontal ruler to the *right* of the guide set at 0. These first two guides are for the outer left and right sides of the menu.

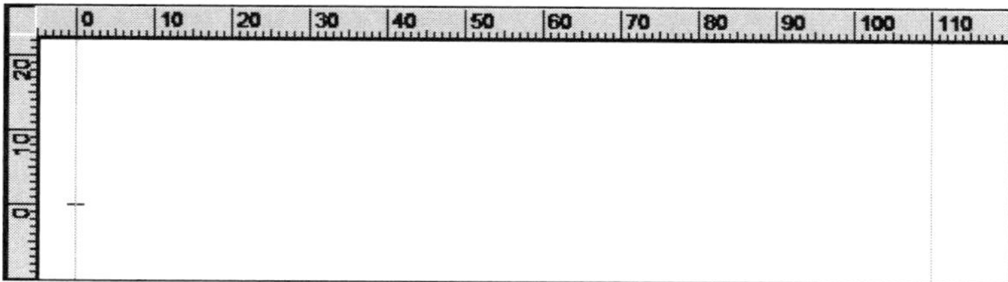

Now you need to set the top and bottom guides. Click and drag a guide from the ruler above the Stage to the 0 pixel on the vertical ruler. Set a ruler for the top of the menu at 17 pixels, *above* the guide set at zero. This value is slightly larger than the 15-pixel height of the final product because you need to erase the rounded top of the menu when you finish the menu. Now create another guide at 15 pixels, *above* the horizontal guide set at 0, which is where you will trim off the top of the menu.

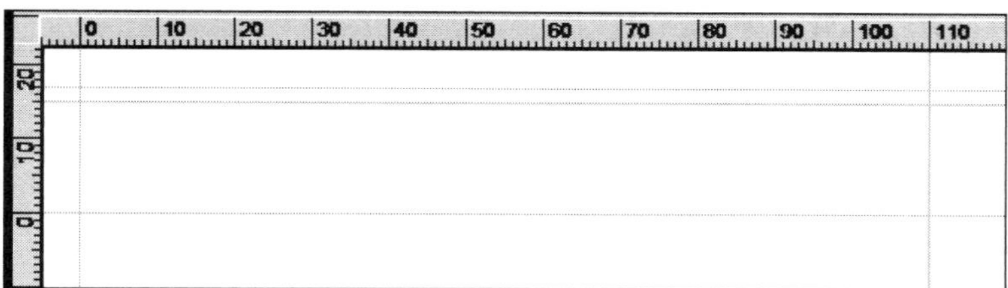

TIP *If you make a mistake and drag too many guides onto the editing area, you can always remove them by dragging them back onto the ruler. This action gets rid of the extra guide you created.*

4) Create three guides at 1-pixel intervals from the sides and bottom of the menu.

In order to accurately line up each layer, you need to create guides for each shape to snap to when you create it. Create three more guides on the left side of the menu: at 1, 2, and 3 pixels on the horizontal ruler, to the *right* of the guide set at 0. Repeat this process for the right side of the menu: at the 107, 108, and 109 location on the horizontal ruler, to the *left* of the guide set at 110.

Only three more guides to place! The final three guides are for the bottom of the menu. Drag guides from the horizontal ruler to 1, 2, and 3 pixels *above* the guide set at 0. You are now finished placing guides. Choose View > Guides > Lock Guides to lock the position of the guides in the editing area. This action prevents you from moving them when you create rectangles in the next step. The editing area should now look similar to the following figure.

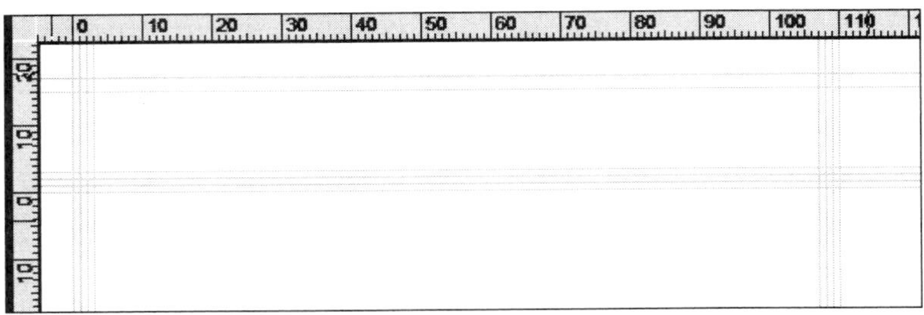

5) Create the menu background on the `outer` layer using the Rectangle tool with a corner radius set to *2* and no stroke color, and a fill color of *#666666*. Create the rectangle within the outermost guides.

You need to create the outer edge of the menu background using a rectangle with rounded corners. Select the Rectangle tool and then click the Round Rectangle Radius button to open the Rectangle Settings dialog box. The Round Rectangle Radius button is found in the Options area of the Tools panel, after you select the Rectangle tool. Enter *2* into the Corner Radius field and click OK. You will use the Rectangle tool with this corner radius for each layer.

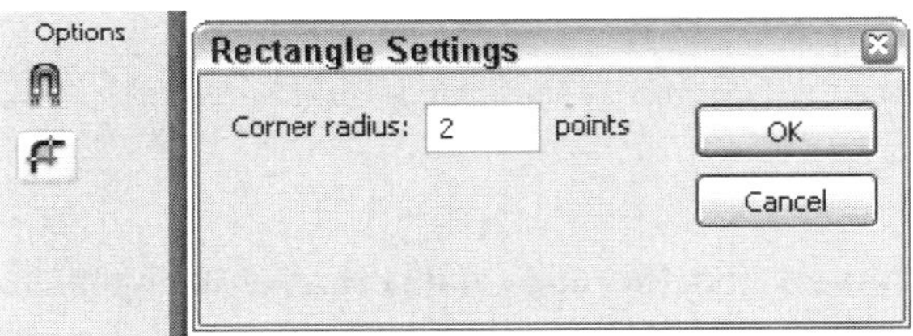

Use the Fill and Stroke controls in the Tools panel to set your fill color to *#666666* and your stroke color to *No Color*. Select the `outer` layer to create the first rectangle. The first rectangle *snaps* to each of the outside vertical guides placed at 0 and 110, and the horizontal 0 and 17 guides. Click the cursor very close to the upper-left corner of the guides and then drag the cursor diagonally to the lower-right corner of these guides. When the cursor is clicked or released close to one of the guides, it snaps right to the line.

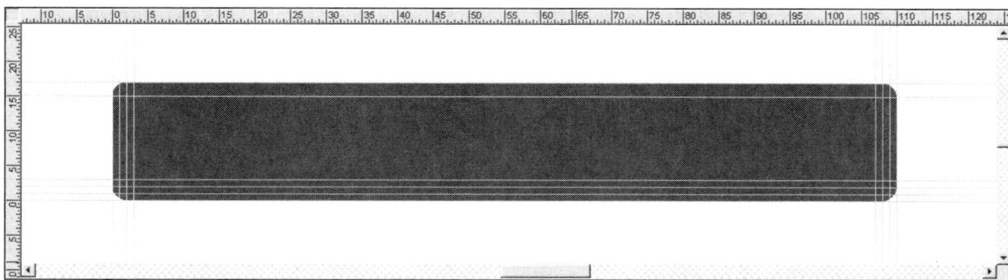

6) Create another rectangle on the `middle` layer, with a fill of *#FFFFFF* and no stroke. Create the rectangle one pixel in from the left, bottom and right sides of the `outer` rectangle.

Now click the `middle` layer to make the next rectangle. Use the Tools panel to set your fill color to *#FFFFFF* (or choose the white swatch) and make sure that the stroke color is still set to *No Color*. Now you need to create a rectangle shape that is inside the rectangle on the `outer` layer by one pixel on the bottom and left and right sides.

NOTE *Use Ctrl-Z or Command-Z if you need to undo and try creating the shape again.*

The third and fourth rectangles are created exactly the same way except for moving in another pixel on each side and the bottom. For the rectangle on the `inner` layer, set the fill color to *#999999* and the stroke color to *No Color*. For the rectangle on the `gradient` layer, set the fill color to *#CCCCCC* and the stroke color to *No Color* for now. In the exercise on gradients later in this lesson, you will fill the `gradient` layer's rectangle with a linear gradient.

7) Trim the top of the menu and then lock the layers in place.

The rounded edges at the top of the menu are not needed. Therefore, you need to select the area at the top and then trim it off. You can use the Selection (arrow) tool to select fills or parts of fills. You can click and drag the arrow to select a rectangular area the same way you created rectangles in the previous step.

Click the Selection (arrow) tool in the Tools panel. Click outside of the rectangle, above and to the left of the upper-left corner. Click and drag diagonally until you select all the shape above the guide line placed at 15 pixels on the vertical ruler. When your selection is exactly at the guide, it turns pink in color. Release the mouse to make the selection when the guide turns pink.

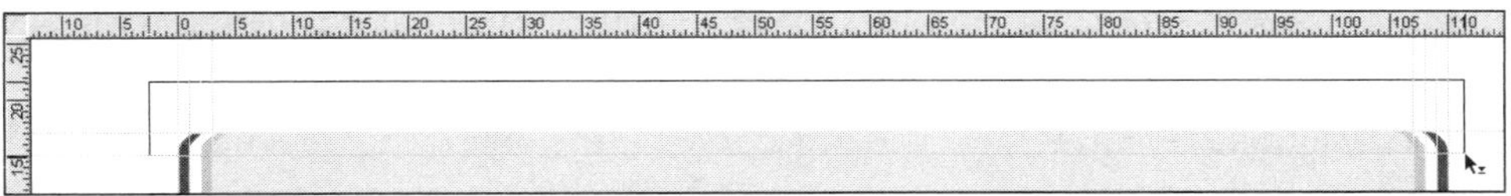

When the area of the graphic is selected, a crosshatch pattern covers the selected area. Press the Backspace or Delete key to trim the rounded top from the graphic. The last thing you need to do is lock the `outer`, `middle`, and `inner` layers by clicking the dot under the Lock Layer icon.

8) Return to the main Stage.

Remember that you are currently in symbol-editing mode? The edit bar is used to tell you where you are when editing an FLA file. In the edit bar, you have a link to Scene 1 and then `menubg_gr`, which is the name you gave to the symbol. The last link in the edit bar list is what you are currently editing. Clicking a link in the edit bar takes you to that particular area for editing. This process is sometimes the quickest and easiest way to navigate through the document and also return back to the main Stage.

Click the `Scene 1` link, which is the main Stage. You are immediately taken back to the Stage and main Timeline. Use the drop-down menu in the edit bar to zoom back out to 100%.

9) Save the FLA before moving on using File > Save from the main menu.

Remember to save the changes you made to the document before proceeding to the next exercise.

CREATING AND USING MASKS

A mask allows you to hide and reveal parts of the Stage. A mask is a lot like a window: Areas that are covered you can see through, but uncovered areas of the Stage are hidden. Using a mask can be a very powerful because some amazing and complex effects can be created by using masks. Masks can remain stationary on the Stage, or you can animate them so they move around. Masks are created by setting a layer to be a *mask layer*, which means that the mask item you create on this layer masks anything on any underlying layers that are linked to it.

In this exercise, you will create a basic shape that is used to mask an area of the Stage. The menus are animated to drop down below the three buttons that are used to control them. You see the menus only in an area below the three buttons that control them as a result of using this mask, because it covers the area beneath those buttons. You should still be using `bookstore5.fla` for this exercise.

1) Add guides to the main Stage by dragging guidelines from the horizontal and vertical rulers.

At this point, you should have a long rectangle on the Stage, but it is not properly put in place. For now, simply double-click the graphic and move it off the Stage to the grey area surrounding it. Repeat this procedure for the other graphics you have on the Stage, such as the oval you created earlier in this lesson for the glow animation.

You need to create some new guide lines, in the same way you created them in the previous exercise. Drag a vertical guide to 115 pixels and a second vertical guide to around 405 pixels. Drag a horizontal guide down to 125 pixels and a second horizontal guide down to 140 pixels.

2) Create a rectangle on a new layer and then change it into a mask.

Select the background layer, and then insert two new layers. Name the lower layer *menu* and the layer above it *mask*. On the `mask` layer, create a rectangle within the guide lines. The edges snap to the guides.

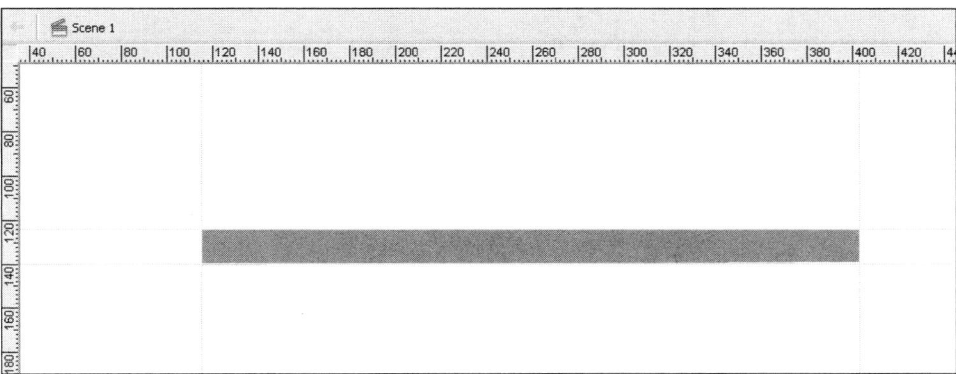

When you finish creating the rectangle, select the `mask` layer in the Timeline. Right-click (or control-click on the Mac) the layer and then choose Mask from the contextual menu. The `menu` layer is automatically indented, which means it is masked.

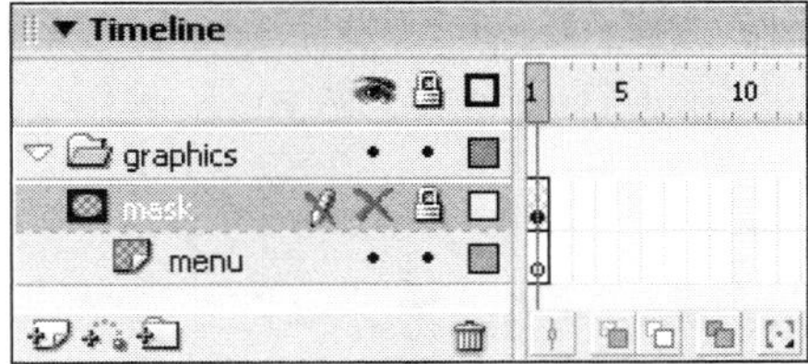

3) Lock and hide the `mask` layer, and delete the guides.

You don't want to move the mask after positioning it accurately on the Stage, so click the dot under the Lock Layer icon for the `mask` layer. Also, you want to hide the layer so you can position other elements on the Stage. To do so, click the dot under the Show/Hide All Layers icon so the layer is not visible. A red *X* appears to signify that it is hidden on the Stage.

You won't need to use the guides for the `mask` layer, so choose View > Guides > Clear Guides to delete the guides you currently have on the Stage.

ADDING STROKES

There are many interesting ways to manipulate strokes using Flash. You have changed the color of your stroke, but not the size or style of it. Select the Rectangle tool again and maximize the Property inspector.

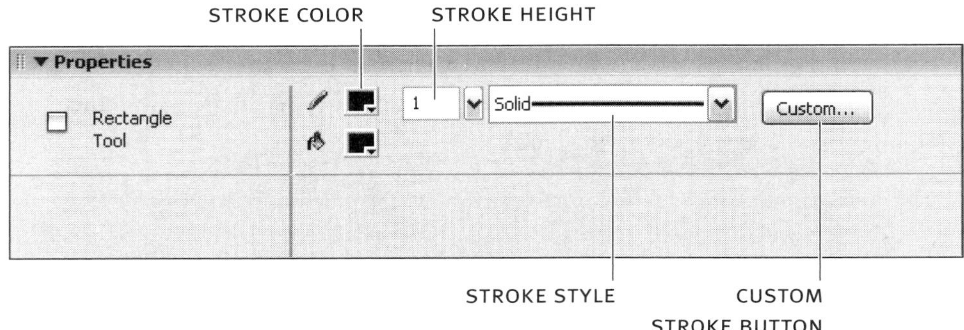

The stroke height controls the thickness of the stroke on the Stage. You can have strokes as small as 0.1 to as thick as 10.

Click the Stroke Style drop-down menu to view some of the stroke styles you can apply. You can set your stroke to *hairline* using this menu. A hairline stroke always stays the same size, no matter how much you zoom into the Stage. A regular stroke appears larger when you zoom into the Stage. So far, you have been using regular "solid" strokes with a height of 1, which is the default setting in Flash.

Take a look at some of the other options in the menu, which include some interesting styles that can be applied. If you click the Custom Stroke Style button, more modifications can be made. Choose a stroke from the menu and then drop-down menus appear, allowing you to customize the stroke. A preview window shows you how the modifications will look on the Stage.

TIP *You should always try to limit the use of special stroke styles in your FLA. These stroke styles (such as dotted or ragged) add more file size to your SWF file. It is a good idea to use as many solid or hairline strokes as possible to help reduce file size when you publish.*

1) Insert a new layer and create another rectangle.

Select the `background` layer and insert a new layer. Rename the layer *outline* and make sure that the `background` layer is locked.

Select the Rectangle tool in the Tools panel and set the Stroke color to *#000000* (black), set the fill color to *No Color*, and make sure that the stroke height is set to the default value of *1*. Click the Rounded Corners button and make sure that the value is set to *0*. Draw a small rectangle anywhere on the Stage.

2) Resize and position the rectangle.

With the rectangle still selected, enter the following values into the Property inspector: *779* (W) and *519* (H). These values ensure that the rectangle is visible all around the edge of the Stage. If you create it the same size as the Stage, some of the rectangle is cut off after you publish the SWF.

Don't close the Property inspector quite yet. Set the X and Y coordinates to *0,0*, which places the top-left corner of the rectangle in the top-left corner of the Stage.

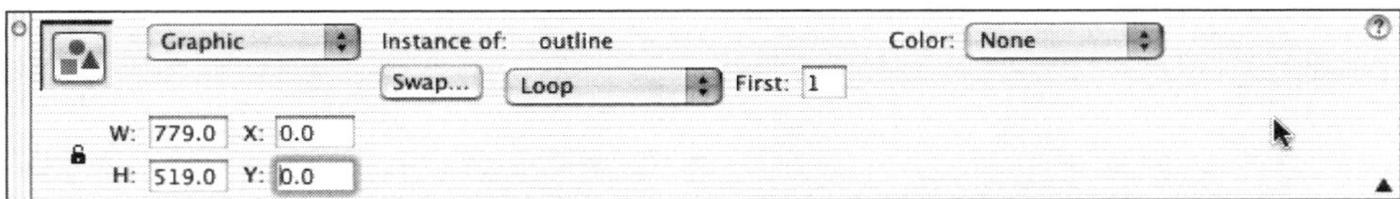

NOTE *Although the right side and bottom of the SWF file might appear to have a double line and be a little rough, the line appears uniform around the edge of the SWF when you publish the SWF file for a browser. If you set the rectangle to be the full size, you do not see your outline at the bottom or right sides of the Stage.*

3) Change the rectangle into a symbol and lock the layer.

The rectangle should still be selected on the Stage. Choose Modify > Convert to Symbol and name the graphic `outline_gr`. Select the Graphic radio button and then click OK. When you finish, lock the `outline` layer.

USING THE LIBRARY

The Library stores the symbols and items that you use in your Flash FLA file. They are stored and organized in the Library, in which you can view, rename, or edit properties. You can also add new items to the Stage from the Library to your FLA by dragging and dropping the symbol onto the Stage.

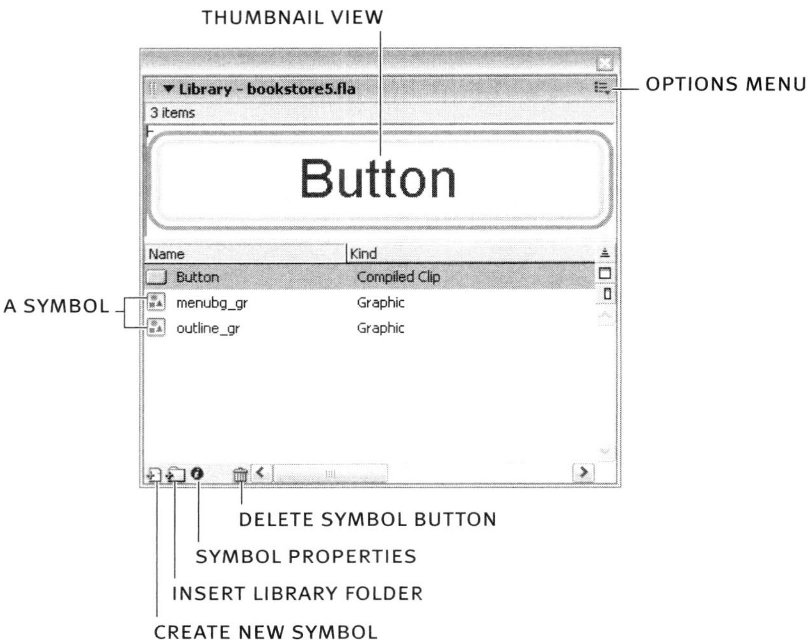

When you add graphics to your document, they are represented in the Library by an icon depicting the type of symbol it is and its name. You can rename items in the Library by double-clicking the name and typing in a new one. The Library also provides information about the item, shows you a thumbnail preview, and allows you to duplicate the item. Take a look at the contextual menu that opens when you right-click an item in the Library. This menu is usually different, depending on what kind of item it is.

In this exercise, you will learn your way around the Library and create some folders to organize the elements you will import into the document. You should still be working with `bookstore5.fla` for this exercise.

1) Choose Window > Library to open the Library.

The Library is just like the other panels: You can minimize and maximize it; and you can dock it to the Stage or leave it floating. It also has an Options menu, on which you can create or modify symbols. Notice that there are several named items in the

Library. The graphic symbol that you created in the previous exercise is in the Library. The graphics that you created on the Stage *without* using the Insert > New Symbol command are called *raw* or *primitive* graphics. If you select a raw graphic, a crosshatch pattern covers the graphic. Anything that is directly drawn on the main Stage is *not* a symbol or represented in the Library until you change it into one. You will learn more about symbols and the Library in Lesson 4.

2) Delete the Button component from the Library.

There should be a Button component in the Library called `Button`, saved from the final exercise in Lesson 1. Even though you finished the exercise by deleting the component from the Stage, it still exists in the Library. The fact the symbol is still left in the Library is useful because it means you can temporarily delete an item from the Stage and then use it again when you need to, instead of having to create it again.

Right-click (or control-click on the Mac) the component and take a look at the contextual menu, which includes options to rename and modify properties for the component.

NOTE *If you have elements in the Library that are not used in the application, they are not exported in the SWF file when you publish a SWF file. Therefore, you don't need to worry about unused elements increasing the file size of the SWF. However, sometimes it is a lot easier to find things in the Library if you remove items you don't intend to use.*

There are a few different ways to delete an item from the Library. You can select the symbol and press the Backspace or Delete key, or the Delete Symbol button, and an alert opens that asks you to confirm the decision. If that symbol is on the Stage, it is replaced with a small white circle where it once was. You can select and delete this circle. You can also choose Select Unused Items from the options menu, which selects all the items in the Library that are not currently being used in the application. Be careful that it doesn't select something that you intend to use because it will permanently delete the items from the Library.

3) Create a new Library folder by clicking the New Folder button and put `menubg_gr` **into the** `graphics` **folder.**

After you use components; create graphics; or import images, sounds, or even video into an FLA file, the Library can end up containing a vast amount of items. Before things get messy, it is a good idea to set up a bunch of folders to organize the Library items into related groups. Library folders are created and serve the same purpose as Layer folders in the Timeline.

Create a new Library folder by clicking the New Library Folder button at the bottom of the Library. A folder is created, and you can immediately type in a name for the folder. Name the first folder *graphics* and press Enter when you are finished. If you want to rename a folder, you can double-click its name to edit it. Create four more Library folders and give them the following names: *components*, *buttons*, *media*, and *movie clips*.

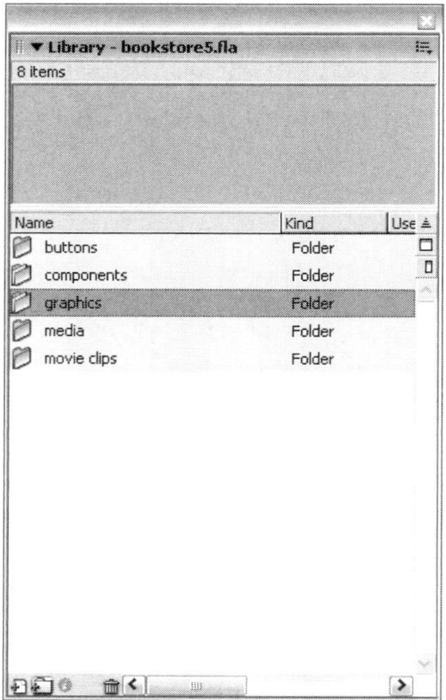

Because `menubg_gr` and `outline_gr` are graphic symbols, you should move them into the `graphics` folder. Click a graphic symbol, drag it over top of the `graphics` folder, and release the mouse button. The symbol is placed within the folder. Double-click the folder's icon to open and close the folder, to either reveal or hide the contents.

4) Open `menubg_gr` from the Library.

Using the Library is a quick way to edit a symbol. When you double-click a movie clip, button, or graphic symbol from the Library, it opens in symbol-editing mode.

Find `menubg_gr` in the `graphics` folder and double-click its icon. Notice that the workspace changes from the main Stage into symbol-editing mode. You need to make your edits in symbol editing mode when you add a gradient to this graphic. Click on `Scene 1` in the edit bar to return to the main Stage.

5) Save the changes you have made to `bookstore5.fla` by choosing File > Save.

IMPORTING AND OPTIMIZING BITMAPS

You have several graphics on or around the Stage at this point. However, there are other images that need to be imported for the buttons, logo, and title area. These images were created using an image editor because the images use certain editing features that are not available in Flash. You might find it necessary at times to use effects and filters in another program and then integrate those features by importing the files into Flash.

NOTE *You have to be careful when you are using bitmap (raster) graphics because they do not always scale well. If you change the size of a bitmap, you probably distort the image. Always try to maintain the same image dimensions as the original that you are importing.*

On the CD-ROM there is a folder called `media`. Inside the `media` folder are several PNG files that were created for you to use.

NOTE *PNG (Portable Network Graphics) is a bitmap image format that is commonly used for adding bitmap images to Flash documents. It is widely used because it is economical on file size and supports both transparency and masking. PNG bitmaps typically add less file size to SWF files than JPG images of the same quality, which is another great reason to use PNG bitmaps instead. If you are working with Fireworks, then you are in luck because the native file format of Fireworks is PNG. You can export PNG bitmaps from most professional image editors.*

Images and graphics can be created using any image editing software, such as Fireworks MX 2004 or even Photoshop, and then imported into Flash. You can even import PSD files (native Photoshop files) directly into Flash with the help of QuickTime. Right-click (or control-click on the Mac) the file in the Library and you can choose to edit the file in Photoshop. Any changes you make in Photoshop are automatically updated in Flash when you save the PSD.

In this exercise, you will import several bitmap files directly into the Library that will be used for the Web site layout. Then, you will check the optimization settings for each image.

1) Choose File > Import > Import to Library to import six PNG files for the buttons. Then organize them in the Library.

When you choose the Import to Library command, the Import to Library dialog box opens. Find the `media` folder on the CD-ROM provided with this book. Inside the `media` folder is another folder called `buttons`, which contains six PNG files that are for the up (regular) and over (hover) states for each button.

Select the six files within this folder by holding down the Ctrl (or Command key on the Mac) while clicking each file. Click the Open button after the six files are highlighted. The six files are automatically imported into the Library.

Now you need to organize the images so they are easy to find. Click and drag each image that you just imported into the `media` folder in the Library.

2) Check the optimization settings for the imported bitmap images.

Flash allows you to have a bit of control over the optimization of the bitmap images that you import. Open the `media` folder and then click the Properties icon at the bottom of the Library panel. The Bitmap Properties dialog box shows you a thumbnail of the image and details the location and size of the image.

Click the test button to find out how much smaller the file size will be from the original bitmap image.

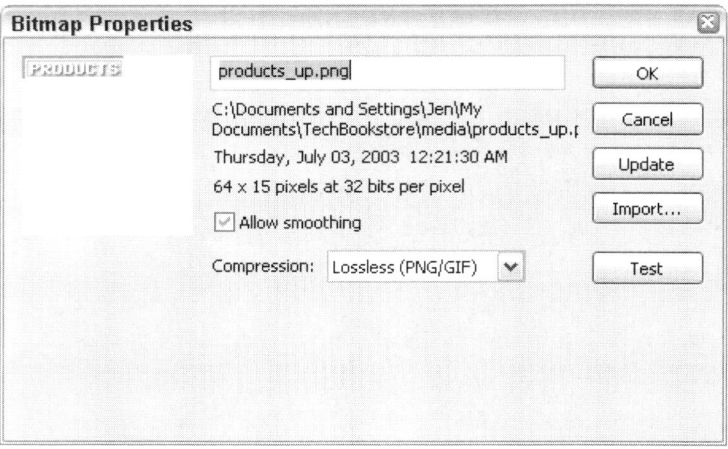

You can also control what kind of compression is applied to the image. Choose from Photo or Lossless compression, depending on what the attributes are in the image. *Photo compression* is good for images that have a lot of detail and different colors, such as photos and gradients. *Lossless compression* is best when fewer colors and simple shapes are used in the image. Because the button images you imported are relatively simple and contain a slight drop shadow, choose Photo compression.

Photo compression allows you to use the document default compression, which is the JPG compression set in your Publish Settings. Or, you can manually set the rate of compression by unchecking the Document default check box. Because you set the document default for compression when publishing the SWF file for the Web in Lesson 13, you can leave this option checked.

Check the Allow smoothing check box if you want to use anti-aliasing to smooth the edges of the bitmap. In most cases, anti-aliasing enhances the look of the image.

3) Import title.png from the CD-ROM, and then change its compression properties.

Choose File > Import > Import to Library and return to the `media` folder on the CD-ROM. Select `title.png` and then click OK to import the file into the Library. After this file is imported, click and drag it into the media folder within the Library.

Select `title.png` in the Library and click the Properties button. Change the compression setting to Photo compression, uncheck the Document default check box, and set Quality to *80*. Now you are ready to add this image to the Stage.

4) Place the image on the Stage and use the Property inspector to enter coordinates to place the image at *0,0*. Lock the `background` layer when you are finished.

Click the `background` layer to make it active and then click and drag the image onto the Stage. The crosshatch outline of the image means that it is a raw image instead of a symbol. This image was created to match the width of the Stage and needs to align with the upper-left corner.

Maximize the Property inspector and select the image. Enter *0* into both the X and Y text fields, pressing the Enter key after each new value is entered. Entering 0 sets the new X and Y coordinates to the upper-left corner of the imported image to that location on the Stage. The image immediately moves to the new location.

TIP *The upper-left corner of the Stage starts the X and Y coordinates at* 0. *When you move horizontally across the Stage, the X coordinates increase; when you move vertically downward on the Stage, the Y coordinates increase. To see how this process works, open the Info panel by choosing Window > Design Panels > Info. Watch the X and Y values as you move the mouse around the Stage—the values update with the current position of the mouse.*

When you finish setting the new location for this graphic, lock the `background` layer so you won't accidentally move the graphic from this precise location or add another element to this layer until you unlock it.

5) Import the logo graphic into the Library and change its properties; then place it on the Stage.

Choose File > Import > Import to Library and open the `media` folder on the CD-ROM. Choose the `logo.png` file and click OK to import it into the Library. In the Library, click and drag the logo into the `media` folder. Open the `media` folder, select `logo.png`, and then click the Properties button. Change the compression setting to Photo compression because this graphic contains gradients.

With the `background` layer still selected, click the Insert New Layer button. Rename the new layer to *logo*. Drag `logo.png` onto this layer and position it in the upper-left corner of the Stage.

Roughly position the graphic as seen in the previous image. You can use your own judgment about where the logo looks best in this corner. Just make sure that it doesn't overlap and obscure much of the title text in the image underneath it. When you finish positioning the image, lock the `logo` layer.

NOTE *To find out how the graphics were made for the Tech Bookstore using graphics editors, go to* `www.TrainingFromThe Source.com/bonus` *for a short tutorial.*

IMPORTING VECTOR DRAWINGS

You can import complex vector drawings into Flash, such as those from FreeHand (.FH7 to .FH11 files) and Illustrator (.AI files). You can maintain the layers in each kind of document, although you have more control when you import documents made with FreeHand. An advantage of using vector drawings is that when they are scaled, you do not lose quality like you do when scaling bitmap images. You do not lose as much quality because vector drawings are made of calculations instead of many pixels on a grid, so distortion doesn't occur when the image is resized.

In this exercise, you will import a file that was created using FreeHand MX. You will choose how and where the assets in this file are placed and then properly place them in the Flash document.

1) Create a new Flash document and change the document properties.

The map area of the Web site is dynamically loaded into the main Web page SWF at run time. When a user visits the map area of the site, the SWF loads into the main Tech Bookstore SWF file. This means that you need to add the map to a new FLA file so you can export the SWF that will be used to load into the main bookstore SWF.

Choose File > New and then click Flash Document from the Type list. Click OK, and a new FLA opens in Flash with its own Document Tab, which makes it easy to switch between open documents when you need to do so.

Maximize the Property inspector. Change the dimensions of the Stage by clicking the button next to Size and entering new values into the W and H text fields in the Document Properties dialog box. Enter a width of *500* and a height of *355*. Then change the frame rate to *21* fps, matching the frame rate you entered for the main bookstore SWF in Lesson 1.

2) Import a vector file that was made in FreeHand into a new Flash file.

One area of the Web site includes a vector drawing of a map. Inside the `media` folder on the CD-ROM is this file, which was created using FreeHand MX. FreeHand files can retain symbols, pages, layers, and text so you can edit the file contents further using Flash.

Select `Layer 1` and rename the layer to *map*. Make sure that it is selected before you import the FreeHand document. Choose File > Import > Import to Stage and navigate to the `media` folder on the CD-ROM. Select the `map.FH11` file and then click Open. After you click Open, the FreeHand Import dialog box opens.

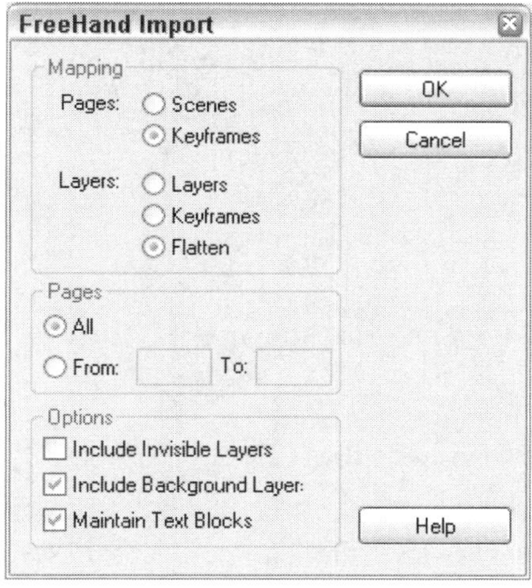

Choose either *Scenes* or *Keyframes* for the Pages setting. This document does not include multiple pages, so it does not matter which one you select. If a document has multiple pages, each page is placed either in a separate scene or ascending keyframes on the main Timeline.

Choose *Flatten* for the Layers section. You don't need to change the placement for the different sections of the map, except for one symbol that you will paste on a new layer.

3) Align the symbols with the Stage.

When you import the file, it doesn't necessarily line up properly with the Stage. Press Ctrl+A (or Command+A on the Mac) or choose Edit > Select All. Open the Property inspector and change both of the values for the X and Y coordinates to *0*. The map shifts to align with the Stage.

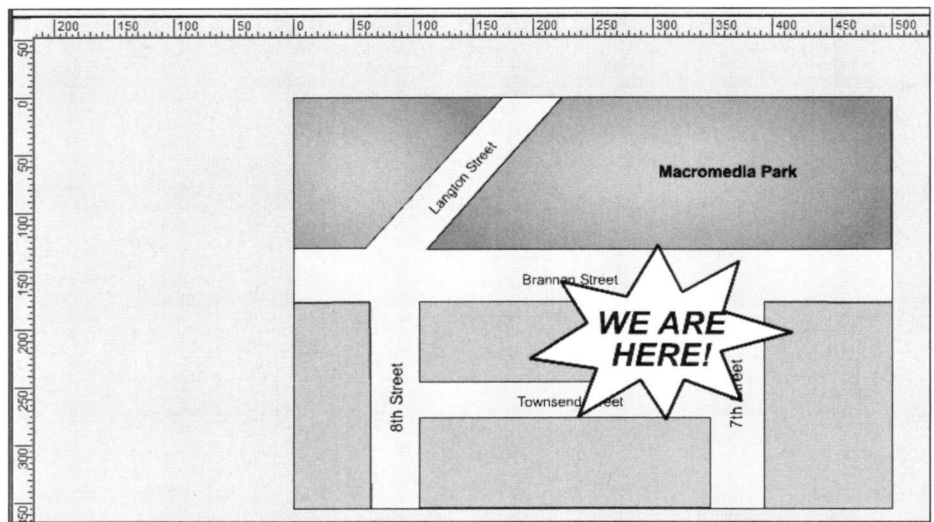

TIP *You see a new FreeHand Objects folder added to the Library. This folder contains the assets that were imported with the FreeHand document. You can work with these symbols the same way as you work with those created in Flash.*

4) Copy and paste a symbol onto a new layer.

With the `map`.layer selected, click the Insert New Layer button. Rename the layer to *map star*.

Select the yellow star symbol on the `map` layer and choose Edit > Copy. This process copies the symbol to the Clipboard. Then press the Backspace or Delete key to remove the symbol from the Stage. Select the `map star` layer and choose Edit > Paste in Place, which pastes the drawing in the same place on the Stage that you copied it from. Lock the `map` and the `map star` layers. You are moving the star to a new layer so you can manipulate it in an upcoming lesson.

5) Save the file as *map.fla* and publish the file.

Choose File > Save to save the file. Navigate to the `TechBookstore` folder on your hard drive. Type *map.fla* into the File name field and click OK. You need to publish a SWF file so you can load it into the main bookstore SWF file. Choose File > Publish Settings so you can modify how the SWF file is published. You do not need to publish an HTML file because you are loading just the SWF into another SWF file. The Formats tab should be active, so just *deselect* the HTML check box so an HTML file is *not* published.

Click the Publish button to generate a SWF file and then click the OK button to exit Publish Settings. The `map.swf` file is created in the `TechBookstore` folder. Click the `bookstore5.fla` Document Tab to return to the main FLA.

You will import other media, such as video and sound, into FLA files for other lessons. For now, you should have a good grasp of the process of importing media. Generally speaking, the process of importing other assets is quite similar. The one process that differs greatly is when you import video content into a document, which Lesson 7 covers in depth.

USING FILLS AND GRADIENTS

You have already used several *fills* in this lesson. The menu background graphic you created used fills without any strokes. You used hexadecimal values to choose fill colors, although you could have also used the color swatches in the palette you opened using the Tools panel. The Eyedropper tool is used to choose the color in the palette. The Color Mixer panel gives you more control over fills than the Tools panel does. This panel should already be open in the `TechBookstore` panel set. If not, open the Color Mixer panel by choosing Window > Design Panels > Color Mixer. You can create gradient and bitmap fills using the controls in this panel.

With *bitmap fills*, you fill an area using a bitmap graphic that was imported into Flash. You should already have several bitmaps in `bookstore5.fla`. Choose Bitmap from the drop-down menu in the Color Mixer panel. The bitmaps currently in the Library are then shown in the Color Mixer panel. If you choose one of these bitmaps, it is selected as the current fill.

NOTE *Bitmap fills are tiled when filling in an area. To resize the bitmap fill, use the Fill Transform tool, which can scale, rotate, and skew bitmap fills. You will use the Fill Transform tool with gradients later in this exercise.*

You can also fill a shape with a *gradient*, which is a gradual transition from one color to another. There are two kinds of gradients in Flash: *radial* and *linear*. A radial gradient makes the transition in a circular pattern, and a linear gradient makes this transition along a straight line.

In this exercise, you will create gradients for several of the assets in the main SWF. You should have a rectangle and a circle that you created in the first exercise of this lesson moved off to the side of the Stage. The fill for both of these elements will be modified.

1) Save a new version of the file as `bookstore6.fla` **in the** `TechBookstore` **folder.**
Choose File > Save As to save a new version of this file, and then type *`bookstore6.fla`* into the File Name field. Click Save when you are finished.

2) Unlock the `background` **layer. Move the rectangle that you created in the first exercise back onto the Stage and create a gradient using the Color Mixer panel.**
In the first exercise, you created a rectangle that was 779 pixels by 15 pixels. Double-click the rectangle's fill to select the entire shape and move it back onto the Stage. Maximize the Color Mixer panel and choose Linear from the drop-down menu. If you do not see a color palette below the drop-down menu, click the arrow in the lower-right corner to fully expand the panel.

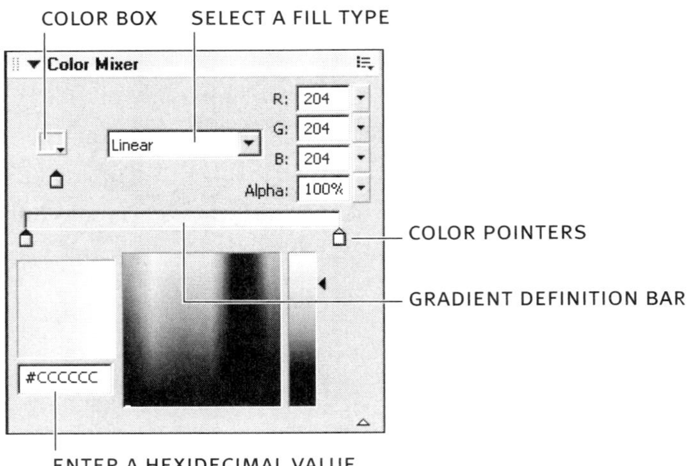

The color box displays the color of the currently selected color pointer beneath the gradient definition bar. The lower area of the panel also allows you to select or assign hexadecimal values to select a particular color.

Click the color pointer on the left hand side of the gradient definition bar. Then enter *#CCCCCC* into the hexadecimal text field at the bottom of the panel and press the Enter key. The color pointer on the right side of the gradient definition bar should still be set to white. If not, click the color pointer on the right hand side of the gradient definition bar. Then change the color to *#FFFFFF*.

TIP *You can change the color using the palette below the drop-down menu or enter color values into the RGB text fields to the right. You can also click the triangle next to the color box to select a swatch.*

NOTE *You can create a gradient with up to eight colors. When you mouse over the gradient definition area, a small "+" symbol appears. Click anywhere, and another color pointer is added to the gradient. You can remove a gradient color by clicking the color pointer and dragging it away from the gradient.*

3) Fill the rectangle with a gradient and use the Fill Transform tool to modify it.

Choose the Paint Bucket tool from the Tools panel. Click the fill area of the rectangle with the paint bucket. A gradient is added to the rectangle. However, the gradient needs to be rotated and resized. You can modify the gradient using the Fill Transform tool so it is visible within the shape.

Select the Fill Transform tool from the Tools panel and then click the gradient fill you just created.

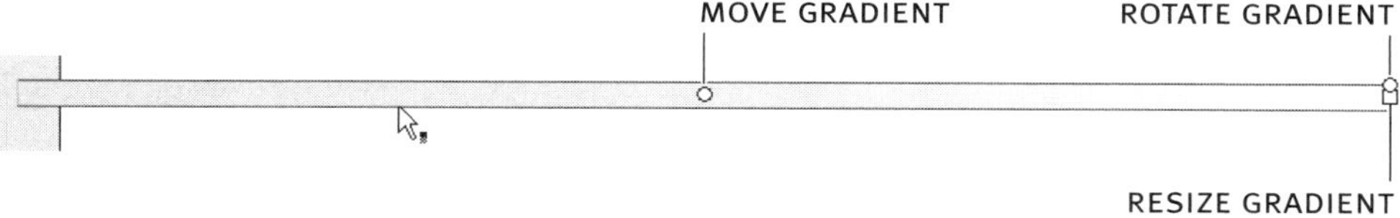

Mouse over the rotation handle at the upper-right corner of the rectangle and click and drag it downward to rotate the gradient 90 degrees clockwise. Thus, the gradient transition is vertical instead of horizontal. However, now the transition is barely visible because of the narrow rectangle. To make the gradient visible, you need to resize the gradient. Click the square editing handle on the Fill Transform tool, which should be below the shape, and then drag it upward. Let the bounding box snap to the sides of the rectangle, so the gradient is the same height as the rectangle.

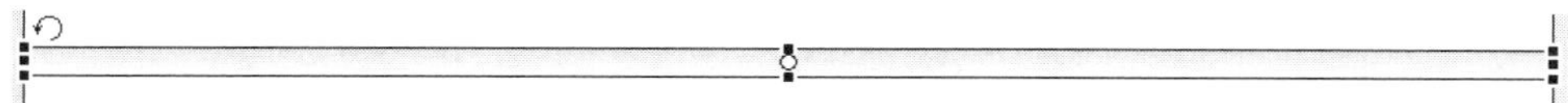

4) Save the rectangle as a graphic symbol, and move it on the Stage directly under title.png.

Using the Selection tool, double-click the rectangle's gradient fill to select the entire shape. Choose Modify > Convert to Symbol and select the Graphic radio button. Enter *bar_gr* into the Name field, which converts the primitive shape into a symbol that is stored in the Library. The *_gr* that you appended to the name signifies that the symbol is a graphic, and sometimes makes things easier to organize in the Library. Select the rectangle and place it directly under the `title.png` image. In the Property inspector, enter *0* for the X coordinate and *109* for the Y coordinate. Notice that the outline of the symbol is blue on the Stage. The outline color is the same for all symbols (unless you change it in the Preferences dialog box) and is referred to as a *bounding box*.

5) Open the `menubg_gr` graphic symbol and fill the shape on the `gradient` layer.

Open the `menubg_gr` graphic symbol by double-clicking its icon in the Library. This procedure opens the graphic in symbol-editing mode, so you can add a gradient to the topmost fill. Make sure that the bottom three layers are locked. Select the `gradient` layer to make it active and then choose the light-grey fill you created on that layer.

TIP *If your guides are still visible and you want to hide them for this exercise, choose View > Guides > Hide Guides. You can delete the guides by choosing View > Guides > Clear Guides.*

You need to create the same gradient that was used for the rectangle. The gradient you created should still be the active fill color. If not, repeat the steps in Step 1 to create a gradient that makes a transition from *#CCCCCC* (grey) to *#FFFFFF* (white).

Select the Paint Bucket tool from the Tools panel, and click anywhere in the fill on the `gradient` layer. Again, you need to change the rotation of the gradient as in Step 2. Select the Fill Transform tool from the Tools panel and click the gradient you just created.

Rotate the gradient 90 degrees clockwise, dragging downward, so the gradient is vertical. Then drag the square editing handle upward to resize the gradient to the same width of the gradient fill.

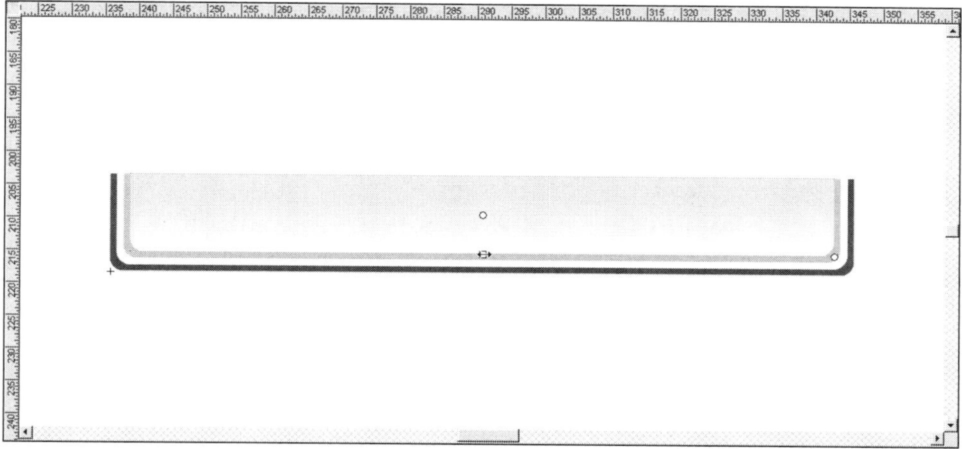

When you finish, click Scene 1 in the edit bar to return to the main Stage.

6) Move the circle that you created onto an empty part of the Stage and fill it with a radial gradient.

You made a circle in the first exercise, and it will be used to create a glow behind the imported logo. Return to the Color Mixer; this time, select *Radial* from the drop-down menu. Click the left color pointer for the gradient and type *#00CC00* into the hexadecimal field at the bottom of the panel; this chooses a bright green color. Although it might not appear too appealing at this point, the glow is mostly hidden, quite transparent and when you are finished creating the site it matches part of the default component set used in the Tech Bookstore.

Select the color pointer on the right side of the gradient definition bar. This time, you set this end of the gradient to fully transparent. Click the arrow button next to the Alpha text field and drag the slider to the bottom, which enters *0%* into the Alpha field.

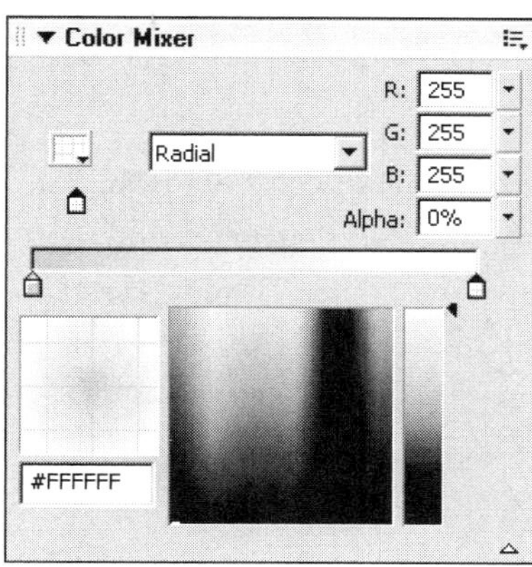

Choose the Paint Bucket tool in the Tools panel and then click the circle fill you created. The radial gradient is applied to the circle. Select the graphic using the Selection tool and choose Modify > Convert to Symbol from the main menu. Enter *glow_gr* into the Name field, select the Graphic radio button, and click OK.

The last step is to place the `glow_gr` symbol on its own layer. Select the `background` layer to make it active and insert a new layer above it. Rename this layer to *glow animation*. Select the symbol and choose Edit > Cut. Select the new layer and choose Edit > Paste in Place.

7) Remember to save the changes you made in this exercise by choosing File > Save from the main menu.

NOTE *You don't want to go crazy with gradients in Flash. They add more file size to your document than solid colors do.*

MANIPULATING GRAPHICS

You have created, imported, and filled graphics for the Tech Bookstore. But there are more ways to manipulate them: You can also rotate, scale, tint, and change the alpha (transparency) of graphics. This exercise will show you how to make some more changes to the graphics you just created using tools and the Property inspector.

1) Create a new layer and call it `bars`, and then move the `bar_gr` symbol onto this layer.

Select the `background` layer and insert a new layer above it by clicking the Insert New Layer button in the Timeline. Rename this layer *bars*. Now you need to move the `bar_gr` graphic that is currently on the `background` layer onto the layer you just created. Select the `bar_gr` graphic that is currently on the Stage and choose Edit > Cut from the main menu. The graphic is cut from the Stage.

Select the `bars` layer and then choose Edit > Paste in Place to place the symbol exactly where it once was.

2) Drag the `bar_gr` graphic symbol from the Library onto the Stage and rotate it.

Drag the `bar_gr` symbol from the Library to the Stage by clicking its name and dragging it onto the Stage. The symbol needs to be rotated so the gradient faces in the opposite direction. With the symbol selected, choose the Free Transform tool in the Tools panel. When the Free Transform tool is active, any selected symbol appears to have handles around its bounding box. You can use these handles to rotate, skew, resize, or move the symbol.

Hover the mouse around the handle in the upper-right corner of the symbol, and a rotation cursor appears. It looks like a circular arrow. Click and drag the mouse downward to rotate the symbol clockwise. Stop when the symbol is vertically flipped (180 degrees). If you hold down Shift while rotating the symbol, it is constrained to 45-degree increments.

3) Place the second `bar_gr` graphic at the bottom of the Stage using the Align panel.
This second bar, which is for the very bottom of the Web site, eventually holds information and links about the site. Maximize the Align panel or open it from Window > Design Panels > Align. Click the To Stage button on the panel so you can align the symbol relative to the Stage.

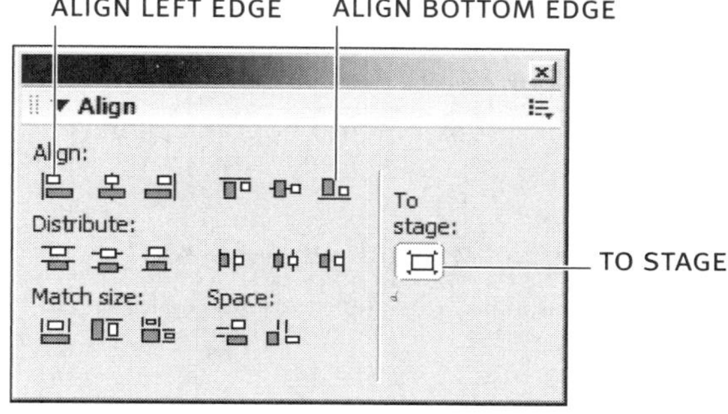

Click the Align Left Edge button under Align so the left side of the symbol aligns with the left edge of the Stage. Click the Align Bottom Edge button under Align so the bottom of the symbol aligns with the bottom of the Stage. Lock the `bars` layer after you finish.

4) Change the alpha and scale of the *`glow_gr`* graphic symbol.
Earlier in this lesson, you imported a logo for Tech Bookstore onto the logo layer and then placed it on the Stage. Make sure that the `logo` layer is locked for this step.

The glow animation is placed beneath the logo and is revealed around the edges of the image because transparency was used in the PNG. Move the `glow_gr` symbol beneath the logo and check to see whether the glow is visible around the edges of the logo. If it isn't visible enough, you might need to scale the `glow_gr` symbol. Select it and then choose the Free Transform tool in the Tools panel. Use the handles on the four corners to resize the graphic by clicking and dragging away from the center. This procedure scales the graphic larger. If you need to make it smaller, click and drag the handles closer to the center.

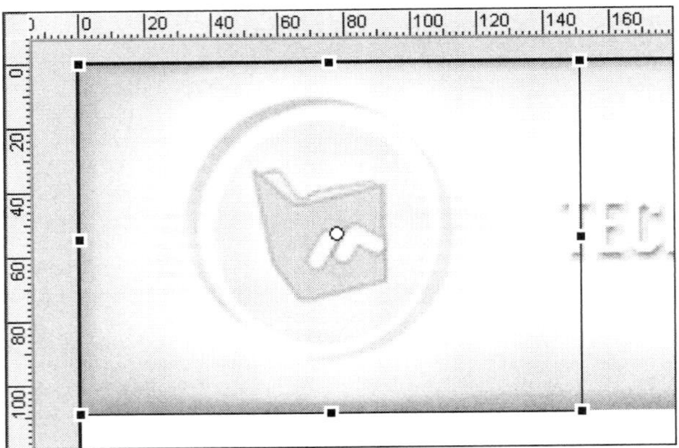

Next, you need to see whether the green color is too bright. If you feel the color is too bright, you can reduce the alpha for the symbol. Select the symbol and maximize the Property inspector. Choose Alpha from the drop-down menu next to Color: A percentage text field with a numerical slider appears.

Enter a value into the text field or use the slider, and watch the Stage to see how the changes look. Test a few different alpha values and choose one that looks right behind the logo.

5) Clean up the Library. Lock the `logo`**,** `glow animation`**, and** `background` **layers when you are done.**

Before you move on to the next lesson, open or maximize the Library. Move all the .PNG files into the `media` folder and move any graphic symbols into the `graphics` folder. You will create more folders in the library after you start using different kinds of symbols.

6) Remember to save all the changes you made to `bookstore6.fla`**!**

WHAT YOU HAVE LEARNED

In this lesson, you have:

- Navigated the tools in the Tools panel (pages 42–47)
- Used tools to draw graphics (pages 47–49)
- Learned how to use guides and snap symbols to them (pages 49–50)
- Created a mask layer (pages 56–58)
- Created and modified strokes (pages 58–59)
- Used the Library and organized items within it (pages 60–62)
- Imported bitmaps and a vector drawing into Flash (pages 63–69)
- Learned more about colors and fills (pages 69–74)
- Modified existing graphics on the Stage (pages 74–76)

using text

LESSON 3

Text is an important part of most Web sites, particularly informational or commercial sites. Flash allows you to have a lot of control over the kind of text you can add to a document and of editing the property settings of the text. Text can be loaded from a server or placed directly on the Stage. Kerning, character spacing, justification, color and anti-aliasing of text can all be controlled by setting properties in the workspace. Text is regularly used in Flash for creative, beautiful, and traditional purposes. In fact, Flash allows you to create many textual effects that are not possible when using HTML or CSS (cascading style sheet).

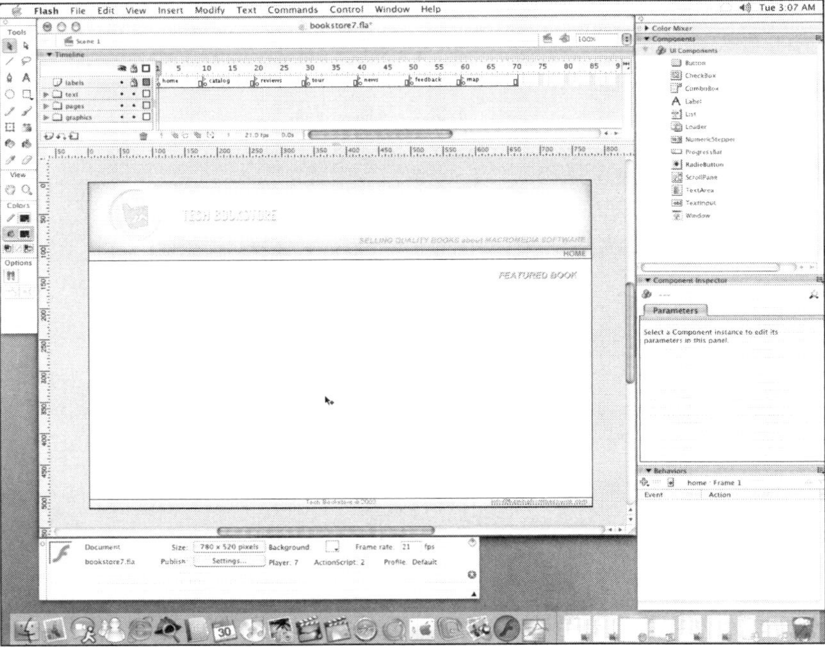

Text fields are added to the Tech Bookstore in this lesson.

In this lesson, you will add and format the properties of many text fields in Flash. You will learn how to add a Timeline Effect to a static text field. You will also spell check the entire document before you finish the lesson. This lesson gives you a foundation in the way text and fonts work and a good basis for using increasingly complex methods of working with text and components in upcoming lessons.

WHAT YOU WILL LEARN

In this lesson, you will:

- Learn about static text and device fonts
- Learn how to use the Text tool
- Learn about embedding fonts and characters in a SWF
- Add text fields to the FLA file and align them on the Stage
- Change text properties in the FLA
- Add a Timeline Effect to text
- Check spelling in the document

APPROXIMATE TIME

This lesson takes approximately 45 minutes to complete.

LESSON FILES

Media Files:

None

Starting Files:

Lesson03/bookstore7.fla

Completed Project:

Lesson03/bookstore7_complete.fla

USING THE TEXT TOOL

There are several different kinds of text that you can use. The three main kinds of text field in Flash are *static*, *dynamic*, and *input* text, and they are used for different purposes. Static text is similar to an image or graphic: It displays any kind of text on the Stage and does not change. On the other hand, dynamic text can change—for example, it might change based on user input or if you load text into the field from a server. Most of the time, dynamic text involves the use of ActionScript to load or change the information. Input text allows a user to type in text when the SWF file is running in the Flash Player. You might use this rather often if you are building a form in which you need to gather a person's name and address. ActionScript is used to capture input text that a visitor types into the form.

NOTE *Flash MX 2004 and Flash MX Professional 2004 ship with several text-based components, which are pre-made assets that you can add to your FLA to add and use text. You are introduced to components at the end of this lesson, and then you will learn how to use the text-based components in Lessons 9 through 12, and you will use them in several areas of the Tech Bookstore.*

There are many text properties that can be edited using the Property inspector. Flash allows you to have control over the font face (a set of characters in a given design), color, size, kerning (adjusts the space between characters for aesthetic purposes), character spacing and position, justification (alignment), and orientation of text fields. You can also control typefaces, meaning that you can set the characters to be regular, bold, and/or italic. Select the Text tool in the Tools panel and maximize the Property inspector. If you don't see properties similar to the following figure, click the Stage once.

NOTE *Throughout this lesson, you will be creating many text fields and altering the properties using the Property inspector.*

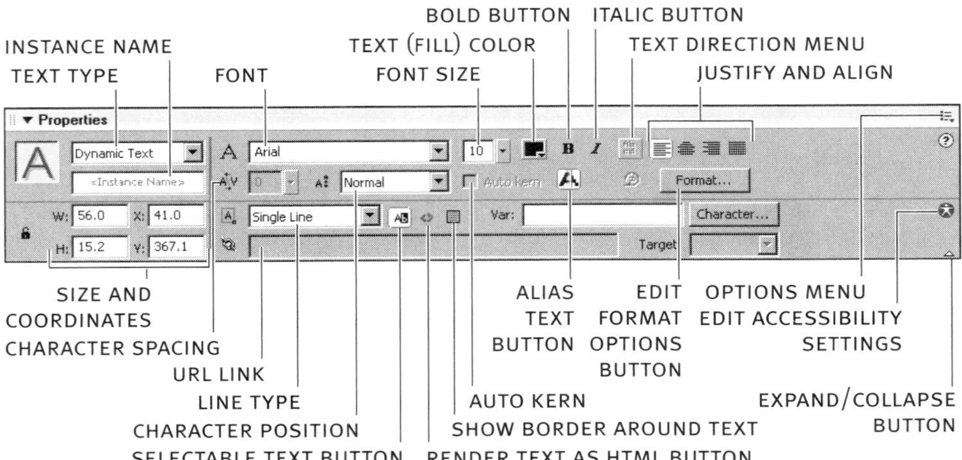

The Property inspector has slightly different options, depending on whether you select Static, Dynamic, or Input text from the Text Type drop-down menu. The Property inspector is where you can select a font to use and then set its color and size or other properties that affect how it is rendered on the Stage.

NOTE *If you send an FLA to someone to edit, that person needs the fonts you used installed on his or her computer in order to see it. A missing font doesn't stop a person from opening and editing the file because any missing font can be mapped to any font currently installed on the system. An alert appears when the file is opened or published, indicating any missing fonts, and allows an available font to be chosen as a replacement. The original correct font is used again if the file is passed on to someone who has it installed.*

Understanding Static text and Device fonts

When you use static text in an FLA file, Flash creates outlines of each character and uses them to display the text. It doesn't matter what kind of static text you use in your document: The characters are visible no matter who views it. You can also be sure the fonts display the same way you see them on the Stage. A pitfall of using static text is that using it increases the SWF's file size because of the additional outline information that has to be included with the file. There is a way around this, though. You can choose to use *device fonts*, which use a system font for text instead of outlines.

Device fonts can be used for horizontal static text fields instead of embedding font outlines in a Flash document. This means that a font on the user's system is used as opposed to rendering outlines on the Stage. There are three device fonts in Flash: _sans, _serif, and _typewriter. The _sans font is similar to Arial or Helvetica, _serif appears like Times New Roman, and _typewriter is similar to Courier.

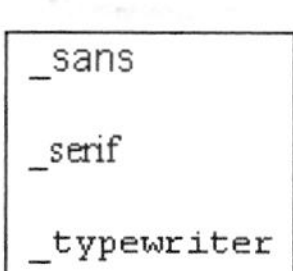

TIP *Because Flash is not drawing outlines for device fonts, it can frequently increase the legibility of 10pt fonts or smaller.*

Remember that device fonts can display differently on the Stage in the workspace from when you view it with the Flash Player. When the SWF plays, Flash uses the first device font it finds on the user's system that is similar to the device font you chose. You can reduce file size slightly by using these fonts because they are not embedded in the SWF file. Device fonts are found in the Font menu in the Property inspector, so you can choose one just as you would any other font. Remember to check *Use Device Fonts* in the Property inspector.

NOTE *One of the issues with using device fonts is that you do not have control over exactly how the fonts look in the SWF. It varies, depending on which font Flash finds on the end user's computer. Use device fonts with some caution, particularly in layout and design. There is also the option of using embedded fonts in your SWF, which allows you to choose any font. Static text fields use embedded fonts by default. We will explain embedded fonts later in this lesson.*

ADDING TEXT TO A DOCUMENT

The first step of learning how to effectively use text in a Flash document is to add some basic static text to the Stage. In this exercise, you will add static text to the FLA. The character outlines are embedded in the file so you can use any font on your computer system, and it is visible to the site's visitors.

1) Open `bookstore6.fla` from the `TechBookstore` folder, and save it as `bookstore7.fla`.

Alternatively, you can open `bookstore7.fla` from the CD-ROM.

2) Add a new layer for static text.

The various pages for the document will be organized along the Timeline. Each of these pages will include a static text field, including the name of the page. Select the `graphics` folder and insert a new layer above it. Rename the layer to *page names*. With the new layer selected, click Insert Layer Folder on the Timeline, and name the new folder *text*. Drag the `page names` layer into the `text` folder.

With the `page names` layer selected, click frame 70 on the Timeline. Press F5 to span the frames across the Timeline, or choose Insert > Timeline > Frame.

3) Organize the layers to form the Web site's pages.

You should add frames to the other layers that include information that needs to be seen on every page of the Web site. If you move the playhead to frame 70, there is nothing on it despite being part of the site. Select the `mask` layer, click on frame 70, and press F5 to insert a frame. Repeat this process for the `background`, `bars`, `glow animation`, `logo`, `menu`, and `outline` layers. Now the Timeline stretches (or *spans*) between frame 1 and 70 in these selected layers. The layers include graphics that need to be displayed throughout the entire Web site, which is why you need to add frames that span across the duration of the FLA. Move the playhead to frame 70. Notice that the frame has many more elements on the Stage.

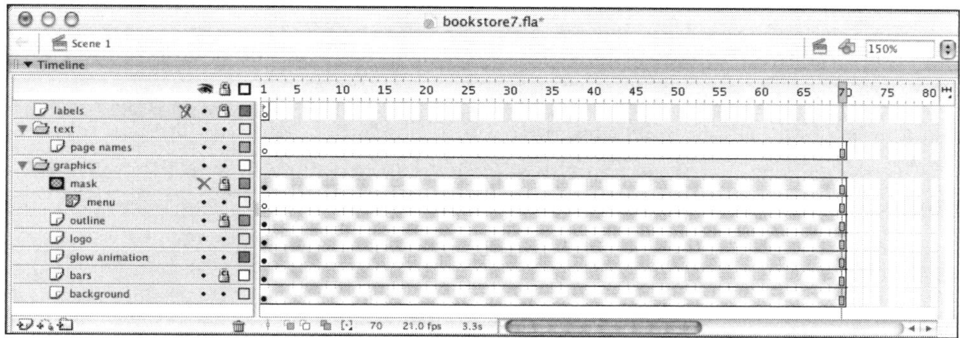

NOTE *If you test the bookstore right now, it plays from frame 1 to 70. In Lesson 5, you will learn how to add an action that uses ActionScript to stop a SWF file from playing automatically.*

Select the `labels` layer and press F5 on frame 70. The reason the layers extend to frame 70 is because you want to be able to view the text for the final label on frame 60. Select frame 10 and press F6 to insert a keyframe. Continue to insert keyframes at frame 20, 30, 40, 50, and 60. Each of these keyframes is labeled with the title of the section.

Select frame 10 on the `labels` layer and then maximize the Property inspector. Type *catalog* into the `<Frame Label>` text field, press Enter, and leave the Label type at *Name*. Repeat this process for the next five keyframes on the `label` layer, entering *reviews*, *tour*, *news*, *feedback*, and *map*.

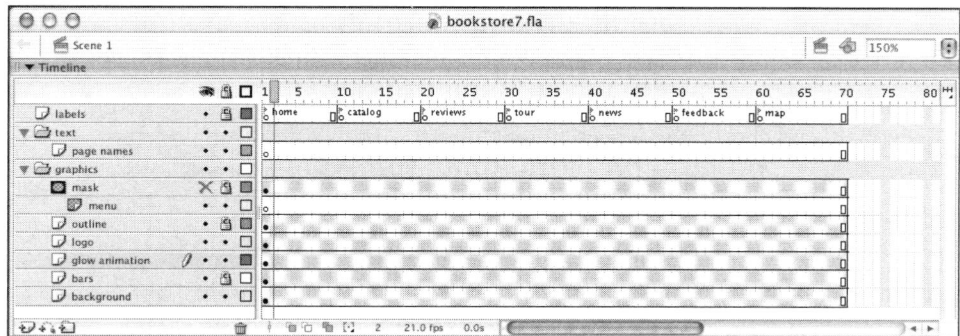

4) Select the Text tool and change the font properties in the Property inspector.

Select the Text tool from the Tools panel and maximize the Property inspector.

Choose Static from the Text Type drop-down menu. Then select Arial from the Font drop-down menu and choose 12 for Font size. Click the Text (fill) color box and enter *#666666* into the Hexadecimal field above the palette. Click the Bold button so the text appears boldface. Finally, click the Align Right button to justify the text field, which ensures that each page name remains consistently aligned with the right side of the Stage area. All of the other settings can remain using the default settings. Your Property inspector should match the settings in the following figure.

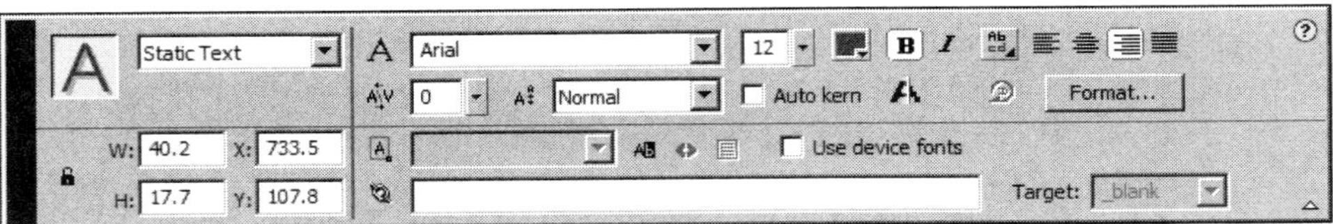

5) Add the page name text to each area of the bookstore site using static text.

Now you need to create the text field on the Stage. The page names are placed on the far right of the bar graphic that sits beneath the title area.

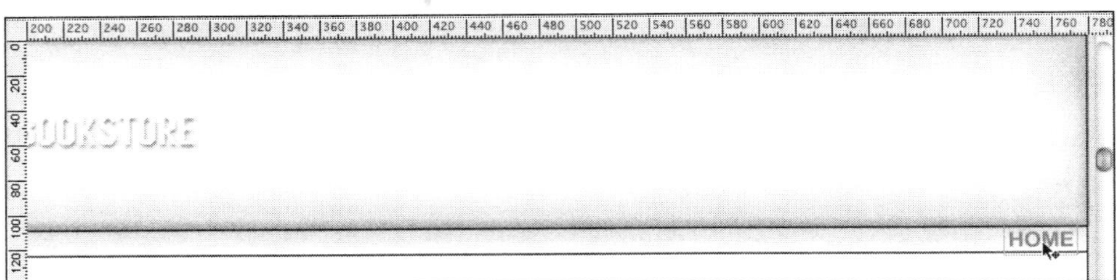

Select frame 1 on the `page names` layer. Remember that the text is right-aligned in the text field. Therefore, click the Stage where you want the text to *end*. Type *HOME* into the text field and choose the Selection tool from the Tools panel after you finish. Select the text field you just created and move it to where you want all the page names on other pages to align to.

TIP *You can create text fields in two different ways. If you want your text field to expand as you type into it, simply click the Stage and start typing. A white circle at the upper-right corner of the field depicts an expanding text field. If you want to set your text field to a fixed width, click the Stage and drag the Text tool to your desired width. A white square at the upper-right corner of the field depicts a fixed width text field. Both of these handles can be used to resize the field as well.*

The frames in the `page names` layer should extend right to frame 70. Select frame 10, which is labeled `catalog`, and insert a keyframe by pressing F6. Continue by inserting keyframes at each labeled frame: 20, 30, 40, 50, and 60.

Now you need to add the actual page names onto each page because currently every one of them says `HOME`! Go to frame 10 and double-click the page name. The text returns to an editable state, so you can change the text from HOME to *CATALOG*. Make sure that you do not move this text field on the Stage or any text properties so it remains consistent and aligned with all of the other text fields.

Repeat this step for all the other pages, giving them the same name (in all caps) as the frame labels you created in the first exercise. All you need to do is double-click the text field and edit HOME to the name of the current label.

Lock the `page names` layer when you finish. The Timeline should look like the following figure.

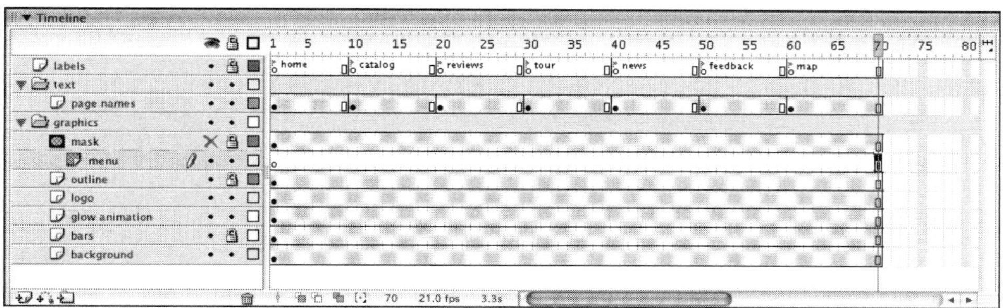

6) Add the bookstore's slogan using static text on top of the title area.

You need to add another text field above the page names. However, you need to create a new layer because the slogan stays the same throughout the Web site, whereas the page names change on every page.

Select the `page names` layer and then insert a new layer. Rename that layer *propaganda*. An empty keyframe and frames should extend right to frame 70 already. Select the Text tool and maximize the Property inspector. All the current settings will be used for this text field, except that you should click the Italic button and change the Text (fill) color to *#999999*.

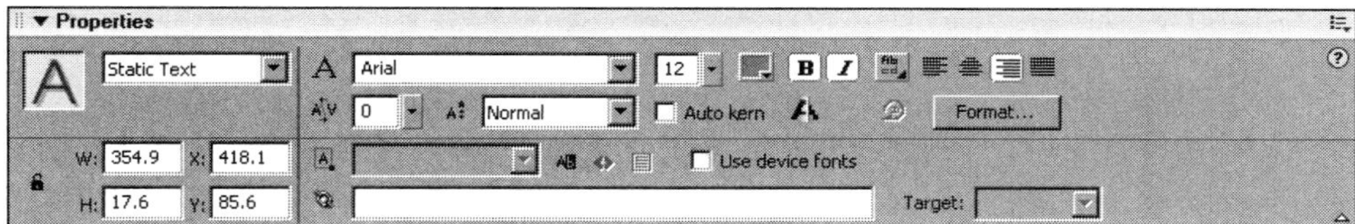

In the `propaganda` layer, click on top of the title area of the layout and type in *SELLING QUALITY BOOKS about MACROMEDIA SOFTWARE*. When you finish, choose the Selection tool and move the text field to a desired location in the general lower-right area of the title area. If you want to align the slogan with the page names, use a vertical guide. Drag the guide from the vertical ruler and align it with the right side of the page name. Then select the slogan and snap the right side of the text field to the guide.

7) Add aliased small text to the bottom of the Stage.

Sometimes, small fonts can be very hard to read in Flash because Flash has to create outlines for the fonts, and it can sometimes cause them to be blurry. However, if you click the Alias text button in the Property inspector, the text is rendered much clearer for many fonts. You will learn more about alias and anti-alias in the next exercise.

TIP *Even when you select the Alias text button, some smaller sizes of text do not display clearly. Flash supports only 8pt and greater text size, although results vary depending on which font you choose to use. You might need to look into "pixel fonts" if Flash doesn't produce the results you need. These fonts typically stay very clear at very small sizes when regular fonts might appear blurry. Refer to Appendix B for a list of links to several sites offering pixel fonts, some of which are specifically made for Flash, for download.*

The next step is to add some more text on the `propaganda` layer. At the bottom of the Web page is copyright and contact information for visitors to use. You should use a very small text size because you probably don't want to make it too distracting.

Select the Text tool and maximize the Property inspector. The text type can stay as Static, and Arial can be the font. However, change the font size to 10, change the text (fill) color back to #666666, make sure that Bold and Italics are *not* selected, and choose the Align Left button.

Click the Alias text button so the text you create renders clearly on the Stage. Using the Text tool, click in approximately the center of the bar on the bottom of the Stage and type *Tech Bookstore © 2003*.

Create a second text field within the bottom bar area. Because this text field has exactly the same properties, you don't need to use the Property inspector before you create the field. Click the Stage and enter the following email address: *`info@trainingfromthesource.com`*.

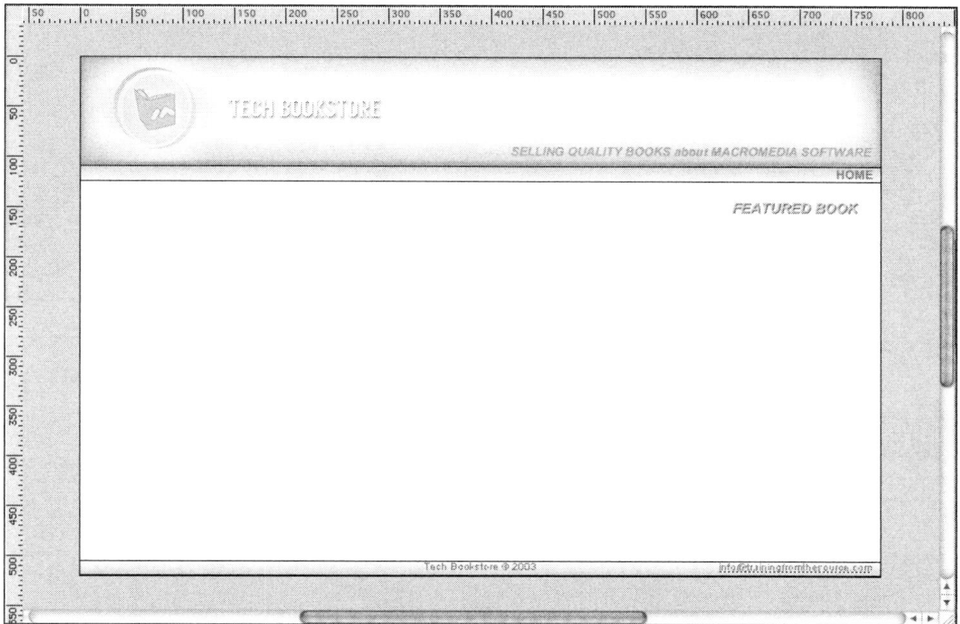

8) Align the small text on the Stage using the Align panel.

When you finish creating both text fields, click the Selection tool and maximize the Align panel. Make sure the To Stage button is selected. Click the first text field you created and then click the Align Horizontal Center button, which centers the text in the middle of the Stage. Use the up and down arrow keys on your keyboard to fine-tune its placement vertically approximately in the center of the lower bar graphic, but depending on where it looks best against the gradient.

Select the second text field that contains the email address and click the Align Right Edge button in the Align panel. This procedure aligns the bounding box around the text field with the right edge of the Stage. If you think it is too close to the edge, select the text field and use the left arrow key to move it a few pixels to the left.

These two text fields are probably already lined up horizontally, but let's make sure that they are aligned perfectly. Select both text fields by holding the Shift key while clicking them with the Selection tool. In the Align panel, click the To Stage button again so it is not selected. Now click the Align Vertical Center button so both fields are vertically aligned. When you finish, the text should look similar to the previous figure.

9) Add a link to the bookstore's email address using URL link in the Property inspector.

There is a really quick way to link the email address so it opens the default email client on the computer the SWF is running on. Select the text field with the email address and maximize the Property inspector. At the URL Link field at the bottom, enter *mailto:info@trainingfromthesource.com?subject=TechBookstore* into the text field. When you finish, the text field has a dotted underline to signify that there is a URL link applied to it.

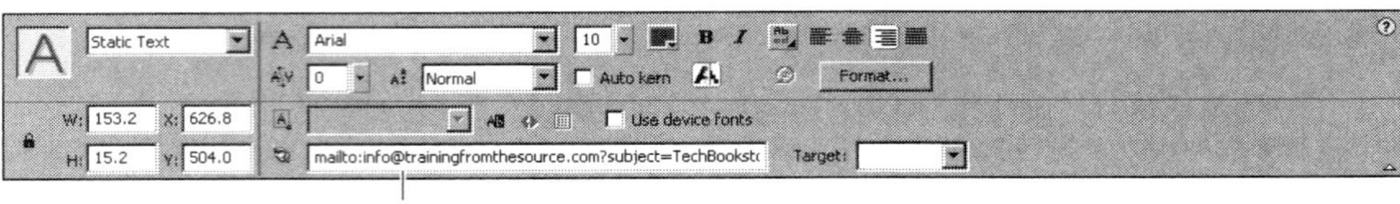

TIP *Remember that not all of your users have a default email client on their machines. Some visitors to the site might be using a shared computer, might not have an email client installed, or might not use the email software that is currently the default. Thus, the Tech Bookstore site uses a built-in contact form, so all users can send feedback or questions from the site.*

If a visitor clicks the link, an email message will open addressed to `info@trainingfromthesource.com`, with *TechBookstore* entered into the subject field. When you finish, lock the `propaganda` layer so you do not accidentally add something else to this layer.

10) Save the changes you've made to `bookstore7.fla`.

The changes you've made in this exercise are saved to the file.

USING EMBEDDED FONTS

You might want to use the option of *embedding* your fonts if you want more control over the exact size and look of your dynamic or input text. Dynamic and input text both rely on system fonts, so whatever font you use for the text field must also reside on the computer the SWF is running on. The SWF contains the name of the font and then looks for a similar name on the end user's computer. If a matching font isn't found on the computer, the user cannot see the correct text in that field. The closest matching font is used instead. In contrast to static text, dynamic and input text fields use device fonts by default, which you learned about near the beginning of this lesson.

You can get around this problem by embedding a font in your SWF file, or at least certain characters of it. The font outlines are stored in the SWF when it is published and ensures proper rendering when the SWF plays on a visitor's computer. The main issue with embedding fonts is that it increases your file size, depending on how much information (how many characters) you choose to store in the SWF file.

1) Create a dynamic text field.

Select frame 1 of the `propaganda` layer on the Timeline. Unlock the layer, select the Text tool, and maximize the Property inspector. Choose Dynamic from the Text type drop-down menu. Click anywhere on the Stage and type *my cat eats chicken* into the text field.

2) Open the Character Options dialog box.

Select the dynamic text field you just created and click the Character button. The Character Options dialog box opens, in which you can specify a range of characters (or individual characters) to embed.

3) Click the Specify Range radio button.

To help reduce the amount of information Flash stores for the font, you can specify for only a particular range of character outlines to be embedded in the SWF. Select the first two options in the list by simply clicking both listings. Press the Ctrl or Command keys while making your selections.

Specifying a range is particularly useful if you want to limit what characters are used, such as numbers only.

4) Deselect the selections under Specify Range and only include specific characters.

Specifying certain characters to embed is a good choice if you do not have much dynamic content in the SWF file and you know exactly what characters you need. Click the Auto Fill button, and the characters Flash needs to embed in the SWF are entered into the field: *my cateshikn*.

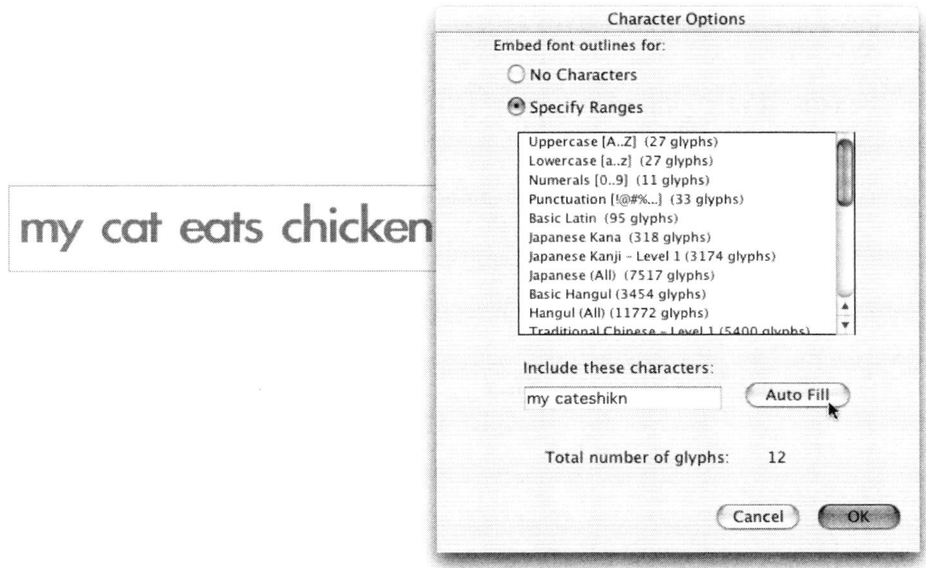

Specifying characters helps decrease the amount of information stored in the SWF. It is not always possible if you do not know what characters will necessarily need to be displayed or typed into a text field. Remember that you can also use a combination of a specified range and specified characters entered into the Include these characters text field.

5) Click Cancel and delete the text field.

Obviously, visitors to the Tech Bookstore don't need to know that my cat eats chicken. Click Cancel at the bottom of the Character Options dialog box to close it. Then delete the dynamic text field from the Stage and lock the `propaganda` layer again.

NOTE *You will learn how to embed a font using a Font symbol in the Library that will be shared across multiple SWFs in Lesson 12.*

LOOKING AT FONT PROPERTIES

In Flash, and in other programs in which you can edit text, there is a wealth of options available for formatting text to change its appearance. At their most basic level, fonts can be divided into two flavors: *serif* and *san-serif*. Serif fonts have small, subtle cross lines at the end of the stems and curves that make up each character. The small stroke in question is called a serif. San-serif fonts do not have those extra lines. Arial, which we are using throughout the Tech Bookstore, is an example of a common san-serif font. Times New Roman is an example of a serif font.

There are many options for text, but so far we have used only the most basic and common of them. In this exercise, you will use some new properties that you didn't use in earlier exercises and learn how they are used and what they do in Flash. You should still be using `bookstore7.fla` for this example.

1) Set the properties for the address text in the Property inspector.

The `map` page will contain some store information and a title, and load a map into a placeholder. Loading content into a SWF is dealt with in Lesson 6, but the address and title are created here. Open the Property inspector so you can set properties for the store information that needs to be placed on the Stage.

Change the Text Type drop-down to static. Choose Arial as the font and then set the font size to 12 and the color to black. Click the Align Center button to set the alignment (justification), which centers the characters you will enter in the text field.

Kerning refers to the spacing between characters; however, it is not uniform like the Character Spacing setting. Kerning is built into the font and determines how two particular letters are spaced. For example, some letters might be spaced closer together based on the way they are shaped. The character *W* is usually placed closer to an *A* character than *O* is. Kerning helps the spacing *look* uniform based on the shape of each character by spacing two characters in varied amounts. Check the Auto Kern check box in the Property inspector to use the built-in kerning information for the font.

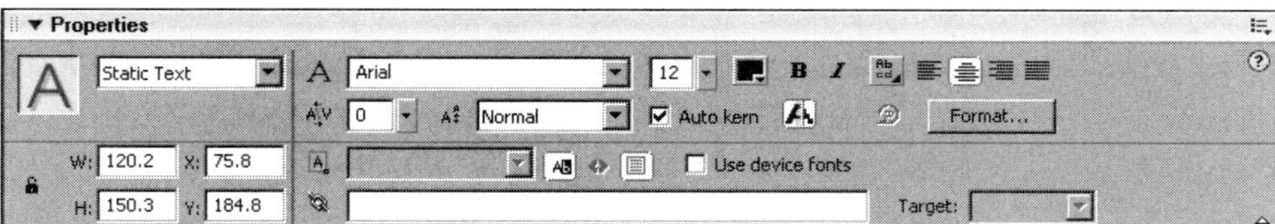

2) Enter the store information and place it on the Stage.

Select the `graphics` folder, insert a new layer, and rename it *map*. Click frame 60, also labeled `map` on the `labels` layer, and insert a keyframe (F6). Choose the Text tool and click on the Stage. Enter the text in the following figure into the text field, using the Enter key to create new lines:

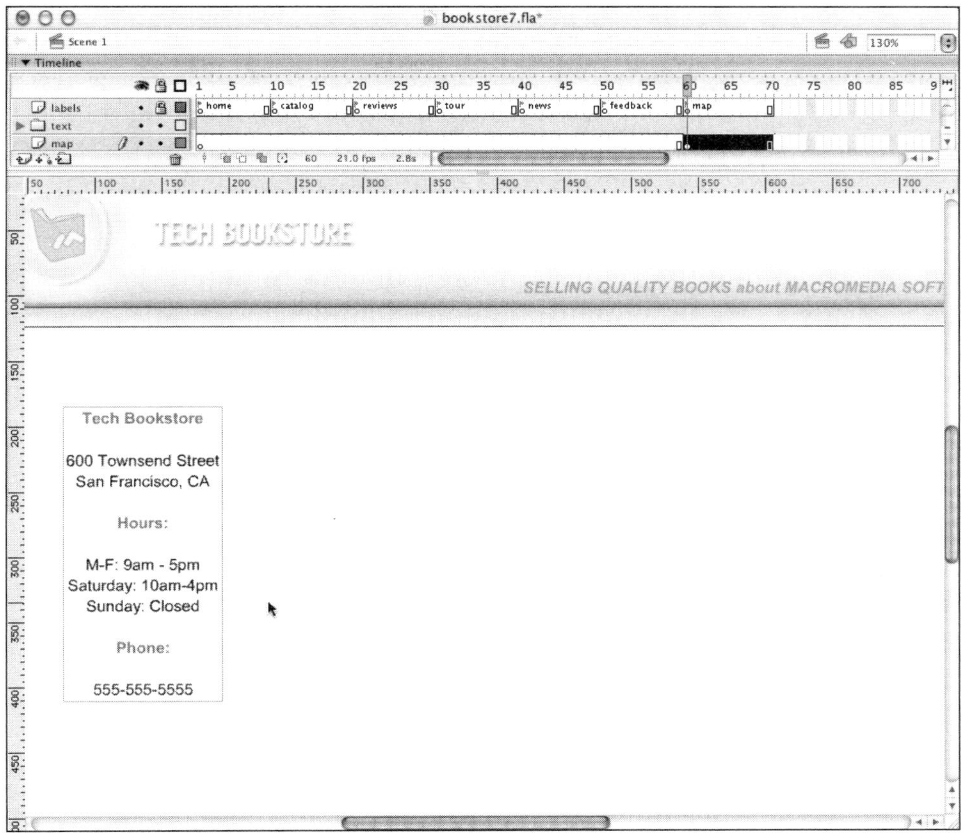

3) Format parts of the address text in the Property inspector.

In the previous figure, you probably noticed that some of the lines are boldface. After you finish typing in the text, go back and highlight the first line: *Tech Bookstore*. With the line highlighted and the Property inspector maximized, click the Bold button and then choose a dark grey swatch from the color control palette for Text Fill. Repeat this step for all headings in the text field.

It is also a good idea to make the address selectable. For example, some of the Web site visitors might want to copy and paste this information into an email, send it to a portable device or save the text. Select the text field and then click the Selectable button in the Property inspector so visitors can highlight and copy this text at run time.

SELECTABLE TEXT

4) Select the Alias text button in the Property inspector.

An aliased image has a hard and definitive edge, and curves tend to appear jagged. Anti-aliasing creates the illusion that lines are smoothed or curved by using blending and shading to smooth the image or lines. Anti-aliasing reduces the jaggedness of aliased text or graphics. Although anti-aliasing is often a good choice for Web graphics, it does not work well with very small text because blending and smoothing usually make small text appear fuzzy and unclear.

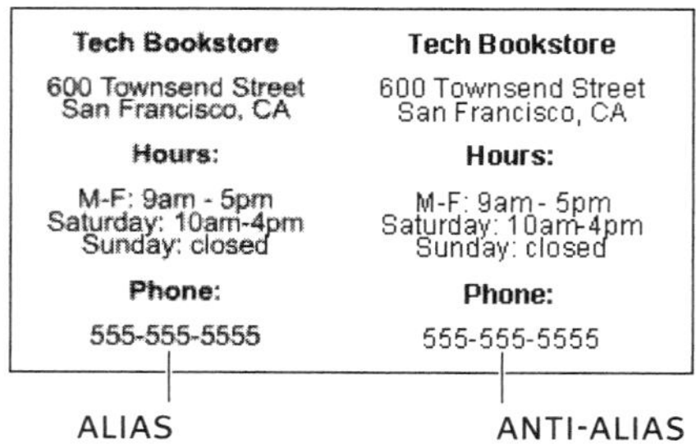

ALIAS ANTI-ALIAS

The Alias text feature takes the outlines of text on the Stage and lines them up with the invisible pixel grid on the Stage. When you use Alias text, all the text within a single text field is affected: You cannot apply alias only to certain parts of a text field.

NOTE *Alias text works for static, input, and dynamic text fields. However, the visitor to your site must have Flash Player 7 or greater to view Alias text in input and dynamic text fields. Static text fields can have the Alias text feature applied and appear correct in earlier players.*

Select the text field you just created in Step 3. Expand the Property inspector and then click the Alias text button. This process should remove the slight fuzziness of the text, and make it much more legible to read.

5) Check that the text is still legible on the Stage.

After you apply Alias text to a text field, it is generally a good idea to make sure that the characters are still legible using the font, size, and properties you have applied to them. Some results are unpredictable. Larger text usually looks a lot better *without* Alias text chosen.

TIP *If Alias text doesn't work for a particular kind of font or size you are using, you might consider creating a bitmap of that text. In your favorite image editor, type the text block and make sure anti-alias is not applied to it. Then save the file and import it into Flash.*

Remember that Flash has a difficult time applying alias to text with serifs, such as Times New Roman and _typewriter. If you are using a serif font, particularly if it is small, make sure that the characters are legible in your text fields.

6) Change the properties for the map title using the Property inspector.

Maximize the Property inspector to change the font properties again. You will use some large text this time, so the first thing you want to do is deselect the Alias text button. Click it again so it is *not* applied to the text field.

You will still use a black Arial font, so don't change those properties. However, change the font size to *26* by typing into the field or using the numerical slider next to it. Make sure that the Bold and Italic buttons are selected. You can leave Auto Kern checked, or deselect the check box. Because you are increasing the Character Spacing in the next step, it doesn't particularly matter.

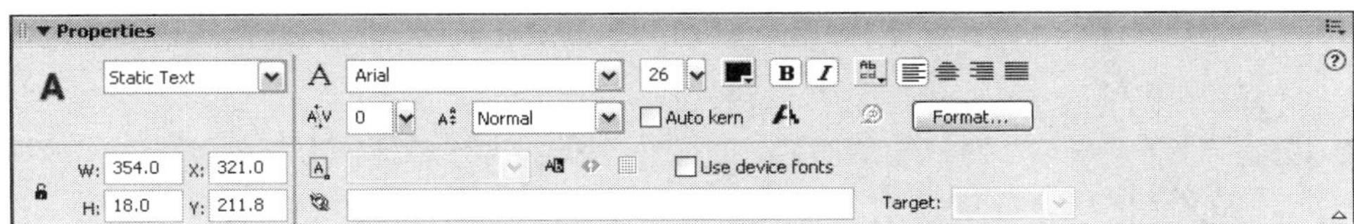

7) Enter the text for the map title and position it on the Stage.

Create a static text field on the Stage, and enter the following text: *How to find us.*

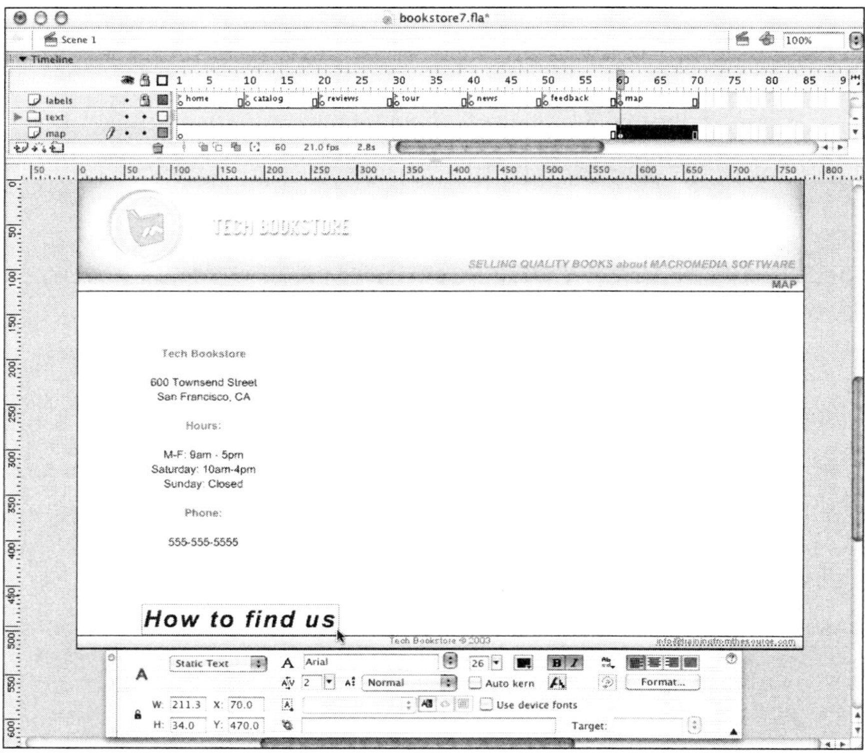

You might need to edit the exact placement later on when you add the map to this page. For now, change the values of the X, Y coordinates in the Property inspector to *70* (X) and *470* (Y).

8) Change the Character Spacing value to *2*.

When you change the character spacing for a text field, a uniform amount of space is set between each character. You can enter a positive value to space the characters further from one another, or enter negative values so they are closer. Select the text field you just created and enter *2* into the Character Spacing text field. Take note of the way the characters change in the text field and adjust the amount as desired.

TIP *You might want to take this opportunity to play around with some of the other settings in the Property inspector. Because the size of this text is so large, it is easy to see how the text is changed. Double-click the text field and select half of the characters in the text field. Try applying changes only to those characters. Remember to remove the changes you make before going on to the next step.*

TIP *You can use HTML markup to format dynamic or input text. If you select the* Render text as HTML *button in the Property inspector, HTML tags can be used to format text. There are some limitations of what tags are supported by Flash. Lesson 11 formats text using HTML tags.*

ADDING A TIMELINE EFFECT TO A TEXT FIELD

Timeline Effects are like filters that you can use to add certain effects to text. Flash installs with several effects made by Macromedia, but you can also find many more on the Web for download to install into Flash. Select third party companies, such as erain and SWiSH, have even created plug-ins you can download and install into Flash that can be used to animate text in various different ways. In this exercise, you will use the drop shadow effect with some static text.

1) Create a new layer and layer folder for the `home` **page on frame 1.**

Move the playhead back to frame 1 on the Timeline, labeled `home`. Select the `map` layer, insert a new layer, and give this layer the name *home*. With it selected, insert a new layer folder and name it *pages*. Drag the `home` layer (and the `map` layer you created in the earlier exercise as well) into this folder. The `pages` folder will eventually hold all of the layers created for each page in the Web site.

Select the `home` layer again. Click just to the right of the final frame on the layer, and drag the cursor back to frame 10 and release the mouse to select the row of frames. Right-click or control-click and choose Remove frames from the contextual menu.

2) Create a static text field with the words `Featured Book`**.**

Open the Property inspector, so you can change some of the text properties. Leave the text as a Static text type and Arial. Change the font color to *#CCCCCC* and the font size to *14*. Make sure that the typeface is set to Bold and Italic, and that Alias text is turned off. You probably need to change Character Spacing back to *0* and make sure that Auto Kern is selected.

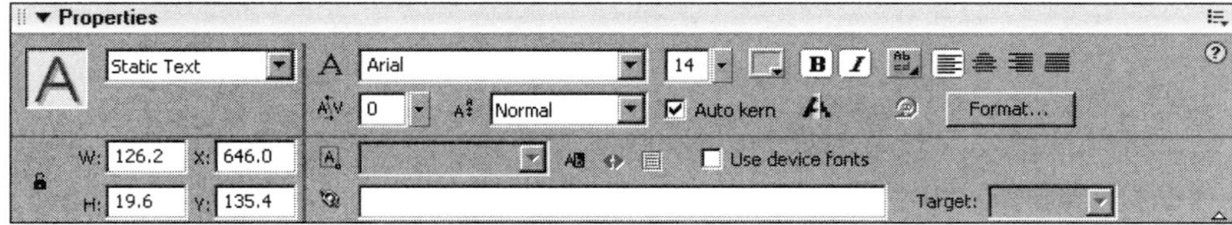

With the `home` layer selected, click the Stage to create a new static text field and type *FEATURED BOOK* into the field. Place the text field on the upper-right side of the Stage under the Home text, similar to the following figure.

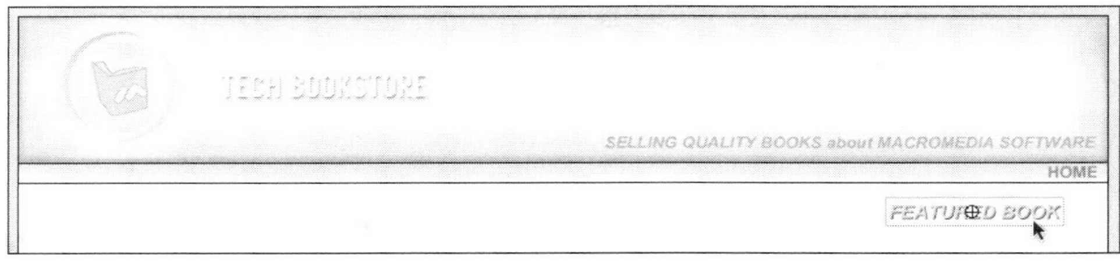

3) Add a Timeline Effect to the text field.

Select the text field you just created and choose Insert > Timeline Effects > Effects > Drop Shadow. A new window opens, in which you can make settings and preview the effect before applying it to the text field.

In this window, change the color control to *black* (#000000), leave the alpha transparency setting at *75%*, and change the shadow offset values both to *1*.

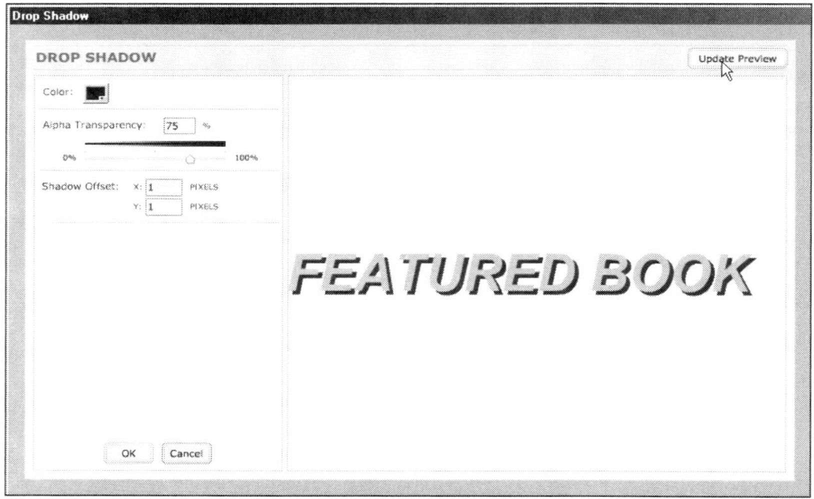

Click the Update Preview button to view the changes you made. If you finish making changes to the settings, click OK to return to the Stage. The effect that you add automatically creates new graphic symbols in the Library and a new folder containing the effect.

4) Rename the new layer, and then save the changes you have made to the file.

The layer is automatically renamed, so you have to double-click the layer and rename the layer `home` again. A new graphic symbol was created in the Library called

`Drop Shadow 1`. Move this new symbol into the `graphics` folder. Remember to save the changes you have made to the file before you go on to the next exercise.

TIP *Many designers also use an image editor to apply various filters or effects to the text and then save the image and import it into Flash. This way, you can have complex text in your SWF with effects you couldn't create using the tools in Flash.*

SPELL CHECK YOUR DOCUMENT

The spell checking tool in Flash allows you to check your spelling in all text in an FLA file. Cleaning up the spelling in an FLA before you publish it for the world to see is a great habit to adopt. The spell check feature in Flash allows you to have a lot of control over how the FLA is checked. You can check the spelling of all text fields and even layer names or ActionScript. Now that you have added a lot of text to the FLA, you should spell check the text you have added.

1) Use the Spelling Setup dialog box to choose your settings.

If you haven't used the spell check feature yet, choose Text > Spelling Setup. You need to open this dialog box before you can use the spell check for the first time. Even if the Spelling Setup has already been run, open the dialog box and explore the settings available. Notice that you can control what text is spell checked in the FLA under the Document heading. The options under Checking options allow you to decide what kinds of words and changes are included or omitted in the spell check. In the Spelling Setup dialog box, check off the selections seen in the following figure before getting started.

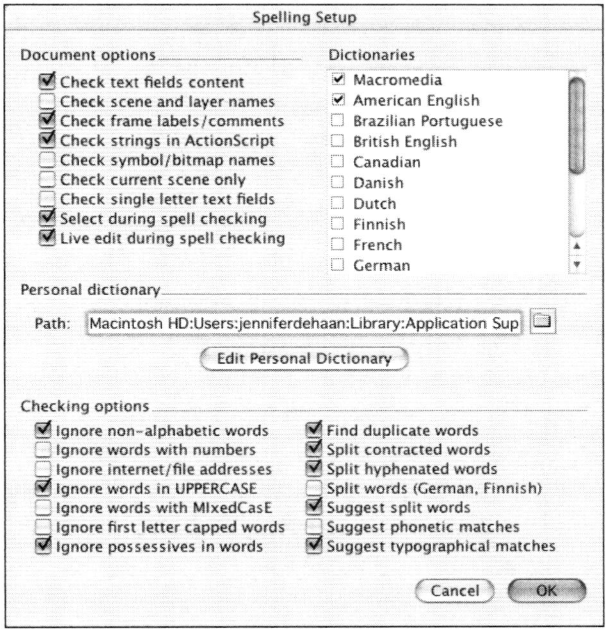

Spelling Setup

Document options
- [x] Check text fields content
- [ ] Check scene and layer names
- [x] Check frame labels/comments
- [x] Check strings in ActionScript
- [ ] Check symbol/bitmap names
- [ ] Check current scene only
- [ ] Check single letter text fields
- [x] Select during spell checking
- [x] Live edit during spell checking

Dictionaries
- [x] Macromedia
- [x] American English
- [ ] Brazilian Portuguese
- [ ] British English
- [ ] Canadian
- [ ] Danish
- [ ] Dutch
- [ ] Finnish
- [ ] French
- [ ] German

Personal dictionary

Path: Macintosh HD:Users:jenniferdehaan:Library:Application Sup

Edit Personal Dictionary

Checking options
- [x] Ignore non-alphabetic words
- [ ] Ignore words with numbers
- [ ] Ignore internet/file addresses
- [x] Ignore words in UPPERCASE
- [ ] Ignore words with MIxedCasE
- [ ] Ignore first letter capped words
- [x] Ignore possessives in words
- [x] Find duplicate words
- [x] Split contracted words
- [x] Split hyphenated words
- [ ] Split words (German, Finnish)
- [x] Suggest split words
- [ ] Suggest phonetic matches
- [x] Suggest typographical matches

Cancel OK

Make any additional selections if desired. All the options are quite self-explanatory and tooltips explain what each option does, as shown in the previous figure. Remember that you can change these settings at any time.

2) Check the document's spelling using the Check Spelling dialog box.

Now choose Text > Check Spelling to open the Check Spelling dialog box and start the spell checker. Currently, it is set to check the spelling of all text fields in the FLA. If a word is correct but is not recognized by the spell check dictionary, you can click Ignore to ignore the word or you can add it to your personal dictionary by clicking the Add to Personal button.

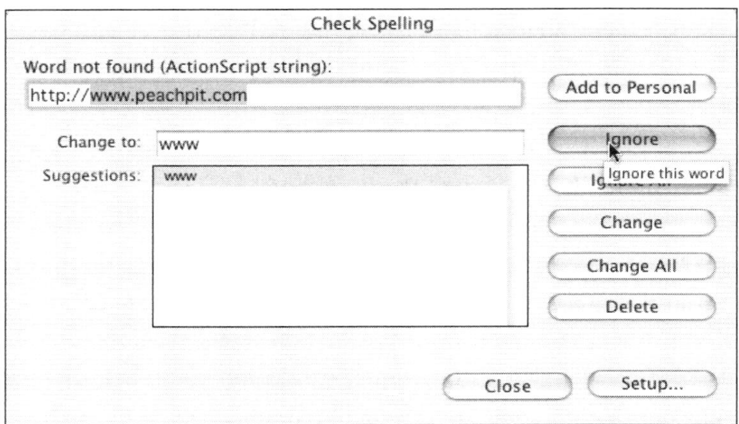

An alert pops up when the spell check is complete. Click OK to exit the Check Spelling feature.

3) Save a new version of the document as `bookstore7_complete.fla`.

Save the new version in the `TechBookstore` folder on your hard drive. If you want to look at the completed file for this lesson, `open bookstore7_complete.fla`, which can be found in the `Lesson03` folder on the CD-ROM.

USING TEXT-BASED COMPONENTS

One of the ways you are going to add text to the Tech Bookstore application in upcoming lessons is by using text components. Text components include the TextArea and TextInput components. TextArea is used when you need to display larger blocks of text that can be scrolled. TextInput is when you need to have users enter data into a text field that can be collected and used. In some ways, these two components are replacements for dynamic and input text fields discussed earlier. A drawback to using TextArea and TextInput instead of dynamic or input text fields is a greater file size, and sometimes you have to write or use more ActionScript to get them to work the way you need them to. The advantage of using these components is the wealth of things you can do using them, and the scrollbars that are automatically attached to the field.

NOTE *Code to load content into these components will be added later on in Lessons 11 and 12. For now, you know where the components will go on the pages you have just added. Later on in the book, you will add TextInput fields to a feedback form that will be created. Users will enter information that will be stored in an XML file.*

UNDERSTANDING DYNAMIC TEXT FIELDS

Dynamic and input text fields are quite different than the static text fields you have worked with earlier. These different kinds of text fields can each handle changing text. This means you can load text into them and change the text based on some kind of event that happens while the SWF file is running.

Dynamic and input text fields can also understand HTML formatted text. This means you can use HTML tags within the text you enter or load into the field, and Flash will display the font type according to the tags within the text. For example, you could enter `<b>` tags to boldface text, and Flash will render text within the dynamic text field as bold. You can also place URLs, images, and paragraphs within a dynamic text field using HTML tags. You will explore these techniques in Lesson 11, except you will use a TextArea component, which works in almost the same way.

WHAT YOU HAVE LEARNED

In this lesson, you have:

- Learned more about static text and device fonts (pages 81–82)
- Used the text tool to add text to the FLA file (pages 82–88)
- Tried embedding characters in a SWF (pages 88–90)
- Changed text properties using the Property inspector (pages 90–95)
- Added a Timeline Effect to a static text field (pages 95–97)
- Learned how to check spelling in your document (pages 97–98)
- Learned more about text-based components and dynamic text fields (pages 98–99)

creating and editing symbols

LESSON 4

Symbols are the primary building blocks of a Flash document: They form a collection of assets that you can use to build an FLA file. Symbols can be static, dynamic, interactive, or even self-contained mini-applications. Movie clips, buttons, and graphics are symbols that you create within the Flash authoring environment.

In order to animate items on the Stage or do any sort of animation, you need to understand what symbols are and what the differences are between each kind of symbol in Flash. Symbols help you reduce file size in a SWF file because you can reuse each symbol more than once without necessarily increasing the size of the file.

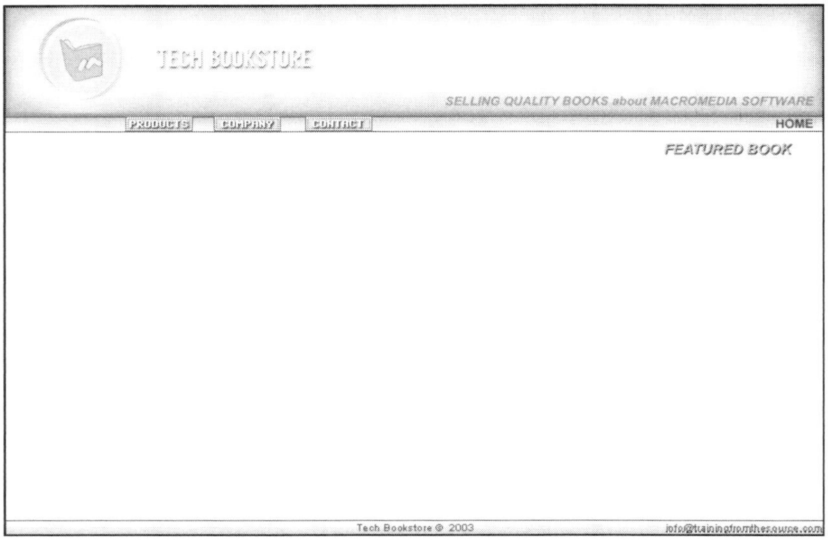

TECH BOOKSTORE

SELLING QUALITY BOOKS about MACROMEDIA SOFTWARE

PRODUCTS COMPANY CONTACT HOME

FEATURED BOOK

Tech Bookstore © 2003

New symbols are added to the Tech Bookstore.

You will begin by looking at how Flash organizes symbols and assets. Then you will learn about the different kinds of symbols in a Flash document. While creating symbols for the Tech Bookstore, you will learn about the different ways you can build and use symbols in Flash.

WHAT YOU WILL LEARN

In this lesson, you will:

- Learn about symbols and how they're used in Flash
- Understand more about graphic symbols
- Create a button and an invisible button
- Define a button's hit area
- Create new movie clip symbols
- Nest symbols within other symbols
- Create a movie clip button

APPROXIMATE TIME

This lesson takes approximately two hours to complete.

LESSON FILES

Media Files:

None

Starting Files:

Lesson04/bookstore8.fla

Completed Project:

Lesson04/bookstore8_complete.fla

UNDERSTANDING SYMBOLS

You worked with graphic symbols in Lesson 2 when you created some of the graphics for the background of the Web site. You took items from the Library and placed them onto the Stage, and found out that the Library is used to store assets you use in FLA files. The Library stores items such as symbols (graphics, movie clips, buttons, and fonts), video clips, bitmap images, sound files, and components. In fact, all items that are stored in the Library are essentially *symbols:* assets you can reuse in the Flash document.

Flash has three primary kinds of symbols that you can build within the authoring environment: *movie clips*, *buttons*, and *graphics*. You created graphic symbols in Lesson 2, and found out the symbols are made from images such as the vector graphics you created using the drawing tools. Buttons are symbols that contain four states that control how the button looks and works in relation to the mouse. You use buttons to create interactive elements in the SWF file, such as navigation, rollovers, and hot spots.

NOTE *You can build* components *within the authoring environment as well. Components are movie clip symbols with pre-defined parameters. You will learn more about using pre-built components in Lesson 9 and 11. You can also create font symbols in Flash, which are stored in the Library. You can find out more about using font symbols and embedding fonts on the book's Web site at* `www.TrainingFromTheSource.com/bonus`.

A movie clip is a lot like a mini-application because it contains a Timeline that runs independently from the main Timeline. An independent Timeline means you can create a looping animation in a movie clip or build an application completely contained within a clip. These multi-frame movie clips can then run and operate on the Stage even if the main Timeline only has a single frame.

TIP *Movie clips can also hold content that is loaded into a SWF file at runtime (when it is played in the Flash Player). You will learn more about loading content into movie clips and components in Lesson 12.*

Symbols always reside in a Library. When you drag a symbol from the Library onto the Stage, it's referred to as an *instance*. An instance is a *copy* of a symbol in the Library (meaning that you can have many instances on the Stage derived from a single symbol). Instances can function as their own entity and can be modified to apply effects, such as changing the instance to a different color or size. You can name button and movie clip instances using the Property inspector so you can manipulate them using ActionScript or a behavior. If you modify the properties of instances using ActionScript or the Property inspector, it does not affect the symbol in the

Library. If you edit the symbol from the Library in symbol-editing mode, all the symbol's instances you have on the Stage are affected.

Reusing symbols within your Flash document by pulling multiple instances from the Library ultimately leads to smaller SWF file sizes because Flash is able to "reuse and recycle" symbols and instances so the file size of your document doesn't increase.

NOTE *Remember that when you import assets such as video clips, bitmaps, fonts, and sounds, they are added to the Library like symbols as well. This means that when the assets are added to the Stage, they are essentially copies (or instances) of the symbol stored in the Library.*

Creating and Editing Symbols on the Stage

There are two ways that you can create a new symbol. You can create a symbol from an item already on the Stage (such as a raw graphic or another symbol). The content you select and press F8 to "convert" into a symbol is actually placed inside of the symbol itself. For example, if you have drawn a square on the Stage, select it and choose Modify > Convert to Symbol. The square is then placed inside of the symbol you create on a new layer, so you are essentially wrapping a symbol around the shape you selected. You could just as easily do the same thing that you did to the square to a bitmap, or even another symbol like a movie clip.

The second way to create a symbol is to start from scratch and add new content into the symbol using symbol-editing mode. As you might remember from Lesson 2, symbol-editing mode takes you to a separate editing area independent from the Stage. You can enter symbol-editing mode by double-clicking a symbol in the Library. While you are in symbol-editing mode, the edit bar (directly above or below the Timeline on Windows and the Mac) reminds you that you are editing the symbol by the links you see on the bar.

You can also edit symbols "in place." This allows you to edit a symbol and still see the placement and size of the symbol in relation to the other elements on the Stage. To edit a symbol in place, double-click the symbol on the Stage. Everything else on the Stage is greyed-out and not selectable while you edit the symbol.

You should always change any vector drawings that you make directly on the Stage (which is raw data) into symbols before publishing the FLA. Vectors that are raw data have a crosshatch pattern over them when they are selected. Raw data placed on the Stage has to be *rendered out* (drawn on the Stage using calculations when the SWF file plays) every time the playhead reaches that frame on the Timeline because the information is not stored in the Library. By changing the raw data into a symbol, you can reduce the SWF file size so the information has to be referenced only once in the Library instead of perhaps many times individually on the Timeline. It also makes the graphic easier to select on the Stage.

NOTE *You can also group raw data to make it easier to select and use in an FLA file. Remember that grouping data does not add the group to the Library. Therefore, grouping does not help reduce SWF file size. You will group several symbols later in this lesson to help arrange the elements on Stage.*

Looking at Symbols in the Library

You can view the symbols within your FLA file in the Library, which is opened using Ctrl+L (or Command+L on the Mac). An icon and name represent each symbol, and you can tell what kind of asset the symbol is by referring to the Kind column. The Use Count column lets you know how many instances of a symbol are used throughout the document. *Linkage* lets you know whether the item is exported, associated with a shared Library, or even linked to something in the FLA file like a component. You will learn more about linkage later in the book.

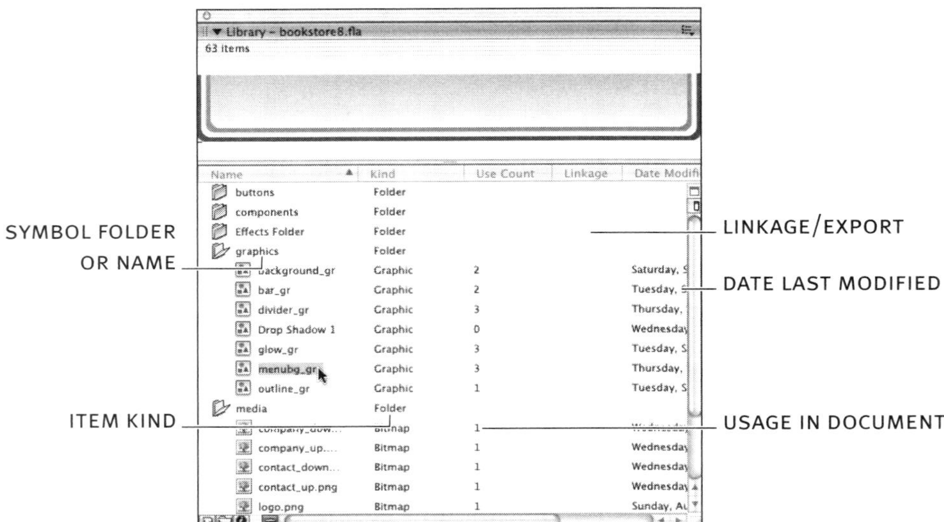

TIP *On Windows, the Library of the current FLA file is white, whereas the Library of an FLA that's not currently being edited is entirely greyed-out. On the Mac, an inactive Library's text is greyed-out instead of the entire background.*

Button and movie clip symbol instances can be named in the Property inspector. These instances are given a unique *instance name* in the Property inspector's `<Instance Name>` field so you can *target* the instance name in ActionScript. An instance name is different from the name you give a symbol when you initially create it. A symbol name can be the same as one of the instance names, but each instance name you create must be unique. You will learn more about naming instances in Lesson 6.

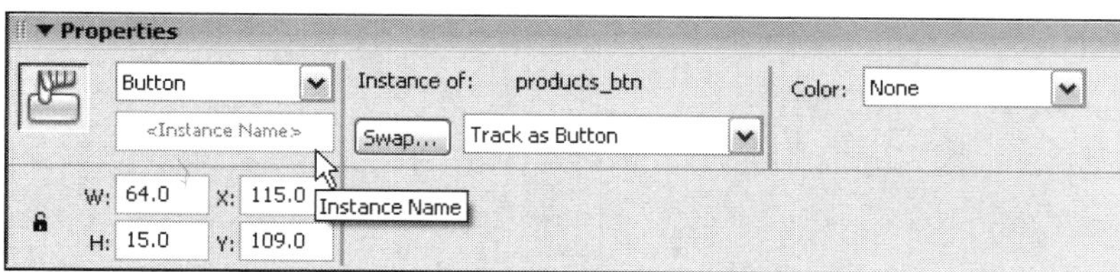

Using ActionScript and an instance name is one way to manipulate properties such as the size, color, or movement of symbol instances on the Stage.

Nesting Symbols and Timelines

Every symbol has a Timeline that can hold other symbols, text, video, and graphics. A button Timeline contains four frames that represent each state of the button: Up, Over, Down, and Hit. You can place graphics or movie clips on each button state that controls how the button works and looks when it's in an application. A graphic symbol has a Timeline that you can use to create layered drawings and animations, although it runs in sync with the main Timeline. Therefore, a graphic that has an animation spanning 50 frames would need 50 frames on the main Timeline to view the entire animation. If you moved the playhead on the main Timeline, the graphic's animation would animate. As was mentioned, the movie clip has a Timeline that is completely independent of the main Timeline, so if the main Timeline only had one frame, the movie clip could still play a 50 frame animation when placed on that single frame. You can do anything inside movie clips that you can do on the main Stage. The biggest difference between a movie clip and a graphic is that you cannot manipulate a graphic symbol using ActionScript. A graphic symbol cannot use or be manipulated by any ActionScript in any way, and cannot be assigned an instance name.

Because you can nest an instance inside of another symbol, you can have many layers of movie clips inside one another. You will nest a few movie clips later on in the lesson. Generally speaking, you shouldn't nest too many symbols within other symbols. Many layers of nested symbols within nested symbols can make a document exceedingly complex and usually creates an FLA that is complicated, intensive, and difficult to work with.

In Lesson 2, you learned about the edit bar. As you work more with movie clips in this lesson, you will find out how important it is to use the edit bar to navigate though documents that contain nested symbols. The edit bar gives you a good idea about what you are editing and where you are within the nested symbols, as you saw in the earlier graphic.

REVISITING GRAPHIC SYMBOLS

You created some graphic symbols when you worked with the drawing tools in Lesson 2. Graphic symbols are useful when you have static bitmaps in the Library and want to place them in your Flash document (and particularly when you want to reuse the images). Graphic symbols don't have instance names, so you cannot control them using ActionScript to manipulate their behavior or appearance. If you need to control the instance using ActionScript, place the graphic symbol inside of a movie clip symbol instead.

You can create animations inside of graphic symbols. Graphic symbols are ideal if you need to view the symbol's animation while working on the main Timeline because the graphic symbol's Timeline works in sync with the main Timeline. So when you move the playhead on the main Timeline (called "scrubbing") you can view the graphic symbol's animation.

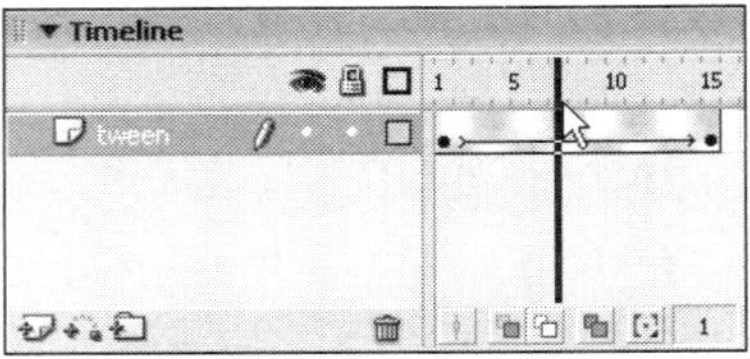

You already added a couple of static graphics to your FLA file. Some of these graphics were graphic symbols, and others were bitmap PNG files that you imported into the document and placed in the `media` folder. Any of these imported bitmaps that were placed on the Stage were stored in the Library when you imported them. Imported bitmap images are treated like symbols: Copies on the Stage are like instances of the imported bitmap.

CREATING BUTTONS

Buttons are used within Flash documents to help create interactivity in the application. As you'll learn in Lessons 6 and 11, buttons can be used to submit forms or execute ActionScript code that controls your Flash document. Buttons also have *events* that are triggered when something happens in the SWF file. An example of an event is when a user clicks a button. Therefore, you could trigger an event (written in ActionScript) when a user clicks the button with the mouse.

The first buttons you need to create for the bookstore are three basic buttons that go under the title area. These three buttons, which are used to trigger the menu below it, are built using the six PNG bitmap images that you imported into the FLA file during Lesson 2.

Every button symbol has four states that determine how the button will look and interact when someone uses a SWF file.

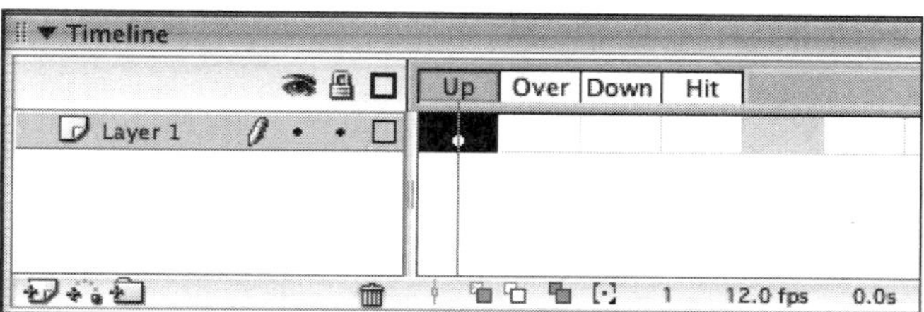

The graphic that you put in the button for the Up state displays when the button is on the Stage. The Over state displays when the mouse cursor hovers over the button's hit area. The Down state displays when the mouse is clicked within the hit area. Any image or drawing that's placed in the Hit state determines the clickable area of the button, which is essentially the region in a SWF file where a user can click the button. In most SWFs, the cursor might change to a hand in this clickable region, notifying the user that the graphic can be clicked and something will happen.

NOTE *The Hit state refers to the fourth state when you are authoring the button, seen in the previous graphic. The hit area is the area you draw where the button is clickable on the Stage when the SWF file runs. The hit area is the area where the user can click the button and something (usually) happens.*

1) Open `bookstore7_complete.fla`**, created in Lesson 3 and found in the** `Lesson03` **folder, and save a new version of the document as** `bookstore8.fla`**.**

Use the Save As command under the File menu and click OK to save a new version of the file to start the lesson with. You can also open `bookstore8.fla` out of the `Lesson04` folder on the CD-ROM.

2) Choose Insert > New Symbol to create a new button symbol called `products_btn`**.**

The Create New Symbol dialog box opens. Type *products_btn* into the Name field and select the Button radio button. This procedure names the button symbol in the Library `products_btn`, but does not give an instance you put on the Stage an *instance name* (which you will do later on). Click OK, and symbol-editing mode opens. The symbol can also be found in the Library.

TIP *Appending* _btn *or* _mc *onto the end of the button and movie clip symbols and instances helps to keep your Libraries organized by giving each symbol an additional text reference as to what kind they are. It also serves as a naming scheme for instances later on in the book.*

3) Open the Library and find the bitmaps that you put into in the `media` **folder.**

Double-click the `media` folder's icon of a folder to open it up so you can find the bitmap files. The bitmaps should still be called `products_up.png`, `products_down.png`, `company_up.png`, `company_down.png`, `contact_up.png`, and `contact_down.png`. These bitmaps will be used for different button states in the bookstore.

4) Select the Up state and add the `products_up.png` **bitmap to the button.**

After you open the button symbol, you will notice in the Timeline that there are four states that you can give the button. These four frames represent the Up, Over, Down, and Hit states discussed at the beginning of this exercise. Select the Up frame on the Timeline and drag `products_up.png` from the `media` folder in the Library into the button symbol.

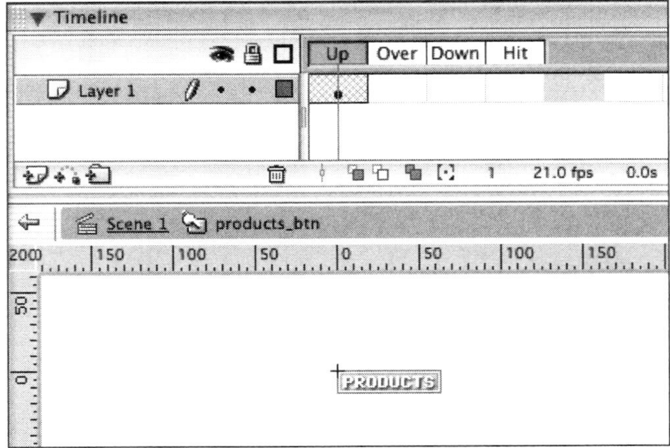

5) Add the `products_down.png` **bitmap to the button symbol's Over state.**

Select the Over state in the Timeline so it is highlighted and then choose Insert > Timeline > Blank Keyframe to insert a blank keyframe onto the Timeline. Drag the `products_down.png` bitmap from the `media` folder into the button for the Over state. This is the image seen by visitors when they hover the mouse over the button. So when they move the mouse over the button, the button changes its appearance.

6) Set the X and Y coordinates of `products_up.png` **and** `products_down.png` **to *0,0* in the Property inspector.**

Setting the X and Y coordinates both to a value of 0 sets the registration point of the button to its upper-left corner. By setting all of the images to 0,0, it is easy to remember where to set each image when it is added. So begin by selecting the `products_up.png` on the Up state, and set the coordinates to *0,0* in the Property inspector. Then select `products_down.png` and set to *0,0* in the Over state. You can also use the Info panel to set the X and Y coordinates.

TIP *A crosshair shows you where the registration point of the symbol is located. Sometimes you want to change the registration point of a button or movie clip, particularly if you are using ActionScript. When you want to change the coordinates of the movie clip, you assign the X and Y coordinates. The registration point is placed at those assigned coordinates.*

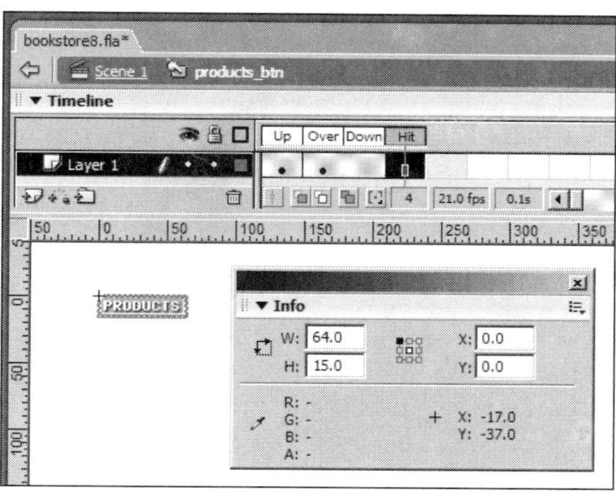

7) Select the Hit frame and press F5 to add frames to the Down and Hit frames.

Pressing F5 applies the `products_down.png` bitmap to both the Down and Hit states, while making sure the bitmap position is the same for each of the frames. The Hit state defines the area where you click the button. Because it is the same image at the same location (which you already set), you know that the clickable area will exactly match the other areas of the button.

NOTE *The hit area is not visible on the Stage. You could substitute a bright lime green rectangle in place of the bitmap image, and it wouldn't be visible to your visitors when they see the SWF file. It's easiest to just use the existing graphic that's already there, which is sized and positioned correctly, to serve as the hit area for the button.*

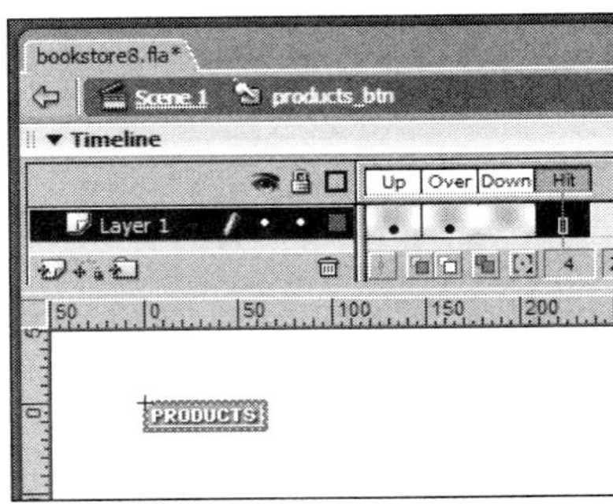

8) You need to create two more buttons and add the symbols to the `button` **folder in the Library in order to organize the new buttons you created.**

You need to create two more buttons for the area beneath the main title area for company and contact buttons. Repeat Steps 2 through 7 to create the `company_btn` and `contact_btn`. When you finish, open the Library and move the three button symbols into the `buttons` folder. Just leave the buttons in the Library for now; you will add the buttons to the Stage in the next exercise.

9) Save your file before moving on to the next exercise.

Choose Ctrl+S or Command+S to save the file. You do not need to create a new version of the file.

PLACING THE BUTTONS ON THE STAGE

You now have three buttons in the Library that should be placed on the Stage before you can progress with adding other elements on the Stage. The three buttons need to be placed on top of the `bar_gr` graphic instance on their own layer. At the end of this lesson, you will create an invisible button that will surround these three buttons and also align menus with these buttons.

1) Create a new layer called `buttons`.

Select the `text` layer folder in the Timeline and click the Insert New Layer button. When the new layer is created, double-click the name and type in *buttons* to rename the layer.

2) Drag the three buttons that you created from the Library onto the Stage.

`products_btn`, `company_btn` and `contact_btn` should all be within the `buttons` folder in the Library. When you drag the buttons onto the Stage, you should notice how the three buttons were created to be about the same height as the `bar_gr`.

3) Move the three buttons into order, and place each button at the correct X coordinate using the Property inspector.

Place the three buttons slightly apart from each other similar to the following graphic in the following order from left to right: `products_btn`, `company_btn`, and `contact_btn`. Now that they're in the correct order, you need to move the three buttons into a correct vertical position. Select the `products_btn` instance, and change the X coordinate to *115* using the Property inspector. Then select `company_btn` and set its X coordinate to *200* in the Property inspector. Finally select `contact_btn` and set its X coordinate to *285*.

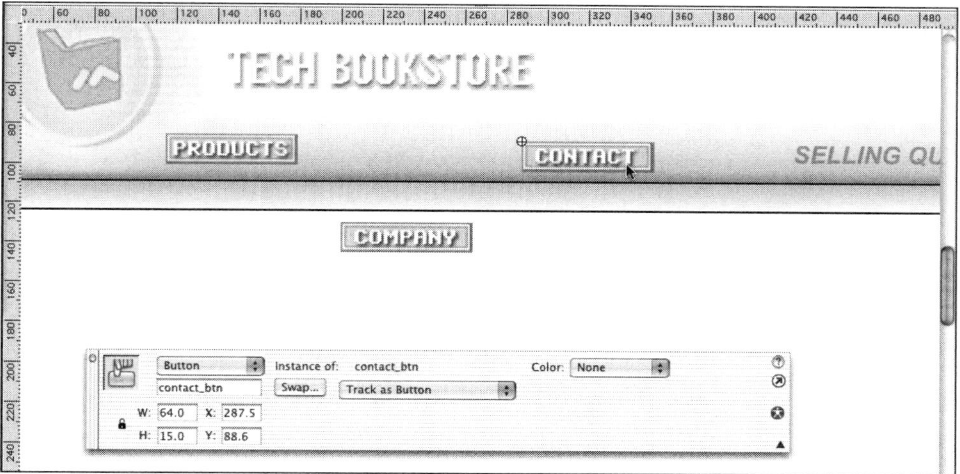

4) Align the three buttons horizontally with each other using the Align panel.

Maximize the Align panel and make sure that the To Stage button is *not* selected. Select the three buttons by holding Shift while clicking each symbol. Then click the Align vertical center button so the buttons align with each other.

5) Group and align the three buttons with `bar_gr` using the Align panel. Ungroup the three buttons and lock the `buttons` layer when you are finished.

You can group symbols so they can be edited together as one object. Sometimes you have a couple of symbols on the Stage that you want to resize, rotate, or move together as one symbol, and you can achieve this by grouping the symbols together.

Select the three buttons by holding the Shift key as you click each symbol. Then choose Modify > Group from the main menu. The three buttons can now be aligned as one object. Then select the group of buttons and move the group *below* the `bar_gr` on the Stage. Unlock the `bars` layer and press Shift to select `bar_gr`. Now the `bar_gr` symbol *and* the group of buttons should both be selected.

In the Align panel, click the Align top edge button to align the grouped buttons to the top of `bar_gr`. Ungroup the three buttons by choosing Modify > Ungroup and then lock the `buttons` layer and the `bars` layer.

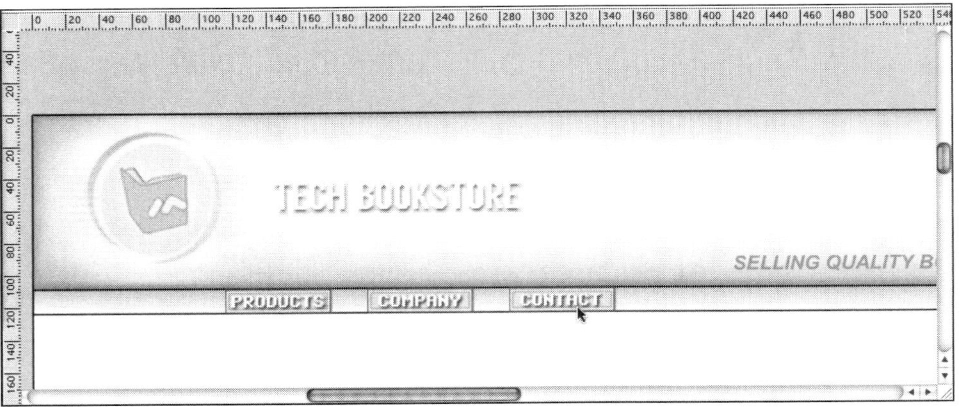

6) Save the changes you made to the file by choosing File > Save from the main menu.

Now you have three buttons on the Stage that are aligned with the bar behind them. The three buttons should align to the top edge of the `bar_gr` and be evenly distributed. They are placed in such a way that when you have the menus attached to each button they lines up fine with the mask you created earlier in the book.

CREATING TEXT BUTTONS

Sometimes you need to create a button that is made out of only text with no background. You will use text buttons like this for part of the menu. You will create text buttons in this exercise and then insert them into the menu later on in the lesson.

One of the more important parts of creating text buttons is properly defining *hit areas* for them. The hit area refers to the area in which a user can click the button. It is particularly difficult to click a text button if you leave text on the Stage without a hit area defined. A person who is trying to click the button would have to click within the small lines defining each character, which isn't easy to do!

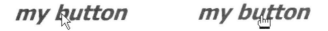

In this exercise, you will create text buttons that will be placed in the menu and define a hit area for each button. Creating a proper hit area for a text button is easy. All you need to do is follow these steps.

1) Select the Text tool and click the Stage to create a text field. In the Property inspector, choose Static text from the drop-down menu, set the font to *Arial*, text color to black *(#000000)*, font size to *8*, and click the Bold button.

After you click on the Stage with the Text tool, maximize the Property inspector and enter the new settings for the font, color, and size. Ensure that you have the correct text type (Static) and that the Bold button is selected.

Select the `buttons` layer on the Timeline (make sure it is unlocked) and then click the Text tool on the Stage and type *CATALOG* (all capitals) into the new text field.

NOTE *It doesn't matter which layer you create the text field on because you will temporarily delete the buttons from the Stage when you finish the exercise.*

2) Select the text field and then press F8 to place it inside a button symbol.

Choose the Selection tool from the Tools panel and then select the text field. Choose Modify > Convert to Symbol to convert the text field into a button symbol. Type *catalog_btn* into the Name field and click OK when you're finished.

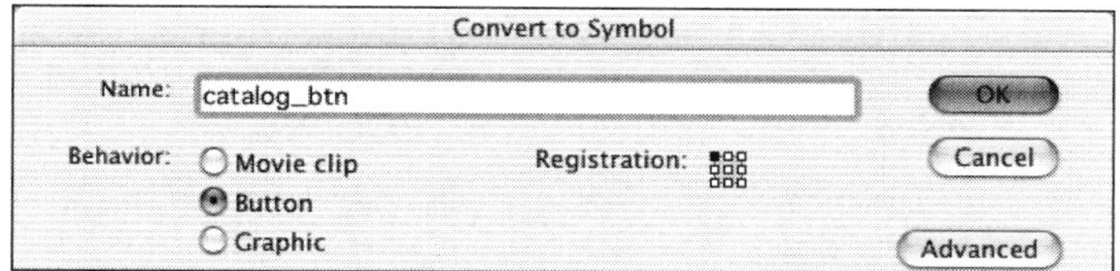

3) Open `catalog_btn` in symbol-editing mode and center the text field in the symbol.

Double-click the button to open it in symbol-editing mode. Select the text field and then use the Align panel to center the text field. Make sure that the To Stage button is selected in the Align panel, and then click the Align Horizontal Center and Align Vertical Center buttons in the panel.

4) Add Over, Down, and Hit states for the button.

Select the Down frame and press F5 to insert a frame. This means that the same text is displayed for the Up, Over, Down frames of the button. This is because you don't need a different visual appearance for each state of these text buttons.

TIP *If you want rollover or click colors for the text, you need to insert a keyframe in the Over frame or Down frame and then select the text field and change the text fill color using the Property inspector. Then the text color changes when a visitor rolls the mouse over the text in these buttons.*

5) Create a hit area for the button in the Hit frame using a rectangle.

Select the Hit frame and press F6 to enter a new keyframe. You can see that the text from the Down frame is entered into the Hit frame. You can use the text field as a reference for where the hit area needs to be created. Select the Rectangle tool and choose any color for a fill color and No Color for the stroke. Then draw a rectangle that completely covers the text that's in the frame. You want to make the rectangle slightly larger than the text area so the button is easy to click.

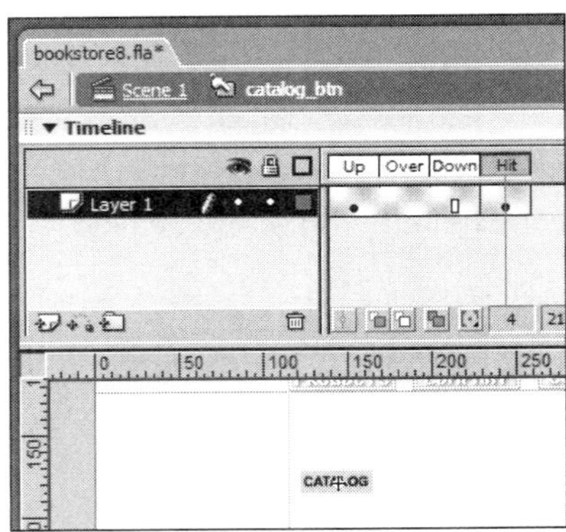

6) Create five more buttons for the menu: `REVIEWS`**,** `TOUR`**,** `NEWS`**,** `FEEDBACK`**, and** `MAP`**. Then delete them from the Stage and lock the** `buttons` **layer.**

Repeat Steps 1 to 5, except add different text (*REVIEWS*, *TOUR*, *NEWS*, *FEEDBACK*, and *MAP*, all in capital letters) for each button. You should have six new buttons in the Library when you finish: `catalog_btn`, `reviews_btn`, `tour_btn`, `news_btn`, `feedback_btn`, and `map_btn`. After you have checked you have the correct number of buttons in the Library, delete the text buttons from the Stage. In the Library, move the symbols into the `buttons` folder. You will add these buttons that are stored in the Library to three menus you create later on in the lesson.

Lock the `buttons` layer when you finish.

7) Save your file using File > Save from the main menu.

Remember to save the changes to the file before moving on.

CREATING AN INVISIBLE BUTTON

You found out that what is entered into the Hit state of a button is not visible when you view a SWF file. You will take advantage of that now and create an invisible button, which contains only a hit area and does not have any graphics. An invisible button is a lot like a "hot spot" when you create Web sites in HTML. When you roll over or click a hot spot, something happens, even if it does not look like a button is there. Invisible buttons do the same thing in a SWF file. You will use an invisible button as a trigger to close the three menus that serve as the main navigation for the Tech Bookstore.

When you roll over one of the three buttons in the bookstore, the menus open by animating downward. Then when you roll over the invisible button, the menus will animate upward so they appear to be closing. Whenever the mouse rolls outside of the menu area, you want the menus to close. The invisible button uses a button symbol's hit area to enable it to serve as a trigger to close the menus.

1) Create a new layer called `invisible button` **below the** `buttons` **layer.**

Select the `text` layer folder and click Insert New Layer. Double-click the new layer and type in *invisible button*. This layer is layered *beneath* the three buttons you created on the `buttons` layer that will be used to open menus. You are layering the invisible button underneath the three buttons so the invisible button does not interfere with opening and closing the menus. If you layer buttons, whatever button on top is the one that works in the SWF file. If the invisible button is layered on top of the three buttons, the menus would not open because the invisible button on top of the three buttons would trigger them to close. Thus, the importance of layer order!

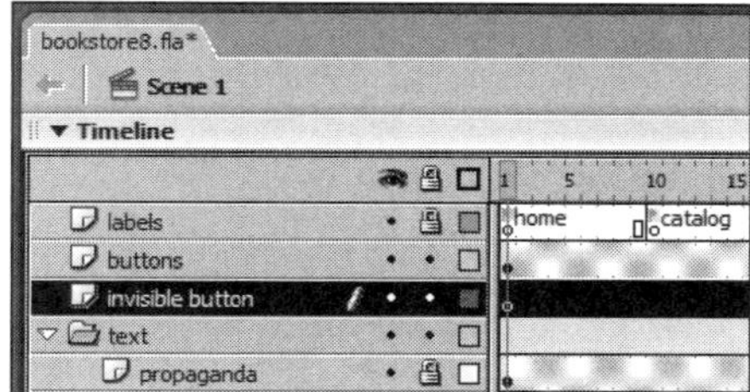

2) Add two horizontal guides to the Stage at 120 and 140 pixels. Create a third guide that is vertical at 450 pixels.

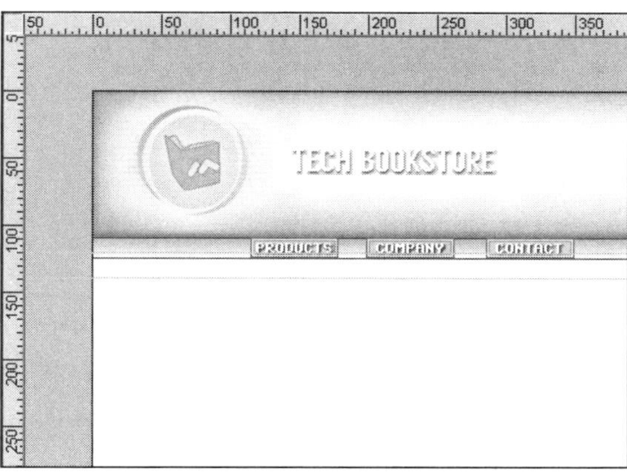

f rulers are not visible, choose View > Rulers from the main menu. Click and drag a ıew guide from the horizontal ruler above the Stage and drag it downward until you each 140 pixels on the vertical ruler. Create a second one that sits at approximately 120 pixels on the horizontal ruler. Then click and drag a guide from the vertical ruler, and drop it at the 450 pixel mark.

3) Select the Rectangle tool, and choose any color for the fill in the Tools panel. Then choose No Color for the stroke. Draw a rectangle in the upper-left corner of the Stage. When you are finished, create a second rectangle below the guide you added in Step 2.

The buttons that trigger the menus are within the `bar_gr`, and the menus extend below it to where the guide is placed. You want to cover all the areas around where the menus will be, but not the area the menus are in itself. You also don't need to cover the rest of the Stage. The button should cover some of the Stage below the menus, which is the area below the guide.

Create a rectangle that covers from the upper-left corner of the Stage that is about 450 pixels wide. The rectangle should stop just about the bottom of the buttons, at the 120 pixel point on the vertical ruler (where you set the guide to in Step 2).

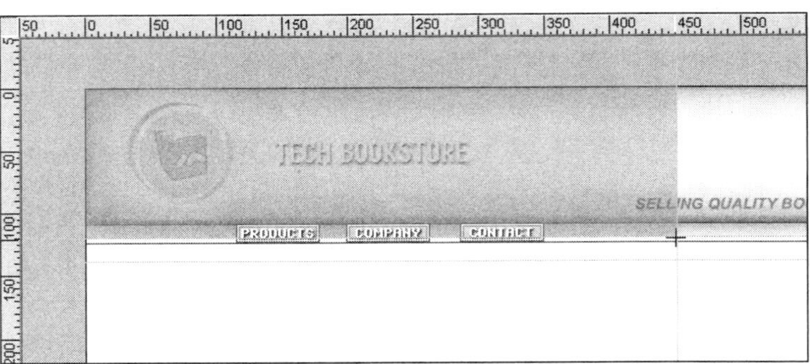

TIP *If you want to be able to see what's on the Stage while creating the hit area for this button, maximize the Color Mixer panel, click the fill color icon, and reduce the Alpha percentage to about 20%. This makes the fill color for the rectangles transparent so you can see through to the Stage, which helps you define the hot spot. If you have already created some of the rectangles, select the shape on the Stage before reducing the Alpha percentage.*

The second rectangle you create below the guide should be the same width of the Stage, and just below where the menus open. Draw a rectangle beneath the guide set at 140 (created in Step 2). This rectangle should be approximately 20 pixels tall. You can see it in the figure in Step 4.

4) Add two more rectangles beneath the `bar_gr` symbol to the left and right of the three buttons on the Stage.

In case a user moves the mouse off the left or right side of the menu, you also need to have two more rectangles spanning either side of where the menus will be.

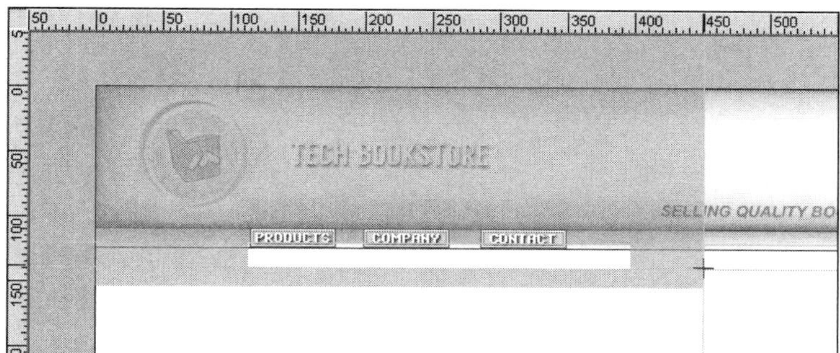

You need to create two rectangles in the empty area between the guide and the bottom edge of `bar_gr`. Create a rectangle that covers that area from the left side of the Stage to the left-lower corner of `products_btn`. Create a second rectangle that begins 45 pixels to the right of the lower-right edge of `contact_btn`. You might need to use a ruler to get the dimensions correct. Refer to the previous figure for reference to where these rectangles should be placed.

NOTE *After you actually build and animate the interactive menus, you might need to slightly modify the invisible button depending on where you precisely place the buttons and menus in your FLA file.*

The height of the rectangles you just created does not matter, as long as they overlap the rectangles above and below them so there are no gaps in between. The empty space between the rectangles is where the drop-down menus will appear.

5) Click the keyframe in the `invisible button` layer to select all the rectangles. Choose Modify > Convert to Symbol and select the Button radio button. Name the button `inv_btn` and then click OK.

After creating the `inv_btn` symbol, the content on the Stage should now have a bounding box around the edge of it. Double-click the symbol to open symbol-editing mode. The rectangles you just drew should all be in the first (*Up*) frame in the button. However, you need content only in the Hit frame because you are only using the clickable part of the button.

6) Drag the rectangles to the Hit frame.

Click the keyframe in the Up frame and then drag it over to the Hit frame.

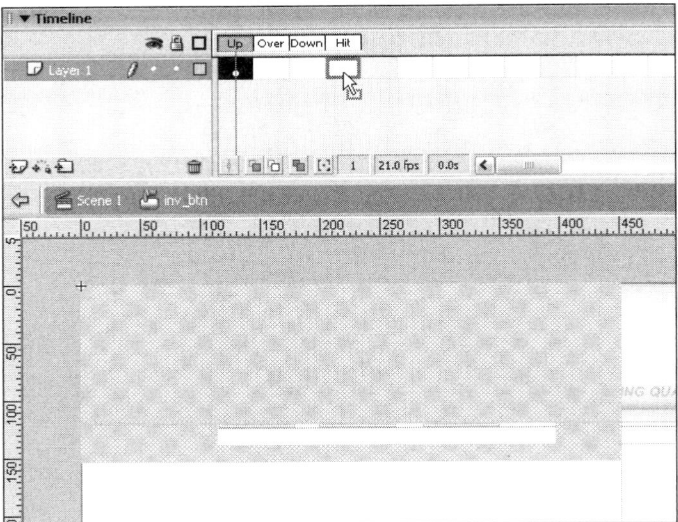

You can just leave all of the other states empty, so the button does not have any states with graphics. Nothing placed in this frame is visible after you publish the SWF file: The button is completely invisible.

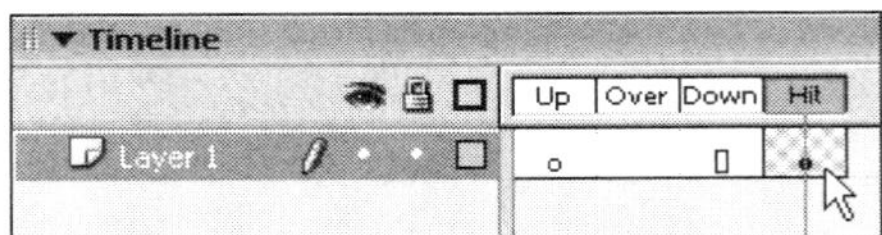

TIP *To quickly convert a selection into a symbol, press F8 or drag the selection into the Library. You have to drag it into the area below the preview pane (under the Name list) and then the Convert to Symbol dialog box opens.*

7) Click on `Scene 1` to return to the main Stage, and hide and lock the `invisible button` layer.

The Stage should now have a large turquoise and slightly transparent area covering a portion of it. The turquoise area is where the invisible button's hit area is. You will use this area as the trigger to close the menus. Even if this transparent turquoise area is *not* visible in the SWF file that you publish, it might interfere with your work in the Flash authoring environment.

Go to the Timeline and click the Hide layer dot (the dot under the large eye icon) in the `invisible button` layer. Also click under the Lock icon to lock the layer. This means that the layer cannot be seen, be selected, or have content accidentally added to it.

8) Find the folder called `buttons` and move all the new buttons into the folder.

You created a new Library folder in Lesson 2 called `buttons`. Move all the button symbols you created in the previous three exercises into the `buttons` folder. In Lesson 11 you will add some ActionScript for the invisible button that makes it target the menus so they close when the mouse rolls over the area.

CREATING AND USING MOVIE CLIPS

Movie clips are arguably the most common type of symbol used by Flash designers and developers. In essence, movie clips are miniature applications themselves. Each movie clip has its own Timeline that operates independently from the Flash document's main Timeline. This means that you can create looping animations while minimizing file size because you can use the Timeline in the same way as the Timeline you find on the main Stage.

You don't have to create long repeating animations: Simply create one loop and then place the movie clip on the Stage. It repeats over and over, independently of the main Timeline. Movie clips don't have to loop, either. You can create a clip and have it animate after a particular event happens. Or, a movie clip could play and then stop at the end.

In the next exercise, you will create several movie clips for the Tech Bookstore. The movie clips in this lesson will be used to contain animations for user interface elements. Later on in the book, you will use movie clips as containers for mini-applications and even to hold content loaded from a server.

You create movie clips in the same way you create graphic and button symbols. However, movie clips enable you to add more functionality to a symbol than button or graphic symbols do. You can also create and manipulate movie clips using ActionScript, which can be a powerful tool in your applications. You assign an instance name to a movie clip instance, which is used in your ActionScript to target and manipulate that instance. You will learn more about ActionScript in Lesson 6 and Lesson 11.

TIP *Movie clips add a bit more file size to your SWF than equivalent button or graphic symbols. If you are able to create the same effect using either a graphic or button then it is wise to do so. Often you will need the additional capabilities that movie clips offer.*

1) Select the `logo` **symbol and press F8 to insert the symbol inside a new movie clip.**

Type *logo_mc* into the Name field, select the Movie clip radio button, and click OK to create the new movie clip. The `logo_mc` will contain a couple of independent animations within it, so you need to insert the `logo.png` bitmap inside of a movie clip so you can nest other movie clips on layers inside one main clip.

TIP *If you cannot select the logo on the Stage, make sure that the* `logo` *layer is not locked.*

2) Double-click `logo_mc`**, rename** `Layer 1` **and then add a new layer to the movie clip.**

You will see the `logo.png` bitmap on `Layer 1` inside the movie clip. Rename `Layer 1` to *logo*. Click Insert New Layer so a new layer is added above the `logo.png image`. Rename the new layer *pageTurn*.

3) Use the Line tool to create a line on the `pageTurn` **layer and then press F8 to place the line inside a new movie clip.**

Make sure that the `pageTurn` layer is selected before you create a line. Click the stroke color control in the Tools panel and change the stroke color to *#999999* in the color pop-up window. Select the Line tool from the Tools panel.

As shown in the following figure, click and drag from one end of the left side of the book cover from the outer to the inner edge of the cover. Position the line so it is the same angle and length as the left book cover edge.

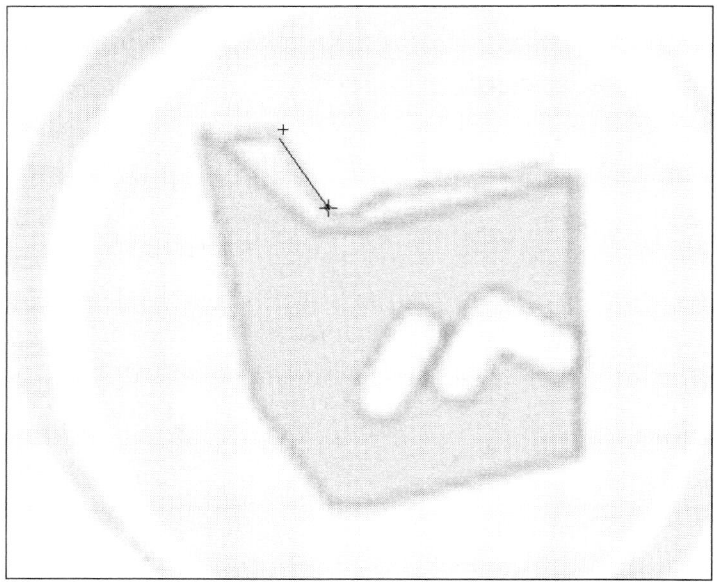

TIP *With the line unselected, mouse over the ends of the lines until you see a cursor containing an "L" shape. If you click and drag the line with this cursor, you can change the position and length of the line. This can help you properly position the line in relation to the logo. If you select the entire line, the cursor changes to a four-way arrow when you mouse over it. Clicking and dragging the line moves the entire line instead.*

4) Place the drawing you made into a new movie clip by pressing F8, and return to the main Stage.

Select the entire line you just created, without moving it. Press F8 to convert the line into a movie clip symbol. Type *pageTurn_mc* into the Name field, select the Movie clip radio button, and click OK. A new movie clip is created *inside* `logo_mc`, so `pageTurn_mc` is nested within `logo_mc`. Look at the edit bar, which shows you a visual representation of where you currently are nested within movie clips.

NOTE *If you double-click* `logo_mc` *and then* `pageTurn_mc`*, you are taken inside of the* `pageTurn_mc` *movie clip, in which you can edit the line you created. The line is left as a raw graphic so you can shape tween the line. You will learn how to create shape tweens in Lesson 5.*

You need to create a movie clip that will eventually be animated within the `logo_mc` movie clip. The animation will loop independently from the main Timeline, which means that it should be placed within a movie clip.

5) Insert a new layer in `logo_mc` and move it to the bottom of the layer stack.

The glow needs to animate beneath the logo itself, so it appears behind that area. Therefore, it needs to be placed beneath the logo itself. Click Insert New Layer to create a new layer and rename it *glow*. Make sure this new layer is on the bottom of the stack in the Timeline.

6) Lock the `logo` layer. Select the `glow animation` layer on the Timeline, copy its contents, and place the `glow` symbol inside the `logo_mc` movie clip.

The `glow_gr` symbol should still be on the Stage from when you created it in Lesson 2. Return to the Stage by clicking `Scene 1` in the edit bar. Select the `glow_gr` symbol and choose Edit > Cut.

Double-click logo_mc in the Library to open it in symbol-editing mode and select the glow layer. Then choose Edit > Paste in Place so the graphic is pasted in the center of the symbol.

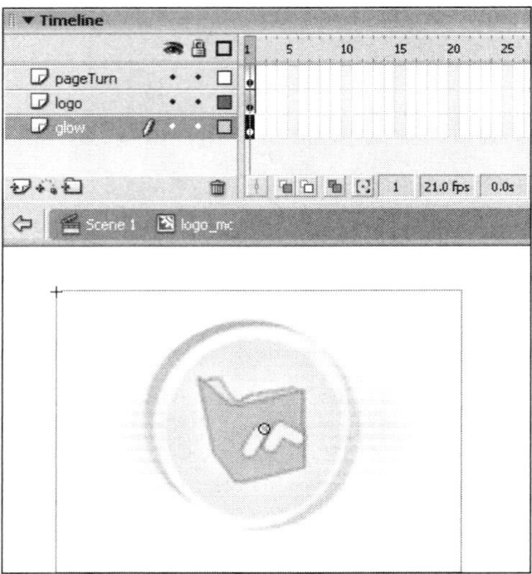

7) Return to the main Stage and delete the `glow animation` layer. Save the changes you have made to the file before moving on.

Click Scene 1 on the edit bar to return to the main Stage again. Notice that the glow animation layer is now empty because you cut and pasted the content from the layer into the movie clip that is on the logo layer. Right-click or control-click the glow animation layer and select Delete Layer from the contextual menu. The layer is permanently removed from the Timeline. Don't forget to save the FLA file before you proceed to the next step.

Now that you have put together the pieces for the logo's animation, you need to create the main menu that controls the Tech Bookstore. In the next exercise, you will create a movie clip to hold both graphic and button symbols.

CREATING THE MENU

You already created the background graphic for the menu in Lesson 2, so you have a good start on creating the menus for the Tech Bookstore. The next steps include nesting menubg_gr into a movie clip symbol, adding a few more graphics, and nesting the text buttons.

1) Drag the `menubg_gr` instance onto the `menu` layer and insert it into a new movie clip symbol; then drag two more instances of `menubg_gr` onto the Stage and also insert them into two new movie clips.

The menu background graphic should be in the graphics folder in the Library, named menubg_gr. Drag three instances of the graphic symbol onto the masked layer called menu in the Timeline.

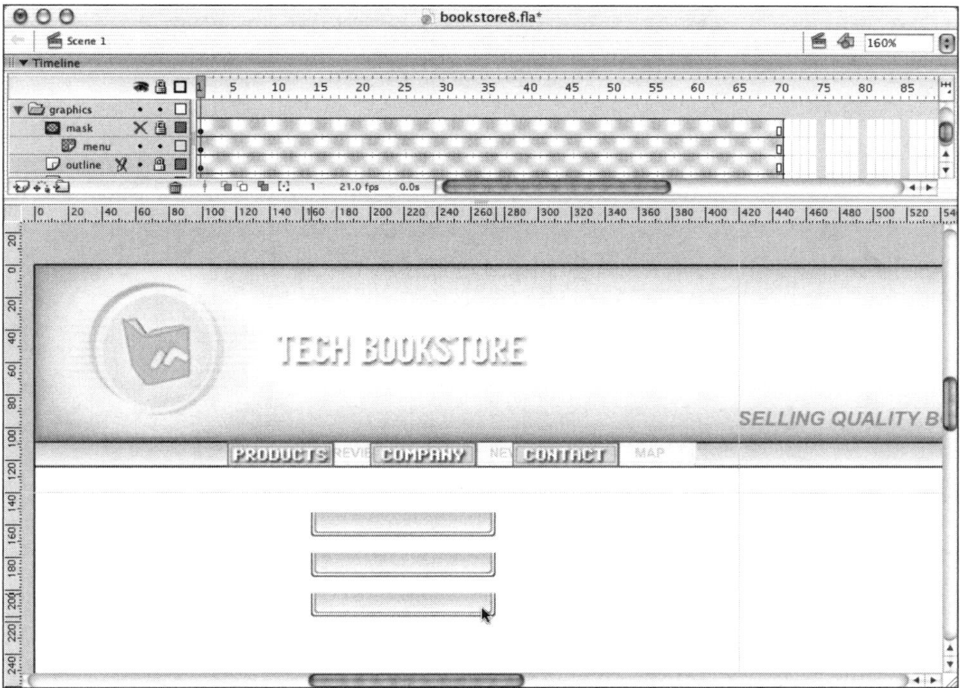

Select the first instance and press F8 to insert the graphic instance into a new symbol. Type *products_mc* into the Name field, select the Movie clip radio button, and click OK. Convert the second instance into a movie clip named company_mc and convert the third instance into a movie clip named contact_mc. You should now have three movie clips created for each menu, sharing a graphic symbol for the background image.

2) Open the products_mc **movie clip by double-clicking the instance on the Stage and rename** Layer 1 **to** bg**. Then insert a new layer and create a vertical line that is *11* pixels high and colored *#666666*.**

The menus need a division down the middle of the background to divide the text buttons on either side of the background. After you rename Layer 1 to bg, insert a new layer inside the products_mc movie clip and name it *divider*. Select the Line tool in the Tools panel and change the stroke color to *#666666*. Create a straight, vertical line on the Stage. With the line selected, open the Property inspector and change the height to *11*.

3) Create a second vertical line on the Stage that is *white* (#FFFFFF) and also *11* pixels tall.

Change the color in the stroke color control and then create a second line of the same length on the Stage to the right of the one you just created. Select the line and use the Property inspector to change the height to *11*.

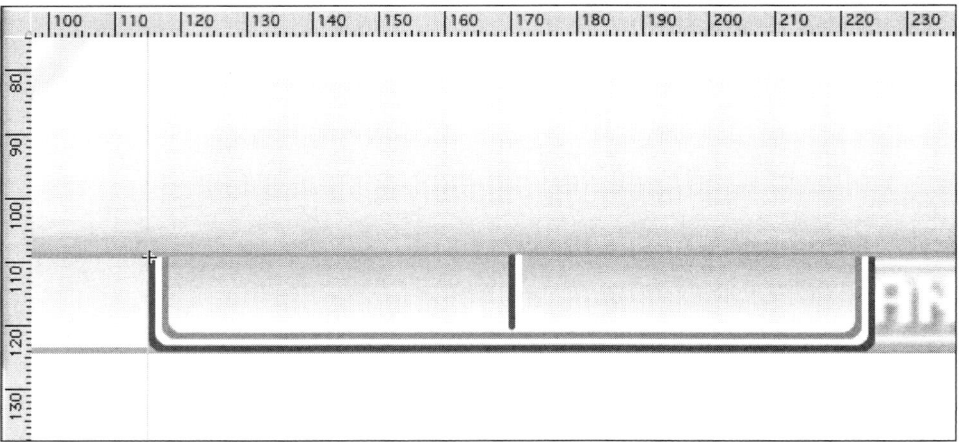

4) Move the two lines together to be next to each other and select both lines. Select and then insert the lines into a new graphic symbol called `divider_gr` and move the symbol to the center of the `menubg_gr`.

Move the lines on the Stage so they are directly next to each other; then select both lines by pressing the Shift key while clicking each line. Press F8 to convert the lines into a symbol. Type *`divider_gr`* into the Name field, click the Graphic radio button, and click OK to create the symbol.

Select `divider_gr` using the Selection tool and move it to the middle of the menu. The symbol should be placed at about 55 pixels to the right of 0 on the ruler.

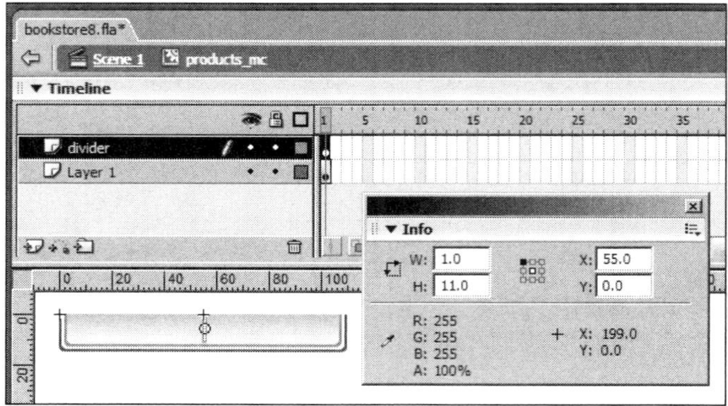

5) Add `divider_gr` to the `company_mc` and `contact_mc` movie clips. Align `divider_gr` so it is in the middle of each movie clip.

Click `Scene 1` to return to the main Stage and open the Library. Double-click `company_mc` to open it up and rename `Layer 1` to `bg` as you did earlier. Then add a new layer called `divider`. Drag an instance of `divider_gr` from the Library onto the `divider` layer and align it in the center of the menu.

In the next part of this exercise, you will insert the text buttons that you created earlier in the lesson into the menu.

6) Open the Library and add the text buttons to each menu.

Find the text buttons you created for the menus in the Library within a folder called `buttons`. Open `products_mc`, insert a new layer above the `divider` layer on the Timeline, and rename it `buttons`. Drag `catalog_btn` to the left of `divider_gr` and then drag `reviews_btn` to the right of `divider_gr`. Center `catalog_btn` between the left edge of `product_mc` and `divider_gr`. Similarly, center `reviews_btn` between `divider_gr` and the right edge of `product_mc`.

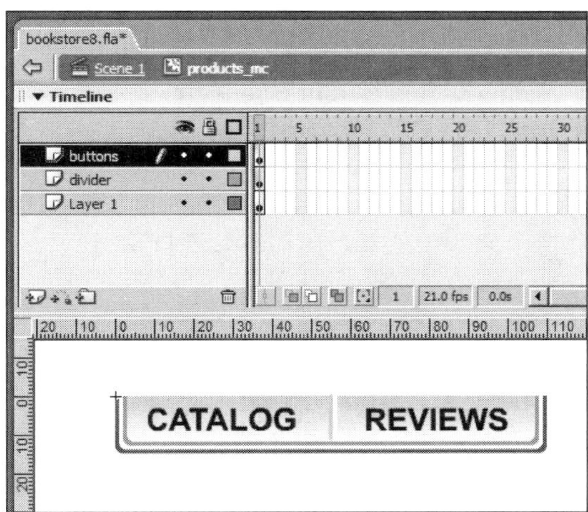

Repeat this step with the other two movie clip menus. Add a new layer to `company_mc` and rename it `buttons`. Drag `tour_btn` and `news_btn` to the left and right of the `divider_gr`. Finally, repeat these steps with `contact_mc`. Drag `feedback_btn` and `map_btn` to the left and right of `divider_gr` and align them on either side of `divider_gr`, as you did with the other menus.

Return to the main Stage. You should now have three menus on the `menu` layer, each containing two text buttons.

7) Clean up the Library and then save the FLA file.

You should now have several movie clips in the Library. Drag the movie clips into the folder called `movie clips` you created in Lesson 2. Then move the `divider_gr` into the `graphics` folder. Save the changes you have made to the FLA file by choosing File > Save from the main menu.

In Lesson 5, you will animate the menu so it appears to be opening and closing, and in Lesson 11 you add ActionScript to make it work when you play the SWF file.

CREATING MOVIE CLIP BUTTONS

There is another way to make buttons in Flash: by using movie clips. Movie clip buttons allow you to create buttons that are more complex than the standard button symbols you made earlier in this lesson. This doesn't mean you should change all your button symbols into movie clips, though! Remember that movie clips are slightly larger in file size than button symbols, and movie clip buttons usually take more time to create than regular buttons. It is beneficial to use movie clip buttons when you want to add extra states to the button, such as a *visited* state (after an area has been visited by the user, similar to HTML pages), or animate them in a unique way.

For this next exercise, you will create a couple of movie clip buttons that will be used in the catalog section of the site. You will create a button used to download sample chapters of a book from the bookstore, and a button that links to a site where you can purchase the book.

The first parts of the movie clip button you need to create are the graphics and text for the button itself.

1) Select the `buttons` layer on the Timeline and then choose the Rectangle tool in the Tools panel. Set the fill color to *#CCCCCC* and the stroke color to *black.*

Click the Round Rectangle Radius button after selecting the Rectangle tool. Make sure that the corner radius is set to 0 before creating the rectangle. Then set the fill color to *#CCCCCC* and the stroke color to *black (#000000).*

2) Create a rectangle and then convert it into a movie clip.

Create the rectangle after you have entered the settings in the Property inspector. Double-click the rectangle's fill to select both the rectangle's fill and stroke. Then change the width of the rectangle to *85* and the height of the rectangle to *15.*

With the rectangle still selected, choose Modify > Convert to Symbol to convert the rectangle into a movie clip. Name the movie clip *samplechapter_mc*, select the Movie clip radio button, and click OK when you finish.

3) Open the movie clip, select the stroke, and place it on a new layer called `fill`.

Double-click `samplechapter_mc` to open the movie clip in symbol-editing mode. Once in symbol editing mode, choose Insert New Layer to add a new layer to the Timeline. Name this layer *stroke*, double-click Layer 1, and rename it to *fill*.

On the `fill` layer, select the rectangle's stroke outline by double-clicking the stroke itself. After it is selected, choose Edit > Cut. Select frame 1 of the `stroke` layer and choose Edit > Paste in Place.

4) Modify the stroke by selecting two of its segments and changing the color to *#999999* and then lock the `stroke` layer.

On the `stroke` layer, press Shift and click the top and left stroke segments. Change the stroke color to *#999999* using the stroke color control in the Tools panel. Changing these two stroke segments creates the effect of depth around the button. When you finish modifying the stroke outline, lock the `stroke` layer.

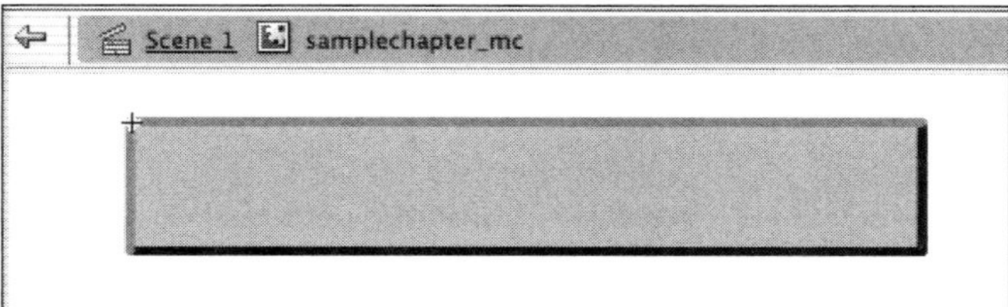

5) Add the text `sample chapter` to the button on a new layer called `text`, and then lock the `text` layer.

So far, the button is not overly descriptive, so you need to add a label to the button using static text. Select the `stroke` layer and insert a new layer on the button's Timeline and rename it *text*. Select the Text tool in the Tools panel and click on the Stage. Change the text properties to Static, Arial, a text size of 10, and black for the text fill color. Select the Alias text button as well, so the text is more legible on the Stage. Type *sample chapter* into the text field on the Stage.

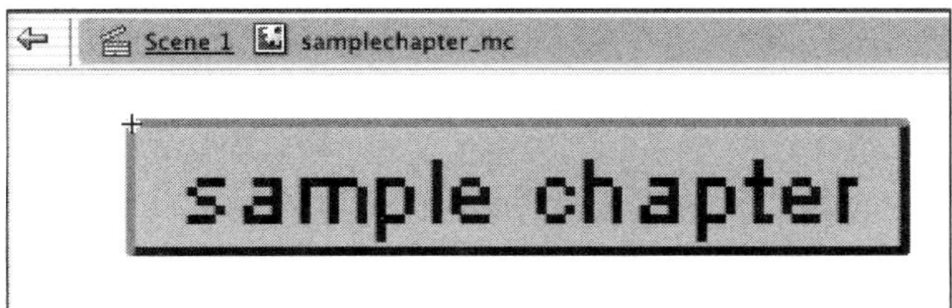

When you finish, lock the `text` layer.

6) Select the `fill` layer, select the shape's fill and convert it into a graphic symbol called `fill_gr`. Then lock this new layer.

This procedure nests a new graphic symbol within the movie clip button. The `fill_gr` symbol will be animated, which is why it was separated onto its own layer and converted into a graphic symbol, because the stroke doesn't need to be animated. Whenever possible, you should always turn a raw graphic into a symbol before animating it and put each animation on its own layer.

Lock the `fill` layer when you're finished.

7) Add a `labels` and `actions` layer to the Timeline.

Add two new layers to the Timeline and name them *labels* and *actions*. These two layers will hold frame labels and frame actions, respectively. It is good practice to keep actions and labels on their own layers so they do not interfere with other aspects of the SWF file.

8) Click frame 25 of each layer and press F5 to insert new frames. Then insert keyframes on the `labels` layer at frame 5 and 15.

The button needs several states, which span across the Timeline. Flash understands the Up, Over, and Down states of a typical button by entering specific frame labels in a movie clip button, which will be added in the following step. Each of these states is treated the same way as in a button symbol's Up, Over, and Down frames. You can then add drawings, graphics, or text at each of these frame labels, just as you did in the button symbols created earlier.

TIP *The hit area is the movie clip itself, unless you define a different hit area manually. If you do, you use a separate movie clip symbol and then set it up as the hit area by using ActionScript. These buttons are solid, so it works just fine for the clickable area to be the visual area of the button. Because of this you don't need to define a separate movie clip to be the hit area.*

Insert keyframes on the `labels` layer at frame 5, and 15. Frame labels will be added to each of these keyframes in the next step.

9) Add frame labels at each keyframe on the `labels` layer. Make sure that each layer is locked and the file is saved before moving on.

If you add frame labels at each keyframe, Flash recognizes each area as a button state. Maximize the Property inspector and select frame 1 on the `labels` layer. Type *_up* into the `<Frame Label>` text field. Select frame 5 and type *_over* into the `<Frame Label>` text field. Finally, select frame 15 and type *_down* into the field.

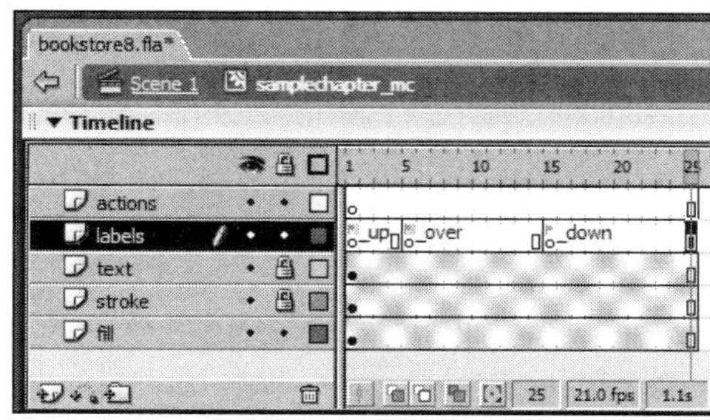

You will add the animation for these buttons in Lesson 5, in which you learn how to animate using motion tweens. You will use motion tweens to animate the button to create an interesting effect.

The button won't work yet if you try to test the SWF file in Flash because Flash needs ActionScript or a behavior to recognize the movie clip as a button. You will add the ActionScript in Lesson 6.

DUPLICATING SYMBOLS AND ADDING SYMBOLS TO THE STAGE

Instead of re-creating a button, it is possible to duplicate the symbol to avoid having to follow all the steps you just went through all over again. It isn't lazy, just economical! By duplicating the button, you can add to or modify the symbol (such as the text contained within it), but you don't have to rebuild the symbol from scratch.

1) Open the Library and find the `samplechapter_mc` you created. Duplicate the symbol by right-clicking or control-clicking the symbol and choosing Duplicate from the contextual menu.

After you choose Duplicate from the contextual menu, the Duplicate Symbol dialog box opens. Name the new symbol `toc_mc` and click OK. The new movie clip is added to the Library.

2) Double-click `toc_mc` in the Library and change the movie clip's text.

After you double-click the movie clip, it opens in symbol-editing mode. Unlock the text layer and double-click the static text field. The same font and text size remain. Enter *table of contents* into the text field.

Choose the Selection tool and use the the tool to center the text over the background.

NOTE *If the text does not quite fit within the rectangle, select the text and change the font size to 9 pt or change the Character Spacing to -0.5. If you do this, remember to open* `samplechapter_mc` *and make the same modifications to the text so both buttons look the same.*

3) Delete the `samplechapter_mc` movie clip from the Stage.

Because you edited `toc_mc` from the Library, it was not added to the Stage like `samplechapter_mc` was. Select the movie clip and press Backspace or Delete to remove the `samplechapter_mc` instance from the Stage. You will add it to a different FLA in a lesson later on, but for now you can leave both of these clips in the Library until you need them.

You have many new symbols on the Stage and in the Library. You should take a moment to lay them out on the Stage before moving on to the next lesson. The `products_btn`, `company_btn`, and `contact_btn` buttons were already placed on the Stage earlier. You still need to place the menus that are associated with those buttons on the Stage.

4) Align the three menus with their associated buttons.

The three menus should still be on the Stage, but they won't be necessarily lined up with their respective buttons. Select the menu with `catalog` and `reviews`, and match up the *lower-left corner* of the menu with the *lower-left corner* of the `products_btn`. You might need to unlock the `menu` layer before you can change the location of the three menus. Lock the `buttons` layer if necessary while you move the menus, because the menu should be directly behind the button. When you move the menu close to the button, by default, you should see a dotted line that helps you align the menu with the button.

NOTE *If you do not see dotted lines to help you align objects on the Stage, select* View > Snapping > Edit Snap Align. *You should set the Snap Tolerance for around the default amount of 10 pixels This means that the objects being moved will snap to other objects that are 10 or fewer pixels away and help align them either horizontally or vertically. This means that you will see a dotted line, and objects will snap when they are aligned along their edges. If you want to also align the vertical or horizontal centers of objects (as you did with the three buttons earlier in this exercise), check both check boxes under Center Alignment.*

Repeat this for the other two menus. The menu containing *tour* and *news* should be aligned with `company_btn`. And the final menu with *feedback* and *map* aligns with `contact_btn`. When you finish, lock the `buttons` layer if it isn't already locked. Then lock the `menu` layer.

NOTE *The* `samplechapter_mc` *and* `toc_mc` *buttons will not actually be used in the main Tech Bookstore Web site. Instead, you will copy these buttons from this file to a new FLA file that is created later on in the book.*

5) Clean up the Library and then save a new version of your file as `bookstore8_complete.fla` **in the** `TechBookstore` **folder.**

In the Library, move all the movie clips you just created into the `movie clip` folder and also move the `fill_gr` graphic into the `graphics` folder. Choose File > Save As from the main menu, type in `bookstore8_complete.fla` into the Save As field, and click Save.

WHAT YOU HAVE LEARNED

In this lesson, you have:

- Discovered the difference between graphic, movie clip, and button symbols (pages 102–106)
- Created buttons and hit areas (pages 107–110)
- Changed the hit area on a text button (pages 112–114)
- Built an invisible button (pages 114–119)
- Assembled movie clip symbols (pages 119–122)
- Nested symbols within other symbols (pages 122–126)
- Learned how to create movie clip symbols (pages 126–129)
- Duplicated symbols (pages 129–131)

creating animation

LESSON 5

Flash has been well known as a program for creating animation for a long time, partly because it does such a good job at animating graphics. Flash is commonly used for Web animation because it allows you to create high-quality animations with a small file size, which is ideal for online content. In more recent years, Flash has even been used to create animations for broadcast, such as television commercials. The reason Flash is found in so many places is because it is a great tool for creating and animating vector graphics.

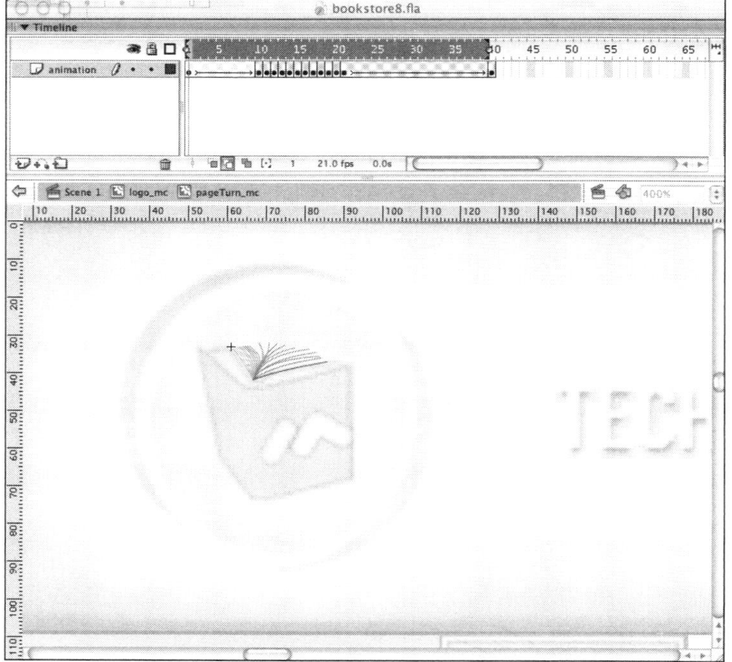

Animation in the Tech Bookstore

Macromedia has made it very easy for beginners and experts alike to animate objects around the Stage without much effort. It is even easier to add motion to a document by using Timeline Effects, which do the animating work for you. With a few clicks of the mouse, you can add effects such as blur, explode, expand, transform, and transitions to the FLA file. Of course, you can create your own custom animations by using *tweening* or frame-by-frame animation techniques. You will learn how to use all of these different techniques for creating animation in this lesson.

WHAT YOU WILL LEARN

In this lesson, you will:

- Learn about the different kinds of animation
- Add motion to the menu system
- Use *easing* to slow down and speed up a motion tween
- Change brightness and alpha levels using a motion tween
- Add a shape tween for animating a shape
- Create a frame-by-frame animation
- Use a motion guide to animate a symbol along a vector path
- Use Timeline Effects to animate instances

APPROXIMATE TIME

This lesson takes approximately two hours to complete.

LESSON FILES

Media Files:

None

Starting Files:

Lesson05/bookstore9.fla

Lesson05/map_starter.fla

Completed Project:

Lesson05/bookstore9_complete.fla

Lesson05/map.fla

UNDERSTANDING ANIMATION

An animation is a sequence of images that create the illusion of movement when viewed in rapid succession. In Flash, these images are formed by content that's placed on frames on the Timeline. You might use drawings, photos, or even ActionScript-generated graphics to create an animation or motion in your FLA files.

There are several different ways to create custom motion or animations in Flash. You can create *motion tweens*, *shape tweens*, or create *frame-by-frame* animation. *Tweening* refers to calculations made by Flash to animate or move or modify the properties or shape of an object in the SWF file. You create a beginning and an end for the particular transition using keyframes. When you apply a motion tween to the set of keyframes, Flash creates the movement itself by filling in the changes that occur between the two frames. Shape tweens are used to change a vector line or shape, such as changing a square into a circle. Motion tweens are used to change properties, such as move objects around the Stage or fade objects in and out. You will create both motion and shape tweens in this lesson.

A frame-by-frame animation is a more traditional way of creating animation. Instead of having Flash create a tween using automatic calculations, you draw each increment of the movement manually allowing you to create more complicated effects, particularly when motion or shape tweening doesn't allow you to create the kind of animation you require. Frame-by-frame animations are usually more time-intensive to create, and they add more file size to the SWF.

NOTE *You can also create scripted animation using ActionScript and (typically) movie clips. There is a part of ActionScript called the Drawing API that is used to script lines and shapes on the Stage, and can be used in very complex ways. Although it goes beyond the scope of this book, it is definitely worth looking into if and when you choose to learn more about ActionScript.*

SETTING UP A MOTION TWEEN ANIMATION

As you just found out, motion tweens are used to change the properties of an object over a certain number of frames. You can change properties such as position, size, alpha, tint, or rotation, and also motion tween along a path. You should always change an object into a symbol before motion tweening the instance, which helps keep your file size lower when exporting the SWF. The file size is kept low because Flash can reuse assets in the Library instead of re-creating the data each time it is encountered on the Timeline.

NOTE *You can shape tween raw data, but you cannot shape tween instances or bitmaps. They have to be broken apart into raw data first by choosing Modify > Break Apart. You will learn how to apply a shape tween to raw data (vector drawings) later on in this lesson.*

There are a few different ways you can add motion tweens to an FLA document, which you will learn how to do in the following exercises. In this exercise, you will be adding a motion tween to the bookstore menus you built in earlier lesson, which causes the menu to open and close when a user clicks or rolls off a menu. You will also add the `stop` action to stop the animation from repeatedly looping when the SWF file plays.

1) Open `bookstore8_complete.fla`**, created in Lesson 4 and found in the** `Lesson04` **folder, and save a new version of the file as** `bookstore9.fla`**.**

In Lesson 4, you created most of the symbols you will animate in this lesson. Save a new version of the file because you will add a lot of new information in this file. By saving a new version, you can always revert to the old one if you want to redo your edits and try again.

2) Find `products_mc` **on the Stage, press F8 to convert it to a movie clip, and name the movie clip** `productsMenu_mc`**.**

This process might seem strange to you. The reason you are inserting the graphic, buttons, and line inside a single movie clip is to animate all these elements together. It would be much too tedious to try animating each element separately, and the way the FLA is set up it is not possible to animate `products_mc` directly on the Stage. This way, you can easily motion tween the entire movie clip as one object and then target it using ActionScript later on because it can be given an instance name.

TIP *If you have difficulty selecting the menus because the buttons are layered on top of them, make sure that the* `buttons` *layer is locked and then hide the layer by clicking the Hide Layer button in the Timeline.*

3) Double-click `productsMenu_mc` **to edit it on the Stage. Zoom in on the menu if necessary.**

After you double-click `productsMenu_mc`, the rest of the Stage is greyed-out so you can concentrate on the symbol you're editing. Editing a symbol this way allows you to animate the menu in relation to the other symbols on the Stage.

NOTE *To zoom in to the menu, select the Zoom tool from the Tools panel. The Zoom tool is set to zoom in if you can see a plus symbol on the tool. If not, select the Enlarge tool in the Tools panel's Options area.*

Click the menu on the Stage using the Zoom tool, and the Stage zooms in while placing the menu at the center. Zoom in a couple of times, but make sure that you can still see the `products_btn` button above the menu. Select the Selection tool from the Tools panel when you finish.

4) Select `Layer 1` and rename it `menu tween`; then insert a new layer and rename it `actions`. Add keyframes to the `actions` layer on frames 11 and 20.

Select the `menu tween` layer, click the Insert New Layer button and rename it *`actions`*. Create new keyframes on frames 11 and 20 of the `actions` layer by selecting each frame and pressing the F6 key. You will change the position of the movie clip in each keyframe. Changing the movie clip position creates the animation after you add the tweens in between each keyframe. You will add the tweens in the following exercise.

If you leave a movie clip on the Stage containing content on more than one frame, it continuously loops unless you stop the movie clip using ActionScript. You will add the `stop` action in the following step so the movie clip does not endlessly loop anymore.

5) Add `stop` actions on the Timeline to control the animation.

Open the Actions panel by choosing Window > Development Panels > Actions from the main menu. The Actions panel opens docked below the Stage on Windows or as a floating panel on the Mac. The Script pane is the large text field located to the right of the Script navigator and Actions toolbox. The following figure shows you the different parts of the Actions panel.

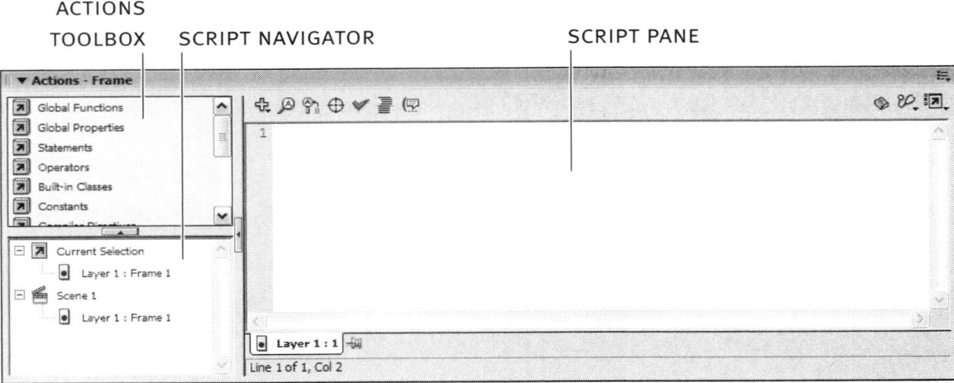

Now you are going to add some ActionScript into the Actions panel. Select the keyframe on frame 1 and type `stop();` into the Script pane. Then select the keyframe on frame 11 and type `stop();` into the Script pane again and then repeat the same for frame 20. The `stop` action stops the playback of the current movie clip at these locations, and in Lesson 11 you will add the ActionScript to make the menu animate properly. The reason you place the `stop` action *before* the keyframe on frame 12 (which you will create in the following step) is so the animation doesn't stop when the playhead is directed to tween the menu upwards. Instead, it stops at the end of the animation when the menu goes downwards. The animation gets confused if you tell the playhead to slide upwards on frame 12, and there is a `stop` action there as well.

When you finish adding the ActionScript, lock the `actions` layer by clicking the dot underneath the Lock Layer icon, which prevents anything being added to the Stage on the `actions` layer. It is a good practice to *never* place any raw data, symbols/instances, components or assets onto a layer that has ActionScript. If you place code on the same layer as objects, such as components or movie clips that contain ActionScript, then sometimes code conflicts can arise in the SWF file. Your FLA file might also more difficult to debug.

6) Insert a new layer and rename it `labels`. Then add new keyframes and frame labels to frames 2 and 12, and lock the layer when you finish.

Create the new layer directly below the `actions` layer and rename this layer *labels*. Create new keyframes on frame 2 and frame 12 by selecting each frame and pressing F6.

Select frame 2 on the `labels` layer and enter a frame label named *slidedown* into the <Frame Label> text field in the Property inspector. Then select frame 12 on the `labels` layer and enter *slideup* into the <Frame Label> text field. When you finish, lock the layer as you did in the previous step to prevent accidentally adding any content to it later on.

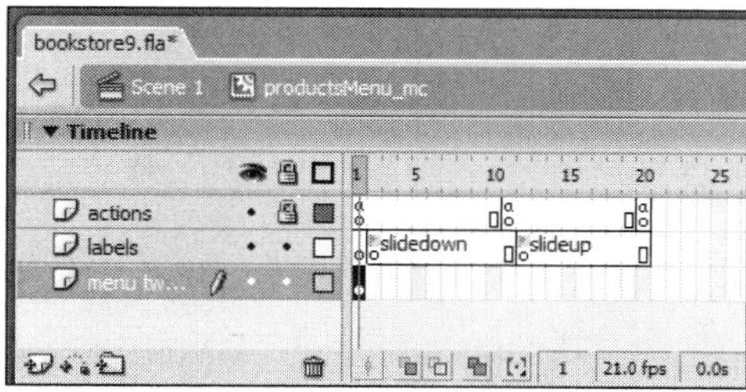

7) Insert new keyframes on frame 12 and 20 of the `menu tween` **layer.**

These frames determine how the menu animates. Frame 12 is the end of the animation for the menu opening and the beginning of the animation for the menu closing.

8) Change the position of the `product_mc` **movie clip at frame 12.**

Select `product_mc` on the Stage at frame 12. Move the movie clip straight downward by holding the Shift key and pressing the Down arrow key until the clip is directly underneath the `bar_gr`, as shown in the following figure.

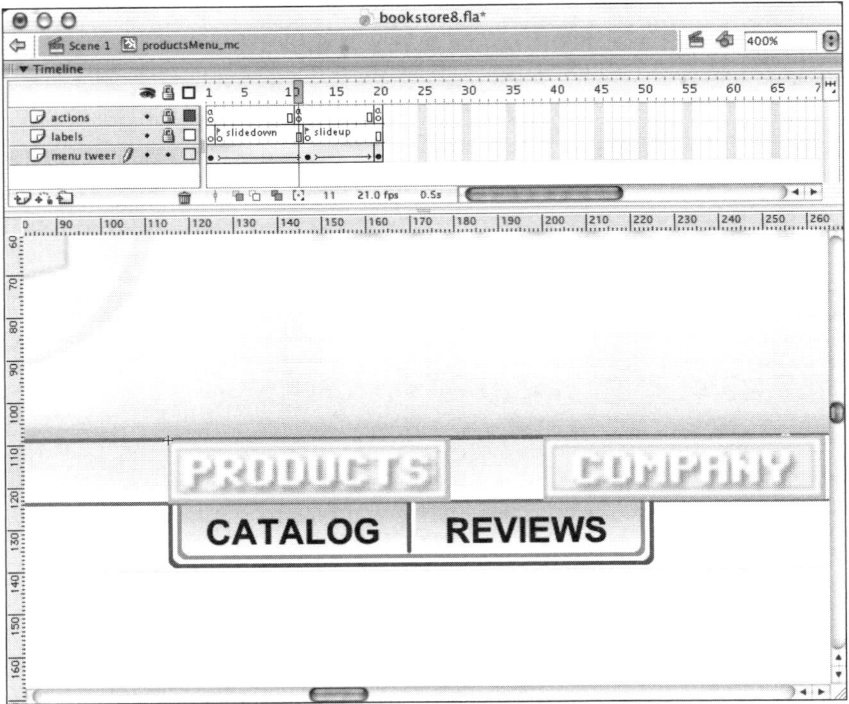

9) Return to the main Stage and repeat each of these steps for the other two menus.

Click Scene 1 in the edit bar to return to the main Stage. Repeat Steps 2 through 8 for `company_mc` and `contact_mc`. When you finish, all three menus are ready to animate using tweening.

10) After you finish, remember to save the changes you have made to the FLA.

You have now set up the menu movie clip so you can easily add motion tweens. Instead of inserting a motion tween and then adding content, you have organized your content before adding a motion tween. Flash is flexible and allows you to use either way to animate content: Add a motion tween and then move the instance, or move the instance and then create the motion tween. In the following section, you will add the motion tweens that make the animation work.

TIP *You can create only one motion tween on a single layer. If you want to tween multiple symbols concurrently, you have to place each symbol on its own layer. To distribute a bunch of separate symbols to their own layers, select the symbols you want to move and choose Modify > Timeline > Distribute to Layers.*

Distribute to Layers is useful when you need to animate individual characters of a text block (that has been broken apart) or if you are importing a group of items onto the Stage while you are creating your FLA. Flash renames each layer for you using the imported file's filename. Distributing to layers also keeps your FLA organized and this speeds up development.

ADDING THE MOTION TWEENS

You can use motion tweens to change an instance's position, brightness, alpha, or tint of an instance on the Stage. The Property inspector's Properties tab has has a drop-down menu called Color, which is used to change the brightness, alpha, or tint of an instance. An advanced option allows you to change both color and alpha values. If you have an instance you are motion tweening, changing the values using this drop-down menu for one of the keyframes creates a transition to or from the new property you have set.

Now that you have set up the movie clip with keyframes and have the beginning and end positions for the instance, you are ready to add the motion tweens that will actually *move* the menus. You will also animate the brightness of the menu using the motion tween and changing a value in the Property inspector.

1) In `bookstore9.fla`, double-click to open `productsMenu_mc` if it isn't already open. Select the `menu tween` layer again.

You will be working with the same movie clip and content as you set up in the previous exercise.

2) Create a motion tween between frames 1 and 12 to slide the menu downward.

Right-click or control-click any frame between frames 1 and 12 on the `menu tween` layer, and choose Create Motion Tween from the contextual menu. The first thing you notice is that the background color for the frames spanning the `menu tween` layer have changed into a purple color and an arrow spans from the beginning to the end of the span of frames. The change in appearance indicates that you have added a motion tween on that layer. The figure following Step 3 shows you a Timeline containing motion tweens.

3) Add a second motion tween to animate the menu upward, and then review the animation by scrubbing the Timeline.

Repeat Step 2 to add a motion tween between frames 12 and 20. Select any of the frames between 12 and 20, right-click (or control-click) and select Create Motion Tween from the contextual menu. When you finish, the movie clip animates downward between frames 1 and 12, and then animates upward between 12 and 20. Click and drag the playhead to view the animation.

TIP *After motion tweens are applied to a series of frames, you can still change the duration of the tween by adding or removing frames in-between the two keyframes. You can add frames by selecting a frame within the tween and pressing F5 (to add more frames), or remove frames by selecting Remove Frames from the contextual menu (to delete frames). Flash automatically modifies the tween for you.*

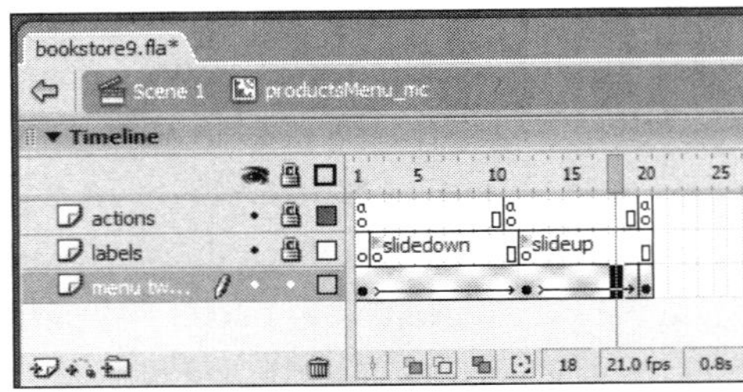

4) Add easing to the menu motion tween using the Property inspector.

The Ease slider is found in the Property inspector when you have your motion tween selected. You can *ease* the animation so it appears to be speeding up or slowing down along the duration of the motion tween. By default, easing is set to 0 (no ease), but by moving the Ease slider to a positive number (between 1 and 100) you are telling Flash to begin the animation quickly and then slow the animation down at the end of the tween. Setting the amount of easing to a negative number (-1 to -100) starts the animation a bit slower, but speeds the movement up towards the end of the tween.

Select frame 1 and expand the Property inspector. Use the Ease slider to set the easing to 100, which means it is easing *out* and gradually slowing down as it animates downward. Then select frame 12 and set the Ease value to -100, which means that the menu is easing *in* toward the end of the animation. The menu gradually speeds up as the menu closes.

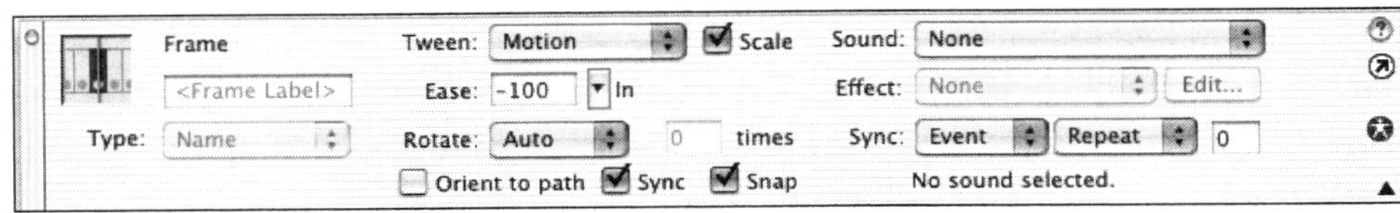

5) Add a brightness tween to the menu, and then test the animation by scrubbing the Timeline.

Select `productsMenu_mc` on frame 1 of the `menu tween` layer. You must select the instance, not the frame, in order to access the Brightness property. Choose Brightness from the Color drop-down menu on the Property inspector's Properties tab and change the value to 85%. Select `productsMenu_mc` on frame 12 and make sure that the brightness is still set to 0. Scrub the Timeline by dragging the playhead back and forth. Take a look at how the animation looks so far.

TIP *You should try to use a brightness tween instead of an alpha tween whenever possible because alpha tweens, particularly over detailed bitmaps, are much more processor-intensive than brightness tweens. Flash needs to perform many more calculations when tweening with transparancy than when you tween the brightness of a color.*

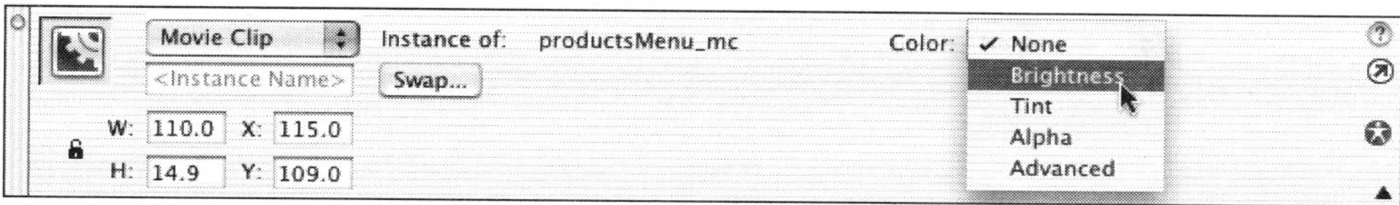

6) Repeat Steps 2 through 5 for the other two menus in the FLA. Scrub over the animation to make sure the animations work correctly.

Repeat Steps 2 through 5 for the remaining two menus in the FLA file so all three menus have animation added to them. When you are finished adding animations for the three menus, click the playhead directly above the frames on the Timeline. Drag it to the right, and you can see the animation play as you drag the playhead. You can also play the animation in the Flash authoring environment by pressing the Enter key, and the animation begins to play right on the Stage and then stops at the end of the animation.

7) Return to the main Stage. Clean up the Library and then save the FLA document.

Click `Scene 1` in the edit bar to return to the main Stage. Clean the Library by moving `productsMenu_mc`, `companyMenu_mc` and `contactMenu_mc` into the movie clips folder in the Library. Save the changes you made to the FLA file.

TIP *When performing a motion tween, there is also an option to set the direction and amount of rotation for the selected symbol. There are four choices for rotation: None, Auto, CW (Clockwise), and CCW (Counterclockwise). If you chose Auto, the item is rotated in the direction that requires the least amount of movement. Clockwise and Counterclockwise rotates the object a specified number of times in either of those directions.*

ANIMATING ALPHA LEVELS AND SIZE

Changing an instance's alpha isn't much different from moving an instance around the Stage and is pretty much the same as changing its brightness level, like you added in the previous exercise. In both cases, you need to have a series of frames to apply the brightness effect to and add a motion tween. As you read in earlier lessons, *alpha* refers to the amount of opaqueness (transparency) that an object has. If an object's alpha is set to 0, it is fully transparent and invisible on the Stage. If an object has a visibility of 100%, it is completely visible.

In the following example, you will use motion tweens to fade the glow that is animated behind the logo and then scale the graphic. You are still working with the `bookstore9.fla` file where you left off from the previous exercise.

1) Select `glow_gr` and convert it to a movie clip symbol named `bookglow_mc`. Then rename `Layer 1` to `glow animation`.

Make sure you are on the main Stage by clicking `Scene 1` in the edit bar if necessary.

Find the instance of the `glow_gr` inside `logo_mc`. Select the `glow_gr` instance and press F8 to convert it into a movie clip symbol called `bookglow_mc`. You need to change the graphic symbol into a movie clip because the animation you add needs to loop repeatedly on the Stage. Make sure the `pageTurn` and `logo` layers are locked so you can select the `glow_gr` instance. Double-click `bookglow_mc` to open the instance and rename the default layer from `Layer 1` to `glow animation`.

2) Create a keyframe on frame 35 and frame 70 of the `glow animation` layer.

Select frame 35 of the `glow animation` layer and add a new keyframe. This procedure copies the contents of frame 1 into the keyframe on frame 35.

Insert another keyframe on frame 70 on the `glow animation` layer. You will change the alpha and size of `bookglow_mc` across the sets of frames later on in the exercise.

3) Resize `glow_gr` using the Transform tool.

Select frame 35 on the `glow animation` layer. Select the Transform tool from the Tools panel and drag one of the corner handles toward the center of `glow_gr` to make the instance smaller. To prevent the symbol from distorting, and to maintain the symbol's aspect ratio while you resize it, press and hold the Shift key while dragging the mouse. Resize the instance so it is mostly hidden behind `logo_gr`, as seen in the figure in Step 4.

4) Change the alpha of `glow_gr` using the Property inspector and motion tween.

You have changed the size of the graphic on frame 35. Now change the alpha of the instance. Select the instance on frame 35 again using the Selection tool. Choose Alpha from the Color drop-down menu in the the Property inspector's Properties tab and move the alpha slider from 100 to 80 percent.

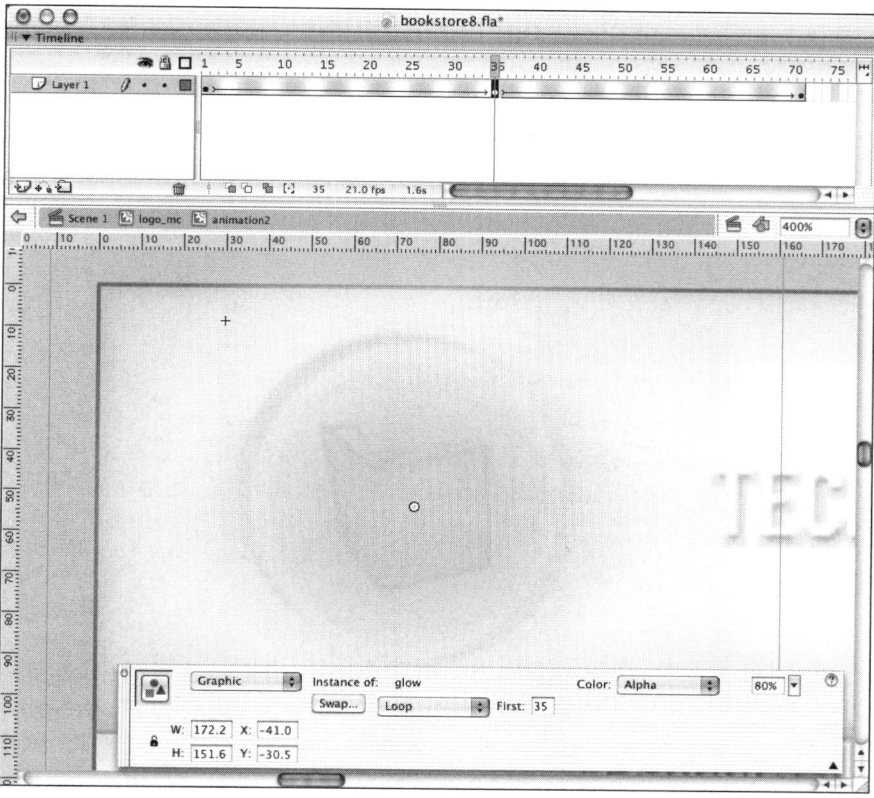

If you find the amount doesn't look quite right on your screen, modify the new alpha value you gave the instance.

NOTE *Remember that the changes you are making to the instance on the Stage do not affect the symbol in the Library. You can pull another copy of* `glow_gr` *from the Library, and it appears on the Stage as it originally appeared before you made the modifications.*

5) Add motion tweens to scale the graphic and then scrub the Timeline to view the animation.

Click on any frame between 1 and 35 and expand the Property inspector. Change the Tween drop-down menu from *None* to *Motion*. Follow the same steps for a frame between frame 35 and 70. The movie clip should now scale the glow larger and fade it out slightly before returning to its original state when you view it on the Timeline. You can also test this individual movie clip (and not the entire SWF file) by moving your playhead to frame 1 of the `bookglow_mc` symbol and selecting Control > Play from the main menu.

6) Move `bookglow_mc` into the movie clips folder in the Library. Save the FLA file before proceeding to the next exercise.

ANIMATING THE MOVIE CLIP BUTTON

In Lesson 4 you created two movie clip buttons: one for a table of contents and the second for a sample chapter. In this exercise, you are going to animate the movie clip button so the fill has a brightness tween with the visitor hovers their cursor over the button. The movie clip buttons use a brightness tween a lot like the three main menus for the bookstore Web site. When the visitor mouses over the button, the button animates, and it also animates when the cursor moves off the button as well. The movie clip buttons use special frame labels so Flash knows to treat each labeled keyframe like a button state instead of as a normal frame label. These special labels you are going to use are `_over`, and `_down` (representing the Over and Down states of a normal button symbol).

You are still working with `bookstore9.fla` in this example.

1) Find `samplechapter_mc` in the Library and double-click the movie clip.

After you double-click the symbol, the movie clip opens in symbol-editing mode. Unlock the `fill` layer and make sure that the other layers are locked before proceeding with the animation, which helps prevent selecting the `text` or `stroke` layers.

2) Select the `fill` layer and insert a keyframe on the `_over` frame, frame 14, and on the last frame in the movie clip (frame 25).

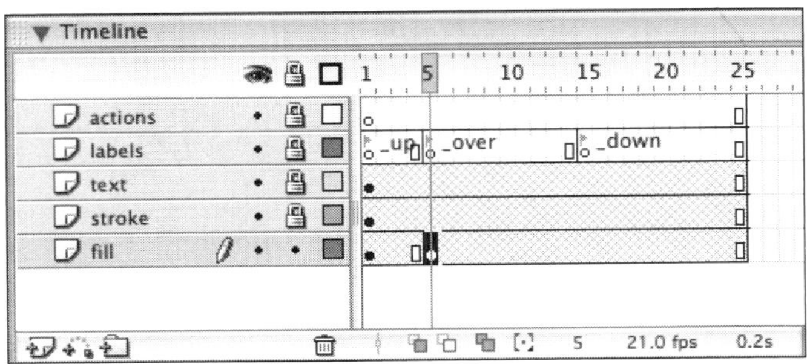

Click to select the frame and press F6 in order to add a keyframe; repeat this process on frame 14 and 25 on the same layer. There are two animations: one for the `_over` state, and a second for the `_down` state. You want to create an animation for the `_over` state that is reversed for the `_down` state, so the beginning of the `_over` animation and the end of the `_down` animation are exactly the same.

3) Add a brightness tween to `fill_gr` and then insert a keyframe on frame 15.
Select the keyframe at the `_over` label, and expand the Property inspector. Choose Motion from the Tween drop-down menu to insert a motion tween. Select `fill_gr` on frame 14, choose Brightness from the Color drop-down menu in the Property inspector, and change the value to *85%*.

When you finish, select frame 15 and press F6 to insert a keyframe. Change the Tween drop-down in the Property inspector to Motion. Scrub the Timeline to view both of the motion tweens you have created.

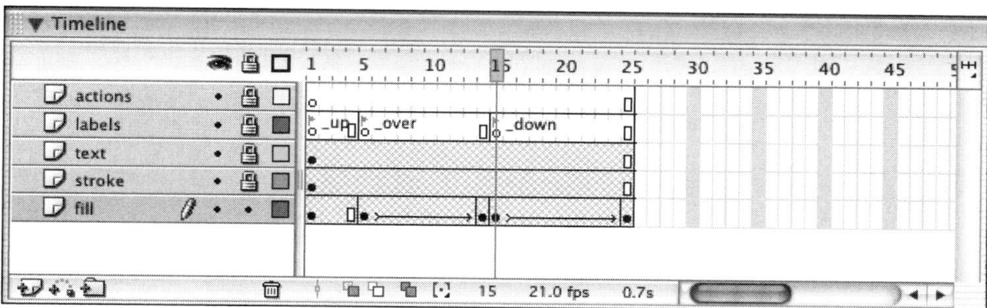

NOTE *If you test the button at this point, you cannot see the brightness tweens. This is because movie clip buttons in Flash are engineered to go to each special frame label and stop. You need to add a bit of additional code to tell it to actually go and play each animation and then stop at the end of the animation. You will do this in Lesson 6.*

4) Repeat Steps 1 to 3 with the `toc_mc` instance.
The `toc_mc` movie clip should also be in the Library. You have to double-click on the `toc_mc` symbol in the Library and it opens in symbol-editing mode so you can edit it. Repeat the same steps you took with `samplechapter_mc` so that each of the buttons animates the same way.

5) Lock the `fill` layer in the Timeline, save the changes, and return to the main Stage.

CREATING A SHAPE TWEEN

Shape tweens allow you to change shapes over a series of frames. Shape tweening allows you to change the length of lines, bend lines, or otherwise change the shape of a drawing and create some very interesting effects. Instead of having to manually create each change in the appearance of the shape, Flash does the calculations to create the animation for you: all you have to do is set the beginning and the end. You can have one or several shapes tween on a single layer, although if you have many shapes they might affect each other. At any rate, the effects you create can be very simple to quite complex.

NOTE *Shape tweens can be applied to raw vector graphics (they show the crosshatch pattern when they are selected) or bitmaps that have had Modify > Break Apart or Trace Bitmap applied to them. This can be a useful way to tween drawings, but to further utilize shape tweening (particularly when you are creating a complex tween), you need to understand how to use shape hints.*

Shape tweening can often produce very unexpected results. The path that a particular part of a shape takes between the beginning and the end of the tween might go all over the place. A *shape hint* allows you to specify corresponding points on tweened shapes (meaning that a particular point on the beginning shape should go directly to a second specified place on the ending shape during the shape tween). Each shape hint has a specific letter. Therefore, wherever shape hint "a" is placed at the beginning of the tween moves to the location of shape hint "a" at the end of the tween.

For example, you might have a cat shape that tweens into a dog shape. If you had a triangle representing the cat's ear with a shape hint "a" at the cat's ear tip, and its corresponding shape hint at the dog's ear tip, the cat's ear should directly tween to the dog's ear instead of taking a more indirect route in the tween between the two locations.

There are two *blend* options when performing a shape tween: *Distributive* and *Angular*. Distributed blending generates a smoother transition that tends to look a bit irregular; whereas Angular blending preserves corners and lines when tweening. Angular is only available when you're working with shapes that have straight lines and sharp corners.

In this exercise, you will be working on building a subtle page-turning effect in the book's logo in the top left corner of the bookstore Web site. You're still working with the `bookstore9.fla` file.

1) Find `pageTurn_mc` **inside the** `logo_mc` **movie clip on the Stage. Double-click** `pageTurn_mc` **to open the movie clip for editing and zoom in to at least 800%.**

You created a movie clip in Lesson 4 that was a single line that was created for a page turn animation. The animation for the page turn is in two parts. The first part of the animation is to create a shape tween, which you will create in this exercise.

2) Rename Layer 1 to `animation`**. Add a keyframe at frame 10 and then modify the new keyframe.**

After you have renamed the layer to `animation` and added a keyframe, you can modify frame 10. Select frame 10 and then make sure that the line is *not* selected. Mouse over the line until you see the cursor, which is shown in the following figure:

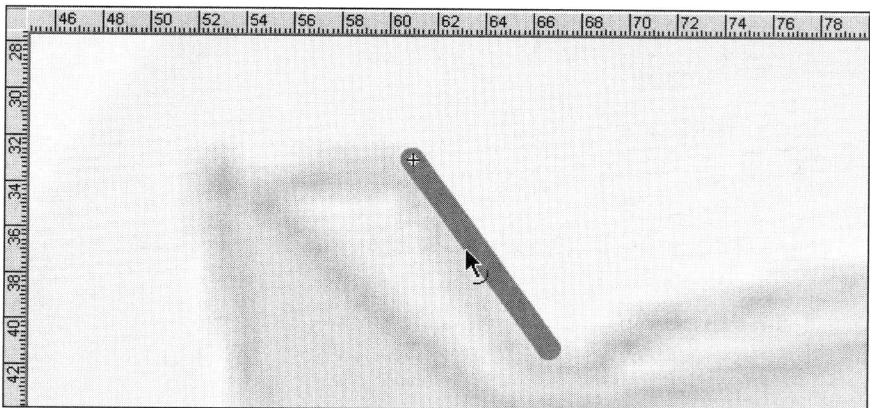

Click and drag the line so it bends. Bend the line until it resembles the following figure.

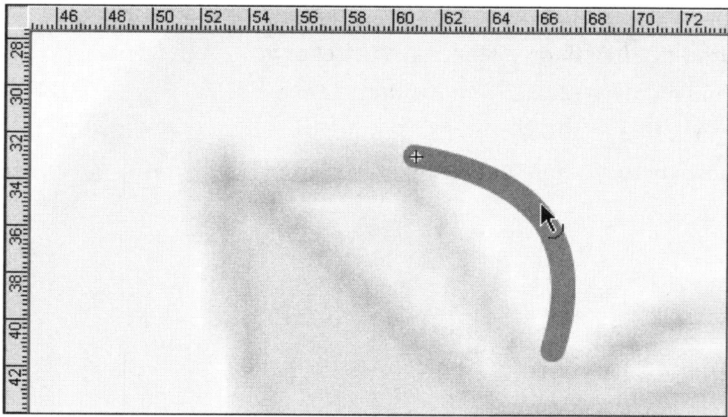

Mouse over the upper end of the line until a cursor appears that has a corner point that's next to the arrow. Click and drag the end of the line slightly to the right until it resembles the following figure.

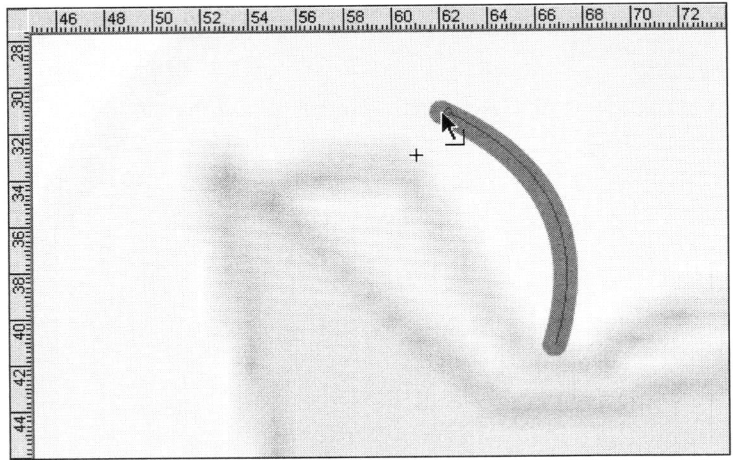

3) Insert a shape tween using the Property inspector, and then check out the animation.

Select frame 1 and expand the Property inspector. Choose Shape from the Tween drop-down menu. A green arrow spans across the `animation` layer, which means that a shape tween has been added to those frames.

Click and drag the playhead across the span of frames and view the animation that has been added to the logo. The lower point of the line should remain in the same place, which is the spine of the book. The page turn animation will be completed in the following exercise.

4) When you finish creating the shape tween, save the changes that you have made to the document by choosing File > Save from the main menu.

In the next exercise, you will add a frame-by-frame animation directly following the shape tween to complete the page turn animation.

CREATING FRAME-BY-FRAME ANIMATIONS

Frame-by-frame animation is the most time-consuming of each of the animation types because every frame of animation must be individually created, manipulated, and tweaked by hand. However, frame-by-frame animation gives you more control over the overall look and feel of the SWF and can be used to create some awesome effects after you spend a bit of time learning animation techniques. Learning a bit about animation definitely is worth the time and effort.

Frame-by-frame animation is best suited to more complex animation sequences where the image must be different for each frame, such as trying to animate facial expressions or create a walk cycle. Because most frames change in a frame-by-frame animation, the penalty is a higher file size because the frames you create have new data that Flash has to store in the exported SWF file.

NOTE *If you are hand-drawing your animations, you might want to try using a pen tablet to create your drawings with, such as those made by Wacom. Flash recognizes pressure sensitivity and pen tilt depending on the features in your tablet.*

In the following example, you will complete the page turn animation that you started in the previous exercise.

1) In `bookstore9.fla`, open the `pageTurn_mc` movie clip where you created the shape tween in the previous example.

You already have a shape tween on the `animation` layer spanning between frame 1 and 10, which begins the first half of the page turn animation. To get the level of detail necessary for the second half of the page turn, you will use a frame-by-frame animation. Although you could certainly create another shape tween to finish the animation, using frame-by-frame animation allows you to have more control over the motion. Obviously it also helps you learn how to create frame-by-frame animation, too.

2) Insert a new keyframe at the end of the shape tween, and then turn on *onion skinning*.

Select the Onion Skin Outlines button to turn on onion skinning, which is a very powerful tool to assist you in creating frame-by-frame animation. Onion skinning allows you to view not only the current frame you are editing, but also the contents of the previous and next frames. This procedure helps you line up your animations and ensure that the animation is smooth. The current frame that you are editing appears in full color (similar to working with onion skinning disabled), whereas neighboring frames appear to be slightly faded out or as an outline. By default, you can edit only the current frame, although you can also choose to edit multiple frames at once as well.

Click the empty frame following the shape tween (frame 11) and press F6 to insert a new keyframe. The contents of the previous frame are added to the new keyframe, which you will modify in the following step. Click and drag the edges of the onion skin markers above the Timeline to see more frames of the animation.

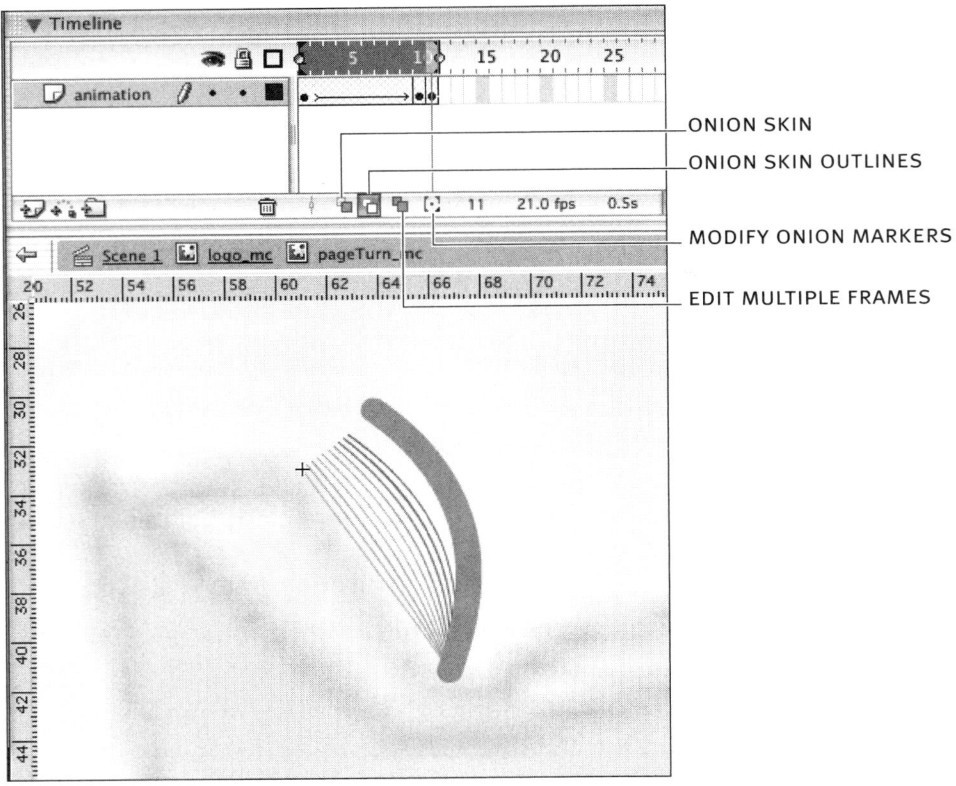

3) Modify the keyframe that you created in Step 2.

In the previous exercise, you bent the line into a curve to create the appearance of a page turning halfway. In this exercise, you will bend the page a little bit further and modify its length on each new frame that you create. All the while you will keep the base of the page (at the spine of the book) stationary.

Each keyframe you select should be an incremental frame in the page turn animation. Select the keyframe you created in Step 2 (frame 11) and then deselect the line on the Stage. Mouse over the upper end of the line, and when the cursor changes, drag the tip of the line the right so the line bends. The frame is now modified from the one to the left.

4) Insert new keyframes and modify the page graphic until the page is on the other side of the bookcover.

When you finish the modifications to frame 11, select frame 12 and press F6 to enter another keyframe. The contents of frame 11 are copied into frame 12, where you can modify the line again. Make the same kind of modifications that you did for frame 11, by dragging the upper tip of the page further to the right. Bend the page if necessary by mousing over the middle of the line and dragging the page to modify its bend. However, most of the modifications can be made by moving the upper tip of the line (or "page"). Just make sure that you do not move the bottom tip of the page by the spine. Only bend the middle of the page, or move the upper tip of the line.

Because the onion skin feature shows you an outline for each frame around the one you are working on, it should help you figure out how the animation will appear while you are editing. You can also scrub the Timeline by dragging the playhead back and forth.

NOTE *Make sure that you do not modify the lower point of the line. If you modify the lower point of the line, it appears as if the page is shifting in the book instead of being bound to the spine!*

Enter as many keyframes as you require until the animation is complete. When you get toward the end of the animation, you probably have to drag the end of the page outwards to make it slightly longer in length.

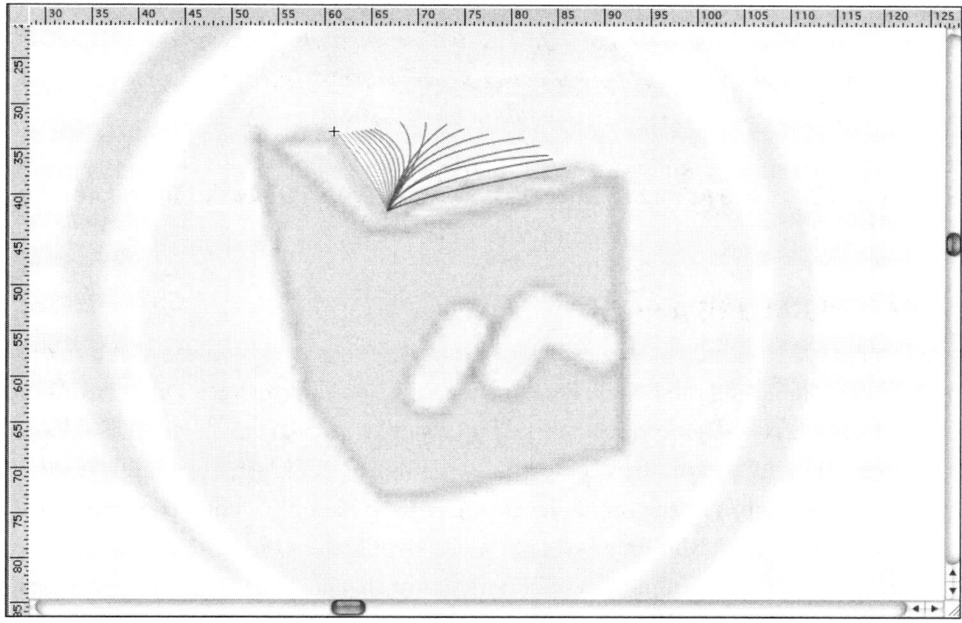

The animation is finished as soon as the page animates all the way to the front book cover. You might have about 9 or 10 keyframes when the animation is complete.

TIP *You can make the animation look a bit better by fading out the page during the frame-by-frame animation. To do this, you can return to each keyframe you created in this exercise, and select a different amount of alpha for the line. You can do this using the Alpha slider in the Color Mixer panel. Select the first line in the frame-by-frame animation using the Selection tool, and then drag the Alpha slider downwards to about 90%. For each frame, gradually fade out the page more until you reach around 10% for the final page.*

5) Insert empty frames at the end of the animation in order to add a pause between the page turns.

Select frame 85 and press F5 to add a frame to the layer, which means that the animation will appear to pause before turning the page again. Remember that because this is a movie clip, it loops on the Stage endlessly. This means that the page will appear to turn over and over again, with a pause in between each one.

TIP *You probably want to make the page turn less uniform. The best way to do this is to use some ActionScript to play this animation at random intervals. Learning how to do this goes beyond the scope of the book, but you can go to* `www.TrainingFromTheSource.com/bonus` *for a tutorial on how to add this functionality to the Tech Bookstore site.*

6) Choose File > Save As and enter `bookstore9_complete.fla` **into the File Name field.**

Click `Scene 1` in the edit bar to return to the main Stage.

ANIMATING ALONG A PATH

You can also use motion tweens to move a symbol along a path. You can make a path by drawing a line using the Pencil, Pen, or Line tools and then attach a symbol to either end of the path. This path must be placed on a *motion guide* layer, which means that whatever you draw will not be visible after you publish the Flash document. It also means that the paths created on the layer can be used to guide an object on the Stage that's being animated. Motion guides allow you to animate objects along the outside of a circle, square, straight line, curve, or any sort of shape you can draw. In these final two exercises you will make some modifications to the `map.fla` file you created in Lesson 2. You are going to use a motion guide to animate a small symbol over the map.

1) Open map_starter.fla **from the** Lesson05 **folder on the CD-ROM and save it into the** TechBookstore **folder on your hard drive.**

You will recognize this file as similar to the one you worked on in Lesson 2. The only difference with this starter file is that there are two graphics in the Library that you need to work with. All of the layers and positioning is the same. At the end of the next exercise (on Timeline Effects), you will save this file as map.fla. That file replaces the map.fla you began in Lesson 2.

2) Select the map **layer and insert a new layer called** car**. Then open the Library and locate** car_gr **and** tree_gr **in the** graphics **folder. Drag an instance of** car_gr **onto the** car **layer and drag an instance of** tree_gr **onto the** map **layer.**

There is a symbol in the Library called car_gr that you can use to animate. The tree_gr symbol will be a static graphic on the Stage. You will probably have to unlock the map layer before you make changes to it.

Move car_gr so it is just beyond the left edge of the Stage on Brannan Street. Move the tree so it is at the right edge of the map at the lower-right edge of Macromedia Park on the map. Refer to the following figure for guidance.

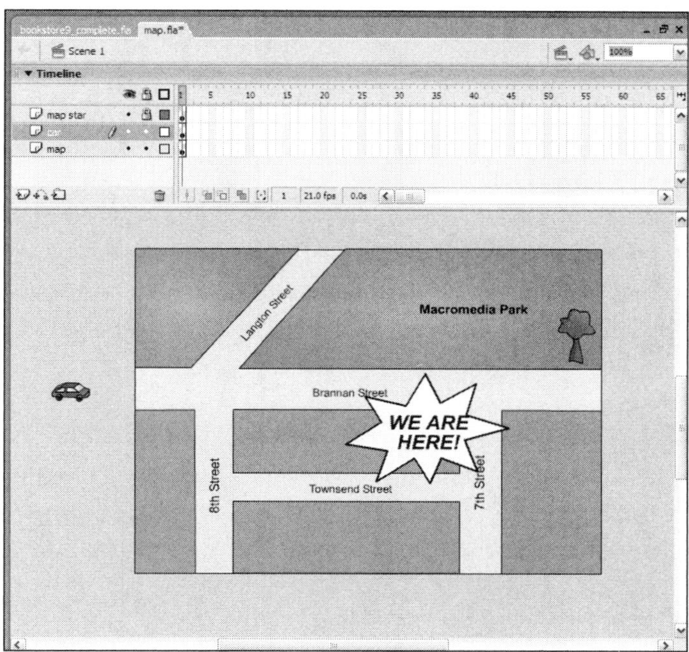

NOTE *You can also use* map.fla *that you created in Lesson 2 (already saved in the* TechBookstore *folder on your hard drive) and make your own graphics to work with for this exercise, and I wouldn't doubt yours to be significantly better than the ones provided.*

3) Create a new motion guide layer and draw a path on the Stage.

Make sure that the `map` layer is locked. Select the `car` layer and click the Add Motion Guide button that's next to the Insert New Layer button. This process automatically indents the `car` layer, so the motion guide will be applied to it. This is a lot like creating a mask layer like you did in Lesson 2. The new layer is automatically called `Guide: car`.

Choose the Pencil tool and make sure that the Smooth modifier is chosen in the Options section of the Tools panel.

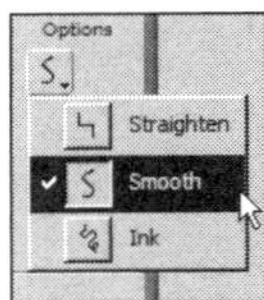

The Smooth modifier helps you draw a path that isn't too ragged, although it still allows you to add a few "bumps" to the path, unlike the Straighten modifier, so the car doesn't have to follow a ruler-straight path! If you find that the path you create is too smooth, choose the Ink modifier instead, which does not alter the strokes you create at all (although the path still appears to be aliased, so it does seem to be smoothed to some extent as well).

Draw a path on the new `Guide: car` layer you just created using the Pencil or Brush tool. The path should be drawn going down Brannan Street from the left side of the Stage to the right side near the tree. The path that you create should follow along the road, bending around the "We Are Here" star, and then curve into the tree at the end of the path. Add a few bumps and curves along the path. When the path reaches the tree, curve the line upwards, similar to the following figure.

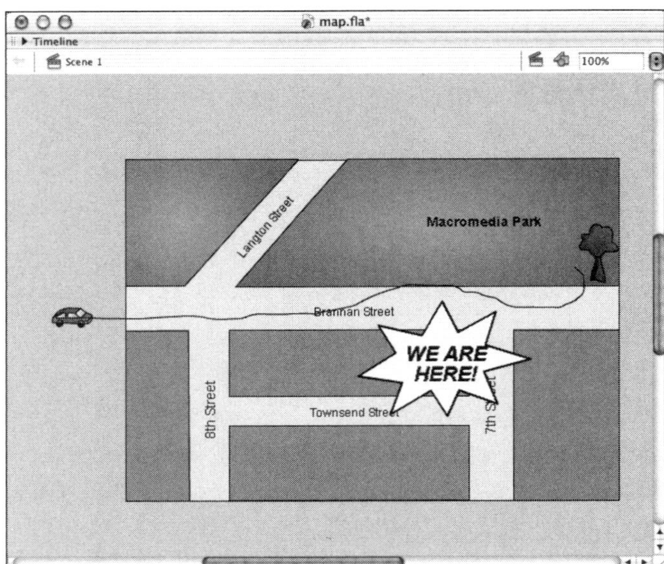

Lock the motion guide layer (`Guide: car`) when you finish drawing the path.

4) Add a keyframe on the `car` layer at frame 70, frames on the motion guide, `map star` and `map` layers at frame 70. Then snap `car_gr` to each end of the path.
Select the `car` layer and insert a keyframe on frame 70 by selecting the empty frame and pressing F6. Then select frame 70 of the `map` layer and press F5 to insert a frame. Repeat this step for the motion guide and `map star` layers.

Choose the Selection tool in the Tools panel and ensure that the Snap to Objects modifier is selected. On frame 1 of the `car` layer, click and drag `car_gr` and snap it to the end of the path near the left side of the Stage. It helps to drag the instance by the registration point, which is in the center of the car graphic.

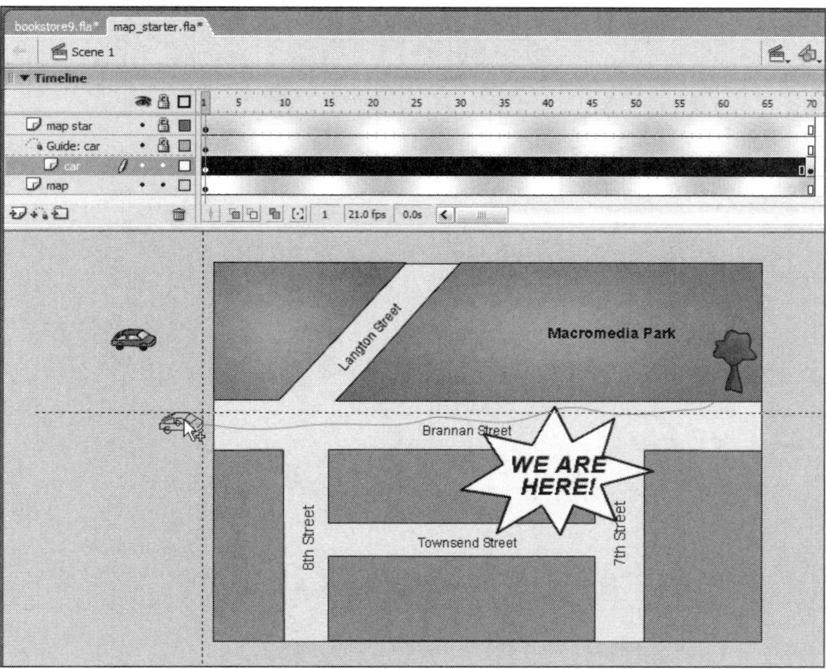

Click frame 70 on the `car` layer and then select `car_gr` by its registration point in the center of the graphic and snap it to the end of the path near the tree.

5) Select the frames on the `car` layer and insert a motion tween.
Select the frames on the `car` layer and expand the Property inspector. Select Motion from the Tween drop-down menu in the Property inspector. When the frames on the layer are selected, make sure that the Snap check box *is* selected and Orient to path

is *not* selected. The car layer changes to a purple color with an arrow spanning the length of the animation, meaning that the motion tween expands across those frames.

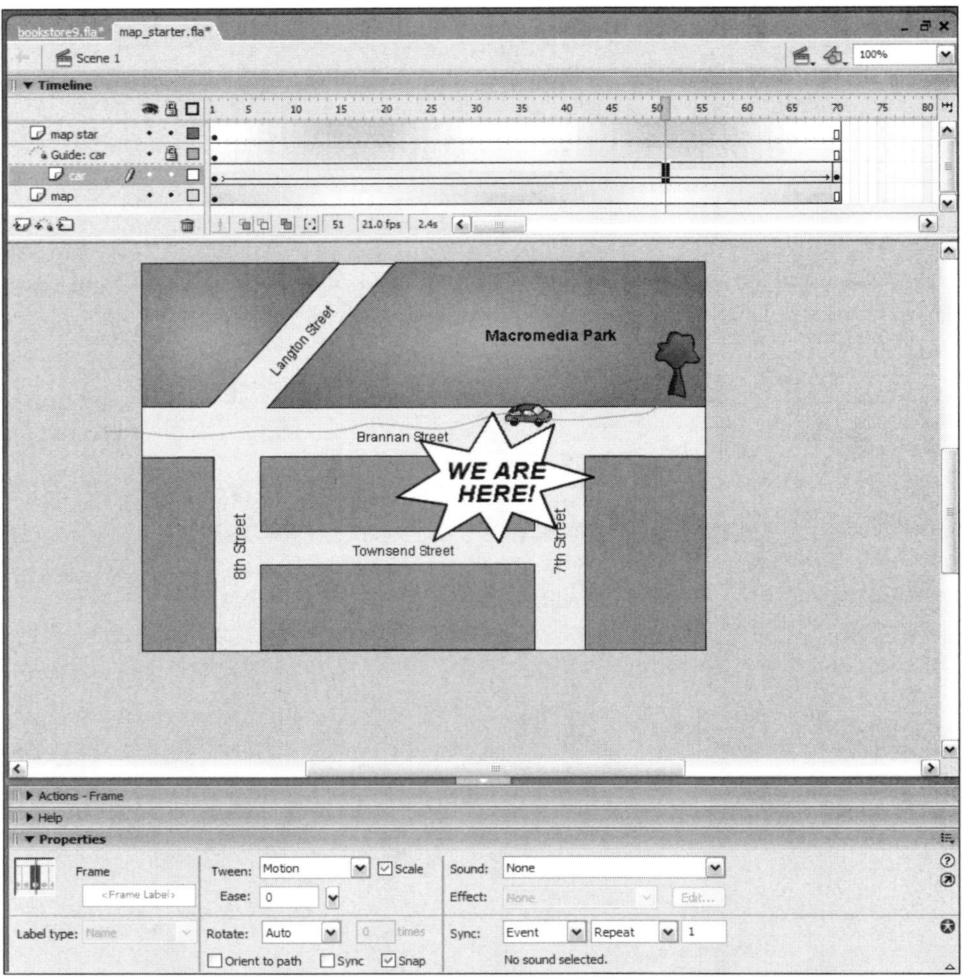

TIP *There are three options on the Property inspector that are related to motion guides and tweening:* Orient to path, Sync, *and* Snap. *Orient to path allows you to point objects in the direction they are moving along the path. The object rotates to align with the curve. Sync allows you to sync the animation in the instance to the main Timeline, and Snap allows you to grab an object by its registration point and add it to the motion guide path.*

6) Add easing to the end of the animation, so the car speeds up while it's tweened from one side of the Stage to the other.

Select the first frame in the animation and expand the Property inspector. Enter *-100* into the Ease text field, which means that the car speeds up between the two keyframes when you play the animation in the Flash player. Choose Control > Test Movie to see the animation in the test player. It loops repeatedly at this point in the exercise.

7) Scrub the Timeline to view the animation and then make a modification to the motion tween.

Click and drag the playhead to scrub the Timeline and see the motion tween along the path you drew. If the car doesn't move along the path, make sure that the car is snapped to each end of the pencil line you drew on the motion guide layer.

You probably notice that the motion path doesn't work properly next to the tree that it is supposed to crash into because it doesn't rotate to appear like it is tilting upwards or crashed. You need to rotate `car_gr` in order to correct the effect. Scrub the Timeline again, find a spot around frame 65 on the `car` layer where the car should begin to rotate, and press the F6 key to insert a new keyframe. This location will be where the new part of the animation will begin.

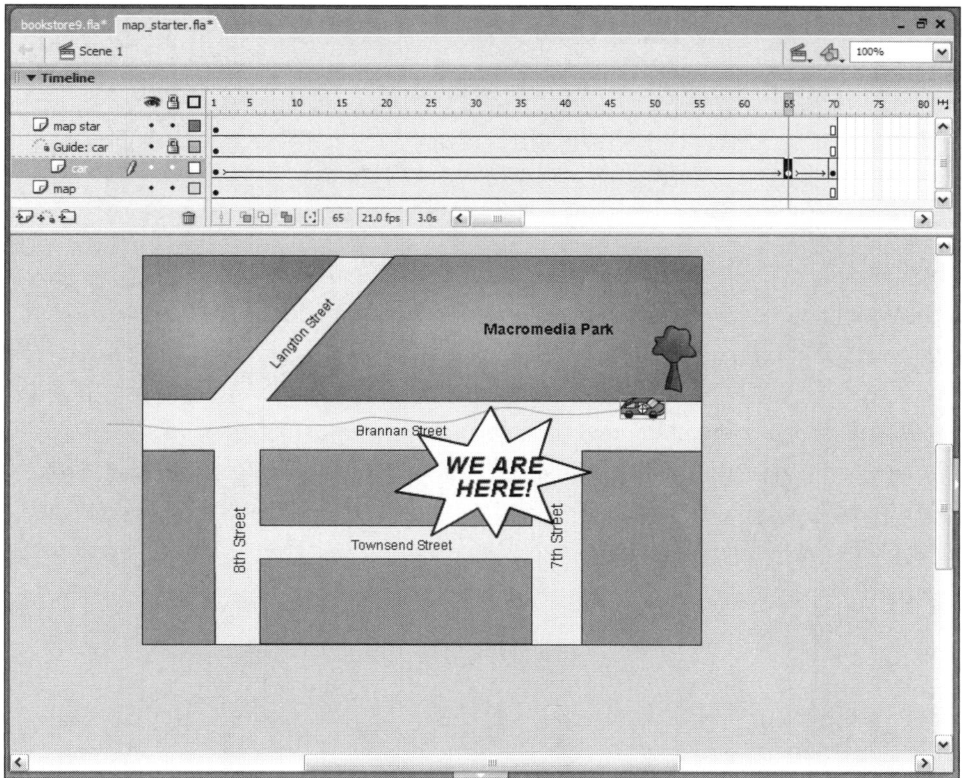

Select frame 70 at the very end of the animation and then choose the Free Transform tool in the Tools panel. Handles will appear around `car_gr`. Mouse over the upper-right corner of `car_gr` until the rotation cursor appears.

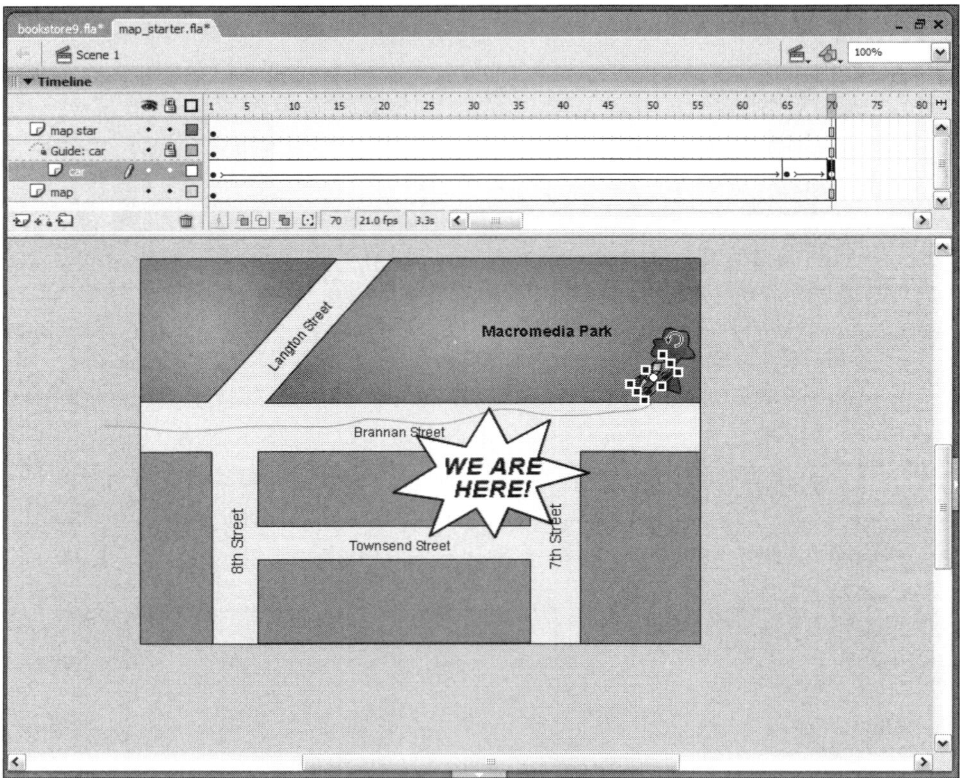

Click and drag the corner to rotate the car until it appears to be leaning against the tree. When you finish, use the playhead to scrub the Timeline again and view the change to your animation.

8) Place a `stop` action on the last frame on a new layer called `actions`.

If you test the animation as a SWF before adding a `stop` action, you will notice that the animation loops repeatedly. To stop the animation at the end, you need to add a `stop` action on the final frame.

Select the `map star` layer and then click the Insert New Layer button. Double-click the name of the layer and rename it *actions*. Click frame 70 (or the final frame in your animation) and press F6 to add a new keyframe. Select the new keyframe and open the Actions panel. Type the following ActionScript into the Script pane:

```
stop();
```

When you finish, press Ctrl+Enter (or Command+Enter on the Mac) to watch the animation in the testing environment.

9) Save the changes you have made to `map_starter.fla`.

You'll add further modifications to this FLA file using Timeline Effects in the following exercise.

USING TIMELINE EFFECTS TO ANIMATE

You added a drop shadow Timeline Effect to some text in Lesson 3. The drop shadow did not animate, but it was added the same way you will add the animated Timeline Effects in this exercise. These animated Timeline Effects allow you to add motion to your Flash documents by clicking buttons and choosing values. A few of the Timeline Effects that are installed with Flash allow you to quickly add blurring effects or a drop shadow, transform a symbol, move and rotate a symbol, or add a fading and wiping transition effect.

In this exercise, you will look at the Expand Timeline effect and see how you can incorporate it into the map you are working on.

1) Open `map_starter.fla` that you were working with in the previous step and select the star group.

Select the star *group* that's currently on the map's `map star` layer, which is the grouping of vector shapes you imported from FreeHand. If you cannot select the group, check that the layer hasn't been locked.

2) Convert star from a group into a graphic symbol called `star_gr`. Then duplicate the `star_gr` symbol on the `map star` layer.

With the star group selected, press F8 to convert the group into a graphic symbol. Enter `star_gr` to name the symbol and click the Graphic radio button.

The Expand effect requires that you use two instances so it can create the particular effect. Therefore, you have to duplicate the `star_gr` instance on the Stage and select both instances before adding the effect. After you have the star effect selected on the Stage, choose Edit > Duplicate or press Ctrl+D on Windows (or Command+D on the Mac). This command creates a second instance about 10 pixels below and to the right of the `star_gr` symbol.

3) Select both `star_gr` instances on the Stage and then apply the Expand Timeline Effect to the instances.

Press the Shift key while selecting both instances of `star_gr` on the Stage. After you have the two star instances selected on the Stage, apply the Expand effect by choosing Insert > Timeline Effects > Effects > Expand from the main menu. The Expand dialog box then opens with the default settings for the effect.

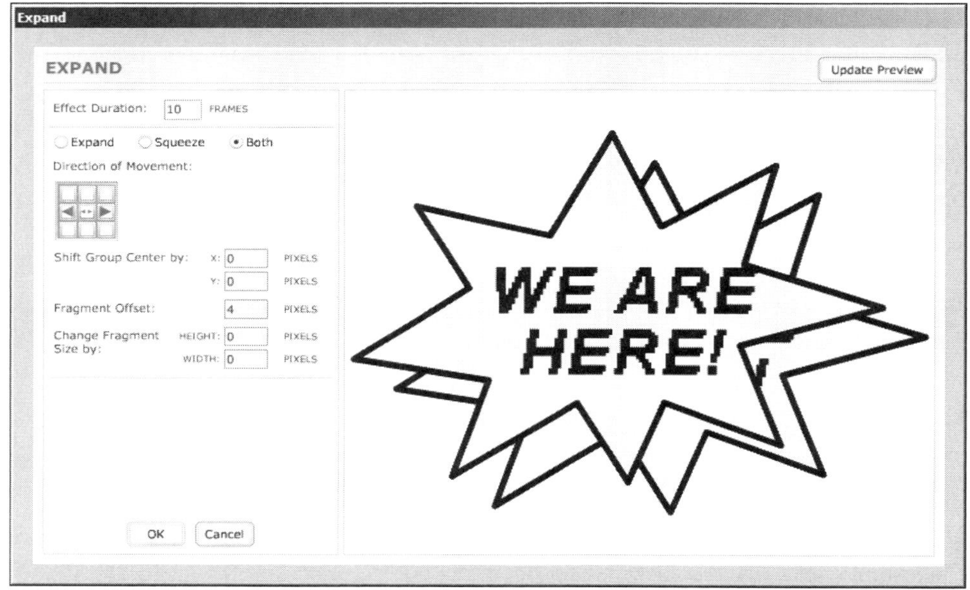

4) Customize the Timeline Effect by changing the settings in the Expand dialog box. Modify the Effect Duration, style, shift, and offset settings.

As you can see, there are a series of options and customizations you can make for the effect and a preview to show you what it will look like before you apply it. On the left side of the dialog box is a series of radio buttons and text fields in which you can change settings such as the type, duration, direction of movement, and offset for the animation. The right side of the Expand dialog box has a preview pane in which you can see the Timeline Effect before adding it to the Stage.

For the map stars, set the Effect Duration to 10 frames. When the effect is added to the FLA, Flash repeats the Timeline Effect's animation every 10 frames. Click the Both radio button so Flash expands and squeezes the `star_gr` instances. Below this, leave Direction of Movement highlighted in the center square, set the fragment offset to *4*, and set the rest of the settings to *0*.

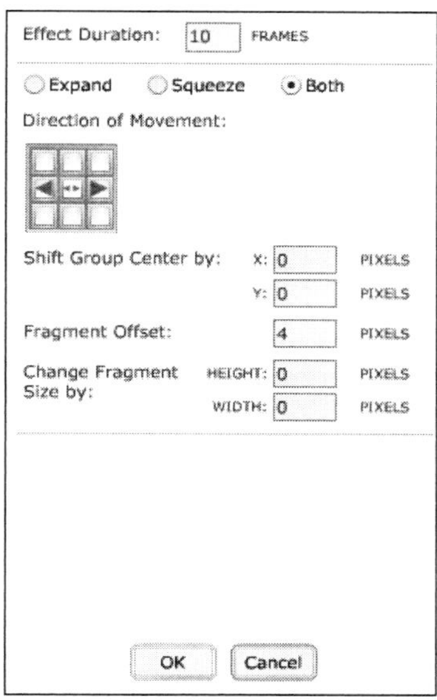

After you make changes to the settings, click the Update Preview button in the upper-right corner of the dialog box, which applies the changes you made to the preview in the window. This feature allows you to tweak your changes accordingly.

5) Apply the effect to the star and modify some of the changes made to the Flash document.

When you press OK, the animation is applied to the graphic symbols, and you return to the main Stage. If you click the Cancel button, the effect is cancelled and you return to the Stage without an effect applied to the selection.

NOTE *The frames on the layer will probably be reduced to 10 frames. You will need to add frames to this layer so it is the same length as the other layers in the FLA file. Therefore, press F5 on frame 70 so the animation is visible for the duration of the animation.*

Also, the map star layer should have been renamed to Expand 1. You might want to rename the Expand 1 layer so it's more descriptive such as back to map star or whatever you feel you want to do.Test the animation so far to see the finished effect by choosing Control > Test Movie from the main menu.

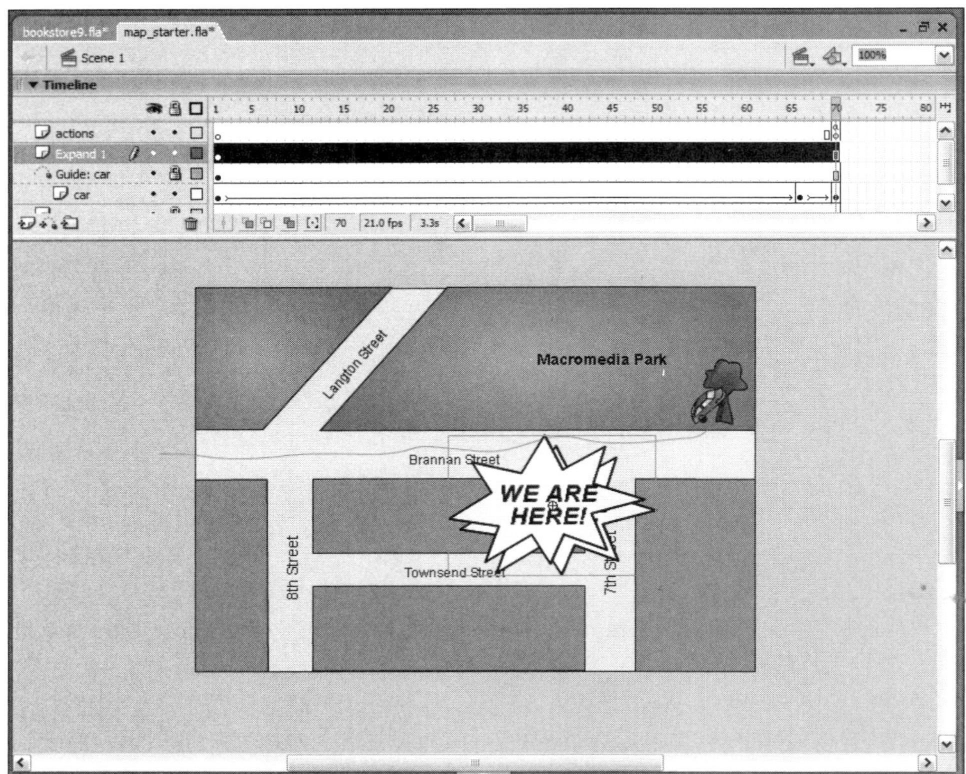

If you aren't satisfied with the effect and want to make different settings, you can edit the Timeline effect by choosing Modify > Timeline Effects > Edit Effect. Alternatively, you can remove the effect entirely by choosing Modify > Timeline Effects > Remove Effect. After applying and removing effects, it might be necessary to rename the layers to help you stay organized.

6) Choose File › Save As and enter map.fla **into the File Name field. Choose to replace the old** map.fla **file in the** TechBookstore **folder. Publish the file when you're finished by choosing File › Publish.**

When you save the file, you are prompted whether you want to replace the old version of the map.fla file that's already saved in the TechBookstore folder. Choose to replace the file. If you do not want to overwrite the existing file, rename the version you made in Lesson 2. Then publish the new file so map.swf is generated in the TechBookstore folder.

WHAT YOU HAVE LEARNED

In this lesson, you have:

- Learned the differences between frame-by-frame animation, motion tweens, and shape tweens (page 134)
- Added motion to a movie clip (pages 134–139)
- Used easing to modify the motion (pages 134–139)
- Added a motion tween to change the brightness of an instance (pages 139–141)
- Added a motion tween to change the alpha level of an instance (pages 142–144)
- Added a shape tween to animate the turn of a page (pages 146–148)
- Created a frame-by-frame animation (pages 149–152)
- Animated a symbol along a vector path (pages 152–159)
- Used animated Timeline Effects to animate instances on the Stage (pages 159–162)

adding basic interactivity

LESSON 6

Although you can make some very interesting and elaborate FLA files that might integrate animation, artwork, sound, and video, eventually you will probably want to add some sort of user interaction. Interaction is what takes Flash beyond a tool that can show animations or display artwork. Interaction adds an element of control and interest to a SWF file. Interactivity might be as simple as asking a user for his or her name, or as complex as creating a full message board system or Flash-based chat room.

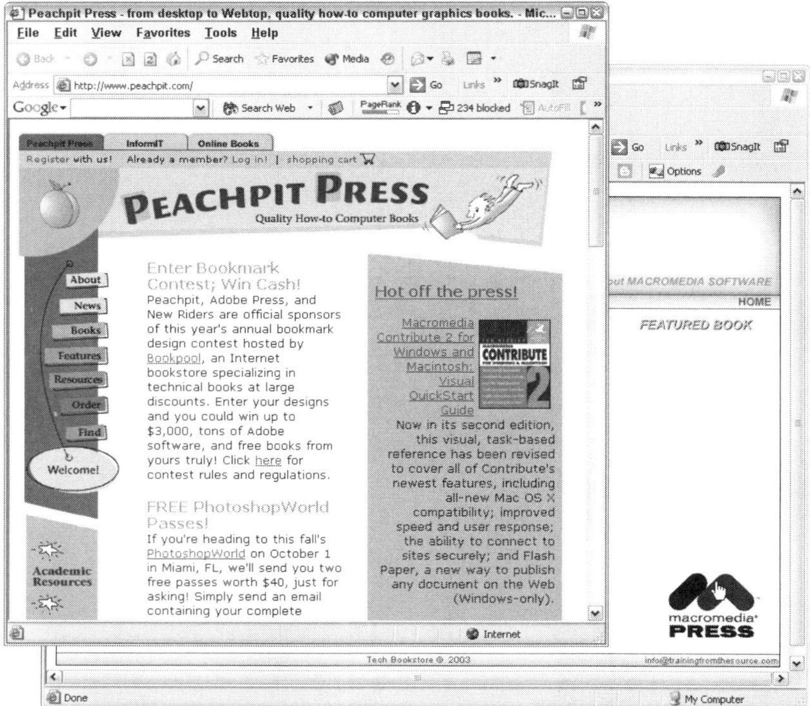

Interaction is added to the bookstore.

Tools found in Flash MX 2004 and Flash MX Professional 2004 make it relatively easy to get started creating Rich Internet Applications (RIAs), uniting data-driven sites with nice user interfaces. You can use *behaviors* that allow you to control the SWF file's playback, trigger data sources, load images, and control embedded video at the click of a button without having to write a single line of code.

WHAT YOU WILL LEARN

In this lesson, you will:

- Add behaviors to a Flash document
- Modify behaviors using the Behaviors panel
- Use basic server interaction to load a JPEG image
- Learn about adding ActionScript
- Find out about the Actions panel
- Learn dot notation
- Start adding ActionScript to the Tech Bookstore
- Use stop actions to control the Timeline
- Add a home button to the bookstore
- Use code to animate the movie clip button
- Learn about the Script navigator and pins

APPROXIMATE TIME

This lesson takes approximately one hour and 30 minutes to complete.

LESSON FILES

Media Files:

media/mmpresslogo.jpg

Starting Files:

Lesson06/bookstore10.fla

Completed Project:

Lesson06/bookstore10_complete.fla

MAKING FLASH DOCUMENTS INTERACTIVE

There are many different ways that you can make your Flash documents interactive. Buttons and movie clips can be used to add simple to very advanced interactions in a SWF. The interaction is powered by actions and behaviors that you add to the FLA, and you can even make a SWF tie into a server for advanced data interactivity. Server interaction involves creating a connection in some way. You can interact with a visitor very simply by loading files (as you do in a couple of different ways in this lesson); or you can use Web Services, Flash Remoting, an XML Socket Server, or the Flash Communication Server. In Lesson 10, you will create a server connection using a Web Service. But for now, let's look at the more basic kinds of interactivity you can add to the Tech Bookstore.

Buttons can add simple interactivity; for example, you click a button (an *event*) and then something happens. Text fields can also add slightly more complex interactivity. You can collect data from a user and send it somewhere by using input text fields or TextInput components, which you will do in Lesson 9. An event occurs when a mouse rolls on to or out of the hot spot, or your SWF files react to the event of keys being pressed on the keyboard.

You do not need to write ActionScript to add interactivity. Behaviors allow you to add interactivity to a SWF file without having to write the code yourself. A behavior can be added using the Behaviors panel. All you need to do is select a frame on the Timeline or an object (such as a button) on the Stage and use the controls and menu options in the Behaviors panel to add the ActionScript. Then you can modify the ActionScript further in the panel. Using behaviors makes adding code very quick and easy, which can add basic interactivity to a SWF file. In the following section, you will use behaviors to add simple actions on frames and instances in the FLA.

INTRODUCING BEHAVIORS

Behaviors allow you to use pieces of ActionScript in your FLA without having to learn the language or to type in scripts to get things working. Behaviors are snippets of code stored in Flash that you can add to your FLA to help it work. The behaviors included with Flash help you add simple functionality to your Web sites. Behaviors are used frequently when you start to use *screens* to build forms and slide presentations using Flash. Screens will be covered in detail when you get to Lesson 8. Undoubtedly you will be able to download additional behaviors that are written by third-party companies and members of the community and install them right into Flash. Watch `www.TrainingFromTheSource.com/resources` for links to sites that offer behaviors for download. Also search the Macromedia Exchange for behaviors as well when they become available (`www.macromedia.com/go/exchange`).

You can add behaviors to the Timeline or directly to instances. Examples of the behavior snippets available are `getURL` (can open a browser window or email client) and `gotoAndPlay`, a method that tells the playhead to move to a particular position on the Timeline and start playing. When you attach a behavior, it adds ActionScript to whatever you attach it to. Using behaviors does not replace ActionScript, and if you only plan to use behaviors exclusively for the code you put in an FLA file, it would limit what you can do with the SWF. There is only a small set of behaviors available in Flash when you install it, and those behaviors probably won't give you all the functionality you need.

NOTE *Many behaviors are written explicitly to add code right on an instance (such as a button or movie clip) in your documents. However, it is easier to find and "debug" (fix) the code if something does not work properly when it is all in one place on the Timeline. Behaviors tend to add bits of code all over an FLA file because so many are added directly onto instances and not the Timeline. This can result in conflicts and make your documents hard to edit. Therefore, you should try to limit adding behaviors directly to instances whenever possible. It is sometimes a better solution to try adding the ActionScript on the Timeline if you know the code in question.*

You should always be careful and conscious when adding code on individual objects, whether or not you are using behaviors to do so. It is always a good idea to try to keep your ActionScript in one place: in most cases, on the Timeline or perhaps after you have more experience, in classes. That said, we will show you how to use them in this application so you have the option of using behaviors later on in your work.

The next couple of exercises will cover how to use behaviors and customize them to suit your application. You will be adding behaviors to the Timeline to control the movement of the playhead and then you will use a behavior to load a JPEG into an instance of a movie clip.

USING A BEHAVIOR TO LOAD A JPEG

Loading JPEG images into a SWF is a very important process to understand. By being able to dynamically load images, site visitors download the images in the gallery only if they click on that specific picture instead of having to download all the data at once, regardless of whether they want to view all of the images or not. Loading makes it much easier for designers and developers to make dynamic applications, such as image galleries, while maintaining low file sizes. It also makes the application a lot more reusable. If an image changes (maybe a product changes or an artist alters the JPEG file), then all you have to do is upload the new picture instead of cracking open the FLA to edit it directly.

After you learn how to load images into a SWF at runtime, you will probably decide to load images this way in many of your applications. The reason it is so important to consider using the loading technique when constructing FLA files is because you do not have to import every image you use into the Library. If you do not use the loading technique, all the images in the Library are downloaded to the end user's computer. Imagine downloading every single JPEG at once in the image gallery mentioned earlier. By loading JPEGs dynamically, the end user needs to download images only on a page of the Tech Bookstore when it is selected. This means that the visitor downloads the content only in the area he or she wants to see, and skips images in the other areas.

As you will discover in this exercise, instance names are necessary to target movie clip or button symbols. You have to give the instances a name so Flash knows what object to manipulate when you add ActionScript to do something. You can add instance names using the `<Instance Name>` field in the Property inspector, or you can provide an instance name when you add behaviors. You will give an instance name to a movie clip so you can load an image file into that movie clip in this exercise.

1) Open `bookstore9_complete.fla` and save a new version of the file as `bookstore10.fla`.

Save the new version of the file into the `TechBookstore` folder on your hard drive.

2) Copy the Macromedia Press logo from the CD-ROM into your `TechBookstore` folder.

There is a file named `mmpresslogo.jpg` located within the `media` folder on the CD-ROM. Copy the image into the `TechBookstore` folder on your hard drive.

3) Select the `home` layer and create a new rectangle on the Stage. Convert the rectangle into a movie clip.

Select the `home` layer that is within the `pages` layer folder on the Timeline. Make sure that the playhead is at Frame 1. Select the Rectangle tool from the Tools panel and set the stroke color to No Color and the fill color to *black* (#000000). Draw a rectangle on the Stage and change its dimensions to *128* pixels wide by *96* pixels high in the Property inspector.

Double-click the rectangle that you created and press F8 to convert to a symbol. Name the symbol `mmpresslogo_mc`, click the Movie clip radio button, and click the OK button. Move the rectangle near the lower-right corner of the Stage, similar to where it is placed in the following figure.

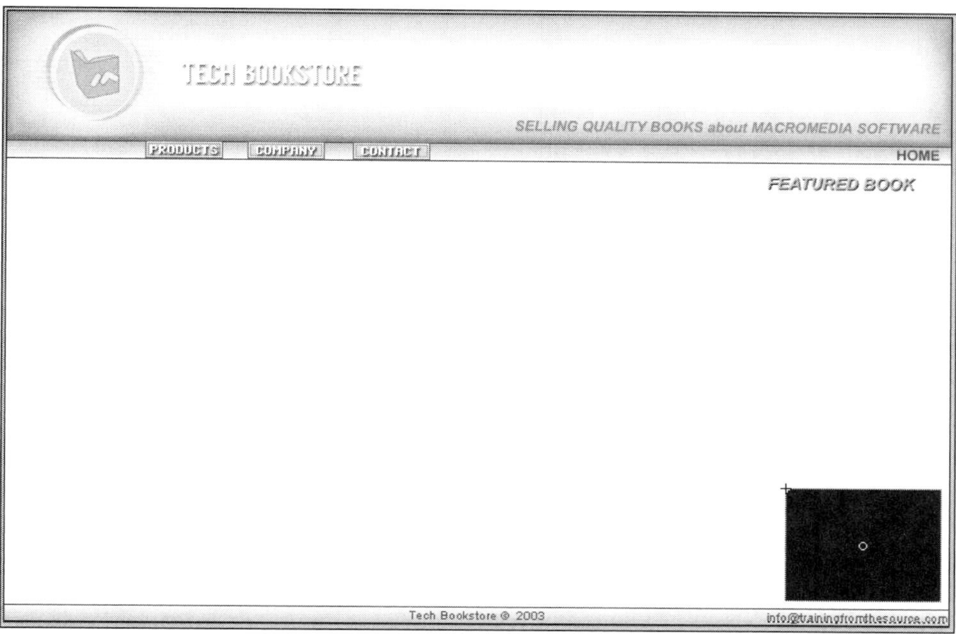

4) Add a new layer called `actions` to the Timeline and add keyframes for each page.
Select the `labels` layer and press the Insert New Layer button. Rename the new layer *actions*. It should be the top layer on the stack of layers in the Timeline.

When you finish creating and naming the layer, select the frame above each label and then press F6 to insert a new keyframe, as shown in the following figure. This is where your actions will eventually be placed for each page. For now, you are concerned only with the actions on the `home` page.

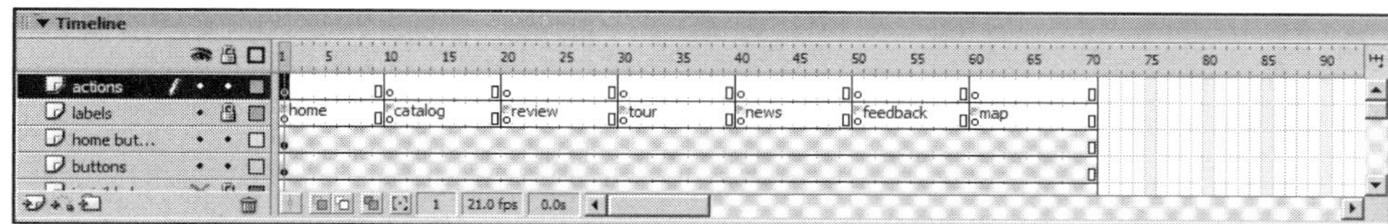

5) Add a behavior by using the Add (+) menu to load `mmpresslogo.jpg` into the SWF.

There are two different places where you can add a behavior: on a frame or on the instance itself. The Add Behavior (+) menu in the Behaviors panel changes depending on what the current selection is. If a frame is selected, you see one set of behaviors in the menu; if an instance is selected, you see a different set of behaviors in the Add menu.

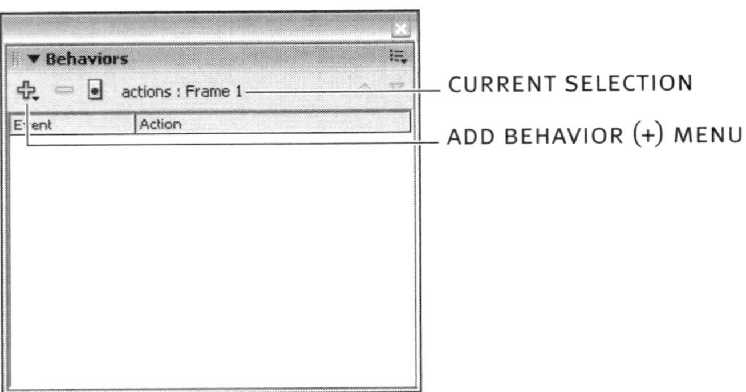

Select frame 1 of the `actions` layer and open the Behaviors panel. If it is not already open, choose Window > Development Panels > Behaviors. With Frame 1 selected, click the Add Behavior button in the Behaviors panel and select Movieclip > Load Graphic from the Add Behavior menu.

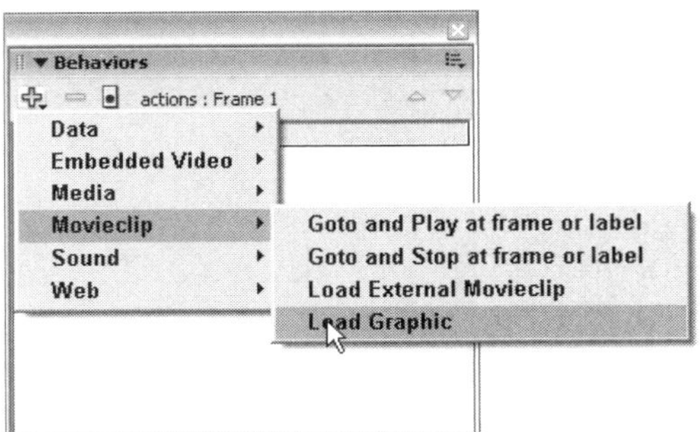

In the Load Graphic dialog box, type *mmpresslogo.jpg* into the upper text field, and select the `mmpresslogo_mc` movie clip from the tree below both text fields listing the instances available. Flash tells you that it requires an instance name to use this object as a target. Click the Rename button, enter an instance name of `mmpresslogo_mc`, and press OK to return to the Load Graphic dialog box. Click the Relative radio button, which refers to the kind of address used to target the image outside of the SWF. You will learn about absolute and relative addressing of instances in Lesson 11. Press OK again to return to the main Stage.

You probably notice that there is still a black square on the Stage instead of the JPEG image you just added the behavior for. Because the image will be loaded in dynamically at runtime, it is not visible on the Stage while you are working on the FLA file.

TIP *One of the restrictions on loading external JPEG images is that the JPEG does not load if it is saved as progressive. You have to make sure that the JPEG image is not exported as a progressive image out of an image editor such as Fireworks or Photoshop. For more information on saving images to dynamically import into a SWF, including descriptive graphics to illustrate the process, go to* `www.TrainingFromTheSource.com/bonus` *for a short tutorial.*

6) Save the changes you made to the document.

You will take a look at the ActionScript being used to do so later on in the lesson. You will also test the FLA file later on in the lesson as well, and you can see the image load into the SWF. Right now if you test the FLA it still runs through the entire Timeline because there is nothing stopping the playhead from zipping through each page. Click the close button to return to the authoring environment.

Choose File > Save to save your changes before moving on.

NOTE *There is more information on loading content into a movie clip at runtime using ActionScript in Lesson 12.*

USING BEHAVIORS TO OPEN A WEB PAGE

You saw how to use a behavior to load in an external JPEG image in the previous exercise. In this example, you will learn how to use one of the behaviors in Flash to open a Web page in a new browser window. In this example, you will be adding a behavior directly to the movie clip instance instead of to a frame in the Timeline. This is sometimes referred to as an *object action*.

You should still be using `bookstore10.fla` for this exercise.

1) Make sure that you are on the main Stage and then select frame 1 of the `home` **layer.**

Using the Selection tool, click the `mmpresslogo_mc` instance that you created in the previous exercise. There is an action in frame 1 of the `actions` layer that references this instance.

2) Add a behavior directly to the `mmpresslogo_mc` movie clip using the Behaviors panel.

With `mmpresslogo_mc` selected, click the Add Behavior button in the Behaviors panel and choose Web > Go to Web Page from the menu. The Go to URL dialog box appears and gives you the option to select a target: _self, _parent, _blank, or _top. Each of these options is the same as the HTML counterparts; change the value to _blank.

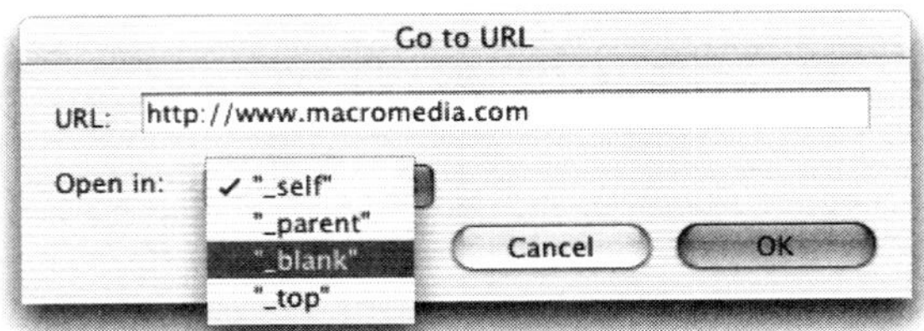

3) Set the target URL for the behavior in the Go to URL dialog box.

Setting the target URL to redirect to is as simple as replacing the default value in the URL text field with your desired target. For this exercise, set the target URL to: `http://www.peachpit.com`. After you type in the URL, press OK and return to the Stage.

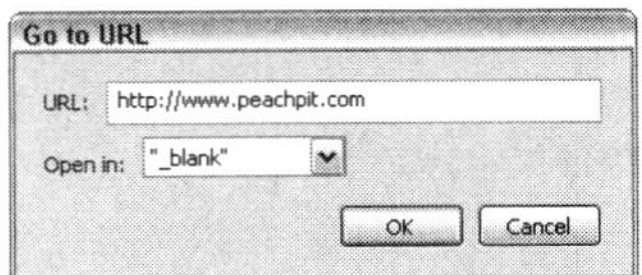

TIP *If you are trying to go to a Web page within a different domain, don't forget to prepend your URL in the Go to URL dialog box with* `http://`*.*

4) Change the behavior's behavior using the Behaviors panel.

Click the `mmpresslogo_mc` instance on the Stage. You can tweak the behavior by opening the Behaviors panel and changing some settings. Open the Behaviors panel and look at the Event and Action lists below the Add Behavior and Delete Behavior buttons.

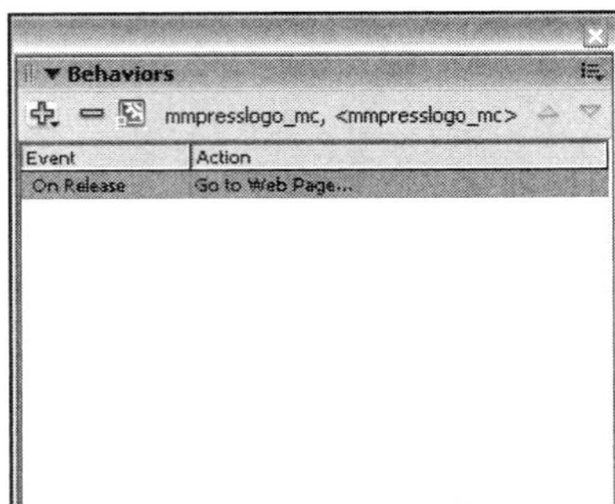

If you click the On Release text to the left of the Go to Web Page action you will see a drop-down list of events to trigger this behavior on. By default, the event is On Release, which means the user presses and releases the mouse button over the `mmpresslogo_mc` movie clip. You can choose a new value from the drop-down list and trigger when the user moves his or her mouse cursor over the instance, or when the mouse cursor moves off the instance entirely. You can also cause the event to trigger when a certain key is pressed.

5) Modify the behavior properties using the Behaviors panel or the Actions panel. Then click OK to apply the changes.

If you want to modify the behavior and redirect the user to a different URL, you can modify the ActionScript directly in the Actions panel. Or, you can double-click on the Action column for the desired behavior in the Behaviors panel, which opens the Go to URL dialog box again so you can make the changes.

Double-click the behavior's action in the Behaviors panel to open the Go to URL dialog box again. Modify the behavior, and click OK to apply the changes or choose Cancel. You return to the main Stage, and can now see the updated code if you look in the Actions panel.

6) Save the changes you made to the FLA.

VIEWING THE BEHAVIORS CODE

It is possible to view the ActionScript code that behaviors generate for you, which is as simple as tracking down where Flash placed the code and then opening up the Actions panel perhaps using the Script navigator (discussed later in this lesson). Ideally, you don't need to edit behaviors in Flash; however, sometimes it is unavoidable if you are trying to accomplish something specific. At times it is easier to write the code yourself instead of using a behavior and then modifying it.

One of the realities of object actions (meaning, placing code directly on a button or movie clip instance) is what's called the `on` event. The `on()` and `onClipEvent()` event handlers are used to attach ActionScript directly to buttons (`on`) and movie clips (`onClipEvent`). Movie clips can also use the `on()` event handler to receive button events, which you will do when you add code for the movie clip buttons you created. The event handlers execute the code you place in the handler when the event occurs. The event is placed in between the two brackets, and the code to execute is placed inside the two curly braces.

NOTE *Although this is an easy way to add ActionScript, please remember that it is not an elegant way to handle adding code to an FLA file. In Lesson 11, you will learn some better ways of adding ActionScript to an FLA file as you develop your skills in writing code.*

1) In `bookstore10.fla`**, select the** `mmpresslogo_mc` **on the main Stage and then open the Actions panel to view the code.**

With the `mmpresslogo_mc` instance selected on the Stage, expand the Actions panel or press F9 to open it. Inspect the code that the ActionScript behavior generated in the Script pane.

```
on (release) {
  //Goto Webpage Behavior
  getURL("http://www.peachpit.com", "_blank");
  //End Behavior
}
```

The previous code is some simple ActionScript that says: *when the user releases the mouse button over this instance, go to the specified URL in a new browser window*. The two lines starting with // are comments and are used only to document the code. Usually, comments are present to tell you what the code is doing, how it is used, how it can be edited, how to disable code, or note what needs to be fixed or added to that particular section of code. Anything placed inside a comment does not execute.

TIP *You might also see several lines of text commented out at once. The beginning of the comment has a /* and the end of the comment is completed with */. None of the lines between these are executed.*

The previous block of ActionScript works exactly the same way if the two comments are removed from the code. However, if you edit the code generated by a behavior, you might be unable to modify the behavior by still using the Behaviors panel.

2) Select frame 1 of the `actions` **layer and view the behavior code that was placed on the Timeline.**

With the Actions panel still open, click on frame 1 of the `actions` layer. You can now see the ActionScript in the Actions panel that was generated by adding the behavior:

```
//load Graphic Behavior
this.mmpresslogo_mc.loadMovie("mmpresslogo.jpg");
//End Behavior
```

Notice that the code is slightly different from the behavior code generated by the Go to Web Page behavior seen in the code in Step 1.

First, an `on (release)` action is not associated with this code. Because you put this code directly on a frame instead of an instance, the code triggers automatically every time the playhead reaches this frame (meaning, if the SWF file loops then the image loads into the SWF each time the playhead reaches frame 1). You can also see that two of the three generated lines of code are comments. The only important line of code in this snippet is

```
this.mmpresslogo_mc.loadMovie("mmpresslogo.jpg");
```

This ActionScript tells Flash to load the specified file (in this case, an image located in the same folder as the FLA file you are working on) into a movie clip with the instance name `mmpresslogo_mc`. You'll learn much more about using methods, and loading files, later on in Lessons 11 and 12. If the image were in a folder called `images`, the code would be this instead:

```
this.mmpresslogo_mc.loadMovie("images/mmpresslogo.jpg");
```

As covered earlier on, an instance is just a copy of a symbol in the Library that has been placed on the Stage. In this particular example, you named the symbol name and the instance name the same thing: `mmpresslogo_mc`. We did this so it was very easy to remember and associate the instances because they're each only used once. You might not want to name your instances the same as the symbol name on your professional Web sites, particularly if you have several instances of the same symbol on the Stage and start to use a lot of ActionScript.

Naming an instance allows you target specific objects in the FLA using code, as you just did in this example.

IMPLEMENTING BASIC SERVER INTERACTION USING A COMPONENT

The previous example demonstrated that Flash MX has the capability to load other SWF files into a SWF on-the-fly (or *dynamically*) at runtime. This kind of interaction involves the user selecting a page to view and then an image is loaded from the server into a component called the *Loader* component.

The Loader component allows you to easily embed SWF files or JPEG images into a SWF file without having to write any code. All you have to do is drag an instance of the Loader component onto the Stage and fill in the `contentPath` parameter with the URL to your SWF file or JPEG image. You can easily scale the content to fit the size of the component or resize the component to fit the content that you are loading.

In this exercise, you will learn how to load a SWF file you created in Lesson 2 into the Loader component. You will be using the Loader component to load `map.swf`, which was initially created in Lesson 2, into the SWF.

1) Select frame 60 of the `map` layer and add a Loader component to the Stage.
On the main Timeline, select frame 60 on the `map` layer which is labeled `map`. The frame is already a keyframe and has a couple of text fields for the address and map title already positioned on the Stage that you created in earlier exercises.

Open the Components panel, and find the Loader component. Drag an instance of the component onto the Stage.

2) Select the Loader component and then look at the component parameters found in the Property inspector.

Select the instance of the Loader component on the Stage and open the Property inspector. Notice that there are now two tabs in the inspector, and both of these tabs contain different content controlling the component you currently have selected.

TIP *You can also control and modify components in additional ways that are not available in the Property inspector by using the Component Inspector panel. Open the Component Inspector panel by choosing Window > Development Panels > Component Inspector panel. You will learn more about using the Parameters, Bindings and Schema tabs in the Component Inspector panel in Lessons 9 and 10.*

For now, you need to be concerned only with the following parameters in the Parameters tab of the Property inspector:

- **autoLoad:** This parameter controls whether the content should load automatically or whether you have to explicitly trigger the content for it to load (using ActionScript). A value of `true` means the content automatically loads; `false` means you need to trigger it before it loads.
- **contentPath:** The text entered into this text field sets the path to the SWF or JPEG that you want to load into the component.
- **scaleContent:** This parameter controls whether the content is scaled to match the size of the component (`true`) or if the component is scaled to match the size of the content (`false`).

3) Set the parameters in the Property inspector for the Loader component instance.

Because you'll just be loading `map.swf` into this component right away, set autoLoad to `true` and then type *map.swf* into the contentPath text field.

NOTE *If you saved `map.swf` into a different folder than `bookstore10.fla`, you have to modify the path. You need to use a relative URL such as `lesson2/map.swf`. This means that you can store certain files in other files in the directory for better organization.*

Set the scaleContent parameter to `false` to make the component resize on the Stage to match the size of the external SWF.

4) Resize the component so it is the same size as `map.fla` and position it on the Stage.

With the component selected, open the Property inspector. Change the width to *500* and the height to *355*.

The map should be aligned to the bottom of the *How to find us* text field and aligned to the right edge of the bookstore's slogan and the page title, similar to the layout in the following figure.

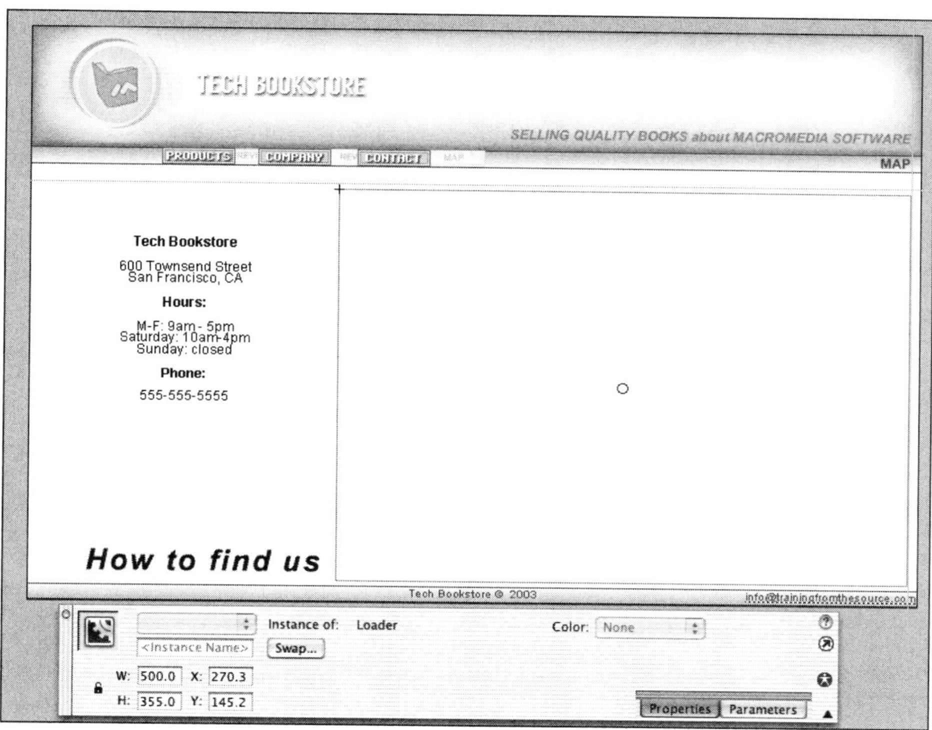

You probably still have guides visible that will help you align the component on the Stage. Just remember to allow enough empty space below the drop-down menus so they do not overlap the map. Make sure that the map either aligns or is (preferably) below the horizontal guide located at 140 on the vertical ruler.

NOTE *Depending on your own layout, you might need to move the "How to find us" text field.*

5) Save the changes you made to the file.

In the next section, you will begin to add more ActionScript to the FLA file. In the following lessons, you will create content to load into other Loader components. When you begin to add actions to navigate through the pages in Lesson 11, so then you can test how each page appears after they are loaded in.

INTRODUCING ACTIONSCRIPT

One of the features making Flash so powerful is its scripting language, ActionScript, which you've already heard so much about. ActionScript allows you to programmatically control the SWF file, position elements on the Stage, manually parse an XML document, change an instance's alpha level, and so on. By learning some basic ActionScript, you can customize the SWF files you create by a large degree, and build increasingly robust applications. You can also create your own custom behaviors, which can then be distributed throughout the large community of Flash users.

The Tech Bookstore uses ActionScript to control the menu system that is used to tell Flash which menus to show and hide when the mouse moves around the Stage. When you use Flash's behaviors, it places ActionScript within the FLA file for you. Although behaviors are fine in many circumstances, there are times when the behavior's code does not fit your specific needs and has to be modified. With a bit of knowledge about ActionScript, you can modify the generated code to work with your specific application.

After you learn some ActionScript, you can take advantage of some of the lesser-known features of components. For example, using ActionScript you can alternate the background colors of the List component, add icons to the List component, or stop the playback of the SWF file using a Button component.

You already used some ActionScript in Lesson 5. You added the `stop` action to a movie clip, which caused the playhead to stop so the movie clip didn't loop. You also went through other basic actions in the behaviors you used in the previous exercise in this lesson. In the following exercises, you will take things a bit further by adding several actions together to control the Tech Bookstore and make something happen in the FLA.

NOTE *Advanced ActionScript is beyond the scope of the book, but learning ActionScript is very useful when developing Flash. We recommend picking up a copy of* Macromedia Flash MX 2004 ActionScript: Training from the Source, *which is a great book for learning more about the ActionScript language.*

You have used behaviors to add ActionScript to parts of the bookstore application. In the following few sections, you cover some of the main concepts that make up the foundation of ActionScript. You are introduced to the parts of the language that make up each line of code, and what they do to help make things work. In Lesson 11, you will continue to learn more about how scripts are put together and construct some of the main sections of the Tech Bookstore. For now, we'll keep things simple and as painless as possible.

Examining What Makes Up ActionScript

There are many things that make up ActionScript, and learning more about some of the terminology making up the language is a great place to start before learning how to put together many lines of code for the FLA file. The terminology found in this section is some of the most common stuff you will encounter.

A *variable* is a container that holds a particular value of any *data type*. A data type is the kind of information that a variable can hold, such as a String (`"cheesy"` is a string data type) or a Number (`15` is a number data type). The variable has a name, such as `myNumber`, and when you create a new variable you are said to be *declaring* it. You want to use a variable when you have a given value in your code that you need to use repeatedly. You *assign* a particular value to a variable so you can use that value over and over during the course of your ActionScript. That value can change during the course of your code, as well. You might have a variable named `myScore` that holds the number value for a team's score in your SWF file. At the beginning of the SWF, the score might be 0, but that value might change to *2* later on if the team scores a couple of points.

The data that a variable contains might be the result of a long or complicated equation that you need to reuse in your code. Instead of typing the equation over and over you can assign it to a variable and just use that short name instead. This saves a lot of typing, and can add up to saving file size by removing a lot of characters of code that can bulk up the SWF file size.

So let's actually take a look at some variables. A variable can have a value assigned to it. For example, you might have a `myScore` variable containing some sort of information, perhaps a score.

```
var myScore = 15;
```

You are assigning a value of `15` to the `myScore` variable (using the *assignment operator*, which is just an equals sign). You have set `myScore` to a certain number, and you can use that same number later on. `var` is a keyword and is used here to declare the variable. You will learn more about both keywords and strict typing variables in Lesson 11. The useful thing you can later do in your code would be to assign the variable to something else.

```
var totalScore = myScore;
```

This code means the `totalScore` is now set to equal the current value of `myScore`. If you change the value of `15`, then `totalScore` uses the new, revised current value of the variable whenever `totalScore` appears in your ActionScript. If you had a different variable set somewhere in your FLA (perhaps `yourScore`), then you could swap `myScore` to `yourScore` to change the value of `totalScore`.

Using variables in your scripts can also be very useful if you are reusing a value frequently throughout the code, and you might end up needing to change it. If the value 15 does change (maybe you need the initial score to be `20` instead), all you have to do is change it in that one line (`var myScore = 15` changes to`var myScore = 20`). Then if you have `myScore` anywhere else in your ActionScript, the value of that variable automatically updates everywhere you use it.

TIP *This can be useful if you are animating or designing a page where you are setting, for example, the alpha value of movie clips throughout your code. You might change your design and then need the alpha value to be increased. To go and find every place in your code where you set the alpha would be a pain. However, if you declared a variable, all you have to do is update that one initial variable.*

There are a few basic ActionScript rules you must follow when you create variables. First and foremost, two variables cannot have the same name. Secondly, variables are *case-sensitive* when you are using ActionScript 2.0, meaning that the variable `Cat` is not the same as the variable `cat`. This is not true if you are using ActionScript 1.0 because there is no case-sensitivity in the language.

But that's not all. The variable's name can contain only letters, numbers, and underscores (_), and must not *begin* with a number or underscore. Variables must not be any word that you find in ActionScript, such as keywords, names of objects, methods, or properties (these terms are all defined shortly.) If you use one of these words, your code just does not work at all because Flash treats the variable like the keyword or action instead, and that breaks your code. These words are known as *reserved words*.

Keywords are words in ActionScript that do one specific thing in particular. A keyword has a specified meaning; for example, the `delete` keyword is used to eliminate variables or objects in your SWF file. Keywords cannot be used as variable names, and you should not use them elsewhere in your FLA files (such as instance names, or the name of a screen). You have already seen the `var` keyword, which is used to declare certain variables. You can look up a list of keywords in ActionScript by using the Help panel and searching the term *keywords*.

A *Boolean* is a `true` or a `false` value. For example, a Boolean can be used to turn something on or off in your SWF. You might have a component on the Stage that you want to be visible only at certain times. So, you would set the visibility of that component instance to `false` and then set it to `true` when you want it to be visible again.

As you found out earlier, a *data type* is the kind of information that a variable can hold. For example, a *String* is one data type, and a *Number* is another data type. The other data types that Flash understands are the following: *Boolean*, *Function*, *MovieClip*, *Object*, *null*, and *undefined*. In the earlier `myScore` example, you saw a variable hold a Number value. A String data type is typically denoted by quotation marks around it. For example, the following `myText` variable holds a String data type.

```
var myText = "My cat eats chicken."
```

Using the Actions Panel

Now that you know a little bit more about what makes up ActionScript, you should find out about the tools you use to add ActionScript to your FLA files. The Actions panel is where you enter all of the code for the Tech Bookstore. Although Flash MX Professional includes a separate interface to write ActionScript called the *Script window*, it is meant for external code files (such as `.AS`, or *ActionScript*, files). Because you won't be using any external files in the Tech Bookstore, the Actions panel is the best place to add your code.

The Actions panel has several excellent features that are available to help you code quickly and efficiently. It also offers you tools to help check your syntax, format your scripts and find help. The Actions panel contains a few main sections: the Actions toolbox, Script navigator, Script pane and a toolbar containing several buttons.

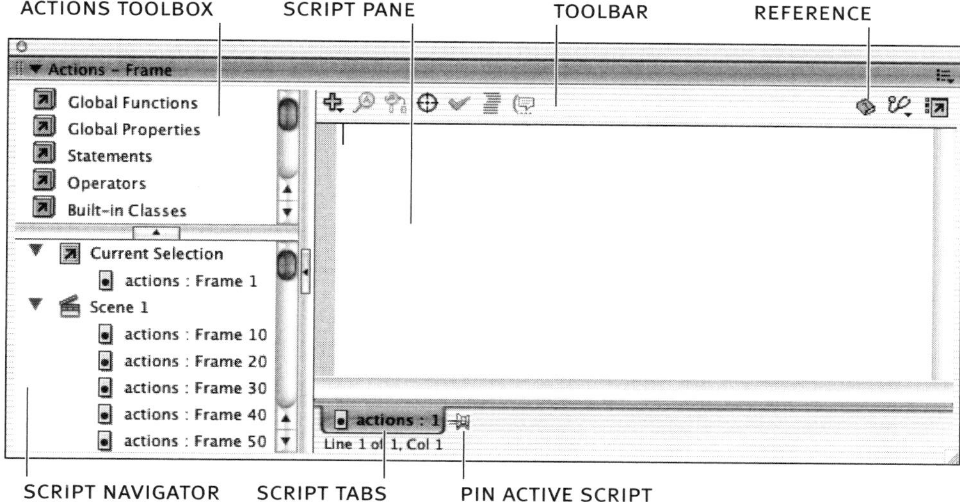

The Script navigator, which is found in the Actions panel, is used to navigate through the pieces of code you have throughout the FLA file. If you have code placed on buttons or a movie clip, the Script navigator helps you locate all that code and modify it if necessary. You will discover more about how to use the Script navigator later on in this lesson.

The Actions toolbox contains all the actions you can use that are built into Flash. The toolbox contains many "books" that you can click and move throughout to find actions, methods and properties. When you double-click a method in the Actions toolbox, for example, it is added to the Script pane wherever the cursor is located.

You can also use the Add (+) button to add new scripts to your code. This useful feature allows you to add pieces of code to the Script pane by selecting an action from the menus. In some cases, after you add the action, the cursor in the Actions panel will be creatively placed so a tooltip appears and provides a guide on how you should go about finishing off the script.

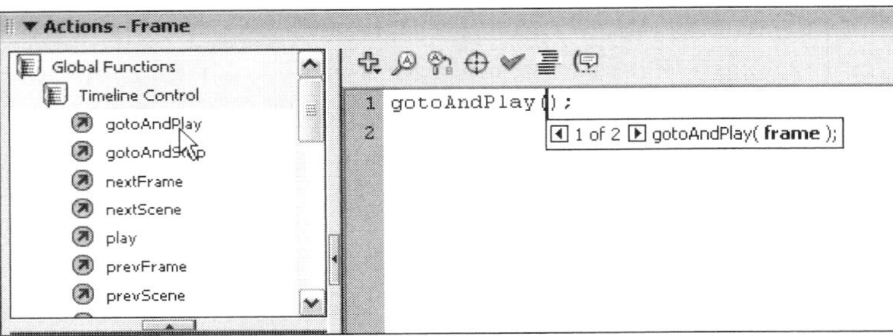

If you highlight a piece of your code that is part of the ActionScript language, such as `gotoAndPlay`, you can click the Reference button in the upper-right corner of the Actions panel. This opens the Help panel and displays the ActionScript Reference entry for that particular action. If something is not working correctly, or you see errors when you publish the SWF file, the Reference is a very useful tool for figuring out what is going wrong. Before you lose all your hair, try clicking this button. You can see where it is if you refer to the previous Actions panel graphic with callouts.

When you publish an FLA file, sometimes the Output panel opens and displays a message about the ActionScript you have written or how the SWF file is working. The Output panel has two main purposes: to alert you to any problems with your ActionScript, and to return values or display information. Sometimes this information is the result of actions in your code that you specifically put there so information would be displayed in this panel. For example, sometimes you will use a `trace` statement in a part of your code. The `trace` statement is used to send things such as values and results to the Output panel that can be used to troubleshoot the SWF file. For example, you might trace the `myScore` variable:

```
trace (myScore);
```

And if the value is `15` for that variable, the Output panel just shows `15`. You might want to check whether a function is working when you click a button. So your button function, placed on a frame in the main Timeline, would look like this:

```
myButton.onRelease = function(){
  trace("I've been clicked!");
}
```

If you click the `myButton` instance, the Output panel displays the text `I've been clicked!` You might be using the `trace` statement to check whether something is working, or what values are being returned from code in the SWF file or information from a server. Therefore, the Output panel is extremely useful in your workflow.

Using Dot Notation to Target Instances

Dot notation (or *dot syntax*) is what ActionScript uses to address certain objects in your SWF file (such as movie clips and buttons) or objects in ActionScript. *Syntax* forms the rules and guidelines for a particular way of writing your code. Dot notation can help create a path to something that you are targeting in your FLA file. Sometimes this is called a *target path*. You need to target things within the FLA file to make them work. In very simple terms, you set a path to target an object, write the name of that object, and then give it a particular action or value to control. Then you can tell the object what you want it to do or give it a particular value. This is exactly what the behavior that loaded content into a movie clip did earlier in this lesson. You will learn a lot more about methods and properties in a later section.

It is most important to remember that you target instances using an *instance name*. As you have learned earlier on, instance names name each individual copy of a symbol or object. When you create a new symbol, you give it a name in the Library but this name doesn't mean you can modify the symbol or instance. When you drag it onto the Stage, you give the instance a name in the Property inspector. The name you enter into the Property inspector is its instance name, which has to be unique from all other instance names in the FLA file.

Let's look at an example of how you might target something. You could have a movie clip that is inside another movie clip on the Stage.

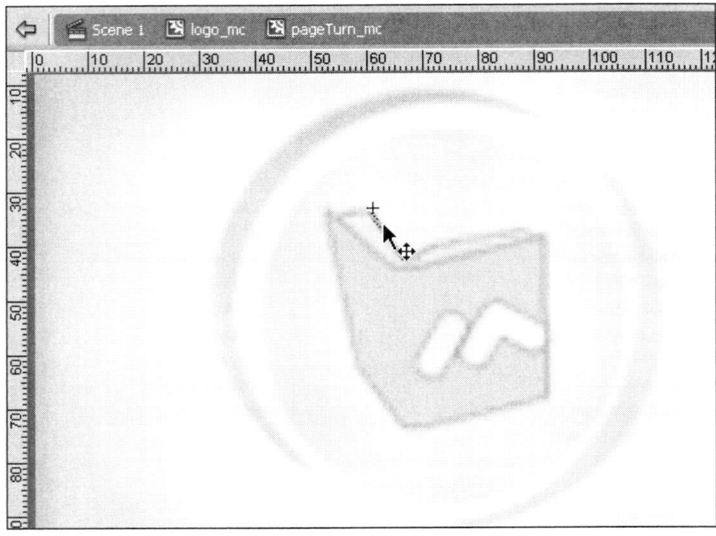

You want to put as much code as possible on the main Timeline (which is actually a movie clip itself) instead of putting it right on a movie clip or button, which would be messy if all of your separate elements had code on them! Therefore, you need to target that movie clip that's nested inside of a movie clip. Without writing any ActionScript yet, the situation you want to occur looks like the following: Main Stage > Movie Clip > Another Movie Clip > (something happens).

So you might want to go to the second frame of the nested movie clip when something happens. But if this is coming from the main Stage's Timeline, you need to target the movie clip from the Stage. Each of the elements (except for the Stage) needs to have an instance name in order to target it. Then you target it in a series of instance names separated by dots, such as the following:

```
myMovieClip_mc.mySecondMovieClip_mc.gotoAndPlay(2);
```

Each movie clip is a special object with a Timeline. You will learn a lot more about classes and objects and what they can do in Lesson 11, but for now you can think of an object as a container that holds data and information. An object can be manipulated if you tell it to do something. For example, you might tell it to be invisible or move to a new location. You do so using *dot notation*. You use a dot (`.`) to follow each object, the objects being the movie clips like you saw previously. If a particular action (really called a method or property, which you'll learn about later) follows that dot, the object directly before that dot is the one that is manipulated. Therefore, in the earlier example, `mySecondMovieClip` is being targeted with the `gotoAndPlay` action, so the nested clip "goes to and plays" frame two.

You target a certain instance, such as a movie clip, and you can make it do something like go to a particular frame using an action or method. You can also assign it a particular value for one of its properties. One of the properties of a movie clip is visibility, which you can set to a value of either `true` or `false` (a *Boolean*).

```
myMovieClip_mc._visible = true;
```

You are using an operator here (the equals sign) to assign the value of `true` or `false` to the `_visible` property of the movie clip.

TIP *You might have noticed by now that many lines are completed using a semi-colon, which is used in Flash to end a statement of some sort. It's a little bit like the end of a sentence being finished using a period. Not all lines in Flash are ended using a semi-colon. If in doubt, use the Auto Format button in the Actions panel toolbar. This adds missing semi-colons to your ActionScript and properly indents your code as well. It's a very valuable tool that you get very used to having available to you at all times when typing in ActionScript.*

You have covered quite a bit so far in ActionScript, just in this short section. In Lesson 11, you will learn a lot more about how to start writing ActionScript so it forms working code that will make the Tech Bookstore work by moving menus and loading in new content.

USING ACTIONS TO CONTROL THE TIMELINE

ActionScript can be used to control instances of symbols, sounds, video, the SWF itself, the timeline, and many other aspects of a Flash document while it is running in the Flash player. In this short and easy example, you will add `stop` actions to the Timeline to stop the playhead at each page in the Tech Bookstore.

You should still be working with `bookstore10.fla` in this example.

1) Select the `actions` layer and then open the Actions panel.

If the Actions panel is not open in the layout, open it using Window > Development Panels > Actions panel or press F9. Expand the Actions panel. In the first exercise in this lesson, you created keyframes for each page of the Tech Bookstore. In this step, you will add a `stop` action on each page.

2) Select each keyframe on the `actions` layer and add the stop action to each keyframe using the Actions panel.

Select frame 1 on the `actions` layer you created earlier in the lesson and type *stop();* into the Script pane. Select the next keyframe on the `actions` layer and enter the same code. The `stop` action causes the playhead to stop once it reaches each of these frames when users navigate through the pages of the Tech Bookstore.

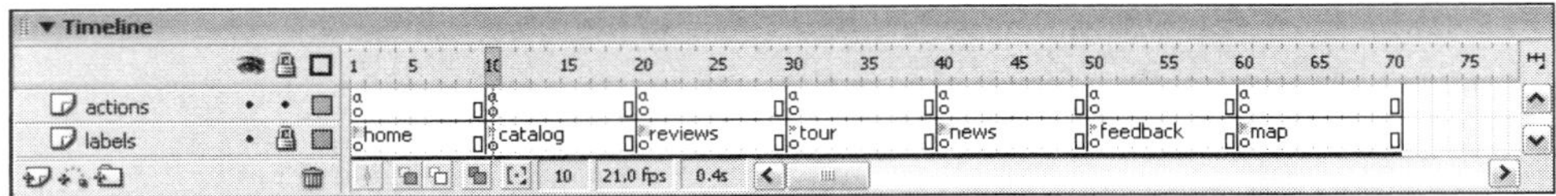

3) Test the FLA and then save the changes you made to the file.

Press Ctrl+Enter (or Command+Enter on the Mac) to test the document in the testing environment. If you tested the bookstore before now, the SWF played through each page. Now, the document stops on frame 1 (the `home` page). Each new page that you navigate to will stop when the playhead arrives at the frame, which will happen when you get the menu buttons working and you can navigate the site's pages. Also notice the JPEG image being loaded into the SWF while in the testing environment. The JPEG is now dynamically loaded into the movie clip holder you created for it in the earlier exercise.

NOTE *You won't be able to navigate through each page yet. You will be able to do so after you add the ActionScript that makes the buttons and menu system work in Lesson 11.*

Select File > Save to save the modifications you made to the FLA.

CREATING A HOME BUTTON

In this exercise, you will create a button to cause the SWF to return to the `home` frame of the Tech Bookstore. You will use an invisible button to be placed over the large logo.

1) Insert a new layer and then create a new invisible button on the new `home button` layer.

Select the `buttons` layer and insert a new layer called `home button` above it. You reason that you need a separate layer for this new button is so you can lock and hide it while not hiding the other buttons on the `buttons` layer.

You will create a rectangular area for the new invisible button. Select the Rectangle tool from the Tools panel, set the stroke color to No Color, and select any color for the fill color. Draw a rectangle that completely covers the `logo_mc` movie clip and the Tech Bookstore text in `title.png` in the upper-left corner and the Tech Bookstore label to the right of the logo.

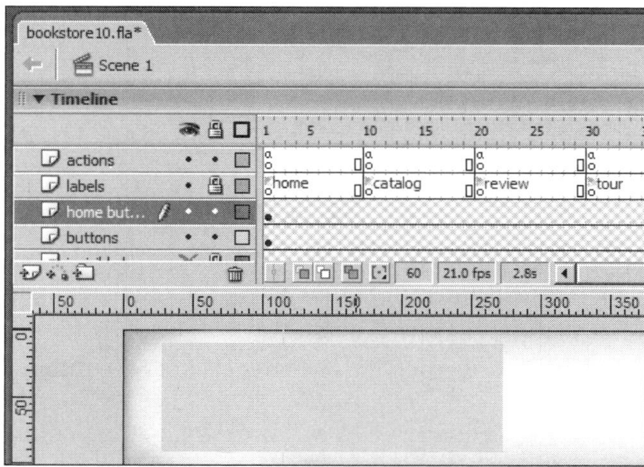

Double-click the mouse within the rectangle to select the shape and press F8 to convert the shape into a symbol. In the Convert to Symbol dialog box, name the symbol *home_btn* and select the Button radio button. Click OK to close the dialog box and return to the Stage.

2) Define the hit area for the `home_btn` button.

Double-click the button on the Stage to open the instance in symbol-editing mode. Drag the keyframe from the Up state over to the Hit state, similar to the way you created the invisible button in Lesson 4. You're interested only in the hit area; the button itself is invisible, so the logo shows through from the layers below. Click `Scene 1` in the edit bar to return to the main Stage.

3) Assign an instance name to the button.

With the Selection tool highlighted in the Tools panel, click the invisible button you just created and expand the Property inspector, in which you can enter an instance name into a text input field where it says `<Instance Name>`.

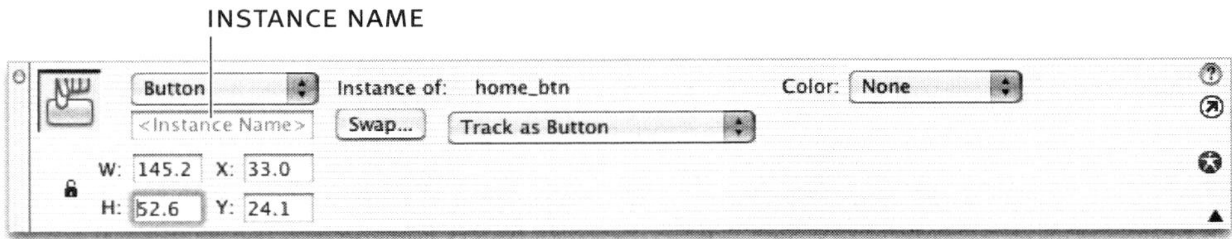

Click your mouse in the `<Instance Name>` text field and type *home_btn*. Now you can use ActionScript to reference that particular instance of the button on the Stage and execute code used to manipulate the SWF in a particular way when the button is clicked (also known as an *event*). In this case, when the button is clicked, you return to the Home page of the bookstore.

4) Write ActionScript that will run each time `home_btn` is clicked.

The ActionScript for the button is fairly simple and requires only three lines of code. The ActionScript you need to use is as follows:

```
this.home_btn.onRelease = function() {
  gotoAndStop("home");
}
```

Select frame 1 on the `actions` layer and enter the code into the Script pane in the Actions panel. This code is placed after the `stop` action that is already on that frame.

The first line of the previous code says: *when the user clicks and releases the mouse button over the* `home_btn` *instance, execute the following function.* The function, which is defined immediately after `onRelease`, is referred to as an *anonymous function*. It is given this particular name because the function doesn't have a name like other functions in Flash do. You will learn how these functions work in Lesson 11. The `gotoAndStop` method is used to send the playhead to a particular frame, and stop at whatever is placed within the brackets. You could either place a number in between the brackets instead, which means the playhead goes to the given frame number on the given Timeline. Or you could place a frame label within quotation marks and the playhead moves to that frame label on the given Timeline.

TIP *You will want to use frame labels instead of frame numbers whenever possible. When your FLA files get larger and more complicated, it is much harder to remember what content was on which frame number. Also, if you ever move content, you would have to change your ActionScript instead of just moving the frame label to a new location. Using frame labels allows you to simplify and give frames a logical name rather than just a number.*

So the question now is how you define that *given Timeline*. It might seem as though this ActionScript references the button itself, sending the playhead to some `home` frame inside the button (which we obviously don't have). That's not the case then - so what is happening here? Whenever you write a function like this for a button, it actually references the Timeline that the button is placed on. Because this `home_btn` is sitting on the main Timeline, that is what the `gotoAndStop` is referencing.

You will learn more about something called *scope* in Lesson 11, which is used to help with referencing and targeting Timelines, instances, and content that you load and so forth. For now you just need to remember that whatever is inside the function is applied to the Timeline the button is sitting on, and not the button instance itself.

NOTE *Just to keep things nice and confusing, ActionScript and movie clips are entirely different. If you were to write some ActionScript for the movie clip, then you'd reference the Timeline inside the clip instead! However, if you were creating a* movie clip button, *then it would behave in the same way described for the button in the previous explanations.*

5) Lock and hide the `home button` layer and clean up the Library.

Lock and hide the `home button` layer by pressing the eye icon and lock icon beside the name of the layer in the Timeline, which prevents you from accidentally adding any instances or moving the invisible button. It also means you can hide the teal blue appearance of the invisible button while you are working on the Tech Bookstore.

It is a good practice to keep the Library clean as you work. Drag the `home_btn` symbol in the Library into the `buttons` folder, move the `mmpresslogo_mc` symbol into the `movie clips` folder, and move the Loader component into the `components` folder.

6) Save the changes you made to the FLA.

As usual, save your changes using File > Save before moving on to the next exercise.

REMOVING THE HAND CURSOR

When you mouse over a button in a SWF, the hand cursor appears. This is typically what you want to have happen because it indicates what part of the SWF is interactive and clickable. However, when you have invisible buttons, usually you don't want the button to have a hand cursor because it really ruins the whole "invisible" thing you have going. In this exercise, you will remove the hand cursor from the invisible button for the button surrounding the menus so users can't tell that it is there. You should still be using `bookstore10.fla` for this exercise.

1) Test the FLA to see how the hand cursor looks.

Press Ctrl+Enter (or Command+Enter on the Mac) to test the FLA file. When you mouse over the upper area of the site, a hand cursor appears. This cursor can be rather distracting and means that the button isn't really invisible at all for visitors to the Web site.

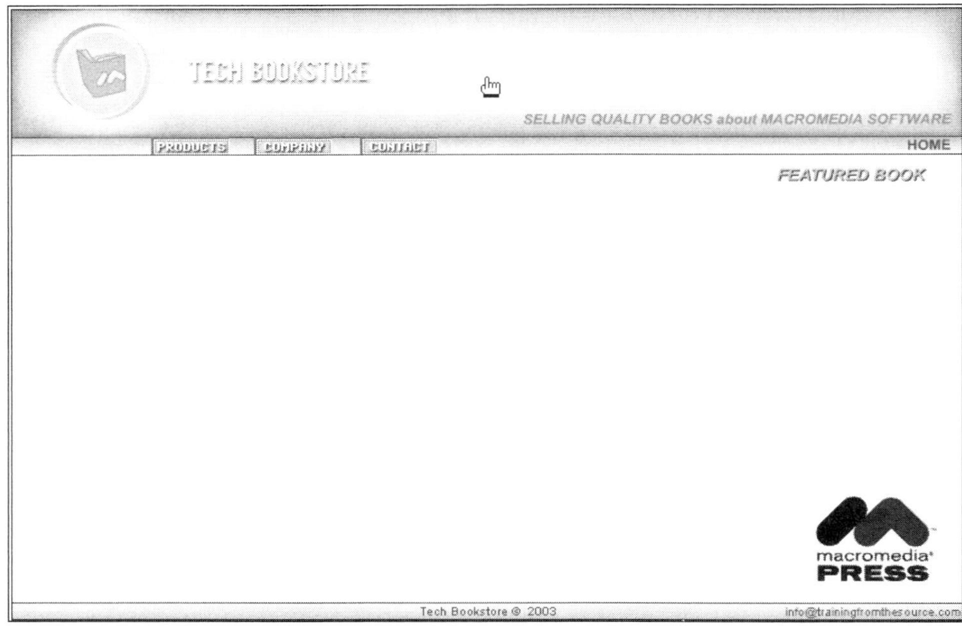

Because this button should not be known to the visitor at all, you need to change the button so the hand cursor does not appear when the visitor's mouse hovers over the area.

2) Add a line of ActionScript to the Actions panel that causes the cursor not to change into a hand cursor when over the invisible `home_btn` instance.

Make sure that frame 1 of the `actions` layer is selected, *not* the `inv_btn` instance. This means you will be applying the code added to the Actions panel to the Timeline instead of the `inv_btn` instance. If you locked and hid the `home button` layer in the previous step, you can't select the instance anyway, which prevents such accidents.

Expand the Actions panel (F9) and enter the following code into the Script pane:

```
inv_btn.useHandCursor = false;
```

This single line of code means that that the `inv_btn` instance does not use a hand cursor when the mouse hovers over the button. The cursor remains as an arrow cursor instead, so the button is truly invisible when a visitor uses the site.

3) Select the `inv_btn` symbol instance. Give the invisible button an instance name.

Select the invisible button surrounding the menus. Open the Property inspector and enter `inv_btn` as an instance name into the `<Instance Name>` field.

4) Test the FLA.

Press `Ctrl+Enter` (or `Command+Enter` on the Mac) to test the FLA. Mouse over the Stage where the invisible button is located and notice that your cursor no longer changes to a hand because of the ActionScript you added in the previous step.

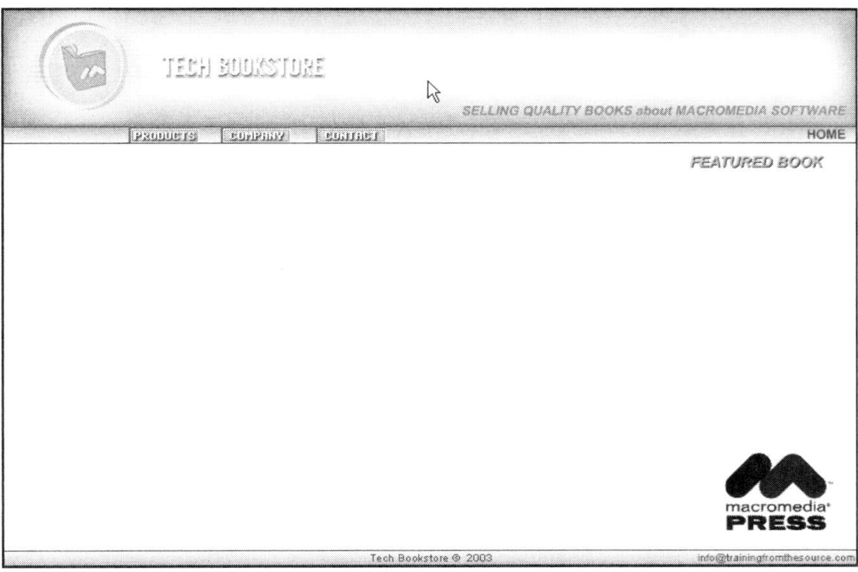

5) Save the changes you have made to the file before moving on to the next exercise.

MAKING THE MOVIE CLIP BUTTON WORK

The movie clip button was built and then animated in the previous couple of lessons. You were even introduced to `stop` actions while building `map.fla`, so the animation did not continuously loop. In this exercise you will complete the movie clip buttons by adding some simple actions that make it animate properly when you click on the buttons themselves. You are still using `bookstore10.fla` for this example.

1) Open the Library and find the movie clip buttons. Double-click the `sample chapter` **button so you can edit the movie clip.**

The buttons you created say *sample chapter* and *table of contents* on the front of the buttons, and you will be able to find them in the Library. Double-click the sample chapter button in the Library so it opens in symbol-editing mode and then refamiliarize yourself with how you structured the button earlier.

2) Select frame 1 in the `actions` **layer and add a** `stop` **action. Continue by adding the** `stop` **actions on frames 14 and 25.**

Select frame 1 and then maximize or open the Actions panel (F9). Type *`stop();`* into the Script pane. Select frame 14 on the Timeline, press F6 to insert a keyframe, and then type *`stop();`* into the Script pane.

Press F6 on frame 25 to insert a new keyframe on the `actions` layer and then type *`stop();`* into the Script pane.

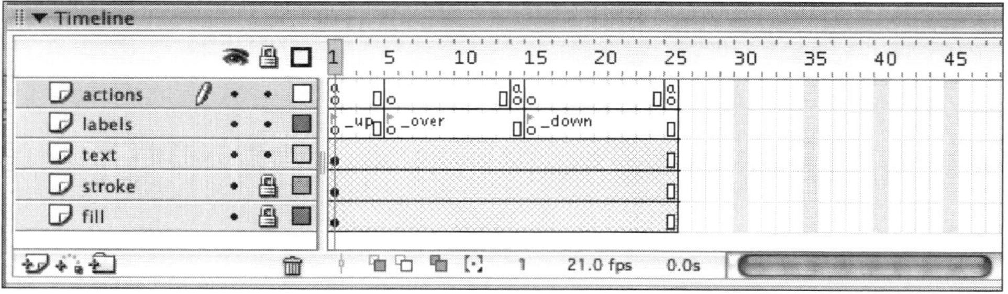

3) Type in *play();* for the `_over` **state on the** `actions` **layer.**

Enter new keyframes on the `actions` layer above the `_over` and `_down` states. Select the keyframe for `_over` and type *`play();`* into the Action panel's Script pane. This action tells the playhead to continue on and play the next frame(s).

The reason you need to add `play();` on the `_over` frame is because Flash is programmed to stop on each frame label when you create a movie clip button. If you allowed Flash to just stop, then the brightness tween animation would not play as a result. Therefore, you need to tell Flash to play the animation instead, which is why you add the `play` action on the frame.

4) Move the playhead to the `_down` **frame and add the** `play` **action on the** `actions` **layer.**

When the user clicks the button, you want another brightness tween to occur. Therefore, you need another `play` action so the button does not stop at this frame label.

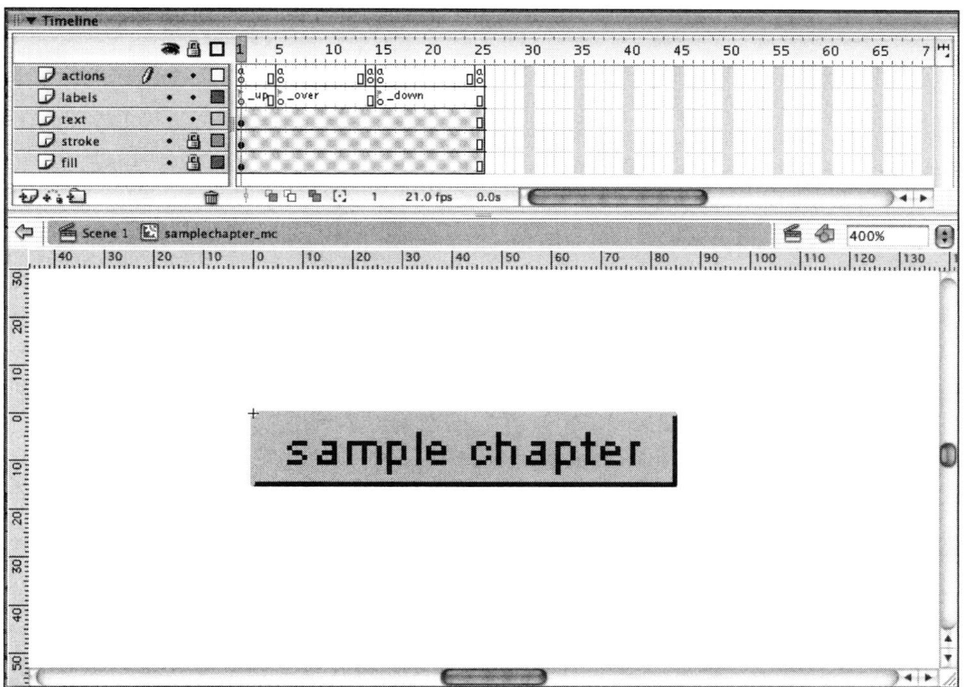

Just to keep you on your toes, there are actually a few different ways you can make the button work. You can select the `_down` keyframe and type in another *`play();`* action into the Script pane, just like you did in Step 3. Or, you can enter either of the following instead:

```
gotoAndPlay.nextFrame();
```

or

```
gotoAndPlay(16);
```

`gotoAndPlay.nextFrame()` tells the playhead to go to and play the following frame on the Timeline, just as it says in the code! `gotoAndPlay(16)` is almost the same as the previous piece of code, except you are instructing the playhead to go and start playing on a designated frame number. You probably wouldn't want to add `gotoAndPlay(16)` because if you change the exact frames your animations or labels are on, you have to go back and change your code as well.

It might be obvious that `play()` is probably the best choice because it is the shortest, simplest, and quickest to add. Therefore, add a blank keyframe on frame 15 of the actions player by selecting it and pressing F6. Open the Actions panel and type *play();* into the Script pane.

5) Return to the main Stage by pressing `Scene 1` on the edit bar. Repeat Steps 1 through 4 for the `toc_mc` button.

Repeat the exact same steps from Steps 1 through 4 for the other movie clip button. When you are finished, return to the main Stage again using the edit bar.

6) Save the changes you made to the FLA file as a new file: `bookstore10_complete.fla`.

After you are at the main Stage, choose File > Save to save the changes to your file, and then choose File > Save As and enter `bookstore10_complete.fla` as the name of the file. Make sure that you save the file in the `TechBookstore` folder. In Lesson 11 you will learn more button events that will be triggered when users roll the cursor on and off of the button.

USING THE SCRIPT NAVIGATOR AND PINS

Now that you added ActionScript in several different places in your FLA file, you should try using the Script navigator to find scripts that you have added to the document. Unfortunately you can't keep your ActionScript all in one place when you're using behaviors, so it is a good idea to familiarize yourself with these tools to help you find where scripts are placed when you need them in your FLA file. The Script navigator can be used to navigate through the scripts you have in a document. It contains a tree where you can navigate through all the different pieces of code in your FLA file. Frame and object actions are all represented in the navigator as part of the tree structure it uses to organize the code in.

You can also *pin* scripts in the Actions panel. If you select a piece of code in the Script navigator, you can either click a pin button to pin the script or double-click the code in the Script navigator. This means the code remains "open" in the Actions panel, like an open document with its own tab.

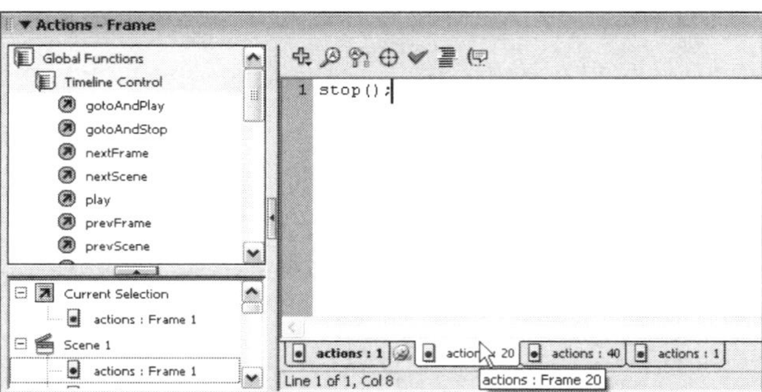

Then all you have to do is click the tab to access the piece of code for editing in the Actions panel. Script pins make it easy to navigate through and edit each piece of code by clicking on different tabs right below the Script pane. You'll find out how to use script pinning in the following exercise.

1) Using `bookstore10_complete.fla` **or** `bookstore10.fla`**, expand or open the Actions panel by pressing F9.**

The Actions panel opens with the Actions toolbox and Script navigator on the left, and the Script pane to the right. A bar separates the two areas, and it can be resized as necessary.

2) Move the bar between the Script pane and the Script navigator to resize each section of the Actions panel.

You can click and drag the bar between each area to resize the Script navigator section of the Actions panel. When you are editing code, you probably want to minimize the Script navigator and Actions toolbox section by clicking on the arrow button in the middle of the bar to close it completely.

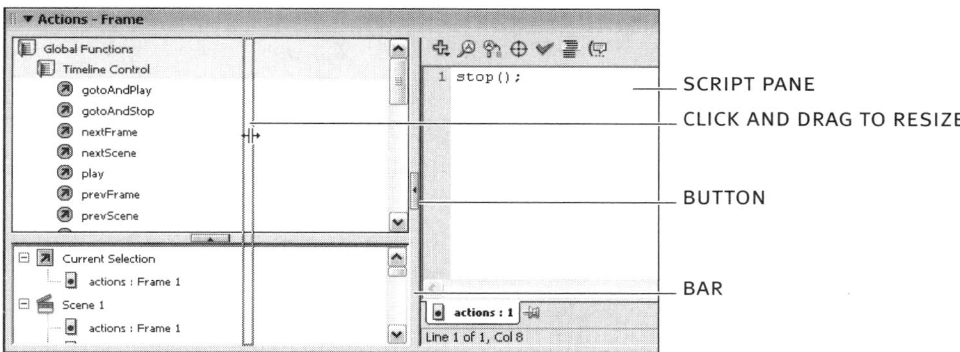

3) With the Script navigator maximized, click `actions: Frame 5` **under the** `samplechapter_mc` **heading.**

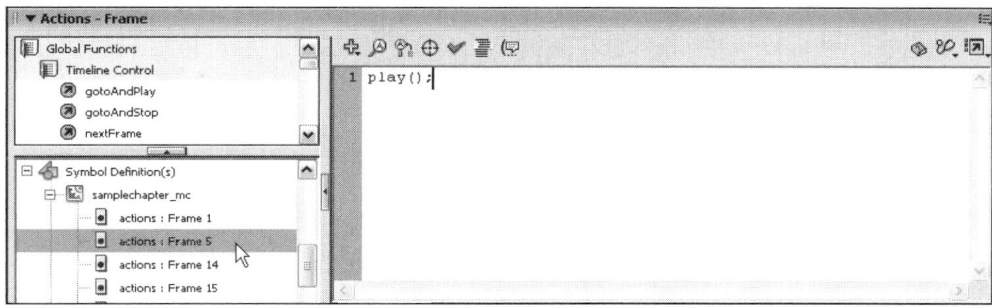

When you click each of these items, you can see the associated code appear in the Script pane. When you click an item in the Script navigator then the document's playhead moves to the frame that the selected script is on. The Script navigator helps you can navigate throughout the code in an FLA file without too much effort. When you find code that you need to edit, you can pin these scripts, as seen in the following step.

4) Select `actions: Frame 1` **in the Script navigator under the** `samplechapter_mc` **heading and click the Pin active script button below the Script pane. Then try pinning a second script in the document.**

After you click the Pin active script button, which looks like a thumbtack, the code stays in the Actions panel until you close the pinned script.

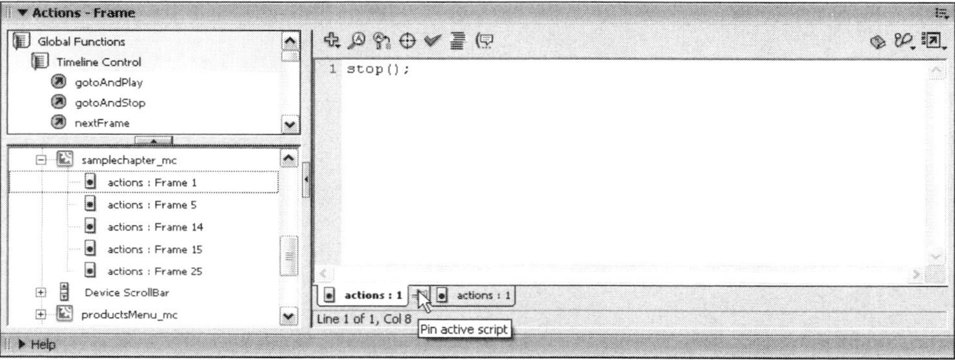

Click `actions: Frame 1` in the Script navigator and then click the Pin active script button. You can also select an instance or frame containing a script on the Stage and then right-click (or control-click on the Mac) the script tab in the Actions panel and choose Pin Script from the contextual menu. This procedure pins the script in the Actions panel and you see a new tab added underneath the Script pane as a result.

TIP *You can also double-click the code in the Script navigator to pin the script in the Actions panel.*

To close a pinned script, select one of the actively pinned scripts either by its tab or the pinned script in the Script navigator. When it is selected, the pinned script thumbtack changes; when you click the button, the script is unpinned.

5) Click through the script tabs for the pieces of code that you have pinned.

Use the script tabs below the Script pane to navigate through the pinned scripts. Navigating through the scripts does not move the playhead in the FLA. Pinned scripts make it much easier to find code than having to hunt through the Flash document to find all the different places you might have placed code. If you use behaviors to place code on different instances, you will probably notice how useful this tool is!

NOTE *If you have too many scripts pinned that the Actions panel is not large enough to hold all the tabs, a double arrow button appears to the right of the panel. If you click this button, a menu appears that shows the additional pinned scripts.*

You do not need to save any changes that you made in this exercise, so just close the document and choose not to save changes when you're finished.

In Lesson 11, you will learn more about the ActionScript language and why it works the way it does. This knowledge will help you understand why you write code the way you do.

WHAT YOU HAVE LEARNED

In this lesson, you have:

- Added behaviors to an instance and the Timeline in an FLA file (pages 167–171)
- Learned how to modify behaviors after they are added to a document (pages 171–173)
- Created basic server interaction by loading a JPEG into a Loader component (pages 175–177)
- Explored the basics of ActionScript (pages 178–185)
- Added stop actions to control the playhead in a SWF (pages 185–186)
- Added a new home button to the bookstore (pages 186–189)
- Used actions to remove the hand cursor from a button (pages 190–192)
- Added code so the movie clip button animates properly as a button (pages 192–194)
- Learned how to use the Script navigator and script pinning to find the scripts in your document and edit them (pages 194–197)

adding sound and video

LESSON 7

Part of creating an interesting Web presence or presentation usually includes adding at least a few media assets such as sound and video. A SWF file is great to use for displaying your videos and for playing sounds and music. Because so many people have the Flash Player installed on their computers, they are likely to be able to see the video when it is placed online. Other audio and video players, such as the QuickTime player, don't have the same kind of player penetration (percentage of people who have installed it) that the Flash Player has. Even though both of these media types (sound and video) can quickly add a significant amount of file size to the bookstore site you are creating, you can progressively load or stream media to help decrease the time visitors have to wait in order to start watching the video.

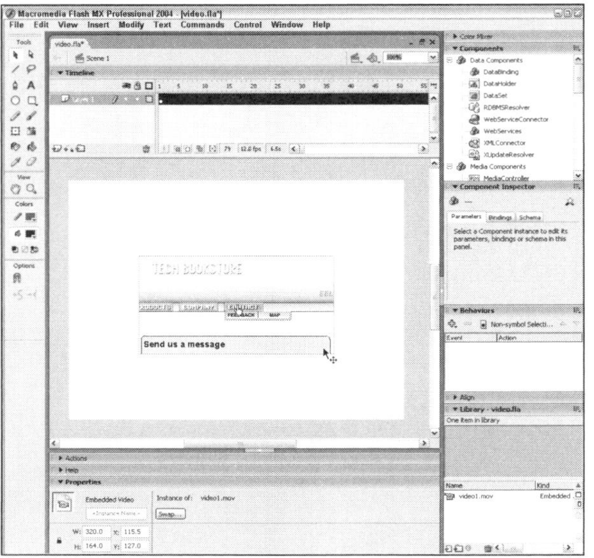

Importing video for the bookstore

Because you can include sound and video in the Tech Bookstore you can add sounds to the buttons and include video right in the application without having to spawn a new browser window. This lesson will begin by providing an overview of some of the issues you will encounter while adding video and audio media to your SWF files and then show you how to import and use sound and video in the Tech Bookstore.

WHAT YOU WILL LEARN

In this lesson, you will:

- Learn more about Flash and media assets
- Add sound to a button
- Find out how to import sound
- Add sound to the Timeline
- Customize your sounds
- Import video
- Edit video
- Encode and compress video
- Export FLV video

APPROXIMATE TIME

This lesson takes approximately one hour to complete.

LESSON FILES

Media Files:

media/video1.mov or media/video1.avi
media/video2.mov or media/video2.avi
media/video3.mov or media/video3.avi
media/sound.mp3
media/click.wav

Starting Files:

Lesson07/bookstore11.fla

Completed Project:

Lesson07/video.fla
Lesson07/sound.fla

USING SOUND AND VIDEO

Sound and video are important additions to many SWF files. You are working with software that can be used to build complete applications, productions, and presentations. Of course, adding interactive and engaging media to enhance the SWF file isn't appropriate for every application you make in the future. Nor should it. However, the presentations you do add sound and video to will change dramatically in the way your SWF files are received by an audience. Sound and video typically make your presentations more engaging, allowing you to express your creativity in different ways. However, you will inevitably have an increased file size in the end. However, your files really become "richer Internet applications," but only if you do it right.

Adding sound can be extremely useful if your site caters to people who are visually impaired. It can be valuable to add audio cues to a SWF file, prompting key press actions or reading text aloud. You can create an MP3 sampler for a freelance musician or add a company's jingle when its Web site loads. Adding tacky or annoying music is fairly easy to do, but detracts from the site. Getting your peers to test your site and provide feedback can help you avoid useless clutter and find subtle, creative, or diverse ways to use sound and video in your SWF files. Because sound and video add a lot of file size to a document, you have to make sure they're worth your bandwidth and the bandwidth of your visitor.

EDITING SOUND AND VIDEO

You can edit sound and video in external editors before you import it, or you can import files and perform basic editing using the Flash video import wizard. Flash MX 2004 is capable of basic video editing. When you import a new video file, you can edit and/or compress the video file. You can create shorter clips from the video, crop the size of the frames, color-correct the footage, and sew it all together. You cannot tween the changes you make over the duration of the footage, though, which needs to be done using a separate piece of software.

This doesn't mean there aren't cheap or free solutions to edit your videos in simple to very complex ways. Windows Movie Maker 2 allows you to quickly and easily edit your video files, and it's also free (but available only for Windows XP). QuickTime Pro is a very reasonable (and useful) piece of software that enables you to perform very simple video editing and compression. These free or nearly free editors are all you need for fade-ins and fade-outs, cross-fades, simple filters, and basic color modification and correction. For more advanced or professional video editing and compositing, look to After Effects, Avid Express DV or Final Cut Pro that allow you to tween effects and perform detailed and controlled color corrections and compositing.

Assuming Responsibility with Your Media

You have to make some important decisions when you are adding sound and video. Consideration for your visitors is important! Some visitors might not want to be forced to hear the music that you are playing (if you are using a loop by the author, this is more than often the case). Your visitor might be in a public setting, have other music playing already. Because of these reasons, you should always offer an "off" button for the sound at the very least. Volume controllers or pause/play toggles also work very well. This kind of responsibility and usability offers a much better experience when someone visits your site. For the bookstore, you will use behaviors to control the background music that will be added for the tour. You will learn how to do this in Lesson 8.

Because sound and video files are often very large, you should try to communicate how much data need to be transferred to the end user by using a progress bar. If the file is large (like our video file), you should give some kind of indication that content is downloading so a visitor doesn't arrive at the page and think nothing is happening. Also, your video might also include an audio track. If so, you should offer the opportunity to control the audio using buttons or sliders.

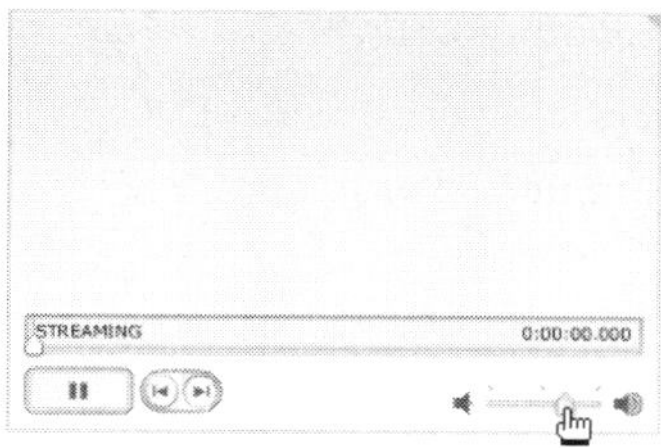

Compression, Codecs, and Plug-ins

Compression reduces the size of a file by using complex mathematical equations that remove information from the content that is not necessary for hearing or viewing it. This means that the video, sound, or file you are working with will be quicker to download online, but you will always lose some quality in the process.

There are several software programs other than Flash that are made to compress video files in particular. You can use professional solutions such as Discreet Cleaner 6 (Mac) or Discreet Cleaner XL (Windows), or you can use a simple solution such as QuickTime Pro. Sorenson Squeeze, which has features that are created with Flash in mind, can compress videos directly into FLV (Flash Video) or SWF formats.

Other programs, such as Windows Movie Maker 2, allow you to compress video when you export a video project. This ability can be particularly useful if you need to edit video in ways that Flash cannot.

TIP *The most important thing you can remember about compression is to always try to avoid recompressing sounds or video after it has already been compressed. Recompressing material leads to a significant loss in quality.*

Codecs are small pieces of software that are used to compress and then decompress files. The file is compressed for placing online and then it is decompressed by the codec again when viewed on the client's computer. Sorenson Video 3, Cinepak, QDesign Music 2 (audio), Mpeg4, and DivX are examples of codecs. If you compress a video using a particular codec, both you and those watching your video would need that codec installed to decompress the video again. Sometimes codecs are already installed into players such as the QuickTime player, but other codecs need to be installed separately by the end user.

NOTE *Flash uses the Sorenson Spark codec, which is a codec that is specifically for importing video into a Flash document. The codec is built into the Flash importer.*

DELIVERING MEDIA ONLINE

When you are delivering media online, you have to think about what the visitor needs to view your files and how long what they need takes to download. File size and how long it takes the visitor to download on different connections should be an immediate consideration when you are working with sound and video files.

You should note that SWF files actually progressively download. This means a SWF file plays as it downloads into a visitor's computer. You can stream sound and video files instead of progressively downloading them like a SWF file. The catch with streaming sound is that when the file is finished playing, it will begin to download the data all over again if you want the sound to loop. The information you already downloaded is not reused—instead, the SWF downloads the data again, and more bandwidth is used. This means that streaming is not overly practical for looping sounds. Another issue with streaming sounds is that sometimes the SWF file will rush to keep up with the streamed sound, so it might start dropping frames to keep up with the music. If there is ActionScript on those frames, your code will be lost.

FILE SIZE CONSIDERATIONS

Even though you are adding great and interesting content to your SWFs, it is important not to go overboard. Sound, video and components can quickly add a lot of file size to applications. You have to make sure that you budget what media you add to the SWF file, and ask yourself if the files are the best use of the file size and bandwidth you will need to devote to the presentation. It might be the best way of communicating a message, but there might be another similar way of getting the same job done that ends up saving you, for example, 800KB.

Some documents have huge file sizes and are just too big to transfer. This is particularly true of a video with a large frame size (the dimensions of the image). For example, never try putting a video that has a frame size of 640 × 480 pixels online. A frame size that is that large will take an incredibly long time to download to the end user's computer because the file size will be much larger than a video that is 320 × 240 pixels. You should always try to stick with smaller frame sizes, such as the aforementioned 320 × 240 or smaller.

ADDING SOUND TO A BUTTON

There are different ways you can handle sound in a SWF file. The main ways that sound can be handled is as an event sound or as a streaming sound. These two different ways affect how you work with the sound when you edit it or manipulate the sound using ActionScript.

Event sounds must be completely downloaded before they start to play, and play independent of the Timeline. Also, each time the sound plays (due to an event, such as a button being clicked), the entire sound plays. For these reasons, event sounds are great for short sounds but not good at all for very long sounds. Event sounds are perfect for button sounds and loops.

Streaming sounds are great for long sounds, because they start playing before the file is completely downloaded. You can set a *buffer*, which means some of the file downloads prior to the sound being played so it plays evenly when streamed to the user. Streaming sounds are tied to the SWF's Timeline, which works to keep up with the streamed sound. As was mentioned in the previous section, streaming sounds are not great for looping or when you have a lot of ActionScript on the Timeline.

In this exercise, you will import a sound file that will be used to add a click to the buttons. The buttons you want to add sound to reside in the Tech Bookstore itself. You will add sounds to `products_btn`, `company_btn`, and `contact_btn` that are present on all of the pages. For this exercise, you will open up the Tech Bookstore file and then add sounds from the sounds common Library to each button.

1) Open `bookstore10_complete.fla` from the `TechBookstore` folder on your hard drive and save a new version of the file as `bookstore11.fla`.

A new version of the bookstore FLA file is saved into the `TechBookstore` folder. You will only make minor modifications to the bookstore in this lesson.

2) Find `click.wav` in the `media` folder on the book's CD-ROM and save the sound file anywhere on your hard drive.

A WAV file is a commonly used uncompressed audio file format. You will import the WAV into Flash where you can set compression settings for when you export the sound as part of the SWF file. Even though WAV is typically used on the Windows platform, QuickTime can be used to play and import `click.wav` if you are using a Mac.

NOTE *You should always try to import uncompressed sounds whenever possible, such as a WAV or AIFF file. This means the sound will not be recompressed when it's made into a SWF file.*

3) Import the `click.wav` into Flash choosing File > Import > Import to Library. Open the Library and locate the sound file you imported (which is again called `click.wav`) and drag it into the Library's `media` folder.

Choose File > Import > Import to Library from the main menu. Locate the WAV file you just saved from the CD-ROM on your hard drive, and click Open (or Import to Library on the Mac). After you import the file, open the Library in Flash, locate the `click.wav` file, and drag it into the `media` folder in the Library.

4) Modify the sound properties by right-clicking (or control-clicking on the Mac) and choosing Properties from the contextual menu.

The Properties dialog box opens where you can choose how the sound is published when you create a SWF file that includes the WAV. Choose MP3 from the Compression drop-down menu. MP3 is an excellent compression for playing sounds on the Web. It is economical on file size while yielding excellent quality. Then choose 8kbps from the Bit rate drop-down menu and make sure Fast is selected in the Quality drop-down menu.

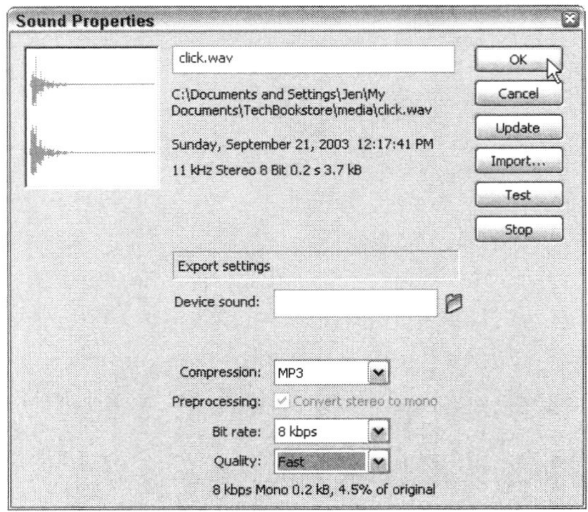

5) Select `products_btn` on the `home` frame on the `buttons` layer and then open the button in symbol-editing mode. Insert a new layer on the Timeline and rename it `sound`.

If the layer is locked, make sure that you unlock it so you can select the button instances.

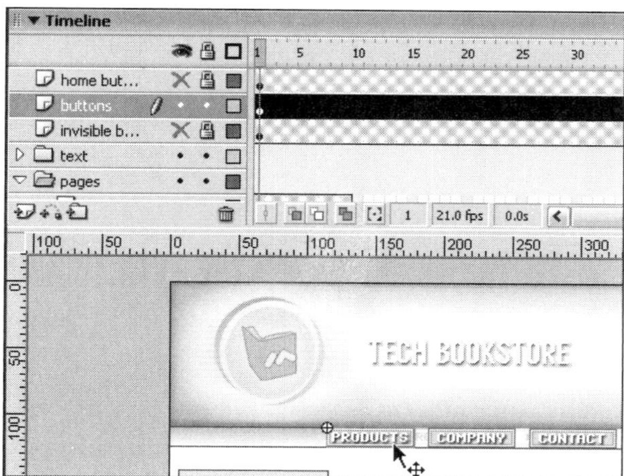

Double-click the button instance so it opens in symbol-editing mode. The `products_btn` symbol opens in symbol-editing mode so you can add the sound to the button. You will see one layer inside the button that has keyframes on each frame. You need to add a new layer to hold the sound for the button, because it's always a good idea to keep sounds on their own layer in the Timeline. So click the Insert New Layer button, and then double-click the new layer's name and rename the new layer *sound*.

6) Add a new keyframe in the Down frame of the `sound` layer.

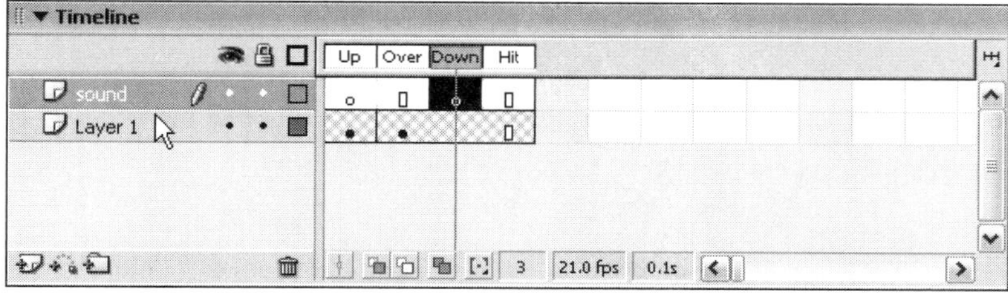

Add a new keyframe to the Down frame by selecting the frame and pressing the F6 key. The down frame is "played" whenever the visitor clicks the button. This means the sound will only play when the button is clicked, not when the visitor rolls over the button.

7) Select the new keyframe on the Down frame, and drag the `click.wav` sound from the Library onto the Stage.

The sound, which is a subtle short click sound, is added to the Down state for the button when you drag it over to the Stage. This means when the button is clicked, the sound will play.

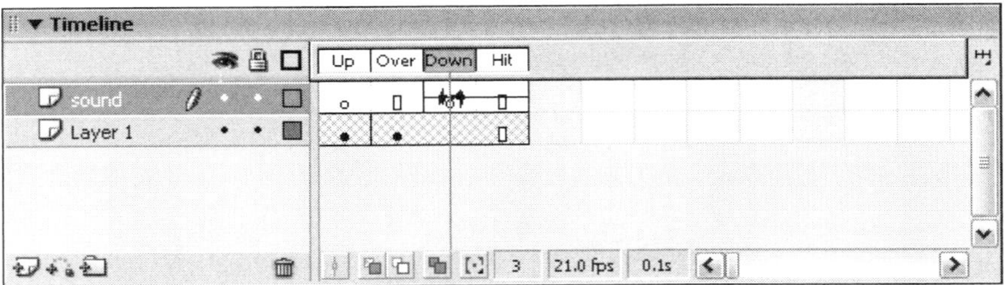

A waveform is seen in the frame, and this indicates that a sound is located on the Timeline. You can access the properties of the sound by right-clicking (or control-clicking) it and choosing Properties from the contextual menu. For example, you can change the export settings. Export settings are discussed further in the following exercise.

8) Repeat the process, adding the same sound to the `company_btn` and `contact_btn` on the main Stage. When you are finished, lock the `buttons` layer again.

After you have added the sound to the `products_btn` instance, press `Scene 1` in the edit bar to return to the main Stage. Double-click each instance to select it and then add new layers and drag the click sound onto a new keyframe on the down frame.

NOTE *When you add code for the menus it causes the menus to open when the three buttons you just added sound to are rolled over. You have probably noticed that this sound was added for when a visitor clicks one of the menus instead of just rolling over it. Really, this makes for a less irritating system*

9) Save the changes you have made to the file.

You have now added the first sound effects to the bookstore.

IMPORTING SOUND INTO A DOCUMENT

There are many different kinds of files that you can import into Flash documents. If you are importing sound files, you can use MP3, AIFF (Mac), and WAV (Windows) files. If you have QuickTime installed on your Mac or Windows computer, you can also import additional file formats, such as Sound Designer II files and AIFF and WAV files on either platform. MP3 files can be dynamically loaded into Flash using ActionScript or the MediaPlayback component in Flash MX Professional.

You can import MP3s into an FLA file or you can dynamically load an MP3 at runtime. You can set the MP3 to streaming or load it as an event sound, as was defined in the previous section. Event sounds can be used as objects, which means that you can control them using ActionScript in additional ways.

Many Flash designers and developers create or find loops to use in their SWF files. Loops are a good way to create the illusion of having a lot of loaded sound, but keep the content small and quick to download. You can find sound loops to download online that are free to use in your projects, or you can create your own loop using audio software such as ReCycle, Cakewalk Plasma or Acid Pro.

TIP *You should make sure to create a loop that loops seamlessly. Loops must begin and end when the waveform crosses the "0 crossing" between the positive and negative waveform where there is no sound. If you trim your music exactly to the beat, so the waveform is crossing the 0 mark, you will not hear the distracting "pop" at the end of your loop. Also, make sure to remove any extra space at the beginning and end of the loop. It helps to create a loop that is an odd number of bars. This means that instead of 4 bars if you are using 4/4 time, create five bars of music. The uneven nature means that it will take the ear a longer time to recognize the sound is a loop.*

1) Create a new FLA document and call it `sound.fla`**. Save the document in the** `TechBookstore` **folder on your hard drive.**

This file will hold the media files, including video and sound files, which will be required for the tour you create in the following lesson. A separate FLA file to hold the media assets is being constructed so you can choose one of two tour versions to build: either using Screens in Flash MX Professional or using the Timeline you are used to in Flash MX 2004.

2) Copy `sound.mp3` **from the** `media` **folder on the book's CD-ROM onto your hard drive.**

You can copy the file anywhere you want on your hard drive, but be sure to remember where it is located so you can find it in the following step. This MP3 file will eventually play in the background of the tour you will create in the following lesson. It is approximately 8 seconds long and will be dynamically loaded in as an event sound in the background.

3) Choose File > Import > Import to Library. Browse to find the MP3 file on your hard drive. Select the file and click Open (or Import to Library on the Mac). Then open the Sound Properties dialog box.

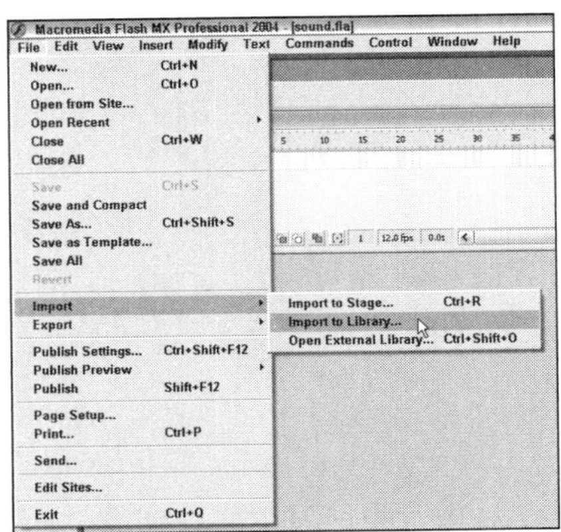

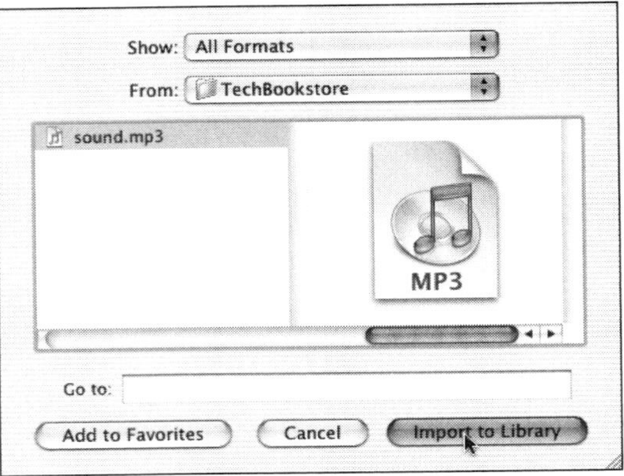

After you choose the MP3 file and click Open, the sound is imported directly into the Library in Flash. Open the Library and find the MP3 sound you just imported. Right-click (or control-click on the Mac) the sound itself and select Properties from the contextual menu. The Sound Properties dialog box opens, in which you can modify the export settings for the sound.

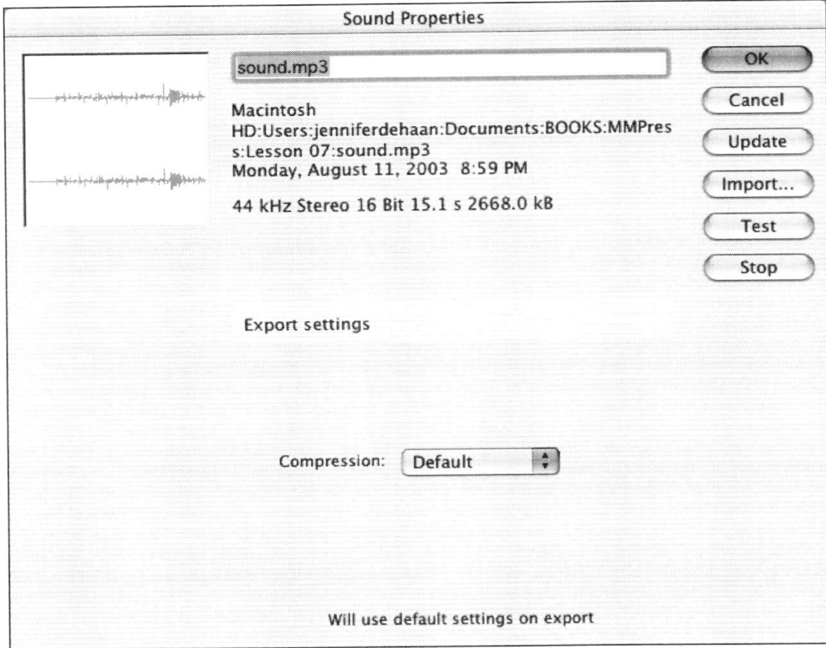

4) Click the Compression drop-down menu and choose MP3.

After you choose MP3 from the menu, several additional options appear below the menu. You can change the bit-rate and the quality of the sound if you want. Just like the previous exercise, MP3 will be a good option for putting this sound on the Web because it offers a good quality sound with a low file size. Choose a bit rate of 16kbps and Medium for the Quality setting.

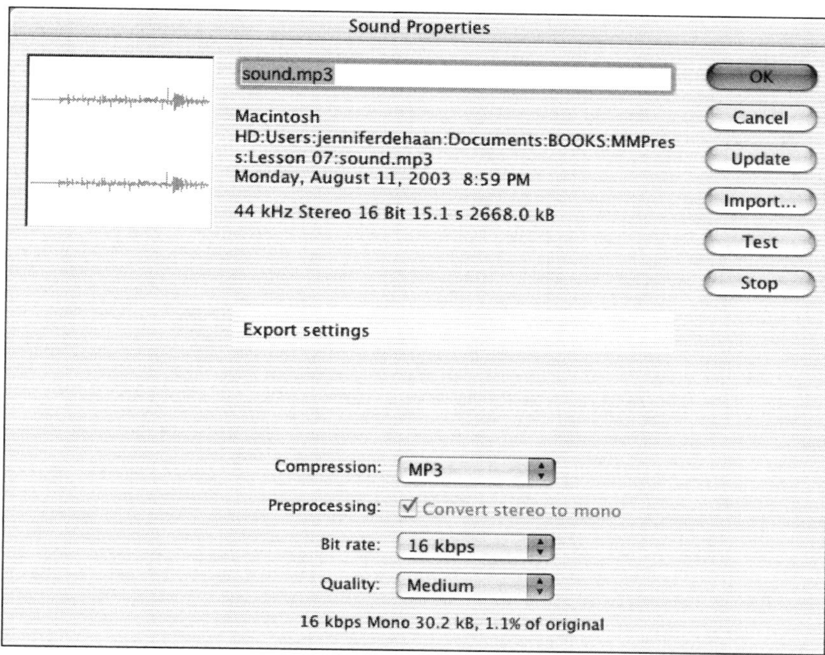

When you are finished, click OK to exit the dialog box.

NOTE *You can set overall export settings in the Publish Settings dialog box (File > Publish Settings), but the properties for an export that you choose in the Sound Properties dialog box override those settings. However, if you choose "Override sound settings" in the Publish Settings dialog box, the settings in Sound Properties are overwritten. You will learn more about Publish Settings in Lesson 13.*

5) Save the file before moving on to the next exercise.

TIP *There are many programs that can be used for audio editing and loop generation, such as Reason, ReBirth, Pro Tools, and Cakewalk. For more information on creating and editing audio, refer to the book's supporting Web site at* `www.TrainingFromTheSource.com/bonus`.

ADDING AND CUSTOMIZING SOUND

You can change the sounds you are using in Flash right in the authoring environment! You should keep in mind that Flash is not an audio editor. It won't replace a dedicated audio editor like those mentioned previously. However, for basic customizations and edits, Flash can help you change the sounds you import into the authoring environment without leaving the workspace.

In this example, you will create a fade-in at the beginning of the sound you imported and modify when the sound starts by trimming off the beginning. You are still working with `sound.fla` for this example.

NOTE *If you copy this sound file to a different Flash document, you will have to reapply this fade-in effect and audio trims to the sound. Your export settings for the file are retained.*

1) In `sound.fla`**, select frame 30 or greater on the Timeline and press F5 to insert a new frame. Then drag** `sound.mp3` **from the Library onto the Stage.**

You will see the waveform span across the Timeline because you added the frames. The waveform represents the sound in the MP3 file. When you are working with a SWF that has many different layers, make sure that you create a separate layer for a new sound.

2) Click a frame containing the waveform on the Timeline and change the Sync drop-down menu in the Property inspector to Event. Then click the Edit button in the Property inspector.

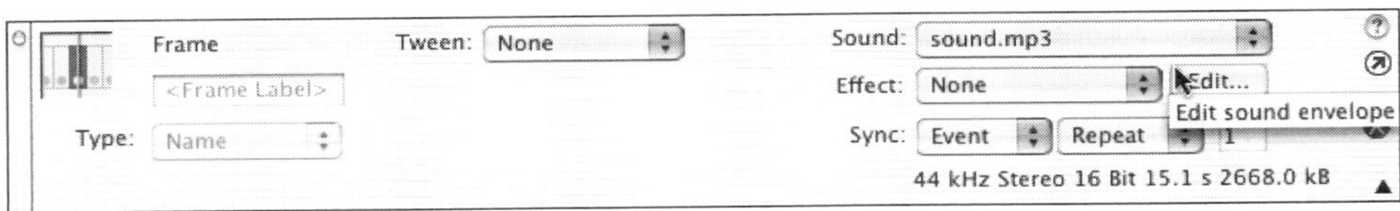

The sound is set to event in the Flash document after you change the Sync drop-down menu. Stream means the sound will play as it downloads. When the sound is set to Event, the entire sound has to download before the sound begins to play. When you click the Edit button, the Edit Envelope dialog box opens.

3) In the Edit Envelope dialog box, click the Zoom Out button on the bottom of the dialog box so you can see more of the waveform.

Zooming out from the waveform allows you to see more of the sound's waveform. You can use the Zoom In button to get a close up view of the waveform, which is useful when you need to accurately trim the beginning or end of the sound.

4) Change the start point and end point for the sound by dragging the Time In and Time Out controls.

The start point refers to where the sound begins, and the end point is where the sound ends. You can define these two points by using the Time In and Time Out controls. You can drag these controls to the left and right to set exactly where the start and end points are. The controls that you drag are small toggles that are located between the two waveforms, as seen in the following figure.

You can drag the Time In control to the right, and the area you trim off is then greyed-out. The loop that you have imported won't have any areas that you need to trim, because the waveform will begin and end with the beginning and ending of the file. If you do have extra area, you need to edit in a sound that you use (like the `click.wav` sound), then you can use these controls to trim the beginning and the ending of the sound. You can see an example of this with a different sound (not `sound.mp3`) in the figure that follows.

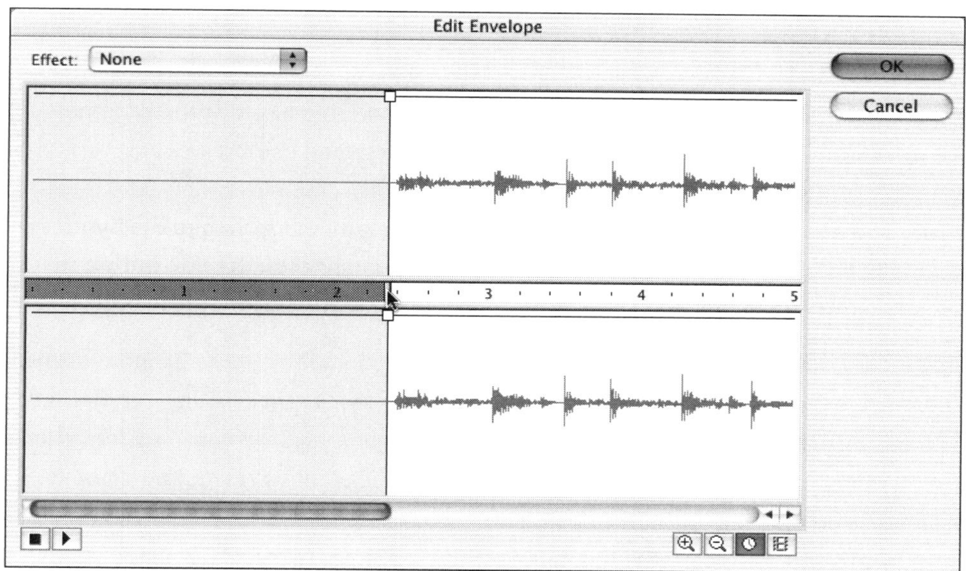

5) Save your changes before moving on to the next exercise.

You will now move on to working with video files. Keep the `sound.mp3` file handy, because you will use it again in Lesson 8 and dynamically load the sound into the tour at runtime using ActionScript.

IMPORTING VIDEO INTO FLASH

Now that you have imported some audio in to the FLA, it's time to switch gears and add some video to an FLA file. Flash MX 2004 allows you to import and embed video, but also edit the video footage as you import the file. You can edit the single video file into several smaller clips or you can import an entire SWF. Either way, you have a lot of control over the compression (or export) settings for the video.

Another critical thing to consider when you import video is how much control you have over editing and compression. The more control you have typically means the better compression you can manage to achieve. However, even with adequate control over compression (and a good codec) video can still be very large because of the amount of data contained in every single frame. Consider the following points about video before you start to edit or compress it:

Trim your video. Remember that blank areas at the beginning and end of the footage add to the file size, so make sure that you use Flash's editing features during the Video Import wizard (used in the following exercises) to trim off any extra video at the beginning and end.

Test your settings. If file size is very important, you should try out different import settings and quality levels. All video footage is different and compresses and decompresses differently, depending on factors such as color, movement, and effects. If your video looks great when you import it, try changing the settings and compress the original file a bit more (perhaps by using a lower-quality setting or fewer video keyframes). It might still look great, but can end up importing with a smaller file size.

Limit fading, noise, and movement if possible. Fading includes fading in and out, and also refers to one clip of video fading into another (known as cross-fading—something you might use if you have edited your video in another program). Noise refers to the speckles over each frame you might see if your footage is dimly lit, and movement (such as a tree blowing in the wind) similarly involves a lot of pixels moving. All these factors usually mean that the footage will be a larger file size. Two video clips that are the same frame size and length, and taken with the same camera, can be a different file size depending on these factors. The footage is also difficult to compress, usually meaning that you need to use more keyframes and a higher-quality setting.

If you cannot avoid using fades, movement, or having a lot of noise in your footage, remember to add more video keyframes when you compress the clip (you'll notice a setting for keyframes when you work with compression later on). The more keyframes you add, the better appearance your video has. However, the clip will also be a larger file size after it's compressed.

Avoid recompressing video that has already been compressed. Every time you recompress your video, more *artifacting* occurs and the quality decreases. Artifacting means you will see blocks and pixilation in the video, which looks bad and of low quality. Because your original footage is already compressed, it probably contains "residue" of blockiness, so this throws off the second compression and the quality level decreases and more of this blockiness occurs. Always try to compress from a video file with the least amount of compression.

If you have the opportunity, consider trying third-party applications such as Sorenson Squeeze for compressing your footage into Flash video. If you own Flash MX Professional and have a recent version of QuickTime installed, you can try out the FLV exporter, which allows you to export FLV video from video editing or compressing software like After Effects and Discreet Cleaner.

NOTE *When you are working with video on a Timeline, remember that it is different from a Flash Timeline. If you're working with normal video imported directly into Flash, you cannot add code or keyframes within the video itself (although, you can insert the video into a movie clip, and add ActionScript to that).*

For this exercise, you will import a video that you will use for the Tour page of the Tech Bookstore site. Following this exercise, you need to import a few other videos, so you will need to revisit this exercise when you do so (unless you remember all the steps!)

1) Create a new file called `video.fla` and save it anywhere on your hard drive.

You will not need this video after this lesson, because you are essentially using it to export video as FLV files. These FLV files will be dynamically imported into the Tech Bookstore. Therefore, you won't need to publish this FLA or revisit it in later lessons.

2) Find `video1.mov` or `video1.avi` in the `media` folder on this book's CD-ROM and copy the file anywhere onto your hard drive. Change the FPS to *15* in `video.fla`.

You must have QuickTime 4 or greater on the Mac, or DirectX 7 or greater on the PC to import video. A computer with QuickTime can import the MOV file, and a computer with Windows Media Player can import the AVI file included on the CD-ROM. Choose one of the files from the `media` folder on the CD-ROM and copy it to your hard drive.

NOTE *This video file does not have any audio. You can expect to see a warning or alert in relation to this. You will be using the audio that was imported earlier to go along with the video files. If you were to import a video with sound, you could not hear it when working with your document in the authoring environment. You could hear it only when you test your document or publish the SWF file.*

Change the FPS setting for `video.fla` to *15* using the Property inspector.

3) Choose File > Import > Import to Library, and find `video1.mov` or `video1.avi` on your hard drive.

Find and select either `video1.mov` or `video1.avi` on your hard drive in the Import to Library dialog box and then click Open (or Import to Library on the Mac). The wizard dialog box opens, which will lead you through the import and editing process.

4) Choose to embed the video file in the Flash document and then click Next.

You have the choice to either embed or link the video to the SWF file you export. If you embed the file, you can edit the video and manipulate it with ActionScript or add buttons that can be used to control the video. When you are finished, click the Next button.

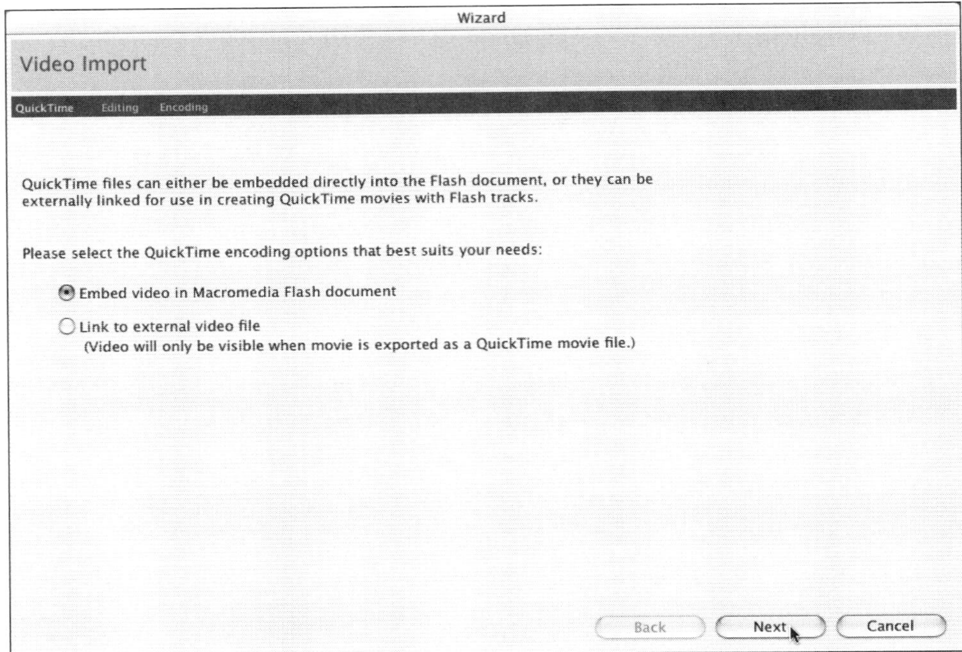

TIP *You can also dynamically load FLV files into Flash at runtime. This means you do not need to embed the file in the SWF file, but instead you can use ActionScript to load it into the SWF when an event occurs (such as a visitor clicking a button). You can then use ActionScript or other controls to manipulate the video file.*

5) Select the Edit the video first radio button and then press the Next button.

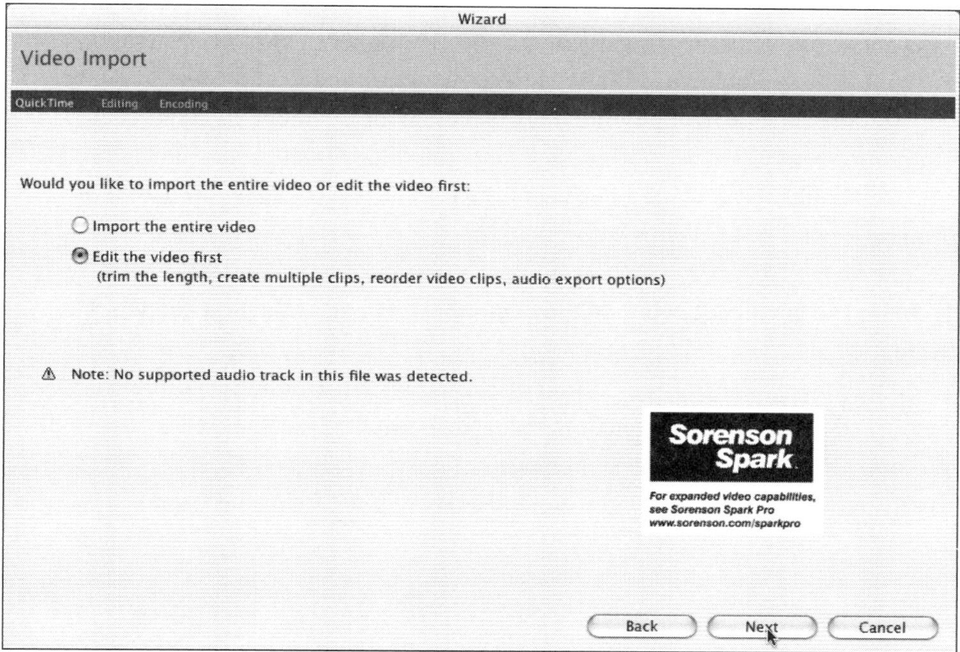

From this point, you can progress directly to compressing and importing the entire video, or you can choose to edit the video first. Editing the video allows you to create smaller video clips from a large video, which is incredibly useful. This means that you do not necessarily need to import the entire video, and you can drop the footage you don't need and save on some file size.

In the following exercise, you will edit this video so it's broken into a few smaller clips using the video-editing features in the Video Import Wizard, so make sure that you don't close the video import dialog box!

Edit the Video

Flash MX 2004 and Flash MX Professional allow you to have a lot of control over the video you are importing. You can edit the length of the video and separate the file into several smaller clips. This means that you can edit out parts of the video you don't want to bring into Flash and avoid having to open and use a separate video editor for a basic function such as this.

`Video1.mov` or `video1.avi` both have several areas that should be cut out of the footage. As you've probably noticed, the video is actually a video screen capture of the bookstore site being used. The video provides some direction and help in using the Web site (or at least it pretends to). The beginning and end include footage that is not useful at all because nothing is happening in the video. You will edit that part out, and should also remove a portion of the middle where the mouse cursor is stationary as well. What clips you actually use are up to you.

1) Move the in and out points to the beginning and end of the first clip you want to create.

You should be on the Editing (Customize) window of the import feature's wizard dialog box. The in and out points are below the scrubber bar. You can use the playhead (the triangle that is above the scrubber bar) to scrub through the video and choose where you want the clip to begin and end as seen in the following figure.

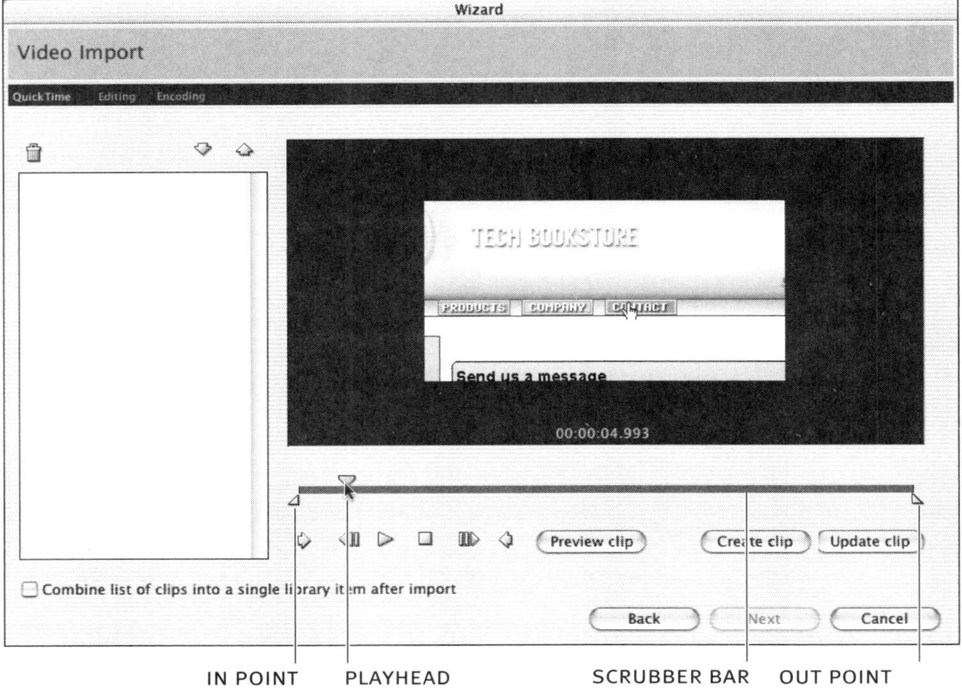

Choose the video clip's in and out points by dragging the in and out points below the scrubber bar and selecting the footage for the first clip to import (the area between the in and out point). Keep in mind that you will make three small video clips from this video file by the end of this exercise. These three clips will combined together into one long clip when you encode and import the video into the FLA file.

2) Click the Create clip button after you have chosen in and out points in Step 1 and rename the video clip to `clip1`**.**

The Create clip button takes the area between the in and the out point and creates a video clip from that selected footage. A new name for the clip is entered into the pane at the left of the video preview. You can rename the clip right after you click the Create clip button. Type in *clip1*. If you cannot type into the pane, then double-click the name and type in *clip1*.

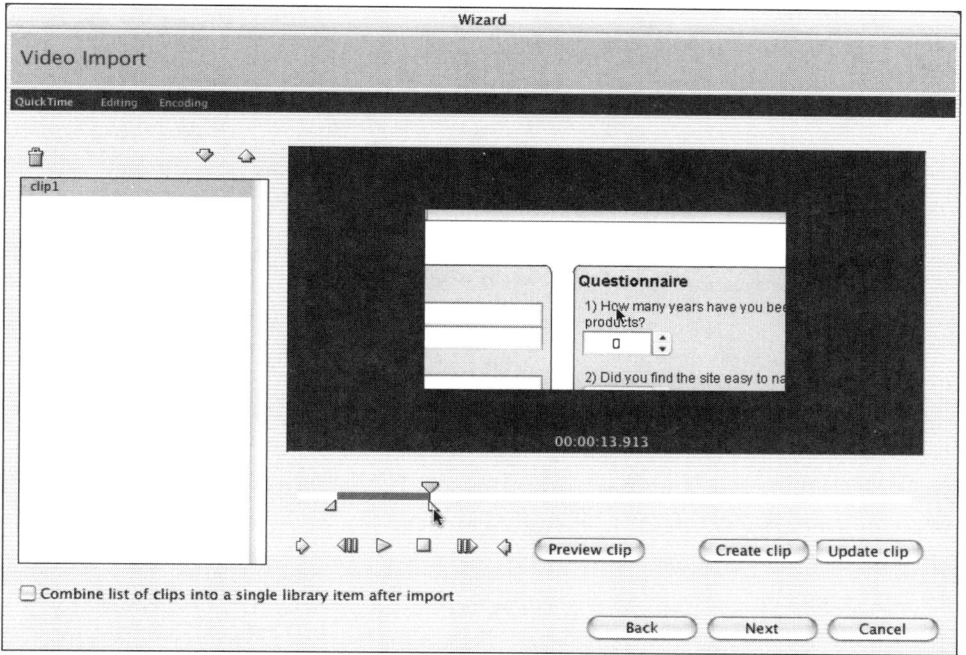

3) Now move the in and out points to determine the beginning and end of a second video clip, and then click the Create clip button. Rename the video clip to `clip2`**.**

Drag the in point on the left towards the out point. This ensures that you will not have two clips with the same footage. Then move the second toggle to where you want the second clip to end. Click the Create clip button and then rename the clip to *clip2*.

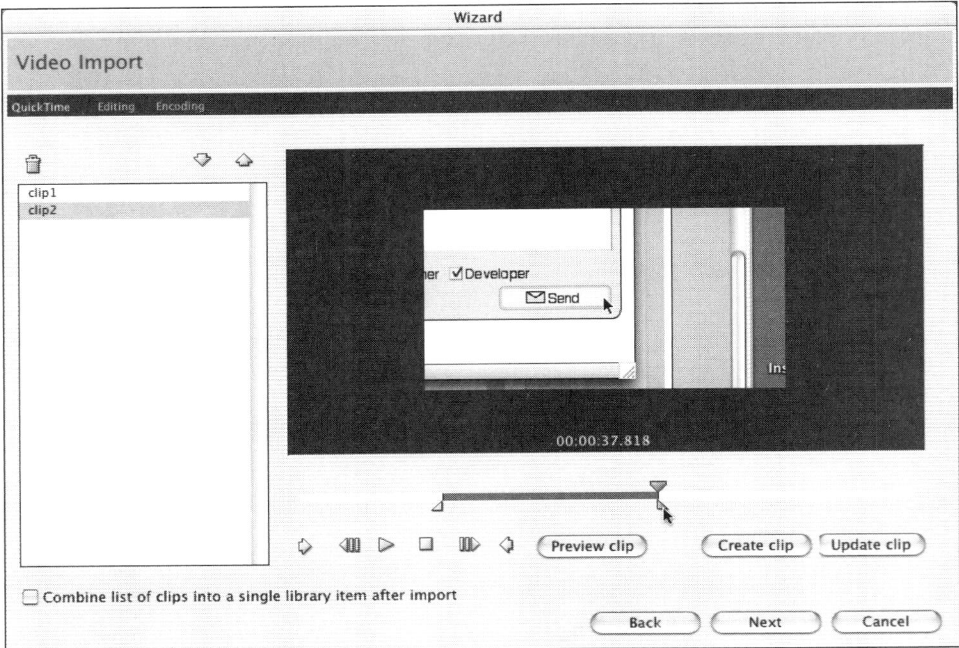

4) Create a third and final video clip by moving the in and out points to the beginning and end of the third video clip. Rename the clip to `clip3`**.**

Drag the in point from the clip you just created to toward the out point that was set for that video clip. Then move the out point to a new location where you want the final clip to end. When you are finished, click the Create clip button and rename the clip to *clip3*.

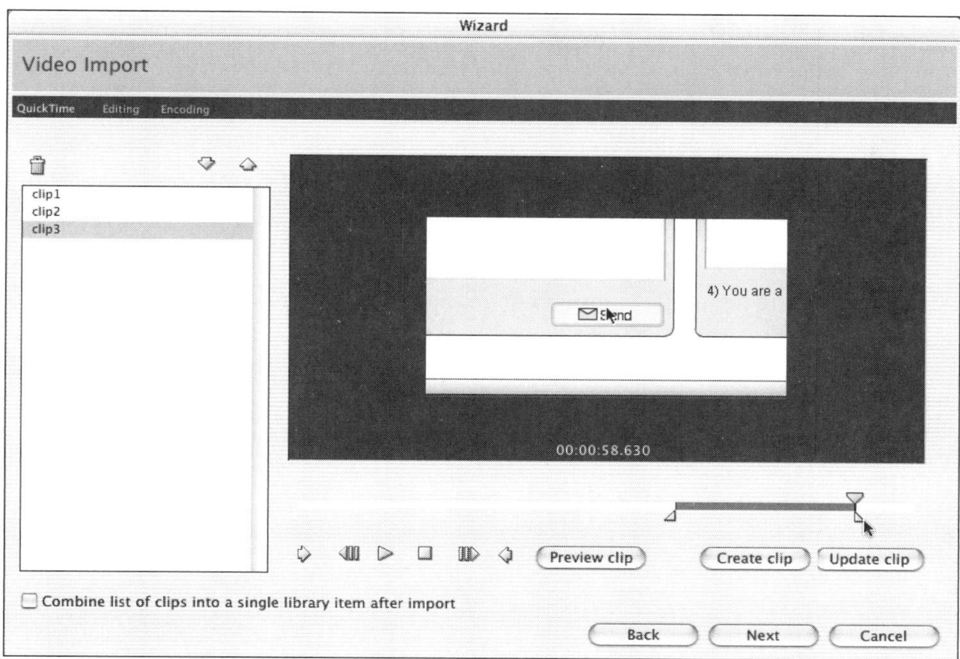

TIP *If you need to change the in and out points of one of the clips, select it in the list of clips and make your changes. When you're finished, click the Update clip button, which updates the in and out points of the clip. You can also click the various clips in the list to review what sections of the video are selected.*

5) Click the `Combine list of clips into a single library item after import` **check box that's located under the list of video clips.**

The three short video clips that you took from the first video will be combined into one single video clip when it is imported into the Library. This means the three clips will play seamlessly as one single video clip after import.

6) Click the Next button at the bottom of the wizard's dialog box.

You are taken to the Encoding step of the import process, in which you will enter settings to compress the video footage in a specific way. Encoding the video is covered in detail within the steps of the following exercise. Don't close your FLA or the Video Import wizard just yet.

ENCODE THE VIDEO

You have some control over the video compression (or encoding) when you are importing video into a Flash document. Flash doesn't give you as much control as other software might allow you to have; for example, Sorenson Squeeze, which contains the Spark Pro codec. Flash uses the Spark codec (the basic version) within Flash, which offers you a limited amount of control over how the video is encoded. If you are importing an FLV file, it is not compressed when you import it into Flash: Flash imports the file at the compression settings that you used when you originally exported the FLV.

TIP *Typically, you cannot make bad video into great video. Sometimes you can use a specialized video editor to make a video much better through creative editing and compression settings, and sometimes you can make small corrections by using some of the more advanced features in the Flash video import. If you are working with poor footage to begin with, it's unlikely you can really fix it using editing. It's much better to invest a bit more time and effort when you are taking the footage to begin with. This will often save you time, money and headaches when you are editing and compressing the footage.*

TIP *Flat areas of color are more difficult to compress well. These areas are typically the first area of a video clip to go blocky when you encode a video because they are difficult areas to compress. Adding a greater number of keyframes and set the Quality slider to a high setting will help.*

1) Select Create new profile from the Compression profile drop-down menu.

After selecting this option, you are taken to the first window of the encoding process which appears like the following figure.

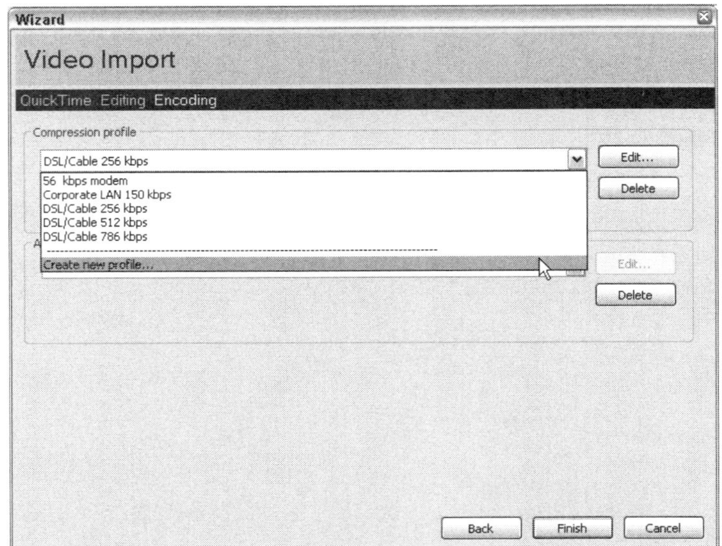

Selecting the Create new profile option immediately takes you to customizable settings, where you can choose specific settings for bandwidth, quality, keyframes, and synchronization (frame rate). Because you are creating a new profile, you can make new settings for a profile without overwriting the default settings in Flash.

2) Click the radio button next to Bandwidth and choose a Bandwidth setting, such as 256. Or you can click the Quality radio button and choose a Quality setting for the video, such as 95 for a high quality video.

You can set the level of compression for the video based on either bandwidth or quality. If you choose to encode the video file based on bandwidth, each individual frame will vary in quality based on the setting you make. If you choose to set the compression to bandwidth then select the radio button next to Bandwidth.

The bandwidth slider ranges between 0 and 750. Lower settings are useful for phone modem connections, but they can go right up to 750 for extremely fast high-speed cable or DSL connections or CD-ROMs. Here you are specifying the download speed in kilobits per second. You could choose a moderate setting (250 or lower) because many visitors might not have high-speed connections (and if they do, they aren't always that fast). Make sure that your bandwidth setting is appropriate for most of your visitors if you know what kind of audience you will have. In this example, we will assume a faster cable modem and choose 256, but the choice is up to you.

Instead of setting a bandwidth setting, you can instead choose a quality setting if you click the radio button next to Quality. This sets all frames to a specified quality setting. After you import the video, you can see how quality affects the video when you place it on the Stage. This setting has a large effect on how the video encodes. While you are choosing a setting at this point, you can scrub the video and see how it will import, which is a very useful feature.

Quality can range between 0 and 100. Most of the time, you'll find that values of 80 and above produce acceptable video quality, whereas values below 80 might not meet the level of quality you would expect. For this video you could choose *95* so the quality is better when you export the FLV in the final exercise.

3) Choose a keyframe interval of *15* and set the Number of video frames to encode per number of frames in Flash.

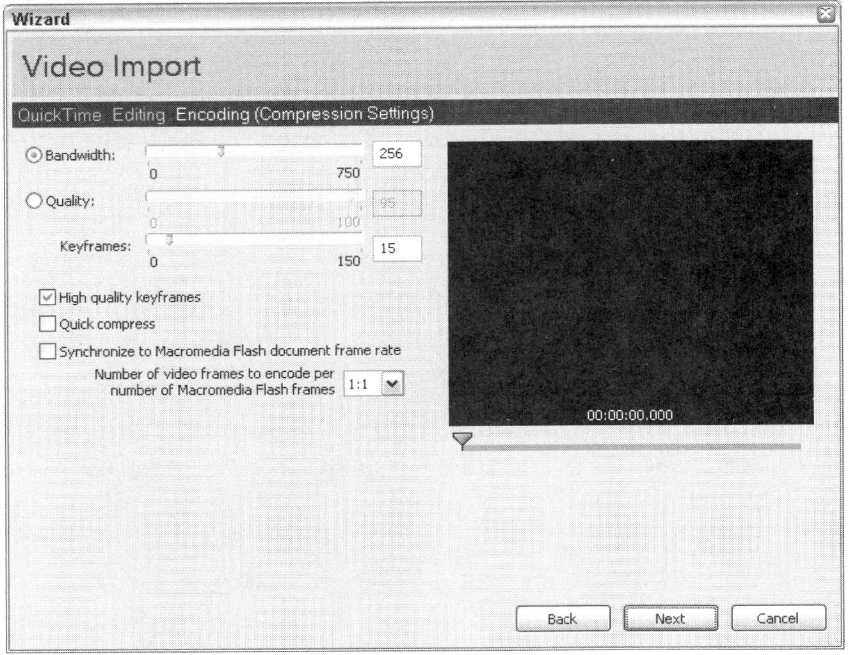

The number of keyframes you choose has an impact over what the video looks like after it is compressed. Video keyframes are different from keyframes in Flash. Each keyframe is a frame that is drawn when the video is compressed. The encoder renders each video frame in-between keyframes by guessing what the pixel changes are, depending on the two surrounding keyframes. Therefore, the more keyframes you choose means the more file size is added to the file, but the better it looks because it is more accurately rendered. For example, if you choose *30* as the value, one keyframe is created every 30 frames. If you choose *15*, one keyframe is created every 15 frames of video, which means a greater file size but slightly higher quality of video because the pixels are more accurate.

Leave the Number of video frames to encode per number of Macromedia Flash frames at 1:1, meaning that for every Flash frame, one video frame is encoded. You are limited to entering a ratio. If you choose one video frame for each Flash frame, the video imports at the same frame rate Flash is currently set at. Earlier, you set the FLA file to 15 fps to match the frame rate. If you choose one video frame for every two Flash frames, the video will import at half of its original frame rate. This is a way to quickly decrease the file size, but it results in a rather choppy playback if you greatly decrease the frame rate. Make sure that you test the resulting footage if you choose to reduce the frame rate.

TIP *You should always encode a video at a frame rate that is a half or quarter of the frame rate than some other number that you pull out of your hat. You will get better results when the video is compressed.*

4) Make sure the option to synchronize to the document's frame rate is deselected, that Quick Compress is also deselected, and select High quality keyframes (if you chose Bandwidth).

Deselect the Synchronize check box so the video does not synchronize to the Flash document's frame rate because this means you will avoid having Flash "drop" frames in the video playback. This means some frames might be skipped when the SWF file plays. If you choose to synchronize the video to the Flash Timeline, the video might drop frames to keep up with what else is going on in the SWF file. Because you don't want this to happen, you can choose to have the video run independently of the SWF frame rate.

Quick compress speeds up the compression time, but it might result in a poor video compression job. Because you don't want to gamble with the quality, make sure that this option is deselected. You can also make sure that the keyframes are created at high quality. You can check this option, but just be aware the file size will increase as a result because each keyframe is rendered at a consistently high quality. If you chose to specify a quality for each keyframe (the Quality radio button) then this option is greyed-out.

5) Click the Next button; a new window opens, in which you can set up an Encoding profile. Type in *TechBookstore* as a name for a new profile and then click Next.

You should save these settings for encoding more videos in Flash so you can use the profile later on. You will use these same settings to import other videos later on in the lesson. After entering `TechBookstore`, and optionally typing in a description, click the Next button.

6) In the following window, choose Create new profile from the Advanced Settings drop-down menu.

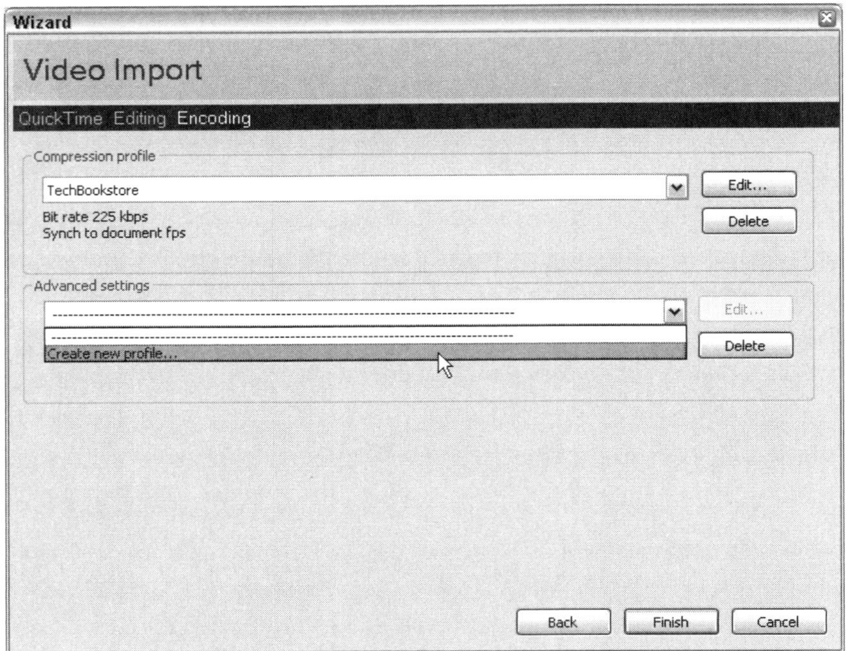

A window for changing advanced encoding settings opens. This window allows you to change the hue, saturation, gamma, brightness, and contrast of the video. It also allows you to scale or crop the dimensions of the video. You do not need to alter any of these settings, although it is useful to try making some changes to them and then see how they will affect video files in general.

7) In the Encoding (Advanced settings) window, try changing the Color properties. This window has several controls for color correction and manipulation. Explore the settings, and change them as you wish, or leave them alone. Sometimes they can achieve some interesting effects, or even make your footage look a little better. You can always restore the default settings you see when opening the window by clicking the Reset button.

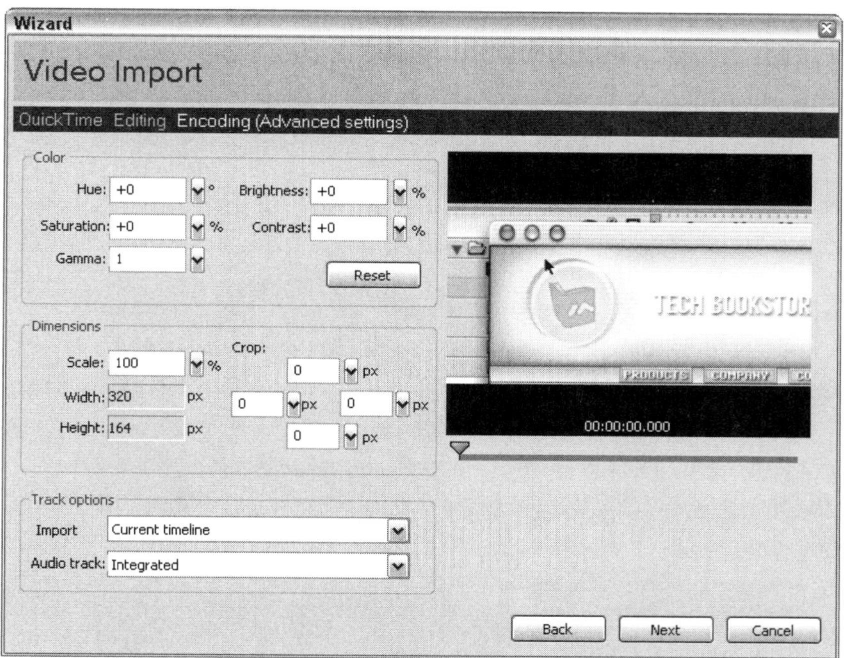

Hue: Changes the color value of the footage. You can add colorful effects or correction using this value slider, which ranges between -180 degrees and 180 degrees.

Saturation: Saturation changes the amount of grey in the video, compared to the amount of color. You can remove or add color (or *hue*) to the video. Desaturate the video by dragging the value slider downwards, which removes all the color and leaves you with video made of varying shades of grey.

Gamma: This setting controls the general lightness of each frame of video in your footage. You can change the values between -0.1 and 1.8. Using gamma can be useful if you want to correct gamma for computer systems (such as Windows machines) that typically do not have built-in gamma correction like Macs do.

Brightness: This setting changes the brightness of a video's color by adding more black or white to the footage. You can have a video that is very light or very dark and ominous by changing this value.

Contrast: This slider changes the amount of contrast between the dark and light values in the video frames. Less contrast is created by dragging the slider downwards, and means you end up with a lovely solid grey video. Higher contrast changes the footage so there is a lot of contrast between the dark and light parts of each frame.

You can scale and crop the video in the Dimensions area. You can scale the video smaller than its original size. You can also crop the top, bottom, left, and right sides by a given number of pixels. When you change these values, a helpful outline appears on the video preview that shows you how the video will be cropped.

You can edit the Track options on this window by choosing to import to the current Timeline, a movie clip, or a graphic symbol. The default value of Current Timeline is fine for now. A video's audio track can be controlled from this window, too. In this case, there is no audio track on the video. If there were, you could choose to import it as Integrated with the video or separate from it. If you choose Integrated, the audio imports as part of the video.

8) Click Next and if you have made any changes to these settings, enter a new name into the Name field. Click Next to return to the Encoding window. Click Finish, and the video imports.

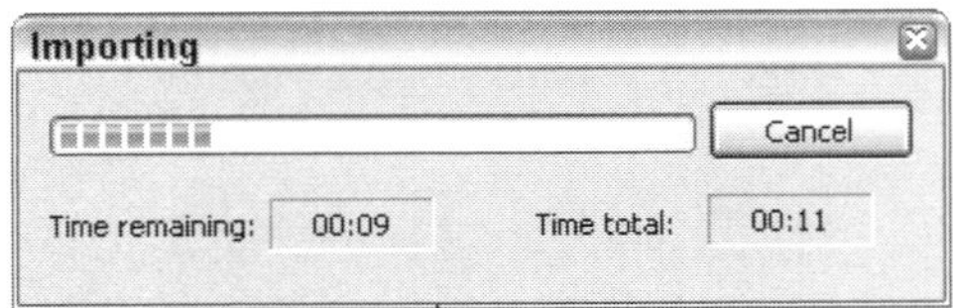

After you click Finish, the video imports using the settings you have made in the earlier steps. When the dialog box disappears, you can open the Library and find the video file. You will notice that it is called *embedded video*.

9) Save the changes you made to `video.fla`**.**

In the following exercise, you will import two more video files into Flash using the settings you made in this exercise and export them all into FLV video format.

EXPORTING FLV VIDEO

As has been already established in this lesson, FLV is a Flash Video file. FLV files can contain video and encoded audio (if the footage has it, ours don't), which can then be imported and exported from Flash. When an FLV file is imported into a Flash document or loaded into a SWF file, no compression takes place. FLV files are economical on file size and can also be dynamically loaded into Flash or streamed from a SWF file. You might remember how dynamic images were loaded into Flash: Loading an FLV file is a similar process, in that you are loading content after a user requests it. It requires very different ActionScript to do so, which you will learn how to do in the following lesson.

In the next lesson, you will create a tour presentation for the Tech Bookstore. These videos will be dynamically loaded into the presentation when it runs. This means that FLV video is required so you can load the video into the SWF file. Because you will need a few different videos to create the presentation, you need to import two more videos into the FLA file and then export them all as FLV.

1) Copy `video2.mov` (or `video2.avi`) and `video3.mov` (or `video3.avi`) from the `media` folder on the CD-ROM onto your hard drive.

Choose the video type that is supported by your computer system, just as you did in the earlier exercise. Copy it from the CD-ROM to any location on your hard drive.

2) Choose File > Import > Import to Library and then choose `video2.mov` (or `video2.avi`) from the hard drive. Click Open (or Import to Library on the Mac).

The wizard dialog box of the Video Import Wizard appears after you click Open.

3) Choose the option to Embed video in Macromedia Flash document and click the Next button. Then choose to import the entire video and click the Next button again.

Just like the previous video, you need to embed the video in your document. You can import the entire video this time because it has already been edited for you, so you don't need to create any new clips. After clicking the second Next button, you bypass the Editing section and are taken immediately to the Encoding section.

4) Choose the `TechBookstore` profile from the Compression profile drop-down menu. Then choose the Advanced settings profile if you made one earlier on.

The TechBookstore profile applies all of the same settings you made for the video you already imported to this document. If you made some color correction changes in the Advanced settings area, you can apply them to the new videos as well by choosing the setting from the second drop-down menu. Click the Finish button when you have made your selections, and the video imports.

5) Repeat Steps 2 to 4 for `video3.mov` or (`video3.avi`).

Apply the same settings to the final video. This is the third video that will be embedded into the document.

6) After the video has imported, open the Library and export all three videos to FLV format using the Embedded Video Properties dialog box.

Each video is placed directly in the Library.

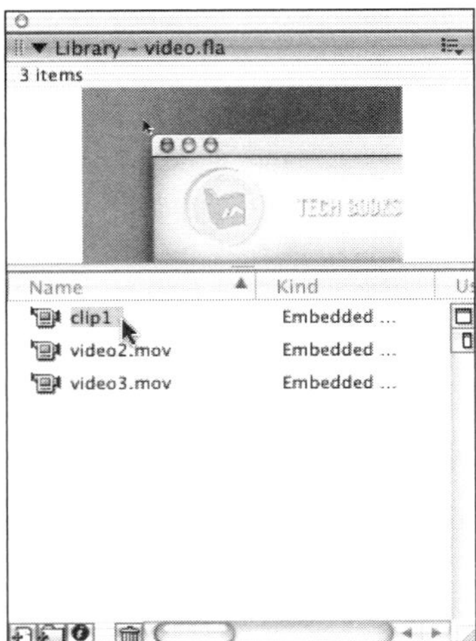

Right-click (or control-click on the Mac) `clip1` in the Library and choose Properties from the contextual menu, which allows you to export the embedded document as an FLV file. Click the Export button, and a new dialog box opens in which you can provide a filename, location and export setting.

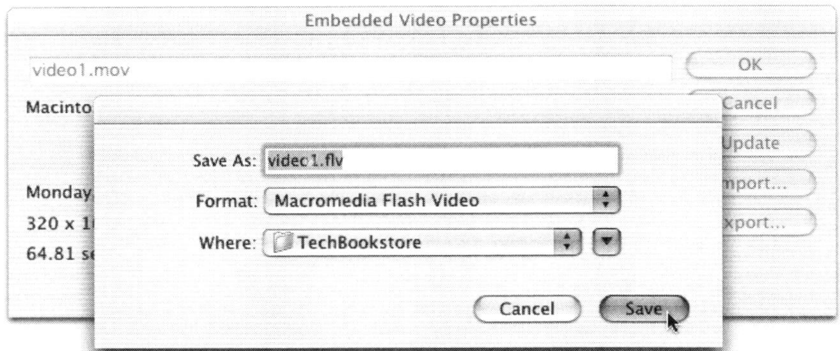

Choose to save the file as an FLV file in the Save as type (or Format on the Mac) drop-down menu. Browse to the `TechBookstore` folder on your hard drive, and type in *video1.flv* for the filename. Repeat these steps for the other two videos. Name them *video2.flv* and *video3.flv*, and also save each of these video files in the TechBookstore folder on your hard drive.

7) Save all the changes you made in the file.

The FLA file is saved in the `TechBookstore` folder, along with your three new FLV files. You will open this file and use it again in the following lesson, and you will dynamically load the FLV files into a SWF that you publish. You will be able to choose whether you want to use the Media components with Flash MX Professional, or use some ActionScript to dynamically load the videos into a SWF file at runtime.

WHAT YOU HAVE LEARNED

In this lesson, you have:

- Learned about using media assets on the Web (pages 202–203)
- Added sound to three buttons (pages 203–206)
- Found out how to import sound files (pages 207–209)
- Added sound to the Timeline (pages 210–211)
- Customized the sound in Flash (pages 210–211)
- Edited a video before it was imported (pages 212–219)
- Learned more about compression settings in Flash (pages 220–226)
- Exported video as FLV files (pages 226–229)

using screens

LESSON 8

Screens are a new way of creating and organizing Flash documents using Flash MX Professional 2004. They allow you to create SWF files quickly and efficiently without necessarily using the Timeline. Screens can make building multi-page documents easier than when you create a file using a regular Flash document. You can add your content to the hierarchical screens, which are organized to the left of the Stage in what's called the *Screen Outline pane*. Each screen is intended to be like a page, layer or section of your document or your form; and either built-in functionality, behaviors, or ActionScript can be used for navigation after the file is published. In this lesson, you will be creating a tour for the Tech Bookstore, so screens will be used to add several pages (or sections) to that tour.

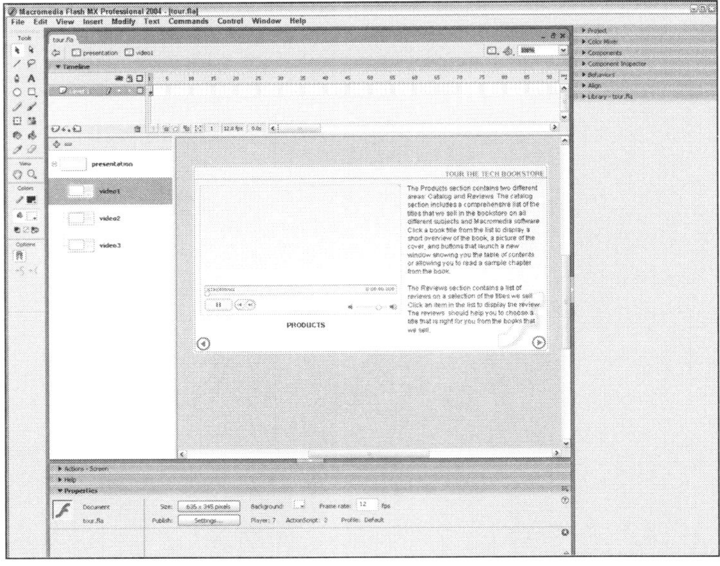

Building a presentation using screens

As you might have noticed by now, Flash MX 2004 does not include screens. For this reason, you will need to manually create each "page" of the tour using layers and frames on the Timeline if you are not using the Professional edition of Flash. You can create the same effect in the SWF file when you are finished, although you have to manually add the pages using keyframes and use ActionScript for the navigation. This lesson includes exercises where you create a tour using either screens, or a regular Flash document instead. The tour will include text, sound, and the FLV videos you exported in Lesson 7. At the end of this lesson you will load the tour you create into the main Tech Bookstore SWF file.

WHAT YOU WILL LEARN

In this lesson, you will:

- Learn about screens in Flash
- Create a new slide presentation
- Add media, components, and content to the presentation
- Control FLA files using the `MediaPlayback` component
- Load sound into the presentation
- Control sound on a Timeline using ActionScript
- Add transitions between screens
- Create the tour in Flash MX 2004
- Dynamically load FLVs using ActionScript
- Load the tour into the Tech Bookstore

APPROXIMATE TIME

This lesson takes approximately one hour to complete.

LESSON FILES

Media Files:

media/video1.flv
media/video2.flv
media/video3.flv

Starting Files:

Lesson08/sound.fla
Lesson08/soundButtons.fla

Completed Project:

Lesson08/tour_fmxpro.fla
Lesson08/tour_fmx.fla

INTRODUCING SCREENS IN FLASH

Flash MX Professional introduces a new way of organizing Flash documents with or without using a Timeline. Screens provide a brand new interface for authoring FLA files, targeted at building either presentations or applications. Screens have an interesting and very intuitive architecture that is used for authoring documents. Screens actually help you understand the way things work in Flash by nesting movie clips in a tree-like format. Screens are very useful for creating presentations or applications because they are organized in this intuitive and visual structure. The drawback is that screens-based files add some file size on top of the compiled ActionScript and the document in order to make the screens' structure work.

Each screen is a movie clip that is arranged in a hierarchical fashion by way of nesting. You can add new screens that are nested within a main container screen (called the *presentation* or *application* screen) and then nest more screens within the new screens that you added. Adding screens and nesting them allows you to create an application that is very complex without introducing new layers or frames on the Timeline. In fact, the Timeline is not open by default in a screens-based file. However, you will sometimes need to use the Timeline to achieve particular effects or add additional ActionScript to the application or presentation you create.

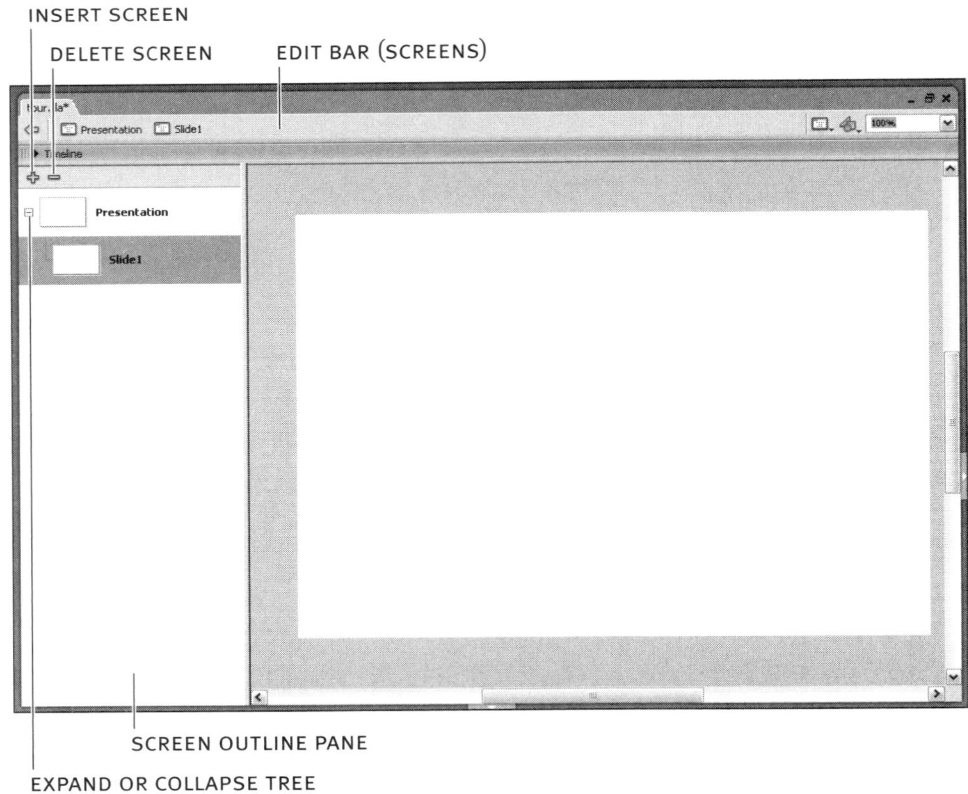

A screen that is nested inside another screen is a *child* screen, and the screen that it's nested within is the *parent* screen. Parent screens are known as *ancestors*, and all nested screens are known as *descendents*. The child screens contain all the information and content of its ancestors.

If you are using Flash MX 2004, you cannot open or create an FLA file using screens like the tour that is created in this lesson. You will instead find a non-screens equivalent to the tour created later on in this lesson. The screens presentation contains some functionality that, to create manually, would be beyond the scope of the book. However, those of you using Flash MX 2004 can skip ahead in this lesson to the special tutorial and starter file called "Creating the Tour in Flash MX 2004," and then proceed with the lesson from that point on. Those of you using Flash MX Professional can skip that particular exercise, and jump ahead to the final exercise called "Loading the Tour into the Bookstore," which is applicable for both versions of Flash.

NOTE *A SWF file made using screens must be saved for the Flash Player 7, and using ActionScript 2. These settings can be made using the Property inspector or the Publish Settings dialog box. Slide-based SWF files cannot be viewed in any earlier Flash Player versions.*

STARTING A NEW SCREEN PRESENTATION

If you are working with Flash MX Professional, you will create a new Slide Presentation document and begin building a presentation for the *tour* page of the Tech Bookstore Web site. Media elements and components are incorporated into the presentation, which use the MediaPlayback component to present the FLV files you exported in Lesson 7. The nice thing about using a slide presentation is that a visitor will be able to navigate between each of the screens using the left and right arrow keys. This is a built-in functionality of a slide presentation FLA file, so you don't have to write code to add key press actions into the FLA file. If you create a Form Application, you have to add the navigation manually using behaviors or ActionScript.

NOTE *If you are using Flash MX 2004, skip ahead to the section called "Creating a Tour in Flash MX 2004." Screens-based documents cannot even be opened without Flash MX Professional.*

1) Create a new Flash Slide Presentation. Change the document's dimensions to *635* px by *345* px. Save the document as `tour.fla` in the `TechBookstore` folder on your hard drive.

To create a new Slide Presentation, choose File > New from the main menu and then choose Flash Slide Presentation from the Type list. A new slide-based document opens, with a Screen Outline pane down the left side of the workspace, and the Timeline is closed. You can add new screens to the Screen Outline pane or remove screens from it. You can view all the slides in your new presentation in this area and select a screen to work on by clicking the screen's thumbnail in this pane.

TIP *You can use the plus (+) and minus (–) icons that are next to the screen names to expand and collapse the tree of screens. You can see these icons in the previous figure. If you are working with a lot of screens, this functionality can be quite useful for viewing the structure of your document. Note that the plus and minus icons above the screen names are for adding or deleting screens instead!*

Click anywhere around the Stage (or press Ctrl/Command+J) and then click the Size button in the Property inspector. Change the width to *635* pixels and the height to *345* pixels. Click OK when you are finished, and save the document as `tour.fla` by choosing File > Save from the main menu.

2) In `tour.fla`, create two new screens using the Insert Screen button.

The screen you see at the very top of the Screen Outline pane called `presentation` is known as the *master* (or *top-level*) screen. The graphics, instances, and other elements that you add to the master screen appear on all the other child screens by default. You will add controls (buttons) to the master screen and then add different videos on three child screens. That means that the controls can be used on all of the children slides.

TIP *There is a very useful contextual menu associated with screens that allows you to insert new screens that are nested or of a given type. It also allows you to copy, cut and paste, delete, or hide screens. To access the contextual menu you can right-click (or control-click on the Mac) the Screen Outline pane.*

To add two new screens, click the Insert Screen button at the top of the Screen Outline pane two times. When you are finished, there will be one `presentation` screen and three child screens nested below it.

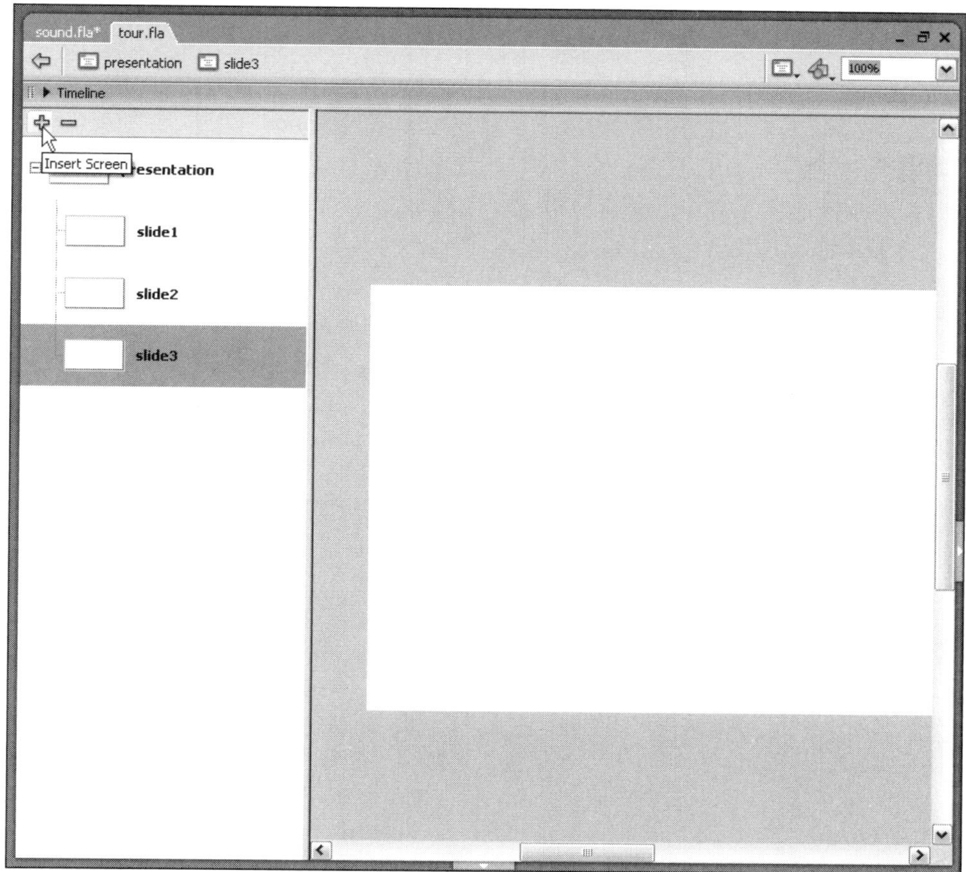

TIP *To remove a screen from the FLA file, all you need to do is select the screen and press the Delete Screen button. The screen is automatically deleted from the Screen Outline pane.*

3) Rename the three child screens to `video1`**,** `video2`**, and** `video3`**.**

It's a good idea to give your screens a name describing what is on that particular screen. The tour will display three videos, which are the FLVs you exported in Lesson 7. Double-click `slide1`, and rename it to `video1`. Then rename the other two screens in the same fashion: `slide2` to `video2` and `slide3` to `video3`.

When you are naming a screen, remember that this name is also used as the instance name when any ActionScript is generated for the slide. If you have any spaces in the screen's name, they are changed to underscores in the code that's generated for the screen. Therefore, you should avoid using numbers at the beginning of the screen name and any special characters (special characters are any characters other than letters, numbers, or underscores). You should also avoid any words or names used in

ActionScript code as a screen name too, because that can cause conflicts in the SWF's code. If you are unsure, do a quick search of Flash documentation using the Help panel to see if there is an entry in the ActionScript Dictionary for that word.

TIP *If you decide to rename the screen after you have added ActionScript, you will need to find the ActionScript and manually update the screen's name in the Actions panel. Therefore, you should try to choose screen names that you will stick with throughout the authoring process.*

4) Add some graphics and text to the `presentation` screen.

You can create graphics and text that might be similar to those seen in the following figure. You can add a rectangle, lines, and text to create a background that is visible on each child screen (the ones that display the FLV video).

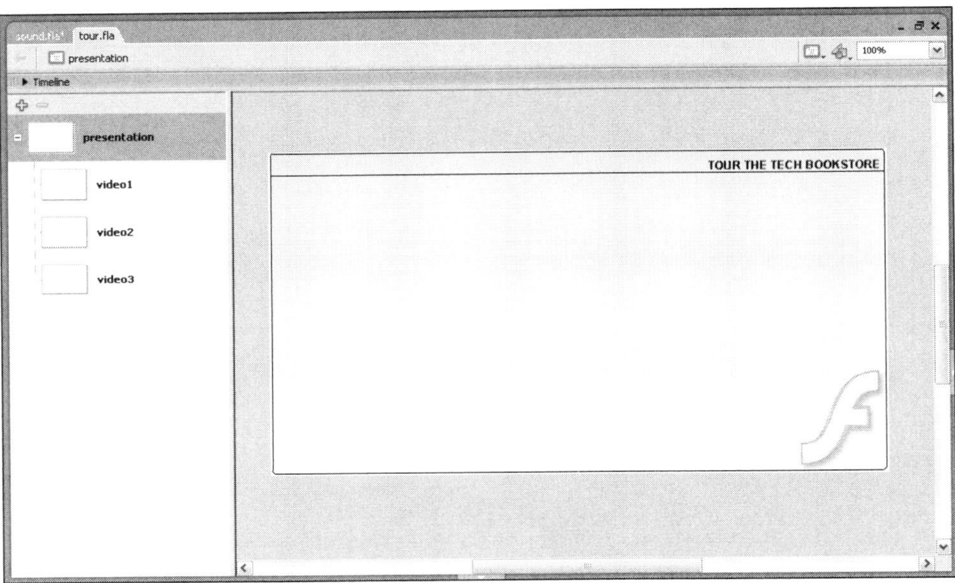

Add a title to the `presentation` screen. As seen in the previous figure, the title in this particular presentation is placed at the upper-right side of the screen. Because you will add MediaPlayback component instances to each child screen, make sure that you keep any text or graphic additions near the edges of the screen. The main area in the center is needed to display the video. You can always return to this screen later on and move the graphics around a bit if they don't fit around the video and text properly.

TIP *If you want to use any of the artwork used in the previous figure, you can open the completed* `tour_fmxpro.fla` *found in the* `Lesson08` *folder on the CD-ROM. Copy and paste the graphics from that file into your own.*

6) Save the changes you have made to the document by choosing File > Save from the main menu.

In the following exercise, you will add the components to the tour you are creating. The components will be used to play and control the FLV files that you exported in Lesson 7.

ADDING SOUND AND VIDEO TO THE PRESENTATION

Now that you have created the screens, you need to add some content to them. The content will primarily include video, although a downloaded MP3 is going to play in the background.

The master screen (named `presentation`) will show or play in the background, and the child screens layer on top of it. As you learned in the previous exercise, the `presentation` screen is a good place to put any graphics or assets that you want to be seen or heard on every page of the tour. Therefore, you will copy some sounds and a movie clip into the tour that will be used and control the sound on the `presentation` screen, so it's available throughout the tour. Then you will prepare the video to be loaded into each page in this exercise.

You are still working with `tour.fla` for this exercise.

1) Select the `video1` **screen and drag an instance of the *MediaPlayback* component onto the Stage. Open the Property inspector, change the instance's size to *360* W by *255* H, and position the instance on the left side of the Stage.**

You have to change the dimensions of the component in order for the video to play at its original size. Changing the instance's dimensions to 360 by 255 means the video will not be resized by the component. If the component is too small, the video shrinks to fit within the component without distorting the video. If the component is larger than the FLV video, and Use Preferred Media Size is selected in the Component Inspector panel (discussed in the next step), it displays at its original size.

When you have finished resizing the instance, align it on the Stage similar to the following figure.

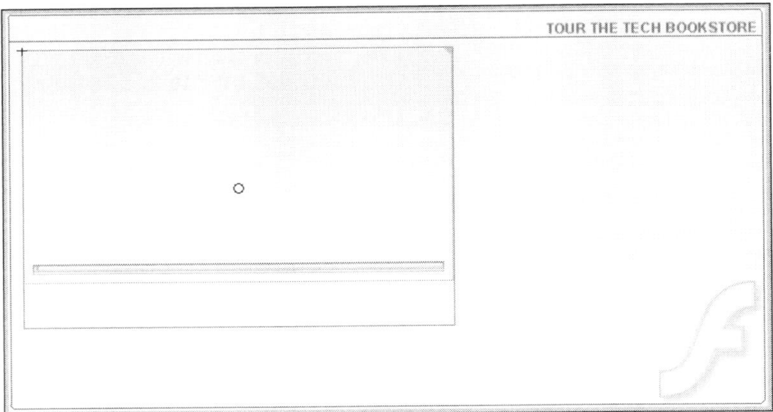

TIP *If you don't want to use any of the Streaming Media components for the presentation, you could always use some ActionScript to stream in an external FLV file. The code and steps are contained later on in this lesson, in the section called "Creating the Tour in Flash MX 2004" and can just as easily be built in a regular FLA file created with Professional.*

2) Select the MediaPlayback instance and change its parameters using the Component Inspector panel. Make sure that the Control Visibility is set to *On* and that the Use Preferred Media Size check box is selected. Type the name of the video file into the URL field. Change the duration to the length of each video file, making sure that Milliseconds is *not* selected. Finally, change the FPS to *15*.

When you set Control Visibility to On, it means that the controller area (including the play and pause buttons and the volume toggle) will always appear onscreen. As discussed in the previous step, Use Preferred Media Size means the video will always appear at its original size or smaller. The video appears smaller only if the component is not large enough for its dimensions. If you want your video to fill the entire area of the component instead of retaining the original size or smaller, deselect Use Preferred Media Size and Respect Aspect Ratio.

Type *video1.flv* into the URL field to target the FLV file you want to load. This means that the FLV needs to be placed into the same folder as the `tour.fla` and the Tech Bookstore SWF when you load the files in. If you are dealing with very short videos measured in milliseconds, you can select that option. However, you do not need the precision that the option offers for the short `video1`.

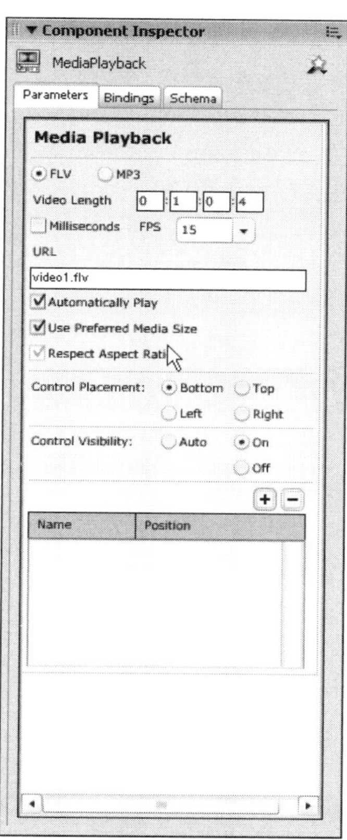

Because you edited video1.flv yourself in Lesson 7, you need to find out how long it is and enter that value as the video's length. Perhaps the quickest way to find out the length is to publish the FLA you're working on to play the video in the MediaPlayback component. When the video finishes playing, note the length of the video by watching the minutes and seconds display at the lower-right corner of the video.

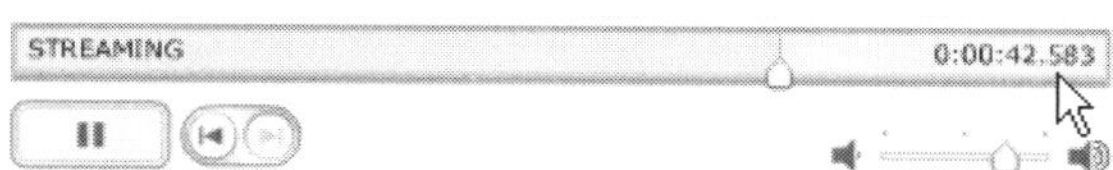

Return to the authoring environment and select the MediaPlayback instance again. Select the FPS drop-down menu in the Component Inspector panel and select 15. This means the video will play 15 video frames per second, regardless of what your FLA file frame rate is set at.

3) Copy the MediaPlayback instance on frame 1 and paste the instance in place in the `video2` **and** `video3` **screens. Change the target video files in the two new component instances to** `video2.flv` **and** `video3.flv`**.**

When the instance is copied (Edit > Copy) and pasted into place (Edit > Paste in Place) onto two other screens, the instance maintains the same size and placement as the others. When the visitor navigates to the next "page" in the tour, the video does not appear to shift in its placement. Remember to use Ctrl+Shift+V (or Command+Shift+V on the Mac) to paste the instance in place on each subsequent screen. Not only is the size and position maintained, but also the other parameters that you set.

Remember to enter `video2.flv` into the URL field in the Component Inspector panel on the `video2` screen, and `video3.flv` for the `video3` screen. Remember that these files should all be in the `TechBookstore` folder from when you exported them in Lesson 7. They are also available in the `Lesson08` folder for your convenience.

4) Enter the duration for `video2` and then enter the duration for `video3`.

Because these two videos were created for you in advance, just enter 23:00 for the Video Length parameter for `video2.flv`, and 40:00 for the length of `video3.flv`. To enter the video length, select the component instance on each screen and expand the Component Inspector panel. Enter each value into the Video Length parameter, while ensuring that the Milliseconds check box is *not* selected.

Entering a video length for each FLV file means that the playhead will move along with the video when it is playing in the SWF file.

5) Add a title on each child screen displaying video content. Optionally add descriptive text about the video that plays or copy it from the complete version of the FLA file.

Each child screen contains a component instance and plays a video when it is tested in the Flash Player. Each of these three pages loads and displays a video about one of the areas of the Tech Bookstore site. Therefore, it's a good idea to describe each different area to accompany the video and add a title underneath the tour's title. Both of these additions are seen in the following figure.

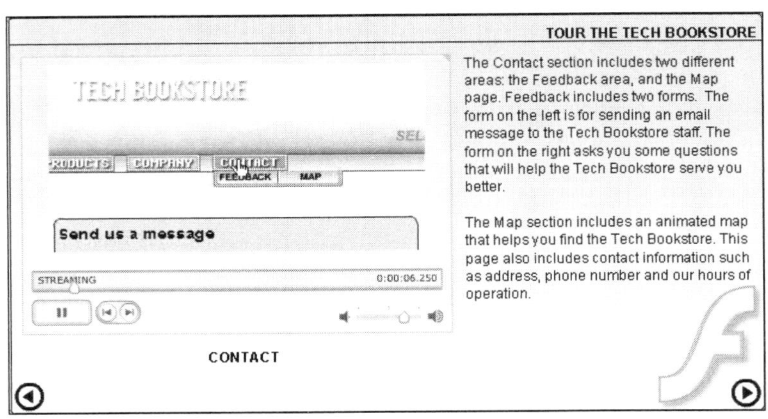

In the presentation for this video, we have written a short description of how to use each different area of the Tech Bookstore site. You can open the completed version of the tour (`tour_fmxpro.fla` from the `Lesson08` folder on the CD-ROM), or you can write your own description. Add these descriptions using static text fields next to the component instances or rearrange the layout to however you think it looks best. You will probably want to choose the Alias text option for the text field as well, which is usually a lot clearer and easier for visitors to read.

TIP *It looks the most visually appealing if you have the text fields on each child screen in the same position. To do this, create your text field on the* `video1` *screen. When you are finished, copy and paste this text field "in place" on the* `video2` *and* `video3` *screens just like you did with each* MediaPlayback *instance using Edit > Paste in Place. Double-click the* `video2` *and* `video3` *instances and type in new text content into each field. Then the top of each field lines up with each other.*

6) Save the changes you have made to `tour.fla`.

In the following section, you will add some ActionScript that is used to control the sound you have already added to the FLA file.

CONTROLLING THE SOUND

It is very easy to control the sound you added to the FLA file. You will download an MP3 sound file (the one you worked with in the previous lesson) into the SWF file at runtime. Then you can control the sound using very simple ActionScript that controls the sound that is downloaded and playing in the SWF file. This is a simple way to work with sound in a Flash SWF file. All of this functionality and ActionScript can be added to Flash MX 2004 FLA documents as well. You should still be using `tour.fla` for this example.

1) Make sure that sound.mp3 is within the `TechBookstore` folder.

You will load the MP3 file into the SWF file at runtime dynamically. That means that it must be targeted in a particular location. Therefore, you should consider keeping the MP3 in the same `TechBookstore` so it is easy to target.

2) Open the FLA file called `soundButtons.fla` from the CD-ROM and drag the movie clip you find in this FLA file into the `tour.fla` Library.

You can find `soundButtons.fla` in the `Lesson08` folder on the CD-ROM. Copy it over to your hard drive, save it in any location, and then open the FLA in Flash.

This file contains a couple of buttons and graphics you can use for the tour, all contained within a movie clip in the file. You could easily create the movie clip contained in this file using the skills you have already learned in earlier lessons. All that the movie clip contains are some simple graphics, a static text field, and two buttons: one for play and one for stop. The play button has the instance name `play_btn`, and the stop button has the instance name `stop_btn`.

3) In `tour.fla`, rename Layer 1 to `background`, and drag the movie clip you just placed in the Library onto the `background` layer. Give the movie clip an instance name of `soundBtns_mc` in the Property inspector.

You will have to expand the Timeline to rename a layer. At this point you should rename `Layer 1` to *background*.

Drag the movie clip onto the `background` layer of the `presentation` screen and position it near the upper-left corner of the screen. It needs to be present for the duration of the tour in order to contain the background music.

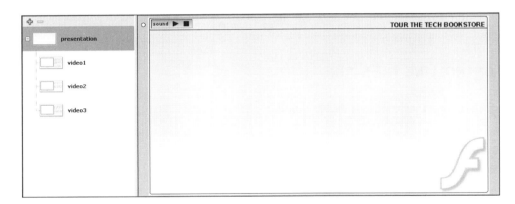

Add an instance name for the movie clip that you dragged onto the `presentation` screen. Select the movie clip instance and type *`soundBtns_mc`* into the `<Instance Name>` field in the Property inspector.

Double-click the movie clip and make sure that the play and stop buttons inside have instance names of `play_btn` and `stop_btn`, respectively. When you are finished, return to the `presentation` screen by clicking `presentation` in the edit bar.

4) Add ActionScript to the presentation's Timeline in order to control the sound.

Expand the Timeline for the `presentation` screen. Insert a new layer above the `background` layer you created in step 3. Rename the new layer *actions*. Then open or expand the `actions` layer, and add the following lines of ActionScript into the Script pane:

```
mySound_sound = new Sound();
mySound_sound.loadSound("sound.mp3", false);
mySound_sound.onLoad = function(){
  this.start(0,9999);
};
```

These several lines of ActionScript create a new instance of the Sound class in the SWF. Then you load a new event sound into the SWF called `sound.mp3`. If you want to load a streaming sound, then you would put "true" instead of the "false" that is there (which tells Flash to load the sound as an event sound). You want to load an event sound because a streaming sound would download over and over again, which is not great when your sound is looping. This way, the sound is loaded one time and does not consume as much bandwidth.

Finally, you can set what happens after the sound loads into the SWF file. You start it playing, and then tell Flash to begin playing the sound at 0 seconds, and loop 9999 times.

When you are finished, write these next lines of ActionScript following the previous ones in the Actions panel. This code will create button functions to control this sound you just loaded.

```
soundBtns_mc.play_btn.onRelease = function() {
  stopAllSounds();
  mySound_sound.start(mySound_sound.position/1000, 9999);
}
soundBtns_mc.stop_btn.onRelease = function(){
  mySound_sound.stop();
};
```

In this example, you are controlling the sound file that you loaded into the SWF file in the previous step. `mySound_sound.start(mySound_sound.position/1000, 9999)` is used to pause the sound you load into the SWF, and resume the sound playing after it's clicked. It captures the position of the sound when it stops, and then starts it up at that given position and again loops the sound 9999 times. `stopAllSounds` does just as it says: stops all of the sounds in the SWF. If you don't use this, then the event sound you load into the SWF file will begin to play over top of itself.

5) Test the SWF file by choosing Control > Test Movie from the main menu. Save the changes you made to the FLA file.

If the sound file works, save the FLA file. Publish the SWF by choosing File > Publish from the main menu, and move on to the next exercise. You will continue to work with the tour file, and add some buttons used to navigate between the screens.

SCREENS AND NAVIGATION

Slide presentations contain navigation that is automatically built into the document's architecture. Visitors can use their left and right arrow keys to navigate to next or previous screens. However, key press navigation might not be intuitive to the user, even if you add some text notifying the user that he or she can use the arrow keys to navigate the presentation. Another option would be to additionally add buttons and use behaviors to add navigation between each screen.

1) In `tour.fla`, open the buttons common library from Window > Other Panels > Common Libraries > Buttons.

You can either use pre-made buttons from the common Library or you can create your own buttons. These buttons will be used to navigate to previous and next screens. Therefore, the buttons should be recognizable to the visitor that they are used to navigate between pages, such as left and right arrows, to denote going to the next or previous page.

Open the `Circle Buttons` folder in the Buttons common library, which contains the buttons you can use for navigation between each screen.

2) Drag the `circle button - next` button and the `circle button - previous` button from the `Circle Buttons` folder onto the `presentation` screen.

Because these two buttons add navigation to the entire tour, you can place them on the `presentation` screen. The ActionScript you will add using a behavior tells the SWF file to jump either to the next or to the previous screen. Therefore, these buttons will work no matter what the current screen is.

Place the `circle button - previous` button in the lower-left corner of the Stage, and the `circle button - next` in the lower-right corner of the Stage. When you are finished, the `presentation` screen looks similar to the following figure.

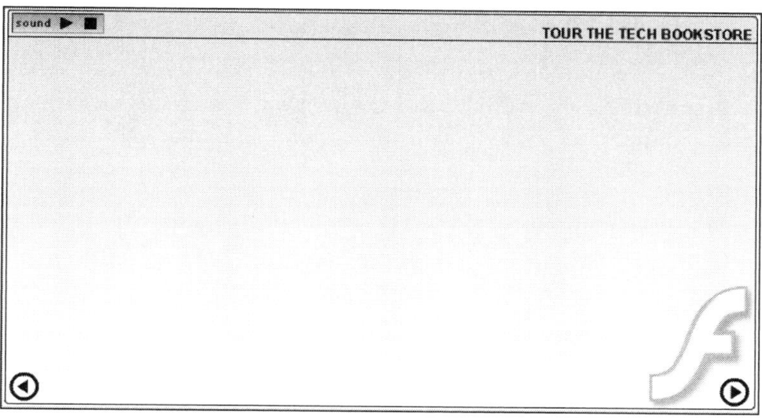

TIP *You can also make your own custom buttons for the tour if you want to have a more customized appearance.*

3) Add the Go to Next Slide and Go to Previous Slide behaviors to the two navigation buttons to enable navigation between screens.

These behaviors will work on each child screen you have within the presentation, no matter what screen the tour is presently at. Expand the Behaviors panel and select the button at the lower-left corner of the `presentation` screen. Click the Add Behavior button in the Behaviors panel and choose Screen > Go to Previous Slide from the drop-down menu.

The behavior is added to the button and is displayed in the Behaviors panel. The default event is `On Release`, which means the event executes after the button is clicked. The behavior adds ActionScript, causing the tour to navigate to the previous slide in the Screen Outline pane when the button is clicked.

Select the `Next` button at the lower-right side of the presentation screen and click the Add Behavior button in the Behaviors panel. Choose Screen > Go to Next Slide from the menu. This adds ActionScript that causes the tour to navigate to the next slide in the Screen Outline pane when the button is clicked.

4) Save the changes you have made to `tour.fla`.

When you are finished, test the Tour in the testing environment or a browser. When you are happy with the results, you can save the file and move on to the next exercise.

ADDING TRANSITIONS AND A MASK

You have created three screens in the presentation that can navigate between each child screen when it is tested or published. However, the presentation currently doesn't do much more than flip through each page without an animation, or *transition*, between each page. A transition is some kind of animation or effect that occurs when a visitor is taken to a new page on a site, or a new part of the presentation. Sometimes a new page slides or fades into view, or sometimes the current page moves off the Stage in an interesting way. Flash contains behaviors that allow you to add many different kinds of transitions without having to write any ActionScript. The transitions are added from the Behaviors panel, and there is even a useful dialog box that shows you thumbnail preview animations of what each transition will look like. You can choose the duration, effect, direction, start location, and easing to customize each transition type.

You are still working with `tour.fla` in this example.

1) Select the `presentation` screen and add a transition behavior to it using the Behaviors panel. Change the event in the Behaviors panel from reveal to revealChild so the transition is applied to the child screens.

Select the `presentation` screen and expand or open the Behaviors panel. From the Add Behavior button, select Screen > Transition, and the Transitions dialog box opens.

In the Transitions dialog box, select Fly from the list on the left side of the dialog box. You can customize that transition with the controls on the right of the dialog box. Leave the default direction In selected and the default duration of 2. Then choose Back In and Out from the Easing drop-down, and a Start Location of Right Center.

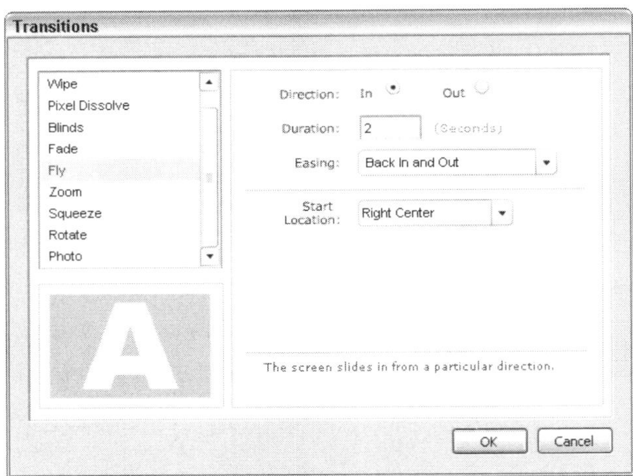

The thumbnail in this panel shows you a preview of what the transition will look like when you publish the FLA file. If you want to change the settings, change the values, and this thumbnail updates to reflect the changes you make.

When you apply the transition to the `presentation` screen, it adds the transition to all of the child screens as well. This means that you do not need to individually add the transition to each screen and only have to apply it to the master screen (`presentation`) instead. However, you will have to modify the ActionScript that was added to make this transition. Open the Behaviors panel, change the drop-down menu under Event from reveal to revealChild.

2) Test the tour and view the transitions you have added to it. Modify the transitions using the Behaviors panel and the Transitions dialog box if you are not happy with the style of transition that has been added.

You may or may not like the transition that was chosen after you test the SWF file and see what it actually looks like with your content, which might leave a very different impression from the thumbnail preview in the Transitions dialog box. If you don't like the effect, expand the Behaviors panel and click one of the screens. You will see one behavior added to the Behaviors panel. If you double-click Transition under the Action column, the Transitions dialog box opens. Make the necessary modifications and click OK when you are finished.

3) Select the `presentation` **screen, and open the Timeline. Insert a new layer above the** `background` **layer. Change the new layer into a mask layer that will cover the entire** `presentation` **screen so the transition is not visible beyond the bounds of the Stage after it's loaded into the Tech Bookstore.**

When you tested the tour, you saw transitions fly into the screen from outside the SWF file. You need to add a mask so the transition is not visible beyond the bounds of the `tour.swf` when it is playing in the Flash Player or loaded into the Tech Bookstore. If you do not add a mask, the content on each screen will be seen "flying" into the `tour.swf` over top of part of the Tech Bookstore SWF. Obviously, this doesn't look very professional.

To add a mask you will have to open the Timeline above the Stage. Expand the Timeline and add a new layer above the `background` and below the `actions` layer. Rename this layer *mask* and right-click (or control-click on the Mac) and choose Mask from the contextual menu. Make sure that the `background` layer indents underneath the `mask` layer, which means the mask will be applied to the contents of the layer.

Select the `mask` layer and then choose the Rectangle tool from the Tools panel. Click and drag the tool to create a new rectangle covering the entire dimensions of the Stage. You will probably have to unlock the layer beforehand.

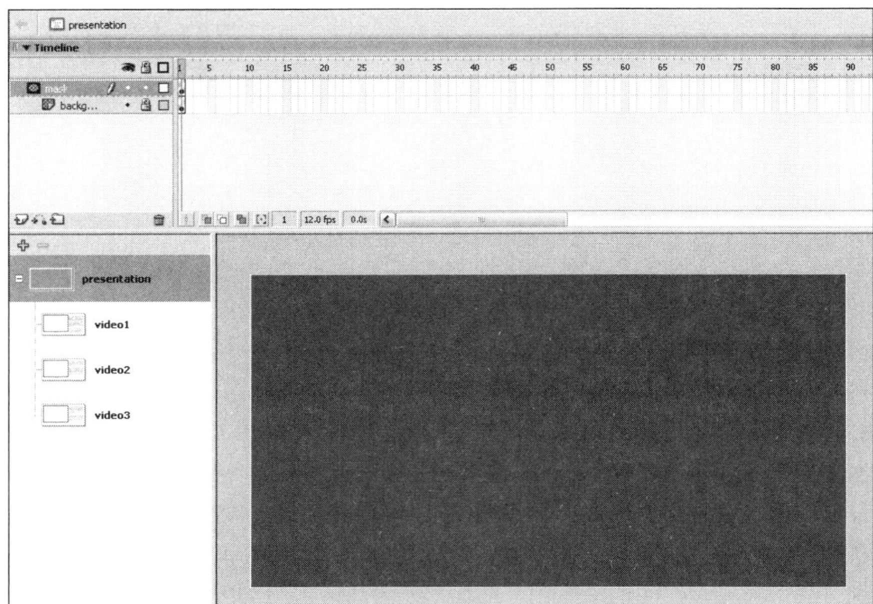

When you finish creating the mask, make sure that the `mask` layer is locked again and hidden by clicking the dot under the eye icon on the Timeline. You can also lock the `background` layer as well.

4) Test the tour in a browser (F12) to see whether the masking works properly. When it works as expected save the changes you have made to `tour.fla`.

Press the F12 key to test the tour. If you notice that the mask doesn't look quite right, return to the `mask` layer in the `presentation` screen, unlock it, and modify it. Save the changes you made to the file when you are happy with the tour.

5) Publish the file by choosing File > Publish from the main menu.

Publish the tour to the `TechBookstore` folder. When you are finished, you will have a `tour.swf` file that will be used to load into the Tech Bookstore Web site in the final exercise in this lesson.

In the following section, you will learn how to create the tour if you are working with Flash MX 2004. If you are working with Flash MX Professional, skip ahead to the section called "Loading the Tour into the Bookstore". However, if you are interested in learning how to work with dynamically loading FLV files without using a component, you might want to follow along and try out the process, too.

CREATING THE TOUR IN FLASH MX 2004

If you do not have Flash MX Professional, you cannot use screens to build a presentation. Although Screens are an intuitive and easy way to build a presentation, they are not vital to making these kinds of files. You can also create a presentation using Flash MX 2004. Even though you do not have the option of using screens, you might want to read over the other exercises in this lesson to better understand the structure of the tour you will create in the following steps. Or, at least take a quick look at the pictures so you know what to expect.

The `Lesson08` folder on the CD-ROM contains a starter file that you can use as a basis for the tour. It includes the tools you need to quickly create the tour similar to how you would use screens in the Pro version of Flash. Some of the layers and parts of the Timeline have been set up for you to follow along with in this exercise. The SWF file will work in very similar ways as the screens-based FLA that was built in the previous exercises. Everything that exists in this file you would be able to build using the knowledge you gained in previous lessons. The rest of it you will create in the steps outlined on the following pages.

Before you begin, make sure that `video1.flv`, `video2.flv`, and `video3.flv` that you exported in Lesson 7 are still located in the `TechBookstore` folder. If you can't find them, they are included in the `media` folder on the CD-ROM.

NOTE *You will be writing ActionScript in this exercise. Although you have not covered some of the concepts that are covered in this exercise, they will be fully covered in Lesson 11. While ActionScript is not necessary to load the video in the Flash MX Professional version, it is necessary to use it in Flash MX 2004. Therefore, it must be included in this lesson. We will provide an overview of what is happening in the ActionScript below, but you will learn much more about the concepts touched upon when you read Lesson 11.*

1) Copy `tour_fmx.fla` from the `Lesson08` folder on the CD-ROM to the `TechBookstore` folder on your hard drive and open the file in Flash.

Take a look at the Timeline and how the FLA file is structured. It is very similar to the Tech Bookstore, although not nearly as complicated. Each area of the tour has its own "page," which is layered according to the content placed on each. Notice that `stop` actions have been placed on each page in the tour on the `actions` layer. The file has been sized to 635 by 345, which properly fits the area of the Stage available in the Tech Bookstore.

2) Select the `background` **layer and drag the** `soundBtns_mc` **movie clip from the Library onto or near the edge of the Stage. Add any graphics to the existing ones on the** `background` **layer if you want to display something particular behind the video. Note that descriptive text has been already added to the file for you on the** `text` **layer.**

The `soundBtns_mc` clip can be used to control an MP3 that is dynamically loaded into the SWF file. Go back to the exercise earlier in this lesson called "Controlling the Sound" and find out how to load MP3 sounds directly into your SWF. You also find out how to use these buttons to control that sound.

NOTE *It is always a good idea to offer visitors control over a sound. Follow the exercise called "Controlling the Sound" earlier in this lesson to learn how to add sound control to this tour. You can replicate the steps in Flash MX 2004 if you substitute the presentation screen for the* `background` *layer in this FLA document. Also, you can find the movie clip that controls the sound file in the Library of* `tour_fmx.fla`*.*

Add any graphics to the `background` layer that you want to display behind the video to the ones seen in the following figure. Don't forget to follow the exercise in this lesson called "Controlling the Sound" and add some sound controls to your Flash document.

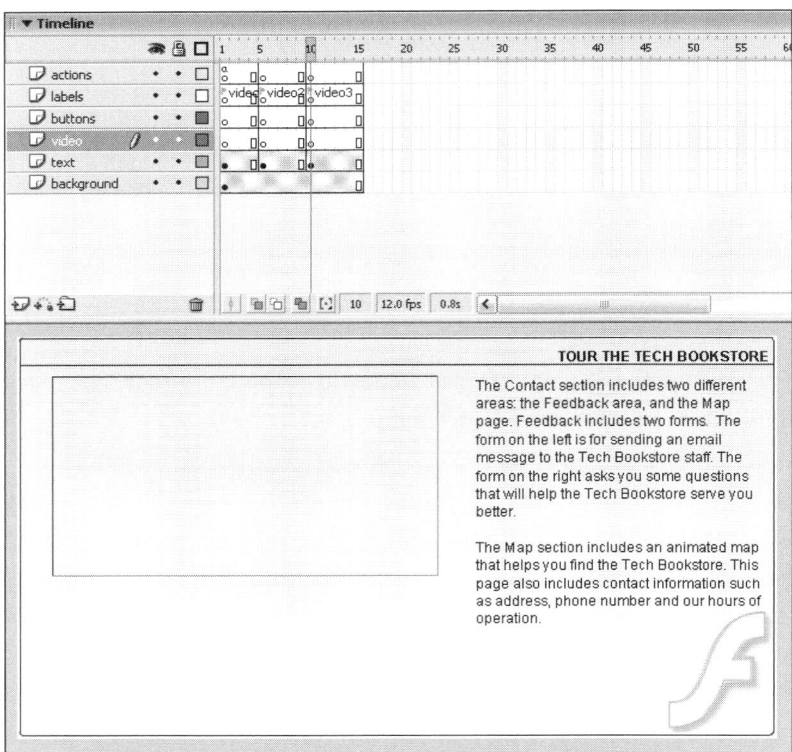

3) Create a new video object using the Library Options menu. Resize the video object and center it on the Stage and give it the instance name `video1_video`. Open the Library and click the Options menu. Select New Video from the drop-down menu.

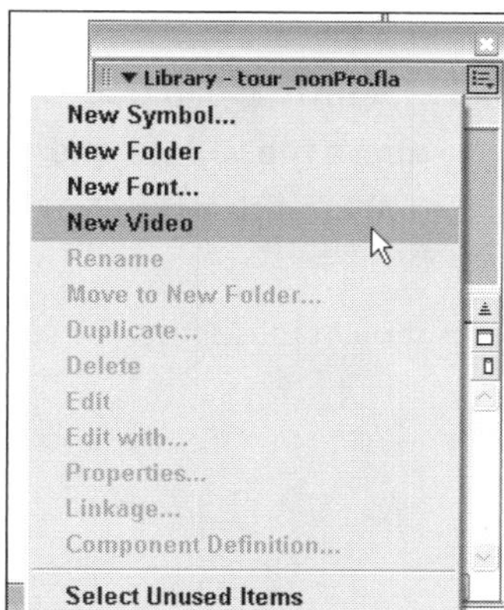

A new video object is created in the Library after you select this menu option: It is called `Embedded Video 1`. Drag the video object onto the Stage on the video layer that was created for you in the start file. When you drag it onto the Stage, it is represented by a square with a large "X" through the middle of the shape.

Resize the video object using the Property inspector so it is 320 by 179, which is the same size as the exported FLV files. When you are finished, position the video on the Stage similar to how it is seen in the previous figure. Then with the video object still selected, expand the Property inspector and enter *video1_video* as the instance name for the object.

4) Copy and paste the Video object onto the `video2` frame and `video3` frame. Change the instance names to `video2_video` and `video3_video`. Then add text titles underneath the video objects for each section, as shown in the figure following Step 6. Select the `video1_video` instance on the Stage, and choose Ctrl+C (or Command+C on the Mac). After you have copied the instance, select the `video2` frame on the video layer, and choose Ctrl+Shift+V (or Command+Shift+V on the Mac). The Video object is pasted in the same position as `video1_video`, so all you need to do is type in an instance name: *video2_video*.

Repeat the same process previously described for `video3_video`. Then you can add titles for each section of the tour underneath each video object. An example is shown in the figure following Step 6. Because each video describes how to use the three main sections of the Tech Bookstore, you can use the same text as that on the three buttons serving as the main navigation: *Products*, *Company* and *Contact*.

5) Select frame 1 of the `actions` layer and add the ActionScript included in this step. Then copy and paste this code into the frames directly above the `video2` and `video3` frame labels on the `actions` layer and make some minor modifications to the ActionScript so it targets and loads the correct video.

Place the following code directly beneath the `stop` action on the `actions` layer.

```
play1_btn.onRelease = function() {
    connection_nc = new NetConnection();
    connection_nc.connect(null);
    stream_ns = new NetStream(connection_nc);
    stream_ns.setBufferTime(3);
    video1_video.attachVideo(stream_ns);
    stream_ns.play("video1.flv");
};
```

This ActionScript is an inline function. You will learn more about functions in Lesson 11. Lesson 11 shows you how to write ActionScript like this, but right now you should just learn what this piece of code is doing. This function begins with connecting to a FLV download on your server (*progressively downloading* the video) instead of truly streaming it from the Flash Communication Server. Progressively downloaded videos will download from the server from start to finish. Streaming videos, which typically require special software to work, open and close a stream without necessarily downloading the entire video.

Next, a new `NetStream` object is created called `stream_ns`. The object contains methods and properties allowing you or the visitor to control the video (such as stop and play the video). A buffer of three seconds is set with the `setBufferTime` method, which means that the FLV video will be buffered for three seconds before it displays in the SWF file. The `attachVideo` method specifies the FLV video you want to load into the SWF file within the video object (`video1_video`) that you created on the Stage. After this, the `NetStream` is attached to the Video object that you added to the Stage. Then the FLV file plays.

NOTE *The frame rate of the FLV video will be maintained when it is loaded into the SWF file. Even if the SWF file has a different frame rate (21), the original frame rate of the video (15) will still be used to display the FLV file. If you are using Flash MX Professional and video editing or compression software such as After Effects or Discreet Cleaner, you might want to try exporting the original video files from those programs using the FLV exporter that Macromedia includes with Professional.*

When you are finished adding the code to frame 1 of the `actions` layer, copy the code in its entirety. Then select the frame in the `actions` layer directly above the `video2` label, which is already a keyframe.

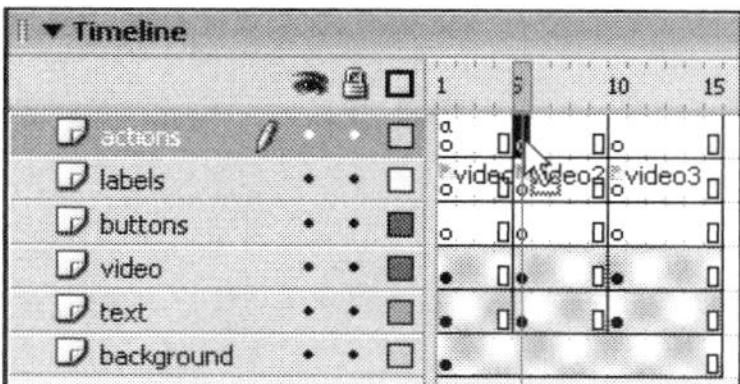

Click in the Script pane in the Actions panel and paste the code in. You will have to modify the instance name and the name of the FLV video in the final lines to `video2_video` and `video2.flv`, so the SWF plays the correct video. The final thing you want to do is to change the instance names for each block of text you pasted. For the `video2` frame, you should change the instance names to `play2_btn` and `video2_video`, and for the `video3` frame they should be called `play3_btn` and `video3_video`. So, in the end, the code on `video2` should be as follows:

```
play2_btn.onRelease = function() {
    connection_nc = new NetConnection();
    connection_nc.connect(null);
    stream_ns = new NetStream(connection_nc);
    stream_ns.setBufferTime(3);
    video2_video.attachVideo(stream_ns);
    stream_ns.play("video2.flv");
};
```

And the code on `video3` should be as follows:

```
play3_btn.onRelease = function() {
    connection_nc = new NetConnection();
    connection_nc.connect(null);
    stream_ns = new NetStream(connection_nc);
    stream_ns.setBufferTime(3);
    video3_video.attachVideo(stream_ns);
    stream_ns.play("video3.flv");
};
```

6) Add two buttons to the `buttons` layer under the `video1` label. Then copy these buttons onto `video2`, and `video3` pages as well.

Drag two instances of the Button component onto the Stage on the `buttons` layer, and position them below the Video objects on the `buttons` layer. Change the label parameter of one button to *Play* and change the second button's label parameter to *Stop*. Then copy these two instances of the Button component onto both of the frames labeled `video2` and `video3` as well.

When you are finished, you should have a Play and a Stop button on all three frames. The buttons won't do a thing yet until you test the FLA document, though so you need to complete a couple more steps before testing the FLA.

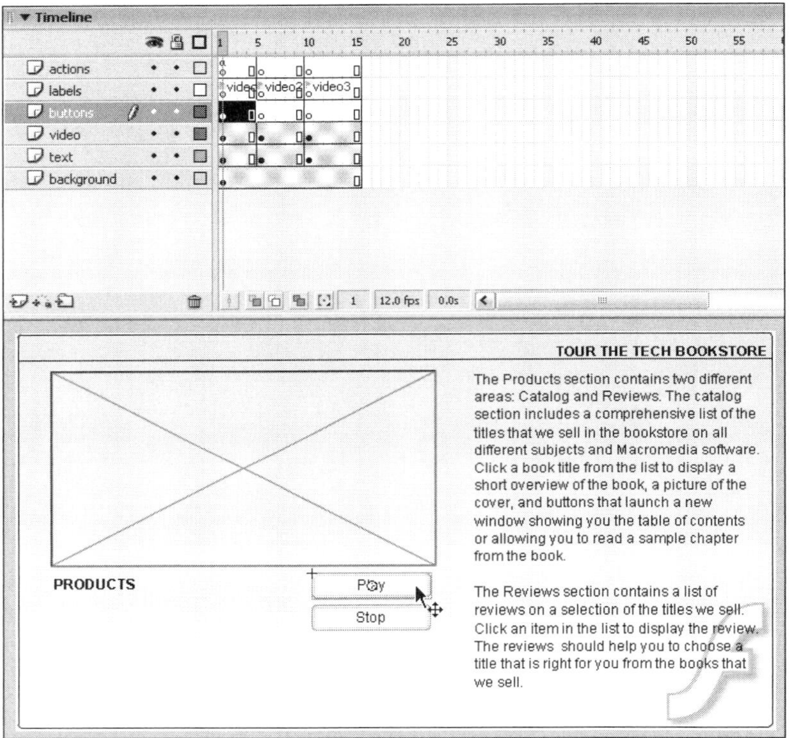

7) Add instance names for all the buttons on the three different pages.

You need to add instance names to all the buttons on all three pages. Change the instance name of each Play button on the `video1` frame to `play1_btn` in the Property inspector. Then change instance name of the *Stop* button to `stop1_btn` in the Property inspector.

Change the instance name of the Play button on the video2 frame to play2_btn and the Stop button on this frame to stop2_btn. Then change the instance name of the Play button on the video3 frame to play3_btn, and the Stop button to stop3_btn.

8) Add the following ActionScript below the code that you added to the actions layer for the video1 page. Copy and paste the ActionScript onto the actions layer for the other pages and modify the ActionScript slightly for the video2 and video3 FLV files so it targets these instances instead.

When you are finished, add the following ActionScript on the actions layer after the code you entered in the earlier step.

```
function stopVideo1(){
    stream_ns.close("video1.flv");
    video1_video.clear();
};
stop1_btn.onRelease = function() {
    stopVideo1();
}
```

This ActionScript triggers when the Stop button is clicked by a visitor, which stops the video stream and playback using two different kinds of function (which are explained in Lesson 11). When the stop_btn instance is clicked, the NetStream connection is closed and clears the image in the Video object on the Stage.

Add this code to all three pages (video1, video2, and video3). Select the frame on the actions layer directly above the frame label. You will need to change the name of the FLV file and the function accordingly in the code, so the ActionScript on video2 page is as follows:

```
function stopVideo2(){
  stream_ns.close("video2.flv");
  video2_video.clear();
};
stop2_btn.onRelease = function() {
  stopVideo2();
}
```

Then the code on the video3 page needs to be added as follows:

```
function stopVideo3(){
  stream_ns.close("video3.flv");
  video3_video.clear();
};
stop3_btn.onRelease = function() {
  stopVideo3();
}
```

9) Drag or paste Button component instances onto to the `video1`,`video2` and `video3` pages. Give unique instance names to each button and add ActionScript to control the instances.

Drag a Button component instance onto the `video1` page, and then select the instance. Expand the Property inspector, change the label parameter to *next*, and give it an instance name of `next1_btn`. Then change the width of the button to *50* pixels. When you are finished, expand the Align panel, click the To Stage button, and click the Align right edge and Align bottom edge buttons. This aligns the button in the lower-right corner of the Stage. If it interferes with your graphics, use the arrow keys on your keyboard to move the button accordingly, as seen in the following figure.

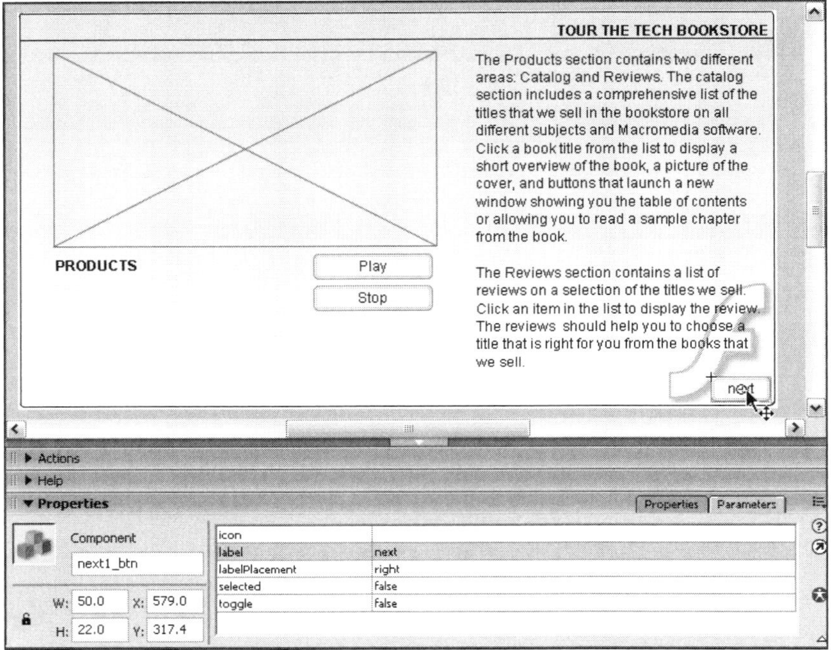

In frame 1 of the `actions` layer, add the following ActionScript to the Actions panel for the `video1` page:

```
next1_btn.onRelease = function(){
   stopVideo1();
   gotoAndStop("video2");
}
```

Select the *next* button on the `video1` page and copy it, use Paste in Place to paste it on the `video2` page. Change the instance name to *next2_btn*. Drag another Button instance onto the Stage, and using the Property inspector, change the label to *back* and add an instance name of *back2_btn*. Change the width of the button to *50* pixels and align it into the lower-left corner of the Stage using the Align panel (and adjust it accordingly).

Select the frame in the `actions` layer below the `video2` page label, as shown in the figure following Step 5. Add the following ActionScript in the Actions panel:

```
next2_btn.onRelease = function(){
    stopVideo2();
    gotoAndStop("video3");
}
back2_btn.onRelease = function(){
    stopVideo2();
    gotoAndStop("video1");
}
```

Finally copy the `back` button on the `video2` page, and use Paste in Place to paste the button on the `video3` page. Then change the instance name to *back3_btn* using the Property inspector.

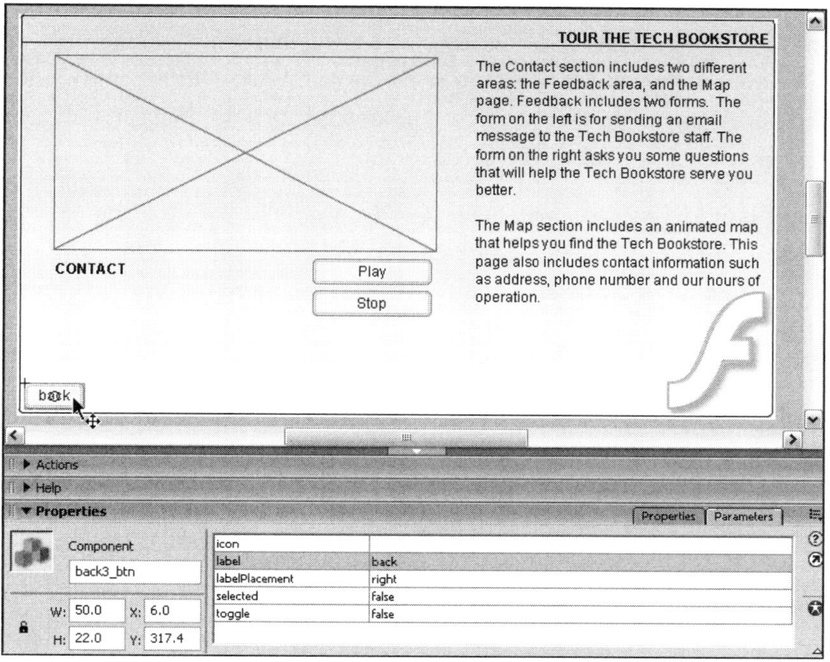

Select the frame in the `actions` layer under the `video3` label. In the Actions panel, add the following code for this page:

```
back3_btn.onRelease = function(){
   stopVideo3();
   gotoAndStop("video2");
}
```

10) Test the SWF file and make sure that it works correctly. If so, choose File > Save As and rename the file `tour.fla`**. Publish the** `tour.fla` **file in the** `TechBookstore` **folder so the** `tour.swf` **file is generated.**

A file called `tour.swf` is generated after you publish the new file. If you also created the `tour.fla` using Flash Professional, then you will have to choose a new file name or save this FLA in a different folder on your hard drive.

This file will be loaded into the main Tech Bookstore in the following exercise using the Loader component. It is somewhat different from the screens presentation in that there are no transitions between the different parts of the tour. However, each of the tours is quite similar, regardless of the version of Flash you use.

LOADING THE TOUR INTO THE BOOKSTORE

Whether you created the tour using screens or on a standard Timeline in Flash MX 2004, you can load the presentation in the same way using the Loader component. Both of the files from each exercise were compiled into SWF files of the same name (`tour.swf`), and both files can be loaded using the same component. You can find a completed version of each tour in the `Lesson08` folder.

If you are using Flash MX Professional, open `tour_fmxpro.fla`. If you are using Flash MX 2004, open `tour_fmx.fla`. Save a new version of either of these files as `tour.fla` after you open them in the authoring environment and publish the file using File > Publish.

If you created the tour in the earlier exercises in this lesson, you only need to make sure you have published the tour and the `tour.swf` file is saved within the `TechBookstore` folder.

1) Open `bookstore11.fla` **from the** `TechBookstore` **folder on your hard drive and move the playhead to the** `tour` **frame label.**

You do not need to make a new version of the file because the changes you make in this exercise are very minor.

2) Insert a new layer for the `tour` page and create and arrange the frames on this layer for the new page.

Click the `map` layer and click the Insert New Layer button. A new layer is added to the Timeline. Double-click the new layer and type in a new name: *tour*. The `tour` layer will just hold a Loader component that is used to load in the SWF file that was published in the previous exercise.

Select the frame on the `tour` layer that is directly under the tour frame label on the `labels` layer. Press F6 to convert the frame into a keyframe. Select all the frames after frame 39 on this layer and remove them from the Timeline by right-clicking (or control-clicking on the Mac) and choosing Remove Frames from the contextual menu.

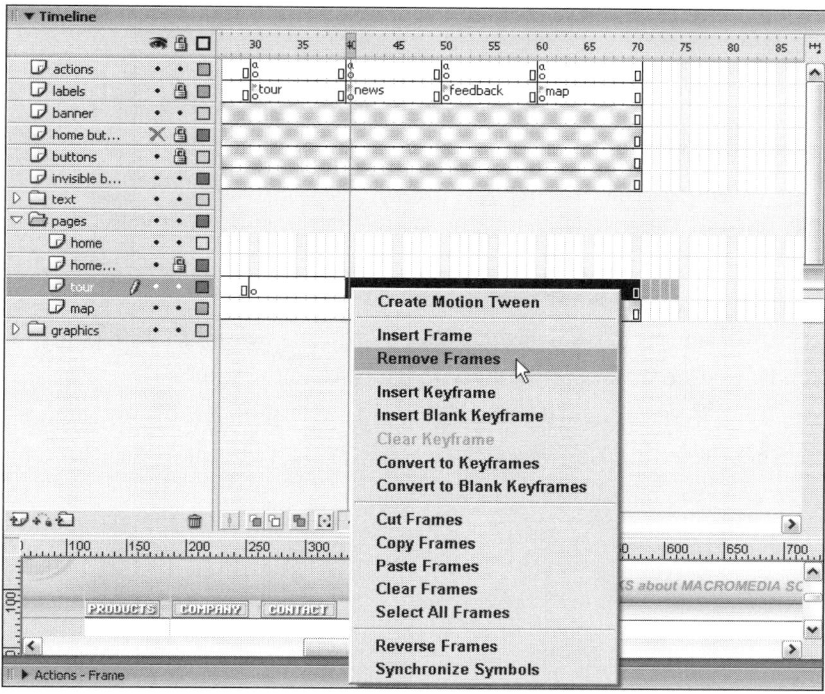

3) Select the keyframe on the `tour` **layer and drag an instance of the** `Loader` **component from the Library onto the Stage. Open the Property inspector and change the component instance dimensions to a width of *635* and a height of *345*.**
The Loader component was used earlier to add a map to the `Map` page. Now it will load the Tour presentation into the Tech Bookstore. The dimensions that you set in the Property inspector match the dimensions of the SWF file you are loading into it.

4) Open the Property inspector and enter `tour.swf` **into the contentPath property. Change the** `scaleContent` **parameter to** `false`**.**
The contentPath property is where you set the location of the file that you are loading into the component instance. If you have the SWF file saved in a different folder, you will have to specify that different location in this text field. Because the SWF is also saved in the `TechBookstore` folder, you only need to specify `tour.swf` as the file location.

Make sure that the scaleContent parameter is set to *false*, or the SWF that you load into the instance could be scaled. This means that the Alias text and the bitmap content might be distorted when it is loaded into the component instance. You should typically only set this to true when you are loading in vector-based content.

5) Save the changes you have made to `bookstore11.fla`**.**
After you add button actions to each of the menu buttons in Lesson 11 and load it into the Tech Bookstore in Lesson 12 you can navigate to the tour and view it loading into the Tech Bookstore. If there are problems with the tour loading you can test and troubleshoot it during Lesson 12. Save `bookstore11.fla` in the `TechBookstore` folder and move on to the next lesson.

WHAT YOU HAVE LEARNED

In this lesson, you have:

- Learned about screen-based FLA files (pages 232–233)
- Created a new slide presentation (pages 233–237)
- Added the *MediaPlayback* component to the presentation (pages 237–241)
- Added and controlled sound in the presentation (pages 241–244)
- Added navigation to the slide presentation (pages 244–245)
- Added transitions to the slide presentation (pages 246–248)
- Dynamically streamed FLV files using `NetStream` and `NetConnection` (pages 249–258)
- Loaded a screen-based presentation into another SWF file (pages 258–260)

creating forms using components

LESSON 9

Flash components are small applications that are created using Flash and compiled into SWC files, and as you know, there is also a large set of them included right in Flash. Components range from simple widgets to robust and complex applications such as photo galleries, polls, charting engines or even text editors. Components are very useful because they can be dropped into a Flash document and instantly add functionality to a Web site merely by changing parameters and sometimes using only a small amount of ActionScript.

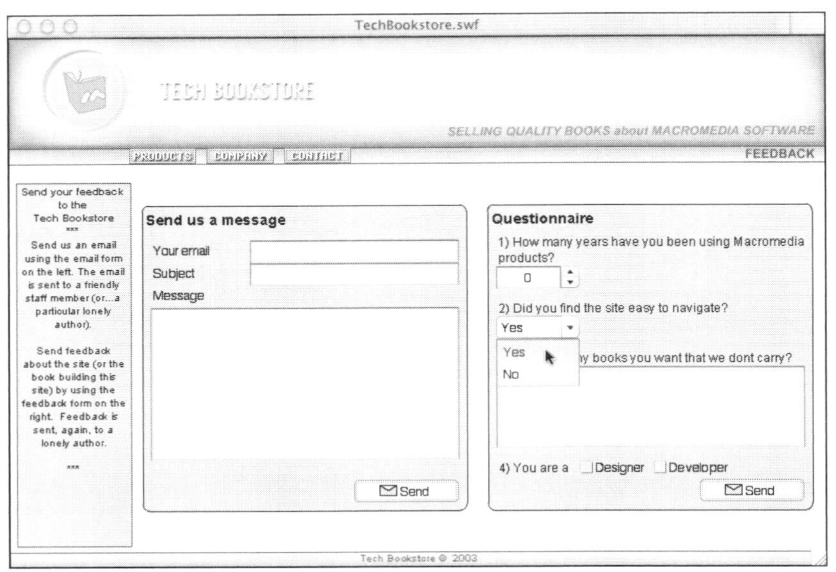

This lesson creates two forms using components for the Tech Bookstore.

This lesson shows you how to use many of the components included in Flash to build forms in which users can enter feedback and fill out a survey. The default UI (User Interface) Components installed with Flash MX 2004 are extremely useful for building forms quickly. You will learn how to use these components to construct a form in which users can select options and enter data that will be sent to a server.

WHAT YOU WILL LEARN

In this lesson, you will:

- Learn about forms and data
- Discover Flash components
- Create a feedback form
- Add an icon to a Button component
- Use FocusManager for tabbing

APPROXIMATE TIME

This lesson takes approximately one hour to complete.

LESSON FILES

Media Files:

None

Starting Files:

Lesson09/bookstore11_starter.fla
Lesson09/mail_icon.fla

Completed Project:

Lesson09/bookstore11.fla

INTRODUCING FORMS AND DATA

Forms are typically a kind of application, sometimes a series of pages, allowing you to collect information from a user. You are probably familiar with forms found on the Internet. You might have filled out a registration form when you activated Flash, or detailed information if you are applying online for a job. You have probably filled out forms to become the member of an online forum. These forms gather the data you enter into text fields and submit this data to a server when you click a button at the end of the form.

Because of components and server integration, Flash enables you to create forms easily and quickly and then create complete applications including search forms, feedback forms, and polls. You could even build complete Web site administration sites, in which you can add, modify, and delete news and manage your content. Using a few short lines of ActionScript and components, you or a developer could easily integrate a Flash application with a server-side language, such as ColdFusion, PHP, ASP or JSP. Server-side languages help you integrate your Web site with an application server. You might want to integrate with a database, XML or other forms data (such as a Web service) that is then used and displayed by the Web site.

If you are using Flash MX Professional, it is even easier to integrate Flash with these technologies using the Flash Data Components. You might have heard about Flash Remoting, which allows you to pass data back and forth between ColdFusion, ASP, or Java by using ActionScript to enable this data transfer. However, Flash MX Professional makes this kind of data transfer easier for you by allowing you to exchange data with the server without having to write large amounts of ActionScript.

Even if you aren't using Flash MX Professional, Macromedia provides a few other technologies that allow you to *easily* talk to a server-side language, such as XML. XML is a mark-up language that you use to format data (for example: names, addresses, and phone numbers) and transfer it to other computers, operating systems, or applications such as Flash—where it can be used in various ways. It is a very simple and intuitive way to organize data, although there are simple to very complex ways used to format and use it online. Both editions of Flash have excellent XML support, meaning that a SWF file can read and parse XML documents and send XML data to a server, although Flash MX Professional also offers the option of using a special XMLConnector component to make the communication easier. Another alternative to using the Data Components is using Flash's `LoadVars` class to load and send data, which you will use in Lesson 10 to send information from the feedback and questionnaire forms you set up in this lesson, if you are using Flash MX 2004.

Form Applications in Flash MX Professional

Flash MX Professional has an option for creating form-based applications. Form application documents are based on screens and use each screen in order to create nonlinear forms. You might need to have several screens that are used likes pages in a Web site. A user might fill out the form in a succession of pages, which can be easily implemented using form-based screens because each screen could serve as a single page.

You used slide-based screens to create a presentation in Lesson 8. Form applications are very similar to slide presentations, except there are different options in the Property inspector. Slide presentations and form applications are each based on different *classes*, which means that each of them has a slightly different functionality when you use the Property inspector and ActionScript. Classes will be defined in Lesson 11. A primary difference between form and slide screens in forms is that you need to write ActionScript to handle the navigation between forms, whereas navigation is built into slides already.

NOTE *You will* **not** *be using form-based screens in this lesson because it is not necessary for the forms being added to the Tech Bookstore Web site. These forms can be easily handled using a single page. Because screens do add a certain amount of file size to an application, you should only use them when they are beneficial to what you are seeking to accomplish.*

INTRODUCING FLASH COMPONENTS

Within the Flash authoring environment are *components* that you can use within a SWF file to add interactivity, effects, or common user interface elements. Components can help designers add functionality in the SWF file that they might not be able to program using ActionScript. Designers can simply drag and drop elements onto the Stage, change parameters, and write a small amount of ActionScript to make the component work in rather complex ways. As you can see, components help Flash users build applications quickly, or create elements that can be reused with relative ease.

TIP *Components are compiled into SWC files, and they can be purchased or downloaded for free from the Web. Distributing components is quite popular, and you will have no problem finding many to work with by searching online. There are many Web sites devoted to distributing components. A database of files is available on the Macromedia Exchange, and there are a number of books aimed solely at Flash Components. See Appendix B orthe Web page at* `www.TrainingFromTheSource.com/resources` *for more information.*

The components found in Flash MX 2004 (and additional components in Flash MX Professional) are rewritten versions of older components or brand new components to Flash. This is why they are sometimes referred to as *V2* UI Components. These components are excellent to use when you are building applications using several components at one time. If you are only using one component, make sure you are aware that it adds a certain amount of file size due to the fact the ActionScript necessary to include with any component must be included with the SWF file. Because this ActionScript is the same for many of the components in the V2 set, it only needs to be included one time so adding additional kinds of components might not bulk up your SWF at all. This is why it's advantageous to include many components, but not as advantageous if you only use one or two. Some components do not include the same architecture, so additional file size might be added, depending on what components you use.

NOTE *If you have installed any V1 components (components built using Flash MX, version 6), you might have difficulty using those components together in a SWF file with components built using Flash MX 2004 (V2 components). If you choose to use both kinds in an application, make sure that you carefully test that there are no conflicts that occur in the SWF file.*

Flash MX 2004 includes many components with the software, including Button, CheckBox, ComboBox, Label, List, Loader, NumericStepper, ProgressBar, RadioButton, ScrollPane, TextArea, TextInput and Window.

If you're using Flash MX Professional, you have additional components, including the Accordion, Alert, DataGrid, DateChooser, DateField, Menu, MenuBar, and Tree components. Flash MX Professional also has several components for connecting to Web Services and XML files, and the Media Components allow you to play back and control streaming FLV or MP3 files as you used in the previous lesson.

The following list outlines some of the components that are included with Flash MX 2004. Maximize the Components panel to view a list of the UI Component set.

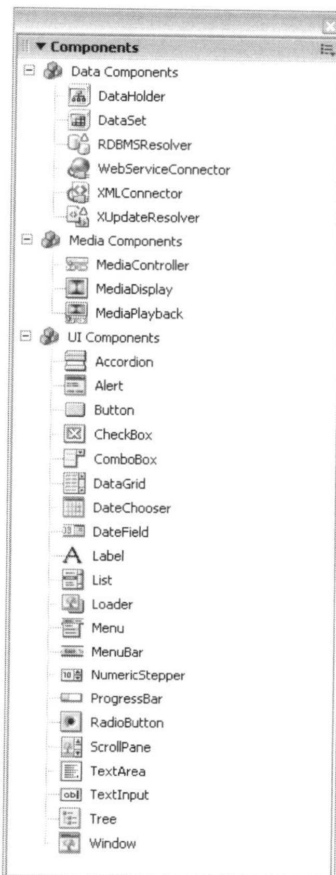

`Accordion`: This component allows you to build complex menu systems with multiple sections. The sections slide up and down vertically, revealing areas of content that you create.

`Alert`: This component allows you to launch an alert window, which is similar to using JavaScript's alert function. These alerts are like the alerts that pop up on your computer when you are cautioned about an error occurring on the system.

`Button`: This component is a customizable button that allows you to define a label (the text that is shown on the button's face) and icon (a small graphic). This component is similar to using HTML's input type of `Submit` or `Button`.

`CheckBox`: Similar to a check box in an HTML page, this component allows you to customize the placement of the label and check box control. It allows a value of either `true` or `false`.

`ComboBox`: This component allows users to make a selection from a drop-down menu. You can control the list and what each menu item associates to.

`DateChooser`: This is a calendar component allowing users to click through months and select a day.

`DateField`: This component displays a text field with a small calendar icon in the field. When a user clicks the instance, a `DateChooser` component appears, and then a day or month can be selected from the calendar.

`DataGrid`: This component displays data that you load into the component. It displays the data using a table-style format.

`Label`: This component is a single-line static text field. The text can be changed at runtime using ActionScript.

`List`: This component is similar to the `ComboBox` component, except it displays multiple lines of data at once. The List component allows multiple items to be selected at once.

`Loader`: A container component that can be used to load SWF files or JPEG images. This component can be customized to allow you to easily resize the content that is being loaded to fit the size of the component. Or you can have the component resize itself to fit the contents being loaded.

`NumericStepper`: You can use this component to select number values. The component is similar to a text input field, but it is restricted to numbers. It also comes with a couple of arrow controls that increment and decrement the current value by a certain number.

`ProgressBar`: This component displays a preloading bar for content that you are loading into a SWF file.

`RadioButton`: This component is similar to radio buttons that you might see on an HTML page. You can group radio buttons so only one button can be selected at one time.

`ScrollPane`: This component allows you to easily scroll content within a window using horizontal and/or vertical scroll bars. They are useful for when you want to load a large amount of content to a small space and help you show a greater amount of content in a limited space.

`TextArea`: This component is a text field that includes scroll bars. This component is a multiline editable text field. You can load plain or formatted text into this field, which will show scroll bars when the text exceeds the display area.

`TextInput`: This component creates a single-line text field. A user can type text into the field, which can be collected and used in a document or sent to a server by using ActionScript.

`Tree`: This component allows you to build a collapsible tree similar to the directory tree interface in Windows Explorer.

`Window`: This component is a draggable floating window that includes a title bar and button that is used to close the window.

NOTE *We have used the TextArea and component for all of our text fields because it has scrollbars to scroll the loaded text. This component can also have data bound to it. There is no ScrollBar component included in Flash MX 2004 or Professional.*

You already encountered components in earlier lessons, but the following exercise will explore a few of the more common UI components. You will also learn how to change component parameters using both the Property inspector and the Component Inspector panel.

BUILDING THE FEEDBACK FORM

In this exercise, you will create a new Flash document that adds a feedback form to the Contact page of the Tech Bookstore Web site. The feedback form gathers information from a visitor and then sends it to an XML page. You create the feedback form in this lesson; then in the following lesson, you will work with data binding, Data Components, and a little bit of ActionScript to make the feedback form work.

1) Open `bookstore11.fla` **from the** `TechBookstore` **folder on your hard drive. Create a new movie clip by choosing Insert > New Symbol and call it** `feedback_mc`**. Rename** `Layer 1` **to** `background`**.**

Alternatively, you can open `bookstore11_starter.fla` from the `Lesson09` folder on the CD-ROM. Insert a new movie clip symbol. After you create the new movie clip called `feedback_mc`, rename `Layer 1` to *background*.

2) Draw a rectangle on the Stage with a fill color of *#E7E7E7* and a *1* pixel black stroke. Add some text to the background. Lock the `background` **layer.**

Select the Rectangle tool from the Tools panel, set the Fill color to *#E7E7E7*, and set the Stroke color to *#000000* (black). Click the Round Rectangle Radius button in the Options area of the Tools panel and set the corner radius to *5* points. Draw a rectangle on the Stage and resize it using the Property inspector.

Double-click the rectangle to select the fill and stroke and maximize the Property inspector. Set the width to *300* px and the height to *300* px. With the object still selected, press the F8 key to convert the object to a graphic symbol and name it `background_gr`. Move the rectangle to the X and Y coordinates of 10, 10.

Finally, add a title at the top of the form on the `background` layer. Select the Text tool and set the Text type to Static, choose Arial for the font, a black fill color, select a font size of 14 points, select the Alias text, and choose Bold face buttons.

Click the Stage and type *Send us a message.* Position the text field near the upper-left corner of the rectangle on the `background` layer. When you finish changing the coordinates and adding the static text, the Stage will look similar to the figure following Step 5. Lock the `background` layer when you're finished.

3) Insert a new layer and then drag the Label component onto the Stage.

The Label component allows you to add captions to text fields. Although you can create labels using the Text tool, using Label instances allows you to keep a consistent look among your components and you can make your application accessible to visually impaired visitors.

Create a new layer and rename the layer *form*. Open the Components panel and locate the Label component from the UI Components folder. Drag three instances of the Label component onto to the Stage near the left edge of the rectangle you created in Step 2.

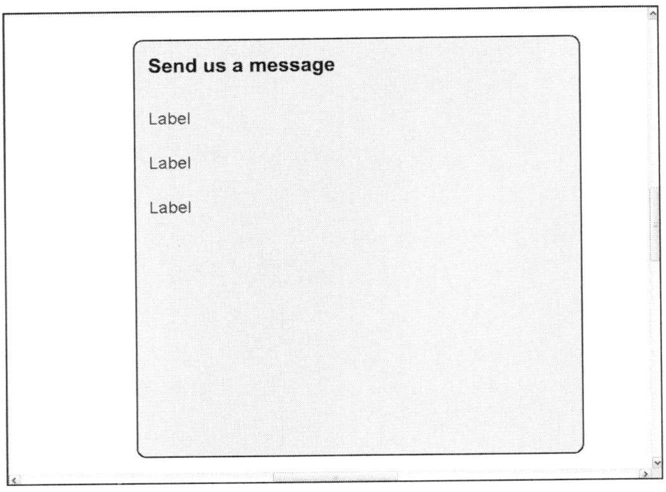

4) Add custom text for each Label instance on the Stage.

Select the first Label instance on the Stage and open the Property inspector. In the Property inspector, make sure the Parameters tab is active and click on the `text` parameter. Type in *Your email* for the `text` parameter, and press Enter or Return. The Stage immediately updates the component's appearance.

TIP *You can also maximize the Component Inspector panel and change the label's* `text` *in the inspector. It contains options that are not available in the Property inspector and are only otherwise accessible using ActionScript.*

Select the second Label instance, change the `text` parameter to *Subject*, and press Enter. Then change the third Label instance's `text` parameter to *Message*.

5) Change the X and Y coordinates of the `Your email`**,** `Subject` **and** `Message` **Label instances on the Stage using the Property inspector.**

Select the `Your email` Label instance on the Stage and use the Property inspector or Info panel to change the X coordinate to *13* and the Y coordinate to *44*. Select the Label instance for `Subject` and change the X coordinate to *13* and the Y coordinate to *66*. Change the `Message` label to an X coordinate of *13* and a Y coordinate of *88*.

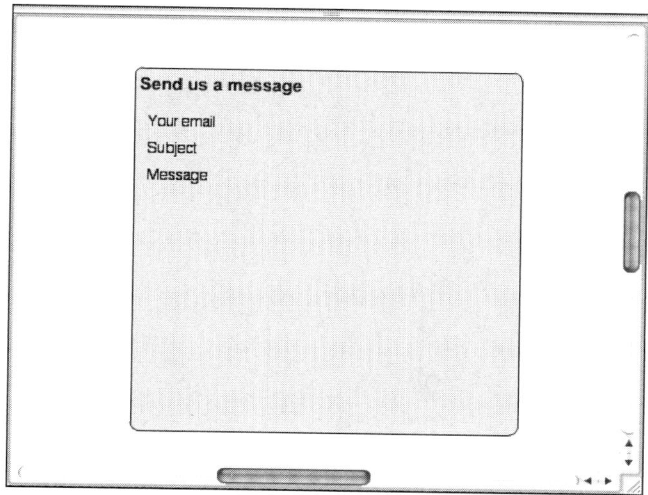

6) Drag two instances of the TextInput component onto the Stage. Then change the width of both instances using the Property inspector.

The TextInput component is similar to using the Text tool and setting the Text type to Input Text. It replicates a text input form field on an HTML page or on your operating system. Each kind of text input field allows a user to input values and data that can then be used in your application.

The TextInput component is limited to displaying only a single line of text. Using the Property inspector, you can set whether or not the text in the component can be modified, whether it is a password (the characters are replaced by symbols such as dots), or whether default text is entered into the field when the page loads. If you maximize the Component Inspector panel, you will see additional parameters that can be used to modify the component. By using the Component Inspector panel you can set a maximum number of characters that can be entered into the component instance, whether or not certain characters are accepted, and whether the component is enabled or even visible on the Stage.

Drag two instances of the TextInput component onto the Stage. Maximize the Property inspector and enter *email_txt* into the `<Instance Name>` field. Resize the component's width by entering *200* into the width field. You can maintain the default instance height of 22 pixels.

Select the second copy of the TextInput component on the Stage and type in an instance name of *subject_txt*. Change the instance's width to *200*, as you did with the previous instance.

7) Position the TextInput instances on the Stage.

With the Property inspector still maximized, select the `email_txt` instance on the Stage. Change the X coordinate to *108* pixels and the Y coordinate to *44* pixels, which will align the TextInput instance with the *Your email* label that was created earlier. Change the X coordinate of `subject_txt` to *108* pixels and the Y coordinate to *66* pixels so it is aligned with the `Subject` label.

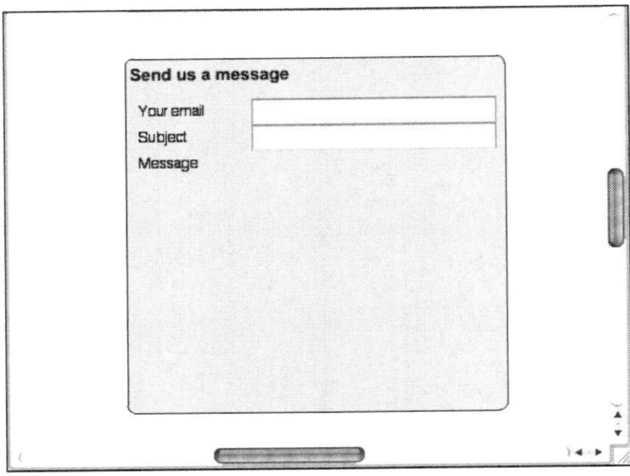

8) Add an instance of the TextArea component to the Stage, change its dimensions, and position the instance among the other elements already on the Stage. Give the new instance an instance name of `message_txt`.

The TextArea component is a *multiline* (more than one line of text) version of the TextInput component, and it has a few additional features that are quite useful. First and foremost, you have the ability to format text that is displayed in the component using Cascading Style Sheets (CSS), which allows you to display text that is much nicer than was possible in previous versions of Flash. Flash has HTML formatting support, and there are more tags now supported than there used to be. Most notably, HTML support also includes embedded JPEG images by using the `<img>` tag. Because TextArea is a multiline component, you can also control word wrapping.

Drag an instance of the TextArea component onto the Stage. Position at the X and Y coordinate of *13* and *110* pixels, respectively, using the Property inspector. While you're at it, set the width of the component to *295* pixels and the height to *150* pixels so the Stage matches the following figure. Then type in an instance name of *message_txt* into the Property inspector.

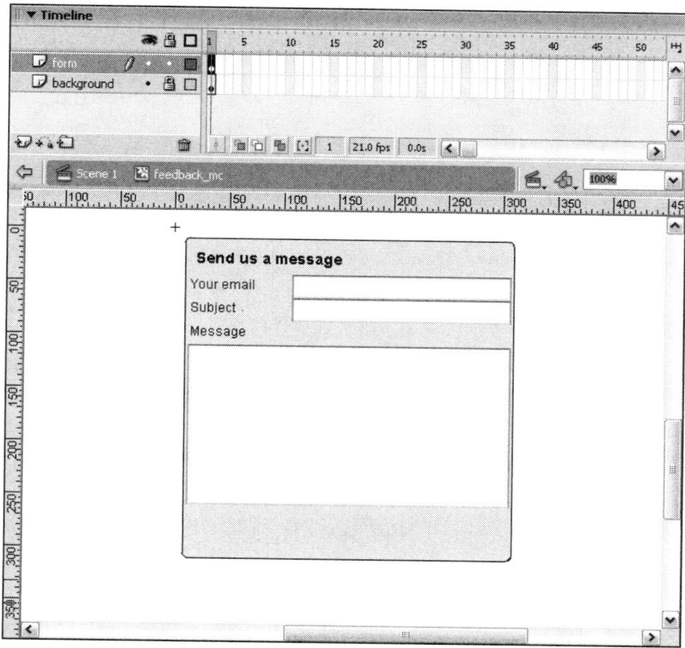

Select the TextArea component on the Stage and open the Component Inspector panel. The Parameters tab in the Component Inspector panel allows you to modify additional properties of the TextArea component. The Component Inspector panel allows you to limit the total number of characters that can be entered into the TextArea by entering a number into the `maxChars` parameter. You can also disable word wrapping, restrict which characters can be entered into the TextArea, mask the text input as a password, or disable the TextArea so that users are not able to enter any text.

You do not need to modify any of these parameters; however, it helps to remember what parameters are available because you will work with and modify them in upcoming lessons.

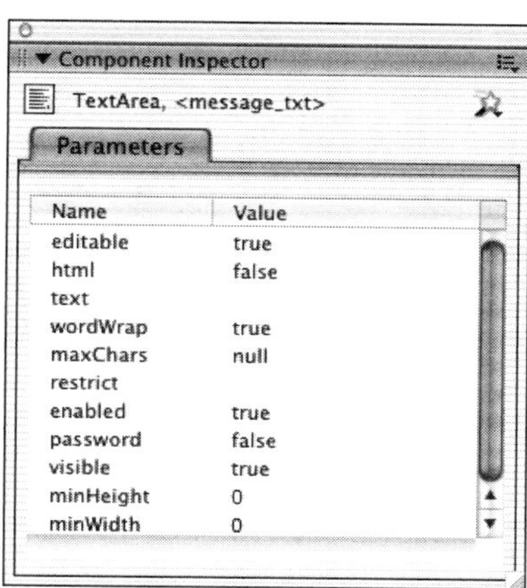

9) Save the changes you made to the file.

You will continue building the form in the following exercise, except that you will be working exclusively with the Button component in the next steps. Make sure that your changes are saved before moving on.

USING THE BUTTON COMPONENT

You can use the Button component in Flash to submit forms when the button instance is clicked. Button instances can be used to trigger events written with ActionScript, such as changing the size or appearance of an instance or opening a new browser window. By binding a behavior to the Button component, you can easily add interaction to any SWF file. Binding means that you are linking two components together, so the data from one component can be used by the other component. They can listen for changes in one component, and then copy that data into the second component. It is essentially a way of getting data into and out of a component, which you will learn the joy of in the following lesson.

NOTE *Button components offer you more functionality than regular button symbols. For example, a component instance is already made for you, it's skinnable (you can customize the look while maintaining the functionality), you can specify themes for it, and Button instances have accessibility features built into the component architecture. You can also set the labels (the text) on the component using ActionScript, and change the Button into a toggle with on and off states.*

This exercise continues where you left off in the previous exercise.

1) In `bookstore11.fla`, open `feedback_mc` in symbol-editing mode, and then select frame 1 of the `form` layer.

You probably still have `bookstore11.fla` open in Flash. Find `feedback_mc` in the Library, and double-click the movie clip to open in symbol-editing mode. Then select frame 1 of the `form` layer inside the movie clip.

2) Add the Button component to the Stage by dragging it from the Components panel and dropping it onto the Stage. Change the text label on the Button instance.

With the `form` layer still selected, drag an instance of the Button component from the Components panel on to the Stage. Select the instance you just added, maximize the Property inspector, and type *send_btn* into the the `<Instance Name>` field. Then select the Parameters tab.

Change the text on the button from the default Button to *Send* by typing in the new value of the label parameter. The Button instance's label (the text on the Button's face) changes after you change the value in this parameter and press Enter.

3) Change the position of the Button instance on the Stage to the lower-right corner of the rectangle graphic.

Move the Button instance to an X and Y coordinate of *207* and *280* pixels, respectively. Use the W and H text fields in the Property inspector to change the location of the instance. The position of the instance is moved to the lower-right corner of the rectangle graphic on the Stage. Leave the dimensions of the button at 100 pixels wide by 22 pixels high.

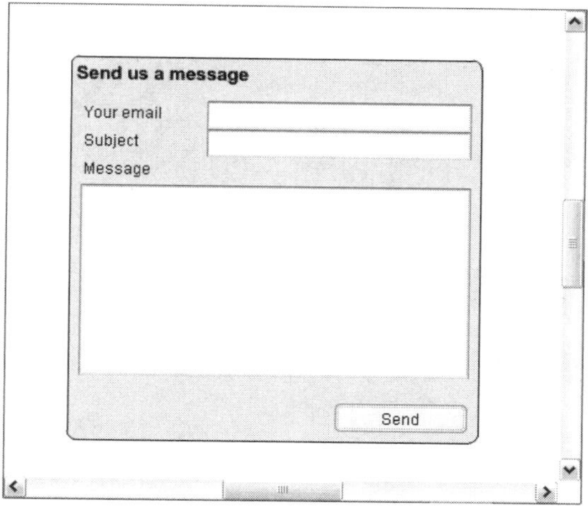

4) Import an icon graphic for the Button instance into a new graphic symbol.

You can customize the Button component by linking an icon to the instance. The icon will be displayed on the face of the Button instance, which allows you to add a nice personal touch to the form and make the form a bit more usable. The icon must be a graphic or movie clip symbol in the library, which you need to *link* to the component instance.

NOTE *Included on the CD-ROM in the finished* `bookstore11.fla` *file is an icon that you can use with the Send button. Alternatively, you could create your own custom graphic or movie clip in Flash that could be used instead.*

Open `mail_icon.fla` from the `Lesson09` folder on the CD-ROM and drag the `send_gr` graphic symbol from the Library into the `bookstore11.fla` Library. The drawing that is made inside this graphic has its X coordinate and Y coordinate set to 0 and 0, respectively.

5) Add a Linkage Identifier to the `send_gr` symbol in the Library.

Before you can use the symbol as a Button icon, you have to assign it a name so Flash can link it to the Button instance. By using the Linkage Properties dialog box, you can assign a Linkage Identifier to the symbol, which allows Flash to uniquely identify the symbol so you can use it in the SWF file.

Maximize the Library for the `bookstore11.fla` document and locate the `send_gr` symbol you copied in Step 4 of this exercise. Right-click (or control-click) the `send_gr` symbol in the Library and select Linkage from the contextual menu. The Linkage Properties dialog box opens.

In the Linkage Properties dialog box, select the Export for ActionScript check box in the Linkage section of the dialog box, which allows you to enter an identifier in the text fields at the top of the window. Enter *send_gr* into the Identifier field and leave the AS 2.0 Class field empty. Click the OK button to return to the Stage.

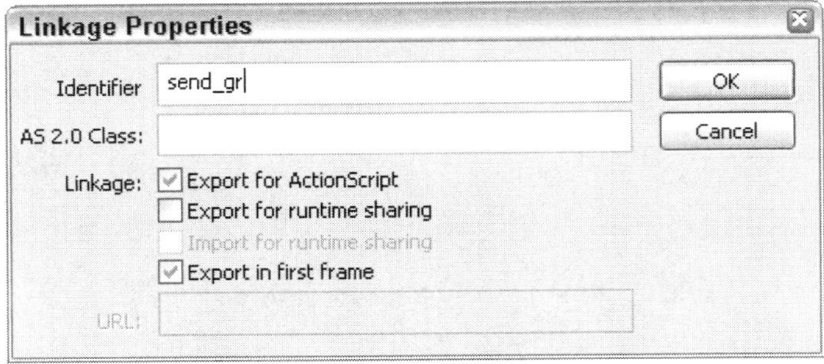

6) Add an icon to the Button component instance.

Select the Button instance in the lower-right corner of the Stage and maximize the Property inspector. Enter the Linkage Identifier, `send_gr`, into the *icon* parameter in the Parameters tab of the Property inspector. When you finish, you will notice a grey box on the left side of the `Send` label of the Button instance.

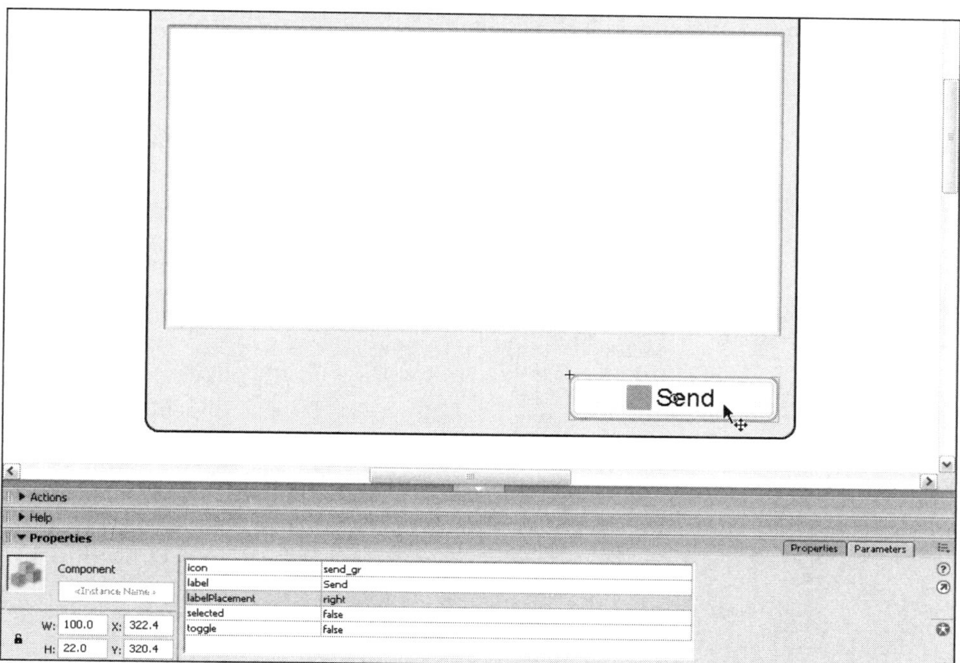

This is where the icon will be located when you publish the SWF file. The icon will not show up in the authoring environment. You will need to test the SWF file in order to view the icon on the instance.

7) Modify the position of the icon on the Button instance.

If you want to change the location of the icon on the Button instance, you can modify the value for `labelPlacement` in the Property inspector. By default, the value for `labelPlacement` is set to `right`, which means that the label appears on the right side of the icon. If you set the `labelPlacement` parameter to `top` or `bottom`, you might need to resize the button's dimensions on the Stage in order to see both the icon and the label.

8) Insert a new layer above the `form` layer and call it `labels`. Then insert a new frame above `labels` and rename it `actions`. Select frame 20 and press F5 for *all* of the layers so they extend to frame 20. Then insert a keyframe on the `actions` and `labels` layer at frame 10, and add frame labels at frames 1 and 10.

Select the `form` layer and click the Insert Layer button in the Timeline to insert a new layer, and rename it *labels*. With the new labels layer still selected, click the Insert Layer button again, and rename the new layer *actions*. When you have the new layers created, press F5 on frame 20 for all four layers. Then select the keyframe on frame 1 of the `labels` layer and type `form` into the `<Frame Label>` field in the Property inspector. Then select the keyframe on frame 10 and type *thankyou* into the `<Frame Label>` field.

Then insert a new keyframe on frame 10 on both the `labels` and `actions` layers. Press F6 to insert new keyframes.

9) Insert a blank keyframe at frame 10 on the `form` layer. Add some text somewhere on the `background_gr` graphic that says "Thank you for your feedback" or similar. Drag a button component and place it below the text.

Select frame 10 and then choose Insert > Timeline > Blank Keyframe from the main menu. Then select the Text tool, set the text to static and whatever font you choose and type in a message that the feedback has been sent. When you're finished, open the Components panel and drag an instance of the Button component onto the Stage. Change the button's label to *Back* using the Property inspector. You will add actions for this button (and more) in the following lesson.

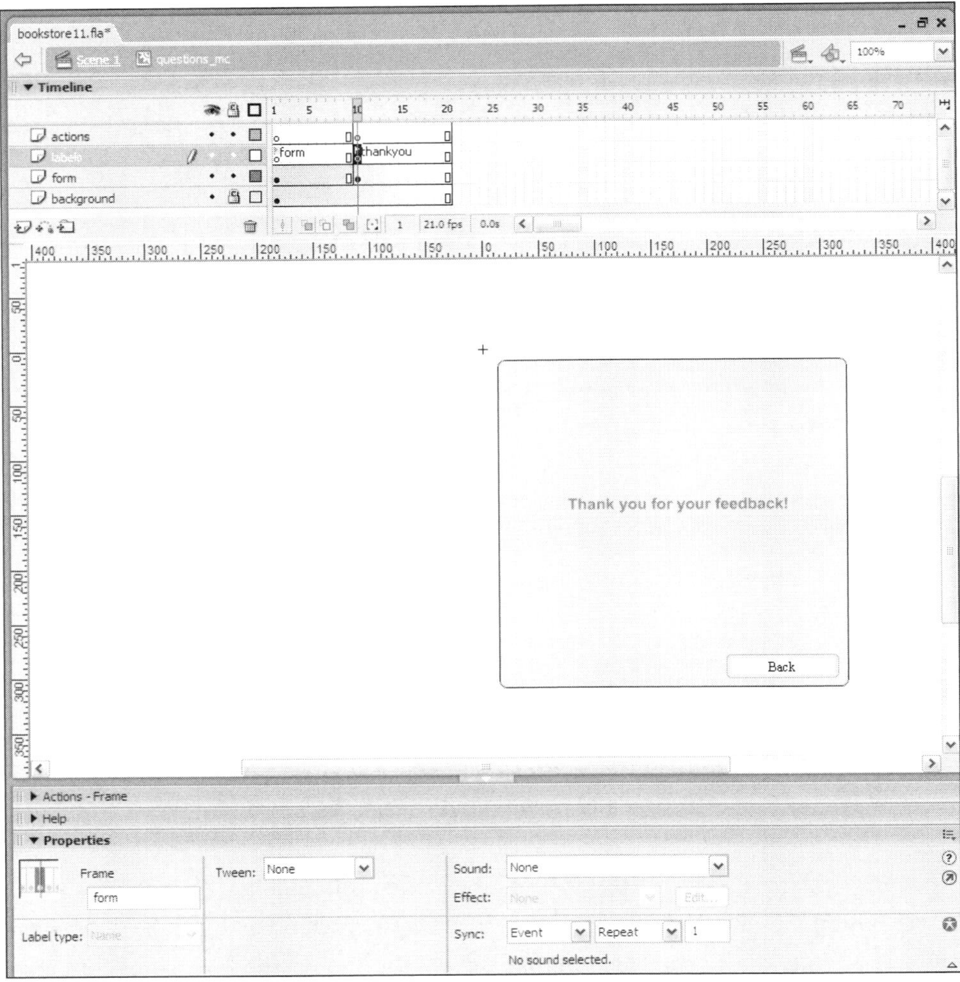

10) Save the changes you made to the feedback form and return to the main Stage.

Save `bookstore11.fla` in the `TechBookstore` folder after you finish positioning elements on the Stage, and you are pleased with the way the icon looks. You will continue working with this file in the next exercise that builds a second form using more components.

BUILDING A QUESTIONNAIRE USING FLASH

In the following exercise, you will create a questionnaire that users will fill out and send to the server by clicking a button. This questionnaire uses several new components not yet covered in this lesson. Because Flash installs many default user interface components, it is very easy to create forms such as these and have them working in no time. You will add ActionScript and data binding in the following lesson to make them collect information and send it online.

The NumericStepper component allows your visitors to click through an ordered set of numbers. The component is a text field showing a number in a text field that's next to small arrowed buttons. When these buttons are clicked, the numbers either step up or down through the set of numbers. You can set the minimum, maximum and the interval amount between each number. The NumericStepper only handles numeric data.

The ComboBox allows users to make a selection from a drop-down menu. You can set a ComboBox to editable, which means that instead of making a selection from the menu, a user can type a selection into a text field first, or select an option from the menu instead. You can set the text that is displayed in the drop-down menu and the associated data for that text, and write ActionScript so something occurs when a selection is made.

1) Open `bookstore11.fla` if it isn't already open. Insert a new movie clip symbol, and rename `Layer 1`. Drag `background_gr` from the Library onto the Stage. Then add a title to the form near the top of the rectangle.

Insert a new movie clip symbol and call it `questions_mc`. Rename `Layer 1` to *background*. In the previous exercise you created a rectangle that served as the background for the feedback form. You can reuse that background for this form as well. Open the Library, and find the `background_gr` graphic symbol and drag it onto the background layer inside `questions_mc`. Place the graphic at the X and Y coordinates of 10, 10.

Select the Text tool from the Tools panel and change the text type to Static Text in the Property inspector. Choose Arial for the font, a font size of 14 points, black for the fill color, and click the Bold and Alias text button. Add a title at the top of the form on the `background` layer. Click the Stage and type *Questionnaire*. Position the text field near the upper-left corner of the rectangle on the `background` layer. When you finish, the application should look similar to the following figure.

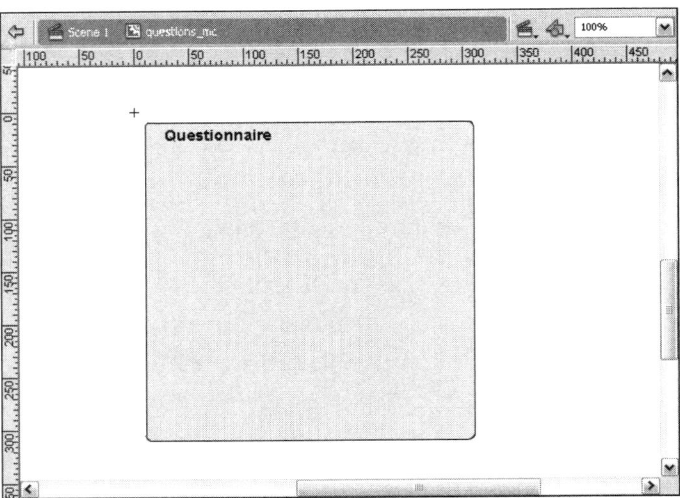

When you finish, lock the `background` layer.

2) Add text fields to a new layer called `form`. Modify those instances using the Property inspector.

Add a new layer above the `background` layer by clicking the Insert Layer button on the Timeline. Double-click the layer name and type in the new name *form*.

Select the Text tool from the Tools panel and change the text type to Static Text in the Property inspector. Choose Arial for the font, a font size of 12 points, black for the fill color, and click the Alias text button. With the Text tool selected, click on the Stage and type in the following text: *1) How many years have you been using Macromedia Products?* Don't worry about the appearance of the text on the Stage right now because you will modify the layout later in this exercise.

Add three more Static text fields to the Stage with the following text: *2) Did you find the site easy to navigate?*; then *3) Are there any books you want that we don't carry?* and *4) You are a*.

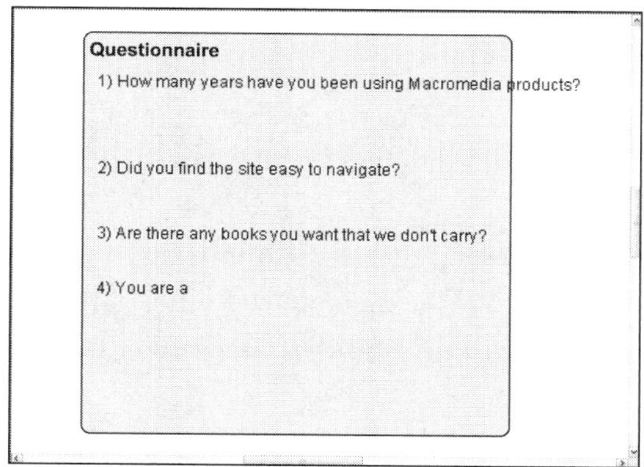

3) Select the `form` layer and add the NumericStepper, ComboBox, TextArea, Button and CheckBox components to the Stage.

Select the `form` layer and maximize the Components panel. Add one instance of the following components to the Stage: NumericStepper, ComboBox, TextArea, Button. Then add two instances of the CheckBox component. Just drag the component from the Components panel onto the `form` layer, as you did in the previous exercise.

Select the text field that contains question 1 and position it near the top of the Stage. Double-click the question's text; you can now edit the size or text of the field. In the upper-right corner of the text field you will see a small white rectangle. Use your mouse to drag the white rectangle to the left so the text doesn't exceed the bounds of the Stage. Notice that the text field automatically resizes and wraps the text as necessary.

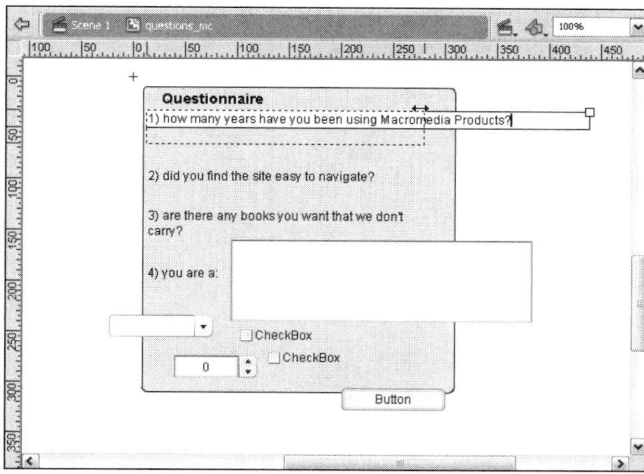

NOTE *Resizing the text field by using the Info panel or Property inspector can lead to text that is distorted. You must use the handle in the lower- or upper-right corners to resize the text field properly.*

4) Modify the parameters of the NumericStepper component using the Component Inspector panel.

Select the NumericStepper component on the Stage using the Selection tool. Position it near the bottom-left corner of the first question. Using the Property inspector, you can modify the following: the maximum and minimum range that can be used in the NumericStepper, the `stepSize` controlling the amount that the current value will be incremented or decremented when the user presses the up or down button in the component instance, and the value parameter defining the current or starting value of the component.

Maximize or open the Property inspector, and make sure you have the Parameters tab selected. Set the *minimum* parameter to *0* and the *maximum* value to *10*.

5) Position question 2 and the ComboBox component instance on the Stage.

Position question 2 below the NumericStepper component and resize the text field as necessary, as you did in Step 4. Move the ComboBox component directly below the text field for question 2. With the ComboBox component selected on the Stage, maximize the Property inspector. Double-click on the data parameter in the Property inspector, and the Values dialog box appears. This is where you can enter new values for the ComboBox component.

Click the plus (+) button at the top of the dialog box twice to add two new values. Change the first value to *1*, change the second value to *0*, and then press OK to close the dialog box and return to the Stage.

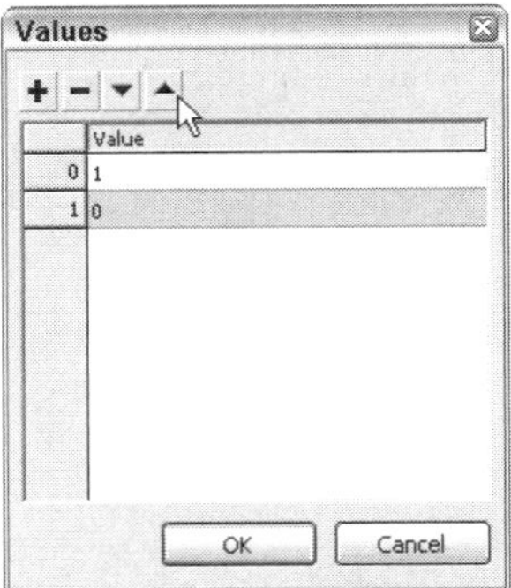

This time, double-click the `label` parameter in the Property inspector to open the Values dialog box again. You are adding labels that will correspond to the data values you added earlier. Add two values, change the top value to *Yes*, change the bottom value to *No*, and click the OK button to return to the Stage.

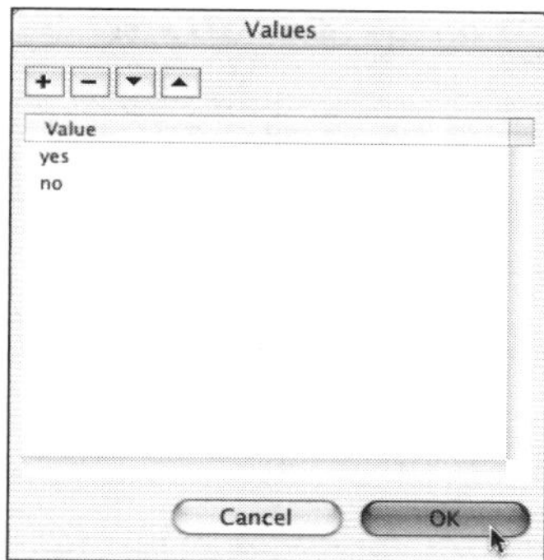

NOTE *When you are adding values, you must be careful to make sure that the values in the* data *property correspond to the values in the* labels *property or your users may experience unexpected results.*

6) Align the third question with the TextArea instance on the Stage.

Position question 3 below the ComboBox component, and resize the text field as necessary, as you did with the previous two question text fields. Then select the TextArea component on the Stage and move it below the question. It will be necessary to resize the TextArea component to fit the width of the Stage. Using the Property inspector, change the width of the component to approximately *290* pixels, depending on how much surplus area you have on the Stage for this instance. Change the height of the component to approximately *80* pixels. You might need to change the positioning of these elements later on if the rest of the form assets don't fit on the Stage.

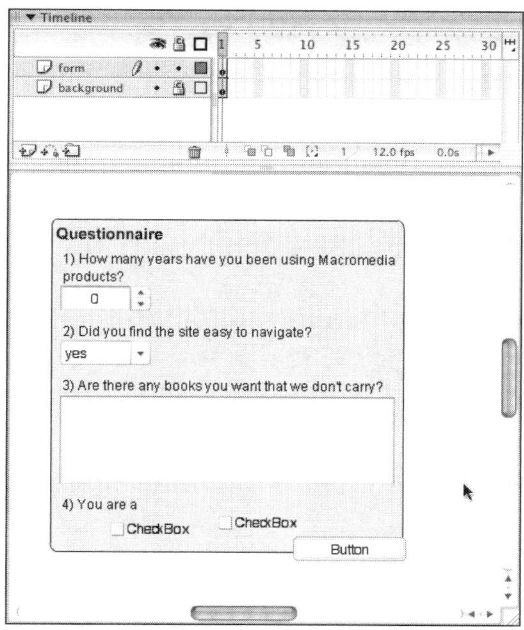

7) Position question 4 and the two CheckBox components on the Stage.

Move the fourth question below the TextArea component and close to the left side of the Stage. With the text in place, drag the first instance of the CheckBox to the right of the text so the text and component are aligned. Select the CheckBox component on the Stage and change the `label` parameter to *Designer* in the Property inspector. Move the second CheckBox component to the right of the Developer checkbox and change the `label` to *Developer* in the Property inspector. If you want to move the label on the other side of the check box, you can use the Property inspector and change the `labelPlacement` from `right` to `left`. Refer to the figure following Step 9 for the way these elements are placed on the Stage.

TIP *Now that you have placed all the questions on the Stage, you might want to select all the instances along the left side of the rectangle and use the Align panel to line them up with precision. Make sure that the To Stage button is deselected first, so they align to the other instances and not to the left side of the Stage.*

8) Position the Button component in the lower-right corner of the rectangle.

Using the Selection tool, move the Button component instance to the lower-right corner of the Stage. Maximize the Property inspector and enter an X coordinate of *207* and a Y coordinate of *280* so the button is placed in the same location as the button in the feedback form. With the button still selected on the Stage, change the `label` parameter in the Property inspector to *Send.* Set the Linkage identifier to *send_gr* and then set the `icon` parameter of the Submit button to *send_gr* in the Property inspector.

When you are finished, your Stage should look similar to the following figure.

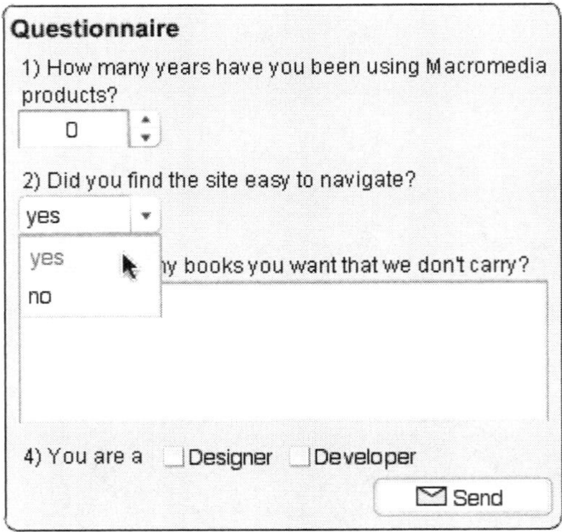

9) Insert a new layer above the `form` layer and call it `labels`. Then insert a new frame above `labels` and rename it `actions`. Press F5 for *all* of the layers so they extend to frame 20. Then insert keyframes on the `actions` and `labels` layer at frame 10, and add frame labels at frames 1 and 10.

Select the `form` layer and click the Insert Layer button in the Timeline to insert a new layer, and rename it *labels*. With the new `labels` layer still selected, click the Insert Layer button again, and rename the new layer *actions*. When you have the new layers created, press F5 on frame 20 to add frames to all four layers. Then select the keyframe on frame 1 of the `labels` layer and type `form` into the `<Frame Label>` field in the Property inspector. Then select the keyframe on frame 10 and type *thankyou* into the `<Frame Label>` field.

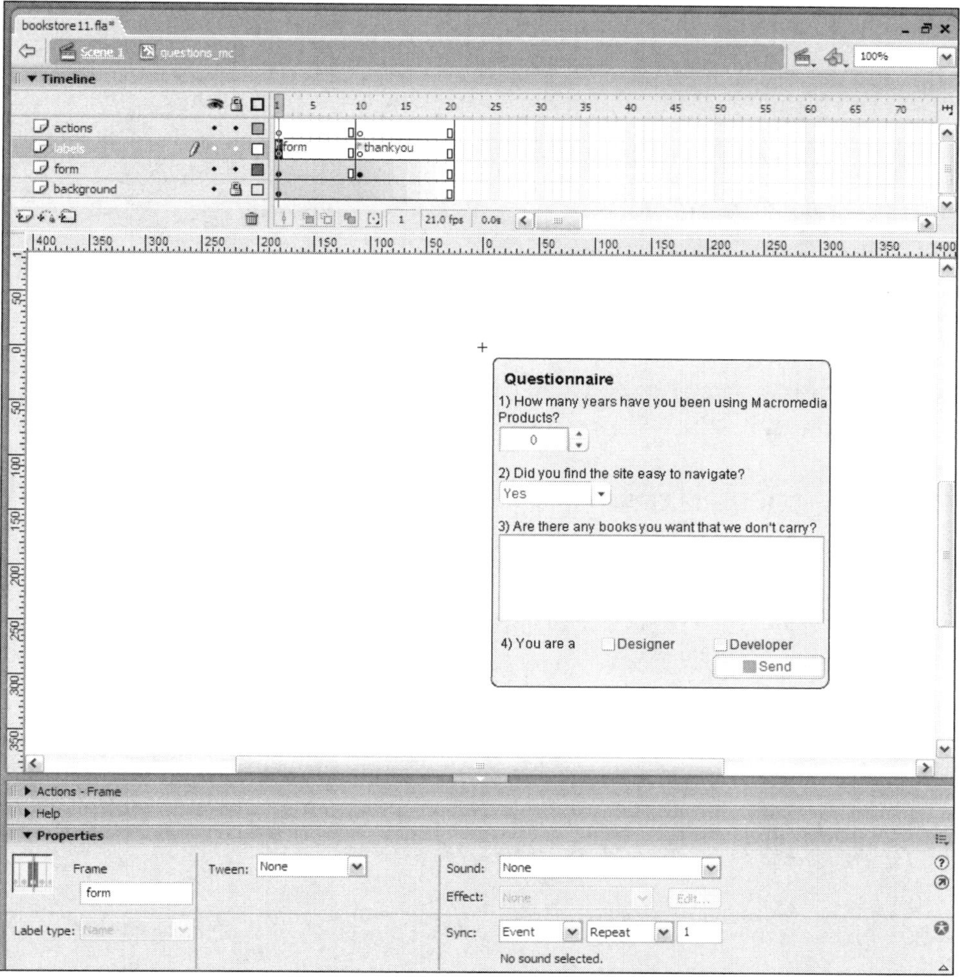

Then insert a new keyframe on frame 10 on both the `labels` and `actions` layers. Press F6 to insert new keyframes.

10) Insert a blank keyframe at frame 10 on the `form` layer. Add some text somewhere on the `background_gr` graphic that says "Thank you for your feedback" or similar. Drag a button component and place it below the text. Lock the `form` layer and save the changes you have made to the file.

Select frame 10 and then choose Insert > Timeline > Blank Keyframe from the main menu. Then select the Text tool, set the text to static and whatever font you choose and type in a message that the feedback has been sent. Type the message "Thank you for your feedback", or something similar.

When you're finished, open the Components panel and drag an instance of the Button component onto the Stage. Change the button's `label` to *Back* using the Property inspector.

After you add ActionScript to the bookstore that controls the menus and allows you to navigate along the Timeline, you will be able to change and store the value of the NumericStepper by clicking the up and down arrow to the right of the number value or by typing in a new value. The NumericStepper allows only values that fall within the minimum and maximum values you defined earlier in Step 5 of this exercise. If you click on the ComboBox component, a drop-down menu will appear allowing you to choose between the *Yes* and *No* values you defined earlier in the exercise. You will be able to select the CheckBox instances by clicking the Designer and Developer check boxes, as seen in the previous figure.

Lock the `form` layer, and then open the Library. Before moving on, save the change you have made to the file.

USING THE FOCUS MANAGER

All the components in Flash MX 2004 automatically support the `FocusManager` class, which supports specifying a tabbing order for components, or it can be used to disable the capability to tab to a form object altogether. Tabbing is very useful for visitors who prefer to navigate forms by tabbing, and for visually impaired users who partially rely on tabbing through forms for their primary or only mode of navigation.

NOTE *It is important to remember that there is no user interface control used to define the properties and methods of the Focus Manager, so you have to enter ActionScript in the Actions panel in order to set tab order or disable tabbing to items.*

In this exercise, you will add tabbing to the `bookstore11.fla` file you created earlier.

1) Open bookstore11.fla**, which is located in the** TechBookstore **folder. Double-click** feedback_mc **to enter symbol-editing mode and select frame 1 of the** actions **layer inside the movie clip.**

Open the bookstore11.fla document saved in the TechBookstore folder and select frame 1 of the actions layer after you have double-clicked feedback_mc and entered symbol-editing mode.

2) Define the tabbing order using ActionScript.

The feedback form has four primary elements in it: the From email address, the Subject, the Message TextArea, and the Send button, which sends the feedback to the server. You will define the tabbing order of the text fields and button from top to bottom, so the email_txt instance will have a tab index of 1, subject_txt will have a tab index of 2, message_txt will have a tab index of 3, and send_btn will have a tab index of 4. Maximize or open the Actions panel (F9) and add the following code in frame 1 of the actions layer:

```
email_txt.tabIndex = 1;
subject_txt.tabIndex = 2;
message_txt.tabIndex = 3;
send_btn.tabIndex = 4;
```

When you test the code in a browser later on you must test the document in a Web browser by pressing F12 on your keyboard.

NOTE *You can't test the FocusManager quite yet, until you add the scripts to enable the navigation in Lesson 11. You can however, copy and paste this ActionScript and your instances into a new Flash document in just a few seconds if you want to test this out now.*

When you press Tab a few times the cursor will tab through each of the instances on the Stage. After the focus reaches the send_btn Button component, if you press Tab again it sets the focus to the email_txt instance because there are no items with a higher tab order than the send_btn, so it returns to the first item in the tab index.

NOTE *Tabbed movie clips and buttons display with a yellow box around the instance. Components display the halo color. Remember that the halo is the green (default color) glow around the components that you see when you mouse over them. To find out how to change the halo color for components, refer to* www.TrainingFromTheSource.com/bonus.

NOTE *In order to use tabbing, the SWF file must be viewed in a browser window. Tabbing does not work with movie clips or buttons in the testing environment or in a SWF file playing in a standalone Player.*

3) Set a default form button using ActionScript.

You can also set a default button instance, which simulates being clicked if a user presses the Enter or Return key while filling out the form (unless you are within the TextArea component). Being able to press the Enter key is similar to a behavior in HTML when you are filling out forms. In the Actions panel, add the following line of code to the bottom of the existing ActionScript:

```
focusManager.defaultPushButton = send_btn;
```

This snippet of code sets the default push button to `send_btn` (which happens to be the only button in the document). If a user presses Enter while they are filling out a form, the click event handler will be triggered for the `sent_btn` button instance. Clicking the Send button will have no effect on the SWF file until some ActionScript is added to the FLA file in the next lesson.

4) Set form focus on the `email_txt` instance.

Imagine that you wanted to set the focus to a certain form instance when the Flash SWF loads into the Tech Bookstore. This is a little bit more user-friendly for your visitors because they won't have to reach for the mouse and click a form field before being able to type in their email address.

Add the following line of ActionScript below the existing code into the Actions panel:

```
focusManager.setFocus(email_txt);
```

This line of code sets the current focus to the `email_txt` instance on the Stage. This method could also become extremely useful if you had form validation in the SWF file and wanted to set the form focus to a TextInput field that was left blank or wasn't a valid value. You could then send the user an alert and also set the focus for the empty text field that needs their attention.

5) Clean up the Library.

You have added a lot of new symbols to the bookstore, so you should take a moment to open and re-organize the Library. Move all of the components you have added into the `components` folder. You will also have a graphic, movie clips and sounds in there. Move the movie clips into the `movie clip` folder and the sounds into the `media` folder.

6) Place the new movie clips on a new layer on the Stage. Give each of the movie clips instance names of `feedback_mc` and `questions_mc`.

Insert a new layer on the Timeline above `map` and rename the new layer *feedback*. Insert a new keyframe on the `feedback` layer below the `feedback` label (frame 50) on the Timeline. Remove all of the frames on the layer greater than frame 60 by selecting them, right-clicking (or control-clicking) and choosing Remove Frames from the contextual menu.

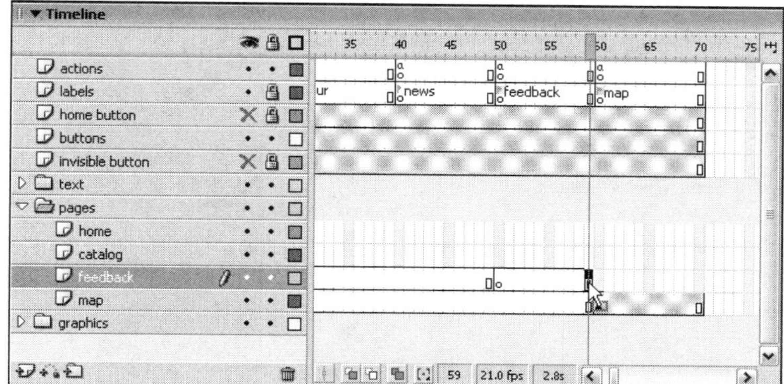

Open the Library and locate the `feedback_mc` and `questions_mc` symbols, and drag them onto this new layer. Place the two symbols on the empty part of the Stage and align the two instances horizontally, similar to the figures at the beginning of this lesson.

Select the feedback form and enter `feedback_mc` into the Property inspector for its instance name. Then select the questionnaire and type in `questions_mc` into the Property inspector.

7) Save the changes you have made to the document.

Choose File > Save to save all the changes you have made to the FLA file. In the next lesson, you will add the bindings between the Flash document and a remote Web Service in the Tech Bookstore. If you are not using Flash MX Professional, you can skip ahead in the lesson and find out how to get these forms working using ActionScript.

WHAT YOU HAVE LEARNED

In this lesson, you have:

- Learned more about forms and data (pages 264–265)
- Discovered the Flash UI Component set (pages 265–269)
- Created a feedback form (pages 269–274)
- Used the Button component (pages 274–279)
- Created a questionnaire (pages 279–286)
- Discovered how to use the Focus Manager (pages 286–289)

incorporating dynamic data

LESSON 10

There are many different ways you can use dynamic data in Flash MX 2004 and Flash MX Professional. You have already used dynamic data in earlier lessons, when you loaded an image into Flash at runtime. However, there are other ways to use dynamic data in Flash that provide a lot more control over what information is contained within the SWF file and what occurs at runtime. Introduced in Flash MX Professional, data binding allows you to establish a connection between components on the Stage. Notably, you can bind Data Components to components that can display and manipulate information such as the List or ComboBox components. Some Data Components help you connect to and load in information from sources such as Web Services and XML, and other components help you manage the data.

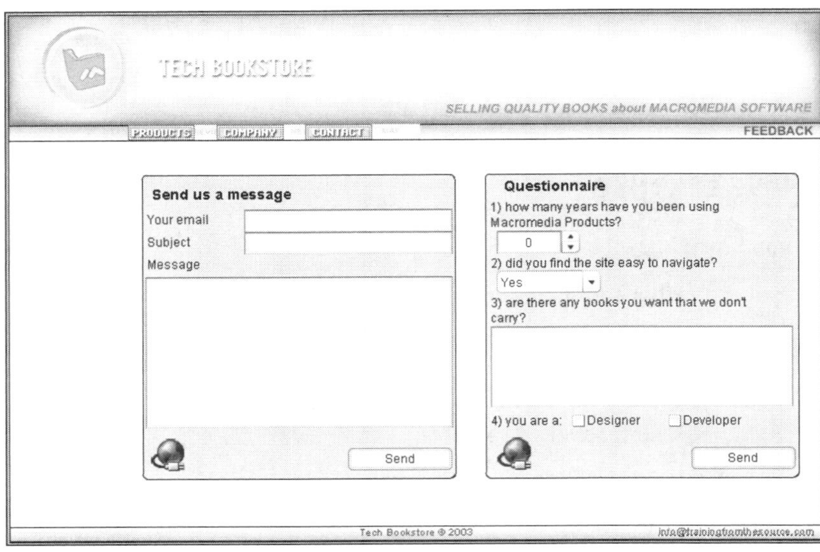

Learn how to load and send data from the Tech Bookstore application.

You will discover that this lesson contains two kinds of exercises: some for use with Flash MX 2004, and others that are applicable if you are using Flash MX Professional. The titles of each exercise let you know what version of Flash is being used in the steps. Go through the lesson, and use the exercises that are applicable to the version of Flash you are working with.

WHAT YOU WILL LEARN

In this lesson, you will:

- Define a Web Service
- Call a Web Service
- Use the WebServiceConnector component
- Use the XMLConnector component
- Bind data to components
- Load dynamic data using ActionScript

APPROXIMATE TIME

This lesson takes approximately 1 hour to complete.

LESSON FILES

Media Files:

None

Starting Files:

Lesson10/bookstore12_starter.fla

Completed Project:

Lesson10/featuredbook.xml
Lesson10/ bookstore12_fmx.fla
Lesson10/bookstore12_pro.fla

INTRODUCING DYNAMIC DATA

Dynamic data refers to the process of sending data between a SWF file and a Web server when the SWF file is playing in the Flash Player. Building dynamic SWF files allows you to customize the file's playback at runtime. You might want to react to information someone enters into a text field, or a choice that is made in a ComboBox, and send the requested data to the SWF file to have it displayed in a certain way.

Flash has many different ways of integrating a SWF file with a Web server by using Web Services, Flash Remoting, Flash Communication Server, XML, and `LoadVars`. Web Services, XML and the `LoadVars` class can all be used in Flash without purchasing additional software.

NOTE *`LoadVars` is a class included in ActionScript that's used to load variables into a SWF file. You will learn more about classes in Lesson 11.*

When you integrate an application with a server, you can allow a SWF file to send and load content from the server on the fly. This means that you can send email from Flash, interact with a database or load charts and graphs into a SWF. Most *Rich Internet Applications* include some amount of dynamic data. You can collect information from a visitor or show them data stored in a database.

There are different ways to work with dynamic data, and it sometimes depends on what version of Flash you are using. Flash MX Professional includes several Data Components helping you quickly create dynamic Flash applications using very little ActionScript. You will discover how easy they are to use in the following exercises. Even though there are no Data Components in Flash MX 2004 you can still build dynamic Flash applications using the software. It just means that you will have to get the job done in a different way, which is also shown in the following exercises! You will need to use more ActionScript to accomplish the same kinds of things, which means it will take you a bit more time to make the forms that you create work. Although this lesson does not show you how to use Web Services or XML with Flash MX 2004, like the exercises using Flash MX Professional (doing so would go beyond the scope of this book), you will find out how to make the questionnaire and email feedback form function using the (ActionScript) `LoadVars` class.

NOTE *If you are using Flash MX 2004 in this lesson, you will use and learn* what *the code is doing in each form. In Lesson 11, you will learn* how *to write code like what is used in this lesson.*

Loading content into a SWF file sometimes involves limitations because of how security and the Flash Player works. You require cross-domain policy files in order to access and use data that is not within exactly the same domain as your SWF file. For example, if you had your SWF file on www.mysite.com/mypage.html, then the data must also be loaded from some other file at www.mysite.com. It could not be located at a virtual domain (http://other.mysite.com) or a completely different domain (www.yoursite.com) unless you placed a cross-domain policy file on the root domain of the site that the SWF file wishes to access.

A cross-domain policy file is a simple XML file that includes information of what sites are permitted to access the data on the domain wanting to load the data. For the most part, you are loading SWF files and data all within the same domain for the Tech Bookstore. Otherwise you are using Web Services to access data. We have placed a cross-domain policy file on the domain hosting the Web Service so you can access the data from the service that we're providing. For more information on cross-domain files and loading, check out this page:

`www.macromedia.com/support/flash/ts/documents/loadvars_security.htm#return`

DEFINING WEB SERVICES IN FLASH MX PROFESSIONAL

Before you can use a Web Service in Flash MX Professional, you need to define the Web Service using the Web Services panel, which is a very useful panel in Flash that can be used to view each of the services you regularly connect to, as well as their methods and properties contained in the Web Service. In this exercise you define a Web Service for the feedback form that you created in Lesson 9.

1) Open the `bookstore11.fla` **document saved in the** `TechBookstore` **folder. Save a new version of the file as** `bookstore12.fla`**. Double-click** `feedback_mc` **to open the movie clip in symbol-editing mode, and then open the Web Services panel.**

You can also open `bookstore12_starter.fla` from the `Lesson10` folder on the CD-ROM and save it to the `TechBookstore` folder to begin.

Double click the `feedback_mc` on the Stage in order to open the movie clip in symbol-editing mode. Before you can use Web Services with your Flash documents, you must define the service within Flash. You accomplish this by using the Web Services panel, which can be opened by going to Window > Development Panels > Web Services or by pressing Ctrl+Shift+F10 (or Command+Shift+F10 on the Mac).

As you can see in the following figure, there has already been a service added to this Web Service panel. When you add a new service in the following steps, it will also be listed in the panel.

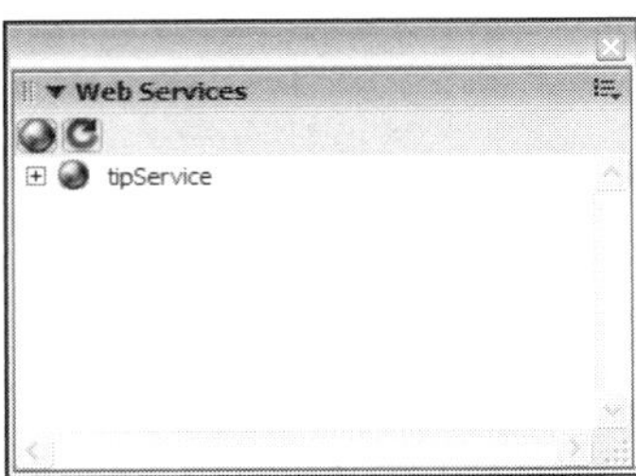

2) Define your Web Service by clicking the Define Web Service button and then click the Add Web Service button. Type in the URL of a Web Service, which is provided in the following description.

To define a Web Service, you can click the Define Web Service button in the panel or select Define Web Services from the Options menu in the upper-right corner. This process opens the Define Web Services dialog box, in which you can click the Add Web Service button to define a new Web Service. Click the Add Web Service button to add a service and type `http://www.forta.com/misc/flash2004tfts/email.cfc?WSDL` into the list of Web Services.

TIP *If you need to edit the service, you can double-click its URL. To remove a Web Service, select it from the list and press the Remove Web Service button.*

After you finish defining Web Services, you can click OK to close the Define Web Services dialog box and return to the Web Services panel.

NOTE *When defining Web Services, you must prefix the URL with* `http://` *or else Flash will not accept the URL and will clear the entry.*

3) View the Web Services' methods and properties using the Web Services panel.

When returning to the Web Services panel, Flash attempts to validate each of the listed URLs and displays an error message in the Output panel if Flash cannot connect to a particular Web Service. When your Web Service successfully registers, it appears in the Web Services panel. View the service's methods and properties by double-clicking the service's name or click the expand control (plus symbol) to the left of the service's name.

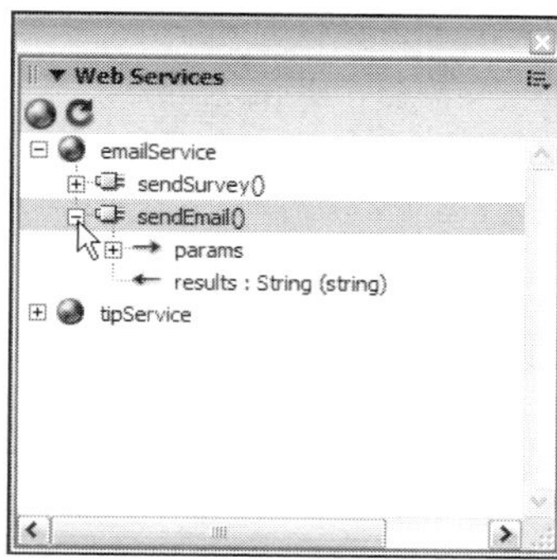

Either double-click the method's name or click the method's expand control (the small plus symbol) to view a specific method's properties. Expand the `sendEmail` method by clicking that small plus symbol or double-clicking the method itself to reveal the input and output parameters. Parameters sent from Flash to the Web Service are denoted by an arrow that points to the right, and parameters returned from the Web Service are denoted by an arrow pointing to the left. The Web Services panel also displays the names and data types of the parameters being passed back and forth.

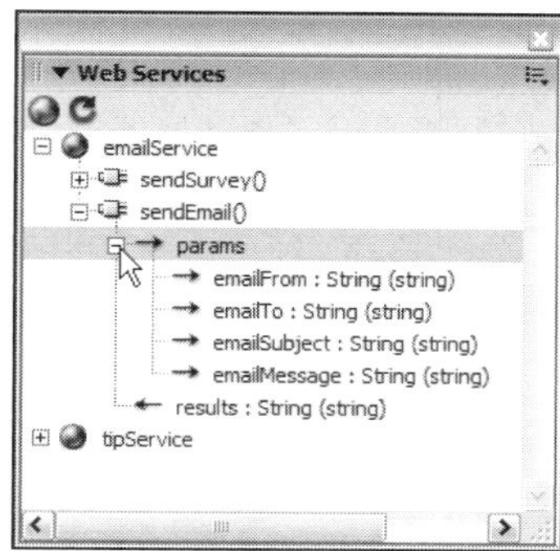

NOTE A parameter *is a value that you are passing to the Web Service, in which it is processed or manipulated by the remote service depending on what the service does. In this case, it sends an email to an address that you specify.*

If a Web Service no longer responds or if the function of it changes, you can refresh the list along with the methods and properties in the following ways: by pressing the Refresh Web Services button at the top of the panel, by selecting Refresh Web Services from the Options menu, or by right-clicking (or control-clicking on the Mac) within the panel and selecting Refresh Web Services from the contextual menu.

4) View the Web Services' source code using the Web Services panel.

To view the source code for the `emailService` Web Service, you can right-click (or control-click on the Mac) the Web Service and select View WSDL in the contextual menu.

TIP *WSDL, which stands for* Web Services Description Language, *is a language that is based on XML. It allows other developers to send and/or receive data that can be used in an application.*

5) Save the changes that you made to the `bookstore12.fla` **file.**

You will continue working with this file in the following exercise, in which you will actually call the Web Service that you defined in this exercise.

CALLING A WEB SERVICE IN FLASH MX PROFESSIONAL

Flash MX Professional introduces an easier method of connecting to Web Services. Although it was possible to consume Web Services using Flash Remoting in Flash MX, the new components now in Flash MX Professional make it much easier to connect to remote servers without having to write nearly as much ActionScript. For more complicated applications—ones in which you want additional control and in most cases consumes less bandwidth—it is good to remember that Flash Remoting is still supported in Flash MX 2004.

In this exercise, you will add a WebServiceConnector component to the feedback form you started working with in the previous exercise. This allows you to send the contents of the form to a remote server, where it can be inserted into a database or emailed to a site administrator.

NOTE *To work with this file using Flash MX 2004, skip ahead to the section in this lesson called "Building the Feedback Form in Flash MX 2004."*

1) Open `feedback_mc` **in symbol-editing mode by double-clicking it in the Library and add the WebServiceConnector component to the** `bookstore12.fla` **document you were working on in the previous exercise.**

Open the `bookstore12.fla` from the `TechBookstore` folder, or continue using the file if you still have it open from the previous exercise. Find the `feedback_mc` symbol in the Library, and double-click it to open it in symbol-editing mode.

You can add the WebServiceConnector component into your Flash document by expanding the Web Services panel and clicking to expand the `emailService` Web Service. Doing this reveals the service's two methods. Select the `form` layer, and then right-click (or control-click on the Mac) the `sendEmail` method and select Add Method Call from the contextual menu.

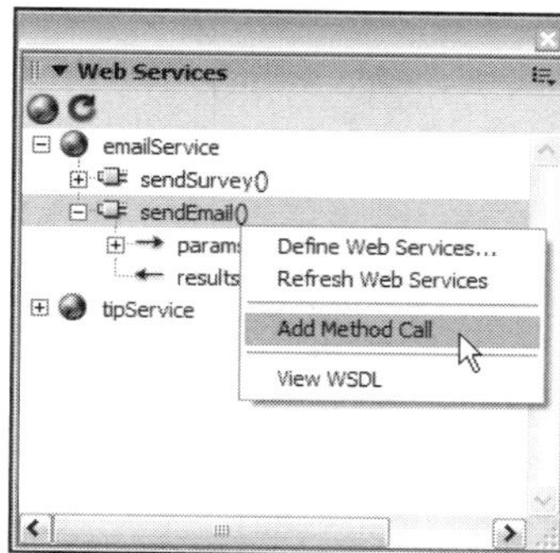

TIP *The WebServiceConnector component must be placed on frame 1 of a Timeline, whether it is the main Timeline or a movie clip Timeline. This is simply the way the component works based on the way its internal architecture has been engineered.*

2) View the WebServiceConnector's parameters in the Property inspector.
After you add the method call to your Flash document, you'll see that Flash has added a copy of the WebServiceConnector component into the Library and a small graphic icon onto the Stage.

NOTE *The WebServiceConnector icon that is added on the Stage will not be visible when the SWF file is published.*

Select the instance's icon on the Stage and open the Property inspector or Component Inspector panel to view the parameters for the WebServiceConnector component. The first thing you'll notice is the URL that you defined in the Web Services panel is listed in the Property inspector. The second important parameter is the `operation` parameter, which holds the name of the method that you're calling.

3) View the Web Service's schema in the Component Inspector panel.
A schema depicts the data hierarchy of a Web Service. To view the variables being passed back and forth between the Web Service and your Flash document, make sure that the WebServiceConnector component is still selected and then click the

Schema tab in the Component Inspector panel. The Schema tab shows you the same parameters and results that were listed in the Web Services panel if you expanded the method, as shown in the previous exercise.

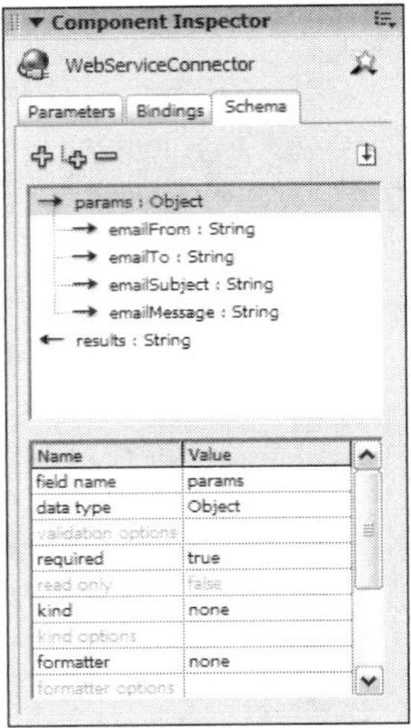

The Schema tab can be useful if you aren't sure which parameters a Web Service expects or if you are unsure what data type a particular Web Service returns. If you need to add any new properties or fields to the schema, you can do so by using the buttons located below the tabs to the left, as shown in the following figure.

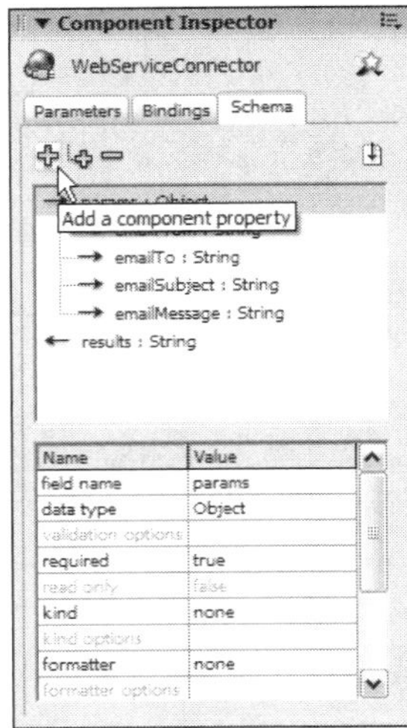

4) Define an instance name for the WebServiceConnector component and create bindings from the WebServiceConnector to text fields in the feedback form.

Actually getting the Web Service to "talk" to the Flash document is a relatively painless process. It usually doesn't require much in the way of ActionScript, which is nice for developing applications quickly. Just click the Bindings tab in the Component Inspector panel and then click the Add binding button below the tabs. Flash displays a dialog box, prompting you to assign an instance name if the WebServiceConnector component does not have one defined. Give the WebServiceConnector an instance name by typing in *wsc* and then click the OK button.

NOTE *An extremely important thing to remember when working with these components and bindings is the following: After you add bindings, you cannot move the component to different frame or into a movie clip, such as by copy and pasting the component. If you do so, you lose all your bindings. Therefore, you should make sure that the component is in the correct location before adding bindings to it.*

In the Add Binding dialog box, select the `emailFrom` parameter and click the OK button. You will notice that a new binding is listed in the Bindings tab. With `params.emailFrom` binding selected in the Bindings tab, double-click the Value column in the `bound to` row. When the Bound To dialog box appears, click the `TextInput, <email_txt>` value in the Component path pane. Select the `text : String` value in the Schema location pane and click the OK button to close the dialog box. Repeat this process binding `emailSubject : String` to the Component path `TextInput, <subject_txt>` and binding `emailMessage : String` to the Component path `TextArea, <message_txt>`.

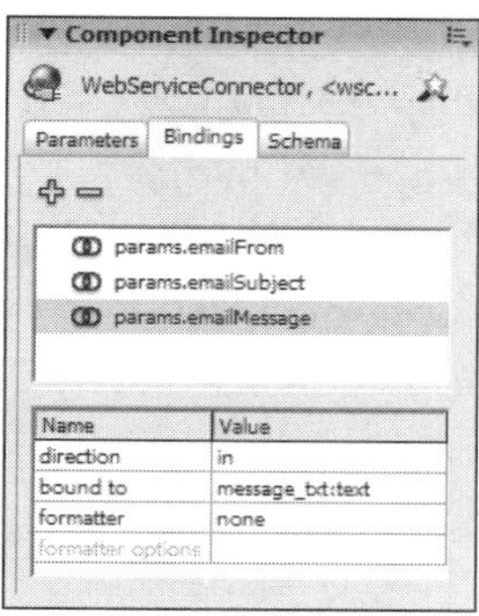

5) Create a binding that binds a constant value to the WebServiceConnector instance.

For the feedback form, you want to use a static `To` email address that specifies where the feedback is emailed to. One way to accomplish this is to bind a constant value to the WebServiceConnector instance. Select the WebServiceConnector component in your Flash document using the Selection tool. In the Bindings tab of the Component Inspector panel, add a new binding for `emailTo : String`. Double-click the `bound to` row to bring up the Bound To dialog box. In the Bound To dialog box, click the check box labeled Use constant value. Type an email address to send the feedback to (such as `you@yourdomain.com`) and click the OK button to close the dialog box. Make sure that you enter an email address that you can access to verify that your file is working correctly. You can now see the constant value listed in the `bound to` parameter of the Bindings tab.

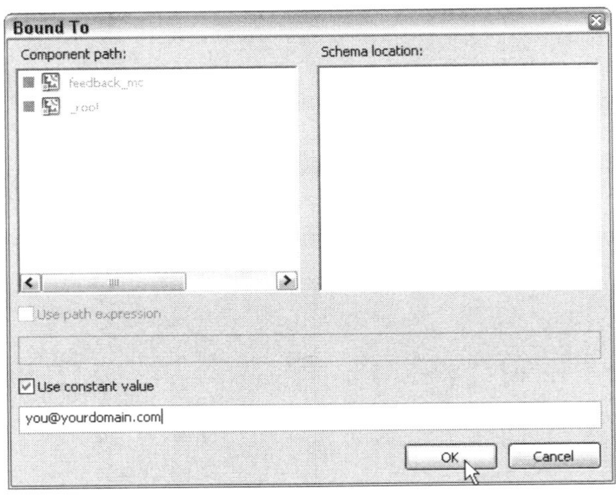

TIP *Another way to set a constant value is to create a hidden TextInput instance that will store the email address. To create a hidden text field, drag an instance of the TextInput component onto the Stage and click on the Parameters tab in the Component Inspector panel. Set the* `editable` *parameter to false, enter an email address to send the data to in the* `text` *parameter, and set the* `visible` *parameter to false. This hides the instance on the Stage. Set the instance name for the TextInput component to* `emailTo_txt`*. Now you can select and move the instance around the Stage, and it won't be visible or editable by users. Next, set up a binding exactly the same way you did in Step 4. Bind* `emailTo : String` *to the Component path* `TextInput, <emailTo_txt>`.

6) Trigger the Web Service using a behavior.

Triggering your Web Service is easy thanks in part to Flash containing a behavior to help you out. Select the `send_btn` Button instance on the Stage and expand the Behaviors panel. In the Behaviors panel, click the Add Behavior button and select Trigger Data Source from the Data menu. This opens the Trigger Data Source dialog box, in which you can select the WebServiceConnector component from the tree control. Click the OK button to close the dialog box when you are finished. Then click `Scene 1` in the edit bar to return to the main Stage.

7) Save the changes you made to the file.

When you are satisfied with the changes you made, publish the FLA file so a SWF is created in the `TechBookstore` folder. Now that you are finished creating the feedback form, skip ahead to the section called "Building the Questionnaire form in Flash MX Professional" to continue with the lesson.

BUILDING THE FEEDBACK FORM IN FLASH MX 2004

If you are using Flash MX 2004, you don't have the WebServiceConnector components that are included with the Professional version. You have to handle all the data a little differently because you do not have access to the necessary components and the Bindings and Schema tabs in the Component Inspector panel. A couple alternative ways of sending data back and forth between a server and your Flash document is to use the `LoadVars` class or XML data, although there are a few other ways of working with data (such as Flash Remoting or the Flash Communication Server, which both require installations and sometimes additionally purchased software).

The following exercise walks you through the steps used to integrate your Flash feedback form with a server-side language (in this case, ColdFusion) that sends the emails. These steps are necessary only if you do not have the WebServiceConnector component available.

NOTE *The ActionScript that is used for this example goes beyond what you learned in earlier lessons. In this lesson, you will learn what the code is doing, but not necessarily about why it is structured in this way. The reason it is included within this lesson is so you can make these parts of the Web site work if you are using Flash MX 2004 and not Flash MX Professional. You will learn how to write this code yourself in Lesson 11.*

1) Open the `bookstore11.fla` **document from the** `TechBookstore` **folder that you created in Lesson 9, or you can use** `bookstore12_starter.fla` **from the** `Lesson10` **folder on the CD-ROM. Save a new version of the file as** `bookstore12.fla`**. Open the** `feedback_mc` **movie clip you created in Lesson 9 in symbol-editing mode.**

Open the bookstore11.fla from the TechBookstore folder on your hard drive, or the bookstore12_starter.fla file from the CD-ROM in the Lesson10 folder. Save a new version of the file as bookstore12.fla.

NOTE *If you want to check out the finished versions of these files, you will need to open up the file that is specifically made for Flash MX 2004 that are appended with _fmx. The Flash MX Professional version will include data binding and additional components that are not included in Flash MX 2004.*

Find the feedback_mc on the Stage and double-click the instance to open it in symbol-editing mode.

Depending on whether you found the exercises Lesson 9 exciting enough to complete, you may or may not have an actions layer created. If you didn't add an actions layer, add the layer now. Select the topmost layer on the Timeline and insert a new layer. Rename the layer actions. Lock the actions layer to prevent you from accidentally adding any symbols to that layer.

2) Add a hidden TextInput instance on the Stage to hold a value for the To email address.

Because you cannot bind a constant value to contain the To email address without Flash MX Professional, one solution to this problem is to add a *hidden* TextInput instance on the Stage.

Drag an instance of the TextInput component onto the Stage. Using the Property inspector or Component Inspector panel, set the text parameter to the email address that you want to email the feedback to, such as you@yourdomain.com. Enter your own email (or an account you can actually check) here.

In the Component Inspector panel, set the visible parameter to false in order to hide the instance on the Stage. Assign an instance name of emailTo_txt to the TextInput instance using the Property inspector.

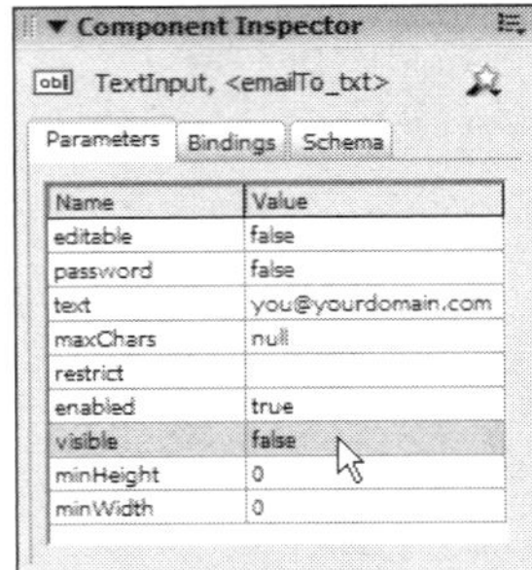

3) Add the following ActionScript into the Actions panel on frame 1 of the `actions` **layer.**

Select frame 1 of the `actions` layer, type in the following code into the Actions panel. This ActionScript is used to send data entered into the form to an email address. An explanation of what this code does follows the listing.

```
send_btn.onRelease = function() {
  var targetLoadVars:LoadVars = new LoadVars();
  var myLoadVars:LoadVars = new LoadVars();
  myLoadVars.emailFrom = email_txt.text;
  myLoadVars.emailTo = emailTo_txt.text;
  myLoadVars.subject = subject_txt.text;
  myLoadVars.message = message_txt.text;
  myLoadVars.sendAndLoad ("http://www.forta.com/misc/flash2004tfts/
  ⇒submit_feedback.cfm", targetLoadVars, "POST");
  targetLoadVars.onLoad = function() {
  trace(this.success);
  };
  gotoAndStop("thankyou");
};
```

This code looks a lot more complex than it really is. You will be using a series of name/value pairs, which are just that: a name that is associated with a particular value, such as Peter/fast. *Peter* represents someone's given name, and *fast* represents a particular attribute or value. Using `LoadVars` limits you to using this name/value structure, whereas different ways of transferring data (such as Flash Remoting) allow you to use complex data structures. Luckily for us name/value pairs are all we need here.

The first step is to add a `onRelease` event handler. This handler is called when a user clicks on the `send_btn` Button instance. Then you create two new variables that are used for sending and receiving the data. The first `LoadVars` variable is used to hold the variables that the server-side script returns. The second `LoadVars` variable holds all the variables that are sent to the server-side script.

Then the code copies the four text field values(`email_txt`, `emailTo_txt`, `subject_txt`, and `message_txt`) into the `myLoadVars` variable. When the `myLoadVars` object is sent to a URL, all these variables are included. Then a server-side script can be used to process the variables. A server-side script is code written using a language such as PHP, ColdFusion, or ASP. The script interacts with Web pages and is used to perform a particular task. The script sits on a server and can be used to load data, interact with a database, and perform other similar tasks—depending on what the code is written to do.

The following line of code is where Flash posts the values within the `myLoadVars` object to your server-side script, generously being hosted by Ben Forta at `forta.com`:

```
myLoadVars.sendAndLoad("http://www.forta.com/misc/flash2004tfts/
⇒submit_feedback.cfm", targetLoadVars, "POST");
```

The values in the `LoadVars` object are sent to `http://www.forta.com/misc/flash2004tfts/submit_feedback.cfm`. Any results sent from the server-side script will be saved into the `targetLoadVars` object. The final parameter in the `sendAndLoad()` function is `POST`. `POST` tells Flash how to send the data to the server-side script. When sending the `LoadVars` object using the `POST` method, all fields are sent to the server-side script as form variables. Form variables are variables that are sent in the HTTP header, which is not visible to the visitor. This is suitable for long sets of variables.

NOTE *The other option for the method is GET instead of POST. The GET method sends the values to your server-side script as URL variables along the query string. The query string, which is the part of the URL in the browser's address bar after the question mark, is suitable for sending short variables. For example, in the URL* `http://www.TrainingFromTheSource.com/index.cfm?name=jtalbot`, *the query string is: name=jtalbot.*

The final section of ActionScript from the code block you typed in is used for debugging in the testing environment only. The `trace` statement appears in the Output panel when the data has been sent from Flash to the server-side script. This lets you know that Flash has sent the data when you are working in the testing environment. The `trace` statements are used only for development and testing purposes, and should be removed before you publish the file and upload it to a server for a Web site (sometimes known as the *production environment*).

Finally, you see the following code:

```
targetLoadVars.onLoad = function() {
  trace(this.success);
};
```

This code is triggered when Flash receives a reply from the server-side script, which sometimes takes a short period of time before it's executed as Flash waits for a reply. Currently, the server returns a string value of success or failure, which will be displayed in the Output panel (again, for testing purposes). You will be able to test this form in Lesson 12 after you have the buttons and menus working for the Tech Bookstore. You could place code in the previous function, which could redirect the user to a thank you page if the email was successfully filled out or to a window informing the unfortunate user that the email couldn't be sent. The success page is targeted in the line: `gotoAndStop("thankyou");` which directs the playhead to the `thankyou` page.

4) Save the changes you have made to `bookstore12.fla`**.**

You can see a finished version of the file on the CD-ROM (that includes finished forms for both the feedback form and the questionnaire) in the file called `bookstore12_fmx.fla`. You will be able to test the document in Lesson 12. The following exercise is intended for those using Flash MX Professional, so skip ahead to the exercise called "Building the Questionnaire Form Using Flash MX 2004".

BUILDING THE QUESTIONNAIRE FORM IN FLASH MX PROFESSIONAL

You created a Flash questionnaire in Lesson 9, asking users for their experience level and skills. In this exercise you will expand upon that FLA and make it work by adding the appropriate bindings to the form to allow users to send the results to a server.

NOTE *If you are not working with Flash MX Professional, skip ahead to the section in this lesson called "Building the Questionnaire Form Using Flash MX 2004".*

1) Open the `bookstore12.fla` **document you created in the previous lesson for creating the feedback form in Flash MX Professional. Find** `questions_mc` **and open it in symbol-editing mode by double-clicking the symbol in the Library.**

Open the `bookstore12.fla` file you worked on earlier in this lesson, which should be saved in the `TechBookstore` folder. Then double-click the `questions_mc` instance *in the Library* to open the instance in symbol-editing mode. The instance must be on the Stage in order to add bindings. Remember that the feedback form and the questionnaire are both at the `feedback` label on the main Timeline.

2) Add an instance of the WebServiceConnector component to the FLA file by selecting Add Method Call from the Web Service panel.

In the previous exercise, you defined a Web Service for the feedback form. The same Web Service has a method called `sendSurvey` that you will use in this exercise. First of all make sure that you select the `form` layer. Then open the Web Services panel and then expand `emailService`. Right-click (or control-click on the Mac) the `sendSurvey` method, and select Add Method Call from the contextual menu. An instance of the WebServiceConnector component is now added to the document. Give the WebServerConnector component instance an instance name of *wsc* in the Property inspector.

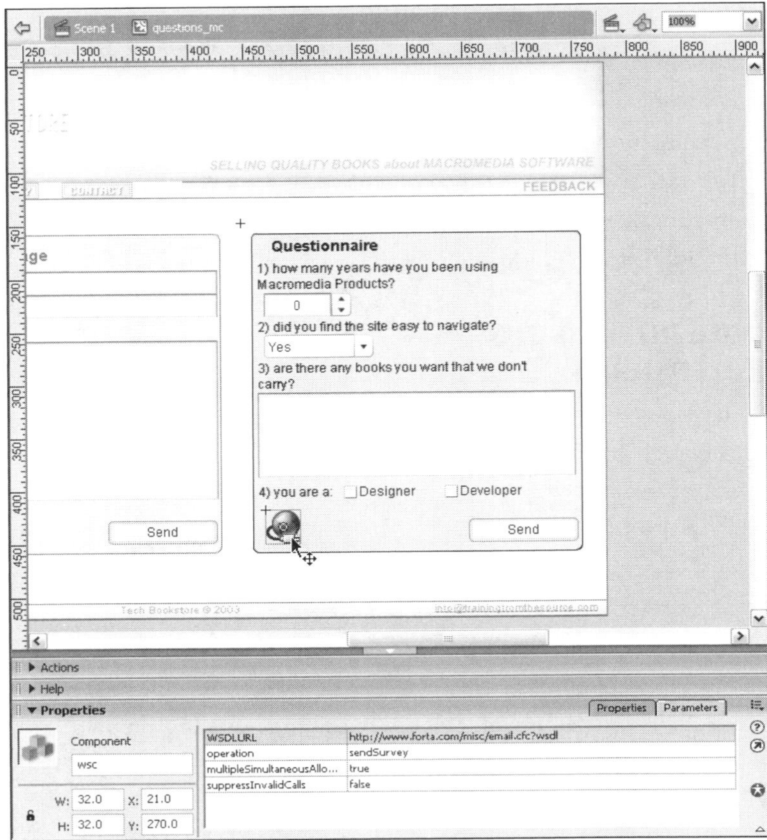

Set instance names for the components that are on the Stage. Give the NumericStepper an instance name of `numyears_ns`, and the ComboBox an instance name of `navigation_cb`. Assign an instance name of `books_txt` to the TextArea component. Then assign the Designer CheckBox an instance name of `designer_ch` and the Developer CheckBox instance an instance name of `developer_ch`. Finally give the Send button an instance name of `send_btn`.

3) Create bindings using the Bindings tab of the Component Inspector panel.
Click on the WebServiceConnector instance and then the Add binding button to add a binding. The button is found in the Bindings tab of the Component Inspector panel. The Add Binding dialog box opens.

In the Add Binding dialog box, select `surveyExperience` from the `params` object and click OK to return to the Bindings tab. Select the `params.surveyExperience` binding and double-click the empty value column beside `bound to` to open the Bound To dialog box.

For Component path, select `NumericStepper, <numyears_ns>`, and choose `value : Number` from Schema location. Click the OK button to close the `Bound To` dialog box and return to the Flash document.

Repeat this process binding `surveyNavigation` to ComboBox, `<navigation_cb>` setting the Schema location to `value : String`, `surveyBooks` to `TextArea, <books_txt>`, `surveyDesigner` to CheckBox, `<designer_ch>` and `surveyDeveloper` to CheckBox, `<developer_ch>`.

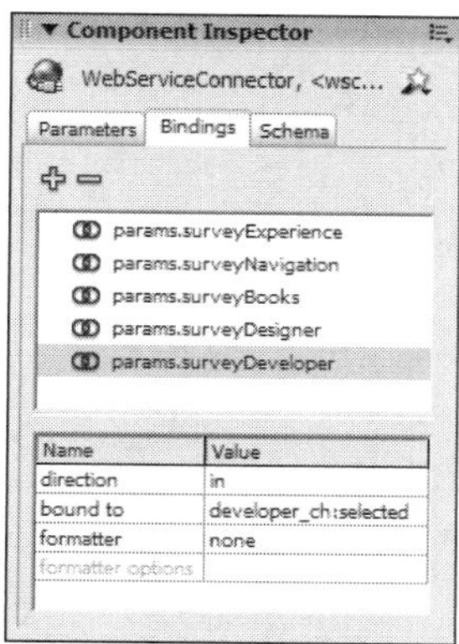

4) Trigger the Web Service using a behavior.

Select the `send_btn` Button instance on the Stage using the Selection tool and open the Behaviors panel. Similar to the previous exercise, click the Add Behavior button and select Data > Trigger Data Source from the contextual menu. Choose the WebServiceConnector component instance from the Select Data Source component control in the Trigger Data Source dialog box.

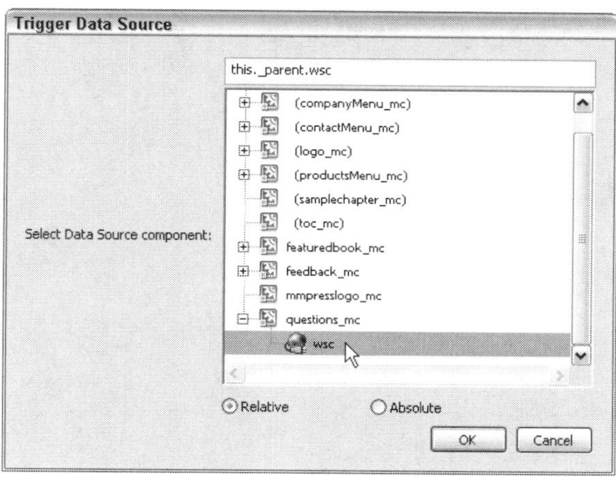

After you have selected the WebServiceConnector instance in the Trigger Data Source dialog box, make sure you have selected the Relative radio button instead of Absolute. The use of an absolute scope, such as `_root` (which you learned about in Lesson 6), is discouraged in Macromedia's ActionScript Coding Standards white paper and the official Flash documentation. Absolute scope is discouraged because it limits the portability of your ActionScript and can cause some problems when you embed one SWF within another Flash SWF file. It might not mean much to you at the moment, but it is a good habit to begin avoiding it now because you will benefit from the practice down the road. There is more information on `_root` and its alternative `_lockroot` at `www.TrainingFromTheSource.com/bonus`.

Click OK to close the Trigger Data Source dialog box and return to the Flash document.

5) Save the changes you have made to `bookstore12.fla`**.**

When you test the document in Lesson 12 and press the Send button, the values will be sent to the Web Service. The Web Service will append the values to an XML document on Ben Forta's server, in which they can be manipulated at a future date. The XML is being created by the Web Service that you are connecting to. If you want to check out the finished bookstore file for this lesson (including the modifications made in this exercise), make sure you open the `bookstore12_pro.fla` version of the file. Now skip ahead in this lesson to the exercise on building the Featured Book using Flash MX Professional.

BUILDING THE QUESTIONNAIRE FORM USING FLASH MX 2004

In this exercise, you will use `LoadVars` to send values to the server, similar to the feedback form you completed in an earlier exercise. The questionnaire is more complex than the feedback form because you are not only dealing with text fields this time. The form has a NumericStepper component, List component, TextArea component, and two CheckBox components that you have to get the values of.

NOTE *The ActionScript that is used for this example goes beyond what you have learned in earlier lessons. In this lesson, you will learn what the code is doing, but not necessarily about why it is structured in this way. The reason it is within this lesson is so you can make these parts of the Web site work if you are using Flash MX 2004 and not Flash MX Professional. You will learn how to write this code yourself in Lesson 11.*

In this exercise, you will use ActionScript to send the variables to a server-side script, which then processes the results so they can be computed later.

1) Open the `bookstore12.fla` **document and double click** `questions_mc` **to open it in symbol-editing mode. Then enter instance names for the component instances that are on the Stage.**

Open `bookstore12.fla` from the `TechBookstore` folder on your hard drive that you worked on earlier in this lesson. Double-click `questions_mc` to open the instance in symbol-editing mode. Lock the `actions` layer to prevent accidentally adding any symbols to that layer.

First of all, you need to give instance names to the components that are on the Stage. Give the NumericStepper an instance name of *numyears_ns*, and the ComboBox an instance name of *navigation_cb*. Assign an instance name of *books_txt* to the TextArea component. Then assign the Designer CheckBox an instance name of *designer_ch* and the Developer CheckBox instance an instance name of *developer_ch*. Finally give the Send button an instance name of *send_btn*.

2) Add ActionScript code to frame 1 of the `actions` **layer using the Actions panel.**

Select frame 1 of the `actions` layer in the `questions_mc` instance and open or expand the Actions panel (F9). Type in the following code:

```
send_btn.onRelease = function(){
  var targetLoadVars:LoadVars = new LoadVars();
  var myLoadVars:LoadVars = new LoadVars();
  myLoadVars.surveyExperience = numyears_ns.value;
  myLoadVars.surveyNavigation = navigation_cb.selectedItem.label;
  myLoadVars.surveyBooks = books_txt.text;
  myLoadVars.surveyDesigner = designer_ch.selected;
  myLoadVars.surveyDeveloper = developer_ch.selected;
  myLoadVars.sendAndLoad("http://www.forta.com/misc/flash2004tfts/
  ⇒submit_survey.cfm", targetLoadVars, "POST");
  trace("send");
  targetLoadVars.onLoad = function() {
    trace(this.success);
  };
  gotoAndStop("thankyou");
};
```

This code is fairly similar to the previous exercise, in which you used `LoadVars` to send the feedback to the server-side script. There are a couple of major differences between the two scripts. Because the questionnaire uses several different component types instead of the `TextInput` and `TextArea`, grabbing the values from the component and adding them to the `LoadVars` object is a bit more complicated.

So the hardest part of writing this code is writing the ActionScript to grab the proper values from each of the components. Each component is different, so they each have a different way to access the value of the component. For example, the `TextArea` and `TextInput` components store the current value in text, whereas the `CheckBox` component doesn't have a value, but instead has a Boolean (Yes/No) parameter called selected and denotes whether the component is checked or not. You access the current value of the NumericStepper component by accessing its value parameter.

The List component uses the parameter selectedItem, which is actually an object within itself and has two values: data and labels. You defined the labels and data values earlier in Lesson 9 after you dragged the List component onto the Stage. The value for labels is simply the label for the currently selected item, and similarly the value for data is the value you defined in the Property inspector or Component Inspector panel for the currently selected instance.

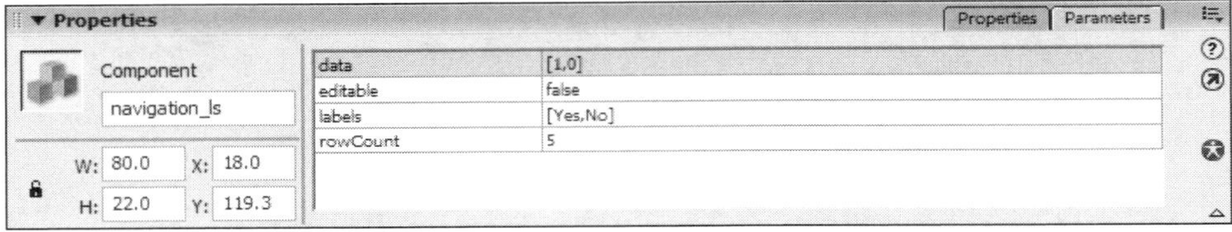

Just like the feedback form, you also have `trace` statements in the code to notify you when the request was sent to the server, and when the server responds it will return success. These two `trace` statements can be safely *removed* when you are convinced that the application is working properly.

3) Save the changes FLA file.

After you have finished, choose File > Save to save your modifications to the file. When you test the SWF file in the testing environment in Lesson 12 you will be able to fill out the form and then click Send. When you click the Send button, the values from each of the components are stored in a `LoadVars` object and are sent to a ColdFusion page. This is where they are stored in an XML file, which can be manipulated and sorted at a later date.

BUILDING THE FEATURED BOOK IN FLASH MX PROFESSIONAL

If you want to add a featured book to the front of the TechBookstore Web site, it can be accomplished by using any of the practices that have been outlined so far in this lesson. You can easily use `LoadVars` to load content in locally, as was done in the Flash MX 2004 exercises. Alternatively, you can use the WebServiceConnector (Flash MX Professional only) or Flash Remoting to load from local or remote servers, or you can use the XMLConnector component (also Flash MX Professional only).

NOTE *If you are using Flash MX 2004, skip ahead to the next exercise called "Building the Featured Book in Flash MX 2004". The XMLConnector component is not included in the Flash MX 2004 edition.*

This exercise walks you through using the XMLConnector component to load remote content into the `TechBookstore`. The XMLConnector makes working with XML in Flash incredibly easy. If you have ever seen the amount and kind of code necessary to work with XML documents in Flash, you will find this a piece of cake in comparison. In this example you will be loading an image and description of a featured book into the front page of the `TechBookstore`. This exercise also outlines how to import an XML schema and bind the values to several different components.

1) Open `bookstore12.fla` and save it in the `TechBookstore` folder. Insert a new movie clip symbol called `featuredbook_mc` and rename Layer 1 to `form`.

Open `bookstore12.fla` that you have been working on throughout this lesson. Choose Insert > New Symbol from the main menu and select the Movie clip radio button. Enter the name `featuredbook_mc` for the new symbol. Then click OK to enter symbol-editing mode.

When you are in symbol-editing mode, rename `Layer 1` to *form*.

2) Drag a Loader component onto the Stage and resize the instance to *90* pixels (width) by *100* pixels (height). Give the instance an instance name of `cover_ldr`, position the instance at the X coordinate of *35* and Y coordinate of *0*, and set the `scaleContent` parameter to `false`.

Open the Components panel and drag an instance of the Loader component onto the Stage. You can use the Property inspector to resize the component to 90 pixels wide by 100 pixels high by selecting the instance and typing new values into the inspector. Position the instance at an X coordinate of 35 and Y coordinate of 0.

Give the component an instance name of *cover_ldr*. The Loader instance will be used to load a JPEG image of the cover of the featured book into your Flash document. With the Loader component still selected on the Stage, expand the Property inspector or Component Inspector panel and make sure that the `scaleContent` parameter is set to `false`.

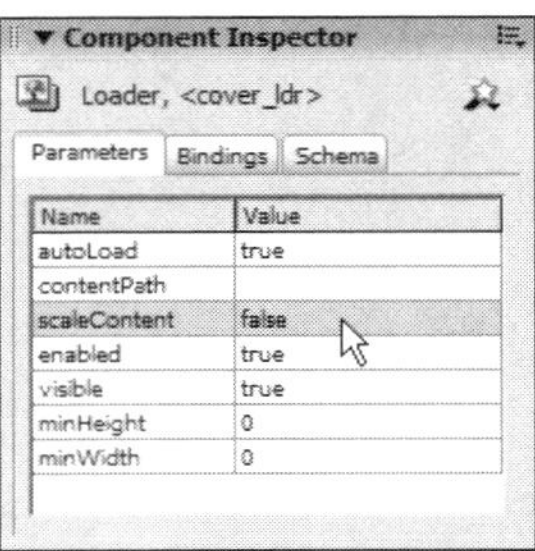

3) Drag a TextArea component onto the Stage and then position and resize the instance.

Drag an instance of the TextArea component onto the Stage and position it directly below the Loader component with an X coordinate of 0 and a Y coordinate of 100. Using the Property inspector, resize the component to *160* pixels wide by *150* pixels high. Rearrange the two component instances as necessary so they fit nicely on the Stage.

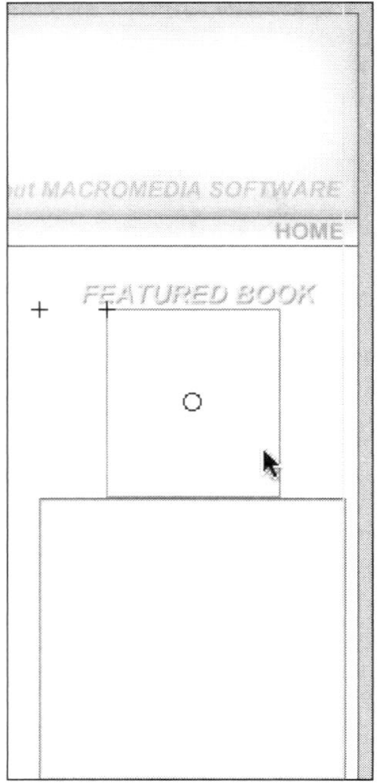

Select the TextArea instance and give the component an instance name of description_txt using the Property inspector. Make sure that the `editable` parameter is set to `false`, `html` is set to `true` and `wordWrap` is set to `true`. The TextArea will display a brief description of the book when it's loaded in. If the text is too long for the TextArea instance, scroll bars automatically appear so users can scroll through the loaded text.

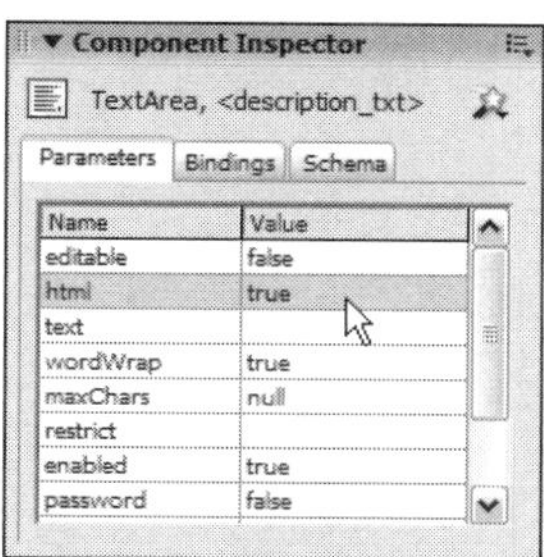

4) Add an XMLConnector Data Component to the FLA document.

Drag an instance of the XMLConnector component from the Components panel onto the Stage. With the component still selected, open the Property inspector and give the component an instance name of `xmlconn`. Set the URL to `http://www.trainingfromthesource.com/featuredbook.xml`, set the direction to `receive`, and make sure that `ignoreWhite` is set to `true`. Remember that the XMLConnector component does not appear in the SWF file when you publish it, so don't worry about where it's positioned on the Stage.

5) Import a XML Schema into the FLA document.

The easiest way to create bindings when working with XML is to import a schema from an existing XML file. This process automatically adds the appropriate fields and properties into the Schema tab of the Component Inspector panel, so you don't have to add the values manually.

When you used the WebServiceConnector component earlier in this lesson, you didn't need to manually import a schema because when you selected Add Method Call from the contextual menu in the Web Services panel, the schema was imported for you. To import a schema, you first need an XML file of sample data. The easiest way to do this is to copy the XML file, `featuredbook.xml`, from the `media` folder on the CD-ROM to your local computer hard drive (if you don't have it already).

Open the Component Inspector panel and go to the Schema tab. In the Schema tab, there is an "Import schema from a sample XML file" button near the upper-right side of the panel, below the tabs. Make sure that the `results` value is selected in the

Schema tab property area and click the Import schema button to open a browse file dialog box. Here you can browse for the `featuredbook.xml` file of sample data, which is stored on your hard drive.

When you find the XML file of sample data you wish to import, select the file and click the Open button to begin importing the fields and properties. You will see that the schema imported and several new properties can be seen in the Schema tab.

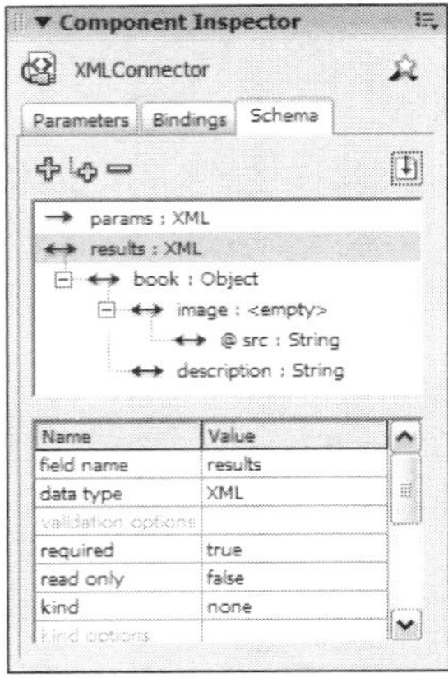

6) Bind the featured book's cover image to the Loader component.

Make sure that the XMLConnector component is still selected on the Stage. In the Component Inspector panel, click the Bindings tab to add a couple of bindings to the Flash document. Then click the Add binding button to add a new binding. In the Add Binding dialog box, select the `src` attribute and click OK to add the binding and return to the Flash document.

Then go back to the Bindings tab. Double-click the value column for `bound to` in order to open the Bound To dialog box and bind the value to a component. In the Component path pane, select Loader, `<cover_ldr>` and select `contentPath : String` from the Schema location pane. Click OK to close the dialog box. This causes the Loader component to load whatever cover image is defined in the XML document in the `src` attribute.

7) Bind the featured book's description to the TextArea component instance.

In the Bindings tab of the Component Inspector panel, click the Add binding button to open the Add Binding dialog box, select the `description` field, and click OK to close the dialog box.

Then go back to the Bindings tab. In the `bound to` field for the results binding, double-click the value column to open the Bound To dialog box. In the Component path pane, select `TextArea, <description_txt>`, select `text : String` from the Schema location pane, and click OK to close the dialog box.

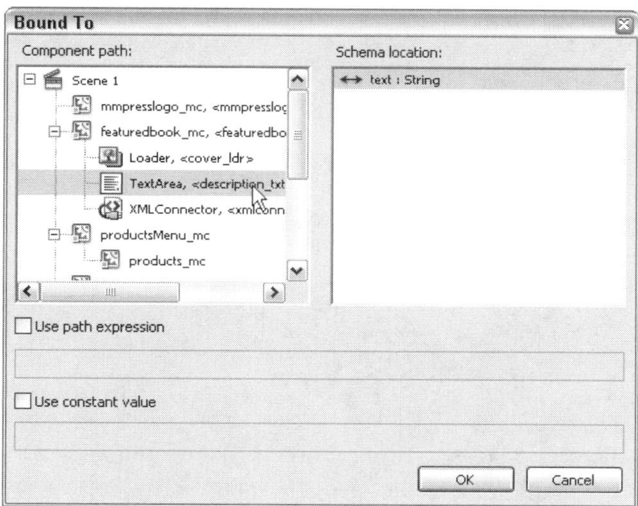

8) Drag the `featuredbook_mc` instance onto the main Stage. Back inside the `featuredbook_mc` instance, add an `actions` layer and trigger the XMLConnector component using a behavior.

You need to trigger the XML to load, which is similar to triggering the WebServiceConnector component when the user clicked the Send button to send feedback or the questionnaire data. However, to add the behavior, you will need the instance to be on the main Stage.

Return to the main Stage by clicking `Scene 1` in the edit bar. Select frame 1 on the `home` layer on the Timeline. Open the Library (F11) and drag the `featuredbook_mc` instance onto the Stage onto the `home` layer. Position the movie clip to the very right of the Stage, under the Featured Book text. You might need to reposition those two elements so they fit properly on the Stage. Select the `featuredbook_mc` instance and expand the Property inspector. Give it an instance name of `featuredbook_mc`.

Double-click `featuredbook_mc` to open the instance in symbol-editing mode again. Insert a new layer called `actions` above the `form` layer and select frame 1 of the `actions` layer. Open the Behaviors panel, click the Add Behavior button, and select Data > Trigger Data Source from the drop-down menu. The Trigger Data Source dialog box opens. In the Trigger Data Source dialog box, expand the `featuredbook_mc` instance and then select the XMLConnector instance (`xmlconn`) from the Data Source component pane. Make sure that the Relative radio button is selected.

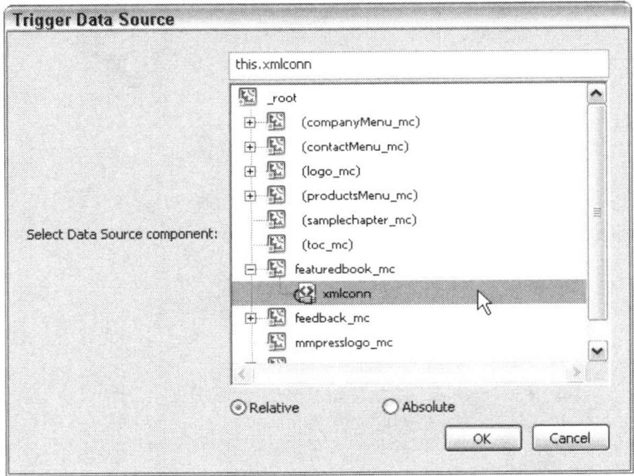

Click the OK button to close the dialog box and return to the Flash document. You now see that Flash has embedded the behavior's code in the first frame of the `actions` layer.

9) Test the FLA file in the testing environment. Save the changes you have made to `bookstore12.fla`.

Return to the main Stage by clicking `Scene 1` on the edit bar. Save your FLA and press Ctrl+Enter (or Command+Enter on the Mac) to test the SWF file in the testing environment. You will see an image of the book's cover and a brief description of the book with some HTML markup below that. If there is enough text, a scroll bar automatically appears in the TextArea component.

If the SWF file works correctly and no modifications are necessary, save the Flash file when you return to the authoring environment.

BUILDING THE FEATURED BOOK IN FLASH MX 2004

Building a dynamic featured book module without the aid of bindings and XMLConnector, as found in Flash MX Professional (and the previous exercise), takes a bit more time. The Flash MX 2004 process typically requires you to write the ActionScript yourself. There are many different approaches you could take. For example, you could use `LoadVars`, as in previous exercises in this lesson. Or, you could use XML, use Flash Remoting, or create multiple SWF files and load them in random files at runtime. Depending on how often you change the featured book, the easiest solution might be to manually type in some text and a URL to an image for the TextArea and Loader components.

NOTE *Again, the ActionScript included in this example jumps ahead a bit to what will be explained in Lesson 11. You will learn what the code does, but not the specifics about how it is structured. The reason this ActionScript is within this lesson is so you can make these parts of the Web site work if you are using Flash MX 2004 and not Flash MX Professional. As you can tell by now, if you are using Flash MX 2004 and not the Professional version, you sometimes need to use a lot more ActionScript!*

1) Open the `bookstore12.fla` you have been working on and insert a new movie clip symbol called `featuredbook_mc` and rename Layer 1 to `form`.

Open `bookstore12.fla` that you have been working on throughout this lesson. Choose Insert > New Symbol from the main menu and select the Movie clip radio button. Enter the name *featuredbook_mc* for the new symbol into the Create New Symbol dialog box. Then click OK to enter symbol-editing mode.

Rename `Layer 1` to *form* in symbol-editing mode for `featuredbook_mc`.

2) Drag a Loader component onto the Stage and resize it to *90* pixels wide by *100* pixels tall. Give the instance an instance name and position it at an X coordinate of 35 and Y coordinate of 0. Set the `scaleContent` parameter to `false` and enter an image URL for the `contentPath` parameter.

Open the Components panel and drag an instance of the Loader component onto the Stage. Change the dimensions of the component to *100* pixels high by *90* pixels wide using the Property inspector and place the instance near the top of the Stage. Enter an instance name of *cover_ldr* for the Loader instance. The Loader instance loads a JPEG image of the cover of the book into your Flash document at runtime. Open the Align panel and make sure that the To Stage button is selected. Position the instance at an X coordiante of 35 and Y coordinate of 0.

With the Loader component still selected, open the Property inspector or Component Inspector panel and make sure that `scaleContent` is set to `false`. Enter the URL to the cover image in the Loader component's `contentPath` parameter. If you're loading images from a remote server (such as `Amazon.com`), you need to type in the full URL (including `http://`) in the `contentPath` parameter. Enter the following value for `contentPath` in the Property inspector: `http://images.amazon.com/images/P/0321213424.01.TZZZZZZZ.jpg`. Different images can be found on `Amazon.com` by changing the ISBN, which in this case is `0321213424`.

If you want, you can also type in the `www.amazon.com` URL into your Web browser and download a copy of the cover art and save it into the `TechBookstore` folder. This means that you can load the file in locally instead of loading it remotely from a full URL. If the file is within the `TechBookstore` folder, you only have to type the image name of the JPEG.

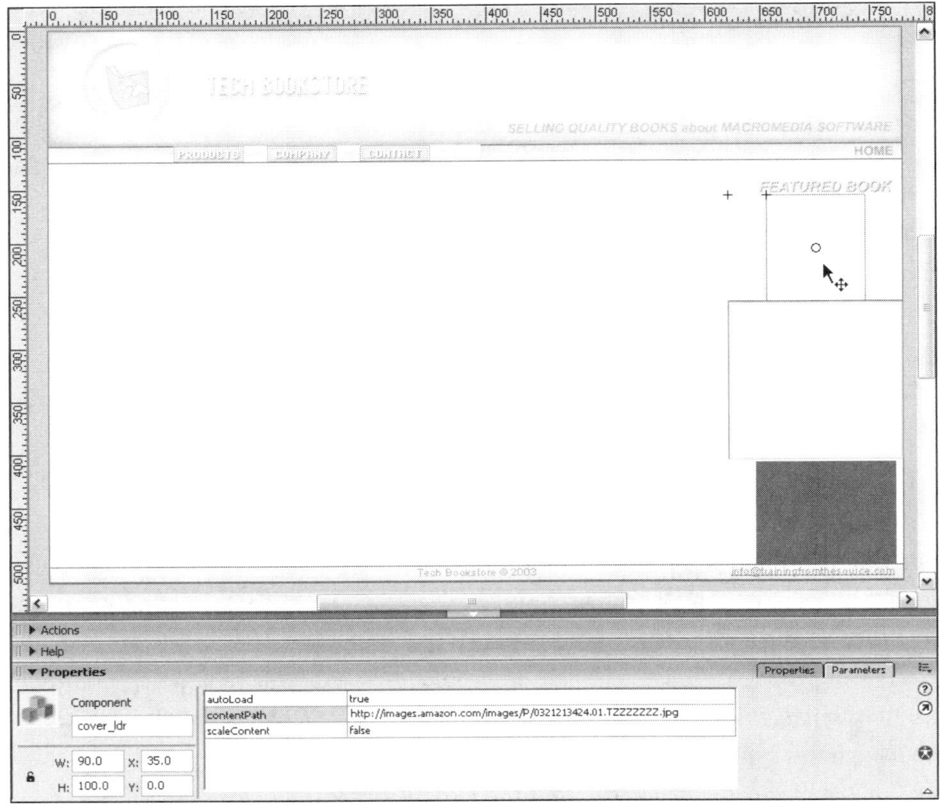

3) Drag a TextArea component instance onto the Stage and position it below the Loader instance. Give it an instance name and set the parameters for the instance.
Drag an instance of the TextArea component on to the Stage and position it directly below the Loader component. Resize the component to *160* pixels wide by *150* pixels high using the Property inspector. Rearrange the components as necessary so they fit nicely on the Stage.

With the TextArea instance still selected, enter an instance name of *description_txt* in the Property inspector. Also make sure that the `editable` parameter is set to `false`, `html` is set to `true` and `wordWrap` is set to `true`. The TextArea will contain a brief description of the book and if the text is too long for the TextArea, scroll bars will automatically appear to allow visitors to scroll through the text as necessary.

4) Add an `actions` layer and type the following ActionScript into the Script pane of the Actions panel.

Insert a new layer above the `form` layer, and rename it *actions*. In frame 1, add the following ActionScript (what this ActionScript does is described following the code listing):

```
var tempString:String = "<span class='title'>Macromedia Flash MX 2004: Training
⇒from the Source</span><br><br>";
tempString += "<b>Synopsis</b><br><br>";
tempString += "Learn Macromedia's Flash MX 2004, a fast solution for developing
⇒rich Internet content and Web applications. The lessons in the book take the
⇒user step-by-step through the creation of a complex Web site - one that
⇒includes movie, sound, interactivity, dynamic text and more.<br><br>";
description_txt.text = tempString;
```

The first line of code simply creates a variable named `tempString`, which holds the text string (just plain HTML-formatted text). The text will be copied into the `description_txt` TextArea component later on. The first time you set the variable, you give it a data type of `String` by appending the `:String` onto the end of the variable name. Data types, and strong typing, will be discussed in the next lesson.

You can also see that the first time you set the variable, you use the equals sign (=) to assign a value to the string. Every subsequent time you set the variable, you need to use the += operator, which Flash calls the *addition assignment* operator. An operator uses one or more values to calculate a new value. The addition assignment operator is often used with strings and to *concatenate* (or *join*) two strings together. It takes the value on the right side of the operator and appends (or *adds*) it to the end of the existing variable that was defined in the left side of the operator.

For example, in the previous code, the `tempString` variable holds the title of the book and a couple of `<br>` tags. The second line of code appends the string `<b>Synopsis</b><br><br>` onto the existing value defined in the `tempString` variable.

NOTE *`<br>` is an HTML tag that is used for a line break.*

Therefore, after the second line of code is executed, the value of the `tempString` variable is:

```
<span class='title'>Macromedia Flash MX: Training from the
⇒Source</span><br><br><b>Synopsis</b><br><br>
```

When the addition assignment operator is used with numbers, it increments the existing value with the value on the right; for example:

```
var i = 12;
// sets the value of "i" to 12
i += 4;
// increments the existing value of "i" by 4, now "i" equals 16.
```

TIP *The double slashes (//) denote a comment, and do not affect the surrounding code. These slashes just help you document your code and leave notes for yourself and other developers who might work on this file at a future date.*

The line of code beginning with `description_txt.text` in this example sets the value of the `description_txt` TextArea component to the value of the `tempString` variable. It is also important to point out that the HTML formatting works only if the TextArea's `html` parameter has been set to `true` in the Property inspector or Component Inspector panel. Otherwise, the code will be displayed as regular text (non-HTML), and you will see the `<b>` and `<br>` tags throughout the text.

5) Add the movie clip instance to the Stage. Test the document by pressing Ctrl/Command+Enter.

Return to the main Stage, and open the Library (F11). Drag an instance of `featuredbook_mc` onto the Stage, and position it underneath the Featured Book text. Reposition the instances if necessary. Then expand the Property inspector and type in *featuredbook_mc* as the instance name.

Because this instance is now on the first page, you can test the bookstore and see the movie clip working. Select Control > Test Movie from the main menu to test the SWF file using the testing environment. Testing the SWF file allows you to see whether there are any problems with the file, meaning that you might need to return and fix any problems with the ActionScript or component parameters.

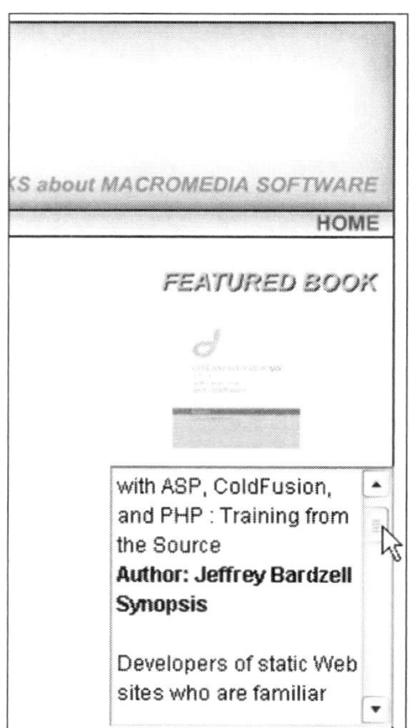

If you have any problems, and there are no problems evident with the ActionScript, you might want to check if your Internet connection is working because it is required to load in the image at runtime. You might also want to check the URL of the image that you are loading in, and whether the image is still available at that location. Remember that you can always save a local copy of a JPEG to the `TechBookstore` folder and load the image from there as well.

6) Save the changes that you have made to the document.

When you are finished, save the changes to your Flash document.

NOTE *To download the server-side scripts that have been used in this lesson for use on your own server or just to take a look at, go to* `www.TrainingFromTheSource.com/bonus/ssfiles`. *You will require ColdFusion MX if you want to run these files on your own server.*

The SWF for this Flash document will be loaded into the `TechBookstore` application in an upcoming lesson.

WHAT YOU HAVE LEARNED

In this lesson, you have:

- Defined a Web Service (pages 293–296)
- Called a Web Service (pages 296–301)
- Sent email using a Web Service (pages 301–305)
- Used an instance of WebServiceConnector in a document (pages 305–316)
- Used the XMLConnector component to organize data (pages 311–316)
- Bound data to components (pages 311–316)

ActionScript basics

LESSON 11

No matter how wonderful tweened animations, Timeline Effects, components, and behaviors might be, they can only take your SWF files and application building so far. There will come a time when you want to add some certain element of interactivity, or perhaps a form built in Flash, and you will need to write your own ActionScript code. You have already been exposed to a fair amount of ActionScript throughout the previous lessons. It's quite likely some of this lesson will look familiar because of several exercises you completed earlier that include similar code, particularly if you are using Flash MX 2004.

In this lesson you will complete the rest of the pages for the Tech Bookstore after you cover some of the fundamental concepts making up ActionScript. This process will help you understand the code you've already written and the code that you're about to write. That might sound like a lot of work to complete in a single lesson! However, you'll quickly discover how similar many of the tasks are to each other, and that it takes only minor modifications for all these different sections to work in unique ways and with differing content. You might end up adopting a similar process, such as recycling common tasks, to save time building the sites you work on after you're finished with this book.

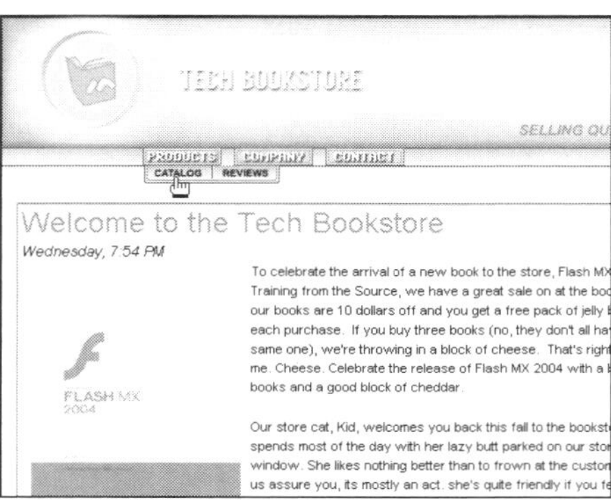

Adding ActionScript allows you to load in content and make those menus work.

WHAT YOU WILL LEARN

In this lesson, you will:

- Learn about the differences between ActionScript 1.0 and ActionScript 2.0
- Learn about objects, methods, and properties
- Learn how to use strict typing with variables
- Learn how to use code hinting to speed up writing ActionScript
- Learn about functions and conditional statements
- Learn about using scope and variables
- Learn more about _root, _parent, and levels
- Work with the `LoadVars` object
- Use events, event handlers,and listeners in your code
- Add CSS formatting to text and load it into a document
- Build the Catalog, Reviews, News, and Home pages
- Make the Tech Bookstore menu animate
- Make the Tech Bookstore menu work

APPROXIMATE TIME

This lesson takes approximately two hours 30 minutes to complete.

LESSON FILES

Media Files:

media/catalog01.png
media/catalog02.png

Starting Files:

Lesson11/bookstore12_fmx.fla
Lesson11/bookstore12_pro.fla

Completed Project:

Lesson11/bookstore13_fmx.fla
Lesson11/bookstore13_pro.fla
Lesson11/reviews.fla
Lesson11/news.fla
Lesson11/catalog01.fla
Lesson11/catalog02.fla
Lesson11/0321213408.txt
Lesson11/0321219198.txt
Lesson11 /home.fla
Lesson11/home.txt
Lesson11/home01.jpg
Lesson11/home02.jpg
Lesson11/styles.css

INTRODUCING ACTIONSCRIPT 1.0 AND ACTIONSCRIPT 2.0

In Lesson 6, you found out about some of the most important terminology and concepts of ActionScript. You learned how dot notation works and how to work with variables and values. In this lesson, you continue with ActionScript and find out how to start putting together code into events and functions, create new instances of an object, and how to write well-formatted ActionScript.

You have probably come across the reference to ActionScript 2.0 many times by now, and perhaps you wonder how it differs from ActionScript 1.0, or what version the language you are or should be writing code in. ActionScript 2.0 is the most recent and updated version of ActionScript available in Flash MX 2004. You don't have to use ActionScript 2.0 in your FLA files built using Flash MX 2004. Depending on the code you use, you might need to publish your FLA files as Flash Player 7 SWF files, but it is also possible to write ActionScript 2.0 for Flash Player 6.

There are several new changes made to the way you format your code using ActionScript 2.0, which is perhaps one of the most noticeable changes between version 2.0 and version 1.0. When you are *strict typing* variables, which you will learn about in an upcoming section, you are using a process that is supported by ActionScript 2.0 and not used in ActionScript 1.0. Another feature of ActionScript 2.0 (sometimes called AS 2.0) is the way *events* are generated and handled in Flash. An event is an action that occurs while an SWF file is playing back and is triggered by events such as keyboard input, a sound file completing, external files being loaded, or a button being pressed. Both of these features are being used in the Tech Bookstore.

Another feature of ActionScript 2.0 is enhanced support for writing object-oriented code that helps you reuse code when building applications. Object-oriented programming (also referred to as OOP) is beyond the scope of this book, and is covered in more depth in *Macromedia Flash MX 2004 ActionScript: Training from the Source*. Basically, OOP allows you to organize your code into external ActionScript files that contain a series of methods and properties related to a single object, such as a Movie Clip, Sound or custom object. These special external ActionScript files are referred to as *classes* and are used all throughout the Flash MX 2004 software. Although creating your own classes does go beyond the scope of this book, classes in general are discussed later in this lesson.

NOTE *When you use any part of ActionScript 2.0 language, you must make sure that you publish your SWF files with ActionScript 2.0 selected as the ActionScript version. This setting is necessary in order for your SWF file to compile correctly. When you publish an SWF file, it is said to be "compiling."*

USING STRICT TYPING AND CODE HINTS

You will reference some variables in a very particular way in the ActionScript you use in this lesson. By naming the variables with specific suffixes or by using ActionScript 2.0's *strict data typing*, it is possible to have Flash give you code hints for each data type or class (which will be discussed in a later section). Strict typing variables helps you avoid errors in your SWF files and also helps you use code hinting in the Actions panel.

NOTE *Classes are referred to a few times in the following section. They will be explained in greater detail following this discussion on code hinting. For now, just think of a class like a* data type *(Number, string, and so on) similar to what was outlined in Lesson 6.*

LEARNING HOW TO USE STRICT DATA TYPING

Strict data typing means that you explicitly tell Flash what data type a variable is when you create it if it's based on built-in or custom classes (which are discussed later in this lesson). If you create (or *declare*) a new variable and strict type it to a particular class (data type), the rules of that class apply. Flash expects a particular kind of data to be stored in that variable, such as the `String` class expecting a string to be contained in the variable. Therefore, if you declare a new variable as in the following code:

```
var myString:String;
```

You are telling Flash to declare a new variable called `myString` that stores a `String` value. You only need to tell Flash what data type to use when you declare the variable; meaning, you only need to strict type initially for each variable you declare. If you try storing a *different* data type in the variable created with strict typing, such as in the following code:

```
var myString:String;
myString = 15;
```

An error occurs when you publish the document. An error occurs because you are assigning a *number* to that variable, which is not accepted by Flash. Flash is expecting a string instead. Therefore, the following code would work only when you assign a string value to the `myString` variable.

```
var myString:String;
myString = "my cat eats chicken";
```

Using Code Hints in the Actions panel

Code hinting is a feature found in the Actions panel (and *Script window* if you are using Flash MX Professional). Code hints help you save time when writing ActionScript and help reduce many of the typos and errors that might break your scripts. When you type in a variable and press the period key, the code hint drop-down menu appears. You are prompted with a list of all the possible properties and methods available for the object that the variable belongs to.

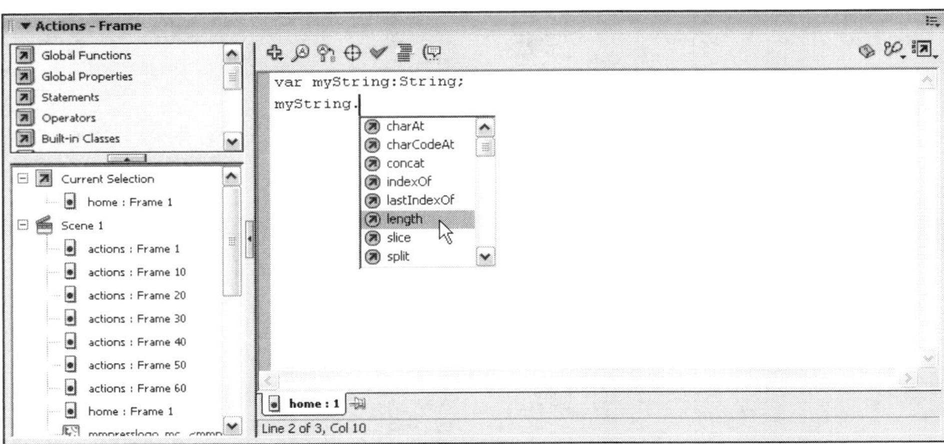

Code hints can be invaluable if you are trying to enter text into a text field and can't remember which property to use. There are two ways you can open the drop-down menu: strict typing the variable or adding suffixes to the variable. You've already seen examples of using suffixes throughout this book.

If you have a variable name, it could possibly be for many different objects because it's just a variable name that could be for anything from a number that's a score, to XML data. Strict data typing or suffixes tell Flash what data type (class) the variable belongs to. If you specify what kind of data that variable is for, the code hints show the correct methods and properties.

The first way you can specify a variable is by using *suffixes*. By ending instance names for objects in your FLA file with suffixes such as `_mc` (MovieClip), `_btn` (Button), `_txt` (TextField), `_str` (String) or `_lv` (LoadVars), Flash provides the proper code hints for that instance. Although not every one of the suffixes provides code hints (notably `_gr` because you cannot write ActionScript for a graphic) one of the other major benefits of following this naming scheme is that it makes it much easier to remember what data type (as you learned about previously) each symbol is within the Library of the FLA. An example of variable suffixing follows:

```
var homeContent_lv = new LoadVars();
homeContent_lv.load("home.txt");
```

Remember that each time you refer to the `homeContent_lv` variable, the `_lv` suffix should be appended because it is part of the variable name. It is important to remember that not every data type has an associated suffix (for example, `Object` has no suffix). Therefore, it might be necessary to use a couple of the methods listed in this section to provide code hints for each of your different variables.

Another way of getting Flash to provide code hints is by what Macromedia calls *strict data typing.* Simply put, strict data typing is when you add `:String` , `:Number`, `:LoadVars`, or any one of a dozen other data types onto the end of a variable name when you create the variable. You saw an example of this in Lesson 10 in the `LoadVars` examples.

The following code creates a `LoadVars` object and provides code hints using strict data typing:

```
var homeContent:LoadVars = new LoadVars();
homeContent.load("home.txt");
```

Notice that this code has `:LoadVars` after the variable name `homeContent`. When you type the `homeContent` on the following line, as soon as the dot (`.`) is typed, a list of methods and properties appears, allowing you to choose `load` without having to type anything else.

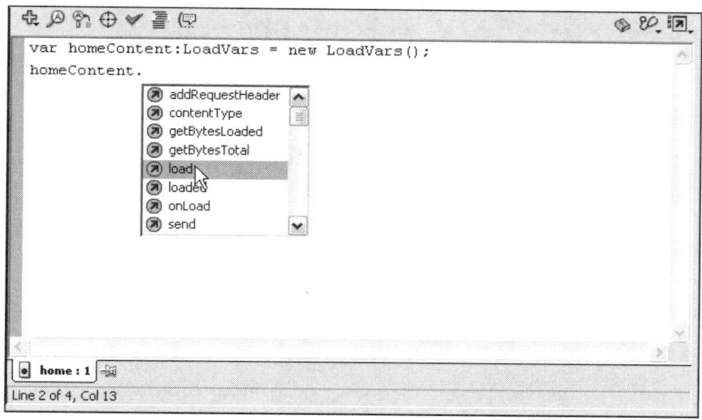

The `:LoadVars` appends onto the variable name when the variable is defined using the `var` keyword. Every future reference to the variable is simply `homeContent`, like you can see in the second line of code. You can also describe an instance on the Stage in a similar way. If you have a movie clip on the Stage with an instance name of `myClip`, you could type the following into the Actions panel:

```
var myClip:MovieClip;
```

and then you will see the appropriate code hints for that movie clip instance when you write ActionScript for it in the Actions panel.

There is a third way to get Flash to display code hints by typing the data type (the kind of data the variable holds, such as a String, Number, Movie Clip, LoadVars, and so on) and variable name within a *comment*, such as:

```
// LoadVars homeContent;
homeContent.load("home.txt");
```

A comment is a message that you type within the ActionScript code, usually to tell you what is happening in the code or as reminders of things to do. Comments do not actually execute any code. However, when you use a comment in this way, as soon as the dot is typed, the Actions panel opens a list of available methods and properties for the LoadVars object, just as in the preceding example.

Whatever way you choose is completely up to you. If you can't make up your mind, you can even combine the methods, as in the following code:

```
var homeContent_lv:LoadVars = new LoadVars();
```

This code has the advantage of using a suffix that can help you remember what the variable is throughout your code, and it also uses strict data typing that makes sure you don't accidentally try setting the variable to the wrong data type such as a Number or String.

LEARNING ABOUT CLASSES, METHODS, AND PROPERTIES

Flash is based on a model that involves classes, objects and instances. You don't need to worry too much about this model or the architecture of it, although it will help you to know a bit about what makes up a class and why it is useful in ActionScript. In a nutshell, a class is a collection of methods and properties that describe objects.

NOTE *Methods and properties are outlined in the following section.*

For example, you could have a computer class. This class might have a bunch of methods and properties describing the computer class. A property might be operatingSystem or diskSize. Methods of the computer class might be restart or shutdown. The class is like a blueprint that describes computers, and you might have several different kinds of computers described by this singular class. To use these methods and properties in your SWF file, you have to create an instance (a copy) of the class like an instance on the Stage—except you create the instance using ActionScript.

NOTE *You do not create classes directly in the Actions panel. Classes must be created in external files that are compiled into the SWF when you publish it. You won't create any classes for this book, but instead just use what are called "built-in classes" that are included right in ActionScript itself.*

ActionScript includes a number of *built-in* classes, which are complex data types that you can work with to make Flash do certain tasks. Examples of built-in classes include the Math class, Button class, and Date class. You have already used the MovieClip class, and some of its methods and properties. These include methods such as stop, and gotoAndPlay. This class also has properties you can change or set for an instance, such as _visible, _width and _height. For example, you could change the location of the instance by changing the _x and _y properties, which you have already done extensively through changing the X and Y coordinates of a movie clip using the Property inspector. You will look at how to use a built-in class shortly.

When you create a new instance of a class, you are creating it using a *constructor*. To create a new instance using ActionScript you would write a line of ActionScript similar to the following:

```
var myColor:Color = new Color();
```

In this example, you are creating (or *constructing*) a new instance of the Color class and storing the instance in a (strict typed) variable named myColor. Just like a movie clip on the Stage is an instance (or copy) of a movie clip symbol in the Library, myColor is an instance of the Color class.

The Color class is an example of a built-in class. "Built-in" means that the ActionScript language has its *predefined* methods and properties that create the class itself, so it's already written into the language for you to use. This means the things that this class can do are already set up in ActionScript. The Date class can be used to grab information from the computer system's clock, for example. And the System class can be used to provide a bit of information about a visitor's computer system.

Looking at Methods and Properties

A class consists of methods and properties. Methods are *functions* associated with that object's class (such as the Color class, discussed previously) and are used to do something with the object, just like functions act upon your SWF file. There are built-in methods in the ActionScript language for the built-in classes you learned about earlier. For example, setRGB() is a built-in method of the Color class. This method sets the hexadecimal color value for an instance you have in your SWF file.

Properties are also built into the class. Properties are like variables or data that is used to *define* an instance, a lot like the variables you use in your SWF file. For example, the code you looked at earlier in Lesson 6:

```
myMovieClip_mc._visible = true;
```

In this code, `_visible` is a property that is used to define whether an instance is visible (`true`) or invisible (`false`). As you can tell, the visibility property is being defined for the `myMovieClip_mc` instance on the Stage.

NOTE *Events and event handlers are discussed later on in this lesson in the example called "Using Events, Handlers and Listeners."*

USING FUNCTIONS AND CONDITIONAL STATEMENTS

Functions are blocks of code that are typically reused many times in an FLA file. Functions can return a value and have parameters passed to them. Parameters (sometimes called *arguments*) allow you to pass an unchanging (or *static*) value or variable into a function. Then the value(s) can be used and manipulated in your function's code. For example, you might want to create a function that takes two date parameters and counts the number of days between the two dates.

TIP *You might notice that components also have parameters. This means that the parameter values that you enter or set using the Property inspector or Component Inspector panel are setting particular values within the ActionScript used by the Components. ActionScript in each component recognizes what to do, based on the values you set in the Flash authoring environment.*

In the following function, two parameters are taken. The second parameter (`_blank`) is an optional parameter, meaning it is not necessary for the function to work. `_blank` specifies the frame or window that the URL should load into. The URL is a static value, which is used to redirect to a given Web page. The URL is loaded in an external Web browser when this function is called.

```
getURL("http://www.trainingfromthesource.com","_blank")
```

The parameters that you pass into a function can be used in that function. For example, in the following function named `welcome`, you are passing two parameters: `firstName` and `hobby`. Then those two parameters are actually used within the function.

```
function welcome(firstName:String, hobby:String) {
 var welcomeText:String = "Hello, " + firstName + ". I see you enjoy " + hobby;
 trace(welcomeText);
}
```

Functions are used all throughout Flash and ActionScript. You've already seen several examples of functions, from the simple `stop`, to the `onLoad` method of the `LoadVars` class. It is also possible to write your own functions to perform specific tasks, or to simplify your code if you find yourself consistently performing the same tasks over and over again. Changing similar code blocks into a single function helps you manage your ActionScript code because now if you need to make changes to that code you only need to modify one place instead of all throughout your Flash document.

A *conditional statement* executes if a particular condition evaluates to `true`. A condition evaluates to a Boolean: either `true` or `false`. Depending on what value is the outcome determines whether code is executed or not, or sometimes *what* code is executed. In the following ActionScript `success` is the conditional and must evaluate to either `true` or `false`. If `success` is `true` then the first statement is executed. If `success` is `false`, the statement beneath `else` is executed. This statement is known as an if/else statement, which means if something is `true`, do this first thing; however, if it is not `true`, do the other specified thing instead.

```
if (success == true) {
   //if success is true, do this
   trace("It's true! That file loaded or something.");
} else {
   //if success is false, trace this
   trace("Rats! Error loading file.");
}
```

Instead of `success`, you could have a value or equation as the condition instead. The equation could just as well be:

```
if (today == 15) {
   //do something
}
```

This means if the value of the variable `today` is equal to `15`, something happens.

NOTE *The double equals seen in the previous code means you are comparing two values. Essentially, you are seeing if one thing equals something else; in this case, if today is equal to the value of 15.*

TIP *As you have seen more than a few times by now, code typically uses varying amounts of indentation in it. This isn't done for any other purpose than to make your code easier to read. Indented code helps you debug, sometimes because it's easier to discover whether you have forgotten to close a bracket. Indentation also helps you clearly separate your statements from the conditionals. You can use the Auto Format button found in the Actions panel toolbar to add proper indentation to your ActionScript.*

UNDERSTANDING SCOPE

In Lesson 6, you learned about some of the things that make up ActionScript, such as variables, keywords, and data types. You also learned about how dot notation works and a bit about how dot notation is used to construct lines of ActionScript. Now you will take a look at *where* ActionScript lives in an FLA file.

One of the most important and sometimes confusing parts of ActionScript is getting a good grasp of how *variable scope* works and how it is used when you are writing code and working with Flash files. A scope is the area of your FLA where a variable can be referenced. That means if a variable exists in a certain place, such as within a function or on a particular Timeline, that is where its scope is. Understanding how scope works (and where your variables are) can take some practice and patience, and a certain amount of experience. As you test many different scenarios with your own personal projects, you quickly get a good grasp about how scope affects a Flash file. It might take some practice to get the hang of scope and see how it affects your code first hand, so don't worry if it doesn't make sense right away.

In Lesson 6 you found out that variables are similar to containers that hold a piece of data, and you learned a bit about how to name them. A very important rule to remember is that two variables cannot have the same name. However, a variable can have the same name if they are in a different *scope*. This indicates how the code lives in different areas of your SWF files. There are three available scopes within Flash, as discussed in the following sections.

Local variables: These variables are available only when a function is called. Local variables are ones inside the two curly brackets of a function, as you just saw in an earlier exercise. Outside of this function (when it's *not* being called), these variables do not exist.

Local variables are defined within a function using the `var` keyword and no longer exist when the function exits. This means that the variables you use inside the function cannot be used in other places on the Timeline or in your code. This is good in a way because it means you won't have conflicts in other pieces of ActionScript with variables that might use the same name. Another benefit is that Flash uses fewer resources because it doesn't have to keep track of a large number of variables, which are no longer being used in your application. The local variables exist only for the life of the function and then disappear.

An example of a local variable is as follows:

```
function myVariable() {
    var myNum:Number;
    //myNum variable exists here
}
//myNum no longer exists.
trace(myNum);    //undefined
```

When you trace the `myNum` variable outside of the function, you have undefined returned, because the variable no longer exists outside of the `myVariable` function. Remember that the trace statement can be used to test your code and send messages to the Output panel when you test a document.

TIP *Although it is possible to use the same variable names in functions and in other scopes without naming conflicts, this isn't always advisable. You will want to avoid using the same names whenever you can because the practice can lead to confusion when editing your code at a future date if you have similarly named variables all throughout your FLA file in different scopes.*

Timeline variables: These variables are available to any script only within the same Timeline. Remember that your SWF can have more than one Timeline, because a Timeline can exist on a different level or in a movie clip or component. Levels will be defined in the following section. If you have more than one Timeline then there can be different Timeline variables in each of these areas, and all have the same name without running into conflicts.

When a variable is defined in a Timeline, that variable is available on frames after the variable has been defined. For example, if the following code is placed on frame 10, it would create a variable named `numUsers` in the main Timeline. That variable exists throughout the Timeline after frame 10. Before frame 10 plays, that variable is not available in the SWF file.

```
var numUsers:Number = 5;
```

Global variables: These variables are available to any of the Timelines, scopes, or functions within the SWF file. Therefore, you can declare a global variable and then use the variables in other SWF files that are loaded into the main SWF file, and also throughout the entire main SWF without making any changes to your ActionScript or file structure. Global variables are slightly different from the first two scopes because they are *not* defined with the `var` keyword and are prepended with the keyword `_global`, as follows:

```
_global.numUsers = 5;
```

You might notice that because you cannot use the keyword `var` when defining global variables, you cannot use strict data typing with global variables. If you want to take advantage of code hinting with global variables, you must use the suffix method (appending `_mc` or `_lv` onto the end of the variable) or the comment method.

USING _ROOT, _PARENT, THIS, AND LEVELS

You might want to target a variable that exists in a different scope or Timeline in your SWF file. If you are writing code that is nested within a movie clip (or a component) and you want to access something on the main Timeline, such as a button, you need to use `_parent` to access the other Timeline. You use these scopes to tell the SWF where to go to access those variables. When using the `this` keyword, you're referring to the current object in the current scope. For example, when you're within a movie clip and refer to `this`, you're telling the movie clip to look at itself. The `_parent` keyword references the parent item of the current object. For example, if you have a movie clip instance on the Stage and within the movie clip object references to `_parent`, you are referring to the Timeline that the movie clip is on. You can combine the use of `this` and `_parent` to reference objects all throughout your SWF files. If you are in a nested movie clip, you can always use code similar to the following to navigate through the hierarchy of the SWF to control other movie clip instances or component values:

```
this._parent._parent.otherMovieClip_mc.stop();
```

Another tricky concept to grasp can be the use of the `this` keyword. Depending on the exact context, `this` can refer to different things. If you use `this` *within* a movie clip instance, `this` refers to the Timeline of the movie clip. If you are using `this` in a button function, the `this` keyword instead refers to the Timeline containing the button instance rather than inside the button itself. If used with an `onClipEvent()` handler attached directly to a movie clip, the `this` keyword refers to the Timeline of the movie clip.

Consider the following code. If you place the following similar code on the main Timeline, it does very different things. Perhaps you have an SWF file playing, and there is a movie clip, called `myClip`, on the Stage that's also playing some content. You can treat movie clips like buttons using ActionScript (which you will do to the movie clip buttons that you created earlier) by giving them the `onRelease` event handler.

```
myClip_mc.onRelease = function() {
    this.stop();
};
```

This ActionScript stops the `myClip_mc` instance itself, if it were animating. The ActionScript inside the function targets the movie clip's timeline using the `this` keyword. However, if you use the following ActionScript instead:

```
myClip_mc.onRelease = function(){
    stop();
};
```

Then the ActionScript stops the main Timeline instead of the movie clips Timeline. This is because the movie clip is being treated like a button, and buttons are made to target the Timeline they are sitting on, and *not* the Timeline of the button itself. Unless of course, as you just saw earlier, you use the `this` keyword.

You will encounter the frequent usage of `_root` when you use Flash and study other people's ActionScript. When someone uses `_root`, it means that they are targeting the main Timeline. It's kind of like your root directory on a hard drive (for example, `C:`) or the root folder for a Web site. You might call this *absolute referencing*. Just like this is not always the best idea to use in a Web site (it's hard to transfer your site to another domain if you use absolute referencing), it's not a great idea to use in Flash because it's hard to move your ActionScript somewhere else, or it causes problems when you load SWF files into other SWFs.

If you use `_root`, problems might occur when you are loading SWF files into other SWF files (just as you did with the Loader component and the Map earlier on). When `_root` is used, it targets the main Timeline of the SWF that loads in all the other SWF files. So if you load the Map into the Tech Bookstore, any references in the Map to `_root` would target the `_root` of the Tech Bookstore and not the `_root` of `map.swf` itself. This can lead to problems that are difficult to track down. Sometimes when your SWF file plays flawlessly on its own, it stops working when it is loaded into a new Flash document. The cause of the problem is the use of `_root` or incorrect paths to symbols on the Stage. This is one of the main reasons to use relative references when you work with instances. If all your instances are scoped locally instead of to `_root`, you'll encounter fewer problems in the long run and have a much easier time debugging your ActionScript. You can use something called `_lockroot` in your ActionScript to bypass this problem although it goes beyond the scope of this book. For more information on `_lockroot`, visit this book's Web site at `www.TrainingFromTheSource.com/bonus`.

You have learned that you have movie clips on the Stage, and with nested code or elements you target the code within them. If you have code within a movie clip, you can use `_parent` to target the main Timeline. However, when you load SWF files into another SWF, you can load it onto a new *level*. Levels have a particular stacking order in an SWF file. The main Timeline is at `_level0`. Then you can load new SWF files onto new levels that are numbered in a stacking order (2, 3, 4, and so on). You layer the content on top of the main Timelines's content, which is visible beneath the loaded SWF's content. It is like layering transparencies on top of the main Timeline.

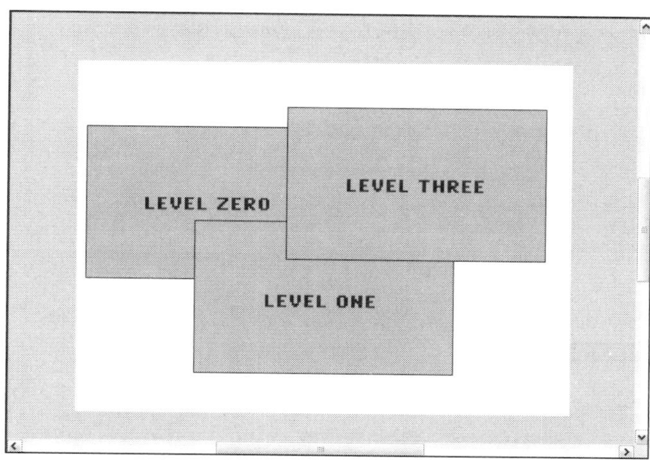

You could also load the SWF file onto `_level0` and replace the main Timeline's content instead.

NOTE *When you load a SWF into a movie clip or a component (such as the Loader), it is not being loaded onto a new level, but instead into the movie clip or component instance itself. Then the content is contained within the movie clip and should be treated like any other movie clip on the Stage.*

If you need to target something on a different level of a loaded SWF, you would use the following ActionScript:

```
_level2.myMovieClip_mc.gotoAndPlay(3);
```

NOTE *Before you call any code targeting a SWF that is being loaded, you should make sure that the content has completely loaded beforehand, or else the code you are executing will not work properly.*

UNDERSTANDING LOADVARS

You will be using the `LoadVars` class throughout the Tech Bookstore. Now that you have a better understanding about classes, objects, methods, properties, functions and conditional statements, you will look at the `LoadVars` class as an example of how to start putting these concepts together in a workable form.

You've already seen a few examples of the `LoadVars` object in previous lessons. `LoadVars` is a simple way to build dynamic Web sites that are easy to update. By placing the data in an external file, the content can be edited using a simple text editor instead of having to open up your FLA file in Flash just to make a few simple text changes or add a new news item. Another benefit of using `LoadVars` is if you're using any server-side language—such as ColdFusion, PHP, ASP or Java—it is possible to have your server-side language query a database and write the latest news articles to a text file that can then be loaded by an SWF file. Then you can create an online administration site where you can add news from a Web site instead of having to download text files, make changes to them, and re-upload the files to the server.

There are three different ways of using Flash and `LoadVars`: `send`, `sendAndLoad`, and `load`. `Send` simply sends data to a server where it can be processed by server-side scripts and entered into a database, appended to an XML document, sent as an email, or however you design the server-side solution to work. Using `sendAndLoad` sends the data to the server, but also accepts a response from the server and places the result in a `LoadVars` object, where the variables can be manipulated or displayed using Flash. Loading and using variables can be useful for the Tech Bookstore if you want to send an ISBN number to a template on your server and have the server-side software query a database, grab a book review or information based on that book, and return the result to Flash to be displayed in the SWF file. The final method, `load`, is what you'll mainly be using throughout the Tech Bookstore site. The `load` method loads variables from a text file, and you'll display the variables in `TextArea` component instances or elsewhere throughout the Tech Bookstore application.

A sample text file, which can be used by Flash, could look similar to the following listing:

```
&name=James
```

By loading in the previous simple text file using the `sendAndLoad` or `load` method, Flash creates a new variable in the target `LoadVars` object named `name` and gives it a value of `James`. You can add as many other variables to the text file by separating each name/value pair with an ampersand (`&`) and equals sign (`=`), as in the following example:

```
&name=James&position=mentor&manager=Nate W.
```

The code here creates three separate variables in Flash: `name`, `position`, and `manager`. The value of `name` is set to `James`, the value of `position` is set to `mentor`, and the value of `manager` is set to `Nate W.` In order to load these values into Flash using the `LoadVars` class, you would save the listing into a text file named `testfile.txt` and add the following ActionScript code to a blank Flash document:

```
var test_lv:LoadVars = new LoadVars();
test_lv.load("testfile.txt");
test_lv.onLoad = function(success:Boolean) {
    trace(this.name);
};
```

Because you're using `LoadVars` for this example, you have to save the Flash document to the same folder as the testfile.txt document before you test the sample code.

The code sets a local variable, `test_lv`, as a `LoadVars` object. You load in the external file using the load method in the `LoadVars` class, which happens in the second line of ActionScript. The method takes a single parameter, which is the path to the file that you want to load. In this case, you're loading in a file named `testfile.txt`, which is in the same folder as the current Flash document.

The next piece of code might be a little tricky to understand. The `LoadVars` class also has a couple of events that Flash triggers when certain things occur. In the code, the event that is being triggered is `onLoad`, which Flash triggers when the text file defined in the load method has been completely loaded into Flash. The code simply says *when the specified text file has finished loading, execute the following code.* After the file has been completely loaded and the `onLoad` event triggers, your three variables defined in the `testfile.txt` file are stored in the `test_lv LoadVars` object. This means you can now trace the value of `test_lv.manager` and see the value `Nate W.` in the Output panel. In the previous code listing, you are using what is known as an *anonymous function*, which is simply a function that hasn't been given a name. Let's look at what that means. You already know that you can create a named function and assign that to the `onLoad` event using the following code:

```
function doOnLoad(success:Boolean) {
    trace(this.manager);
}
test_lv.onLoad = doOnLoad;
```

The anonymous function does the same thing as this named function. A named function is a bit longer to type, but perhaps a bit easier to read.

First, you create a named function called `doOnLoad` that has one parameter: a flag telling you if the file has successfully loaded. When Flash triggers the event (after the file has loaded), the value of the `success` variable holds whether or not the file successfully loads. This is just a simple example, and therefore you can assume that the file loads without incident. If you are using this on your Web site, you should check the value of `success` and write ActionScript depending on this outcome. If the file wasn't loaded, you would either want to display an error message for the user or perhaps write more complex code that would connect to your server-side application and send an email notifying you of the error.

The body of the function just traces the value of the name variable from `LoadVars` to the Output panel. Also make sure that when you set the value of `test_lv.onLoad` event to the `doOnLoad` function, you don't place any brackets after the `doOnLoad` function name.

NOTE *One final important aspect to point out is that when you refer to the `this.manager` from within the `doOnLoad` function or the anonymous functions in the previous listings, you're actually referring to the `test_lv LoadVars` object. Instead of using the `this` keyword, you could instead use the following code:*

```
trace(test_lv.manager);
```

CREATING THE REVIEWS PAGE

Now it's time to start working with Flash, and add some ActionScript to make the FLA files do some work. In this exercise, you will look at how to write a custom function that loads text into a TextArea component. This page creates the Review page containing a List component, which you can click to choose a review to look at. When you click the review's title, it appears in a TextArea next to the List. You will be using components to set up the structure of the Review page. You create a brand-new FLA document to form the body of the review and then publish a SWF file that will be loaded into the Tech Bookstore later on.

Before you start writing any ActionScript, open the Actions panel in Flash (F9). Click the Options menu in the Actions panel and choose View Line Numbers from the drop-down menu. Then click the Options menu again and select Word Wrap from the drop-down menu.

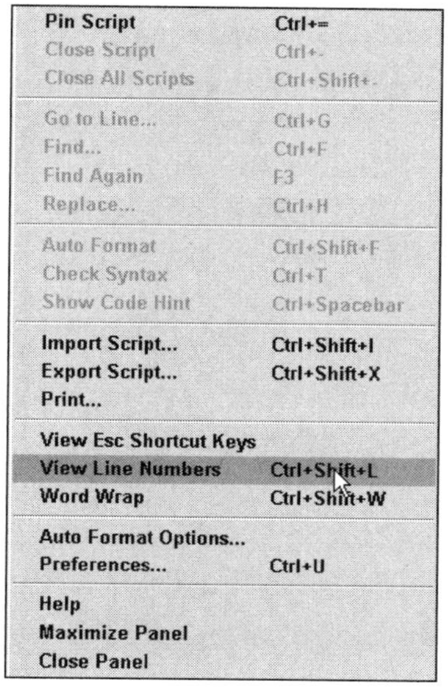

Pin Script	Ctrl+=
Close Script	Ctrl+-
Close All Scripts	Ctrl+Shift+-
Go to Line...	Ctrl+G
Find...	Ctrl+F
Find Again	F3
Replace...	Ctrl+H
Auto Format	Ctrl+Shift+F
Check Syntax	Ctrl+T
Show Code Hint	Ctrl+Spacebar
Import Script...	Ctrl+Shift+I
Export Script...	Ctrl+Shift+X
Print...	
View Esc Shortcut Keys	
View Line Numbers	Ctrl+Shift+L
Word Wrap	Ctrl+Shift+W
Auto Format Options...	
Preferences...	Ctrl+U
Help	
Maximize Panel	
Close Panel	

Line numbers help you find any ActionScript errors that appear in the Output panel when you test the document because the Output panel tells you the line number containing the error. The error is a lot easier to find when you have line numbers turned on in the Actions panel!

1) Create a new Flash document, resize the Stage to *720* pixels wide by *345* pixels high, and rename Layer 1 to `form`. Open Publish Settings and deselect the HTML check box in the Formats tab. Save this document as `reviews.fla`.

Create a new Flash document and change the size of the Stage by clicking the Size button in the Property inspector, or by pressing Ctrl+J (or Command+J on the Mac) to open the Document Properties dialog box. In the dimensions text input fields, type in *720* pixels for the width and *400* pixels for the height. Rename the `Layer 1` to `form` using the Property inspector.

When you publish the document, you don't need to generate an HTML page. You only need to use the SWF file that is created when you choose to publish the document. Therefore, choose File > Publish Settings. Deselect HTML under the Formats tab and click OK. Then choose File > Save to save the new file as `reviews.fla` in the `TechBookstore` folder on your hard drive.

2) Drag a List component instance onto the Stage, resize it, and enter a new position for the instance using the Property inspector.

Open the Components panel and drag a copy of the List component onto the Stage. With the List component still selected on the Stage, open the Property inspector and change the component's width to *200* pixels and change the height to *325* pixels. Enter a value of *10* pixels for both the X and the Y coordinates to position the component near the upper-left corner of the document. Give the component instance an instance name of *reviews_ls*.

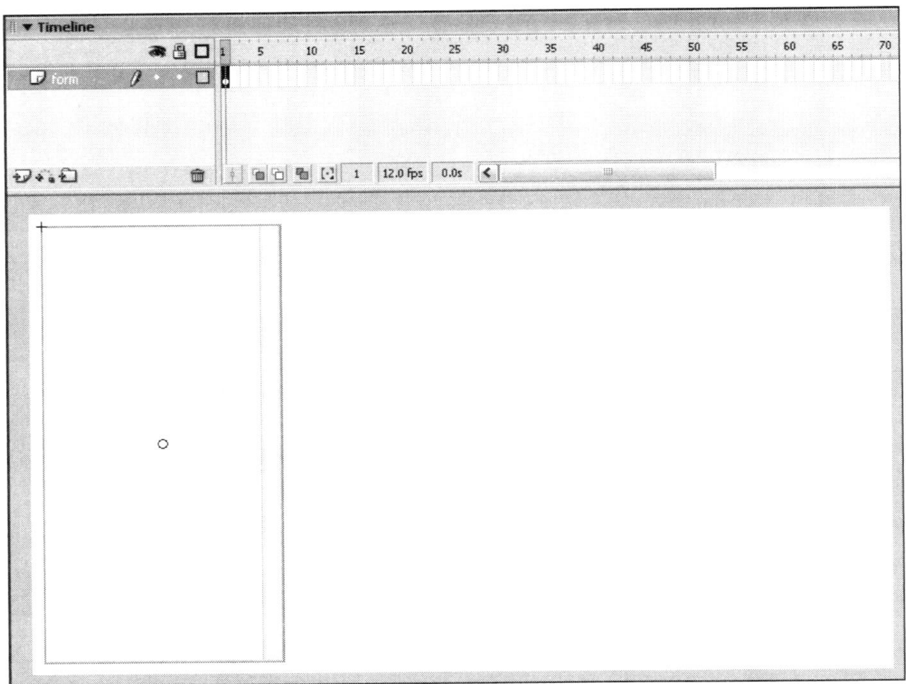

3) Copy the two review files onto your hard drive. Configure the List component using the Property inspector. Add data and labels for two reviews to the List component using the Values dialog box.

There are a few different ways to populate List or ComboBox components, but perhaps one of the simplest ways is to manually enter the information into the component using either the Property inspector or the Component Inspector panel. You already saw how to do this in a previous lesson when you created the survey.

Make sure the List component instance is selected on the Stage and expand the Property inspector if it isn't open. You will add a couple of sample book reviews from the CD-ROM for this example. To keep the reviews organized, create a new folder inside the `TechBookstore` folder on your hard drive called `reviews`. Save the two sample reviews that are provided on the CD-ROM in the `Lesson11` folder into this new folder.

TIP *You want to place all of the reviews inside its own folder because if you add dozens of reviews in the root folder it would be messy and difficult to navigate. All of these reviews are simple text files. You could create more reviews if you want, and then add them to the* `reviews` *folder. You could even add your own by opening up one of the text files in question and copying the format of the simple HTML formatting.*

In the Property inspector, click the data row and then click the magnifying glass on the far right of the row to open the Values dialog box.

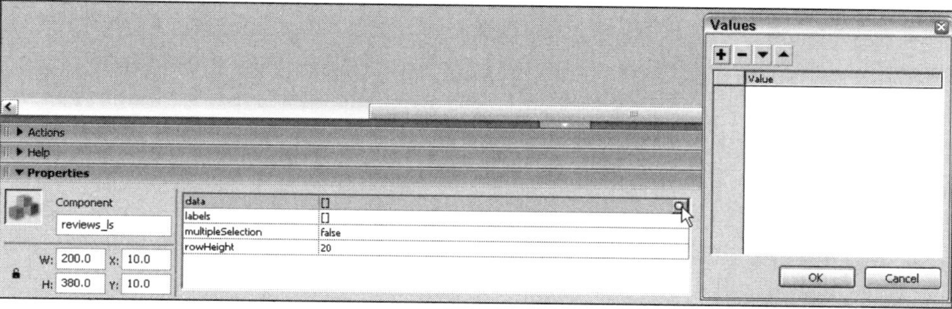

Click the plus (+) symbol twice to add two values. In order to keep the reviews organized, we decided to name each file after the ISBN number of the book. This way, if you need to locate a specific book in the list at a later date, you have to search only for its ISBN instead of scanning through each text file looking for the specific book. In the first value, change the value to *`reviews/0321213408.txt`* . Note that the directory name is appended to the file so that Flash knows that the file is not in the same directory as the SWF. Click the second value and enter *`reviews/0321219198.txt`*. Click the OK button to close the dialog box and return to the Property inspector.

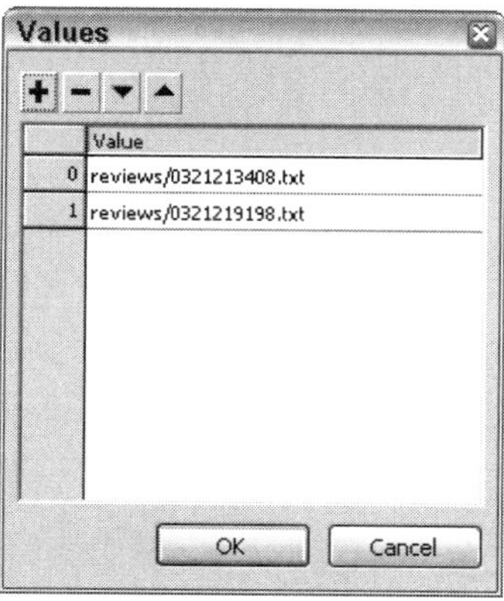

Click the labels row and again on the magnifying glass on the far right of the row to open the Values dialog box again for the labels in the List component. Click the plus symbol two times to add two values, just as you did for the data parameters. In the top value, change the default value to *Fireworks MX 2004: TFS*, which is the title of the book. In the second value, change the value to *Dreamweaver MX 2004: TFS*. It is very important that you pay special attention to enter the values in the same order when adding data and labels; otherwise, a user clicks on one book title and the bookstore returns the review of a completely different book. Click the OK button to close the Values dialog box when you are finished.

4) Add a TextArea component to the Stage and position the component using the Property inspector.

Drag an instance of the TextArea component onto the Stage and align its top-left corner near the List component's upper-right corner. With the TextArea component still selected on the Stage, go to the Property inspector, change the width to *490* pixels and the height to *325* pixels, and give this instance an instance name of *review_txt*. Set the X coordinate of the TextArea component to *220* pixels and the Y coordinate to *10* pixels. In either the Property inspector or Component Inspector panel, set the `editable` property to `false` so users can't change the review text and set the `html` property to `true` so you can use text with embedded HTML tags.

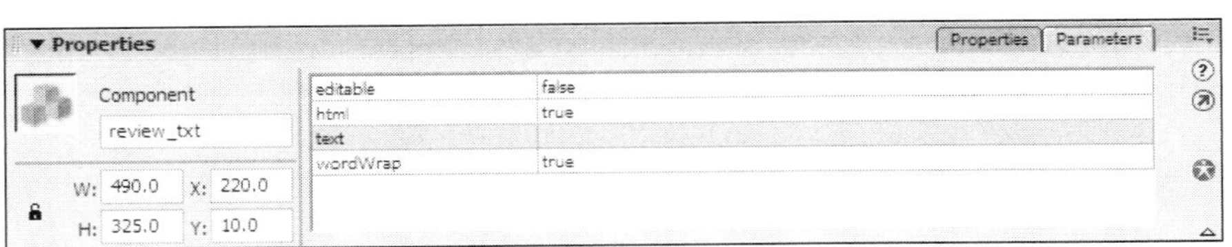

5) Insert a new layer on the Timeline and rename it `actions`. Write a function to load the selected book's review.

Insert a new layer on the Timeline and rename it *actions*. Expand the Actions panel. Select frame 1 of the `actions` layer and then add the following function into the Script pane in the Actions panel:

```
function loadReview(evt) {
  var review_lv:LoadVars = new LoadVars();
  review_lv.load(evt.target.selectedItem.data);
  review_lv.onLoad = function(success:Boolean) {
  if (success) {
    review_txt.text = this.content;
  } else {
    trace("unable to load text file.");
}
    };
}
```

Here, you are creating a function by using the function keyword followed by the function's name. After you define the function's name, which in this case is loadReview, you define any parameters that your method takes inside the brackets. This function takes a single parameter named evt. Everything between the {curly brace and the} curly brace is considered the function's *body*, and executes when the function is called.

The first thing this function does is create a local variable (using the var keyword), which you use to hold the results of the LoadVars call. The next line of code is another example of a function within Flash. The load function takes a single parameter, which is the URL of the file to load. In this case, the value is taken from the data field of the selected item in the reviews_ls List instance. The value of evt.target is the path to the reviews_ls instance, as you will see in the following exercise.

The review_lv.onLoad is an example of a different type of function. The onLoad function is actually an *event* that is triggered when the file has been completely loaded by Flash. Flash executes the function listed after the review_lv.onLoad code when the event triggers. This is what is known as an *inline function* (or *anonymous function*—same thing) because it doesn't have a function name and can be triggered only when the onLoad event is triggered.

TIP *You could also rewrite the inline function as a regular named function instead, as you might have done in Lesson 8 when you were loading FLV videos into the tour.*

The inline function takes one attribute called success, which tells you whether or not the file was successfully loaded. If the value of the success attribute is true, the file has been loaded. Therefore, Flash sets the text property within the review_txt TextArea to the value of the content variable within the LoadVars document. However, if the value of success evaluates to false, the file was unable to load and therefore you display a message in the Output panel.

This example code has several different function types defined in only a few lines, but understanding how methods and events work is imperative when developing applications using LoadVars, XML, Web Services, or Flash Remoting

6) Press the Check Syntax button in the Actions panel toolbar and check that the syntax of your ActionScript does not generate any errors. Save the changes you made to the file.

Click the Check Syntax button in the Actions panel to see whether there are any syntax errors in the code you just wrote.

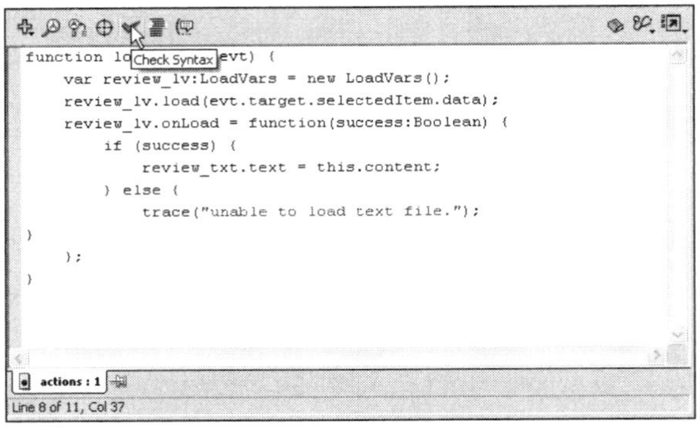

```
function lo Check Syntax evt) {
    var review_lv:LoadVars = new LoadVars();
    review_lv.load(evt.target.selectedItem.data);
    review_lv.onLoad = function(success:Boolean) {
        if (success) {
            review_txt.text = this.content;
        } else {
            trace("unable to load text file.");
}
    };
}
```

actions : 1

Line 8 of 11, Col 37

If everything works correctly, save the changes you made to your FLA file by choosing File > Save. You will continue working with this file in the next exercise.

USING EVENTS, HANDLERS AND LISTENERS

The previous exercise looked briefly at an *event* in Flash. Events are like flags that are raised when something happens within Flash. An event is an action that occurs at runtime in a SWF file. When the SWF is playing, events occur when a movie clip or an XML file loads, a button is clicked, and so on. *Event handlers* and *listeners* are actions that help manage those events. You've seen a couple examples of events already with the `LoadVars` class. When the file has been loaded by Flash, the `onLoad` event is generated by Flash and any function defined for that event is then executed. A simple example of this happening is when a button is clicked (the event), the SWF file goes to and plays a designated frame.

An example of what you've already seen is when a file is loaded, either successfully or not, `LoadVars` triggers the `onLoad` event—telling Flash that the operation has completed. This is necessary because Flash continues processing code instead of halting the SWF file to wait for the operation to complete. This is what is known as *asynchronous communication*. In the previous exercise, you ask the SWF file to load the contents of a text file. When the SWF file receives a result, the SWF either displays text in the TextArea component or displays an error in the Output panel (if you are in the test environment). Because `trace` statements are not sent to the user when you publish the FLA, users do not see the contents of any `trace` statements in your SWF file.

There are all sorts of different events for many items within Flash. If you are loading an MP3 at runtime using Flash, three different events can occur: `onID3` triggers when the ID3 data (information about the MP3 file) is available, `onLoad` triggers when the MP3 has finished loading, and `onSoundComplete` triggers after the MP3 has finished playing. When something triggers, it means that Flash executes any function that might be defined in the event handler for these three events. You can see an example of this happening in the following code:

```
var intro_sound:Sound = new Sound();
intro_sound.loadSound("Tool - disgustipated.mp3", true);
intro_sound.onID3 = function(success:Boolean) {
   trace(success);
};
intro_sound.onSoundComplete = function() {
   trace("sound has completed");
};
```

This code first defines a new instance of the Sound object and then loads in an MP3 into the Sound object using the loadSound method. The true after the MP3 filename tells the SWF file that you want to stream the MP3 rather than waiting for the entire MP3 to load before beginning playback. Then you create event handlers for the onID3 event and for the onSoundComplete event. As each of these events occurs at runtime, the SWF file executes each function that's defined in the event handler automatically. That means that when any sort of ID3 information is available in the SWF, the onID3 event triggers, the function executes and the SWF traces the value of the success attribute. The trace tells you if the sound was successfully loaded into the SWF file.

When the MP3 finishes playing, the onSoundComplete event triggers and the SWF displays a message in the Output panel in the testing environment. The onSoundComplete function can be very useful if you want to load a new MP3 when the current MP3 finishes playing.

Using Listeners

You use listeners a lot in this lesson when you are using components in the interfaces. Listeners are very similar to event handlers because they both wait for events to happen in a SWF file and then perform an action when the event occurs. There are two important distinctions between events and listeners: listeners are caught by listener objects. Listener objects are objects with methods that are defined to catch specific events differing from events where the event handler is assigned to the LoadVars or Sound objects. The other difference is that you associate an instance and a listener object using the addEventListener method and specifying the event to receive and the listener object that handles the event. You can see an example of listeners in the following code:

```
var listenerObject:Object = new Object();
listenerObject.click = function(evt) {
  trace("you clicked the button.");
};
myButtonInstance_btn.addEventListener("click", listenerObject);
```

The first thing that happens here is you create an object to receive the events. Then you define a function handling the event and assign it to the evt function. Flash uses the name of the event that the function catches as a *property* of the function. By doing this, you can have a single object catch several different events.

The last thing you do is add the event listener to a button on the Stage with an instance name of myButtonInstance_btn. Then you tell the SWF file which event you are listening for (in this case, click, which triggers when the user presses and releases the button) and then pass the listenerObject as a parameter.

ADDING A LISTENER TO THE REVIEWS PAGE

The LoadVars class has two events available: onData and onLoad. The onData event triggers when a result has been returned from the server, but before the results have been parsed by Flash. The onLoad event triggers if you call the load or sendAndLoad method of the LoadVars class, but it triggers after the results have been parsed by Flash. Each event is useful in different circumstances, and they each take different parameters.

NOTE *It is important to remember that if you are using the* onData *event in your code, the* onLoad *event no longer triggers unless you specifically call it from within your code.*

The following exercise focuses on handling an event that is triggered when the user changes the value of the List component. You should still be using reviews.fla for this example.

1) Add an event listener to the List component instance using ActionScript.

Select frame 1 of the actions layer, and open the Actions panel. Add the following code to the Script pane, below the function that's already there:

```
reviews_ls.addEventListener("change", loadReview);
```

This code adds an event listener to your reviews_ls List component instance, which triggers when the user clicks a new book title. The addEventListener method takes two parameters: the event that it listens for (in this case, change), and the function to trigger when the event is triggered (in this case, the loadReview function you defined in the previous exercise). There is another option for the addEventListener method, allowing you to pass an object containing a function that is used to handle the event.

2) Test that the document works properly by choosing Control > Test Movie. Then save and publish the document

Test the FLA by selecting Control > Test Movie. Each time you click a book title in the reviews_ls Component instance on the left of the Stage, Flash calls the loadReview function, which in turn loads that book's review into the TextArea instance. You also should notice that when the contents of the external text files display in the TextArea instance, the external files containing HTML formatting such as bold (using the <b> tag), italics (<i>) and images (<img>) tags affect the look of the text. If the TextArea component displays the actual HTML source code, including tags, check that the html parameter is set to true in the Component Inspector panel. If you look at the contents of the text files, you'll see that the images are actually loading from the Amazon.com servers for this exercise. In reality, you would want to load images from your server locally instead of from the servers at Amazon.com. You could save the image files locally and change the URL in the text files you're loading in.

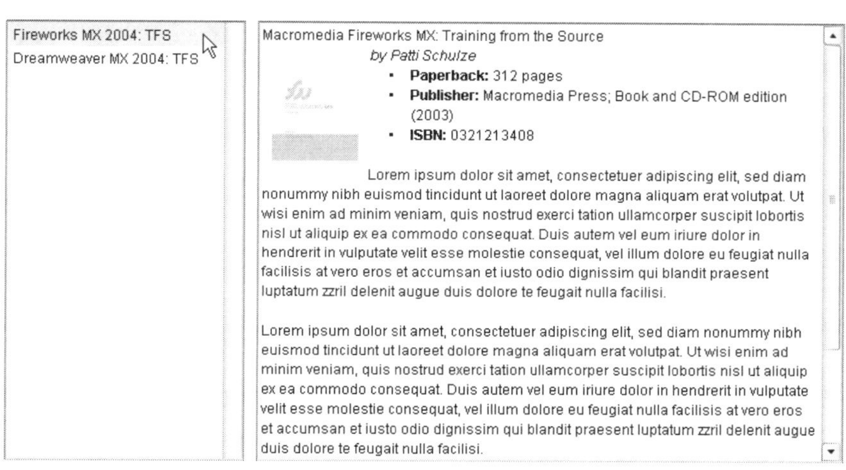

Return to the authoring environment and save the changes you have made to reviews.fla. Publish the FLA file by choosing File > Publish to generate the SWF file. You will load this file into the main Tech Bookstore SWF file in a later lesson.

The file is generated in the TechBookstore folder. If you want to add more reviews, you can copy the text within an existing review and make changes as necessary. Save the new file into the reviews folder after you have finished editing them. Remember that you'll also need to modify both the data and labels parameters in the Property inspector for the list component and add new values similar to Step 3 of the previous exercise.

ADDING CASCADING STYLE SHEET FORMATTING TO THE REVIEWS

Cascading Style Sheets (CSS) is a method to define styles that can be applied to text and other elements within an HTML page to help format the style. CSS documents contain rules defining which fonts a block of text should use, what kinds of spacing should be around certain elements such as images or table cells, or what colors are used with particular elements. When you use a style sheet, you can apply a single set of rules to every page within your site and have the site look consistent while maintaining the ability to change the rules and have the changes appear on every page you have applied the style sheet to immediately.

Flash boasts support for CSS1 as a way to format text within a SWF.

NOTE *There are different versions of the CSS. CSS2 boasts additional properties for formatting, although Flash does not support CSS2. Refer to* `www.w3.org/TR/REC-CSS1` *for the CSS1 specification.*

Although Flash supports only a subset of CSS1's properties, it is an excellent feature, allowing you to easily format a block of text and have it look consistent with the rest of the site. There are two ways of adding style sheets to your Flash document: loading in a style sheet at runtime and defining the style sheet using ActionScript. Because you'll be using the same styles throughout the entire Tech Bookstore application, which is contained within several different SWF files it is easier to use an external style sheet and load it into each of the separate SWFs. You can also use the same style sheet in the HTML pages you might also create, to help maintain consistency throughout your site regardless of whether the page contains a SWF or is only HTML code.

1) Open the `reviews.fla` document again from the previous exercises, and lock the `form` layer.

Open the `reviews.fla` document you worked on in previous lessons and lock the `form` layer. Select frame 1 of the `actions` layer where you will add ActionScript in the following step.

2) Add ActionScript to `reviews.fla`, which will load a CSS file into `reviews.swf` at runtime.

In frame 1 of the `actions` layer, add the following code before the existing code:

```
var flash_css = new TextField.StyleSheet();
flash_css.load("styles.css");
flash_css.onLoad = function(success:Boolean) {
  if (success) {
    review_txt.styleSheet = flash_css;
  } else {
    trace("Error loading CSS file.");
  }
};
```

You should notice that the code listed is similar to using `LoadVars` in earlier exercises. The first thing you do is create a new Timeline variable named `flash_css` to contain the new style sheet and then load an external CSS file called `styles.css`. The next block of code triggers when Flash receives an `onLoad` event, and takes a single parameter (`success`) specifying whether or not the style sheet has successfully loaded. If the style sheet loads, the code assigns the style sheet to the `reviews_txt` TextArea instance. If it wasn't loaded successfully, an error is sent to the Output panel notifying you that it has failed.

If you test the SWF file now by pressing Ctrl+Enter (or Command+Return on the Mac), you see that Flash displays the error message in the Output panel, saying that the SWF couldn't find the CSS file. This occurs because you currently don't have the style sheet in the `TechBookstore` directory yet.

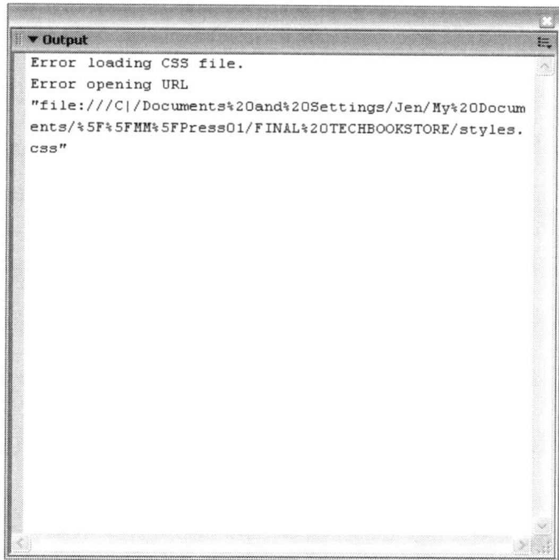

3) Create a Cascading Style Sheet file called `styles.css` to define the text styles. Save the file into the `TechBookstore` folder.

Open any text editor on your computer, or even an editor such as Dreamweaver that has specific support for CSS. If you are using a PC, you probably have Notepad installed; if you are on a Mac, you should have TextEdit installed. Enter the following code and save the file as `styles.css`.

```
p {
  font-family: Arial,Helvetica,sans-serif;
  font-size: 11px;
  color: #000000;
}
.headline {
  font-family: Arial,Helvetica,sans-serif;
  font-size: 24px;
  color: #999999;
}
```

The style sheet defines two styles. One style applies to the <p> tag, and another style is a custom style called `headline`, which you will apply to the book's title in each review. The `headline` style will be grey text and 24 pixels in size to help differentiate the headline from the rest of the text making up the review. Save the file into the `TechBookstore` folder on your hard drive and close the text editor.

4) Test `reviews.fla` again. If everything works correctly, save the document and publish the FLA file to generate an updated SWF file.

Test the Flash document by pressing Ctrl+Enter (or Command+Return on the Mac). Now if you click on the title of a book, Flash loads in the book's review and applies the style sheet to the TextArea. Save the file and republish the Flash document to update the SWF file in the `TechBookstore` folder.

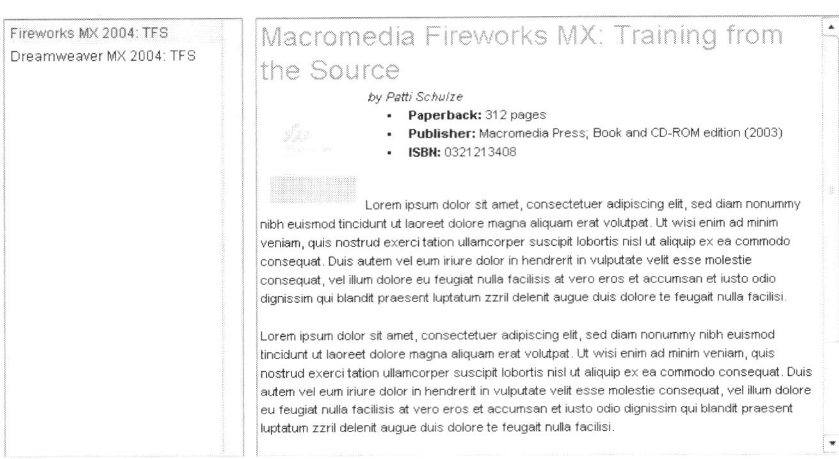

CREATING THE CATALOG PAGES

In this section, you create two new catalog pages that will import into the `catalog.fla` you will create in the following exercise. The catalog pages are fairly simple pages containing information on each book that is sold in the Tech Bookstore. You need to make only a couple of books for the catalog, but you can make many more if you want to.

Each catalog page uses a couple of buttons to open additional pages: one button opens a table of contents, and the second button opens a sample chapter. You created these buttons earlier in this book out of movie clips. The catalog pages also include an image of the book's cover and a short description of its contents. You can add whatever graphics you want to make the catalog pages look and feel customized.

1) Create a new folder in the TechBookstore **folder called** catalog**. Open** bookstore12_pro.fla **or** bookstore12_fmx.fla **(whatever file you saved at the end of Lesson 10), and save a new version of the file as** bookstore13.fla**.**

First, create a new folder called catalog on your hard drive that's *inside* the TechBookstore folder. This is where you will save a couple new FLA and SWF files you create in this exercise, that will ultimately be loaded into the main Tech Bookstore application.

Use File > Save As to save a new version of bookstore12_pro.fla or bookstore12_fmx.fla depending on what edition of Flash you are using. Save the new FLA into the TechBookstore folder.

2) Create a new document called catalog01.fla **and save it in a** catalog **folder within the** TechBookstore **folder. Open the Publish Settings dialog box and turn off the HTML check box under the Formats tab.**

When you publish the document, you don't need an HTML page generated. You only need to use the SWF file that is created when you choose to publish the document because eventually the SWF will be loaded into another SWF file. Therefore, choose File > Publish settings and deselect the HTML option in the Formats tab and click OK when you're done. Using the Property inspector, resize the Stage to 490 by 325.

3) Drag the two movie clip buttons from the Library in bookstore13.fla **into the Library of** catalog01.fla**.**

You have a couple movie clip buttons intended for the catalog within the Library of bookstore13.fla. One of the easiest ways to move assets from one Library to the other is to open both files in Flash and open each of their Libraries. With both Libraries open, simply navigate to the movie clips folder in the Tech Bookstore's Library and drag the samplechapter_mc and toc_mc symbols from the bookstore13.fla Library into catalog01.fla's Library.

4) Delete the Table of Contents and Sample Chapter buttons from the Tech Bookstore Library and close the FLA file.

When the samplechapter_mc and toc_mc symbols are in the catalog01.fla document, you can delete them from bookstore13.fla's Library by selecting each symbol and dragging them over the trash can icon located at the bottom of the Library.

TIP *You always want to delete any symbols that are not being used in an FLA so you can attempt to keep the FLA file size to a minimum. Deleting symbols does not affect the size of the published SWF file because any unused symbols are not compiled into the SWF when you publish the Flash document.*

5) Copy `catalog01.png` and `catalog02.png` from the `media` folder on the CD-ROM onto your hard drive. Import `catalog01.png` into the `catalog01.fla` Library.

Located within the `media` folder on the CD-ROM are files called `catalog01.png` and `catalog02.png` containing images of *Training from the Source* book covers. Copy both of these files onto your hard drive. In `catalog01.fla`, select File > Import > Import to Library in order to add the PNG image into the Library.

6) Rename `Layer 1` to `pages` and drag `catalog01.png` onto the layer. Insert a new layer above `pages` and rename the new layer `buttons`. Select the `buttons` layer and drag the two buttons onto the Stage. Using the Text tool, create a new static text field on the Stage and then lay out all of the items on the Stage.

First rename Layer 1 *pages*. With the Library open for the `catalog01.fla` document, drag an instance of `catalog01.png` on to the Stage and position it near the upper-left side of the Stage similar to the following figure. Create a new layer above `pages` and rename it *buttons*. With the `buttons` layer selected, drag the two movie clip button instances from the Library onto the Stage. Position the two movie clip buttons under `catalog01.png` on the Stage. Position the second movie clip button underneath the first button.

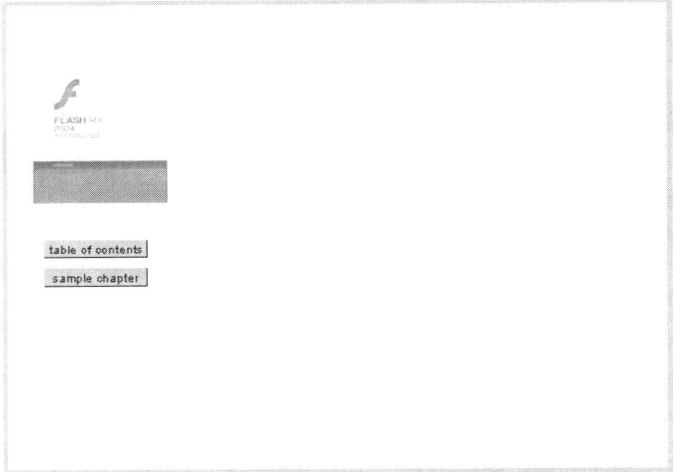

Finally, click the Text tool in the Tools panel and open the Property inspector. Set the Text type to *static* and the font to *Arial 10 pt black*. Select the Alias text button. Select the `pages` layer and create a text field on the Stage that is the correct width of the field by clicking and then dragging. When you enter text into this field, it will create additional lines vertically. Type some text into the static text field you created (it doesn't matter what you type). You can use *lorem ipsum* text as placeholder text, open the completed catalog01.fla, and use the text you find in the finished FLA, or find the actual book description online.

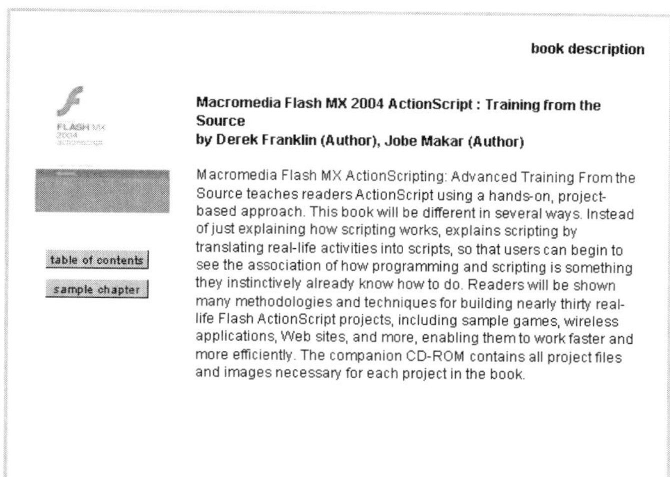

7) Give the two movie clip buttons new instance names. Then insert a new layer called actions **and add functions to make the two buttons work.**

Using the Selection tool, click each of the buttons near the top of the Stage and give them instance names. Enter an instance name of *toc_mc* for the *table of contents* button. Then enter an instance name of *samplechapter_mc* for the *sample chapter* button. Select the top layer in the FLA and insert a new layer. Rename the new layer actions, expand the Actions panel, and add the following ActionScript to the Script pane:

```
stop();
samplechapter_mc.onRelease = function() {
    getURL("http://www.trainingfromthesource.com/flashTFS/samplechapter.html",
    ⇒"_blank");
}
toc_mc.onRelease = function() {
    gotoAndStop("toc");
}
```

This ActionScript stops the playhead on the current frame and defines two functions. One will move the playhead to a specific frame label, and the other opens a browser window. If the user clicks the *sample chapter* button, the browser opens and goes to a page containing a sample chapter; if the user clicks the *table of contents* button, the playhead moves to the frame that will be labeled `toc` in the following step.

8) Insert a new layer and rename it `labels`. Then add a frame labels `toc` on frame 5, and `home` on frame 1. Insert new blank keyframes on the `pages` and `actions` layers under the frame label, and add a `stop` action on frame 5 of the `actions` layer.

Insert a new layer and move it directly below the `actions` layer. Rename the layer *labels*. Right-click (or control-click on the Mac) on frame 5 of this new layer in the Timeline, select Insert Blank Keyframe from the contextual menu, and give that frame a label of *toc* using the Property inspector. Select frame 1 on the layer and add a frame label of `home`.

Then insert a new blank keyframe (F6) on frame 5 in the `actions` layer and type `stop();` into the Actions panel. Then add a new keyframe on frame 5 of the `pages` layer by pressing the F6 key. The text field from frame 1 is copied onto frame 5.

NOTE *You don't need to extend the `buttons` layer to frame 5 because you are making a page that's exclusively used to display the table of contents, and not necessarily to open the sample chapter.*

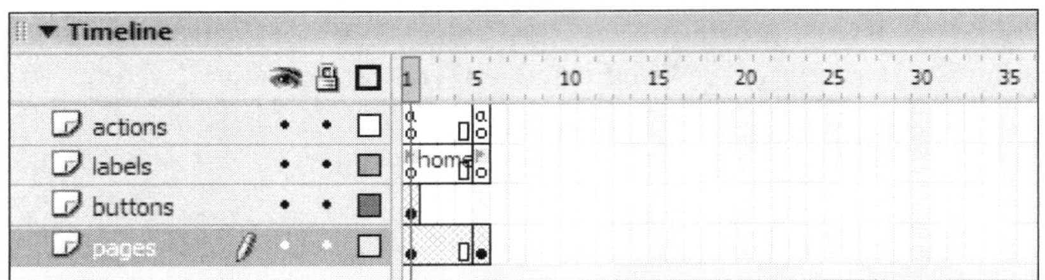

By adding a keyframe on this layer instead of a blank keyframe, you can change the text in the static text field on the Stage and be able to maintain the same positioning of the text field. It also allows you to keep all the elements in exactly the same place so the items don't shift when visitors navigate to the second area. Modify the text fields, so now it displays a table of contents instead of a book description. Finally, add a back button on the Stage onto the `toc` keyframe on the `pages` layer. Either create your own button or drag a Button component instance from the Components panel onto the `pages` layer.

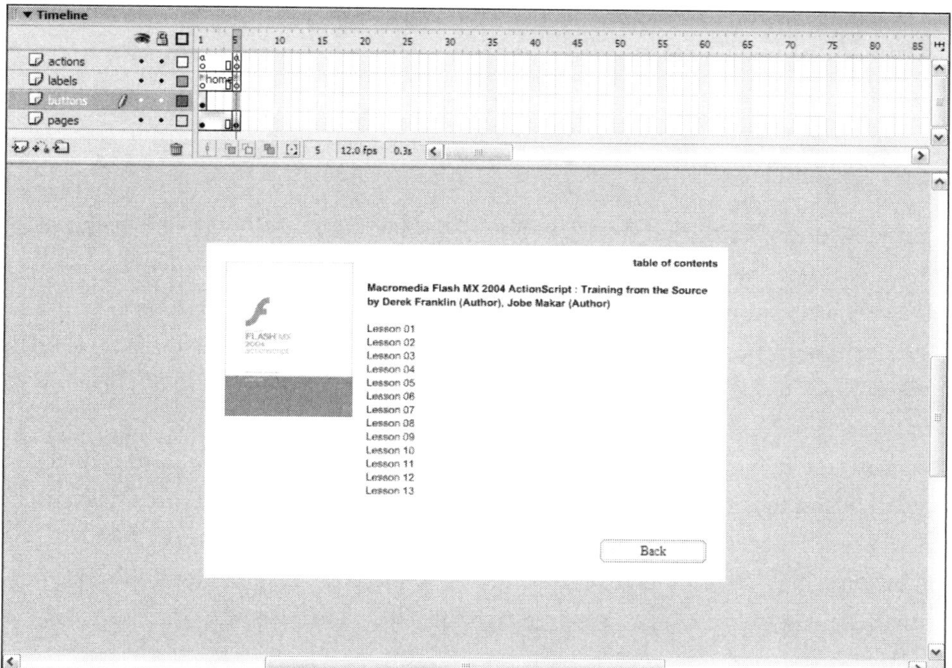

If you use a Button component instance, change the label parameter to *Back* and the instance name to *back_btn*. Select frame 5 of the `actions` layer and type the following code into the Actions panel.

```
back_btn.onRelease = function() {
    gotoAndStop("home");
}
```

9) Test `catalog01.fla` and then save and publish the file if there are no problems. Then save a new version of `catalog01.fla` by selecting File > Save As and name the new file `catalog02.fla` and make sure it's saved in the `catalog` folder. Import `catalog02.png`, swap it with `catalog01.png`, and modify the catalog's text fields.

Test `catalog01.fla` to make sure that the document works as expected. If there are no problems, then save the file, and publish it by choosing File > Publish. After you have saved a new version of `catalog01.fla` as `catalog02.fla`, you only need to make a few minor modifications (detailed below) to the FLA file and then republish it.

TIP *If you don't want to create a second catalog page, you can always save `catalog02.fla` from the `Lesson11` folder on the CD-ROM into the `TechBookstore` folder on your hard drive and publish that file instead.*

Usually, the quickest way to rebuild any file (such as the `catalog01.fla`) while maintaining a consistent layout and feel is to save a new copy of `catalog01.fla` and then modify certain elements or swap them out. This way, you can save a few steps by not having to re-create the entire file from scratch and then worry about positioning each element the same way.

Open the Library for the `catalog02.fla` file, right-click (or control-click) `catalog01.png`, and select Properties from the contextual menu. Flash opens the Bitmap Properties dialog box where you can preview the current image and modify compression settings. Click the Import button on the right side, and the Import Bitmap dialog box appears, in which you can locate the `catalog02.png` image on your hard drive that you copied over from the CD-ROM in Step 5. Select the image and press Open to swap the old PNG with the new one. Click the OK button to close the Bitmap Properties dialog box and return to the Stage. You'll notice that Flash automatically replaces the bitmap image on the Stage and replaces the image in the Library as well. Modify the existing text for the table of contents text field. You do not need to change the URL that was given in step 7—there's only one sample chapter file to open.

10) Test `catalog02.swf` in a browser window. If the page works correctly, return to the authoring environment, save the FLA file, and publish it to create `catalog02.swf` in the `catalog` folder.

Test the `catalog02.swf` file in a browser window by pressing F12 in the authoring environment. If everything looks OK and you can navigate to the different sections of the SWF and open a new browser window, save the file and publish the FLA to generate the new `catalog02.swf` file. You should now have two SWF files in the `catalog` folder that you will import into the Tech Bookstore later in this book.

BUILDING THE MAIN CATALOG

The Catalog section of the `TechBookstore` is very similar to the Reviews section built in the earlier exercises. The main catalog file has a List component with the names of several books. When you click one of the books in the List, it updates content on the Stage by loading in the catalog pages you created in the previous exercise. The main difference between the Catalog section and the Reviews section is that the Catalog page loads an external SWF file into a Loader component instead of using `LoadVars` and a TextArea component that the Reviews section used to display content.

1) Create a new Flash document and resize the Stage to *720* pixels wide by *345* pixels high. Open the Publish Settings dialog box (File > Publish Settings) and deselect the HTML check box under the Formats tab. Then save the file as `catalog.fla`.

Create a new Flash document by choosing File > New and selecting Flash Document. Resize the Stage to 635 pixels by 345 pixels using the Property inspector. When you publish the document, you don't need an HTML page generated. You need to use the SWF file that is created only when you choose to publish the document. Therefore, choose File > Publish settings. Deselect HTML under the Formats tab and click OK.

When you are finished, save the FLA as `catalog.fla`.

2) Rename Layer 1 to `form` and add a List component to the Stage on the `form` layer. Resize the List instance to *200* pixels wide by *325* pixels high using the Property inspector and move the instance to the upper-left corner of the Stage. Give the List an instance name of `catalog_ls`.

The catalog section has a List component that includes names of books in the catalog that will update content on the Stage when they are clicked. Change the name of Layer 1 to *form*, open the Components panel, and then drag an instance of the List component onto the Stage.

Change both the X and Y coordinates of the List instance to *10* pixels in the Property inspector. Change the width of the instance to *200* pixels and the height to *325* pixels, and type in an instance name of *catalog_ls* for the component instance.

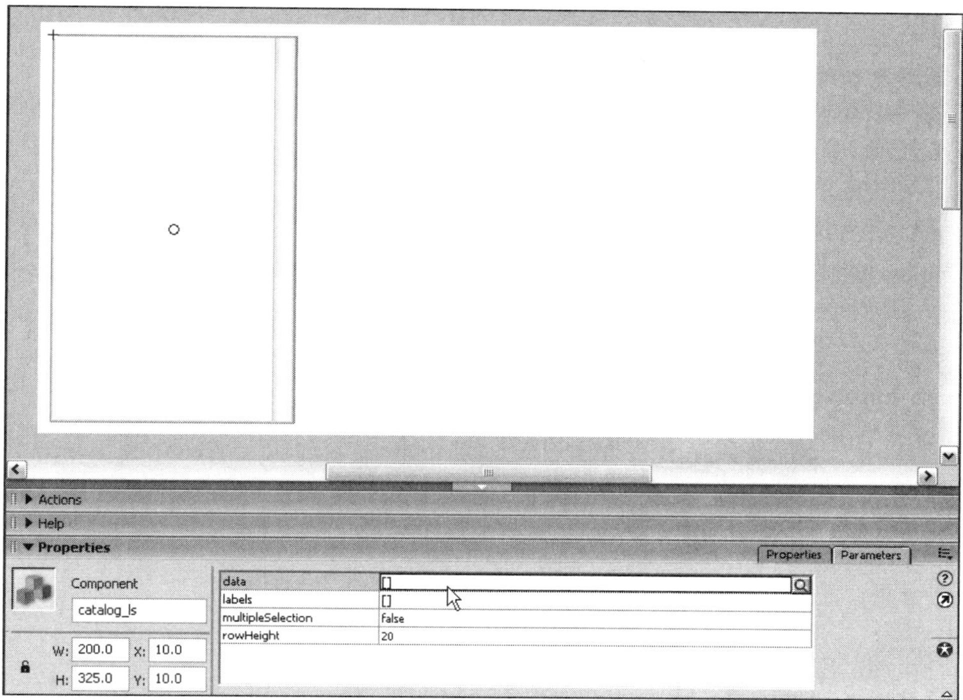

3) Set the values and labels for the List component using the Values dialog box.

With the List component still selected on the Stage, open the Property inspector or Component Inspector panel and click the data row. Click the magnifying glass to the right of the data row to open the Values dialog box. Add two new values by clicking the Add (+) button twice and enter *catalog/catalog01.swf* for the top value and *catalog/catalog02.swf* for the bottom value. Note that each of these values is prefixed with `catalog/`, which tells Flash that it should look for the SWF in a subfolder named `catalog`.

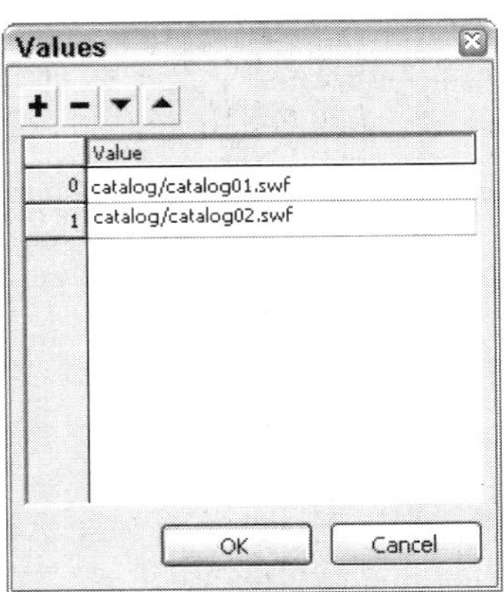

Click the OK button to close the Values dialog box and select the labels row in the Property inspector. Click the magnifying glass again for labels to open the Values dialog box and enter values for the List component. Add two new values, setting the top value to `Flash MX 2004 ActionScript: TFS` and the bottom value to `Dreamweaver MX 2004: TFS`. When adding values, you always have to exercise caution that you add the data in the same order as you add the labels; otherwise, your users click a title and receive information on a different book.

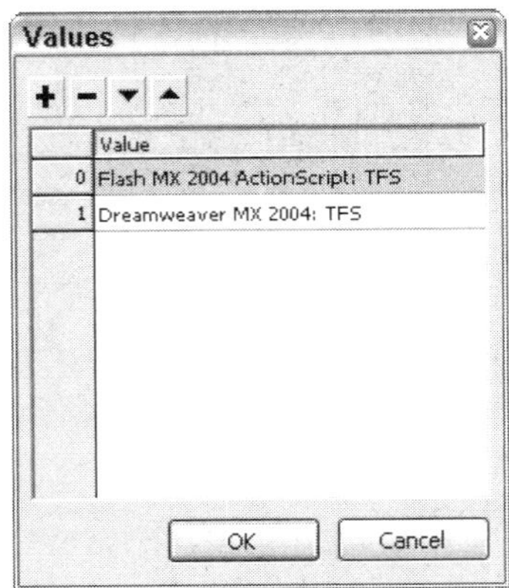

4) Add an instance for the Loader component to the Stage, and then position and resize the instance using the Property inspector.

Expand the Components panel and drag an instance of the Loader component on to the Stage. Set the width of the component to *490* pixels and set the height to *325* pixels, and then position the component at an X coordinate of *220* pixels and a Y coordinate of *10* pixels. Give the Loader component an instance name of *catalog_ldr*. Use either the Property inspector or Component Inspector panel to set the `autoLoad` parameter to `false` and the `scaleContent` parameter to `false`.

5) Create an `actions` layer and add ActionScript to load a catalog SWF based on the currently selected book in the List component.

Insert a new layer in the Flash document and rename the new layer *actions*. Make sure that the new layer is above the other layers in the Timeline stack. Select frame 1 of the `actions` layer and add the following code into the Actions panel:

```
function loadCatalog(evt) {
    catalog_ldr.load(catalog_ls.selectedItem.data);
}
catalog_ls.addEventListener("change", loadCatalog);
```

This code defines a function named `loadCatalog`. The function loads the value of the currently selected item's data property, which is the location to a SWF. The function loads that particular SWF file into the Loader component instance on the Stage.

The component's instance name is `catalog_ls` . You add a listener at the end of this ActionScript that waits for the catalog's List instance to be clicked by the visitor. When an item in the List is selected, the `loadCatalog` function is called. The function tells the `catalog_ldr` to load the value of the currently selected item in the list. The value is defined in the Values dialog box and contains the path to the SWF.

6) Test the FLA to make sure it works correctly. If so, save the changes you have made to `catalog.fla`. Then choose File > Publish to publish the SWF file into the `TechBookstore` folder.

In the previous exercise, you created a subfolder called `catalog` inside the main `TechBookstore` folder where you saved `catalog01.swf` and `catalog02.swf` (also provided in the `Lesson11` folder on the CD-ROM). So when you test the file, it should load those two SWFs from the `catalog` folder into `catalog.swf`. If the files don't load, open the `catalog` folder and make sure that the SWF files (and the folder itself) are there and named correctly. Also check you added the values correctly into the Values dialog box in Step 3.

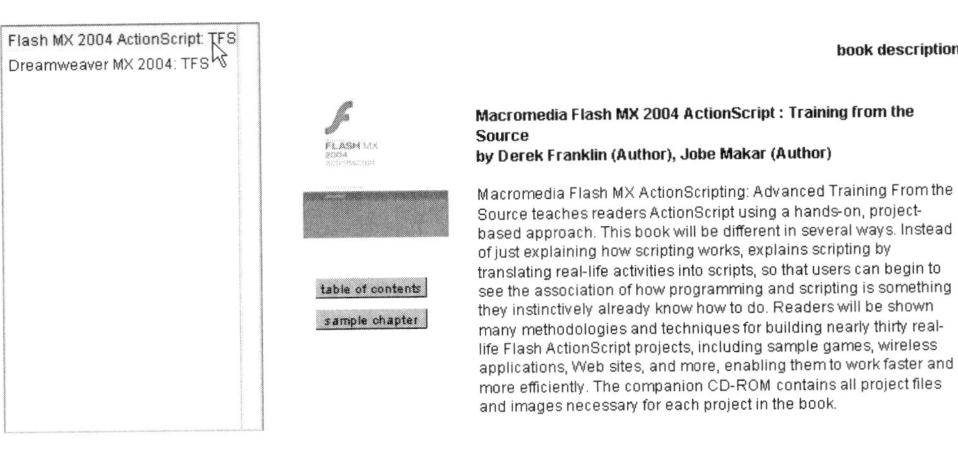

When everything works correctly, save the FLA file and then publish the file so an SWF file is generated in the `TechBookstore` folder.

CREATING THE NEWS PAGE

The News section of the Tech Bookstore is fairly straightforward because it is very similar to the Reviews page you have already created. The News page consists of a TextArea component, CSS formatted text and a `LoadVars` statement to load the text content from a remote file. You use some text files that are provided for you on the CD-ROM.

1) Create a new document and resize the Stage to *635* pixels wide by *345* pixels high. Open the Publish Settings dialog box and deselect the HTML check box. Click OK, return to the main document, and save the file as `news.fla`.

Create a new Flash document and resize the Stage by opening the Property inspector. Set the new dimensions of the Stage to *635* pixels wide by *345* pixels high. Save the Flash document to the root of the `TechBookstore` folder and name the new document `news.fla`.

When you publish the document, you don't need an HTML page generated. You need to use the SWF file that is created only when you choose to publish the document. Therefore, choose File > Publish settings, deselect HTML under the Formats tab and click OK.

2) Drag an instance of the TextArea component onto the Stage and resize it to *615* pixels wide by *325* pixels high. Position the TextArea instance on the Stage.

Drag an instance of the TextArea component onto the Stage from the Components panel. Expand the Property inspector. Resize the TextArea component instance to *615* pixels wide by *325* pixels high. Position the instance on the Stage at an X and Y coordinate of *10* pixels. This should give the component a 10-pixel border on every side of the Stage. Give the TextArea an instance name of *news_txt*. Don't worry about setting the `editable` or `html` parameters in the Property inspector. You'll set those manually using ActionScript in a later step.

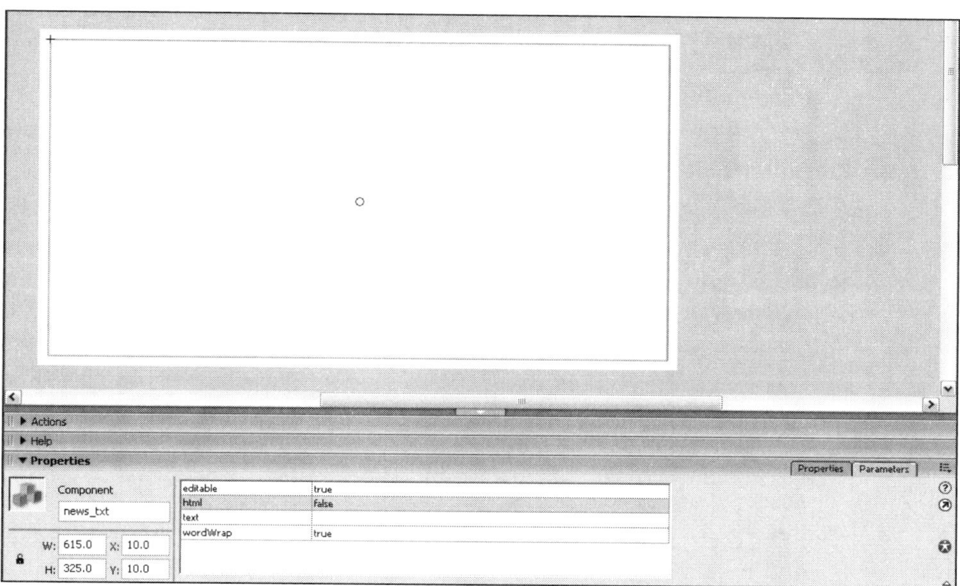

3) Rename `Layer 1` in the Timeline to `form` and add an `actions` layer.

Double-click `Layer 1` in the Timeline and rename the layer to *form*. Insert a new layer above the `form` layer and name it *actions*. Lock each of the layers to prevent accidentally adding any symbols to either layer. Because you won't be adding any more symbols to the Stage, you can lock layers and still add ActionScript.

4) Add ActionScript to import the cascading style sheet into the SWF file.

You learned how to import style sheets in an earlier exercise (CSS). By using an external style sheet, you can reuse the same style sheet throughout each of your Flash documents and maintain a consistent look. Select frame 1 of the `actions` layer and add the following code into the Actions panel:

```
var flash_css = new TextField.StyleSheet();
flash_css.load("styles.css");
flash_css.onLoad = function(success:Boolean) {
    if (success) {
        news_txt.styleSheet = flash_css;
    } else {
        trace("Error loading CSS file.");
    }
};
```

This ActionScript is exactly the same as in the previous exercise, but with one exception. Instead of binding the style sheet to the `review_txt` instance, you're assigning the style sheet to the `news_txt` instance.

5) Load the news text file and set the TextArea properties.

Add the following ActionScript below the style sheet code on frame 1 of the `actions` layer. This code is used to load in an external text file using `LoadVars`:

```
var news_lv:LoadVars = new LoadVars();
news_lv.load("news.txt");
news_lv.onLoad = function(success:Boolean) {
    if (success) {
        news_txt.text = this.content;
    } else {
        trace("unable to load text file.");
    }
};
```

This ActionScript should also be familiar from earlier exercises.

6) Set the `html` and `editable` properties for the TextArea instance using ActionScript.

Instead of setting the `html` and `editable` properties using the Property inspector, you will set them using ActionScript. This is accomplished using the following code, which can be placed below the existing `LoadVars` code:

```
news_txt.html = true;
news_txt.editable = false;
```

The first line sets the `html` property value to `true`, enabling you to display HTML-formatted text in the TextArea instance `news_txt`. The second property, `editable`, ensures that the user can't modify the text and change the content in the TextArea. Even if you set `editable` to `true` (or if you left the line out altogether), and the user did change the content within the field, it wouldn't ruin your site. The changes would display only on his or her computer screen and not be visible to anybody else.

7) Test `news.fla` **and make sure that the SWF works properly. If so, save the FLA and then go to the Publish Settings dialog box and uncheck the HTML option for publishing. Publish the document so** `news.swf` **is generated in the** `TechBookstore` **folder.**

Test the SWF in the testing environment to make sure that the text loads properly. When you are satisfied everything is working, save the document (name the document `news.fla` if you didn't already save the file in Step 1) and publish the FLA file so the SWF file can be loaded into the main `TechBookstore` site.

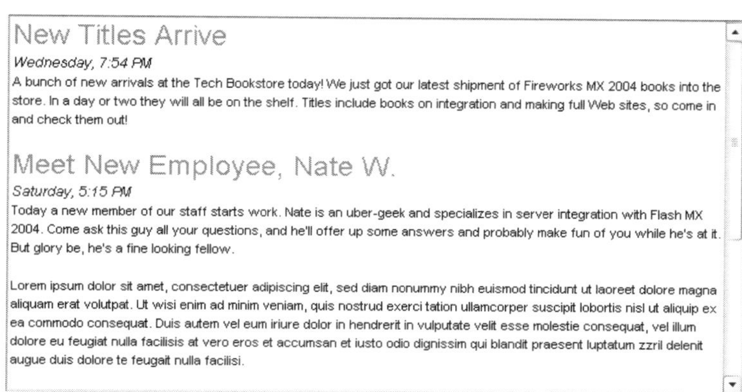

BUILDING THE HOME PAGE

The Home section is also a block of formatted text that loads into the Tech Bookstore using `LoadVars`. The text is loaded into a TextArea component instance. In this section, you create a SWF file that loads into the front of the Tech Bookstore Web site. You reuse some of the content that you already created in earlier exercises. Because reusing assets makes for fast development, it is easiest to simply make a copy of the News section and modify it as needed rather than starting from scratch. So, in this exercise, you duplicate the News page and convert it into the Home page.

1) Open `news.fla` **(created in the previous exercise). Save a new version of the file as** `home.fla` **in the** `TechBookstore` **folder.**

By using the `news.fla` as a starter file, you can skip a lot of steps while you create the new file, and you save having to retype out the ActionScript code from scratch. All you need to do is resize the Stage and TextArea component and modify the instance names and ActionScript slightly, thus saving some time.

Open up the copy of news.fla you created in the previous exercise. Choose File > Save As from the main menu. Type in *home.fla* as the new filename for the document and then click the Save button. Save this file into the same TechBookstore folder as the previous document.

2) Resize the dimensions of both the Stage and TextArea instance in the document.

Because the Home page on the TechBookstore site already has a featured book module, it is necessary to resize the home.fla document so it fits the bookstore properly. Using the Selection tool, click the TextArea component instance on the Stage and use the Property inspector to set the width of the component instance to *570* pixels. Leave the height at 325 pixels and the X and Y coordinate at 10 pixels. Click on the Stage and change the dimensions of the document to *580* pixels by *345* pixels.

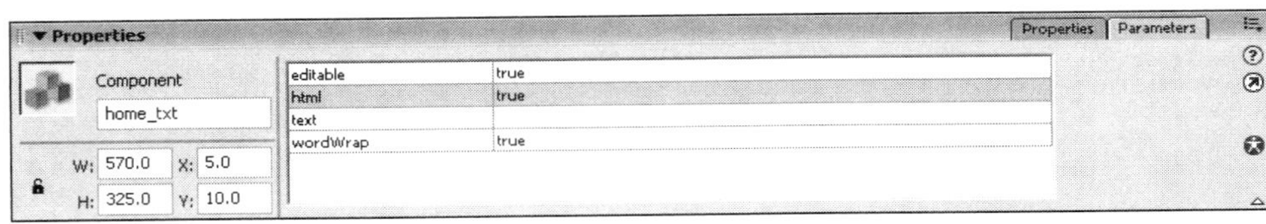

3) Enter a new instance name for the TextArea instance and change the ActionScript on the actions layer.

Select the TextArea component instance on the Stage and type in a new instance name of *home_txt* into the Property inspector. Because you changed the instance name for the component instance, you have to change the references to the TextArea in your ActionScript. You also have to change any references to news_lv to home_lv. Your finished modified code should look like the following:

```
var flash_css = new TextField.StyleSheet();
flash_css.load("styles.css");
flash_css.onLoad = function(success:Boolean) {
    if (success) {
        home_txt.styleSheet = flash_css;
    } else {
        trace("Error loading CSS file.");
    }
};
var home_lv:LoadVars = new LoadVars();
home_lv.load("home.txt");
home_lv.onLoad = function(success:Boolean) {
    if (success) {
        home_txt.text = this.content;
    } else {
        trace("unable to load text file.");
    }
};
home_txt.html = true;
home_txt.editable = false;
```

This ActionScript is almost identical to that of the news.fla. The only thing that needed to be changed was the instance names and the file name of the external text file that's being loaded.

The second to last line of ActionScript makes sure that the home_txt instance on the Stage displays HTML-formatted text correctly. This allows you to use images, bold text, italics, and bulleted lists to give your text some extra formatting. The final line of code sets the editable property to false so that users can't modify the text on their screen.

4) Copy home.txt, home01.jpg, and home02.jpg from the Lesson11 folder on the CD-ROM to the TechBookstore folder.

Before you can properly test your Flash document, you need to either copy or create a text file that can be loaded in using LoadVars. A text file is adequate for the front of the Tech Bookstore, and can be found on the CD-ROM, so you don't have to type in a whole bunch of content for the front page. Naturally, you can create whatever it is you want for the front of the Tech Bookstore if you so choose and want to type in the text. Or you can use the home.txt file from the CD-ROM. Locate the Lesson11 folder on the CD-ROM and copy the home.txt file and the two images home01.jpg and home02.jpg into the TechBookstore folder on your hard drive. Open the text file and look at the HTML markup.

TIP *The two image files are used within the HTML formatted text and are loaded into the SWF using the <img> tag in the home.txt file.*

If you're creating your own text file to load into the Tech Bookstore, you can make the HTML and formatting as simple or as complex as you like. Flash supports a small subset of HTML tags that include the following:

Anchor <a>: allows you to add links to your Flash text fields. The <a> tag also supports the use of the target attribute, which allows you to specify the frame or window in which the link should open. If you're using a style sheet, you can also specify colors and attributes for a:link, a:hover, and a:active.

Bold <b>: displays the text in bold.

Break
: adds a line break at the specified point.

Font <font>: allows you to change the current font, size, and color. This tag is very useful if you're not using style sheets and want to add some formatting to your text.

Image <img>: allows you to add images to your text fields. This tag supports loading local or external image files, SWF files, or even symbols from the Library (by assigning the symbol a Linkage Identifier).

Italics <i>: displays the text in italic.

List Item <li>: slightly different from HTML, the <li> does not appear between a pair of <ol> (ordered list) or <ul> (unordered list) tags. Flash's <li> tag allows you to easily create bulleted lists.

Paragraph <p>: allows you to add a new paragraph.

Span <span>: allows you to assign styles to a block of code.

TextFormat <textformat>: allows you to build simple tables in Flash.

Underline <u>: underlines a section of text.

Although Flash supports only about a dozen tags, combining them can lead to some fairly impressive results when it comes to formatting text for your sites.

TIP *When you load an image only into the TextArea, and the image is larger than the TextArea instance dimensions, scrollbars do not appear. You must have some text following the image in order for the scrollbars to activate. You have to use a ScrollPane component instead.*

If you want to use this file as is, close it. Otherwise, make any modifications to this file now that you know how it is being formatted.

5) Make sure that everything works properly in the Flash document. Save the file and then publish `home.fla` **so an SWF file is generated in the** `TechBookstore` **folder.**

Make sure that the FLA file works properly by selecting Control > Test movie to test the file in the testing environment.

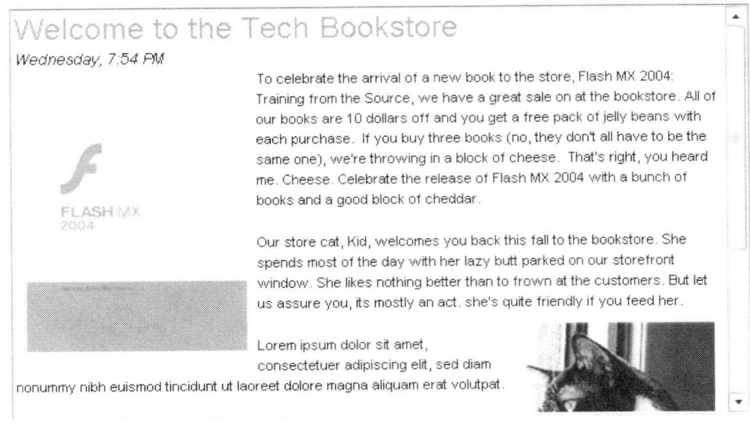

After you confirm that everything works in the SWF file and your formatting works correctly, return to the authoring environment and then save and publish the FLA file. A SWF file generates into the `TechBookstore` folder.

ANIMATING THE MENU

In this exercise, you will animate the menus that slide down in the Tech Bookstore when each button is clicked. You can see the functionality of them at the sample Web site at `http://flash.TrainingFromTheSource.com`. When a button is clicked, the menu slides down, and when the visitor rolls off the menu, the menu slides up. You created the animation that the menu actually uses earlier in this book. Now you will write the ActionScript that causes the animations to play when a visitor clicks the three buttons or rolls off the menu.

1) Open `bookstore13.fla` from the `TechBookstore` folder on your hard drive, if it isn't already open.

The file should have the edits that you made earlier in this exercise when you deleted the two buttons from the catalog page.

2) Name all the instance names in the menu so you can control the buttons and movie clips using ActionScript later in this exercise.

You have to add instance names for the three buttons at the top of the authoring environment and then the three menus sitting behind them.

Name the three buttons at the top of the main Stage, unlocking the `buttons` layer if necessary. Type in an instance name of *products_btn* to the Products button, *company_btn* to the Company button and *contact_btn* for the Contact button. Lock the `buttons` layer when you are finished.

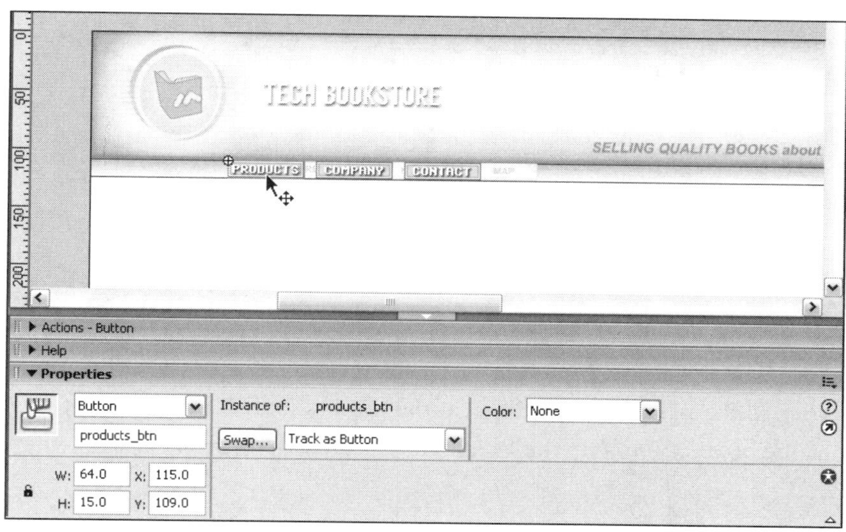

Now you need to give instance names to the three menus that are sitting behind the three buttons. They should be on the menu layer, which you need to unlock if it is locked. Click the menu behind the Products button and give it an instance name of *productsmenu_mc*. Then give the menu behind the Company button an instance name of *companymenu_mc* and the menu behind the Contact button the instance name *contactmenu_mc*.

Note the suffixes that have been added to each of the instances, so you can use code hinting when you start writing ActionScript. Then inside of the menu movie clips is another movie clip that you have to name. Double-click productsmenu_mc and select the menu inside that movie clip. Expand the Property inspector and give that clip an instance name of *menu1_mc*. You might first have to unlock the layer that the instance is on. Then select the second instance on this layer in the menu tween. Give it the same name *menu1_mc*. Repeat this for the third and final keyframe in this tween.

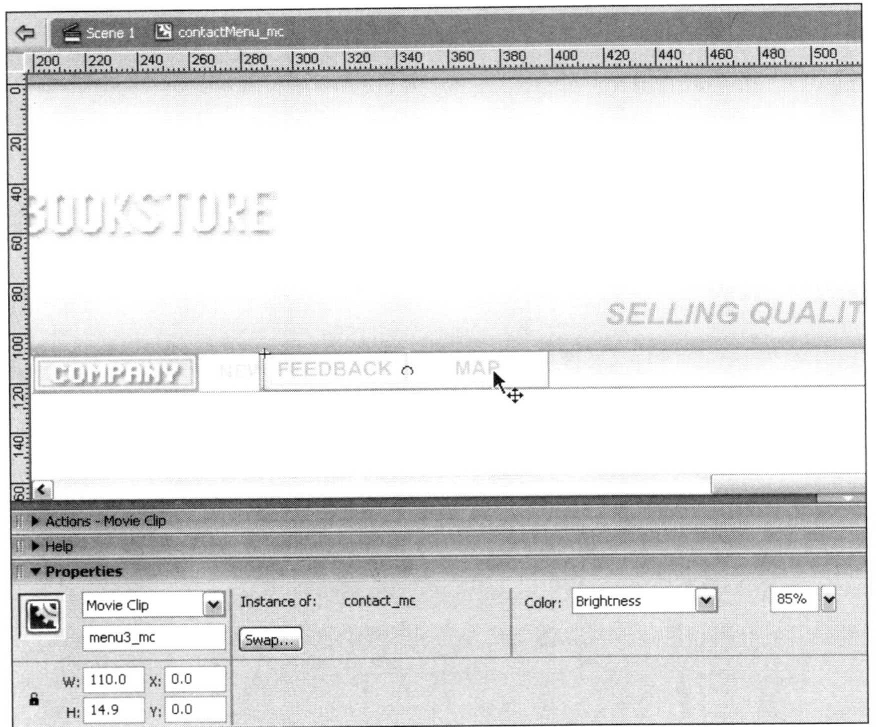

Use the edit bar to click back to the main Stage. Double-click companymenu_mc and give an instance name of *menu2_mc* to the clip inside companymenu_mc. Use the edit bar to navigate back to the main Stage, and repeat the process for the final menu, typing an instance name of *menu3_mc* into the Property inspector. Lock the menu layer when you're finished.

3) In frame 1 of the `actions` layer, add the following ActionScript into the Actions panel. This code initializes the menu's variables. You also want to add a line of ActionScript removing the menu when the visitor right clicks on the Stage.

You should already have a `stop` action entered on this frame. Following this action, you need to add the following three lines of code. These three variables are flags that you use to track which of the three menus are currently open (if any). If the value is set to 0, the sliding menu is up or closed (inactive); if the variable is set to 1, it tells you that the menu is currently down or open (active) and visible on the Stage.

```
var prodmenu:Number = 0;
var compmenu:Number = 0;
var contactmenu:Number = 0;
```

Then add the following line of ActionScript after the variables:

```
Stage.showMenu = false;
```

When you add this ActionScript to the document, visitors will not see most of the menu options when they right-click or control-click on the SWF file after the file is published. The contextual menu that opens typically includes a number of options such as *zoom* and *play*. However, all of these options are removed from the menu if you add this ActionScript - except for *Settings* (which allows the visitor to control their Flash Player settings).

4) In frame 1 of the `actions` layer, enter the following code that closes any menus that are open when the mouse rolls out of the menu's area.

The invisible button closes all the menus when a visitor roll over it. Earlier in the book, you created an invisible button around all the menus when they are open.

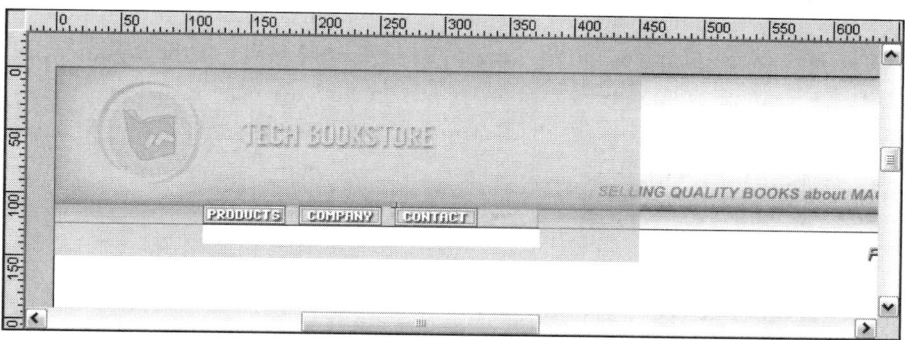

Then you need to add some ActionScript that tells the SWF file when to call the function to close the menus whenever the mouse rolls over this invisible button. When the mouse rolls over the button, ActionScript is used to close any open menus.

TIP *The following code in this example could be replaced by something in ActionScript called a for..in loop. Although this goes beyond the scope of the book, if you continue on in ActionScript, you might want to investigate and update this ActionScript accordingly. What happens is that you could place the three variables defined in the previous step into an Object. Using the for..in loop, you can loop over each item in the Object and execute a block of code. This would allow you to shorten the amount of code necessary and also make the ActionScript more flexible.*

Because the ActionScript you are adding to the Tech Bookstore is not major, it is OK to use repetitive ActionScript. Right now, learning how to properly use these few parts of the language is the most important part of the process.

```
//invisible button
this.inv_btn.onRollOver = function() {
  if (contactmenu == 1) {
    contactmenu_mc.gotoAndPlay("slideup");
    contactmenu = 0;
  }
  if (compmenu == 1) {
    companymenu_mc.gotoAndPlay("slideup");
    compmenu = 0;
  }
  if (prodmenu == 1) {
    productsmenu_mc.gotoAndPlay("slideup");
    prodmenu = 0;
  }
};
```

This function is placed within an `onRollover` event handler for the `inv_btn` instance, which means it executes every time a user moves the mouse onto the `inv_btn` instance (the invisible button on the Stage). The code looks at each of the menus and checks if the value is 1, 1 meaning that the menu is open in the SWF file. If the value of the variable is 1, the menu is open (has fully animated downward) and needs to be closed (animated upward). Therefore, you change the playhead of the corresponding movie clip (`productsmenu_mc`, `companymenu_mc`, or `contactmanu_mc`) to the frame labeled `slideup` to animate the menu so it is closed.

Also, note the path to the nested movie clips that are being closed in the previous code. Because the code is being written for the `inv_btn` instance, the menu movie clips can be addressed `contactmenu_mc.gotoAndPlay("slideup")`. This is a button code referencing the Timeline that it is placed on, which is the Stage. From the Stage, you can directly reference the `contactmenu_mc` instance and its `gotoAndPlay` method.

5) Now that the invisible button code has been added, follow it with the code for all the menus themselves.

Now that you have the menus closing when you roll over the invisible button, it is time to add the ActionScript that animates the menus when you click the main navigation. The code is very similar to the code for the `inv_btn` instance, except now you will be closing two of the menus if they are open and open the one that was clicked.

```
//products menu
this.products_btn.onRollOver = function() {
  if (contactmenu == 1) {
    contactmenu_mc.gotoAndPlay("slideup");
    contactmenu = 0;
  }
  if (compmenu == 1) {
    companymenu_mc.gotoAndPlay("slideup");
    compmenu = 0;
  }
  if (prodmenu == 0) {
    productsmenu_mc.gotoAndPlay("slidedown");
   prodmenu = 1;
  }
};
//company menu
this.company_btn.onRollOver = function() {
  if (prodmenu == 1) {
    productsmenu_mc.gotoAndPlay("slideup");
    prodmenu = 0;
  }
  if (contactmenu == 1) {
    contactmenu_mc.gotoAndPlay("slideup");
    contactmenu = 0;
  }
  if (compmenu == 0) {
    companymenu_mc.gotoAndPlay("slidedown");
    compmenu = 1;
  }
};
//contact menu
this.contact_btn.onRollOver = function() {
  if (compmenu == 1) {
    companymenu_mc.gotoAndPlay("slideup");
    compmenu = 0;
  }
  if (prodmenu == 1) {
    productsmenu_mc.gotoAndPlay("slideup");
    prodmenu = 0;
  }
  if (contactmenu == 0) {
    contactmenu_mc.gotoAndPlay("slidedown");
    contactmenu = 1;
  }
};
```

Although the code looks very overwhelming at first, it is actually quite simple because it is very repetitious. There are three menus in the navigation: `products`, `company`, and `contact`. For each menu item, you have to check to make sure that the other two are not already open, which you can tell because of the three variables you set earlier (`prodmenu`, `compmenu`, and `contactmenu`). If the values of these variables equal 1, you know that the menu is already open and therefore needs to be closed before you can display the menu that needs to open.

The code is broken down into three major sections, one for each menu item. When the `products_btn` is pressed, Flash executes the inline function checking whether the `compmenu` variable or `contactmenu` variable equal 1, meaning that the menu is already open. If a menu is already open, the variable is set to `0` and the menu is closed, similar to the code for the `inv_btn` earlier.

Finally, you check whether the menu you need to open, in this case `products`, is open or closed. If it is closed, you animate the menu opening up. This code doesn't need any `else` statements because if the menu you want is already open, the work is done and you can just go to the next menu item to check if its open or closed. The logic is the same with the `company_btn`, except you're checking making sure the `prodmenu` and `contactmenu` are closed.

TIP *Again, for the sake of simplicity, you aren't using the most elegant code possible for the menus. What is most important to take away is not only the process, but how the menus are being targeted and the general idea of* if *statements. This code could be shortened, although the complexity would increase accordingly and it would be more difficult to understand how it works. Perhaps one of the best ways to simplify the code is to create a function that takes two parameters: a menu item to expand and an array of menu items to hide. By converting the logic into a function, you would be able to reuse the code for all three cases and have to adjust only the parameters that get passed into the function.*

6) Check the syntax of your code and format it in the Actions panel. Then test the menu animation in the testing environment.

Press the Check Syntax button at the top of the Actions panel. If there are problems with your ActionScript, such as a missing bracket, a message will be displayed in the Output panel and you'll have to return and check your code against the ActionScript in Steps 3 to 5. When there are no errors, click the Auto Format button in the Actions panel toolbar, which formats the ActionScript with proper indentation and adds any missing semi-colons at the end of a statement.

Press Ctrl+Enter (or Command+Enter on the Mac) to see whether the menus animate properly in the SWF file. If you run into problems, you want to first double-check that the ActionScript matches the code in Step 3 to 5. If it seems to be related to the masking or invisible button, ensure that the mask is properly covering where the menu drops down and that the invisible button is properly surrounding where the menu drops down.

TIP *When you test the menu, you might find that the masking is slightly out of place. If the menus exceed the mask, you need to return to the mask and resize it appropriately so it doesn't obscure the menu. You might also find that the invisible button's hit area (the one that closes the menu) does not quite work properly. That means that you need to slightly resize the menu.*

7) If the menu animation is correct, save the changes you made to the FLA file.

Save the changes you made to `bookstore13.fla` and then move on to the next exercise, in which you add code so the buttons inside the menu work.

CONTROLLING THE MENU'S BUTTONS

Compared to the previous exercise, the menu's buttons are a walk in the park. Remember that a button's scope means that event functions affect the Timeline the button is on, not the button's Timeline. That means that the buttons control the main Timeline unless you specify otherwise. In this exercise, you will need to specify otherwise because you want to control the main Timeline from a Timeline that's nested inside a couple of movie clips. That's about as tricky as it gets for this exercise, and it really isn't too bad at all if you remember the section on *scoping* that was covered earlier in this lesson.

When one of the buttons in a menu is clicked, a message goes back through a couple of Timelines to the main Timeline. Then the playhead moves to a new page.

1) Add instance names for each of the buttons inside the menu using the Property inspector.

These buttons need instance names so you can target them with your ActionScript. Each of the menu's buttons, as you might remember, are nested inside the movie clip menu that's nested inside the main menu movie clip. So click `productsmenu_mc` and then `menu1_mc`, and inside you find two buttons. Select the button that says catalog and type the instance name *catalog_btn* into the Property inspector. Then click the button on the right and give it the instance name *reviews_btn*.

Navigate back to the main Stage using the edit bar, and repeat this process for the other two menus. The names you are giving them should be fairly intuitive. Give the buttons inside `menu2_mc` the instance names *tour_btn* and *news_btn*. Then give the `menu3_mc` buttons the instance names *feedback_btn* and *map_btn*.

2) Add ActionScript that is used to control the six buttons you find in the drop-down menus you just created. Enter this code following the code you added in the previous exercise.

You initially created these buttons to help visitors navigate throughout the Tech Bookstore, and you just gave them instance names so you can target them using ActionScript. The ActionScript targets the button so the function is called when the button is clicked; then the function tells the playhead on the main Timeline to move to the correct page in the Tech Bookstore.

TIP *Remember that wherever a button is placed, the Timeline that the button is placed on is affected. Therefore, even though you are writing code for a button that is nested way inside a movie clip, the function you are writing affects the current Timeline. So you need to tell Flash where to look for the button, but do not need to scope back to the correct Timeline to move the playhead.*

Select frame 1 on the actions layer of the main Timeline. Expand the Actions panel and enter the following ActionScript into the Script pane.

```
this.productsmenu_mc.menu1_mc.catalog_btn.onRelease = function() {
  gotoAndStop("catalog");
};
this.productsmenu_mc.menu1_mc.reviews_btn.onRelease = function() {
  gotoAndStop("reviews");
};
this.companymenu_mc.menu2_mc.tour_btn.onRelease = function() {
  gotoAndStop("tour");
};
this.companymenu_mc.menu2_mc.news_btn.onRelease = function() {
  gotoAndStop("news");
};
this.contactmenu_mc.menu3_mc.feedback_btn.onRelease = function() {
  gotoAndStop("feedback");
};
this.contactmenu_mc.menu3_mc.map_btn.onRelease = function() {
  gotoAndStop("map");
};
```

You should recognize button functions from code that you already entered for other buttons in the FLA files you have created. Although the structure might be familiar, targeting the button might not be. In this context, the `this` keyword refers to the current Timeline, which is the main Stage. Although this code works without it, it can be useful at times if you are moving your ActionScript around. Following this, you target `contactmenu_mc`, which is sitting on the main Stage and then inside this clip target `menu3_mc`. Inside `menu3_mc` is the button, so continue with the instance name `map_btn`. Because you have now targeted the instance you want to manipulate, you can type in the `onRelease` event handler and the rest of the inline function.

You already have labels on every frame that a new page begins in. These frame labels are used to navigate throughout the Tech Bookstore. The `gotoAndStop` action targets `"map"` (which is the name of the frame label). Frame labels must be placed within quotation marks (which mean a *string*).

Amazingly, you have now finished the main bulk of ActionScript that you find in the Tech Bookstore. The remainder of the work involved on the Tech Bookstore is integrating the FLA files you built in this and previous lessons into the main site. You will also optimize the Flash site, which is described in Lesson 12.

3) Test the buttons by selecting Control > Test Movie to see if the buttons work correctly.

When you click a button to open a menu, it animates downward. When you roll off the menu area onto the invisible button, it should then animate upward to "close" the menu. If you click a button in the menu, it should take you to a new page in the Tech Bookstore and stop. If the menus don't animate properly, go back and double-check your instance names and quickly check the code in this lesson. Make sure that each button in the three menus takes you to the correct page as well. If you still cannot get the menu working, locate the finished file on the CD-ROM and compare your file against what you find in the completed FLA.

4) Save the changes you made to the FLA file.

You can find a copies of the finished products, called `bookstore13_pro_complete.fla` and `bookstore13_fmx_complete.fla`, in the `Lesson11` folder on the CD-ROM. If you are having any problems with the code you have typed in, you can find a copy of it in this file on the main Timeline.

In the following lesson, you start out by loading in all of the SWF files you created in this lesson. Then you test and debug the Tech Bookstore site and add a progress bar (the ProgressBar component) for each of the sections in the application.

WHAT YOU HAVE LEARNED

In this lesson, you have:

- Learned about the differences between ActionScript 1.0 and ActionScript 2.0 (page 324)
- Learned how to use objects, methods, and properties (pages 328–330)
- Found out how to use strict typing with variables (page 325)
- Used code hinting to speed up writing ActionScript (page 326)
- Used functions and conditional statements (pages 330–331)
- Learned about scope and variables (page 331)
- Found out about using `_root`, `_parent`, and levels in your ActionScript (pages 333–336)
- Extensively used the `LoadVars` object (pages 336–338)
- Added events, event handlers, and listeners to your code (pages 344–347)
- Incorporated CSS to format text that's loaded into a document (pages 347–350)
- Created the Catalog, Reviews, News, and Home pages (pages 338–367)
- Added code so the Tech Bookstore's menu could animate (page 367)
- Added ActionScript so the Tech Bookstore menu works (pages 373–376)

optimizing flash content

LESSON 12

It is very important to consider how you organize Flash documents when you work with a lot of content. Loading as many SWF, JPEG, FLV video and MP3 files into a base SWF file as possible on demand helps minimize what your end user has to load all at once. It also means that your visitors do not have to download a lot of content from the Tech Bookstore that they might not be interested in seeing. If every visitor had to download the Tour each and every time that they arrive at the Web site, it's unlikely they would revisit the site again! The same goes for your own sites that you create later on. Organization and consideration of your visitors is very important if you are building a site based on a single FLA file.

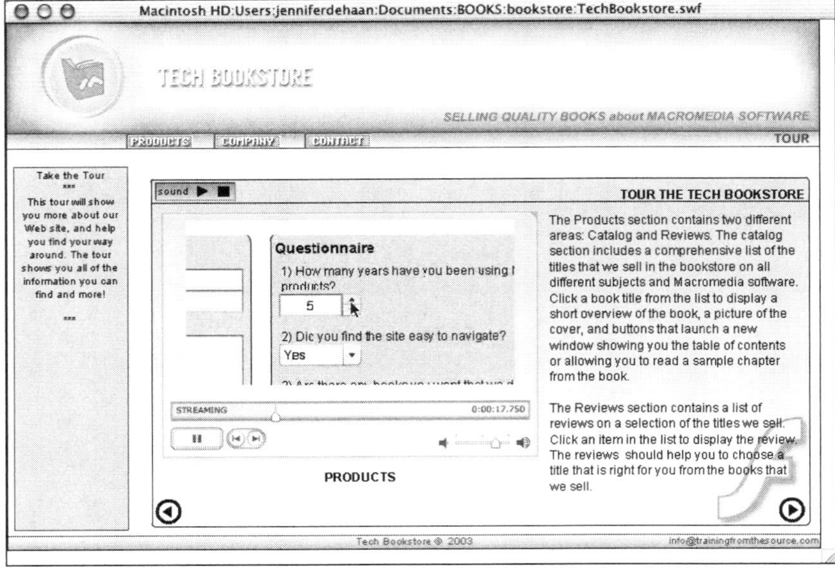

Loading content into the Tech Bookstore site.

This lesson explains why the Tech Bookstore has been created the way it has, and also finishes off loading some of the final pages into the main site. Progress bars indicate the status of files that are loading into the Tech Bookstore. You will also add progress bars onto some of the files you are loading and then create a custom one to load the main Tech Bookstore FLA file. You will debug the application and make sure that everything is working properly before you move on to publish the Web site and put it online in the next lesson.

WHAT YOU WILL LEARN

In this lesson, you will:

- Learn about how to optimize Web sites
- Learn how to organize Flash projects
- Load content into the Home, Catalog, Reviews, Tour, and News pages
- Add progress bars to content that is loading in
- Use `MovieClipLoader` to load in the Tech Bookstore
- Test and debug the Tech Bookstore

APPROXIMATE TIME

This lesson takes approximately one hour 30 minutes to complete.

LESSON FILES

Media Files:

None

Starting Files:

Lesson12/bookstore14_fmx.fla
Lesson12/bookstore14_pro.fla

Completed Project:

Lesson12/techbookstore_fmx.fla
Lesson12/techbookstore_pro.fla
Lesson12/loader.fla

OPTIMIZING FLASH DOCUMENTS

If you are building an entire Web site using Flash, or even a complex element for an HTML site in Flash, file size can quickly become a concern. When you are importing bitmaps using a lot of text, video, components or sound, the amount of data you are working with can grow quickly. And if you're adding video or sound, you have to consider how you will organize the Flash documents.

You have followed steps to build the Tech Bookstore in a particular way during the lessons you have completed so far in this book. The way you are building the bookstore is simple, yet it takes into account some of the easiest ways you can optimize an FLA file on the Web by loading assets at runtime, adding progress bars to inform visitors, and separate the content into smaller SWF files instead of adding everything into one large document.

UNDERSTANDING PROCESSORS AND SWF FILES

SWF files are handled differently by different computers. First of all, the operating system might handle a SWF file in its own way, but also browsers might differ in the way they play back a SWF file. For the most part, regardless of the platform or browser, your SWF will play the same way for those who view the document. The differences are infinitesimally small compared with something like an HTML page with style sheets, JavaScript, and so forth. However, there are small inconsistencies that are good to be aware of. First of all, a Mac will play your SWF back a little bit slower than on a Windows-based machine. This has to do with the operating system and the Flash Player; however, it has been greatly improved with the Flash Player 7, so the differences are quite insignificant if this Player is what your visitor has installed.

TIP *A Mac and a PC handle colors differently. A Windows-based machine will appear darker than one on the Mac. This has nothing to do with the SWF file itself; it has to do with gamma correction differences between the machines. This inconsistency occurs no matter what you are using to create your Web site.*

Sometimes it is quicker to create an animation using ActionScript than it is to painstakingly motion tween and animate movie clips. Using ActionScript sometimes (but not always) decreases the file size and workload when you have to animate something, but the code can increase how intensive the SWF file is on a visitor's processor and this might slow down the playback. Different processor speeds can also affect the playback of a SWF file. Older processors might play the SWF back at a snails place compared to a fast, modern processor. The best things you can do are test the SWF file on several different computers and examine how the SWF runs on each machine. Some older computers will have a difficult time playing a SWF file regardless of whether you use ActionScript or tweening to create animations. Something fading in or moving might play back very slow and choppy on these machines.

TIP *If you have a SWF file that continually calls functions or runs code on every frame (for example, if you were using an* `onEnterFrame` *event handler to check something or execute code every single time a frame plays), a SWF file might slow down considerably. If you have a SWF set to 21 fps, the code executes 21 times a second. Again, it is a good idea to delete the event handler when it is not needed, and get your friends to test the file on several different machines.*

Understanding Bandwidth and File Size

Bandwidth refers to the amount of information that is transferred between client computers and a Web server. For example, a busy Web site might use 5 gigabytes of bandwidth in a month. Every time visitors arrive at your Web site, some bandwidth is consumed when they download the pages and media from it. Depending on the number of visitors you have and how big your Web site is, bandwidth quickly adds up over time on a site with some traffic. Therefore, you want to try and minimize how much information your visitors download on each page! Limiting bandwidth consumption affects the way you build your FLA file in many different ways that are outlined in the following sections. You want your visitors to download only the information they need and limit the surplus information they might not be interested in.

The first thing you can do to minimize bandwidth is go through all your vector drawings, bitmap images, and sound files and check their publish settings for when the SWF file is generated. For your vector drawings you can choose Modify > Shape > Optimize to optimize the vector drawing. This can reduce (or smooth out) the vectors in the shape. If you have a lot of ragged edges, optimizing the shape reduces the number of calculations that are required by Flash to render the drawing. This in turn reduces overall file size and even improves the performance of the SWF file. You can right-click (or control-click) on the asset and choose Properties just as you did in earlier lessons for other media assets in the Library (such as sound and images). You can change properties in the Publish Settings dialog box, too. Finally, you can use the Bandwidth Profiler in Flash to analyze and work on minimizing the file size and manage how the SWF is downloaded to the visitor. The Bandwidth Profiler is discussed later in this lesson, and you will learn about the Publish Settings dialog box in Lesson 13.

ORGANIZING APPLICATIONS AND USING GOOD PRACTICES

There are many different kinds of Web sites when it comes to how information is arranged. Some people might build a Flash site in which all of the information downloaded by the users when they arrive at your site is contained in one large file. The entire FLA file and everything associated with it (including JPEG images, sounds, and so forth) is contained in one SWF that is progressively downloaded from beginning to end. Then the visitors can click through each page. Whether the user looks at all the content or not doesn't determine how much he or she has to download. The visitor downloads the entire Web site regardless of what they want to see.

Instead of creating an FLA file that contains all the content of your site in one large file, you should create a site that dynamically loads most of the content at runtime (when the SWF file plays in the Flash Player). This is mostly how the Tech Bookstore is working, in a basic way. There are ways to make an application dynamic, such as hooking it up to a database or extensively use XML, Flash Remoting, or Web Services. Or you can just load JPEGs, MP3s, text, and other SWF files into your document. All of these ways mean you are working with dynamic content and improving the way your Flash documents work.

You also have to consider the usability of your Flash file, and consider how easy it is for visitors to navigate your site. Is the size of your text large enough to read? Is the font legible? Does the visitor have the font installed, or are you embedding it? Are the buttons big enough, easy to find, and easy to understand as buttons; and is your site easy to navigate between each of the different sections? Sometimes you might create an "artistic" site where you specifically want the visitor to not really know how to navigate right off the bat. Weird navigation can be perfectly acceptable in certain situations, but just make sure you have considered who your intended audience is and what it can expect to find at your site. If you are creating a shopping cart application for a business to sell its pet supplies, you wouldn't want to have three tiny + symbols at the bottom-right corner of the Stage for the main navigation! This is fine for an experimental Flash site, but not usable for a mainstream business application.

You might have heard of Flash and the *skip intro* phenomenon. In older Web sites that use Flash, you might remember how many of them had introductions play when you first arrived at the site. Many of these introductions included a bunch of flying text, tweening images, and music playing. Although some of them were quite interesting to watch and were well done, many of them were not. One big issue with intros was how common and irritating they were and how they muddied the name of Flash for awhile. However, another main issue regarding intros was how many of them forced visitors to sit through a long introduction without the option to skip it (hence, the infamous *skip intro* button).

You won't see as many Flash intros anymore, thank goodness, partly because of the backlash against them. Many people hate intros and share that information with anyone who will listen. This said, many clients and individuals still love intros and create them for their Web sites, so they haven't completely disappeared yet. You might even be commissioned to make one yourself. A good rule of thumb to follow is "always do what the paying client wants you to do." But what this skip intro phenomenon has taught us is how important usability and following good or standardized practices is when you create Web sites. If you must have a Flash intro, just make sure you remember to have a skip intro button or link *in the HTML portion* of your Web site. The link immediately moves the user on to the main part of the Web site and stops the intro from downloading and consuming more bandwidth.

What you should take away from the *skip intro* idea is to always remember to give your visitor control. If the visitors don't want to download something, allow them to stop it and move on. If they don't want to hear your music, give them the option to turn it off. And it is always a bad idea take over the visitor's computer by changing the site to full screen! Dynamically load your bandwidth heavy content whenever possible, giving your visitor the control over whether they want to download the information in the first place.

LOADING IN NEW CONTENT

You have created a lot of the content that will load into the Tech Bookstore site. This decreases the amount of information you have to store in the main Web site, particularly some of the components that can quickly bulk up the size of your SWF. So let's add the rest of the content into the Tech Bookstore.

1) Open `bookstore13.fla`, if it isn't already open, and save a new version of the file by selecting File > Save As. Save the new document as `bookstore14.fla`.

Make sure that this file is saved in the `TechBookstore` folder on your hard drive. You can also find a copy of `bookstore14_fmx.fla` on the book's CD-ROM if you would rather begin with that file instead. If you are using Flash MX Professional, then use `bookstore14_pro.fla` instead.

NOTE *When you are placing the content in this exercise on the Stage, make sure that you leave enough room for the menus to drop down. Drag a horizontal guide to approximately 140 pixels on the vertical ruler. Place all new content below this guide.*

2) Add a Loader component instance on the `home` layer. Resize the component instance to *580* by *345* and give it an instance name.

This Loader instance is to load in the content for the Home page. Expand the Components panel and drag an instance of the Loader component onto Frame 1 of the `home` layer, which is within the `pages` folder. Give the component an instance name of *home_ldr* and position it on the left side of the Stage under the navigation, similar to the following graphic.

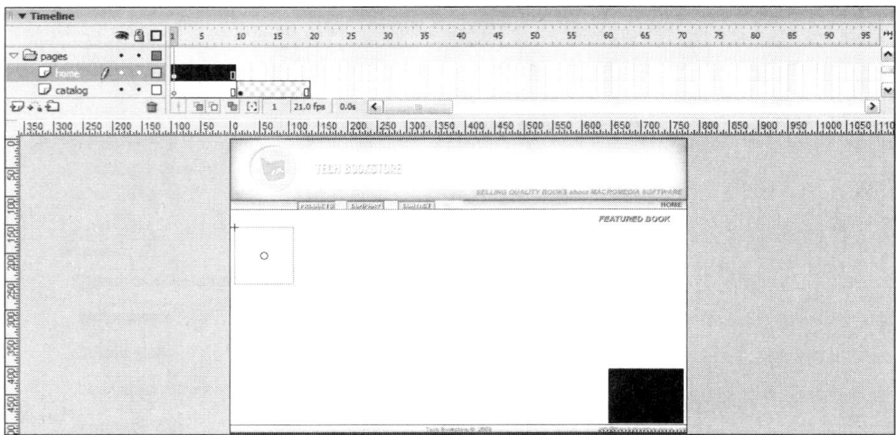

You can either resize the component to the size of the `home.swf` document (which is 580w by 345h) or leave the component at its default size and let Flash resize the instance when the content loads in. Often, it is easier to size the component manually because it allows you to see where the content will load in relation to the other instances on the Stage.

NOTE *If you choose not to resize the component, place the Loader's upper-left corner where you want the upper-left corner of the loaded SWF to be located. Also make sure that* `scaleContent` *is set to false. If it is set to true, your content will resize and this can end up distorting it. Text can look horrible after it is scaled.*

Set the `contentPath` for the Loader component to `home.swf` in either the Property inspector or Component Inspector panel. This is the URL of the content you want to load into the component.

There are three properties you can change for the Loader component using the Property inspector:

`autoLoad`: Determines whether or not the content should load automatically when the frame is loaded (`true`). If not, you have to explicitly call the `load` function (`false`).

`contentPath:` The URL pointing to the content that should be loaded. This field accepts both relative and absolute URLs.

`scaleContent:` Boolean (`true` or `false`) value that determines whether the Loader component should resize itself to fit the content being loaded (`false`) or whether the content should be scaled to fit the size of the existing Loader component (`true`).

For each of the sections in the Web site, you want to make sure the `autoLoad` is set to `true` and the `scaleContent` is set to `false`.

3) Insert a new layer called `catalog`. Add a Loader component instance to the Catalog page. Resize the instance, set the `contentPath`, and position it on the Stage.

Insert a new layer directly below the `home` layer. Rename the new layer *catalog*. Insert a new keyframe on frame 10, and delete all of the frames on the layer after frame 19 by highlighting them with the mouse, right-clicking (or control-clicking), and selecting Remove Frames from the contextual menu.

Click frame 10 of the `catalog` layer in the Timeline and drag an instance of the Loader component onto the Stage. Give the component an instance name of *catalog_ldr*. Expand the Property inspector and set the `contentPath` to `catalog.swf` and then set the `scaleContent` property to `false`. Resize the component to the same dimensions as the `catalog.swf` document, which is 720 (width) by 345 (height).

Position the component so it is roughly in the center of the main content area, as seen in the following graphic.

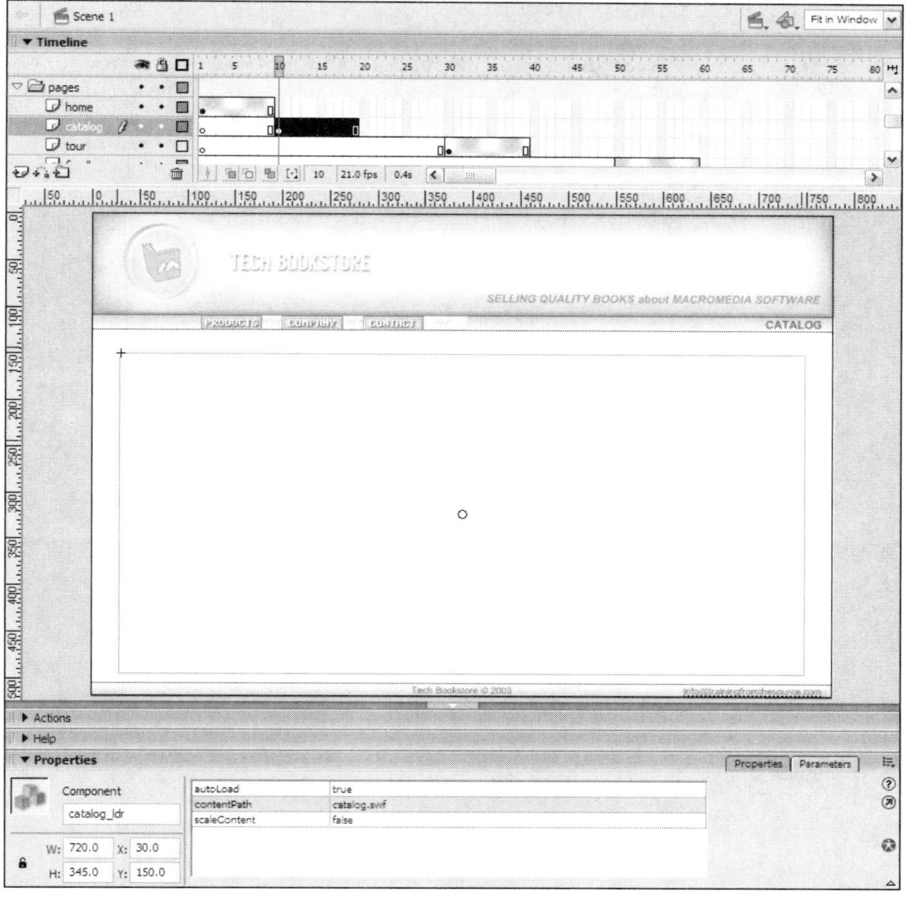

4) Insert a new layer called `reviews`**. Add a Loader instance on the Reviews page to load in** `reviews.swf`**. Resize and position the component as well as change its parameters.**

Insert a new layer directly below the `catalog` layer. Then insert a new keyframe on frame 20 of the layer by pressing F6 and delete all the frames greater than frame 30 on the layer. Highlight the frames with the cursor, right-click (or control-click), and select Remove Frames from the contextual menu.

Click on frame 20 of the `reviews` layer and drag an instance of the Loader component on to the Stage. In the Property inspector, set the instance name to `reviews_ldr` and set the `contentPath` property to `reviews.swf`. Then set the `scaleContent` property to `false`. Resize the component to *720* by *360* and position it in the middle of the Stage.

5) Insert a new layer called `news` **and add a Loader instance to the Stage. Give the instance an instance name and then resize and position it on the Stage.**

Insert a new layer and rename it *news* and make sure it is directly below the `tour` layer. Click frame 40, insert a new keyframe by pressing F6, and then remove all the frames on the layer that are greater than 49.

Click frame 40 of the `news` layer and add a Loader component. Give the component an instance name of *news_ldr*, set the `contentPath` to `news.swf` and set `scaleContent` to `false`. Resize the Loader instance so it is *635* wide by *345* high and place it in the horizontal center of the News page.

When you are finished, the Timeline should look similar to the following figure.

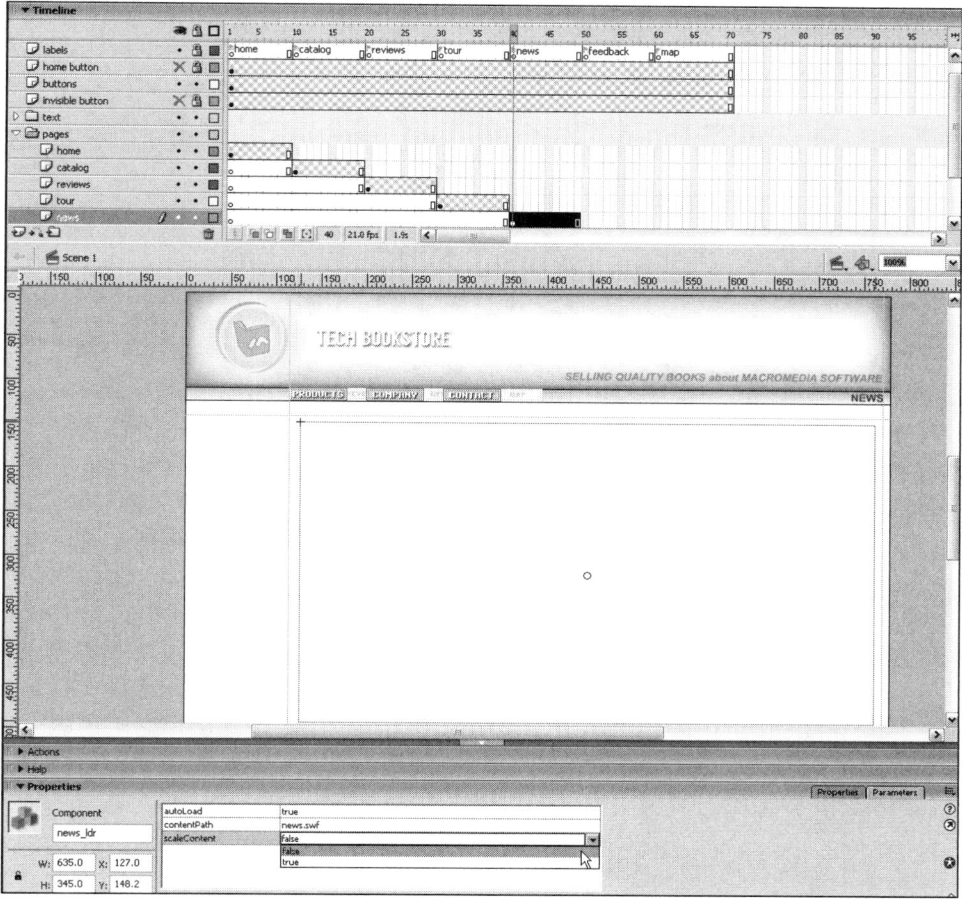

6) Give the Loader instance already on the `map` layer a new instance name, and the Loader on the Tour page an instance name. Then make sure that a mask is drawn over the Loader instance on the Map page.

The Map page already has a Loader component on the Stage from a previous lesson. Click the instance and in the Property inspector give it an instance name of *map_ldr* and set the `scaleContent` property to `false`. Do the same thing for the Loader component on the Tour page. Select the instance and type in an instance name of *tour_ldr*.

The next thing you need to do is create a mask over the Loader instance. A mask is necessary because you animated the car in the mask SWF file to animate beyond the edges of the map. When the map loads into the bookstore, the car will also appear beyond the Stage itself after it's loaded in.

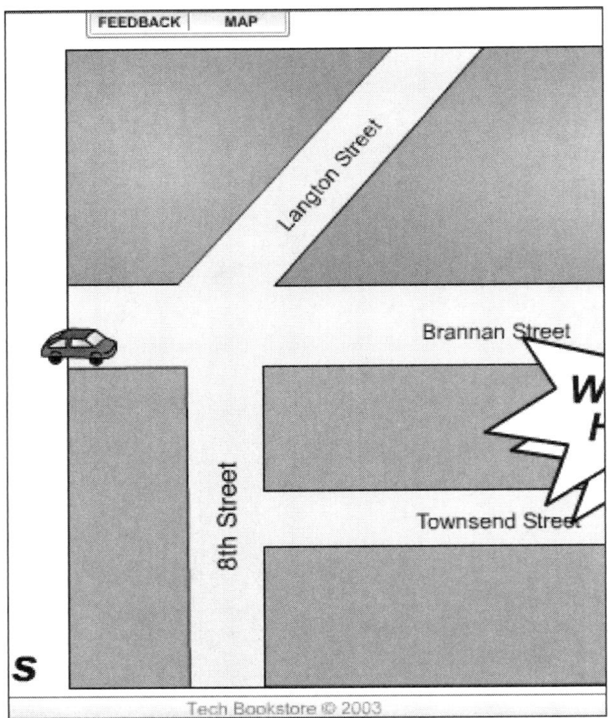

To solve this problem, you can create a mask layer to hide the car when it's outside of the map. Create a new layer over the `map` layer and insert a keyframe directly over the keyframe on the `map` layer. Convert the new layer to a Mask layer by right clicking the layer in the Timeline and choosing Mask from the contextual menu. Rename this new layer *map mask*. Draw a square on the `map mask` layer that covers the map's Loader instance. You might need to draw guide layers in order to show where the edges of the map instance are so you can make a mask the same size and in the same position on the Stage. You will also need to draw squares on the mask layer over where all of the text appears on the `map` layer so it is still visible when the SWF is published. You could alternatively make a new layer for the text that is not masked and it will appear as well.

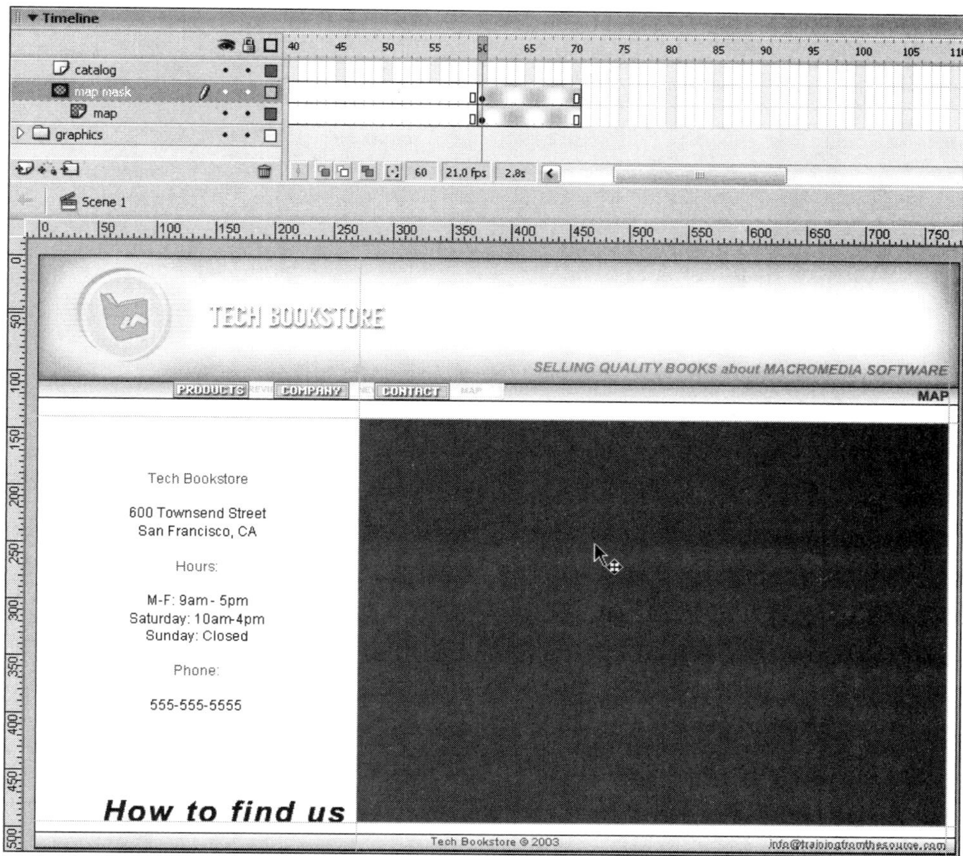

Lock both layers (`map` and `map mask`) when you are finished.

7) Add any additional graphics or text to the Tech Bookstore site

Before you finish up, you might want to add some static text on some of the individual pages. You could feel it is necessary to give directions on what to click or do to make the site work. Look at the following figure for an example of some of the additional text that we have added to the Tech Bookstore. You might need to move the assets around the Stage a bit to accommodate for the additions you make.

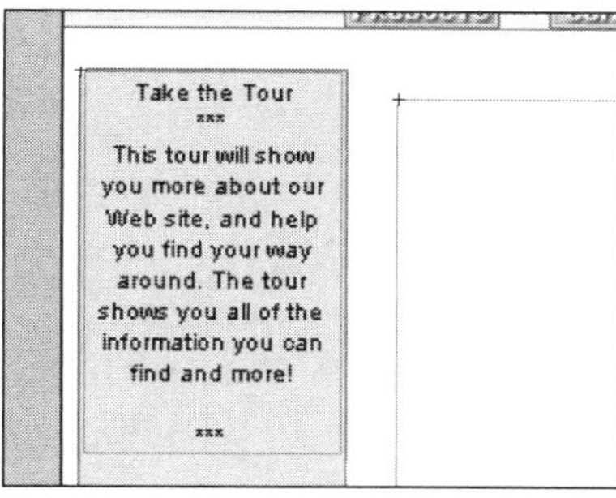

8) Clean up the Library. Then test and save the changes that you have made to the FLA file.

Move any of the new graphics or symbols you might have created, and the new components into their respective folders in the Library.

At this point, you can test the entire Tech Bookstore application. Press Ctrl+Enter or Command+Enter to test the SWF file in the testing environment or in a Web browser window by pressing the F12 key. Each of the sections should now have content load when you click one of the menu buttons to navigate to each page.

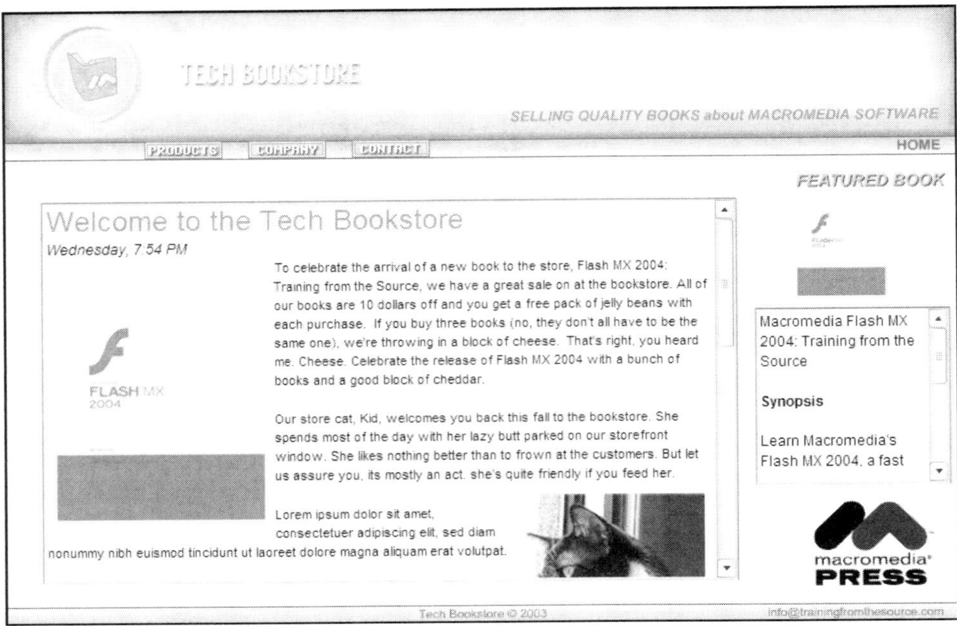

If one of the SWF files does not load, make sure that it is saved in the `TechBookstore` directory, and that the SWF's filename is entered correctly (without typos) into the Property inspector for the particular Loader instance.

ADDING THE PROGRESSBAR COMPONENT

Progress bars are an important part of many larger Flash documents, particularly ones using video, audio, or complete sites built using Flash. In this case, you're dealing with all of the above! When you load in content, it is important to display indication on the screen that loading is taking place. You might have visitors using dial-up phone modems to view the Web site, or you might have a large video file that even visitors on the fastest broadband connections will have to wait to start viewing. In these cases, a progress bar tells the visitor that content is in progress of loading. If you do not use a progress bar or preload content, your users might think something is wrong with the site because they do not see anything happening. A visual indication is quite important to let them know to hold on a second while the SWF file loads.

Now that you have added the Loader components to `bookstore14.fla`, you can add some progress bars to show visitors that something is loading into the application. You will also have to add a progress bar for the entire application, which happens in the following exercise.

1) Open `bookstore14.fla` from the `TechBookstore` folder on your hard drive.
You are still working with the same FLA file you used for the previous exercise.

2) Select frame 1 of the `home` layer. Expand the Components panel and drag an instance of the ProgressBar component on to the Stage.
Position the progress bar over the middle of the Loader component and give it an instance name of *home_pb*.

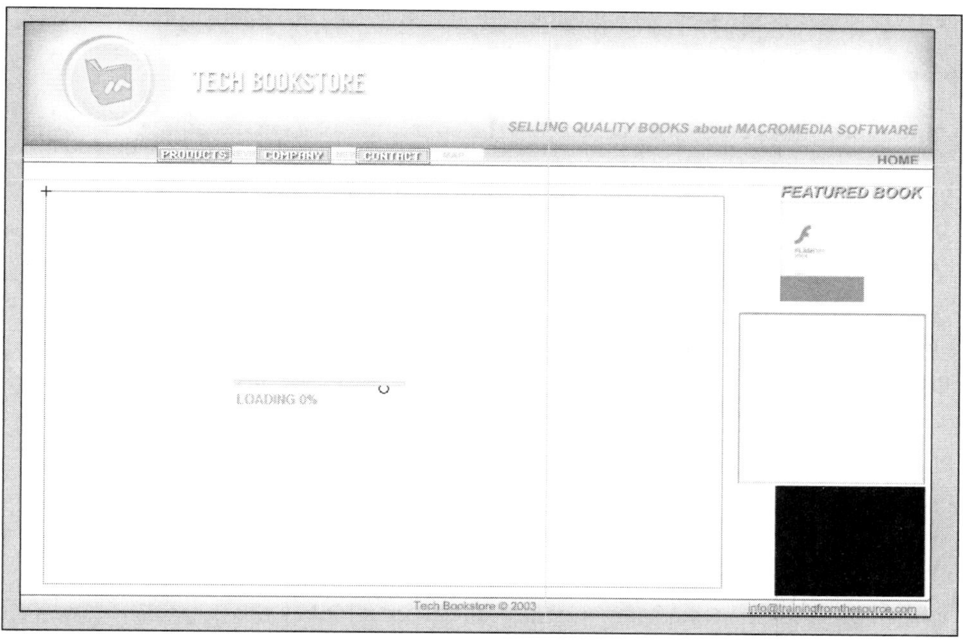

In the Property inspector, set the mode to `polled` and set the source to the instance name of the Loader component, `home_ldr`. If you were to test the SWF file, the progress bar increments while the content is loading until it's fully loaded. If the content you load has a small file size or if you're loading the content directly off your hard drive, the counter might quickly progress from 0% to 100%. You might not even see it happening!

3) Add the event listener Object ActionScript. Add this code on frame 1 of the `actions` layer.

When the content displays in the Loader component, the ProgressBar remains visible and stays at 100%. You need to create an event listener that waits for content to finish loading and then hides the ProgressBar component.

Select frame one on the `actions` layer and add the following ActionScript below the existing code in the Actions panel:

```
var pbListener:Object = new Object();
pbListener.progress = function(evt) {
  evt.target._visible = true;
};
pbListener.complete = function(evt) {
  evt.target._visible = false;
};
```

This ActionScript creates a new `Object`, which you use to handle the events that are generated by the ProgressBar component. The ProgressBar has two events generated:

progress: This event is triggered while content is being loaded

complete: This event is triggered when the content has finished loading

You use these events to toggle the *visibility* of the ProgressBar component. When the external SWF file is actively being loaded into the Loader component, the ProgressBar is visible on the Stage. It displays what percentage of the file has been loaded. When the `complete` event is caught, the content is fully loaded and the ProgressBar component can be hidden on the Stage because the Loader instance already displays the loaded content.

4) Create an event listener for the `home_pb` ProgressBar component to hide the ProgressBar instance.

In order to hide the `home_pb` progress bar on the Stage when the content in the Loader component has finished loading, you need to add the following ActionScript code to the bottom of the actions layer. Add this code below the ActionScript you entered in Step 3:

```
home_pb.addEventListener("progress", pbListener);
home_pb.addEventListener("complete", pbListener);
```

This ActionScript adds two event listeners to the `home_pb` instance on the Stage. Now when the `home_pb` ProgressBar receives the progress event, it executes the function defined in the `pbListener.progress` property.

When the complete event is triggered by Flash, the `pbListener` event handler sets the visibility of the target component (the component that generates the event—which in this case is `home_pb`) to `false`. The event hides the symbol on the Stage. You can substitute `evt.target` with `home_pb` in the code in Step 3, and the code would work the same way. One drawback to *hard coding* (setting a definite single value instead of a variable that could change the value) `home_pb` into the function is that the function works only with that one component instance. By keeping the function dynamic and using the `evt.target`, you can reuse that same ProgressBar listener object on each of the ProgressBars instances throughout the entire FLA.

5) Add new ProgressBar instances for the remaining SWF files that need to be dynamically loaded into the site. Give each new instance a new instance name.

Repeat the process of adding ProgressBar components onto the Stage for the Loader component instances that load in the *Reviews*, *News*, *Catalog*, *Tour*, and *Map* sections. Give each new ProgressBar component instance a unique instance name.

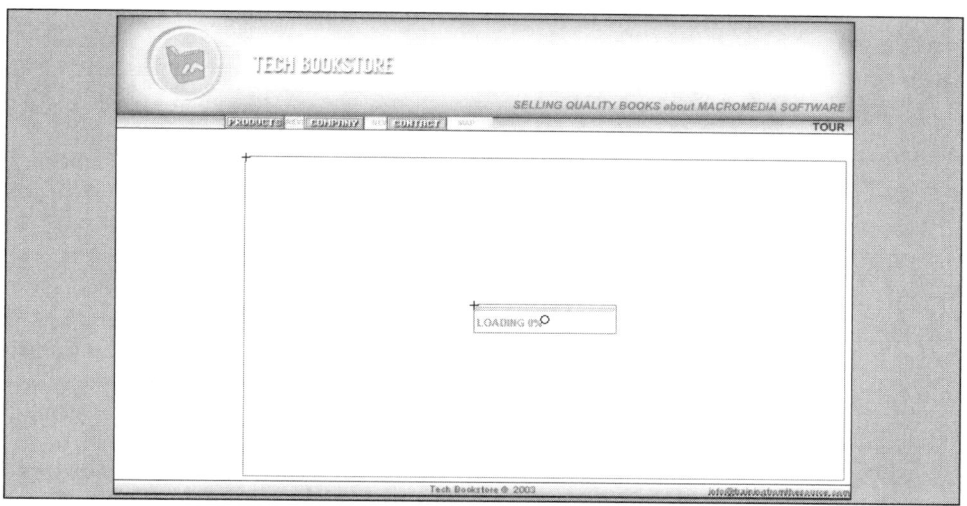

TIP *Make sure that you add each ProgressBar to the layer for each page these Loader instances are on. If you choose a layer that spans multiple pages, your ProgressBar instance is visible on pages where it doesn't belong.*

6) Add an event listener to every page containing a ProgressBar component. Add the code onto the `actions` layer. Change the instance name in the code to match the instance name of the ProgressBar instance on that particular page.

You'll also need to add the two lines of event listener code from Step 5 to each frame with the ProgressBar components. Each listener can reuse the same `pbListener` event handler object defined on Frame 1 of the FLA, but the listeners must be added to the same frame as the component instances. For example, the code on the frame labeled `news` (frame 40) you would need to add the following code on the `actions` layer, assuming that your ProgressBar component had an instance name of `news_pb`:

```
news_pb.addEventListener("progress", pbListener);
news_pb.addEventListener("complete", pbListener);
```

As mentioned, ActionScript needs to be added to each frame that has a ProgressBar. There are already keyframes with the `stop` action on each page. You want to add this code following each `stop` action, and remember to modify the instance name in the code with the instance name of the particular ProgressBar component on that particular page.

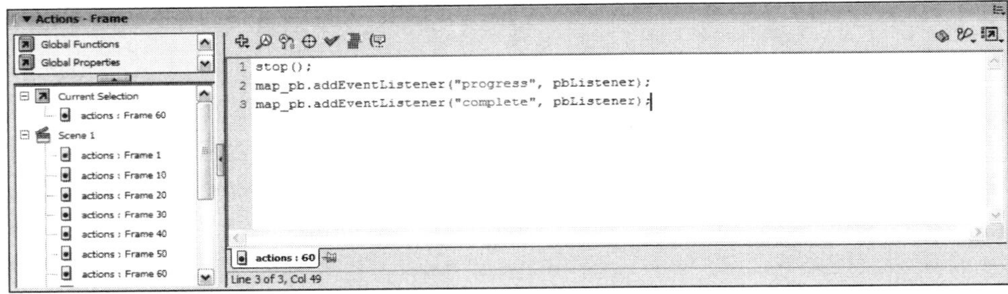

LOADING THE TECH BOOKSTORE

The Tech Bookstore is not a massive file because a lot of its content is being loaded into Loader movie clips. However, it would take too long to load on phone modems *not* to have a progress bar for the entire site itself. Therefore, you will create a special SWF file that loads in the entire Tech Bookstore. This is not the only way to handle this process, but it is probably one of the easiest ways and, more importantly, it shows you how the `MovieClipLoader` class works to load in external content into a movie clip. You will find the `MovieClipLoader` quite useful for this purpose and other sites that you build in the future.

1) Create a new FLA file called `loader.fla` and save it in the `TechBookstore` folder. This file will load in the Tech Bookstore online and contain a progress bar that you create yourself to load the bookstore using the new `MovieClipLoader` class.

The `MovieClipLoader` class can track the successful loading of content into movie clips, such as images and SWF files like the many `bookstore.fla` files you have created. Because the ProgressBar component adds about 30KB in its own right, you will build a very lightweight SWF file so visitors with dial-up connections don't see a blank SWF file while waiting for the ProgressBar component itself to load in.

TIP *You might want to add a graphic or animation to entertain visitors while they wait. Now, you won't want to make the animation too intensive or the visitor will have to wait for that to load as well!*

2) Change the FPS speed of the new FLA to *21fps* and the dimensions to *780* (width) by *520* (height). Rename Layer 1 to `progress`.

These dimensions and the frame rate match those of the Tech Bookstore. This means that your SWF file will not slow down after it is loaded into the `loader.swf` file.

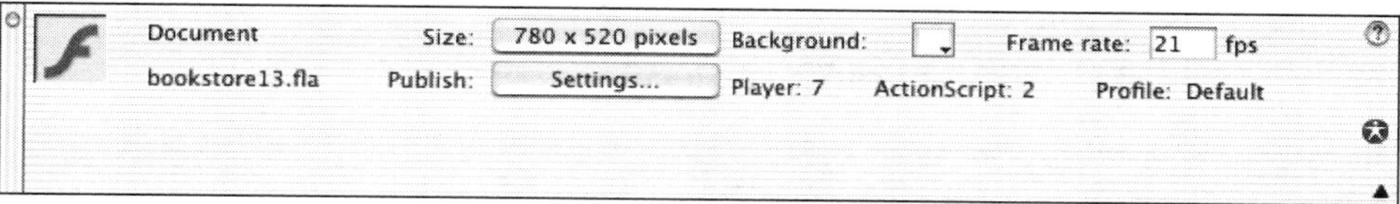

3) Create a rectangle on the Stage with a fill color of your choice. Resize the rectangle to approximately *150* pixels wide and a height of about *10* pixels.

The rectangle serves as a progress bar like the component you used earlier on. You can make the rectangle a different size, but try to maintain the same ratio and shape of the rectangle in the following figure.

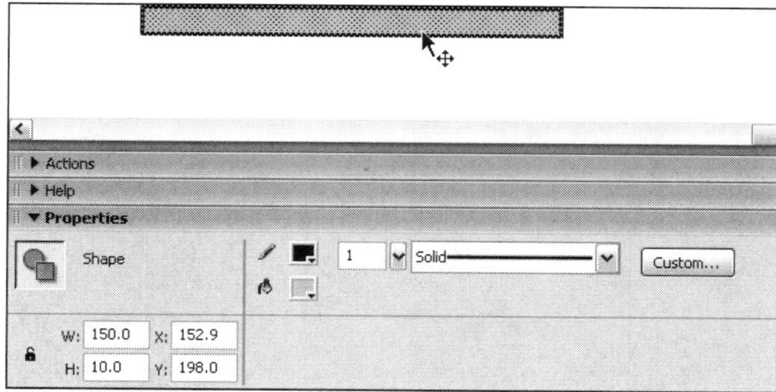

The fill color will be the actual progress bar that grows in size as the SWF file loads, and the stroke around the edge will contain the progress bar, showing visitors a depiction of how much more data the SWF has to load in.

4) Select the fill itself and convert it into a movie clip. Give this clip an instance name of `bar_mc`. Then select the stroke, convert it to a graphic symbol, and select Modify > Arrange > Bring to Front.

Select the fill on the Stage and press F8 to convert it into a movie clip. Open the Property inspector and type *bar_mc* into the `<Instance Name>` field.

When you convert the fill into a movie clip, it overlaps the stroke that surrounds that movie clip. Therefore, you need to select the entire stroke (double-click the stroke to select all of the segments) and press F8 to convert it into a graphic symbol. Select the Graphic radio button, name the symbol `graphic_gr` and click OK. Then when the stroke is a symbol and still selected, choose Modify > Arrange > Bring to Front. This changes the location of the symbol so it is visible in front of the `bar_mc` again.

5) Create a dynamic text field on the Stage and enter the text *loading*. Set the text to black, 12 pt Arial font and select the Alias text button. Set the justification for the text field to right, and resize the text field so there is leading space. Then position the field near the rectangle and give it an instance name of `pctLoaded_txt`.

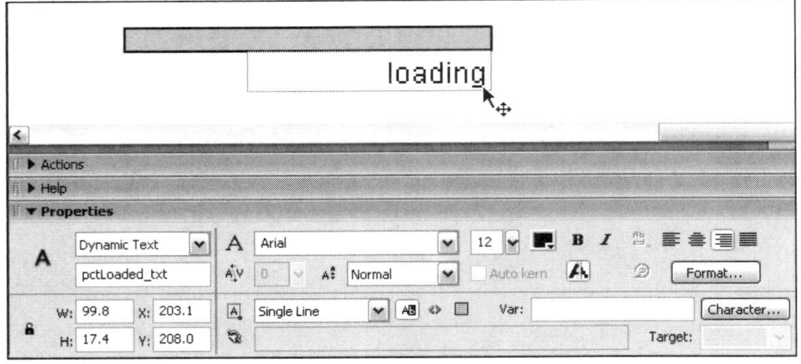

The text displays the percentage of the loaded SWF file and changes as the percentage of loaded content updates because it is set to be a dynamic text field. Change the justification of the field to `right` so you can align the text to the right of the progress bar if you want. Because the text on the left side changes and the "loading" text remains stationary, the text field looks better when the SWF file loads.

You need to add some leading space so the text that is dynamically entered into the text field has some room to change size because of the dimensions of text as the numbers change in the text field. As you can see in the previous figure, this just means making the text field quite large so it can hold all the text you are assigning to the text field. Double-click the text field so you see a white square in the lower-right corner. Click and drag the square to resize the text field.

Then make sure that you add an instance name of `pctLoaded_txt` using the Property inspector to assign a text value to it using ActionScript.

6) Select the rectangle and the text field and then convert them into a new movie clip by pressing F8. Give it an instance name of `loader_mc`.

Select both instances by pressing the Shift key while you click each one. Then press F8 and select the Movie clip radio button. Type in *loader_mc* as the symbol name for the new movie clip and click OK. Then select the instance on the Stage and open the Property inspector. Enter *loader_mc* into the Property inspector as the instance name of the movie clip.

7) Insert a new layer above the `progress` layer and rename it `actions`. Enter this ActionScript onto frame 1.

Select frame 1 of the `actions` layer, and open the Actions panel. Enter the following code into the Script pane. A description of this ActionScript follows the code listing.

```
var myLoader_mcl:MovieClipLoader = new MovieClipLoader();
var mclListener:Object = new Object();
mclListener.onLoadProgress = function(target_mc:MovieClip) {
   var prog:Object = myLoader_mcl.getProgress(target_mc);
   var pctLoaded:Number = Math.round((prog.bytesLoaded/prog.bytesTotal)*100);
   bar_mc._xscale=pctLoaded;
   pctLoaded_txt.text = pctLoaded+"% loaded";
};
myLoader_mcl.addListener(mclListener);
myLoader_mcl.loadClip("bookstore14.swf", 0);
```

This ActionScript should be a familiar to you after going through Lesson 11. There are a few new things going on in this ActionScript, though. The `MovieClipLoader` class is used to find out the progress and status of files being loaded into a movie clip. You create a new instance of the `MovieClipLoader` object and a new listener object to listen for events generated by the `MovieClipLoader`. You add a new listener for the `mclListener` object using the `addListener` method and then load the SWF file using the `loadClip` method. The `loadClip` method works as follows:

```
MovieClipLoader.loadClip("url", clip);
```

The *URL* path (either relative or absolute) is to the file you are loading in, and the *clip* is the movie clip instance (Loader instance, or level) you are loading the file into. This works the same way as the `MovieClip.loadMovie` method.

The onLoadProgress listener is invoked when new content is downloaded onto the visitor's computer, so it is used to show the progress of the download (and helps you use the bar_mc to display that progress). The MovieClipLoader class has a getProgress method that takes a parameter which is the target movie clip that you are loading the SWF file into. This returns an object that we are calling prog. prog has two properties called bytesLoaded and bytesTotal. Then you are rounding it and multiplying by 100 to get the percentage that the clip has loaded. You are saving the percentage loaded in a variable called pctLoaded.

You are scaling the bar_mc movie clip using the _xscale MovieClip property by the percentage that is loaded using the pctLoaded variable. _xscale refers to the scaling (resizing) of an instance along the X axis, which is horizontal. Then you are setting the value of the dynamic text field to display that percentage as well, and adding (or *appending*) on a bit of text as well (the % loaded text).

TIP *Because your SWF file is loading into level 0, that means it will "kick out" or discard any existing content there. That means as soon as the SWF file has completed loading, the loader SWF file (including the progress bar) disappears. If you are loading content into a movie clip, then you could use the following few lines of ActionScript in your FLA:*

```
mclListener.onLoadComplete = function(evt) {
  loader_mc._visible = false;
};
```

You would place these lines directly above myLoader_mcl.addListener(mclListener); *When the* onLoadComplete *listener is invoked, the file has completely downloaded. So when this happens, the* loader_mc*'s (the progress bar) visibility is set to false. This is so it doesn't sit there behind the loaded Tech Bookstore, which would look pretty bad, of course.*

8) Test the FLA file.

When you test the FLA document, you might not be able to see the file loading just because it is loading so fast off of your hard drive. You will probably notice quite a difference as soon as you put the files online and test the loader. In the next exercise, you will test all of the files to make sure they work correctly.

9) If everything works as expected, change the final line of ActionScript. Then save the changes you made to the file.

Because you won't be loading `bookstore14.fla` into the final version of the file, you need to change that final line, in which you are loading in the current version of the Tech Bookstore FLA. Change the final line of the code on the `actions` layer to the following.

```
myLoader_mcl.loadClip("TechBookstore.swf", 0);
```

This means you will instead load in `TechBookstore.swf`, which will be the final version of the Tech Bookstore FLA file. The `TechBookstore.swf` file overwrites any of the existing contents because it is loading into level 0. If you are using a Linux or Unix server the file will be case sensitive so make sure you type in the correct case.

TESTING AND DEBUGGING THE TECH BOOKSTORE

At this point, the Tech Bookstore should look somewhat complete. You can navigate between each page because of the menus and buttons that you added ActionScript to in Lesson 11. The content loads into each page because of the Loader components you added in the previous exercises, and you even have preloaders for the content that's loading (even if you don't see the progress because your hard drive is too fast!). Now it's time to test each of the areas and make sure your content loads in and the ProgressBar component instances work correctly.

At this point, you might have some modifications to make if things don't work exactly as you expect them to or if something is not loading in. The first thing you want to do is check that all of your files are in the correct place in the `TechBookstore` folder and any other folders that you created within. You might have added new folders yourself and need to modify where the URLs point, or you chose not to create folders at all and have everything in the `TechBookstore` folder (a bit messier, but easier when you're just starting out, which is why we chose to do it this way).

The Bandwidth Profiler allows you to determine the download performance of your SWF file by simulating what the SWF will look like when it's loaded in using different bandwidth settings (such as phone modems and so forth).

NOTE *When your file is cached, sometimes it appears to load in quicker than the bandwidth profile you have set. You might also run into problems with the SWF file not showing up if you choose to simulate a download (by pressing Ctrl+Enter or Command+Enter a second time), which occurs intermittently.*

The Profiler shows you the amount of data stored on each frame in the SWF file. This shows you how much information you should preload before displaying the content of the SWF. If a SWF is "streaming," it might stall out at a frame with more content than the others. This causes the playback to not be as smooth as you may want it to be. As we have mentioned earlier, remember that your content is always *progressively downloading* from the server instead of truly streaming. You will find out more about the Bandwidth Profiler later in this exercise.

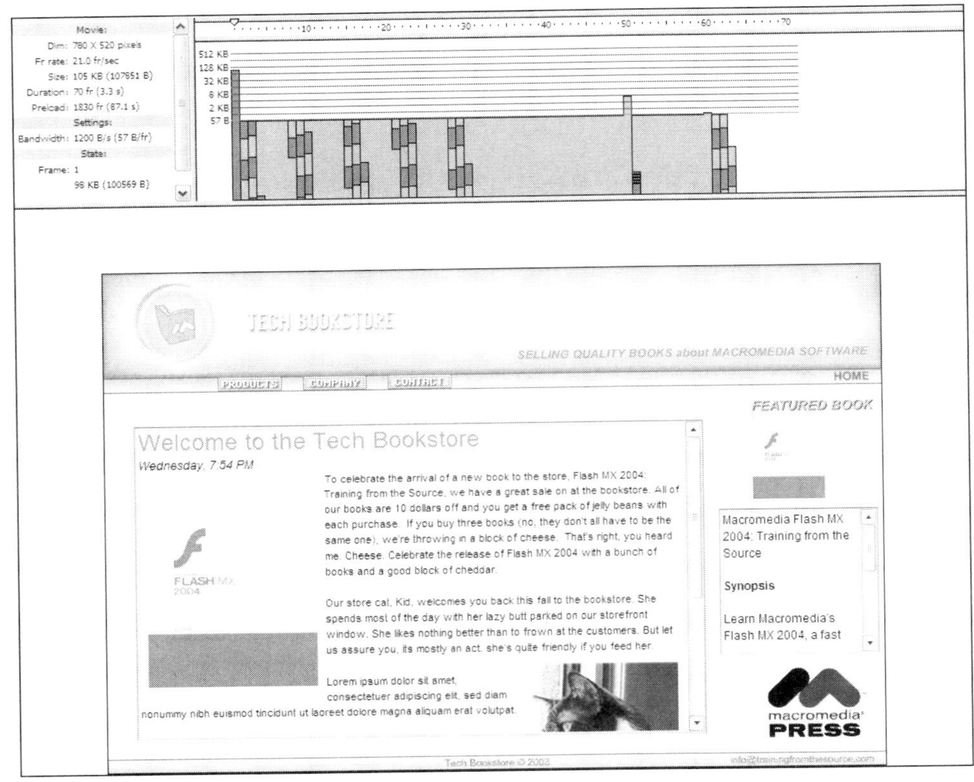

1) Open the `TechBookstore` **folder and double-click** `loader.html` **or** `loader.swf` **to test the Tech Bookstore application.**

When you double-click the HTML file, it opens in your default Web browser unless you specify otherwise. If you choose to open the SWF file, it opens in the Flash Player 7.

2) Check that the menu animates and works correctly.

If you aren't quite sure why your menu is not animating correctly or if something in the Tech Bookstore just doesn't jive, you might want to dig through the sample file from the CD-ROM and compare it to the FLA you're working on. It's very easy to miss a single piece of ActionScript or have one button out of place and not have the application work properly. That's just the way it is when you are building applications. In fact, studies say that 80% of the time you spend building something will be spent debugging! Welcome to the joy of creating things for the Web.

One common problem with the menu and its animation is the invisible button. Because you have the invisible button underneath your buttons, you might run into a problem if the menu doesn't line up exactly with each button above it. If there is even a small amount of the invisible button peeking through between the three buttons and the menu that drops down, the menus will close before you can mouse over or click them. To avoid this happening, you might need to trim some of the invisible button from the area between the three buttons and three drop-down menus. Open the invisible button (you might have to unlock and make this layer visible first). Select the Hit frame and then use the Selection tool or Lasso to select some of the invisible button's hit area in the region between the buttons and the menu and trim it off. This is depicted in the following figure.

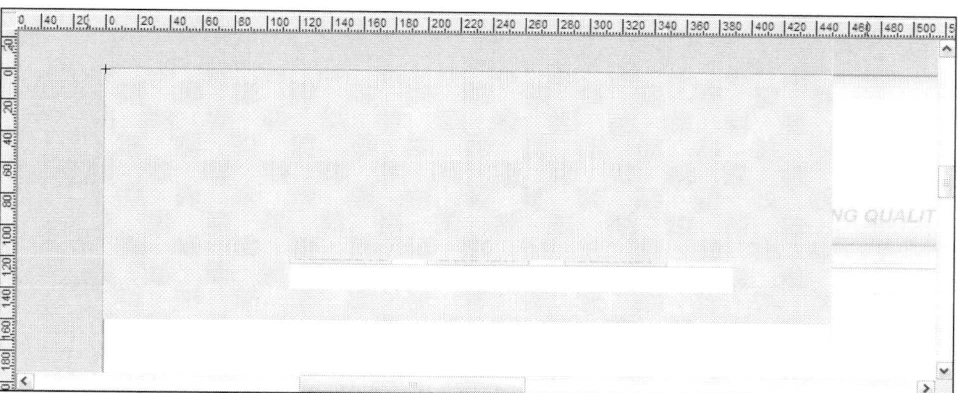

3) Make sure that the ProgressBar component instances are working correctly.

Click through each section on the Web site. Does each section load properly? Do the progress bars disappear when the Loader component has finished loading and displays the content? If the content doesn't load, make sure that the path to the SWF is correct in the Loader component's `contentPath` property.

If the content loads into the Loader and the ProgressBar doesn't proceed higher than 0%, confirm that the Loader component has an instance name and that it matches the value in the source parameter for the ProgressBar. Also check that you gave an instance name to the ProgressBar component instance and that it matches the instance name that you're adding the event listener to. Another potential problem could arise if you forget to change the `mode` parameter for the ProgressBar from `event` to `polled`. When the `mode` is set to `event`, the ProgressBar remains on the Stage, even though the Loader component displays the content.

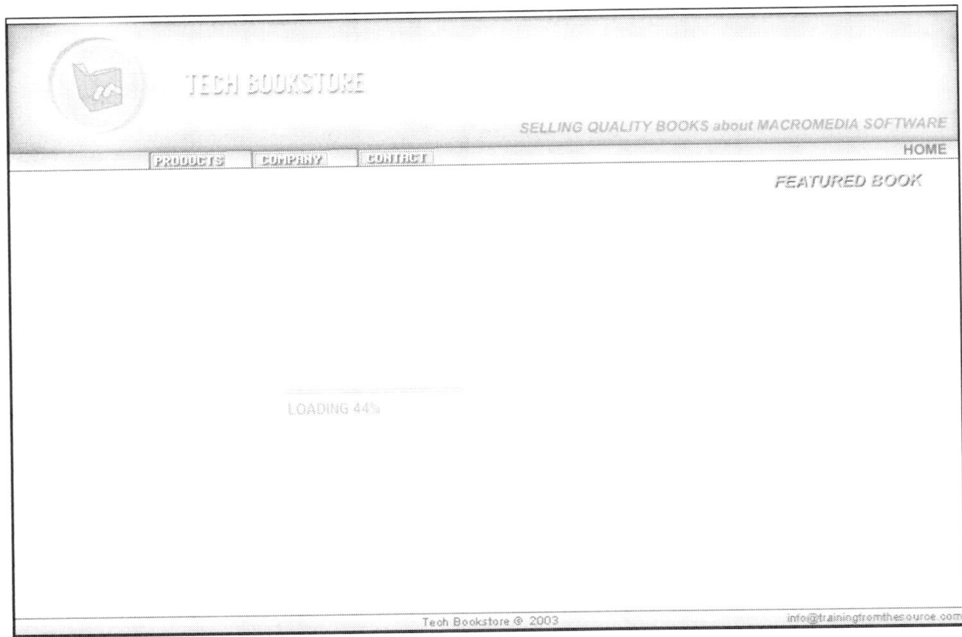

4) Click the Company button and then click the Tour button. Make sure that the masking is correct for the Tour that loads into the bookstore.

You created the Tour in Lesson 8, but you have not yet tested it in the Tech Bookstore. If you built the tour using Flash MX Professional, make sure that the Tour loads correctly into the SWF and that the mask you drew over the main presentation screen covers the entire tour. You will need to test the bookstore in a browser window to do so. The mask should properly mask the transitions between each screen after it's loaded into the bookstore. If the mask doesn't mask properly, you might want to return to the `tour.fla` and modify the mask accordingly. This probably involves resizing the mask or repositioning it on the Stage. You also might check the Timeline and make sure that the layer is appropriately set to Mask.

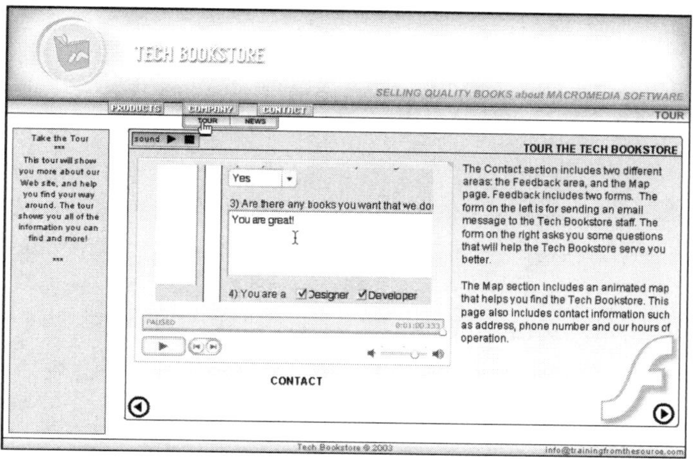

5) Test the Feedback and Questionnaire forms.

The feedback form and questionnaire are both in the Feedback area of the Tech Bookstore. Try sending your feedback using the forms when they have loaded in. You should receive an email to whatever address you specified as the constant value when you built the feedback form. The questionnaire will send data to an XML form instead.

6) Test that the SWF files for Featured Book, News, Reviews, Tour, Map, Home, and the Catalog all load into the bookstore properly. Also make sure that the text and images load in as well.

Each of these pages loads into the Tech Bookstore in almost the same way because a Loader component is being used in the Tech Bookstore to import all of them. Make sure that each of these page's content loads in completely and behaves as expected. Sometimes, when you load external files into Flash problems can arise if you've been using scopes such as `_root` in your SWFs. Luckily, you have avoided this entirely in the Tech Bookstore.

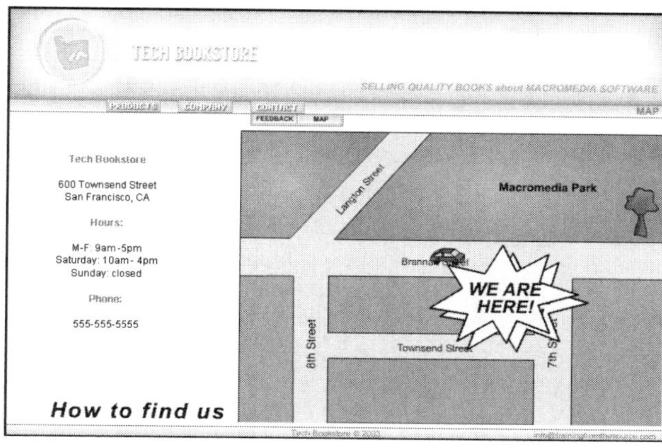

Regardless, the `techbookstore_fmx.fla` or `techbookstore_pro.fla`, depending on which version of Flash MX 2004 you are using, on the CD-ROM (in the `Lesson12` folder) file is complete with ActionScript, Library elements and all the graphics in place. And at least when it was placed on the CD-ROM everything worked correctly. There's always the chance that an update in the Flash Player (such as a security update) and so forth might cause some small element to change the way it works in the Tech Bookstore. Typos might do the same! Any updates and examples on how to modify the FLA file will be available on this book's Web site at `www.TrainingFromTheSource.com/errata`. So feel free to take a dig through that FLA that's on the CD-ROM, and if you still have problems or questions, don't hesitate to look for some assistance at `www.TrainingFromTheSource.com` and the forums linked from that address.

7) Open `bookstore14.fla` and check the SWF file in the Bandwidth Profiler.

The Bandwidth Profiler can be accessed while testing the SWF file in the testing environment. Select Control > Test Movie or press Ctrl+Enter, and when you're in the testing environment you can select View > Bandwidth Profiler from the main menu or press Ctrl+B.

The Bandwidth Profiler displays lots of useful information, such as the dimensions of the Stage, the current Frame rate, the size of the SWF file in kilobytes (as well as bytes), the number of frames in the SWF file, and how many seconds it takes to play the SWF file back to a visitor.

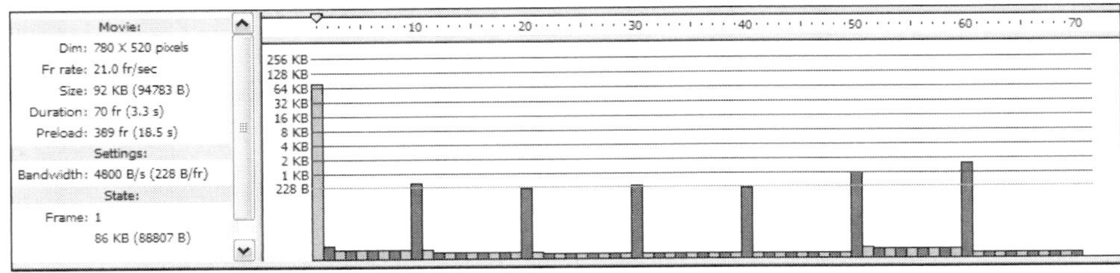

The Bandwidth Profiler also includes a graph showing how much data is being sent by each frame. This helps you optimize the SWF. If one frame has too much information and ends up slowing down the playback, you might want to move some of that data onto another frame containing much less. Another feature closely tied to the Bandwidth Profiler is the ability to simulate download times within the Flash testing environment. By using View > Simulate Download, you can simulate the playback of your Flash SWF file when a visitor is using a slower modem. This helps you see how the SWF plays back at on computers with slower Internet connections (such as dial-up access) and determines how long it takes before users are able to see content.

You can modify the speeds you want to simulate playback at by selecting a setting from the View > Download Settings menu. Speeds range greatly, from 14.4 dial-up access at 1.2 KB per second to a significantly faster T1 connection at 131.2 KB per second. If there are specific speeds you want to test at that aren't present in the list, you have the option of adding up to three custom download settings that you can set the number of bytes per second to test at. Testing your SWF at several different speeds is always a good idea because it gives you a general concept of how long it takes before the visitor sees content. This can greatly affect the general Web site "experience," and as Macromedia says, "Experience Matters." If users have to wait for a long period of time for your SWF to load, often they will give up and leave the site before even seeing any of your Flash content at all.

8) Save a new version of the `bookstore14.fla` as `TechBookstore.fla`.

That's right, a new filename to complete all of those bookstore files. Indeed, you are finished building the Tech Bookstore FLA files and all of its many associated and assorted SWFs. The only thing that's left to do is go through publishing the files and then putting them online. The hard part is over, and really you should be proud of all the assorted things that you've covered so far.

WHAT YOU HAVE LEARNED

In this lesson, you have:

- Learned about Web site optimization (pages 380–382)
- Found out how to organize Flash projects and why you should do so (pages 382–383)
- Loaded SWF files for each of the remaining pages in the Tech Bookstore (pages 383–390)
- Added instances of the ProgressBar to view content loading into the site (pages 390–393)
- Used the `MovieClipLoader` class to load in a SWF file (pages 394–399)
- Tested and debugged the Tech Bookstore (pages 399–405)

publishing flash documents

LESSON 13

The way that most Flash documents are presented to the world is by embedding them in an HTML page on the Web. Therefore, getting your document online and in an attractive page is very important in order to successfully complete the Tech Bookstore. You do not need to necessarily upload the site to the Web to complete this lesson. You can create the HTML page embedding your Flash site and even try the player detection, all on your hard drive without going online.

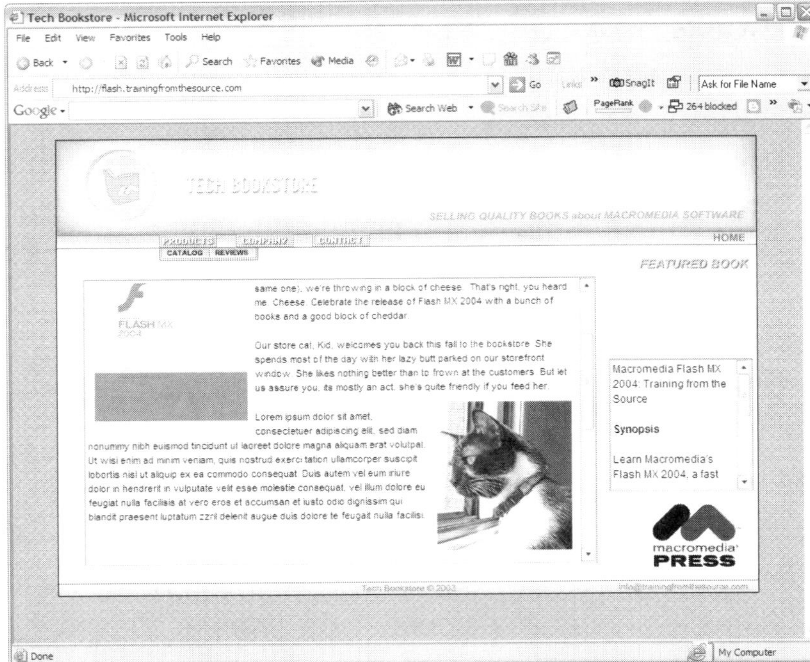

The Tech Bookstore is embedded in an HTML page.

In this lesson, you will create the HTML page containing the Tech Bookstore by adding some simple HTML tags and a background image for the site to an existing document that Flash creates for you. You will also create a publish profile in Flash and learn more about the available publish settings, create a Flash Player detection system, and put together a customized page embedding the bookstore.

WHAT YOU WILL LEARN

In this lesson, you will:

- Create a new publish profile
- Learn how to change your publish settings
- Detect a visitor's Flash Player and redirect them as necessary
- Learn how to embed a SWF file
- Create an HTML page for the Tech Bookstore
- Upload your files to a server, and view the bookstore online

APPROXIMATE TIME

This lesson takes approximately 1 hour to complete.

LESSON FILES

Media Files:

tile.gif

Starting Files:

Lesson13/TechBookstore_fmx.fla
Lesson13/TechBookstore_pro.fla
Lesson13/loader.fla

Completed Project:

Lesson13/complete/TechBookstore.fla
Lesson13/complete/index.html
Lesson13/complete/bookstore_content.html
Lesson13/complete/bookstore_alternate.html
Lesson13/complete/bookstore/ (All Files)

PUBLISHING SWF FILES

To put a Flash document on the Web you have to start by publishing a SWF file. You have already published SWF files so they can load into the `TechBookstore.swf`. However, you have to embed the `TechBookstore.swf` (and `loader.swf`) into HTML pages for the Web. When you publish a Flash document, the Publish Settings dialog box allows you to control many settings that determine the size, compatibility, and kinds of files that you export from the authoring environment.

In this lesson, you will publish the Tech Bookstore and `loader.swf` with particular settings and loader SWF file and then embed the documents into a Web page.

1) Open the `TechBookstore.fla` file that you created in Lesson 12. Open the Publish Settings dialog box by choosing File > Publish settings.

Additionally you can open `TechBookstore_fmx.fla` or `TechBookstore_pro.fla` (if you are using Professional) from the `Lesson13` folder on the CD-ROM. There are tabs in the Publish Settings dialog box that allow you to control the files that are generated by Flash.

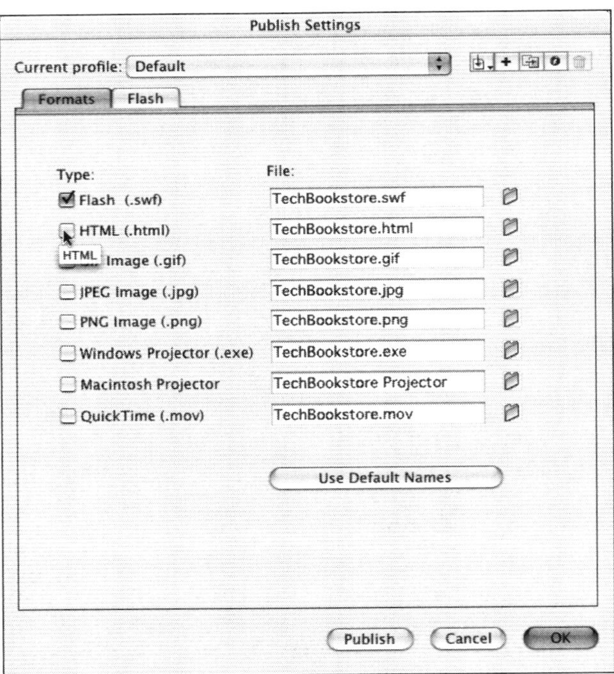

You used the Formats tab throughout several lessons to deselect the HTML option so the document is not published along with the SWF file (because you don't need it). This tab allows you to add additional file formats to publish as well, including an EXE, which is usually known as a Flash projector file. These files are useful for creating CD-ROMs and kiosk presentations. The Flash Player is embedded right into the executable file, so there is no need to worry about whether your end user has the latest Flash Player. Other file formats include image file formats and even the MOV video format.

2) Click the Create New Profile button at the top of the Publish Settings dialog box. Type in a name for the publish profile and click the OK button.

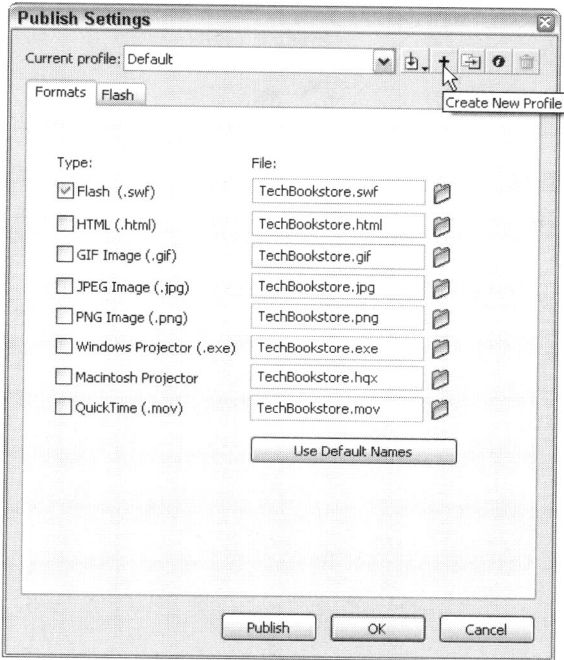

A Publish profile saves a profile on your hard drive that's based on whatever publish settings you make in the Publish Settings dialog box. This is handy if you always use the same settings for many documents (like all the SWF files you are loading into the Tech Bookstore file). You don't necessarily need a publish profile for this document, but at least you know how to make one now. You will use this profile in the next exercise, but you will modify it to fit the necessary publish settings for `loader.fla`.

After you click the Create New Profile button, the Create New Profile dialog box opens. Type in *TechBookstore* or something similar into the text field as the new name for the publish profile and click OK when you are finished.

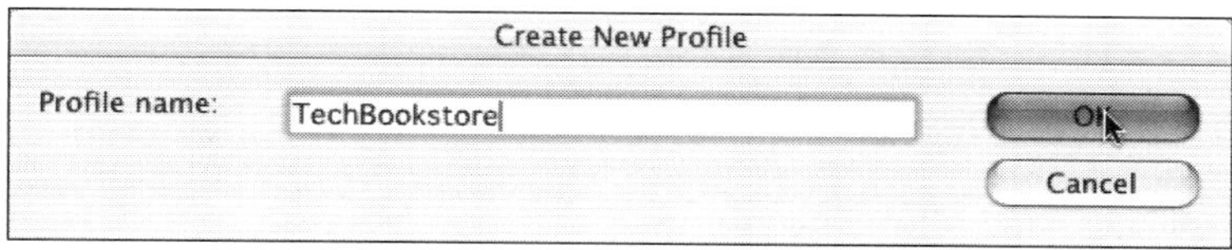

The new name is added to the Current profile drop-down menu when you return to the Publish Settings dialog box. Now you can modify the settings of the publish profile as required. These settings are saved into the profile.

3) Make sure that the HTML format is still deselected, and that the SWF format is selected.

You are loading the `TechBookstore.swf` file into the `loader.swf` file so there is a progress bar for the site; therefore, you don't need an HTML page for the bookstore and you can deselect this check box. You will need the HTML page for the loader SWF file, which you will amend in the following exercise.

4) Click the Flash Tab and make sure the document is set to Flash Player 7, Bottom up Load order, and ActionScript 2.0 as the ActionScript version. Then make sure the Compress movie check box is selected. Also select the Protect from import and Omit trace actions check boxes.

All these settings are shown in the previous figure. The Flash tab enables you to modify what version of Flash Player you are publishing the file to. You can change the version of ActionScript you are using (this includes the default components, which use ActionScript 2.0). Leave the document at the default ActionScript 2.0 setting for the document.

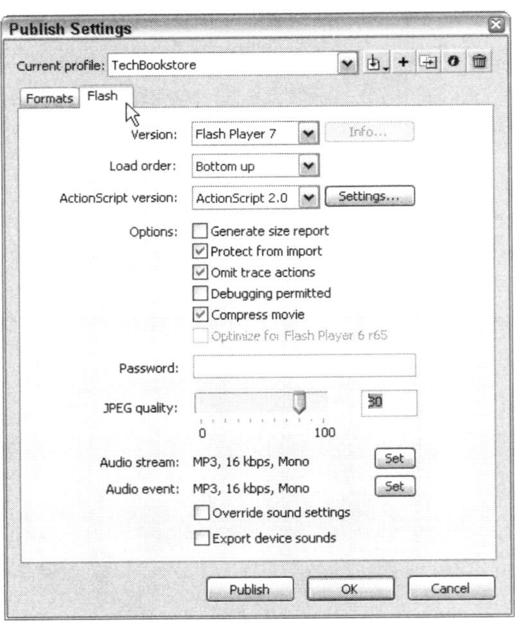

The player version must be determined based on the parts you have in the Flash document. If you have ActionScript that does not work with the version of the player you have selected the errors are shown in the Output panel. When you use certain components that require the Flash Player 7, you need to set the player version to Flash Player 7 (and ActionScript 2.0). Other components can be set to Flash Player 6 and use ActionScript 2.0.

TIP *If you are unsure what Flash Player or ActionScript version you need, you can try testing the SWF file by pressing Ctrl+Enter and viewing the results in the player. If you don't see the element in your SWF file, you know you have to modify the settings.*

Load order specifies the order that the layers in your FLA files load into the Flash Player at runtime. If you choose Bottom up (default setting), the layers load from the lowest to highest. This is evident when someone with a slow Internet connection views your site because the items on the Stage appear in the layer order that you specify. It also can affect your ActionScript as well because the actions on lower layers (if you have them there) will be loaded before those on higher layers if you use this particular setting. The Load order affects only the first frame of your SWF file.

There are many additional options available to you in this tab. *Generate size report* means the Output panel shows the amount of data in the final SWF file, broken down into content: frames, symbols, text characters, actions, and bitmaps. If you *Omit trace actions*, you won't see anything traced to the Output panel when you publish the SWF file. This is a good setting to go and check if you think something should be tracing, but it isn't. It's also a good idea to select this option before publishing the SWF file for the Web because it helps performance a little bit.

When you protect an FLA file from import (the *Protect from import* option), the setting prevents other people from importing your SWF file into their own FLA documents. Remember that SWF files import as a series of frames, bitmaps, and graphic symbols. Importing a SWF file does not preserve any ActionScript, layers or components. If you lose an FLA file, importing the SWF doesn't "get your FLA back." It does help you get the images, but you'll have to reconstruct other aspects of the FLA over again.

TIP *You should be aware that even if you do protect your SWF from import, there are tools available online that can undo this option. There are also tools online available to open your SWF files and see the ActionScript that you use. Never, ever place sensitive information (such as passwords or similar) in a SWF file.*

If you select *Debugging permitted*, you can remotely debug the SWF file. You can access the file when it is online and enter a password when prompted, which also helps protect the SWF file. If someone downloads the SWF file then they must use the password when they import it into Flash.

And finally, the *Compress movie* option allows you to compress the SWF file so it's a smaller size. This works only for the Flash Player 6 r65 and greater (*r65* refers to a minor release of the Flash Player 6), so your visitors must have at least this version of player installed on their system to view the SWF. This is fine because you are creating a SWF file for the Flash Player 7.

5) Set the JPEG quality setting to *85* and select the Override sound settings check box. Leave the default Audio stream and Audio event settings at their default settings.

The JPEG quality compresses the images to different amounts. A higher value on the slider means a better quality image because the JPEG is not compressed as much. If you set the quality too low, the SWF file size is smaller, but the images might end up distorted.

Select the Override sound settings check box. This means whatever properties for each sound that you individually set using the Library and Properties dialog box in the authoring environment are overridden by these settings for the entire SWF file. This helps decrease the overall file size of the SWF when it's published. You can change the compression, sample rate, and whether the sound is an event or streamed sound if you click the Set buttons. The default settings (MP3 with a bit rate of 16kbps and Mono) is adequate for the Tech Bookstore.

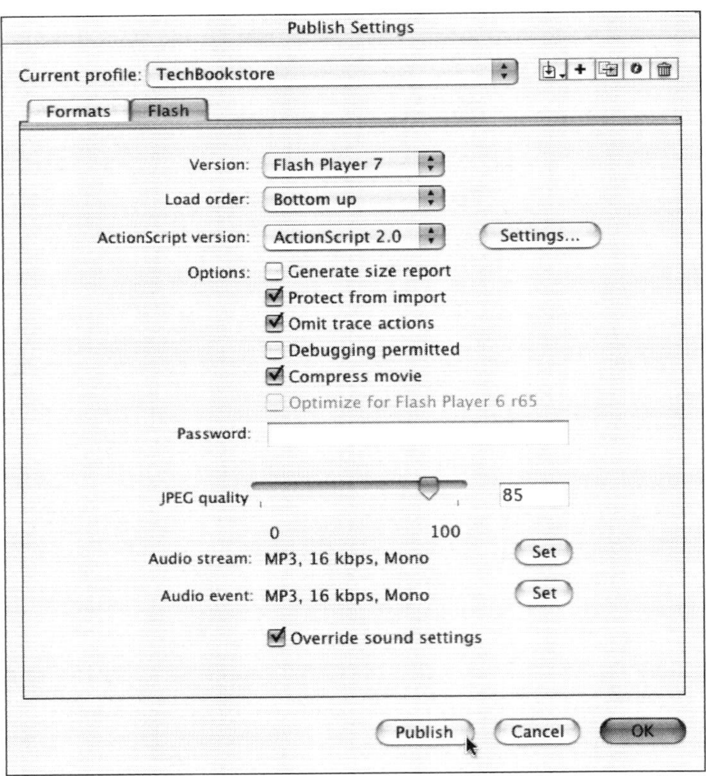

TIP *To publish a file in one step, all you need to do is choose File > Publish from the main menu. This automatically publishes the FLA file using whatever the current Publish Settings are. The files are created in whatever directory the current FLA file is in.*

6) Click the Publish button to publish the file. Then click the Import/Export Profile button and choose Export from the menu that appears to export the Publish profile you just created.

After you click Publish, `TechBookstore.swf` is generated into the `TechBookstore` folder. Now you need to export the Publish profile in order to use it in other FLA files. The profile is saved as an XML document on your hard drive. The XML file contains your settings, which can then be imported into the Publish Settings dialog box when you create another FLA where you need the profile.

Choose Export from the drop-down menu that opens when you click the Import/Export Profile button. The Export Profile dialog box opens where you can type in a file name to save the profile as (or leave it as `TechBookstore`.) Click Save to export the Publish profile. Now you are able to import the profile into other FLA files that you create.

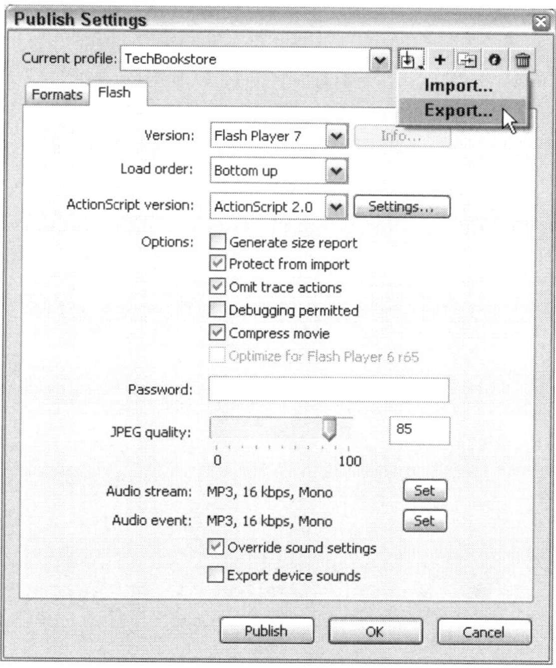

7) Click OK to close the Publish Settings dialog box. Save the changes you have made to the Tech Bookstore by selecting File > Save.

After you have published the bookstore SWF file and exported the Publish profile, you are finished with the bookstore.

DETECTING THE FLASH PLAYER

When a visitor arrives at your site, you don't necessarily know whether they have a Flash Player installed on their system, or whether it is the correct version that can be used to visit the site. The Tech Bookstore requires that visitors have the correct version of the Flash Player in order to see the content of the SWF files that are loading into the Tech Bookstore (such as the tour), and the bookstore itself. Detecting the Flash Player is a complex process to do well. However, you can let the Flash publishing process do the hard work for you by creating a player detection system instantly when you publish the file. Here's how.

1) Open `loader.fla` and open the Publish Settings dialog box by choosing File > Publish Settings. Import the Publish Profile you just created in the previous exercise.

Import the Publish profile that you created in the previous exercise called TechBookstore. Click the Import/Export Profile button and choose Import from the drop-down menu. The Import Profile dialog box opens where you can choose a profile to import. Click `TechBookstore.xml` and then click the Open button.

Now the `TechBookstore` profile is available in the Current profile menu. Select the `TechBookstore` profile. The profile maintains the same settings that you used for the previous SWF file that you modify in a few areas in the following steps.

2) Make sure that the Flash and HTML check boxes are both selected on the Formats tab.

Selecting this option means that the HTML page is created when you select the check box. You need to publish both HTML pages and a SWF document. One of the HTML pages will be modified later in this lesson. You do not need to modify any settings on the Flash tab. You can leave the default settings from the publish profile you made earlier.

3) Select the HTML tab. Select the Detect Flash Version check box, and deselect the Loop and Display menu options in the Playback section. Click the Settings button next to the Detect Flash Version check box and enter new filenames for the HTML pages you will publish. Click the OK button when you're finished.

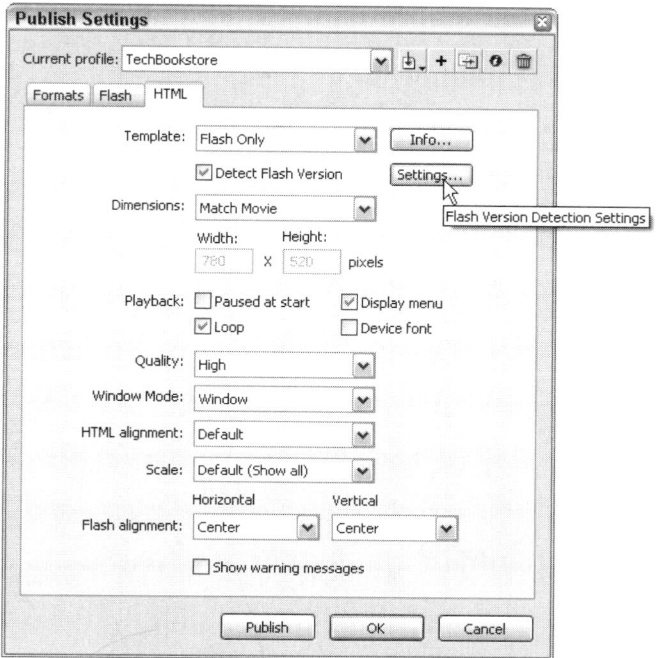

You need to make some changes on the HTML tab. Select the Detect Flash Version check box to create a Flash Player detection system. Three HTML files, a GIF file, and a couple SWF files are generated when you publish the FLA. You will learn more about this setting in the following exercise.

Click the Settings button to open the Version Detection Settings dialog box. This dialog box allows you to specify the specific version of Flash Player that you want to detect and change the filename of HTML files you want to create for each file. This is useful if you do not want to have the HTML pages with the same name as the SWF file, such as an index page for the root file.

Enter *index.html* into the Detection File field. This file is the first page your visitors encounter when entering the Tech Bookstore site, and it is used to detect the version of Flash Player that is installed on their system.

Change Content File to *bookstore_content.html*, which is the main page that will hold the entire Tech Bookstore site. This is where visitors are directed if they have the required version of the Flash Player. Change the Alternate File field to *bookstore_alternate.html*. This page is what visitors are directed to if they do not have the minimum requirements for a Flash Player.

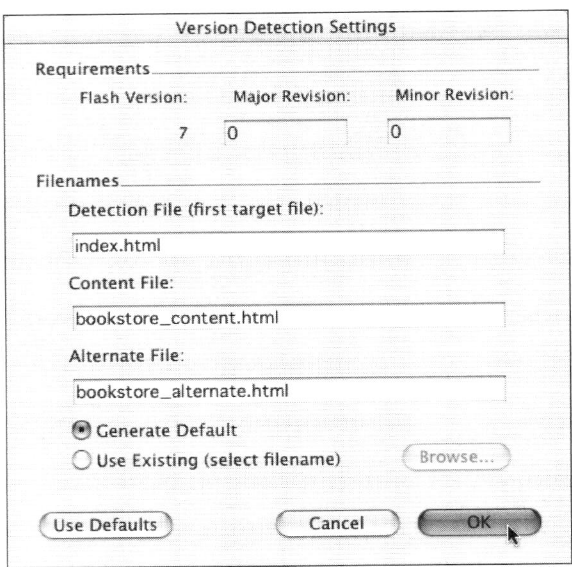

You are renaming the filenames that appear online when the user goes to each page. It doesn't matter what the names of each file are, as long as they are unique. You can use an existing page for the `bookstore_alternate.html` if you have one that is created. This is the page asking users to go download the latest version of Flash Player if they do not have the minimum required Player to view the site. It is nice to sometimes have a customized page matching the look and feel of your Web site, however it is not necessary, and you can just use the default page Macromedia provides. If you choose to use your own page and already have it created, select the Use Existing radio button. Then you are prompted to find a file on your hard drive when you click the Browse button.

When you are finished making edits, click the OK button to return to the Publish Settings dialog box. Make sure that you have deselected the Loop option under the HTML tab, and click the Publish button when you are finished.

TIP *You can use Flash Player detection only if you publish to the Flash Player 4 or greater.*

The other settings that were available under the HTML tab do not need to be modified, but here is a brief breakdown of what the settings under the HTML tab are used for:

Template: This setting specifies a kind of template to use for publishing the HTML portion of the movie. Click the Info button next to this setting to find out more about each kind that is available.

Dimensions: You can set the dimensions for the Flash SWF file that will be embedded in the document. The default "match movie" size is the current dimensions of the Stage, although you can set a different size measured either in pixels or a percentage.

Playback: The playback options control how the SWF file plays at runtime. Loop means the SWF returns to frame 1 and plays again after it reaches the final frame on the Timeline. You can pause the SWF when it begins using the *Paused at start* option, and control the playback manually or use the contextual menu. You can choose whether to display a contextual menu by selecting or deselecting the Display menu option. You can also choose whether to use *device fonts* in the SWF file (as were defined in Lesson 3 on using text.) Select the Device font option to use device fonts with static text. Note that the static text must be specifically set to use device fonts.

Quality: You can set the SWF quality from "Low" to "Best" in this menu. Low doesn't use anti-aliasing and affords the fastest playback, however Auto-Low will attempt to use better quality when possible but also attempts to play back the SWF file quickly. High is the default, which we use, and will always use anti-aliasing but if there is animation, bitmaps are not smoothed (smoothing looks better but slows down the SWF playback).

Window Mode: You can control the `wmode` attribute in the HTML file using this option. The *Transparent Windowless* option sets the background of Flash documents to transparent and removes the browser window around it (including the title bar). For example, you would use this mode if you were making one of those ads appearing to float over an HTML page. *Opaque Windowless* leaves the background in the Flash document, but still removes the browser around it. You should always remember to offer some kind of button to close the SWF somewhere in the SWF. *Window* is the normal default mode where the Flash document appears in a normal browser window.

NOTE *Not all browsers support windowless mode. As for major browsers, recent Netscape browsers now support the windowless mode (NS 7+), as do IE 5 (Win) and IE 5.1(Mac) and above.*

HTML alignment: Helps position the SWF file in the HTML page to the various sides of the browser window.

Scale: This option scales the SWF file if you changed the dimensions of the file in the dimensions setting. Default maintains the aspect ratio of the original SWF file, whereas Exact Fit displays the document without keeping the aspect ratio, but will fill the dimensions you set. No Border scales the SWF file while keeping the aspect ratio, but it crops the Stage if necessary. No Scale stops the SWF from scaling when the user resizes the browser window.

Flash alignment: This option aligns the SWF file in the browser window and determines cropping if it is necessary. This affects your SWF in particular when you choose different dimensions and the Stage is cropped.

4) Save the changes you made to the FLA file. You can close the FLA, and Flash for that matter, when you are finished.

You are finished publishing the file. All you have left to do now is edit the HTML files that were generated and put all of the files online (or in a single place, so you can locally test the Web site).

EMBEDDING A SWF IN AN HTML PAGE

When you place SWF files online, you typically embed them in an HTML page. You do not have to learn HTML in order to do so because Flash generates the code for you. However, in this exercise, you will slightly customize the HTML document that Flash creates so you can add a background tile and center the SWF file on the page.

You will create an HTML page in this exercise, embedding the Tech Bookstore SWF file within it. SWF files are embedded into an HTML page using the `<object>` and `<embed>` tags. When you created the Flash Player detection files, you specified for the HTML pages to be created with the names `index.html`, `bookstore_content.html`, and `bookstore_alternate.html`. The `bookstore_alternate.html` page contains information that directs users who don't have the required Flash Player to the Macromedia Web site, where they can download and install the most recent player. And the `bookstore_content.html` page contains the actual bookstore on it that users who have the Flash Player are directed to. Therefore, this page is the one that you actually want to edit.

1) Open `bookstore_content.html` in an HTML editor or text editor of your choice.

It doesn't matter if you are using a fully featured editor such as Dreamweaver or a simple text editor such as Notepad for this exercise. The changes you will make are very minimal to the file that already exists, so you don't need anything fancy to make your modifications.

2) Rename the name within the `<title>` **tag in order to name the site.**

This name appears within the title bar of the Web browser. You can rename this title to whatever you want the site to be called in the title bar. We have chosen Tech Bookstore, so this line is written as:

```
<title>Tech Bookstore</title>
```

3) Delete `bgcolor="#ffffff"` **from the** `body` **tag. Change this attribute to** `background="tile.gif"`.

Underneath the title and head tags is the `body` tag. The `bgcolor` attribute sets the background color of the Web site. However, instead of a background color, you might want to set a background image. On the CD-ROM is a file called `tile.gif`, and you can find it in the `media` folder. Copy this file into the `TechBookstore` folder and then change the `<body>` tag to the following.

```
<body background="tile.gif">
```

Adding a background image means that the image will tile over the entire background of the Web site, which will appear "behind" the SWF file. This particular GIF file is small and unobtrusive, creating a subtle pattern in the background.

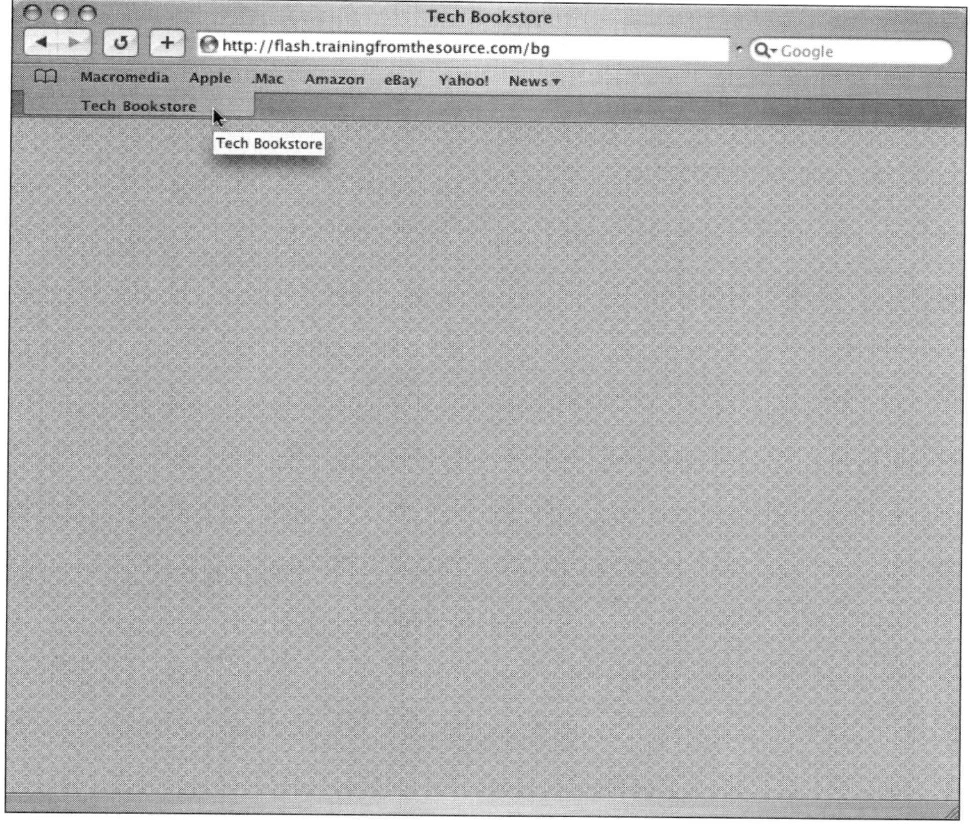

4) Add a table to contain the Tech Bookstore and center it horizontally on the page.

Under the `<body>` tag, you sometimes see a lot of commented-out text. When the HTML document contains text like this, it is quite similar to the commented-out code you might have in a Flash file in that it can provide directions to coders and explain what the code does. The text that is commented-out in these generated HTML files contains the text that is found inside the SWF file, which helps index the content better for search engines.

TIP *You might hear that search engines can't search SWF files; however, this situation has changed. Some engines can search the URLs inside of SWF files, and others can search all the text inside a SWF.*

Add the following lines below the `<body background="tile.gif">` tag:

```
<table width="100%">
    <tr>
        <td align="center">
```

After these lines come the `<object>` and `<embed>` code that embeds the SWF file so all browsers can see it. However, now that you have created an HTML table, you need to close it. Add these lines directly following the `</object>` tag:

```
        </td>
    </tr>
</table>
```

When you are completely finished, the entire HTML file for the `bookstore_content.html` page should look similar to the following:

```
Edit | Browse
<!DOCTYPE html PUBLIC "-//W3C//DTD XHTML 1.0 Transitional//EN"
"http://www.w3.org/TR/xhtml1/DTD/xhtml1-transitional.dtd">
<html xmlns="http://www.w3.org/1999/xhtml" xml:lang="en" lang="en">
<head>
    <meta http-equiv="Content-Type" content="text/html; charset=iso-8859-1" />
    <title>Tech Bookstore</title>
</head>
<body background="tile.gif">
<!--url's used in the movie-->
<!--text used in the movie-->
<!--
loading
-->
    <table width="100%">
        <tr>
            <td align="center">
            <object classid="clsid:d27cdb6e-ae6d-11cf-96b8-444553540000"
codebase="http://download.macromedia.com/pub/shockwave/cabs/flash/swflash.cab#version=7,0,0,0" width="780"
height="520" id="loader" align="middle">
                <param name="allowScriptAccess" value="sameDomain" />
                <param name="movie" value="loader.swf" />
                <param name="quality" value="high" />
                <param name="bgcolor" value="#ffffff" />
                <embed src="loader.swf" quality="high" bgcolor="#ffffff" width="780" height="520"
name="loader"   align="middle" allowScriptAccess="sameDomain" type="application/x-shockwave-flash"
pluginspage="http://www.macromedia.com/go/getflashplayer" />
            </object>
            </td>
        </tr>
    </table>
</body>
</html>
```

TIP *After you have finished editing the HTML file, make sure that you go back to the Publish Settings dialog box for the* `loader.fla` *file, and deselect the HTML option under the Formats tab. This way you won't overwrite the changes to any of the HTML documents if you republish the FLA file.*

5) Save the changes that you have made to the HTML file and then open the HTML page to view it in the default browser.

Save the HTML file and then you can close the file. Three HTML documents, two SWF files and a GIF file are published into the `TechBookstore` folder. Find the file in the `TechBookstore` folder and double-click the `index.html` file that was published to open the bookstore using the default Web browser. If your computer defaults to a text editor instead, choose to open it in a browser instead. Click through the file and explore the different areas.

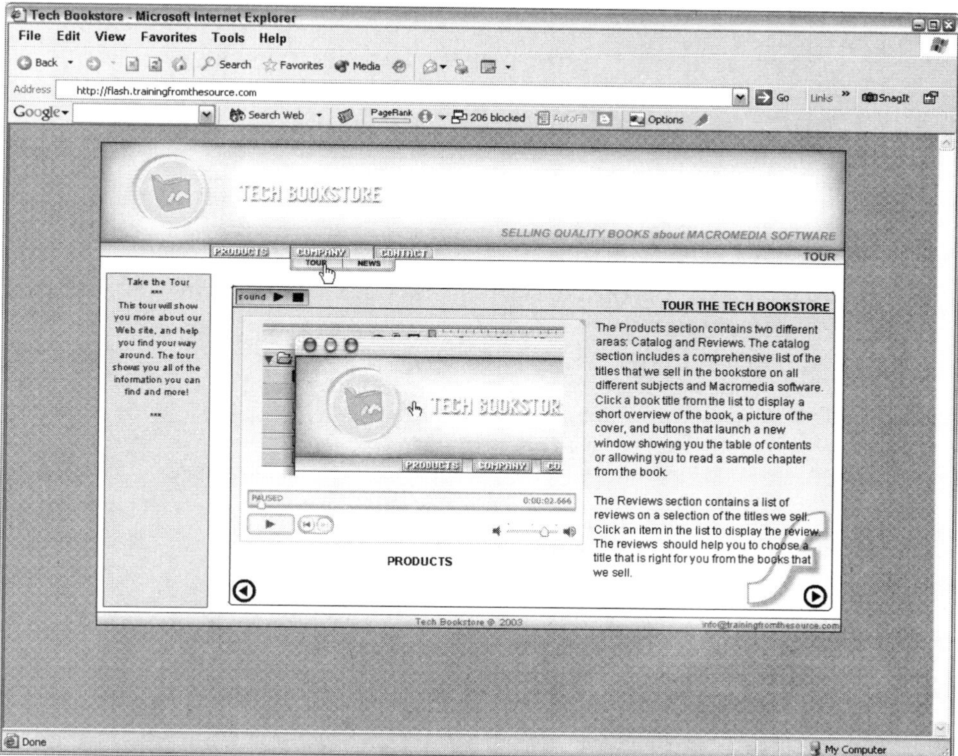

In the following exercise, you will upload all the files to a server or you will organize the ones you need neatly into a single folder.

UPLOADING THE TECH BOOKSTORE TO THE WEB

If you have access to upload files to the Web, the next step is to upload the Tech Bookstore so it can be viewed online. Because you do not need all the files you have created during the book for the Web site, you need to organize all the files specifically for the bookstore into a single folder and then upload them to the server. If you do not have Web space, you should stop at the step that uploads the files and test the site locally off your hard drive. But if you want to put your site online, follow these simple steps right to the end.

1) Open the `TechBookstore` **folder on your hard drive. Then create a new folder on your hard drive where you will move (or copy) the files for the Tech Bookstore site.**

Because you have been saving most of the files inside the `TechBookstore` folder, there are a lot of files stored in the folder, including ones that shouldn't be uploaded. You do not need to upload all the files because you do not need the FLA files or the imported images online for the Web site. You need to upload only some of them: the HTML files, SWF files, and files that you are dynamically loading or linking to the site.

The new folder you create can be called whatever you want, such as `bookstore`.

2) Move the following files into the folder you just created.

You need to move all the files that you need for the site into a single location. These include the SWF files and media files loading into the SWF files, as well as the HTML documents you published in this lesson. For your convenience, the files you need are in the following list:

```
index.html
flash_detection.swf
loader.swf
bookstore_content.html
bookstore_alternate.html
alternate.gif
tile.gif
TechBookstore.swf
home.swf
catalog.swf
reviews.swf
tour.swf
news.swf
map.swf
video1.flv
video2.flv
video3.flv
mmpresslogo.jpg
home01.jpg
home02.jpg
styles.css
home.txt
news.txt
sound.mp3
```

You also need to move the `catalog` folder and the `reviews` folder into this folder alongside these other files.

TIP *If you do not have a Web server to upload your files to, open this new folder you created and double-click the* `index.html` *file. This should open the completed Tech Bookstore site in a Web page. And you're done! Congratulations!*

3) After you moved all the files required for the Tech Bookstore into a single location, connect to the Web server where you want to host the material, and upload the documents to the Web.

You are probably using FTP to connect to a Web server, or you might be using another file transfer method (perhaps even hosting off of your own computer). At any rate, you need to transfer the files to a server so you can put them online. Transfer all the files that are inside the folder you created in the previous step. You don't need to transfer the folder as well, although it's likely you want to create a folder on the server to hold all of these files.

TIP *Make sure that you do not overwrite any existing files on the server. Creating a folder to hold all the files is an easy way to make sure you don't overwrite existing files, such as an index file you might already have on your site.*

TIP *If you are using Flash MX Professional, you actually have access to an FTP inside of Flash itself. This is via the Projects feature built into Flash. Although this book doesn't cover that feature, there is more information on the book's supporting Web site. Go to* `www.TrainingFromTheSource.com/bonus` *for more information.*

4) Open the Tech Bookstore in a Web browser.

Type the location to the bookstore's index page into your browser of choice. Usually you do not need to type in the `index.html` file (depending on how your server is set up), just the folder name (such as `www.yoursite.com/bookstore`). Because you have the Flash Player installed, you are automatically directed to the content page after the `index.html` page detects the player and redirects you to the Tech Bookstore.

If one of your visitors does not have the correct Flash Player installed (perhaps it is older than Flash Player 7), or no Flash Player is installed at all, he or she will be directed to an HTML page that notifies them of this fact and tells them where the player can be downloaded from.

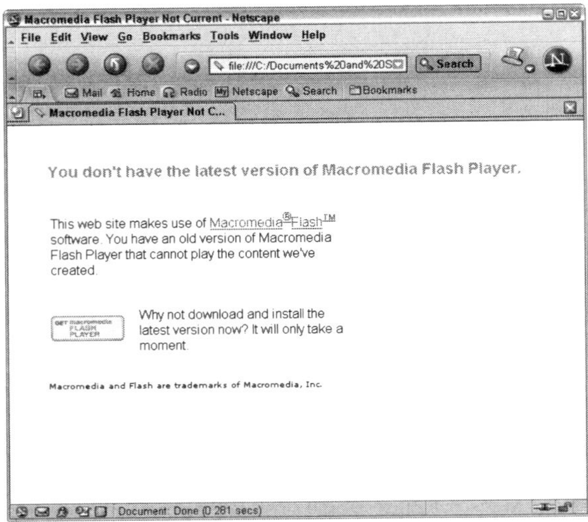

You can view the page by opening `bookstore_alternate.html`. Or if the visitor has Internet Explorer, a pop-up window asks them if they want to download and install a new version of the Flash Player.

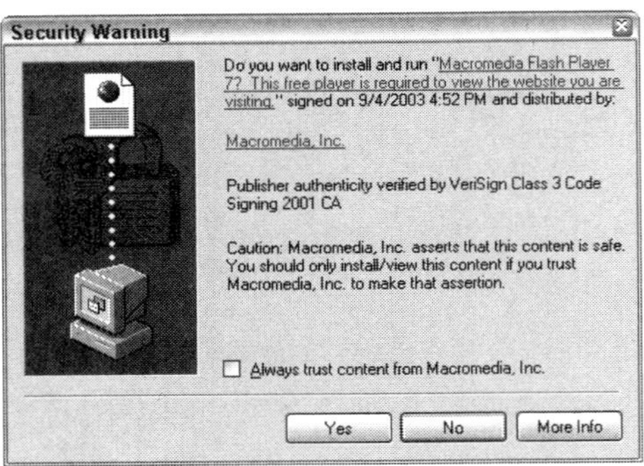

It's always easy to forget to publish a file, or perhaps even save one in the wrong directory on your hard drive. If you are missing any SWF files from this list, open the FLA file again and publish the FLA so a SWF file is saved in the `TechBookstore` folder. Then upload this new file to the server into the correct directory. You might also want to check that you have remembered to upload the `catalog` and `review` folders as well.

The complete published Tech Bookstore can be found in the `Lesson13` folder on the CD-ROM. The finished Tech Bookstore site is in the `complete` folder, in another folder called `bookstore`. This folder contains the completed SWF files and HTML files for the Web site.

NOTE *Microsoft has recently released information regarding some significant changes that are being introduced into the next version of Internet Explorer (due to a law suit) that is going to affect how you embed SWF files in an HTML page. Although there is not sufficient information to offer at the time this book is going to press, you will be able to find information and links at* `www.TrainingFromTheSource.com` *in the next few months as it becomes available. Macromedia is developing tools that will help make the transition easy for you.*

WRAPPING IT ALL UP

You have successfully completed the Web site (we hope)! It's important to go take a break and put your feet up after a major undertaking, so that's your final step in this book: Go take a break.

Hopefully, you have found out how much fun Flash can be, and just how easy it is to get started using the software. Obviously, it doesn't end here. But hopefully this is what you might call a firm foundation in Flash. Now that you have created an entire Web site, you can start creating your own projects using Flash while continuing to learn new tips and tricks along the way.

Make sure you come by and visit the forums for this book at `www.TrainingFromTheSource.com/forum`, where there is a specific forum dedicated to getting help with the book, and information on add-ons. Unfortunately, it's usually not possible to write a perfect book or create perfect software, and from time to time there are updates to the software or to the player that might mean changes to the bookstore application must be made. If something like this occurs (or anything else), your questions can be answered on the forum. You might find an answer even faster by checking the errata, forum and FAQ pages on the supporting Web site I've mentioned many times throughout the book: `www.TrainingFromTheSource.com`.

You will probably have questions left over about ActionScript, because a tutorial format just doesn't allow a person to clarify everything you probably want to know about the ActionScript language (even what's included in the lessons). There is a lot of help in the community, which is one of the best parts of using Flash MX. So thanks for reading, best of luck with your future projects, and I hope to see you out there!

WHAT YOU HAVE LEARNED

In this lesson, you have:

- Created a new publish profile (pages 408–414)
- Changed the publish settings (pages 408–414)
- Detected the Flash Player version (pages 414–418)
- Embedded a SWF file in an HTML page (pages 418–422)
- Created an HTML page for the Tech Bookstore (pages 418–422)
- Put the Tech Bookstore online (pages 422–425)

installing extensions

APPENDIX A

You can install *extensions* into Flash that include components, effects, tools, screen types, behaviors, and commands. You can install extensions using Macromedia's Extension manager or by manually placing the extensions within the Flash directory on your hard drive. You can also manage existing extensions that you have installed from a single interface when you use the Extension Manager. Download the latest Extension Manager from the following URL: `www.macromedia.com/exchange/em_download`.

NOTE *You need the Macromedia Extension Manager 1.6 (or greater) to install extensions for Flash MX 2004. You can also install extensions for Dreamweaver MX 2004, Fireworks MX 2004, Flash MX, Dreamweaver MX, and Fireworks MX.*

After you close any Macromedia software you have running after downloading the Extension Manager, you can run the installer that you downloaded. After the Extension Manager installs, it will open like any other standalone program.

You can open the Extension Manager using the Start menu on Windows, in your `Applications` folder on the Mac. You can also access the Extension Manager right in Flash by choosing Help > Manage Extensions.

INSTALLING EXTENSIONS AND COMPONENTS

Components are distributed by using MXP files, which are installed using the Extension Manager. You double-click the MXP file, which opens the Extension Manager that installs the extension, so it is available within Flash. Then you can access the extension directly in Flash. Other extensions might be distributed as EXE, SWC, or even FLA files. The SWC and FLA files have to be placed in the correct directory in order to work properly.

TIP *You might also encounter plug-ins, which are sometimes installed using EXE files. These extensions take you through an installation process, perhaps requiring you to enter a serial number. Where the extension appears in Flash depends on what the extension is for. For a Timeline effect extension, the extension is found alongside the other Timeline effects you have in Flash (Insert > Timeline Effects).*

To install an extension on your computer, open the Extension Manager and then choose File > Install Extension to open the Extension to Install dialog box. You can also click the Install New Extension button. The Select Extension to Install dialog box opens, and you can select any MXP file on your hard drive that you want to install and then read and accept the disclaimer.

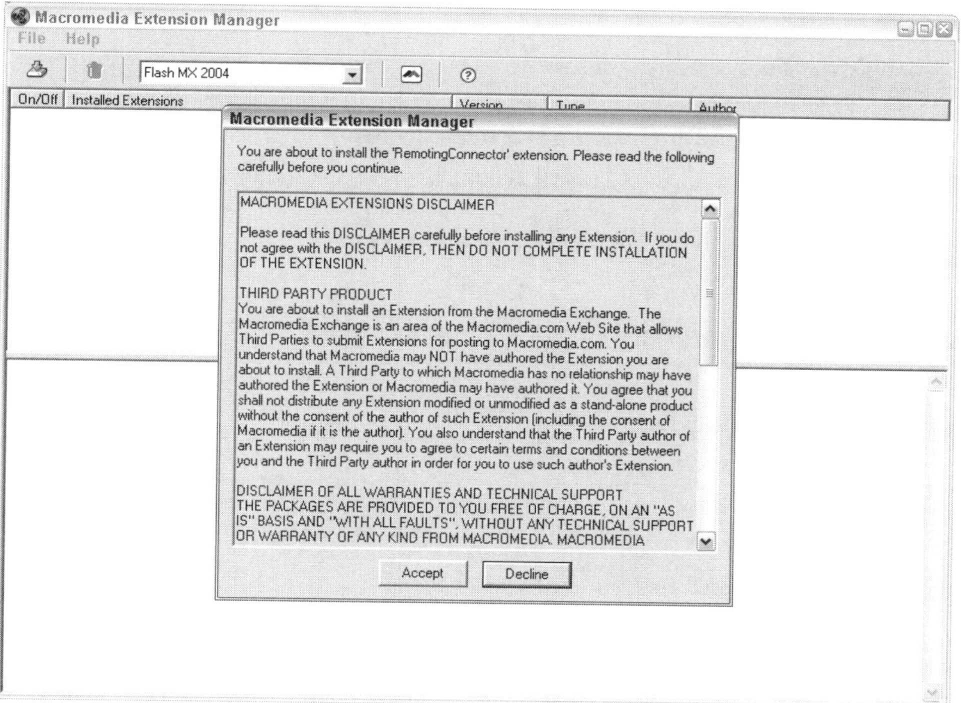

After the component installs, you see a message similar to the following, notifying you that it has successfully installed.

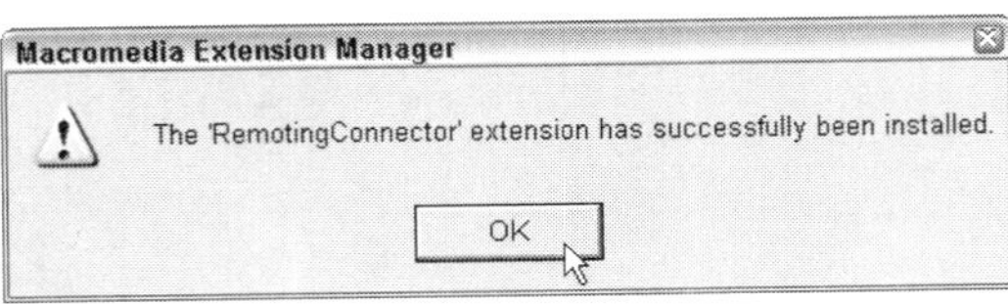

After extensions are installed on your system, they can be toggled, sorted, or removed by using the Extension Manager. Selecting an extension from the list enables you to see a brief description of the extension and as well as additional information by the author on the extension, and how to use or access it in Flash. When you install an extension in a multiuser environment (Windows NT, 2000, XP, or Mac OS X), the Extension Manager installs components and extensions only for the logged-in user.

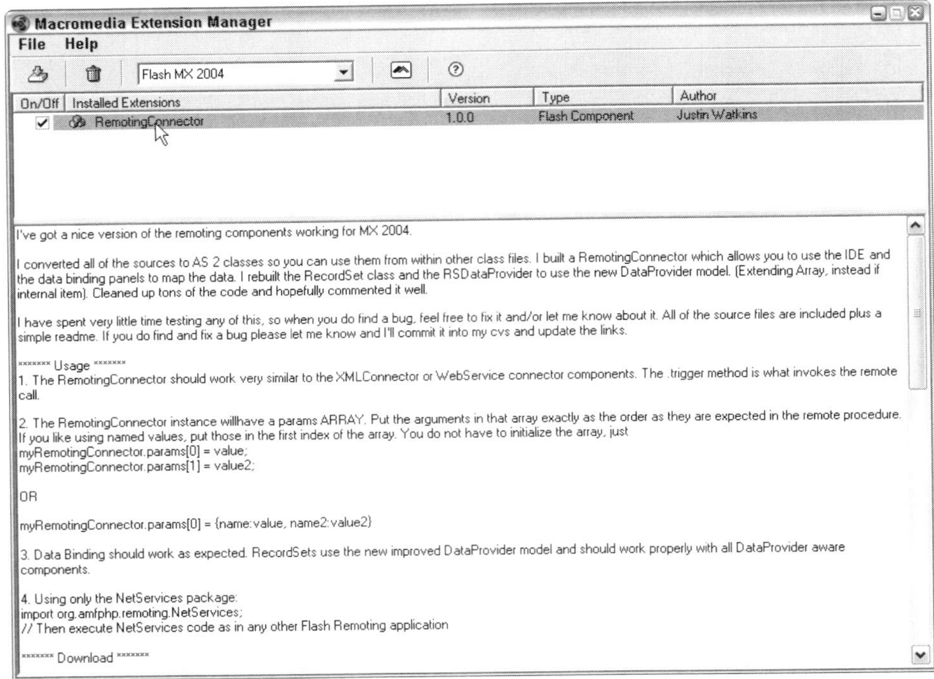

You can manually install components if you have an FLA or SWF. On a Windows-based system, find the user configuration folder in the following folder: `C:\Documents and Settings\<USERNAME>\Local Settings\Application Data\Macromedia\Flash MX 2004\en\Configuration` (or `<username>\Library\Application Support\Macromedia\Flash MX 2004\en\Configuration` on the Mac). The path is a bit different if you change the location of the Documents and Settings folder or your default settings.

NOTE *To see all the folders listed previously, it might be necessary to modify your folder options so Windows Explorer displays hidden files. Do this by choosing Tools > Folder Options from Windows Explorer's main menu. Then click the View tab in the Folder Options dialog box; and in the Advanced settings pane, make sure that "Show hidden files and folders" is selected from the "Hidden files and folders" folder.*

Many directories, including `Behaviors`, `Components`, `Effects`, `Libraries`, `Panel Sets`, and `Templates` are found in the `Configuration` folder. Do remember if you install components by directly placing them in the user's folder, you can't manage them via the Extension Manager.

NOTE *After you have installed new components or behaviors, you must choose Reload from the Components panel or you must restart Flash. The component is available in the Components panel.*

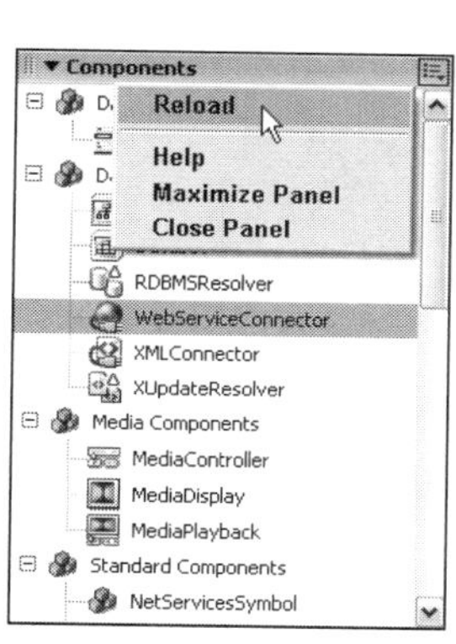

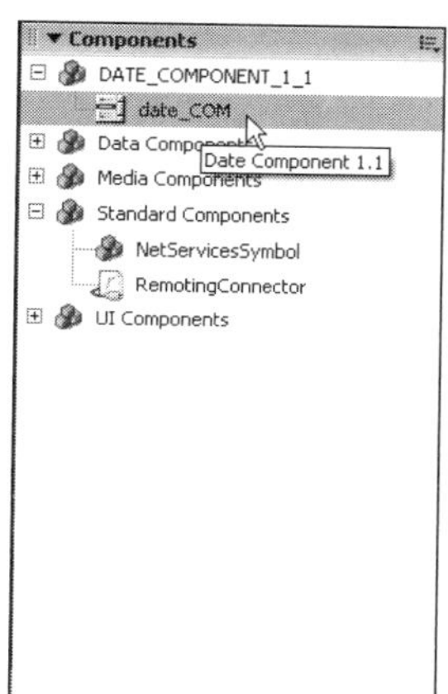

Extensions might appear within the Components panel, Common Libraries, Commands menu, or the Behaviors panel. Extensions might be installed using the Extension Manager instead of an EXE file or require you to manually place it in a particular directory. If you installed the extension using an MXP and the Extension Manager, there will be an On/Off check box to disable the extension if you need to. There is also a File > Remove Extension option available.

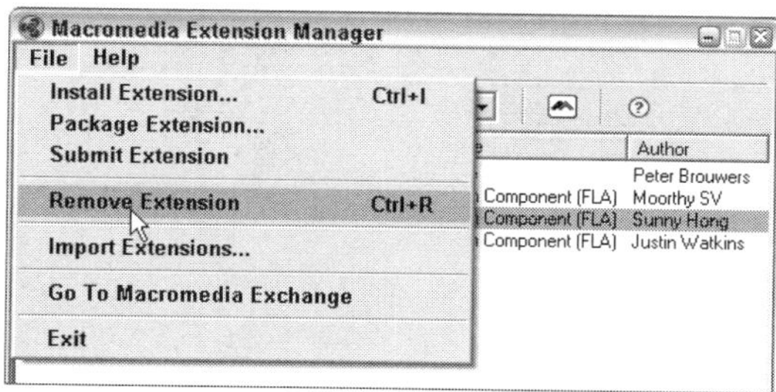

ADDING COMMANDS AND BEHAVIORS TO FLASH

Commands are used to repeat tasks numerous times. You can download commands from the Flash Exchange or create them yourself by saving steps from the History panel. Commands and behaviors can be installed using the Extension Manager as well.

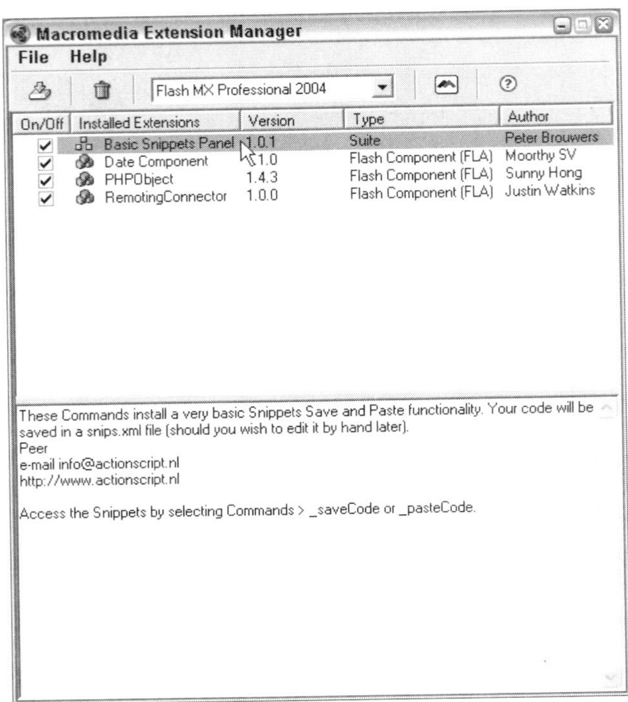

You can also create your own custom commands very easily by following these steps:

1) Open up the History panel.

Choose Window > Other Panels > History to open the History panel.

2) Do a common task in Flash.

A common task might be creating an actions layer. Do anything that is registered by the History panel and that you might want to repeat as some kind of task in Flash.

3) Select the steps that should be saved as the command in the History panel.

These are the steps that will be reproduced when you choose to run the command.

4) Within the History panel, right-click (or control-click on the Mac) and choose Save As Command from the contextual menu.

A dialog box appears and prompts you for a name for this command.

5) Assign a name to the command.

You can replay the command after you have assigned a name to it. All you need to do is select the command name from the Commands menu or Commands > Run Command from the main menu. If you choose the latter, the Open dialog box pops open, and you need to select a specific command to run from the hard drive. Commands are saved as Flash JavaScript files and have a JSFL extension. If you create your own custom commands using the History panel, the JSFL file will most likely be saved to the following directory: `C:\Documents and Settings\<USERNAME>\Local Settings\Application Data\Macromedia\Flash MX 2004\en\Configuration\Commands` (or `<username>\Library\Application Support\Macromedia\Flash MX 2004\en\Configuration\Commands` on a Mac).

Behaviors are used to make your SWF files more interactive without having to write ActionScript code yourself in the Flash authoring environment, and you have used many of them throughout the exercises in this book. You can install a behavior using the Extension Manager or place it directly in a folder on the hard drive. Place the behavior in the following folder: `C:\Documents and Settings\<USERNAME>\Local Settings\Application Data\Macromedia\Flash MX 2004\en\Configuration\Behaviors` (or `<username>\Library\Application Support\Macromedia\Flash MX 2004\en\Configuration\Behaviors` on the Mac). After you put a behavior in the `Behaviors` folder, you need to restart Flash or choose Reload from the Options menu in the Behaviors panel. To delete a behavior, you need to delete the behavior's XML file from the user's folder above.

WHERE TO FIND EXTENSIONS

One of the best places (if not *the* best place) to find Flash extensions is at the Macromedia Exchange at `www.macromedia.com/go/flash_exchange`. Accessing the Exchange is easy. You can reach the site from Flash by selecting Help > Flash Exchange or by selecting Macromedia Flash Exchange from the Start page.

Extensions (including components, code snippets, or plug-ins) are created by Macromedia themselves as well as members of the Flash community. Many extensions are free of charge, although some are for sale. Sometimes, you will be required to pay for extensions or components before you are allowed to download them, although this sometimes means that you get a higher-quality component or extension with some level of customer support as well. Some extensions are available from personal or commercial Web sites, blogs, or even forums.

Macromedia has published a list of companies, which have created third-party extensions in the form of plug-ins for Flash MX 2004. A list of select companies offering plug-ins is found at: `www.macromedia.com/software/flash/extensions`. The extensions include plug-ins that create text effects, charts, image effects, and an extension that converts your 2-D art and text into 3-D animations.

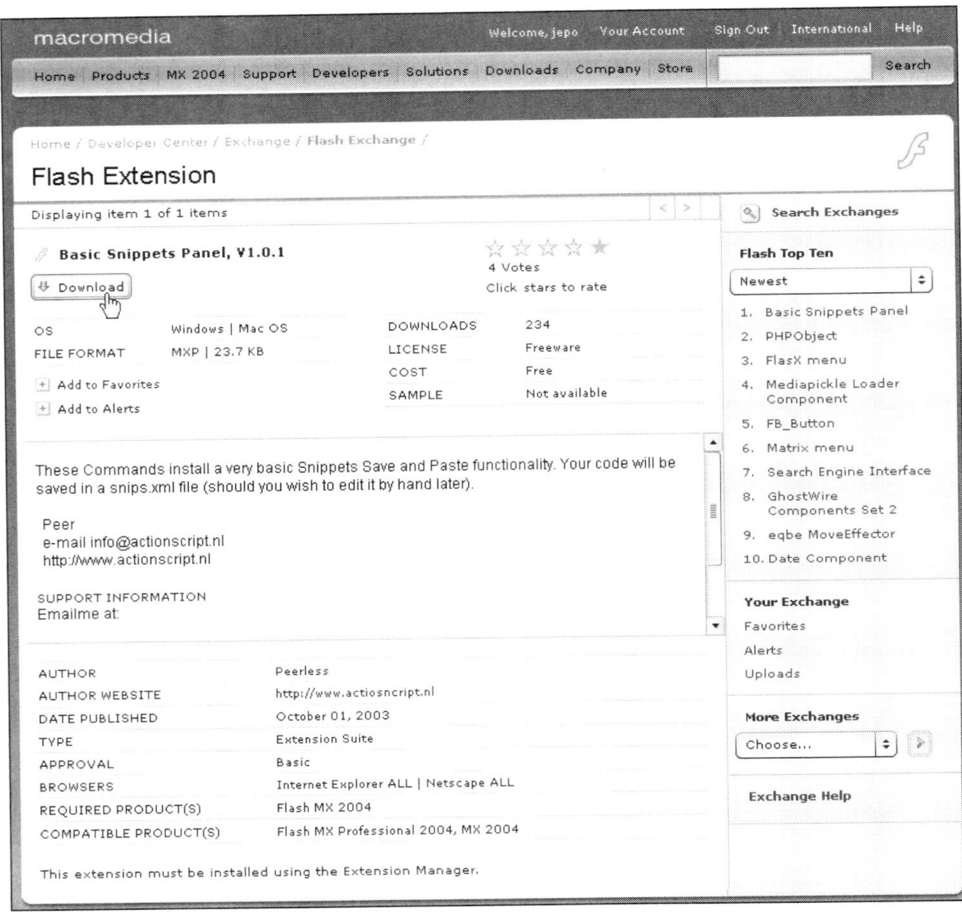

NOTE *You can find a more detailed list of where to find third-party tools and extensions in Appendix B.*

You can also find more commands on the Flash Exchange by choosing Commands > Get More Commands from the Command menu in Flash.

resources

APPENDIX B

Online resources are extensive and useful when it comes to answering very specific needs to your Flash-related queries. Forums, email lists, blogs ("weblogs"), and tutorial-based Web sites are important parts of the Flash community. In recent years, the Flash-related blogs have popped up everywhere. These Web pages journal the experiments and learnings of many great Flash minds in the community. Searching the Flash blogs is a great way to find out about others who are going down the same path you are and learn a bit more each day. Most of them even allow you to comment on each entry that is made.

In the following pages, I will list some of the sites I have found most useful. Of course, this is by no means a complete list, and I'm sure I have forgotten some great sites. You can also visit `www.TrainingFromTheSource.com/resources` for an up-to-date list that includes all these links, and more.

FLASH TRAINING FROM THE SOURCE

A lot of effort has been made to create a support network for this book. Please don't be discouraged if you don't get a personal reply right away because there's only one girl behind this site. However, I will make every effort to help as quickly as possible. Perhaps try to post your questions on the forum before email, so everyone can take advantage of the answer. As I figure out what the most frequent questions are, I will create a "Frequently Asked Questions" page. The FAQ and the forums will be good places to start—you might find out an answer right away instead of having to wait.

TrainingFromTheSource: `www.TrainingFromTheSource.com`
This book's Web site. You can find the entire set of bonus tutorials, forums, contact information, and more linked from the main page.

Tech Bookstore: `http://flash.TrainingFromTheSource.com`
See the Tech Bookstore site in action.

Forums: `www.TrainingFromTheSource.com/forums`
Go to the forums to ask questions, or when you need some help or guidance in building the application in this book. Updates and corrections can also be found in the forums. Search the forums to try and find an immediate answer to your problem.

FAQ: `www.TrainingFromTheSource.com/faq`
An FAQ will be developed over time, depending on what questions are asked the most.

Errata: `www.TrainingFromTheSource.com/errata`
Updated errata can be found on this page.

TUTORIAL AND RESOURCE SITES

Tutorial and resource sites are plentiful; however, you will probably have to do a bit of searching to find what you are looking for. That said, there is a lot of opportunity to become involved in the Flash community. Surf around and find your "spot." There are many friendly people out there who are more than willing to help you as you learn the ropes. Many of these sites also offer forums and a related community.

Flash MX: `www.flash-mx.com`
This Web site is dedicated to Flash-based tutorials, news, and book and software reviews.

flash2004.com: `www.flash2004.com`
This Web site is dedicated to Flash MX 2004 and Flash MX 2004 Professional. Resources include tutorials, reviews, and more.

Macromedia Developer Center: `www.macromedia.com/devnet`
The Developer Center (also known as DevNet) contains resources for all of Macromedia's product line. Each product has an area devoted to resources on development using the software.

Inform IT: `www.informit.com`
This is a large resource site for Web designers and developers. Contains a section devoted to Flash.

ActionScript.com: `www.actionscript.com`
Flash reference and online community. The site even offers a growing reference of the ActionScript language that you can contribute to using a commenting system. The ActionScript Reference is like a nonofficial Macromedia LiveDocs system.

ActionScript.org: `www.actionscript.org`
An extensive reference and tutorial site.

Studiowhiz: `www.studiowhiz.com`
Studiowhiz offers tutorials, reviews, and a forum on everything to do with Web design and development. This Web site includes a lot of content on Flash MX.

UltraShock: `www.ultrashock.com`
An online community for Flash that includes resources for learning the software.

ActionScript Toolbox: `www.actionscript-toolbox.com`
Tutorials and resources on Flash MX and 2004.

Flash Zone: `www.flzone.net`
Resources and information about Flash MX, including tutorials, extensions, and news.

Tip of the Day: `www.flash2004.com/tipoday`
A Flash (or Studio MX) tip of the day provided daily by numerous members of the Macromedia online community.

What is Flash: `www.whatisflash.com`
A wiki-style Web site whose purpose is to discuss and help promote a standardized way of working with Flash. Also moves to promote the use of good Flash on the Web.

Flash the Future: `www.flashthefuture.com`
Information on creating Flash content for mobile devices.

Flash Enabled: `www.flashenabled.com`
Information on creating Flash content for mobile devices.

SwiftDev: www.swiftdev.com
Online community and resources for those working with Swift.

Person 13: www.person13.com
Includes articles and information primarily on Flash Remoting and ActionScript 2.0, written by the jovial Joey Lott.

Lionbich Studios: www.lionbichstudios.com/tutorials.html
Tutorials on the entire Studio MX 2004 suite, including beginner to advanced tutorials on Flash.

FullAsAGoog: www.fullasagoog.com
An excellent Flash blog aggregator.

MX Developers Journal: www.sys-con.com/mx
A magazine devoted to the MX product family.

FORUMS

Forums are plentiful out there. Flash forums exist in many languages and many sizes. There are high traffic forums, and smaller ones where you can get to know the regulars. Whatever you're looking for, you'll probably find it.

Flash MX 2004 forums: www.flashmx2004.com/forums
These forums are exclusively dedicated to working with Flash MX 2004. The first MX 2004-dedicated forum of its kind on the Web.

Were Here forums: www.were-here.com
A busy online community (forums) for Flash designers and developers.

Macromedia Web Forums (Flash): http://webforums.macromedia.com/flash/
Official Macromedia Web forums. Also available in newsgroup format (news://forums.macromedia.com)

Flash Move: www.flashmove.com/board/index.php
An online community for Flash.

FlashKit: www.flashkit.com
One of the biggest and the oldest, this established community is also probably the busiest.

Flash MX Files: www.flashmxfiles.com/phpBB2/
Busy forum with a wide range of Flash-related subjects.

EMAIL LISTS

If you aren't partial to forums, perhaps you want to join some email-based lists. These email lists range from high-traffic to moderate- and low-traffic. There are many out there to join, and sometines you happen across the best ones by chance. This list contains some of the more common (public) ones out there, although there are many more.

Flashcoders: `http://chattyfig.figleaf.com/`
An advanced list discussing the finer aspects of coding ActionScript. Discussion is limited to intermediate to advanced topics involving ActionScript. This is a high-traffic list.

Flash Newbie: `http://chattyfig.figleaf.com/`
Flash novice list run by the fine people that bring you Flashcoders.

Flash Lounge: `http://chattyfig.figleaf.com/`
A great "on-topic and clothing optional" list run by the fine people who bring you Flashcoders.

Flash MX 2004: `www.flash2004.com/list`
Discuss anything pertaining to Flash MX 2004.

Flasher: `www.chinwag.com/flasher`
General Flash discussion.

DevMX: `www.devmx.com/mailing_list.cfm`
Mailing list that focuses on discussing dynamic flash.

EXTENSIONS AND FONTS

Third-party extensions might include components, plug-ins, behaviors, and commands. The following Web sites offer free extensions for the community. See the following section on Macromedia links for extensions available on the Macromedia Web site. At the time of writing, there were not many tools online making use of the extensibility layer in Flash. Go to `www.TrainingFromTheSource.com/resources` for the latest links available.

NOTE *Remember that the extensions you find in these sites might not be compatible with the components found in Flash MX 2004. If the components you download are built using ActionScript 1.0 (for Flash MX), they might not work with the ActionScript or components you use in your Flash sites.*

Flash Component.com: www.flashcomponent.com
Free components for download, although mostly Flash MX at this time. Components are free, and you can provide or read feedback on each one. At the time of writing, content available was for Flash MX.

Flash Components.net: www.flashcomponents.net
You can download free components from this site. You can preview components and also use the tutorials on the site describing how to build and use components in Flash. At the time of writing, available content was for Flash MX.

Dovelop Extensions: www.dovelop.com/extensions/default.asp.
Flash, Dreamweaver, and Fireworks extensions available for download from this site.

Ghostwire component set: www.ghostwire.com
An excellent set of version 1 components that serve as an alternative to the default set of components that come with Flash MX. Lightweight and extremely useful.

Flash DB Components: www.flash-db.com/Components
Component libraries available for download.

Flash Components.com: www.flashcomponents.com
A subscription-based service. A monthly fee allows you to download components from this site.

Miniml: www.miniml.com
Long-time, respected source for pixel fonts.

Fonts for Flash: www.fontsforflash.com
Many interesting and unique pixel fonts are available from this source.

THIRD-PARTY TOOLS AND INTEGRATION

Third-party tools are very important for exploring different ways to integrate special content, such as 3D or video. Explore some of your options through downloading trial versions. These third-party tools are built specifically with integrating with Flash in mind. Also, integrating server-side software is sometimes necessary depending on what you need to get done. The following links include some good reference sites for application server software.

Toon Boom Studio: www.toonboom.com
Professional animation and drawing tool primarily used by animators and then directly imported into Flash.

Swift 3D: www.swift3d.com or www.erain.com
A standalone 3D program that is used to create content that can be imported into Flash. You can also use an exporter to save SWFs from 3D Studio Max.

Sorenson Squeeze: `www.sorenson.com`

Software that's used to compress media that can be imported into Flash. You can output as video, SWF files, or FLV files (among others) that can then be used in your Flash applications.

Wildform Flix: `www.wildform.com`

Flix compresses your video so it can be imported into Flash. Much like Squeeze, Flix can be used to create many different kinds of video files, including SWF and FLV. There are several different versions of this software available. Wildform also offers other tools that can be used in conjunction with Flash.

SWiSH: `www.swishzone.com`

Create animations and more, easily and without having to create an FLA in Flash. Many interesting effects are available from the Web site.

ActionScript Viewer: `www.buraks.com/asv`

This software is incredibly useful if you have ever lost an FLA. ASV allows you to view inside a Flash document and view the code that is used to make it work. You can also view Timeline placement of instances and grab graphics from inside of the SWF file. It does not re-create the FLA for you (this is simply not possible).

Flash Jester: `www.flashjester.com`

Tools used to extend the capabilities of Flash.

SWF Studio: `www.northcode.com`

Tool used to extend the capabilities of Flash Projector files.

Ming: `http://ming.sourceforge.net/`

This is a C library for generating SWF files, and is a series of wrappers for Python, C++, PHP, and more.

Flash Remoting: `www.macromedia.com/software/flashremoting`

The official word on Flash Remoting MX. Remoting components that you can install with Flash MX 2004 are included in this area of the site. Flash Remoting includes support for ColdFusion MX (included with the server), .NET and Java. Flash Remoting for .NET and JAVA is not free.

AMFPHP: `www.amfphp.org`

Official site for Flash Remoting with PHP. This is a third-party tool that's not supported by Macromedia, although it is free.

Flash Communication Server: `www.macromedia.com/software/flashcom/`

The official part of Macromedia's site for the Flashcom server.

ColdFusion MX: `www.macromedia.com/software/coldfusion/`

The official word on ColdFusion MX: an application server that works very well with Flash. The Web Services you use in this book were written using CFML, the markup language for ColdFusion.

ASP.NET: `www.microsoft.com/net`

Get started learning ASP.NET. This site is a good jumping point for learning how to use this server-side language.

PHP: `www.php.net`

The place to start learning or using PHP for your work that integrates with a server.

RELATED MACROMEDIA PRESS BOOKS

Other Macromedia Press books that might interest you as you continue to learn Flash MX 2004.

Macromedia Flash MX 2004 ActionScript : Training from the Source

0-321-21343-2

Written by Derek Franklin and Jobe Makar.

Studio MX 2004: Training from the Source

0-321-24158-4

Written by Jeffrey Bardzell.

Macromedia Flash MX Professional 2004 Application Development: Training from the Source

0-321-23834-6

Written by Jeanette Stallons.

Object Oriented Programming with ActionScript 2

0-735-71380-4

Written by James Talbot.

MACROMEDIA.COM

There are many great resources on `Macromedia.com` just waiting to be found. Here are some useful links from the site that will help you when working with this book—and more so when you're finished with it.

Download software: `www.macromedia.com/downloads`

Download trial versions or purchase software from this location.

Developer Center for Flash: `www.macromedia.com/devnet/mx/flash`

The Flash Developer Center offers many great articles and resources for you each and every week. From articles to tutorials, to papers and sample applications, you will never run out of great things to read and try for yourself.

Tech Notes (Flash): `www.macromedia.com/support/flash/technotes.html`
The Tech Notes are a great resource if you're running into problems or want to find out some tips and tricks for Flash. Think of the Tech Notes like a great big FAQ in a way. If you have "issues" with Flash, this is the place to go for some support.

Macromedia Exchange: `www.macromedia.com/cfusion/exchange/index.cfm`
The Macromedia exchange is where you can either upload your own components and extensions, or find them for download. Although many are free, some are for purchase.

Third-Party Extensions: `www.macromedia.com/software/flash/extensions/`
This is a list of Macromedia's latest third-party extensions. This page links to extensions you might want to try installing or purchasing. Macromedia teams up with companies that develop useful extensions that help you get more out of Flash.

Wish List: `www.macromedia.com/software/flash/contact/wishlist/`
The Wish List is where you can go to either report bugs or send a note saying what you most want to see added to Flash. If you have great ideas for the software—or find a bug to report—fill out this form, which is sent to the Flash team for examination.

User Groups: `www.macromedia.com/cfusion/usergroups/`
User Groups are a great way to meet other people developing content using the Macromedia product line. Find a group in your local area or start your own.

MXNA: `www.markme.com/mxna`
MX News Aggregator for Macromedia and community blogs. Start here for the extensive Flash blog circuit and find the latest news on everything Macromedia-related.

keyboard shortcuts

APPENDIX C

FILE MENU		
Command	**Windows Shortcut**	**Mac Shortcut**
New	Ctrl+N	Cmd+N
Open	Ctrl+O	Cmd+O
Close	Ctrl+W	Cmd+W
Save	Ctrl+S	Cmd+S
Save As	Ctrl+Shift+S	Cmd+Shift+S
Publish Settings	Ctrl+Shift+F12	Option+Shift+F12
Publish	Ctrl+F12	Shift+F12
Print	Ctrl+P	Cmd+P
Exit	Ctrl+Q	Cmd+Q
Import to Stage	Ctrl+R	Cmd+R
Open External Library	Ctrl+Shift+O	Cmd+O
Export Movie	Ctrl+Alt+Shift+S	Cmd+Option+Shift+S
Default Publish Preview (HTML)	F12	F12

EDIT MENU

Command	Windows Shortcut	Mac Shortcut
Undo	Ctrl+Z	Cmd+Z
Redo	Ctrl+Y	Cmd+Y
Cut	Ctrl+X	Cmd+X
Copy	Ctrl+C	Cmd+C
Paste in Center	Ctrl+V	Cmd+V
Paste in Place	Ctrl+Shift+V	Cmd+Shift+V
Clear	Backspace	Delete
Duplicate	Ctrl+D	Cmd+D
Select All	Ctrl+A	Cmd+A
Deselect All	Ctrl+Shift+A	Cmd+Shift+A
Find and Replace	Ctrl+F	Cmd+F
Find Next	F3	F3
Edit Symbols	Ctrl+E	Cmd+E
Cut Frames	Ctrl+Alt+X	Cmd+Option+X
Copy Frames	Ctrl+Alt+C	Cmd+Option+C
Paste Frames	Ctrl+Alt+V	Cmd+Option+V
Clear Frames	Alt+Backspace	Option+Delete
Remove Frames	Shift+F5	Shift+F5
Select All Frames	Ctrl+Alt+A	Cmd+Option+A
Preferences	Ctrl+U	Flash › Preferences

VIEW MENU		
Command	**Windows Shortcut**	**Mac Shortcut**
Go to First	Home	Home
Go to Previous	Page Up	Page Up
Go to Next	Page Down	Page Down
Go to Last	End	End
Zoom In	Ctrl+=	Cmd+=
Zoom Out	Ctrl+-	Cmd+-
Magnification: 100%	Ctrl+1	Cmd+1
Magnification: 400%	Ctrl+4	Cmd+4
Magnification: 800%	Ctrl+8	Cmd+8
Show Frame	Ctrl+2	Cmd+2
Show All	Ctrl+3	Cmd+3
Outlines	Ctrl+Alt+Shift+O	Cmd+Option+Shift+O
Fast	Ctrl+Alt+Shift+F	Cmd+Option+Shift+F
Antialias	Ctrl+Alt+Shift+A	Cmd+Option+Shift+A
Antialias Text	Ctrl+Alt+Shift+T	Cmd+Option+Shift+T
Work Area	Ctrl+Shift+W	Cmd+Shift+W
Rulers	Ctrl+Alt+Shift+R	Cmd+Option+Shift+R
Show Grid	Ctrl+‘	Cmd+‘
Edit Grid	Ctrl+Alt+G	Cmd+Option+G
Show Guides	Ctrl+;	Cmd+;
Lock Guides	Ctrl+Shift+;	Cmd+Shift+;
Edit Guides	Ctrl+Alt+Shift+G	Cmd+Option+Shift+G
Snap to Grid	Ctrl+Shift+‘	Cmd+Shift+‘
Snap to Guides	Ctrl+Shift+;	Cmd+Shift+;
Snap to Objects	Ctrl+Shift+/	Cmd+Shift+/
Hide Edges	Ctrl+H	Cmd+Shift+E
Show Shape Hints	Ctrl+Alt+H	Cmd+Option+H

INSERT MENU		
Command	**Windows Shortcut**	**Mac Shortcut**
New Symbol	Ctrl+F8	Cmd+F8
Frame	F5	F5

MODIFY MENU		
Command	**Windows Shortcut**	**Mac Shortcut**
Document	Ctrl+J	Cmd+J
Convert to Symbol	F8	F8
Break Apart	Ctrl+B	Cmd+B
Optimize	Ctrl+Alt+Shift+C	Cmd+Option+Shift+C
Add Shape Hint	Ctrl+Shift+H	Cmd+Shift+H
Distribute to Layers	Ctrl+Shift+D	Cmd+Shift+D
Convert to Keyframes	F6	F6
Clear Keyframe	Shift+F6	Shift+F6
Convert to Blank Keyframes	F7	F7
Rotate 90 degrees CW	Ctrl+Shift+9	Cmd+Shift+9
Rotate 90 degrees CCW	Ctrl+Shift+7	Cmd+Shift+7
Remove Transform	Ctrl+Shift+Z	Cmd+Shift+Z
Bring to Front	Ctrl+Shift+Up	Option+Shift+Up
Bring Forward	Ctrl+Up	Cmd+Up
Send Backward	Ctrl+Down	Cmd+Down
Send to Back	Ctrl+Shift+Down	Option+Shift+Down
Lock	Ctrl+Alt+L	Cmd+Option+L
Unlock All	Ctrl+Alt+Shift+L	Cmd+Option+Shift+L
Align Left	Ctrl+Alt+1	Cmd+Option+1
Align Horizontal Center	Ctrl+Alt+2	Cmd+Option+2
Align Right	Ctrl+Alt+3	Cmd+Option+3
Align Top	Ctrl+Alt+4	Cmd+Option+4
Align Vertical Center	Ctrl+Alt+5	Cmd+Option+5
Align Bottom	Ctrl+Alt+6	Cmd+Option+6
Distribute Widths	Ctrl+Alt+7	Cmd+Option+7
Distribute Heights	Ctrl+Alt+9	Cmd+Option+9
Make Same Width	Ctrl+Alt+Shift+7	Cmd+Option+Shift+7
Make Same Height	Ctrl+Alt+Shift+9	Cmd+Option+Shift+9
To Stage	Ctrl+Alt+8	Cmd+Option+8
Group	Ctrl+G	Cmd+G
Ungroup	Ctrl+Shift+G	Cmd+Shift+G

TEXT MENU		
Command	**Windows Shortcut**	**Mac Shortcut**
Plain	Ctrl+Shift+P	Cmd+Shift+B
Bold	Ctrl+Shift+B	Cmd+Shift+P
Italic	Ctrl+Shift+I	Cmd+Shift+I
Align Left	Ctrl+Shift+L	Cmd+Shift+L
Align Center	Ctrl+Shift+C	Cmd+Shift+C
Align Right	Ctrl+Shift+R	Cmd+Shift+R
Justify	Ctrl+Shift+J	Cmd+Shift+J
Tracking Increase	Ctrl+Alt+Right	Cmd+Option+Right
Tracking Decrease	Ctrl+Alt+Left	Cmd+Option+Left
Tracking Reset	Ctrl+Alt+Up	Cmd+Option+Up

CONTROL MENU		
Command	**Windows Shortcut**	**Mac Shortcut**
Play	Enter	Enter/Return
Rewind	Ctrl+Alt+R	Cmd+Option+R
Step Forward One Frame	.	.
Step Backward One Frame	,	,
Test Movie	Ctrl+Enter	Cmd+Enter
Debug Movie	Ctrl+Shift+Enter	Cmd+Shift+Enter
Test Scene	Ctrl+Alt+Enter	Cmd+Option+Enter
Test Project	Ctrl+Alt+P	Cmd+Option+P
Enable Simple Buttons	Ctrl+Alt+B	Cmd+Option+B

WINDOW MENU		
Command	**Windows Shortcut**	**Mac Shortcut**
New Window	Ctrl+Alt+K	Cmd+Option+K
Project	Shift+F8	Shift+F8
Properties	Ctrl+F3	Cmd+F3
Timeline	Ctrl+Alt+T	Cmd+Option+T
Tools	Ctrl+F2	Cmd+F2
Library	Ctrl+L or F11	Cmd+L or F11
Align	Ctrl+K	Cmd+K
Color Mixer	Shift+F9	Shift+F9
Color Swatches	Ctrl+F9	Cmd+F9
Info	Ctrl+I	Cmd+I
Scene	Shift+F2	Shift+F2
Transform	Ctrl+T	Cmd+T
Actions	F9	F9
Behaviors	Shift+F3	Shift+F3
Components	Ctrl+F7	Cmd+F7
Component Inspector	Alt+F7	Option+F7
Debugger	Shift+F4	Shift+F4
Output	F2	F2
Web Services	Ctrl+Shift+F10	Cmd+Shift+F10
Accessibility	Alt+F2	Option+F2
History	Ctrl+F10	Cmd+F10
Movie Explorer	Alt+F3	Option+F3
Strings	Ctrl+F11	Cmd+F11
Hide Panels	F4	F4

HELP MENU		
Command	**Windows Shortcut**	**Mac Shortcut**
Help	F1	F1

ACTIONS PANEL		
Command	**Windows Shortcut**	**Mac Shortcut**
Pin Script	Ctrl+=	Cmd+=
Close Script	Ctrl+-	Cmd+-
Close All Scripts	Ctrl+Shift+-	Cmd+Shift+-
Go to Line	Ctrl+G	Cmd+,
Find	Ctrl+F	Cmd+F
Find Again	F3	Cmd+G
Replace	Ctrl+H	Cmd+Shift+H
Auto Format	Ctrl+Shift+F	Cmd+Shift+F
Check Syntax	Ctrl+T	Cmd+T
Show Code Hint	Ctrl+Spacebar	Cmd+Spacebar
Import Script	Ctrl+Shift+I	Cmd+Shift+I
Export Script	Ctrl+Shift+X	Cmd+Shift+X
View line Numbers	Ctrl+Shift+L	Cmd+Shift+L
Word Wrap	Ctrl+Shift+W	Cmd+Shift+W
Preferences	Ctrl+U	Cmd+U (only in Actions)

DEBUGGER PANEL		
Command	**Windows Shortcut**	**Mac Shortcut**
Continue	F10	F10
Stop Debugging	F11	F11
Step In	F6	F6
Step Over	F7	F7
Step Out	F8	F8

OUTPUT PANEL		
Command	**Windows Shortcut**	**Mac Shortcut**
Copy	Ctrl+C	Cmd+C
Find	Ctrl+F	Cmd+F
Find Again	F3	F3

index

A

D

E

G

H

M

N

O

P

Q

R

S

T

W

X – Z

Macromedia Tech Support: http://www.macromedia.com/support

LICENSING AGREEMENT